Legal Training Handbook

Other titles available from Law Society Publishing:

Anti-Money Laundering Toolkit
Alison Matthews

Career Planning for Solicitors
General Editor: Sue Lenkowski

Complaints Handling Toolkit
Vicky Ling and Fiona Westwood

Compliance and Ethics in Law Firms
Tracey Calvert

Data Protection Toolkit
Alison Matthews

Equality and Diversity Toolkit
Mark Lomas

Financial Stability Toolkit
Peter Scott and Andy Poole

SRA Handbook (Version 15)
Solicitors Regulation Authority

The Solicitor's Handbook 2015
Andrew Hopper QC and Gregory Treverton-Jones QC

Titles from Law Society Publishing can be ordered from all good bookshops or direct (telephone 0870 850 1422, email **lawsociety@prolog.uk.com** or visit our online shop at **www.lawsociety.org.uk/bookshop**).

LEGAL TRAINING HANDBOOK

Melissa Hardee

The Law Society

All rights reserved. No part of this publication may be reproduced in any material form, whether by photocopying, scanning, downloading onto computer or otherwise without the written permission of the Law Society except in accordance with the provisions of the Copyright, Designs and Patents Act 1988. Applications should be addressed in the first instance, in writing, to Law Society Publishing. Any unauthorised or restricted act in relation to this publication may result in civil proceedings and/or criminal prosecution.

The author has asserted the right under the Copyright, Designs and Patents Act 1988 to be identified as author of this work.

Whilst all reasonable care has been taken in the preparation of this publication, neither the publisher nor the author can accept any responsibility for any loss occasioned to any person acting or refraining from action as a result of relying upon its contents.

The views expressed in this publication should be taken as those of the author only unless it is specifically indicated that the Law Society has given its endorsement.

© The Law Society 2016

Crown copyright material is reproduced with the permission of the Controller of Her Majesty's Stationery Office

978-1-907698-84-2

Published in 2016 by the Law Society
113 Chancery Lane, London WC2A 1PL

Typeset by Columns Design XML Ltd, Reading
Printed by CPI Antony Rowe, Chippenham, Wilts

The paper used for the text pages of this book is FSC® certified. FSC (the Forest Stewardship Council®) is an international network to promote responsible management of the world's forests.

Contents

Foreword   xiv
Introduction   xvi
Acknowledgements   xx
Abbreviations   xxii

PART A: MANAGING TRAINING IN THE BUSINESS

1   The training investment   3

    1.1   Introduction   3
    1.2   The case for training   3
    1.3   Where the investment in training needs to be made   6
    1.4   Challenges to the case for training   7
    1.5   Maximising the investment of training   8
    1.6   Developing the right culture   10

2   The structure and ownership of training within the firm   14

    2.1   Introduction   14
    2.2   Structure   16
    2.3   Ownership   17
    2.4   Management responsibility   18
    2.5   Responsibility of the training function   19
    2.6   Interaction of training and knowledge management   20

3   Developing and implementing the training strategy   21

    3.1   Introduction   21
    3.2   Understanding the firm's business strategy and objectives   21
    3.3   Developing a competence framework   22
    3.4   Carrying out a training needs analysis   23
    3.5   Writing the training strategy   26
    3.6   Developing a training programme   28
    3.7   Evaluating the effectiveness of training   30

CONTENTS

4	**Financial management of training**		**33**
	4.1	Introduction	33
	4.2	The financial structure for training	34
	4.3	Financial planning and budgeting for training	35
	4.4	The training budget	36
	4.5	Measuring the investment in and return from training, in financial terms	40
	4.6	Ways of maximising the financial investment in training	41

PART B: QUALIFICATION AS A SOLICITOR IN ENGLAND AND WALES

B1: REGULATION OF LEGAL EDUCATION AND TRAINING — 47

5	**Regulatory authority**		**48**
	5.1	Introduction	48
	5.2	The Legal Services Board	48
	5.3	The Law Society of England and Wales	49
	5.4	Solicitors Regulation Authority	49

6	**Reform of legal education and training**		**53**
	6.1	Introduction	53
	6.2	The Legal Education and Training Review	53
	6.3	Reforms	60
	6.4	Consultations	63
	6.5	Proposed consultations and reforms	79
	6.6	The SRA Training Regulations	82

B2: ROUTES TO QUALIFICATION — 83

7	**Domestic routes**		**86**
	7.1	Introduction	86
	7.2	The law degree route	86
	7.3	The non-law graduate route	87
	7.4	Non-degree routes	87
	7.5	Equivalent Means	88
	7.6	Proposed changes	89

8	**European directive routes**		**90**
	8.1	Introduction	90
	8.2	Registered European Lawyer status	90
	8.3	Recognition of Professional Qualifications Directive	91

8.4	Partially qualified European lawyers	93
8.5	Foreign lawyer status	94

9 Qualified Lawyers Transfer Scheme routes — 96

9.1	Introduction	96
9.2	The scheme	96
9.3	Requirements	97
9.4	Variations in requirements	103
9.5	The QLTS Assessment	106
9.6	Application for the QLTS	109
9.7	Appeals	110
9.8	Admission and qualification	111
9.9	Proposed changes	112

10 Equivalent Means — 113

10.1	Introduction	113
10.2	What is meant by 'Equivalent Means'	114
10.3	Eligibility	114
10.4	Exemptions	116
10.5	Applying for exemptions	122
10.6	Proposed changes	123

11 Legal Apprenticeships — 124

11.1	Introduction	124
11.2	Background	125
11.3	The apprenticeship standards in law	126
11.4	The Solicitor Apprenticeship	128
11.5	Proposed changes	134

B3: THE ACADEMIC STAGE REQUIREMENTS — 135

12 Qualifying Law Degree — 136

12.1	Introduction	136
12.2	The degree	136
12.3	Requirements	137
12.4	Exempting Law Degree	143
12.5	Proposed changes	143

13 Conversion course — 144

13.1	Introduction	144
13.2	The course	144
13.3	Requirements	145

CONTENTS

13.4	Integrated Course	148
13.5	Proposed changes	148

B4: THE VOCATIONAL STAGE REQUIREMENTS — **149**

14 Legal Practice Course — 150

14.1	Introduction	150
14.2	The course	151
14.3	Requirements	151
14.4	LPC outcomes	154
14.5	Course structure	154
14.6	Course assessment	157
14.7	Quality assurance	158
14.8	Proposed changes	158

15 Period of Recognised Training — 160

15.1	The course	160
15.2	Governing regulations	161
15.3	The PRT and the Training Contract	161
15.4	Exemption from the PRT	165
15.5	Authorisation as a Training Provider	165
15.6	Training Principal	167
15.7	Employing trainees under the PRT	170
15.8	Eligibility to commence a PRT	175
15.9	Notification requirements	177
15.10	Support requirements	180
15.11	Training requirements	183
15.12	Supervision, review and appraisal requirements	192
15.13	Monitoring	199
15.14	Summary of responsibilities	202
15.15	Proposed changes	204

16 Professional Skills Course — 206

16.1	Introduction	206
16.2	Governing regulations	207
16.3	Requirements	207
16.4	Course content	209
16.5	Authorisation as PSC Provider	215
16.6	Proposed changes	227
	Annex 16A: Compulsory Core subjects – summary of requirements and features	228

B5: THE REQUIREMENTS FOR QUALIFICATION AND ADMISSION		**239**
17	**Education and training requirements for admission**	**240**
	17.1 Introduction	240
	17.2 Requirements	240
	17.3 Rights of appeal against SRA decisions	242
	17.4 Proposed changes	243
18	**Character and suitability requirements**	**246**
	18.1 Introduction	246
	18.2 The test	246
	18.3 DBS disclosures	247
	18.4 Self-disclosures under the SRA Suitability Test 2011	248
19	**Admission process**	**252**
	19.1 Introduction	252
	19.2 Issue of certificate of satisfaction	252
	19.3 Admission application	253
	19.4 Practising certificate	254
B6: POST-QUALIFICATION REQUIREMENTS		**255**
20	**Continuing Professional Development**	**256**
	20.1 Introduction	256
	20.2 Governing regulations	256
	20.3 Who is subject to the CPD Scheme	257
	20.4 CPD year	257
	20.5 CPD requirements	257
	20.6 Waivers	260
	20.7 Monitoring compliance with CPD requirements	261
	20.8 Minimum hours option – reg.3.1(a)	261
	20.9 Continuing Competence approach option – reg.3.1(b)	268
	20.10 Confirmation of compliance with requirements	279
	20.11 Sanctions	282
	20.12 Proposed changes	282
	20.13 Management Course Stages 1 and 2	283
21	**Competence Statement**	**285**
	21.1 Introduction	285
	21.2 Statement of Solicitor Competence	286
	21.3 Threshold Standard	292

21.4	Statement of Legal Knowledge	294
21.5	Proposed changes	299

PART C: OTHER QUALIFIED LAWYER QUALIFICATION REQUIREMENTS

22 Lawyers under the Legal Services Act 2007 — 303

22.1	Introduction	303

23 Barristers — 306

23.1	What is a barrister?	306
23.2	What a barrister does and is permitted to do	307
23.3	Regulation of barristers	308
23.4	The barrister qualification	308
23.5	Maintaining qualification as a barrister	310
23.6	Ongoing CPD and other training obligations for barristers	311
23.7	Costs of maintaining the qualification	315
23.8	Professional conduct requirements	316
23.9	Proposed changes	316
23.10	Source	316

24 Chartered Legal Executives — 317

24.1	What is a Chartered Legal Executive?	317
24.2	What a Chartered Legal Executive does and is permitted to do	317
24.3	Regulation of Chartered Legal Executives	319
24.4	The Chartered Legal Executive qualification	319
24.5	Maintaining the Chartered Legal Executive qualification	327
24.6	Ongoing CPD and other training obligations	327
24.7	Costs of maintaining the qualification	331
24.8	Professional conduct requirements	331
24.9	Requirements for a Chartered Legal Executive to qualify as a solicitor	332
24.10	Sources	332

25 Licensed conveyancers — 333

25.1	What is a licensed conveyancer?	333
25.2	What a licensed conveyancer does and is permitted to do	333
25.3	Regulation of licensed conveyancers	334
25.4	Requirements for qualifying as a licensed conveyancer	334
25.5	Maintaining the qualification	335
25.6	Ongoing CPD and other training obligations	335
25.7	Costs of maintaining the qualification	337

	25.8	Professional conduct requirements	337
	25.9	Source	338

26 Intellectual property practitioners — 339

	26.1	What is an intellectual property practitioner?	339
	26.2	What IP practitioners do and are permitted to do	339
	26.3	Regulation of IP practitioners	340
	26.4	The qualifications	341
	26.5	Maintaining the qualifications	343
	26.6	Ongoing CPD or other training obligations for IP practitioners	343
	26.7	Costs of maintaining the qualifications	345
	26.8	Regulation of the professional conduct of IP practitioners	346
	26.9	Sources	347

27 Costs lawyers — 348

	27.1	What is a costs lawyer?	348
	27.2	What a costs lawyer does and is permitted to do	348
	27.3	Regulation of costs lawyers	350
	27.4	The qualification	350
	27.5	Maintaining the qualification	351
	27.6	Ongoing CPD or other training obligations	351
	27.7	Costs of maintaining the qualification	352
	27.8	Professional conduct requirements	352
	27.9	Sources	352

28 Notaries — 353

	28.1	What is a notary?	353
	28.2	What a notary does and is permitted to do	353
	28.3	Regulation of notaries	354
	28.4	The Notary qualification	355
	28.5	Maintaining the qualification	356
	28.6	Ongoing CPD or other training obligations	356
	28.7	Costs of maintaining the qualification	360
	28.8	Professional conduct requirements	360
	28.9	Sources	360

PART D: MEETING TRAINING NEEDS WITHIN THE BUSINESS

29 Pre-period of recognised training — 365

	29.1	Introduction	365
	29.2	Recruiting during the academic stage	365

CONTENTS

	29.3	Sponsoring on the CPE/GDL and/or LPC	368
	29.4	During the CPE/GDL and/or LPC	373

30 Trainee solicitors — 381

	30.1	Introduction	381
	30.2	Understanding the firm as an organisation and the trainee's role	382
	30.3	Legal technical knowledge for the particular practice area	385
	30.4	Peripheral knowledge	387
	30.5	Business awareness	387
	30.6	Management skills	388

31 Qualified solicitors — 389

	31.1	Introduction	389
	31.2	Training for newly qualified solicitors	389
	31.3	Training for qualified solicitors	393
	31.4	Training for senior assistants and leading to partnership	401

32 Partners — 403

	32.1	Introduction	403
	32.2	New partners	403
	32.3	Partners generally	404
	32.4	Re-deployment of partners	406
	32.5	Partner relocation	406

33 Training for non-lawyer employees — 407

	33.1	Introduction	407
	33.2	SRA Code of Conduct and entity-based regulation	407
	33.3	Benefits of training	407
	33.4	Induction	408
	33.5	Types of training	408
	33.6	Projects	409

34 Overseas offices and overseas qualified lawyers — 410

	34.1	Introduction	410
	34.2	Overseas qualified lawyers	410
	34.3	Overseas offices	411

35 Clients — 416

	35.1	Introduction	416
	35.2	Issues to consider	416

35.3	Types of training	417
35.4	Practical arrangements	418

PART E: DELIVERING THE TRAINING PROGRAMME

36 How to design training — 423

36.1	Introduction	423
36.2	Forms of training	424
36.3	E-learning	434

37 How to deliver training — 440

37.1	Introduction	440
37.2	Presentation skills	441
37.3	Facilitation skills	441
37.4	Questioning skills	443
37.5	Feedback skills	444
37.6	Managing skills	445

38 How to organise and run training — 447

38.1	Introduction	447
38.2	Developing the training in the training programme	447
38.3	Organising the training session	461
38.4	Recording training information	470
38.5	Collecting and collating feedback from training	472
38.6	SRA administration requirements	473

39 How to evaluate training — 475

39.1	Introduction	475
39.2	Feedback about the training	476
39.3	Performance feedback	479

Index — 485

Foreword

How will the future providers of legal services be trained? That is the fundamental question which this book addresses. It does so at a time when legal education and training has been and is currently the subject of review. Moreover, the legal services market itself is changing faster than ever before.

In 2011 the Solicitors Regulation Authority (SRA), Bar Standards Board (BSB) and CILEx Regulation (then called ILEX Professional Standards) commissioned a fundamental review of the education and training requirements of individuals and entities delivering legal services. This review was known as the Legal Education and Training Review (LETR).

Together with Sir Mark Potter, I chaired the LETR's Consultation Steering Panel. The LETR Report, 'Setting Standards', was published in June 2013. Since then, regulators have been responding to its contents and publishing proposals for change, such as those from the SRA in its 'Training for Tomorrow: Assessing Competence' consultation paper.

Given that legal education and training is in a state of flux, I very much welcome this book which seeks to bring together all of the different facets of legal education and training for the benefit of those involved in this topic from day to day. It offers valuable guidance and is essential reading in a time when the legal services market is undergoing fundamental change.

The Legal Services Act (LSA) 2007 defined new regulatory objectives for a market which was already facing pressures from a number of sources – advances in technology, globalisation, demographic and social changes, demands for better value for money and the rise of consumerism. Now regulatory models are being questioned and certain regulators are seeking to move towards a more flexible, less prescriptive and more accessible form of regulation.

Some of these pressures will in due course affect how legal education and training is delivered.

For example, the long-term effects of the advances in technology on education and training have yet to be seen. Some commentators forecast that tasks previously carried out by highly trained humans may be carried out by less qualified individuals or by the latest technology. If this comes to pass, there will be many questions for those involved in legal education and training. How will legal experts acquire their expertise in their early careers? Will legal apprenticeships (see **Chapter 11**) become more popular? How will e-learning evolve? How will clients' increasingly demanding views on costs affect the cost of and manner of training? How important will ethics be, if the law is practised in new ways?

The need to maintain the quality of legal services delivered both nationally and internationally will remain. A high standard of education and training is crucial if the worldwide reputation of the current legal system and its lawyers is to be maintained. This reputation results in billions of pounds being contributed to the nation's economy. A deep understanding of training requirements and the ability to deliver them successfully, obtainable through reading this book, will support this overall objective of ensuring the quality of legal services.

A continuing challenge will be that of ensuring that the current system of education and training is fit for purpose and affordable for both the trainer and the trained. Growing numbers of students, escalating costs of qualification and difficulties in finding employment after qualification continue to cause concern. There is also the ongoing debate about how those who meet the required standards for practice should be identified and what routes to qualification should be followed. At the same time, ensuring the education and training options remain flexible will be essential if the widest possible pool of talent is to be available.

Generally, the existing regulatory framework will no doubt continue to be kept under review. There are at least twelve pieces of primary legislation, including LSA 2007, which govern the regulation of lawyers in England and Wales. It is not surprising, therefore, that one possible future change may be the consolidation of these. In addition, the case for reform of the Legal Services Act itself has recently been made by legal regulators following cross-regulator discussions facilitated by the Legal Services Board.

Meanwhile, the task of training the future providers of legal services remains. This book provides an essential route map for navigating a complicated and continually evolving legal landscape.

Dame Janet Gaymer DBE QC (Hon.)
2016

Introduction

The purpose of this book is to provide a resource for anyone involved in, or responsible for, training in a law firm or other organisation which provides legal services. For convenience, though, 'firm' is used as the generic term throughout the book to include private law firms, in-house legal departments, ABSs and so on.

It is intended as a guide – not an encyclopaedia or a text book – for anyone who needs to know something or to do something about training; whether they are new to training or an 'old hand'; whether they are in a dedicated training role or are a fee earner who has been corralled into giving training; and whether they are in a large law firm with a dedicated training department, a small firm which just needs a secretary to book CPD courses, or an in-house legal department with limited internal resources.

The book aims to provide guidance on all aspects of training that a firm may need to know about, all in one place. It does not need to be read from cover to cover, not least because different sections will be of use or interest to different people, and it can also just be 'dipped into' to find an answer.

Most importantly, it is not intended solely for training managers, those in dedicated training roles or those with any of the words 'training', 'development' or 'talent' in their job titles. Senior partners, managing partners, CEOs, COOs, finance directors, practice group heads, training partners, Training Principals, graduate recruitment partners, human resources – all are the intended readership of the book, as well as the training managers and training department staff. The reason? To have successful training in a firm requires the involvement of all these people.

Training is an investment. Even if no money passes hands and the training is done in-house, it is still a financial investment, simply because of the time invested by both the person attending the training and the person giving the training. Like any other investment a business makes, it should provide an identifiable return. How many firms, though, actually measure their return on investment (ROI) from training? How many firms understand that, just because the firm has a training programme, that does not guarantee a return? The ROI should be a workforce which can be utilised in the way that is needed for the business at a given time, and redeployed when the business need changes. That means that training should be informed by the firm's business strategy and aligned to its business plan. To achieve its objectives, the training also needs to be effective: that means being appropriately designed and delivered, not to mention efficiently administered so that it actually takes place and the intended attendees actually turn up. After all that, the effectiveness of the training needs to be evaluated, ideally against financial parameters, so that the ROI can be confirmed if not measured. If a firm is not doing this then it is wasting its investment in training, or to put it more bluntly, it is probably wasting its money.

To be fair, there is another reason for training: regulatory requirement. The Solicitors Regulation Authority (SRA) requires training at various levels in firms – trainee solicitor and post-qualification – and any organisation regulated by the SRA must train its staff to a level of competence appropriate to their work and level of responsibility, as well as complying with Principle 5 of the SRA Handbook to provide a proper standard of service to one's clients.

Understanding the regulatory requirements is not always easy, it has to be said – testament to which is the length of that section of the book! There has been a lot regulatory change in legal education and training since the Legal Education and Training Review, with more yet to come, and much confusion consequently. Understanding the new and proposed regulatory requirements is essential for good business planning. In fact, the way regulatory reform is going, the next edition of this book might be a lot slimmer!

There is another facet of training that may also be relevant for firms. In the post-Legal Services Act 2007 world, firms are able to employ non-solicitor lawyers, which can enhance the legal services the firm is able to offer its clients by the addition of that specialist expertise. However, employing a barrister, Chartered Legal Executive, licensed conveyancer, costs lawyer, patent attorney, trade mark attorney or notary gives rise to other training requirements in the firm, as well as regulatory and professional conduct obligations to add to the picture.

HOW TO USE THIS BOOK

This Handbook is divided into five distinct parts, with different audiences in mind.

Part A: Managing training in the business

The effectiveness of the training in a firm can either be assured or undermined by the commitment of management. This section is therefore geared to those responsible for managing the firm, and discusses: the training investment and the cultural challenges that may need to be overcome; the structure and ownership of training within the firm; how to develop and implement the training strategy; and the financial management of training.

Part B: Qualification as a solicitor in England and Wales

This rather large section deals with all the regulatory requirements in relation to qualifying, and maintaining the qualification, as a solicitor of England and Wales. It is divided into six sub-sections, as follows.

INTRODUCTION

- **B1: Regulation of Legal Education and Training** explains the regulatory authority and governing regulations for the qualification requirements. It also provides a summary of all the regulatory reforms of legal education and training since the Legal Education and Training Review, as well as the proposed future reforms known at the time of publication.
- **B2: Routes to qualification** describes the various routes to qualification available to aspiring solicitors at the time of publication: domestic, European directive, Qualified Lawyers Transfer Scheme and Legal Apprenticeships, as well as exemptions available by way of Equivalent Means.
- **B3: The academic stage requirements** explains the requirements for and features of the various options for satisfying the academic stage – Qualifying Law Degree, Exempting Law Degree or Conversion Course (Common Professional Examination or Graduate Diploma in Law).
- **B4: The vocational stage requirements** explains the requirements for and features of each of the components of the vocational stage: Legal Practice Course, Period of Recognised Training and Professional Skills Course.
- **B5: The requirements for qualification and admission** describes the education and training requirements and character and suitability requirements for qualification and admission, as well as the admission process itself.
- **B6: Post-qualification requirements** describes the requirements of the current CPD scheme, including the Continuing Competence option, as well as the SRA's Competence Statement and how the SRA intends it to be used.

Part C: Other qualified lawyer qualification requirements

For firms that employ or are considering employing a barrister, Chartered Legal Executive, licensed conveyancer, costs lawyer, patent attorney, trade mark attorney or notary, this section explains what each qualification means, what work (including reserved and regulated work) is permitted under the qualification, the regulatory authority, the requirements for the qualification, the CPD and professional conduct obligations which attach to the qualification, as well as the cost of (and requirements for) maintaining practising rights under the qualification.

Part D: Meeting training needs within the business

This section covers the different training needs in a firm at the various levels (from trainee, new qualifier or qualified assistant, to partnership, new partners and experienced partners) and how those training needs can be met. Given that a firm's investment in training actually starts before its trainees start in the firm, if it sponsors them on the Legal Practice Course, Common Professional Exam or Graduate Diploma in Law, Part D also considers how firms can maximise the benefit of that investment as early as possible. The section also covers training for non-lawyer employees, for overseas offices and overseas qualified lawyers, and also training for clients, which increasingly firms are expected to provide.

Part E: Delivering the training programme

This section is about the design and delivery of training, and is primarily intended to be of use to the firm's lawyers. Lawyers, being experts in law, often tend to presume that they are experts in everything – including training. Delivering effective training, however, is not something taught at law school. Since training delivered by a firm's lawyers can be the most valuable training, it is unfortunate if, through poor design or presentation skills, the training is less than effective. This section, therefore, provides a practical guide for anyone who has to design a training session or deliver training, particularly where they are not a training professional. For training managers and administrators, the section also provides guidance on how to manage the trainers, and on how to evaluate the effectiveness of the training delivered.

SECTIONS OF INTEREST ACCORDING TO JOB ROLE

Depending on the reader, the following sections might be of particular interest.

Senior partner/managing partner/CEO/COO	**Part A**; **Part B**, especially **Chapter 6**
Finance director	**Part B**, especially **Chapter 4**
Training Principal	**Section B1**; **Section B4**, especially **Chapters 15** and **16**; **Section B5**; **Part D**, **Chapter 30**
Practice area head	**Part A**; **Part B**, especially **Chapter 21**; **Part D**
Training partner	**Part A**, especially **Chapter 3**; **Part B**, especially **B5**, **B6** and **Chapter 6**; **Part D**; **Part E**
Solicitor supervising a trainee	**Part B**, especially **Chapter 15**
Solicitor delivering and/or designing training	**Part E**, especially **Chapters 36** and **37**
Solicitor	**Part B**, especially **Chapters 20** and **21**
Human Resources/Personnel/Talent Management	**Part A**; **Part B**, especially **Chapters 6, 20** and **21**; **Part C**, as applicable; **Part D**, especially **Chapter 29**
Training director/manager	**Part A**, especially **Chapter 3**; **Part B**; **Part C**, as applicable; **Part D** and **Part E**
Training administrator	**Part B**, as applicable; **Part D**; **Part E**, especially **Chapter 38**

Acknowledgments

I have been very fortunate in writing this book to have benefited from the wisdom, experience and expertise of many experts in legal education and training, in not only the solicitors' profession but also other lawyer professions, as well as in higher education. Without the generosity of these people in helping with my research, and in some cases also taking on the burden of reading and reviewing, this book would be a far leaner offering.

I must give special thanks to Dame Janet Gaymer for being so kind in writing the foreword to the book. Special thanks are also due to Simon Howley of CMS Cameron McKenna, David Day of King & Wood Mallesons, and Penny Newman of Lewis Silkin, each of whom has been an invaluable 'critical friend' – sounding board, critic and reviewer – and to Robert Mowbray of Taylor Mowbray for allowing me to base **Chapter 4** on his own work on budgeting for training.

I am very grateful to the many firms who have been so generous in giving me the benefit of their thoughts and ideas so that I could understand current training practices in firms, the issues that firms have to grapple with and what would be useful to them in a legal training handbook. In particular, I would like to thank: John Cook of Bird & Bird; Kevin Bell of Clifford Chance; Jean Young of Goodman Derrick; Patrick McCann of Herbert Smith Freehills; John Muncey of Wedlake Bell; Suzanne Todd of Withers; Catherine Innes of Trowers & Hamlins; Charles Clarke and Wendy Tomlinson of Linklaters; and Hannah Kozlova Lindsay of Berwin Leighton Paisner.

The chapters in **Part B** have been reviewed by a number of people whose experience and expertise have been invaluable in making sense of what at times has seemed like a regulatory quagmire. They are: Iain Miller of Bevan Brittan on the regulatory framework; Alison Wells of BPP Law School on Legal Apprenticeships (the funding regime in particular); Professor Jane Ching of Nottingham Law School on the legal education and reforms; Graham Ferris of Nottingham Law School on the academic stage; Amanda Fancourt of City University London on the LPC; Jenny Crewe of the Law Society on the Qualified Lawyers Transfer Scheme route to qualification; Julie Mamou of the Law Society on EU lawyer routes to qualification; and Julie Brannan, the SRA's director of education and training, for her help with my queries on the training regulations and the chapter on Legal Apprenticeships. Any errors remaining must be laid entirely at my own door.

ACKNOWLEDGMENTS

In writing **Part C** I could not have done without the generous input of a number of individuals who helped me to understand their particular profession and its qualification requirements. Although many read and commented on my drafts, I do not mean to infer that these chapters have been signed off or endorsed by the relevant body, and any errors remain my responsibility. Nonetheless, I am extremely grateful to: Vanessa Davies and Christopher Adiole of the Bar Standards Board; Patrick Maddams and Struan Campbell of the Honourable Society of the Inner Temple; Noel Inge of CILEx Law School; Stephen Ward of the Council for Licensed Conveyancers; Simon Cooper of Adamson Jones; Andrea Brewster of the Chartered Institute of Patent Attorneys; Mark Anderson of Anderson Law; Lynn Plumbley of the Costs Lawyer Standards Board; and Neil Turpin, clerk in the Court of Faculties. Writing these chapters gave me enormous respect for what is required to gain these qualifications.

I would like to say a special thank you to Ashley Atkins, a modern-day 'Q', for his help, knowledge and insight on all things technological, and to Janice Barnes for her unstinting patience in typing what turned out to be a (very) long book, and for her exceptional skill in deciphering my hieroglyphic amendments.

I am also very grateful to the team at Law Society Publishing: Janet Noble and Paul Milner, who made it a pleasure to write the book; and Josephine Gibbons and her excellent team of copy editor, proof-reader and indexer, who actually got the book to publication.

Lastly, I could not have completed what turned out to be a much bigger project than I had thought without the unfailing patience and support of my long-suffering husband, Peter – thank you!

Melissa Hardee
2016

Abbreviations

ABS	Alternative Business Structure
ACL	Association of Costs Lawyers
APL	Accreditation of Prior Learning
BIS	Department for Business, Innovation and Skills
BLP	Business Law and Practice
BPTC	Bar Professional Training Course
BSB	Bar Standards Board
BVC	Bar Vocational Course
CILEx	Chartered Institute of Legal Executives
CIPA	Chartered Institute of Patent Attorneys
CLC	Council for Licensed Conveyancers
CLSB	Costs Lawyer Standards Board
COIC	Council of the Inns of Court
CPD	Continuing Professional Development
CPE	Common Professional Examination
CRB	Criminal Records Bureau
DBS	Disclosure and Barring Service
ECJ	European Court of Justice
ELD	Exempting Law Degree
ETC	Education and Training Committee
FHEQ	Framework for Higher Education Qualifications in England, Wales and Northern Ireland
FSA	Financial Services Authority
FSMA 2000	Financial Services and Markets Act 2000
GDL	Graduate Diploma in Law
GFTD	Graduate Fast-Track Diploma
HEI	higher education institution
IELTS	International English Language Testing System
IIP	Investors in People
IPReg	Intellectual Property Regulation Board
IPS	ILEX Professional Standards
ITMA	Institute of Trade Mark Attorneys
IVA	Individual Voluntary Arrangement
JASB	Joint Academic Stage Board

ABBREVIATIONS

KM	knowledge management
KPI	key performance indicator
LETR	Legal Education and Training Review
LMS	learning management system
LPC	Legal Practice Course
LSA 2007	Legal Services Act 2007
LSB	Legal Services Board
LSET	legal services education and training
MCQ	multiple choice question
MCT	Multiple Choice Test
MLR	money laundering regulations
MCS1	Management Course Stage 1
MCS2	Management Course Stage 2
NLH	notional learning hour
NPP	New Practitioners' Programme
OLC	Office of Legal Complaints
OSCE	Objective Structured Clinical Examination
PCR	Professional Conduct and Regulation
PCRE	Practising Certificate Renewal Exercise
PDP	personal development plan
PEB	Patent Examination Board
PHDL	Professional Higher Diploma in Law
PLP	Property Law and Practice
PRB	Patent Regulation Board
PRT	Period of Recognised Training
PSC	Professional Skills Course
QAA	Quality Assurance Agency
QCF	Qualifications and Credit Framework
QLD	Qualifying Law Degree
QLTR	Qualified Lawyers Transfer Regulations
QLTS	Qualified Lawyers Transfer Scheme
QLTT	Qualified Lawyers Transfer Test
REL	Registered European Lawyer
RFL	Registered Foreign Lawyer
SAR	Solicitors' Accounts Rules 2011
SLA	service level agreement
SQE	Solicitors Qualification Examination
SRA	Solicitors Regulation Authority
SWOT	strengths, weaknesses, opportunities and threats
T4T	Training for Tomorrow
TLST	Technical Legal Skills Test
TMRB	Trade Mark Regulation Board
TTC	time to count
UK NARIC	UK National Recognition Information Centre

PART A

Managing training in the business

Those who manage law firms these days are only too aware that managing a law firm is nothing more nor less than running a business. Whether the firm has the traditional flat partnership structure or something more innovative, such as an Alternative Business Structure, the bottom line is the same: everyone involved in the business needs to have a clear financial focus. Activities such as training can sometimes seem peripheral – even unimportant in the greater scheme of things. If those involved in managing the business have no experience of training (the days of their own training probably having receded into the mists of time) or, worse, no interest, then the attitude of management might be to 'leave it to the training department' at best, or 'do we need to worry about it?' at worst, particularly given the imminent removal of a minimum Continuing Professional Development hour requirement.

If a firm is going to make any sort of investment in training, it should make that investment in the way it makes any other investment: by identifying the benefit the investment is intended to bring, carrying out the necessary analysis and 'due diligence' first, and then making sure that the investment that has been made brings the required return. In other words, investing in training should be a way of addressing business needs and the return on that investment should be able to be measured.

Part A discusses the considerations for firms in investing in training:

- the reasons for investing in training (**Chapter 1**);
- how training should be structured and 'owned' within the firm (**Chapter 2**);
- how to develop and implement an appropriate training strategy (**Chapter 3**); and
- the financial management of training (**Chapter 4**).

CHAPTER 1

The training investment

1.1	Introduction	1.4	Challenges to the case for training
1.2	The case for training	1.5	Maximising the investment of training
1.3	Where the investment in training needs to be made	1.6	Developing the right culture

1.1 INTRODUCTION

Why should a firm invest in training? It is not a foregone conclusion. A firm could quite easily recruit 'fully-formed' qualified lawyers and avoid the need to train. And given that Continuing Professional Development (CPD) requirements can now be satisfied without having to meet any minimum hours requirement, the question needs to be asked.

1.2 THE CASE FOR TRAINING

One reason a firm should invest in training, even if it does recruit only fully-formed lawyers, is because the law that they practise changes. So, at the most basic level, the firm's lawyers would need to keep up to date with the law. The lawyers could do this by taking responsibility for their own learning, and doing any necessary reading, which is fine but only up to a point. If the firm wants to present a 'seamless' front of consistent expertise, however, can it be sure that all its lawyers will read what will keep them up to date and that they will understand it correctly and interpret the impact or significance of the change in the law for that practice? What if some of the firm's lawyers do not do this? Can the firm be sure it is meeting its responsibilities under Principle 5 of the Solicitors Regulation Authority (SRA) Handbook to provide a proper standard of service to the firm's clients? If not, the firm is then at risk.

Just to expand this scenario: when would the firm expect its busy lawyers to do the reading? In their own time, might be the answer. But what if the amount of reading that keeping up to date requires imposes a strain on lawyers, which then has an impact on their performance? What if the lawyers have questions about what they are reading, and if they are doing the reading in their own time – who is there to ask (other than Google ...)? They could ask someone in the office the next day, but that would take away from the fee-earning time of both the lawyer and the colleague being asked ... and therein lies the dilemma.

Extending this scenario may appear contrived, which of course it is, but the point it is making is that, even at the level of keeping up with the law, there are issues of consistency, as well as time- and cost-efficiency, that a training session on the topic of the new development in the law can address conveniently and cost-effectively, and give the firm comfort that everyone who needs to be has been brought up to speed.

However, training is not just about keeping up to date with changes in the law: it is also about acquiring the knowledge and skills needed to do the job, to remedy poor or under-performance, to take on new or further responsibilities to develop one's career and realise one's potential, and to develop the attitudes and behaviour to be a professional and a 'good citizen' of the firm.

A myth that should be dispelled is that training is a formal training session. It is not. In fact, any of the training aims just listed, whether developmental or remedial, could be achieved without any formal training session at all. It is just that firms think that that is what training is, and then waste money only doing training this way.

In an ideal world there would be no need for training in the formal training session sense for law firms. No need for training departments, training managers or training programmes, because lawyers would learn on the job. They would observe role models, emulate and practise what they observe, and receive instruction, guidance and feedback. This is how it worked previously when not even a law degree was required, just five years of articles. Training then was a proper apprenticeship, with few aids other than case reports, legislation, reference books and role models. Were the lawyers who went through this training any the worse for it? On the contrary. Interestingly, we have nearly gone full circle with the introduction of Legal Apprenticeships as a route to qualification as a solicitor.[1]

1.2.1 The reality of practice

The world of legal practice has changed dramatically since the time of five-year articles. The lot of the generalist is in decline, with a simultaneous rise of the specialist. And a completely technology-driven way of working has arisen, not to mention the explosion in the size and international dimension of some law firms. What all this means is that one-to-one training just does not work for a lot of law firms, not only because of gearing levels but also because of the shortened timescales and increased expectations brought about by technology. Another consequence of technology is that meetings with clients are fewer because so much is able

---

[1] See **Chapter 11**.

to be done by email or conference call, which means the training opportunities that trainees and junior lawyers had from attending client meetings with partners or senior lawyers and learning by observing are far fewer.

Email has made response times immediate, which the use of Blackberries and smart phones has only exacerbated. A more competitive legal services market has put a downward pressure on costs, so overheads have to be kept lean, and time is the one luxury that few solicitors have. So, how does a firm train its lawyers in this frenetic, financially hard-pressed environment, with a constant nagging concern of protecting the firm's professional indemnity cover?

1.2.2 Training divorced from practice

The solution for firms to these challenges has been to move from the one-to-one training to 'mass', often generic, training, as the most time-efficient and cost-effective way of providing lawyers with instruction in what they need to know and be able to do. The benefits are that supervisor time is freed up; consistency is assured (not all supervisors will be as good as each other in supervising, or will teach the same things). However, there is a flaw in this as a solution, which is the increasing distance of training from the job, and from those in the firm with knowledge and experience of the firm's practice, and of how to practise. Assistants are being trained, but not necessarily by those for whom they are working or by those who have recent experience (if any) of legal practice. If the training is delivered by someone outside the firm, the firm's lawyers may not necessarily be trained in the way the firm actually works.

Does it matter? It does if you believe that a firm's most valuable asset is the knowledge and expertise of its lawyers. Not passing on the knowledge and expertise residing in the firm, but relying on the more generic knowledge and expertise of someone outside the firm to do the training, means that the training is not going to be as effective or as valuable as if it had been delivered in-house. (The interaction of training and knowledge management (KM) is discussed further at **2.6**.) The counter-argument to this is that in the absence of anything else some training, even if not bespoke, is better than no training at all.

1.2.3 Imperatives

Principle 5 of the SRA Handbook requires solicitors to provide a proper standard of service to clients and Outcome 7.6 of the SRA Code of Conduct 2011 requires solicitors to 'train individuals working in the firm to maintain a level of competence appropriate to their work and level of responsibility'. Even aside from these regulatory imperatives, from the practical consideration of the firm's professional indemnity cover it is essential that a firm is sure that all its lawyers are of an appropriate and competent standard, and have the wherewithal to carry out the work at the level at which they are expected to perform. Consequently, it is very difficult to ignore the reality that focused, timely and effective training is an important way for a firm to ensure competence.

It is these adjectives describing the training that is needed which are key: focused, timely and effective. A firm in which training is not focused, not timely or does not achieve its objectives is wasting its investment.

Having said that, there will be training which a firm has to invest in, whether it likes it or not, because of regulatory requirements. Admittedly, these regulatory requirements are fewer, due to the SRA's 'Red Tape Initiative'[2] in recent years, which has seen the demise of the Management Course Stage 1, for example. However, for the training that the SRA does still require – the Professional Skills Course, for example – the trick is not merely to tick the box, but to think about how to fit the training as closely as possible to the firm's business plan, so that the firm's business is being benefited at the same time as it is meeting its regulatory responsibilities.

It is also true that sometimes a firm needs to invest in training which its employees expect the firm to provide, or as incentives for recruitment or retention. However, recruiting and retaining good trainees and assistants should be key business objectives of any firm. What a firm needs to avoid is using training as 'window-dressing', which can backfire and damage a firm's credibility if the reality turns out to be different from the blurb and ends up being a disincentive for potential recruits, or a reason for leaving for those already in the firm.

1.3 WHERE THE INVESTMENT IN TRAINING NEEDS TO BE MADE

The greatest investment in training is likely to happen at the trainee and junior assistant level. The Period of Recognised Training, like the Training Contract before it, is an apprenticeship and is concerned with training and development.

The best way to understand where the investment in training needs to happen is to picture a pyramid, or even a wedding cake:

- In terms of the legal technical knowledge needed for practice, the greatest training need at the base of the pyramid is for trainees; the next greatest need is for new qualifiers; the legal technical training needed for assistants who have two years' post-qualified experience or more is smaller still, and so on until the top, where the technical legal training needs for partners is an apex rather than a layer – miniscule and probably just a requirement for updates on legal developments.
- Similarly, practice skills (i.e. the skills needed to apply legal technical knowledge to practise) have the greatest training need at the trainee level and the least at senior assistant and partner level.
- In terms of management skills and more business-focused knowledge and expertise, the required investment in training is the reverse: most of the training

---

[2] See **Chapter 6**.

will be needed at the partner level, where the training becomes more bespoke, with least at the trainee level, where it is more about creating business awareness and threshold self-management skills, and can be more generic.

Figure 1.1 – Investment in training

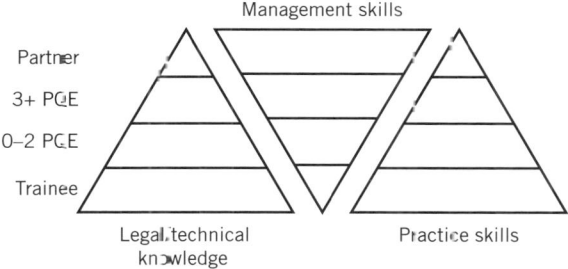

1.4 CHALLENGES TO THE CASE FOR TRAINING

1.4.1 The challenge of no CPD hour requirement

As is explained in **Chapter 20**, solicitors currently have an alternative option to satisfying the CPD requirements without undertaking a minimum number of hours of CPD activity, and from 1 November 2016 this will be the case for all solicitors under a new Continuing Competence regime. The prospect of not having to undertake 16 hours of CPD activity may make the hearts of many law firm managers sing. However, as the old adage goes, 'be careful what you wish for': although solicitors may not need to do 16 hours of CPD activity, it would be a mistake to think that Continuing Competence is a carte blanche for doing no training at all. Principle 5 of the SRA Handbook is what the SRA is 'hanging its hat on' to ensure that firms will continue to provide training for their lawyers – and other members of the firm. What all firms will need to have under the new Continuing Competence regime – and need to have now if they are adopting the Continuing Competence approach leading up to 1 November 2016 – is the culture to support the discipline and systems that a Continuing Competence approach requires.

Any solicitors who think that Continuing Competence means no training are going to have to be able to justify to the SRA that they are nonetheless delivering a proper standard of service to their clients, and their firms are going to have to be able to demonstrate that as well.

1.4.2 The challenge of an economic downturn

In an economic downturn, the confident commitment to invest in things such as training and KM can quickly disappear, and anything that is not fee earning becomes a luxury or non-essential. Proper business planning, which should include proper financial management of training (see **Chapter 4**), should inform any decisions to cut functions and services arising from difficult economic times. It is simplistic to regard anything non-fee earning as expendable. For example, giving in to the temptation to cast off a training officer may mean that the firm then no longer has anyone who knows or understands anything about the firm's regulatory obligations regarding trainees.

Resisting this temptation is most difficult in the traditional law firm environment where fee earning is the bread and butter of the firm. However, expertise in more than fee earning is needed if a firm is going to be successful. Of course, there is always the 'never waste a good recession' ethos – an opportunity to do some culling that might have been needed for some time. However, if a firm will not get rid of its best rainmakers, who would be difficult to replace, it should be just as wary of dispensing with other talented experts in the firm, be they in training, KM or marketing, just because they are not fee earners. A particularly 'Neanderthal' view is the one that, if fee earners have to be made redundant, so should support staff. A better approach is to look at what training the firm cannot afford *not* to have, and then ensure it has the resources needed to deliver that training. This is discussed in **Chapter 4**, as well as the importance of having and using training business plans and training budgets as management tools. If used properly, these tools can prevent a firm shooting itself in the foot by offloading the very people it needs to carry out its 'vital' functions. Without appropriate metrics to measure the effectiveness (or not) of the training programmes, training can be an easy target for cutbacks.

What also needs to be remembered is that employees who need training (and trainees and junior assistants immediately spring to mind), but whose training is stopped because of budget cuts, become a moribund resource. Apart from the fact that compulsory regulatory training requirements (see **Part B**) do not stop just because there is an economic downturn or recession, training within the firm generally should not cease if the firm is to recoup the investment it has already made in recruiting its trainees and junior assistants, who need to be trained and developed in order to be able to work profitably. If anything, running training when the firm is less busy can provide an ideal opportunity to train those who need training – making a virtue out of necessity.

1.5 MAXIMISING THE INVESTMENT OF TRAINING

A firm can invest in top-class training which will achieve the training and development needs of its business; it can recruit competent and talented individuals to design, run and even deliver training. However, if its lawyers do not turn up to the training, or when they do turn up approach it negatively, then the investment is not going to achieve what it could or should.

There has to be a commitment to training within the firm, and at all levels, as well as a culture which supports and promotes training. Quite simply, if the managers of the business do not take training seriously (they just 'sign the cheques'), why should anyone else?

A firm would not pay lip service to billing or client care, so why would it pay lip service to training that has been identified through a proper training needs analysis as necessary to take forward the firm's business objectives? Yet firms do, and the evidence of this can be seen at all levels:

- **At assistant level**: Assistants who believe (because this is the culture of the firm) that the only thing that matters is billable hours, and that time away from their desk for a training session is 'dead time' and not in their interest to do it. It is only because the firm pays lip service to training that they put down their name for the training session in the first place – but then either do not turn up or cancel at the last moment because of 'client work'. This may be quite genuine: 'client work' may have come up. However, how often is it that a person cannot be unavailable for an hour, half a day or even a full day? Assistants take holidays and they have other commitments which can make them unavailable – even client meetings. Why then can they not be 'unavailable' because they are attending training? It should be a similar commitment: only a reason that would make them cancel a client meeting should justify cancelling training.
- **At supervisor level**: The senior assistant or partner who is supervising the assistant who is due to attend training, and tells the assistant that he or she just cannot be spared from whatever job it is that he or she is working on – on principle. It is from this 'role model' that assistants learn and develop the same agnostic attitude to training (and probably to KM, marketing and any other 'non-fee earning' activity). The likelihood is that the senior assistant or partner was pulled out of training him or herself at the last minute when he or she was junior – a self-perpetuating attitude.
- **At manager level**: The practice area or department head who refuses to deal with the serial offenders within the practice area or department when the frazzled training manager/Professional Support Lawyer (PSL) raises the problem that, yet again, there were only two attendees for the training session out of the planned 16 or whatever number had confirmed attendance. Another scenario is the practice area or department head who takes to task the senior assistant or partner whose billable time is down because he or she has been spending 'non-fee earning' time in giving training.

A variation is the partner who is a Trainee Supervisor but who refuses to 'waste' time talking to the trainee at all about the trainee's performance, problems and so on, on the deeply disturbing pretext that 'I was thrown in at the deep end and had to survive; why should it be any different for you?'

There is the management team or managing partner or even chief executive who will not agree to have 'non-fee earning' time recognised as something beneficial to the firm's business and given its own classification for time-recording; who will not take account of contributions made to things like training and KM in the calculations of bonuses or promotion criteria – just billable hours and perhaps client activities.

MANAGING TRAINING IN THE BUSINESS

There is also the training partner, responsible for deciding what training goes on, who recognises that a certain group of assistants need drafting training but decides that the full-day session proposed by the training manager is beyond the pale, and possibly the budget, and that the drafting training will have to be done in an hour because the loss of fee-earning time cannot be justified. Learning how to draft in an hour? Might as well save the time and the money.

The tendency to see training as a necessary evil rather than a serious development tool which adds to the firm's profitability may be generational: those in senior management posts in firms may have been thrown in the ubiquitous deep end but managed to float to the surface. However, times – as well as training needs – have changed.

Where it all starts and ends is with management: if those who are responsible for managing the business do not lead, no one else will follow, and who, wanting a career in the firm, is going to be brave enough to strike out against the accepted lines of rewarded behaviour within a firm's culture? If any of these attitudes exist in a firm the investment in training is going to be compromised, and to a fairly considerable extent.

1.6 DEVELOPING THE RIGHT CULTURE

If a firm is serious about ensuring that it obtains the benefits from its investment in training, then it needs to tackle these sorts of attitudes on several levels, starting at the top in order to develop the right culture.

1.6.1 At management level

The managers of the firm's business need to be explicit about their commitment to the firm's training strategy and training programme (discussed in **Chapter 3**), both to the partners themselves as well as to the firm's employees as a whole. Words are not going to be enough – there is always the risk of pronouncements and commitments being seen as pseudo-management if there is nothing more. So, the words need to be underpinned by various policies and actions. Depending on the general management culture of the particular firm and the appetite of those with management responsibility, the options range from the benevolent to the authoritarian as outlined below.

1.6.1.1 Rewarding commitment to training

Rewarding commitment to training can be done in various ways, for example by:

- having 'non-fee earning' codes in the time-recording system for giving training, attending training, coaching and mentoring, Why not go further and, instead of giving it a 'non-fee earning' code, classify training as 'investment'

time, in the same way as may already be done for practice development, client entertaining and so on? The code could also be used for KM and similar activities;
- including 'non-fee earning' time in any calculations for bonuses or other financial and other rewards;
- setting targets of a certain number of hours per annum to be spent in giving and receiving training;
- including evidence of commitment to training in the criteria for promotion within the firm and within the firm's competence framework, if it has one.

1.6.1.2 Changing performance measurement

Change the measurement of performance so that:

- training is regarded as a natural part of a partner's role – be it delivering formal training sessions, supervising trainees or coaching and mentoring assistants – or junior partners for that matter;
- it is not just whether a partner attends or gives training that is taken into account in the partner's own appraisal, but also whether the partner releases and supports those who work for him or her to attend training, for instance;
- giving training is built into the firm's competency framework at the appropriate levels of senior assistant looking to partnership, and partner level;
- any 'senior' partner who believes he or she does not need training is required to pass on his or her knowledge and expertise by giving training sessions, giving one-to-one training in a coaching role or contributing to the firm's KM systems.

1.6.1.3 'Punishing' lack of commitment to training

A lack of commitment to training can be redressed by implementing policies to:

- recoup from practice area or department budgets the cost of cancelled training, or of training where assistants or partners did not turn up without justifiable reason (what 'justifiable' encompasses is determined by a predetermined list of acceptable reasons);
- have individual training records considered in performance appraisals, and to have lack of attendance by an individual without justifiable reason (see above) treated as unacceptable behaviour – as bad citizenship.

1.6.1.4 Imposing responsibility

The heads of practice areas can be required by management to:

- take responsibility for ensuring attendance at training by the practice area or department's members, and to deal with offenders (a 'cancellation fee' charged against the department's budget could help to avoid serial offending);

- set up a mentoring scheme, so that each member of the practice area or department has a mentor who meets with their mentee on a regular basis. This is not just about making the most of the investment in training; it is also about making the most of the firm's investment in its people: staff retention is very important to this, and mentoring may be the difference between someone who is disgruntled leaving because he or she feels that no one cares, and staying because someone took the time to talk to him or her.

1.6.2 At practice area level

Practice areas need to implement the directives from management described above. To encourage a culture within the practice area or department itself, however, the head of the practice area or department can also:

- set regular training sessions for updates on legal or practice developments or to discuss particular issues that have arisen in the practice area's work, which everyone attends, from partner to trainee;
- require or encourage (depending on their position on the management spectrum) partners and senior assistants to give practice area-specific training wherever possible, as opposed to using external trainers;
- ask for regular reports on training attendance – and look at them to identify any serial absentees, and then speak to the offender to ask why he or she has not been attending. If the offender is unable to give a satisfactory reason, then it could be put on his or her Human Resources (HR) record, or set for discussion at his or her next appraisal or a sooner discussion with his or her supervisor;
- require partners or senior assistants who wish to pull a trainee or assistant off training because of client work, to clear it with the head of the practice area first.

1.6.3 At partner level

Apart from implementing the policies which management might impose, partners individually and collectively can also foster the appropriate culture by:

- encouraging and promoting training within the firm and within their practice area;
- taking their supervising responsibilities seriously – and undertaking training themselves in how to supervise, how to coach and how to give feedback should they need training;
- taking on a mentoring role – and taking it seriously – and undertaking training in how to mentor, if that is needed;
- agreeing to give training sessions in their area of expertise – and undertaking 'train the trainer' training, if needed;
- making sure when they do an appraisal, that they look at and discuss the appraisee's training record since the last appraisal: what the appraisee should

have done, what in fact the appraisee has done and if there is a deficiency in performance notwithstanding training, finding out why.

The point is that people should be taking individual responsibility for their own learning and development if they are being a 'good citizen' of the firm. If they need training and development, and are not undertaking it, then quite simply they are not fulfilling their obligations to their employer. Equally, a firm as an Authorised Body, as well as its managers and employees, 'must at all times ensure that they act in accordance with the requirements of the SRA's regulatory arrangements as they apply to them'.[3] Under entity-based regulation this means a firm is responsible for training 'individuals working in the firm to maintain a level of competence appropriate to their work and level of responsibility'.[4]

1.6.4 Firm-wide

Even if there is a commitment to attending training, lawyers possess human frailty like anyone else, and therefore with the best will in the world may need to be protected from themselves, for which reason policies along the following lines might be useful:

- compulsory attendance at training unless prior consent has been given by a manager, who is in turn answerable to management, not to attend;
- non-attendance only allowed for sickness, holiday, unexpected delay over which he or she has no control (not the cappuccino machine in Starbucks being slow; but perhaps the tube line shutting down because of a security alert) or urgent client work, which is then approved by the practice area head, permission to be sought in advance where possible;
- where giving notice in advance is not possible apologies are given, with the reason, as soon as possible afterwards;
- the appraisee's training record must be produced at appraisal (under the Continuing Competence regime being introduced from 1 November 2016,[5] all solicitors will be required to keep a record of the training and development needs they have identified, how they have met those needs and how effective the steps taken to address those needs were);
- attendance at external seminars or functions will not be authorised if the individual is a habitual non-attender at internal training.

The aim is not to impose a police state but to effect a change in attitude and behaviour.

---

[3] SRA Code of Conduct, Outcome 7.6.
[4] SRA Practice Framework Rules, rule 19.
[5] See **Chapter 20**.

CHAPTER 2

The structure and ownership of training within the firm

2.1	Introduction	2.5	Responsibility of the training function
2.2	Structure		
2.3	Ownership	2.6	Interaction of training and knowledge management
2.4	Management responsibility		

2.1 INTRODUCTION

The solicitors' profession is nothing if not diverse: in type of firm, size and focus; the range of areas of practice; the types of in-house legal departments, which range from those in large companies to national or local government legal departments; the range of vehicles for delivering legal services, from the traditional law firm partnership to the externally-owned, and even listed, Alternative Business Structures (ABSs). Meeting the training needs arising from this diversity is a challenge, and not easily met by 'a one size fits all' approach, which is a particular dilemma for the regulator that regulates a diverse but nonetheless single generic qualification.

2.1.1 Law firms

The following are huge generalisations, but they aim to highlight how differences in training needs can arise:

- For the small or 'high-street' firm, resource is usually the main issue. This sort of firm may have a generalist or a specialist practice. Because of resource issues (time and staff), such a firm may not recruit trainees, or, if it does, it does so on an 'as needed' basis.
- For medium-sized firms, resources will not normally have an impact so much on trainee recruitment as on whether to have dedicated support, such as training

managers or a training department. These firms will also not necessarily have the critical mass to justify focused training for, say, trainees or newly qualified assistants.
- For large firms, such as City firms, large national firms and international firms, recruitment of trainees will usually take place up to three years in advance, and the firm will normally sponsor its future trainees through the Legal Practice Course (LPC) and even a conversion course,[1] as well as perhaps paying something towards living expenses. This type of firm has the size of practice and number of staff which can justify dedicated support functions: training, knowledge management (KM), and marketing, to name a few. The large firm is also likely to outsource training more than small or medium-sized firms, simply because it can afford to do so.

2.1.2 In-house legal departments

In-house legal departments vary in their training structure and support, depending on the organisation to which they belong: corporate, government department or local authority, for example. Like the smaller partnership, in-house lawyers tend to be more general practitioner than 'specialist', although this depends on the organisation. For many in-house legal departments, it is not feasible to recruit trainees for the simple reason that the prescribed range of experience may not be able to be provided within the department. One way in-house legal departments are able to obtain more junior 'hands' is by secondment arrangements with the firms that act for them: as part of the firm's service to the client, the firm will send its trainees to the client for a period. This means the in-house legal department (unless it is authorised as an Authorised Training Provider – see **Chapter 15**) has the benefit of having trainees but without the burden of the regulation. A further liberation that in-house solicitors may have compared to their colleagues in practice, and which is relevant to training resources, is that in-house solicitors who do not practise reserved areas of law and do not hold themselves out as solicitors do not need to have practising certificates. Without a practising certificate, regulator-imposed training requirements, such as Continuing Professional Development (CPD), do not apply.

2.1.3 Alternative Business Structures

ABSs have similar training needs to those of the small, medium or large firm model, depending on the size of the ABS. However, they may also have specific training needs arising out of the composition of the legal and other services they deliver and the scope of their business.

---

[1] Common Professional Examination or Graduate Diploma in Law (see **Chapter 13**).

2.2 STRUCTURE

For training to be successful and achieve its learning objectives it needs not only to be well designed and competently delivered, it also needs to be properly managed and supported by efficient administration and support. Lawyers can be dismissive of management and administration, and think that these are things that can be done in a matter of minutes, or 'on the back of an envelope'. If a firm is going to get the most out of its investment in training, however, it has to have an effective training function. This can range from a 'one-man band' – a secretary in a small firm – to a dedicated training department which, in addition to looking after training administration, may also take responsibility for the development, design and delivery of training within the firm – and everything in between.

What a firm's management must decide is the best structure for delivering and supporting training in the firm. This is going to depend on resources, the firm's ethos and culture, and what is there already. A firm may not be able to justify a dedicated training department, but if it has a committed Training Principal who is able to look after the strategic and tactical responsibilities and a competent administrator who has the capacity to deal with the operational aspects, then that should be all that is needed. However, a large firm with a number of offices may need a central training department to look after delivery of training across the firm.

Whatever structure is used, there are certain issues that bear consideration:

- Split function: In some firms, the training function can end up being a bit of a hybrid, with the HR department or graduate recruitment team taking some responsibility for skills training because of its involvement with trainees, and a training manager, training department or even individual practice groups looking after legal technical training. Hybrid structures are fine if the areas of responsibility are clearly demarcated, and there is coordination of the two areas with training responsibility. If, however, the reason for the split function is simply because the managers of the business have not been able to decide who should 'own' training in the firm because it is too political and too fraught (post-merger is a common scenario for this happening) then there can be potential for territorial warfare. Failing to structure training responsibility appropriately in this sort of situation is nothing other than a cop-out on the part of management.
- Satellite model: In some firms, individual practice areas will take responsibility for the training of their assistants, and do it very well too. Any attempt to centralise control of training may therefore meet with resistance. However, the satellite model, without more, does not lend itself to a coherent firm-wide strategy – the 'more' being the need for consistency with the firm-wide approach, while still meeting individual practice area need. It can also be difficult to assure prudent spending if the practice area has its own training budget to spend as it wishes. Again, this is a difficult decision for the managers

of the business because it is likely to put someone's nose out of joint – but that is not a reason for not making a decision.

If there is to be a split of responsibility between soft skills and legal technical training or between centrally-led and practice area-led training, then management should at least ensure that there are effective channels of communication which bridge the split, so that each side of the split is co-operating and delivering what the firm needs. If the split becomes more of an issue than the training, the firm has a problem – and the wrong structure.

What a firm should want to have is a structure that provides an overview of all training taking place in the firm, in order to ensure appropriate and effective deployment of training resources, not to mention best use of training budgets. The structure should also support localised training in practice areas or departments, and encourage 'local' initiatives which meet the specific needs of individual practice areas, and therefore keep training close to practice. As lawyers are not going to be training experts, there also needs to be appropriate expert support available to fee earners who are designing and delivering training. So, in simple terms, what the training structure needs to provide is:

- oversight for training planning and budgetary purposes;
- practice involvement and delivery;
- training expertise for design and delivery.

There is no one model which will be right for every firm, and much depends on the resources already available, as well as the culture of training – and co-operation – within the firm. However, if there is no overview in the first place to check that the training which is happening is in line with the firm's training programme (which, in turn, is in line with the firm's training strategy and training business plan), time and money can be wasted. Equally, if practice areas are not involved in designing and/or delivering training, the training may be out of context, and there is a risk of the training having little relevance for practice. Likewise, if there is no training expertise available in order to assist with the design and delivery of training, then there is the risk that the training may be ineffective or at least less effective than it could – and should – have been.

As a minimum, a firm needs someone to keep central records, to book training, make logistical arrangements, arrange payments, liaise with regulators, and so on. It may also need dedicated expertise to oversee the operational, and carry out the strategic, responsibilities involved in managing and running training in the firm.

2.3 OWNERSHIP

If a firm has more than one office, an important issue is going to be who 'owns' training in the firm, or who drives it. In other words, is the firm a single unit for training purposes, with the firm's training needs being addressed as a whole; or is it a collection of independent satellites, each doing their own thing? Which it is will be determined by whether:

- each office has its own business strategy and objectives (i.e. a sort of franchise situation); or
- the firm is a homogeneous whole in terms of its business strategy, perhaps with slightly different permutations in different offices to take account of local needs and jurisdictional differences.

If the former, then each office will need to carry out its own training needs analysis (see **3.4**) to develop its own training programme and deliver its own training; if the latter, there will need to be agreement about a common approach to training, agreement as to where the driver for this should be, and agreed differences, if appropriate.

Even where a firm has only one office, 'ownership' as between the centre and the practice areas will still need to be worked out.

2.4 MANAGEMENT RESPONSIBILITY

This ties in to the question of who should have management responsibility for the training function within the firm: should it be those who manage the business (in a non-training expert sense) in the form of a training partner, or should it be a training expert in the form of a training professional such as a training director or training manager or the head of Human Resources (HR)? This will really depend on the culture of the firm (does it have non-partners sitting at the 'top table'?) and the calibre of the training professional (is he or she capable of sitting at the 'top table'?). If the answer to the second question is 'yes', then he or she should be able to join the 'top table', even if this has not been done before. The worst situation is to have an extremely able professional – whether director of training, director of KM, or director of HR, for example – who is prevented from taking a proper place at management level purely because he or she is not a partner, and then for him or her to be given a reporting line to a less competent or perhaps uninterested 'training partner' who does sit at the 'top table' but is inadequate in making and arguing the non-partner professional's case. This issue has become less relevant with non-solicitor 'Managers' in ABSs, but the problem has not gone away in non-ABS firms.

If, however, the firm has a partner who has the passion and commitment to take on responsibility for training, then that should be harnessed, particularly if the firm does not have the sort of training professional who is able to be involved at the management level.

The advantage of a training partner who is engaged and committed is that he or she already has authority within the firm and, with luck, the ability to encourage buy-in from his or her fellow partners. However, where a partner may suffer in that scenario is in a firm with a strong fee-earning ethos, where a partner who demonstrates an interest in anything non-fee earning may earn the title 'eccentric' or 'maverick', and then be disadvantaged in progression and bonus allocations if no proper account is taken of his or her non-fee earning contribution.

That is not to say that everyone in the firm should just be left to get on with it if they show any initiative with regard to training – that is not going to maximise the firm's investment. Whoever has management responsibility for training needs to know what is going on in different parts of the firm (the need becomes more urgent the larger the firm) and this means ensuring there is effective liaison with all parts of the firm in order to bring their training activities into the firm's training strategy and training programme. The managers of the business also have a role in this.

To be frank, it doesn't really matter whether a firm gives management responsibility for training to a training director or a training partner, so long as the decision is clear, the individual is treated seriously and is fully supported (and valued) by management, and management itself is committed to having best practice in training. Equally, whether responsibility is given to a training director or training partner, he or she needs to drive training initiatives in line with the firm's business strategy and objectives, and ensure the following responsibilities are carried out:

- to identify the competencies required for the firm's business in all roles and at all levels;
- to carry out a training needs analysis;
- to draft a training strategy for the firm;
- to identify the learning objectives, and then develop and identify the appropriate training to achieve the firm's strategic objectives, and the most effective means of delivery;
- to develop a training programme to achieve the firm's training strategy and to provide the basis for producing the training budget;
- to deliver the training as planned; and then
- to evaluate the effectiveness of the training in meeting the training objectives.

2.5 RESPONSIBILITY OF THE TRAINING FUNCTION

Irrespective of the level of responsibility – strategic, tactical or operational – anyone involved in the training function must build relationships within the firm – with the various practice areas, as well as with the support departments, if there is going to be the co-operation needed to run training effectively and efficiently.

Equally, those involved in the training function should use those relationships to promote the firm's training strategy. It is not enough for management to be committed: those involved in the training function also have to do their bit by promoting what the training function does, so that it gains both credibility and respectability as a necessary function of the firm. What is important is for the training function to be seen as responsive, supportive, expert, professional, effective and necessary. Much of this comes from personal relationships rather than budgetary and other empirical measures, and needs to happen at all levels in the firm.

Another responsibility of those involved in the training function which is important to the success of the firm's training strategy, is to understand the legal education and training market and to keep up to date with changes and developments – including proposed and prospective developments in legal education and training outside the firm. This is important so that changes which may have an impact can be anticipated, and so that the firm benefits from developments in best practice, as well as from new initiatives and technology. On the regulatory side, this means keeping up to date with Solicitors Regulation Authority (SRA) developments (see **Chapter 6**) and its Training for Tomorrow (T4T) website.[2] On the commercial side, it means networking with those involved in training in other firms through training and HR organisations, and relevant conferences. The legal press reports developments in training, as well as carrying articles on training at different times. The important thing is that the training function does not sit in splendid isolation with a purely internal focus and no awareness of what is going on outside the firm.

2.6 INTERACTION OF TRAINING AND KNOWLEDGE MANAGEMENT

Training is but one form of knowledge dissemination. So, there is an inextricable link between training and KM. However, the traditional way firms have tended to structure both training and KM is as distinct rather than integrated, or even related, functions. So, a firm may have a KM function, perhaps headed by a head of KM, and supported by a bevy of Professional Support Lawyers (PSLs). Then it may have the HR department which is charged with looking after, say, skills training, and then individual practice areas which look after their own legal technical training. Although this may be the structure in theory, in practice it becomes much less clear, and the PSL who sits within the KM structure may in fact also be doing the job on the ground in the department of dealing with the practice area's training. This would make sense because, if there is an important new legal development, for example, which the PSL would be expected to disseminate to the practice area, the PSL could choose to do this by way of a practice note – or by arranging a training session. However, in terms of reporting lines, responsibility and ownership, this split structure also has the potential to create confusion, inefficiency and ineffectiveness.

A lot of firms put the two together – training and KM – and therefore may have a head of both KM and training, so that the 'synergy' between the two is more effectively harnessed and utilised.

The critical issue for management is to recognise that KM and training are just different facets of the same thing: the firm's intellectual capital – its protection, deployment and utilisation. Having one without it interacting with the other is wasting the investment and endangering the firm's assets.

---

[2] www.sra.org.uk/t4t

CHAPTER 3

Developing and implementing the training strategy

3.1	Introduction	3.5	Writing the training strategy
3.2	Understanding the firm's business strategy and objectives	3.6	Developing a training programme
		3.7	Evaluating the effectiveness of training
3.3	Developing a competence framework		
3.4	Carrying out a training needs analysis		

3.1 INTRODUCTION

The underlying theme in this book is that the training that a firm invests in is the training which supports the firm's business strategy by developing the human resources in which the firm has invested, namely its employees, in line with business need. If training is not doing this, then aside from compulsory training required by the regulator, it is questionable whether the investment in that training can be justified. That is not to say that all training must go to profitability: some training may be a 'loss leader' in direct financial terms, but still fulfil a business objective – such as training for clients to build client relationships, training programmes which may assist in recruitment or even retention of staff. These examples still achieve a business objective, and the investment can therefore be justified. What a firm therefore needs to do is to have a training strategy on which its investment in training is based.

3.2 UNDERSTANDING THE FIRM'S BUSINESS STRATEGY AND OBJECTIVES

The starting point, therefore, in developing a training strategy has to be the firm's own business strategy and objectives: what does the firm wish to achieve, and what is it committed to achieving, as a business?

What the person with strategic responsibility for training (see **Chapter 2**) must do is know and understand the firm's business plan and what it is aiming to achieve in the short term, medium term and long term. To do this effectively means having involvement in the firm's management and with those who are responsible for developing the firm's business strategy and business plan.

3.3 DEVELOPING A COMPETENCE FRAMEWORK

The next step is to look at the firm's human resources and to identify the gearing and ratios needed for the business generally but also the business needs of the individual practice areas: what competencies does its staff need to have to deliver not only the firm's business objectives, but also Principle 5 in the Solicitors Regulation Authority (SRA) Handbook: to provide a proper standard of service to one's client. Under entity-based regulation, firms have responsibility to train staff to maintain a level of competence appropriate to their work and level of responsibility.

This is best explained by illustration: take a small regional firm with a predominantly conveyancing practice. The competencies required would be the obvious ones of knowledge and expertise in property law and conveyancing transactions. However, as a small firm, skills in client relationship building and in marketing are also going to be important. It may be that the firm has decided on a gearing which uses a larger number of junior assistants than senior assistants because of the high turnover of conveyancing work that it handles, supported by a number of paralegals who are supervised by junior assistants. Consequently, the junior assistants, in addition to needing conveyancing knowledge and transaction skills (writing, drafting, research, client interviewing, verbal communication, time management, transaction management, to name a few), will also require supervision and delegation skills because of the paralegals they supervise. The senior assistants in the firm, in addition to the knowledge and transaction skills they would be expected to have, may also require team leadership and appraisal skills if they have responsibility for the junior assistants, and trainee supervision skills, including feedback and mentoring, if they have responsibility for the trainees the firm takes each year. If they are also going to be required to do their share of marketing, they will need marketing and possibly networking skills as well.

There is also a philosophical side to this analysis, which is whether a firm takes a generalist approach (i.e. everyone is expected to do everything) or a specialist approach (i.e. each individual's strengths are identified and the individual is deployed to do what he or she is best at).

This is an important distinction: for instance, does a firm require every lawyer to be involved in recruitment and therefore provide training for everyone in interviewing skills – the generalist approach – or does the firm want those who are good at, and particularly interested in, recruitment to be trained to do this, while others who may be more focused on business development take responsibility for that, and those with particularly good technical skills concentrate on the technical legal work – a specialist approach?

Neither approach is right or wrong, nor is one approach preferable to the other. It is a case of being clear about what the firm as a business needs and expects of its lawyers. The generalist approach is likely to involve a heavier investment in training – training everyone to a level of competence in everything the firm requires – than the specialist approach. However, the specialist approach risks missing those who may, with some training and development, prove themselves to be particularly adept. The reality may be, however, that a firm expects both: a general level of competence across the board so that people can be deployed and re-deployed as necessary, and additional specialist focus to enhance performance in the relevant areas.

By identifying what it is in terms of knowledge, skills and attitudes that the firm's business strategy requires, it is possible to be quite specific in describing the competencies needed in the various roles within the firm. Putting together the competencies for all the roles creates a competency framework which can then underpin the training programme the firm needs to deliver. It can also assist in performance evaluation for each individual, something that also helps in assessing the effectiveness of training which has been provided.

Integral to the SRA's Continuing Competence approach (see **Chapter 20**), is the use of the SRA Competence Statement (see **Chapter 21**) to identify training and development need. The SRA Competence Statement is actually a real boon for firms which do not already have their own competence framework and can be used as the basis for developing a competence framework for the firm. Once the Continuing Competence regime is introduced on 1 November 2016, all solicitors will be expected to use the Competence Statement in this way. So, if a firm does not already have a competence framework, it would be well advised to develop one, ideally using the SRA Competence Statement. The SRA Continuing Competence toolkit can provide assistance with this.

3.4 CARRYING OUT A TRAINING NEEDS ANALYSIS

Identifying the competencies that are needed by individuals in different roles and at different levels in the firm is not the end of the exercise. One does not, at that point, just decide to buy in team leadership training for all senior assistants in the firm, for instance – not if the firm wants to use its training investment wisely, that is. It may be that all senior assistants are very competent in their team leadership skills, or it may be that there are only one or two who are not as competent as they should or need to be. What the firm needs to be able to do is measure actual competence against the required competencies set out in the competence framework for knowledge, skills and attitudes, in order to identify any knowledge or performance gaps. This is known as a training needs analysis.

There are two levels on which a training needs analysis can be carried out: the first is at a strategic level, which means looking at the firm overall and at the training needs that arise from its business objectives, with a view to formulating a training strategy for the firm as the basis of an annual training plan and programme.

The second is at a more tactical level, and identifies training needs as and when they arise. Even though a particular training need may be ad hoc, it must still be tested against the firm's business objectives. In other words, a business case needs to be made in order for the training to be required. Ideally, training needs should be identified through appraisals, as well as through an individual's personal development plan. Both provide effective ways of pinning training needs to the firm's business plan, particularly if the personal development plans are underpinned by a competency framework.

3.4.1 Identifying knowledge and performance gaps

Identifying knowledge and performance gaps can be done in a number of ways and should involve the individual's own input as well as 'objective', or third party, observation. This is easier to understand if the way performance or knowledge gaps can arise is considered. Performance and knowledge gaps are not all to do with poor performance, nor are they always related to an individual or even individuals. Rather gaps can be:

- **Firm-wide**: A firm might introduce a new IT system, for example, or a new procedure for time-recording or billing or as a firm it might identify that improvement is needed in client care, or that as a result of new legislation all staff need to be trained in new anti-money laundering procedures.
- **Practice area-specific**: In a practice area or other specific group, gaps may arise from a change in the law or other legal development relevant to the area, or through a change in procedure which affects only a particular group of employees.
- **Individual**: It may be that an individual has recently joined the firm from another firm and does not have the necessary level of knowledge or experience, which needs to be developed. For existing members of staff, it could be that an individual is performing perfectly competently but has been given new tasks or responsibilities for which he or she does not have the required level of competence. Similarly, it could be a case of 'stepping up' – such as a trainee moving to qualification; a senior assistant moving up to partnership; a partner moving into a management position. Of course, an individual may also have a performance gap because of a lack of motivation or some other reason where he or she is simply not performing to the level of which he or she is capable. Ways in which these gaps can be identified, depending on whether they are firm-wide, group-specific or individual, are many and varied. They include:

Extent of gap	Method of identification
Firm-wide gaps:	• staff attitude surveys • client surveys or questionnaires • staff focus groups • staff recruitment and retention statistics
Group-specific gaps:	• job descriptions • questionnaires to members of the group • focus meetings • business plans • management reports
Individual gaps:	• performance appraisals • supervisor/manager observation • interview • questionnaire

3.4.2 Causes of knowledge and performance gaps

A word of caution: just because a knowledge gap or performance gap has been identified, it does not mean that it will give rise to a training need. For one thing, the gap may not be important enough to 'fix' – 'sledgehammer to crack nut' scenario – or the cause of the gap may be something that training may not be able to 'fix': training may change behaviour, develop knowledge or improve skill; it will be unlikely, however, to change personality or to change attitudes which are deeply, even if inappropriately, held. So, the cause of the gap needs to be considered:

- Is the individual being asked to do something for which he or she has had no training and which is new for him or her to perform? If this is the case then training may be the answer.
- Is it that the individual knows how to do what he or she is required to do, but just does not do it? This may be more of a behavioural problem, and may go to issues of morale, supervision, incentive – none of which is necessarily a training issue for the individual.
- Is it something that the individual has been able to do before but is not able to do now? If so, what has caused the individual not to be able to do it now? Is it because the individual does not need to use the knowledge or to practise the skill as often as he or she did before (in other words, a case of being out of practice)? If so, refresher training may be appropriate, or it may be that the job itself needs to be looked at, and perhaps more feedback provided.
- Is it because the individual's attitude has changed? This may be a behavioural problem, possibly related to morale, supervision, incentive and so on, none of which is related to training.
- Is it faulty equipment or flawed procedures in the firm causing the problem? In this case it may be the performance of others – those who maintain equipment or carry out procedures – whose performance may need to be looked at.

- Is it as a result of poor management or supervision? This may point to a training need for the manager or supervisor (and possibly also training in communication or assertiveness for the individual).
- Is it something that the individual has the ability to do but has not been required to do? If so, it may be a case of giving instructions on how/what to do, or perhaps providing training, and changing the role description.

Do not underestimate the impact of morale or incentives (or lack thereof) on performance, let alone poor management and supervision. These do not give rise to training needs for the individual so much as for those involved in the individual's personal management and supervision, or that of the department – or even a firm's management.

3.5 WRITING THE TRAINING STRATEGY

Having identified the firm's training needs against the firm's business objectives, it is possible to start writing the training strategy. Perhaps more easily said than done. How does one write a training strategy? Answer: in the same way that the firm writes its business strategy.

There are plenty of books on management which cover business plans, business strategies and the like, some even on managing law firms specifically, and any of these will provide sensible and detailed guidance. In summary:

- A strategy is not a budget or business plan, both of which are to do with planning for the coming year and are discussed in **Chapter 4**. A strategy, however, is something which looks to the future and is aspirational, although the aspirations need to be specific and achievable. The strategy needs to provide the foundation for a programme of training which will meet the firm's business objectives, as well setting out how better and more profitable training can be delivered in the firm.
- Time-wise, the strategy should address the next 12 months, and possibly a longer period depending on the firm's own strategy, which may be a three-year or five-year strategy plan.
- The skills and resources which will be needed to deliver the training strategy should be identified. If it is the first training strategy the firm has produced, and the firm is setting up a new training function, then those who manage the business need to consider the structure of the training function and issues related to its relationship intra-firm as discussed in **Chapter 2**.
- The strategy should start with an analysis of where training in the firm currently stands, and where it needs and wishes to be at a particular point in the future

(aligned with the firm's business strategy). This could take the form of the first part of a SWOT analysis.[1] identifying the strengths and weaknesses of training in the firm.
- The strategy should set out the main training goals, and identify what the key indicators will be for measuring the strategy's success.
- The main steps that will need to be taken, and by whom, in order to achieve the strategic goals need to be identified.
- The strategy should spell out the implications for the firm and its business, and the strategic gaps which could arise potentially if the firm does not follow the training strategy.
- There should be an analysis of any risks arising at a strategic or business level (the second part of the SWOT analysis) that could have an impact, and which need to be anticipated. Also, any anticipated changes in either the regulatory or practice environment which could also have an impact should be identified. The point is that there will be things that happen and over which the firm has no control. Because of this, the strategy has to be amenable to review and change; it should not be set in stone as permanent and immutable.
- Any assumptions that have been made upon which the strategy relies (e.g. that there will be no changes to the regulatory framework in the next year) need to be stated.
- Expected expenditure, where that expenditure is likely to arise, and some idea of its order of magnitude should also be included. However, remember that the strategy is neither a budget nor a business plan.
- Most importantly, the strategy should identify who has 'ownership' of the strategy, and who has specific responsibility for its different aspects, as well as for delivering the strategy overall.

Once the strategy has been produced and approved through the appropriate channels and made known to those to whom it needs to be made known in the firm (this could be all members of the firm, or just management and those with responsibility for training), the strategy should be kept under regular review to ensure it continues to meet the firm's business objectives.

The strategy can then be used as the basis for the training programme, and the design and/or procuring of appropriate training.

Putting the training strategy into effect involves:

- producing a training programme that sets out the specific training which will take place, how, where and when;
- putting in place systems to obtain feedback; and
- overseeing the administration of the training programme.

This necessarily encompasses responsibility for overseeing the operational support, which is responsible for ensuring training is delivered and also relies upon gaining co-operation from:

---

[1] An analysis of strengths, weaknesses, opportunities and threats.

- the people who need to deliver the training;
- the people who need to attend; and
- the people whose co-operation are needed to support the training,

and is discussed in **Chapter 38**.

Having developed the firm's training strategy, and from that a training programme, the training programme needs to be implemented. This means providing efficient administration and support. Lawyers can be dismissive of management and administration and think it is something that can be done in a matter of minutes. This is probably because good administration is not usually visible; good administration avoids problems and anticipates and deals with the unexpected. If the firm is going to get the most out of its investment in training, then its training function has to be effective at an operational level.

Operational responsibilities include:

- organising training (so that it takes place);
- recording training information;
- collecting and collating feedback from training;
- complying with SRA requirements, e.g. for authorisation

and are discussed in **Chapter 38**.

3.6 DEVELOPING A TRAINING PROGRAMME

While developing a training strategy is important to managing training (see **Chapter 4**) within the firm, what is equally important is implementing the training strategy, and doing so effectively. This involves:

- producing a training programme that sets out the specific training which will take place, how, where and when;
- putting in place systems to obtain feedback; and
- overseeing the administration of the training programme.

This necessarily encompasses responsibility for oversight of the operational support that arranges the delivery of training. Putting the strategy into effect also relies upon gaining co-operation from:

- the people who need to deliver the training;
- the people who need to attend; and
- the people who are needed to 'champion' training in the firm.

3.6.1 Preparing the training programme

Having decided on the training that is required in the firm either through a training needs analysis (see **3.4**) or identification of training needs through appraisals and personal development plans (PDPs) (see **39.3.4**), and having set the budget for training (see **4.4**), there is the task of turning this into a viable training programme. The training programme has to work for the firm, so that people attend training and, by attending training, achieve the training and development objectives the firm has identified it needs in order to meet its business objectives.

The training programme should take account of much of the training delivery issues discussed in **Part E**:

- the optimum time for the training;
- the resources which are both available and required;
- the training methods;
- the urgency of the training;
- the trainers;
- the attendees and so on.

From the administration point of view, it is also important to identify who is responsible for each training course or session in the training programme. This is sensible management – ensuring ownership.

If these details have not been decided, then the considerations set out in **Part D** need to be addressed so that a comprehensive programme of all of the firm's training may be produced. There may be resistance to a firm-wide training programme where, for example, training in the firm is delivered by and within individual practice areas. The intention of the training programme, however, is not to stymie innovation or initiative, or to emulate 'big brother'. If the firm is serious about ensuring it is obtaining the best return from its investment in training, then it does need to know just what training is taking place within the firm, and whether it is in line with both the firm's training strategy as well as its business strategy, and whether the investment is justified for the fiscal year.

A further advantage of having a firm-wide training programme is that it makes it possible to utilise training which may already be planned, thereby avoiding duplication and lack of consistency. Equally, training in other practice areas that could be relevant or useful in terms of strengthening 'peripheral' knowledge can be more easily identified.

3.6.1.1 Responsibility for identifying training needs

This in fact raises a related issue to that of the ownership of training in the firm (discussed in **2.3**): who has responsibility for identifying training needs in the firm? Is it the training function, which then needs to persuade the firm's management or budget holder; or will training needs be identified within practice areas and through performance appraisals, and then passed to the training function to deliver? The difference between the two approaches is important: in the first, the training function is going to have to make the case for training, which is likely to mean making a financial case as well (see **4.5**), with the challenge of achieving management commitment; the second presupposes management commitment and the financial case having been made if the practice area has its own training budget. The latter approach leaves the training function with the task of producing a training programme which will achieve the necessary attendance but minimise disruption and time away from fee-earning work. The former involves a strong strategic element; the latter, more of a tactical approach (see **Chapter 2**).

3.7 EVALUATING THE EFFECTIVENESS OF TRAINING

A firm's management needs to have an idea, and a fairly accurate one, of whether there is a return on its investment in training. This means evaluating the effectiveness of the training that has been, and is being, delivered.

All training which is delivered should be evaluated. This is quite simply to ensure that the training has achieved its objectives. How individual training sessions which make up a training programme are evaluated is part of the administration of training. However, from a strategic perspective, once the individual feedback and evaluation exercises have been carried out, the whole needs to be pulled together in order to produce a coherent overview of the effectiveness of the firm's investment in training. There is no one simple empirical exercise which is going to give this measure and, as change in performance rarely happens overnight, the time it is likely to take for training to achieve its objectives should also be factored in.

Evaluating training is not a science, nor does it lend itself easily to empirical measurement. However, if the firm is to justify its investment in training, including investment in training personnel, then measures which show that training has enabled work to be delegated, has improved financial performance or reduced write-offs, are going to be very important. This is where key performance indicators come in.

There is also the fact that evaluation will mean different things to different people, and will have different relevance for different people.

3.7.1 Metrics

In order to evaluate the effectiveness of training, there are a range of metrics that can be used (provided that information is captured in the first place). Which metrics are appropriate will have a different relevance for different people. For example:

- From the point of view of those running training in the firm, it may be important to know the proportion of training run (i.e. not cancelled) from the training programme, and the attendance rate for training – these are indicators of the effectiveness of the way training is being run.
- For attendees, it could be the proportion of training they were able to attend in relation to the training needs identified in their personal development plans,

and the degree to which the improvements they perceive in their own performance are matched by similar observations by their manager/supervisor. The simple fact of an individual being promoted or 'stepped up' would be another positive indicator.
- For managers or supervisors in practice areas, it may be whether an individual has been able to be deployed more usefully and profitably in fee-earning work, and can be trusted with more responsibility after he or she has undertaken training.
- For management, it will be a combination of an increase in the intellectual capital of the firm, as well as a related increase in the firm's profitability.

None of these metrics is easy to demonstrate. Even the key performance indicators for the training function in measuring attendance and delivery, which one might think would be straightforward, are not: there may be good reason why people were not able to attend or why training was not able to be delivered, which have nothing to do with the effectiveness or performance of how training is run in the firm. Somehow, this consideration also needs to be added to the pot if the evaluation is to be meaningful.

3.7.2 Capturing feedback

Related to how a firm evaluates training, it also needs to have in place mechanisms and procedures for capturing feedback about the training itself, and feedback about improvement in performance of the individual attendee following the training. The different methods for doing both are discussed in detail in **Chapter 39**. However, capturing the information is not enough: it then also needs to be analysed by drawing on indicators of improved performance, effective delivery and any trends which may need investigating.

A government-like approach of 'targets' or 'league tables' pure and simple is a highly unsophisticated measure, and a lazy and often self-serving management tool. It does not actually evaluate effectiveness, and by reason of its lack of sophistication can be misleading, not to mention damaging to the morale of those whose performance has been brought into question by the unrefined statistics.

3.7.3 Analysing feedback

The most common feedback for training comes from feedback sheets. How this feedback can be converted into data is explained at **Chapter 39**. The data can then be used in a number of contexts, including:

- **To evaluate performance**: Data relevant to an individual's performance should be used in his or her performance appraisal as the basis for discussion with the individual.

Take as an example the senior assistant who has delivered several training sessions as part of a firm-wide training programme which has specific PowerPoint slides. However, the senior assistant did not use the PowerPoint slides, and there have been complaints from attendees that they could not follow the session because of this. Is this proof of a lack of commitment by the senior assistant, or an inability or refusal to follow instructions? It may turn out that the reason the assistant did not use the PowerPoint slides is simply because the projector kept breaking down and, although the her or she reported it, the person responsible in the firm for dealing with breakdowns did not deal with it (one could argue that he or she should have reported this to his or her line manager or the training function after the second time nothing happened to fix the projector, and this would be a performance development issue ...). So, data alone is not conclusive of the effectiveness or otherwise of that senior assistant without anything more.

- **To identify trends**: Attendance records may indicate a falling off in attendance at certain times, such as when trainees are required to attend a Professional Skills Course (PSC). This can be helpful in deciding the optimum timing for training so that there is no clash, and attendance is not adversely affected. Equally, attendance records might indicate a constant problem with attendance at training starting at 5 pm, compared to training that starts at 8.30 or 9 am. It may be that, because of the way a particular practice area works, 5 pm starts do not fit with the client work, particularly if the practice area does work with or has an office in the US. Knowing this can inform planning of future training.

- **For comparative analysis**: It may be that comparison of the feedback from different peer groups, or performance levels, may point to management issues. For instance, if attendance by assistants in one practice group of the firm is better than attendance by assistants in another, this could point to an agnostic attitude in the latter practice group which demonstrates a lack of commitment to training. It may be that the issue needs to be addressed with whomever is responsible for managing the practice group. However, before escalating the problem, it would be important to look at the reasons for non-attendance, even speak to some of the non-attendees, to make sure that the reason is not just that the whole practice group has been involved in a mega-deal requiring seven days a week working for the past few months.

The point is that data alone is not reliable: it also has to be placed in context.

CHAPTER 4

Financial management of training

4.1	Introduction	4.5	Measuring the investment in and return from training, in financial terms
4.2	The financial structure for training		
4.3	Financial planning and budgeting for training	4.6	Ways of maximising the financial investment in training
4.4	The training budget		

4.1 INTRODUCTION

Whatever the potential benefits of well-structured and organised training, there still needs to be sound financial management of training. This goes to the question of whether training should be treated as an expense or an investment. The answer is that in the short term it is an expense to the firm, while over a longer period it should represent a sizeable investment in the development of a firm's human resources so that those resources can be more effectively deployed to meet the firm's business needs, as well as providing a better service to clients, all of which are important to the firm achieving its business objectives and enhancing profitability.

Various challenges to the case for training are described in **Chapter 1**. There is a further challenge that is sometimes made to the financial investment in training, which is that there is no point in the firm investing in training because, having trained people, they then leave. The response to this challenge is to ask: but what if the firm does not train people – and they stay?

If those managing the business do not see how training is adding value, then budgets may be cut and/or the training function may be outsourced to a third party which appears to deliver an equivalent service at a lower cost.

This chapter therefore considers:

- the financial structure for training;
- financial planning and budgeting for training;
- measuring the investment in and return from training, in financial terms;
- ways of recouping and protecting the financial investment in training.

4.2 THE FINANCIAL STRUCTURE FOR TRAINING

Lawyers do not necessarily understand training, and as a consequence in a firm large enough to have a training department, they may not get best value from their training because they do not understand that the training department is in fact a service department and not simply a part of the firm that organises training courses (see **Chapter 2**).

If a firm runs its training through a dedicated training department, then the training department is one of the business support departments in the firm, in the same way as departments which deal with accounts, business development and IT, and will be part of the business support financial structure, with the same financial responsibilities and oversight. Consequently the training department needs to be 'client-focused', and structured to provide training which is not only cost-effective but adds value to the business.

What can waste the firm's investment is if people do not turn up to training that has been booked, and equally if the training does not meet actual need and is neither cost-effective nor cost-efficient. What can help is to consider using a service level agreement (SLA) between the training department and the firm.

To use an SLA means having the training department set up as a profit centre which then charges practice areas and other departments by re-charging the costs it incurs in running training for the practice area or department.

The SLA would set out in commercial terms how the relationship between the rest of the firm and the training function would work. SLAs are common practice in large companies, and outsourcing arrangements are based on an outsourcing contract that sets out the arrangements by which the two parties agree to act.

Where practice areas 'own' their training but the actual sourcing and running of the training is being carried out by a central training department (see **2.2**), there could be SLAs between the training department and each practice area which wishes to use the services of the training department.

The practice area would specify in the SLA:

- the training it requires, the needs of attendees and the expected outcomes from the training;
- how many people require training and in what sort of group size;
- when training needs to be provided and how long it should last.

The training department, however, would specify in the SLA:

- the price of its training;
- the quality of that training;
- what input the practice area needs to provide, and when, to enable the training to be most effective.

The SLA would then provide the basis for the training budget (see **4.4**). However, even without an SLA, the same information is required for budgeting purposes.

Where one firm does not have a dedicated training department or has the training function split (see **2.2**) between practice areas and, say, the Human Resources (HR) department, the position is a bit more complex. For instance, an immediate question is whether practice areas have devolved budgets for the training they organise and deliver, or are they allocated funds from a central training budget controlled, for example, by the HR department?

The advantage of using an SLA is that it provides a basis for identifying non-commitment or non-performance on the part of practice areas, other business support departments or the training department itself, which can aid the financial management of both training and the business (see **Chapter 3**).

4.3 FINANCIAL PLANNING AND BUDGETING FOR TRAINING

There can be a tendency in any business, but law firm businesses in particular, to look at short-term horizons and fail to keep an eye on the horizon in the distance, or even to contemplate what might be lying beyond that horizon. This means that sometimes the short term is better managed than the long term.

A firm which is purely concerned with meeting budgets is likely to take a short-term approach and is unlikely to measure the return on investment properly, and is also likely to regard training, and any related expenditure, as unnecessary expense in times of financial pressure.

A firm which takes a longer-term approach is likely to accept the length of time it takes to achieve change, and will recognise that investment is needed in order to obtain a return down the line. Such a firm is more likely to use budgets as an early warning system, rather than as an alarm, and what will be important for the firm's management is that the firm is achieving its longer-term and business objectives.

An enlightened management will actually understand concepts such as 'intellectual capital' and the fact that a firm's profitability is not determined by fee-earner returns alone. This will be the firm which has non-fee earning codes in its time-recording system, and which talks of 'investment time' rather than 'non-fee earning' time; which regards training in every sense of the word, including coaching and mentoring, as de rigueur for all partners and senior assistants, and treats those who do not take this responsibility seriously as committing a dereliction of duty. An ideal world ...

However, as a minimum, management needs to make sure it is doing its part to provide those who have responsibility for training in the firm with the tools to be able to carry out the necessary measuring and analysis so that management can then assess the return on its investment (see **4.5**).

If a firm's management sees support functions such as training as an expense rather than a strategic investment which only delivers full value if it is undertaken consistently over a long period of time, then the training budget is vulnerable to cutting, as are those in the training department. Although cutting the training budget can improve results in the short term, the long-term consequences could be damaging to the firm's ability to optimise its investment in its human resources. This is why it is important to develop a training strategy (see **Chapter 3**) which supports the firm's business plan, and which forms the basis for the training programme. In this way, the money being spent in the budget is no longer an unnecessary expense, but a necessary cost in helping the firm to implement its business plan.

4.4 THE TRAINING BUDGET

There are three structural issues which need to be considered in putting together a training budget:

- whether there should be a central budget for the cost of training which is treated as a central expense or if the budget should be split between the various departments of the firm;
- whether it is better to resource all of the trainers from within the business or to use external trainers;
- what expenses should be included in the training budget.

4.4.1 Centralised versus de-centralised budgets

This is going to depend very much on the ownership and structure of the training in the particular firm (see **Chapter 2**). The risk with allowing each practice area to organise its own training is that, if practice areas do not have the expertise to do this, there will be inefficiencies which a well-run central function might have avoided. It is also probably the case that a central function might also be able to achieve larger discounts by being able to buy in bulk. If a centralised model is used, then relevant parts of the budget can be re-charged to practice areas, which means practice areas can more easily assess their true level of profitability, which might otherwise have been concealed by having training expenses borne centrally. Although most expenses can easily be re-charged to other departments or practice areas, there will probably be some expenses that cannot be re-charged, which are to do with longer-term strategic initiatives. Other parts of the firm might discourage or even resist these longer-term initiatives if they knew the cost was being charged to their budget for the current year.

4.4.2 Internal versus external resourcing of training and trainers

This is discussed in more detail at **38.2.1**. There are arguments for both strategies. However, from a financial perspective, using internal trainers has no marginal costs, unlike external trainers who have a real cost. When a firm does the training itself, there is fee-earner time used in preparing and delivering the training, but this is not usually included in the budget. It may therefore appear that it would be cheaper to use external trainers who do not have as high an hourly charge-out rate. However, cost is obviously not the only issue and it is also important to measure the value of the training to try and determine the value added benefit. Having training delivered by partners and senior assistants in the firm both protects and increases the firm's intellectual capital (see **2.6**).

4.4.3 Direct versus indirect costs

The obvious expenses which should be included in the budget would be:

- the gross salary cost of those working in the training department;
- the cost of buying in external trainers;
- the cost of hiring training venues and associated accommodation costs;
- the costs associated with preparing and printing course materials;
- the cost of online training products.

There are, however, other costs which probably should also be taken into consideration, including:

- a fair share of the accommodation and IT costs attributable to the training department; and, arguably
- a re-charge of the salary cost of fee earners who help with the delivery of training.

When these additional costs are added, the cost of training may look higher. However, at least the true cost of training is being reflected, which is what needs to be managed.

4.4.4 Expenses incurred or services provided?

What is also important to ensure when putting together the budget is that it is not presented merely as a list of expenses but instead as a list of services. The following shows how a list of expenses might be converted into a list of services:

Budget for the year ending 30 April 20XX – Expenses

Training manager	45,000
Training administrator	23,000
External trainers	
– PSC	8,000
– CPD	46,000
Course materials	6,000
Share of property and IT costs	9,000
	137,000

If one then makes the following assumptions:

1. Eighty days of Continuing Professional Development (CPD) are organised each year, of which 25 are presented by external trainers, 20 by the training manager and 35 by fee earners. The training manager also presents 25 days of courses to business support staff. There are six days of the Professional Skills Course (PSC) presented by external tutors.
2. The training manager spends his or her time as follows: 40 per cent management of training within the firm; 10 per cent dealing with external trainers and organising their courses; 30 per cent presenting and developing CPD courses; and 20 per cent dealing with fee earners over the presentation of their courses.
3. The training administrator spends: 10 per cent of his or her time on PSC courses; 60 per cent supporting the CPD programme; 10 per cent managing the training function; and 20 per cent on business support staff training.
4. The course materials are all for CPD courses.
5. The property and IT costs are allocated to the different services provided in accordance with the number of days of training that are provided.
6. There are 100 fee earners (including 20 trainees) and 100 support staff working in the firm.

It is now possible to re-write the budget as a list of services being provided as follows:

Expense	PSC	CPD	Business support	Management	Totals
Training manager		13,500	13,500	18,000	45,000
Training administrator	2,300	13,800	4,600	2,300	23,000
External trainers – PSC	8,000				8,000
External trainers – CPD		46,000			46,000
Course materials		6,000			6,000
Property and IT costs	486	6,486	2,028		9,000
	10,786	85,786	20,128	20,300	137,000

This can then be simply summarised as an annual budget for training services as follows:

Trainee PSCs	10,786
CPD courses	85,786
Business support staff training	20,128
Management of training function	20,300
Total budget	£137,000

When the budget is presented in this way it looks completely different. It is clearer where the main costs of the training budget are allocated. It is also obvious that, if the budget is cut, then a service will be cut. The above budget can be broken down into far more detail – for example, the CPD element of the budget could be split between legal, IT, personal skills, finance and management skills.

4.4.5 Benchmarking the budget

4.4.5.1 Measures of performance

The next issue to address is whether this budget represents good value for money. A good way of considering the effectiveness of the expenditure is to do benchmarking against other firms which are trying to provide similar types of training, if this is possible. There is not a great deal of benchmark information available.

However, even without benchmarking the following measures can be used to assess the cost-efficiency of the training being offered:

- **Training budget as a percentage of annual fee income**: In some other industries the training budget might be calculated as a percentage of salary costs. This is a similar sort of calculation, because presumably as a firm grows it will employ more staff and require more training. The benchmark number that comes out of various surveys for this is 0.67 per cent. So, if a firm has annual fees of £1 million, it might spend just under £7,000 on training. It may therefore be useful in the business plan to state the minimum spend in each year at, say, 0.5 per cent to ensure that the investment is maintained.
- **Cost per training day delivered**: In the above budget the total cost of training was £137,000 and there were 111 days of training delivered. This means the cost per training day delivered was £1,234.
- **Cost per day per person attending**: If in the above example it was assumed that, on average, 15 people attended each day of training, then the cost becomes £1,234/15 = £82. This number can be compared with the cost of sending people individually on external courses. If class sizes are higher, the number will fall, but so too may the quality of the training. For this reason, a firm could stipulate its required class sizes, and use class size to control costs without there being a drop in quality.
- **Cost per employee**: In the above example, excluding the management cost of training, the cost per staff member of the training was:
    - fee earner CPD: £85,786/80 = £1,072 per fee earner;
    - trainee PSC: £10,786/20 = £539 per trainee;
    - business support staff: £20,128/100 = £201 per support staff.

As with the training budget as a percentage of annual fee income, a firm may wish to set longer-term plans by setting minimum levels of spend per employee

type. Surveys in larger firms have indicated that it is not unusual to budget to spend about £2,000 per fee earner on training each year.
- **CPD hours per fee earner**: If there were 80 days of CPD training and each day had six hours of training with 15 people attending, then there were 7,200 hours of CPD delivered. This means that, for each of the 80 qualified lawyers, there were 90 hours of CPD, which is well in excess of the current Solicitors Regulation Authority (SRA) requirements.[1]

If it turns out that the cost-per-employee figures seem to be the same whether the firm runs all the training itself or uses a training manager to buy all the training in, the deciding factor should be quality.

4.5 MEASURING THE INVESTMENT IN AND RETURN FROM TRAINING, IN FINANCIAL TERMS

Once the cost of providing training has been determined, what needs to be identified is the value that training is delivering. If the value added is less than the cost of the training, then the training should be questioned. If the training is adding significant value, then the investment in training has been justified.

Firms have always struggled with how to determine the exact value of training delivered in financial terms. The value could perhaps be identified as the higher of:

- the cost of buying in the training from outside; and
- the 'added value' to the firm.

To put it another way, the profit generated by the training function is the higher of the cost of buying training in and the 'added value' to the firm, less the cost of the training function. This makes it possible to show the profitability of the training delivered, as illustrated in the following table where the costs determined are compared with the assumed value of the training services.

	Cost £	Value £	Profit/loss £
Trainee PSC courses	10,786	8,525	(2,261)
CPD courses	85,786	124,500	38,714
Support staff training	20,128	24,500	4,372
Management of training function	20,300	42,000	21,700
Total budget	137,000	199,525	62,525

The figures used in the value column are necessarily subjective. It is not always possible to work out what it would have cost to buy in the service from outside, but it is normally possible to make a reasonable estimate. Determining the 'added value'

---

[1] SRA Training Regulations 2011 Part 3 – CPD Regulations, reg.3.1(a).

may be even more difficult for training which develops soft skills or which is designed to change attitude, but again some measure could and should be established when the training is being designed (see **Chapter 36**).

The above table suggests that the trainee PSCs would be better done externally, while the other parts of the training budget are adding value to the firm and are best retained. Even though these other areas are profitable, how they can be made more profitable by controlling costs and attempting to add further value should always be kept under consideration.

It is possible, as has been done in other professional service firms, to set the training department up as a profit centre which then charges other departments the 'value added' rather than just re-charging the costs incurred. The effect of this would be to reduce the aggregate profit of the fee-earning departments by an amount equal to the profit now recognised in the training department.

4.6 WAYS OF MAXIMISING THE FINANCIAL INVESTMENT IN TRAINING

4.6.1 Consortia

For smaller firms, organising training through consortia arrangements with other firms can be a cost-effective way of investing in the training needed for the firm. The benefits of this are that consortia can still organise the training that they want but it reduces the cost per head by sharing the costs with other firms.

There are additional benefits with these arrangements, in that having more delegates means that they raise more issues and it gives them the opportunity to discuss issues with people working in similar firms. If the firms are all based in the same area then there are further efficiencies in cutting down on travel time and costs which may be associated with travelling to larger public courses. This sort of arrangement is really only appropriate for generic training such as regulator-required courses, courses for basic knowledge, and skills-based courses – not anything which might actually differentiate firms to their clients. However, for generic training it is not just smaller firms which can benefit, and larger firms may also find the consortia approach useful for certain types of training which do not need to be customised to the particular practice or requirements of the firm.

4.6.2 Client training

If a firm has developed expertise at designing and delivering training, then it could turn this into another income stream by offering training to clients. This could be viewed as an additional source of income for the firm or it could be viewed as a credit to be off-set against the training budget.

As discussed in **Chapter 35**, many firms offer training to clients, and indeed many clients expect a certain amount of training to be provided as part of the service from the firm. However, this training does not need to be provided free of charge, and clients might be happy to attend high quality seminars open to a range of clients. There is perhaps a fundamental difference between an event that is designed specifically to generate business, which a client might expect to be free, and an event which is designed to educate the client and for which a client might be happy to pay.

It would not need many well-attended seminars to be organised before significant amounts of revenue were generated. Seminars could also be offered to non-clients, perhaps at a slightly higher price, as a way of attracting new clients and generating some marginal revenue in the process. There is also no longer a requirement to be authorised to offer courses which attract CPD points. However, on 1 November 2016 the requirement for a minimum number of CPD hours will be removed, so the main driver for clients needing their lawyers to attend CPD courses will evaporate, if it has not done so already with the Continuing Competence option under the SRA Training Regulations 2011 Part 3 – CPD Regulations.

4.6.3 Other savings on training

There have always been firms which consider the cost of training trainee solicitors to be too high once the cost of the Legal Practice Course (LPC), the compulsory PSC and other necessary training for new recruits to a firm are added together with the trainee's salary. Such firms might therefore resource themselves in a different way, by using a number of paralegals to cover the work that would otherwise be performed by trainees, for example, or by recruiting only newly qualified solicitors at the qualification stage.

Clearly there have to be firms who take and train trainee solicitors if the profession is to continue (although the SRA's proposals for removal of prescription of pathways to qualification discussed in **Chapter 6** may solve the problem), but this does not mean that all firms have to provide traineeships. The obvious problem with buying people in once they are qualified is that they have not been trained in the practice of that firm and may have trained in a firm with a very different culture. Re-training in this situation can take a large chunk out of a training budget.

Another way of trimming the training budget is to make best use of compulsory courses, such as PSC Electives that will help trainees post-qualification.

4.6.4 Recouping the cost of training

The cost of training people well can be considerable. However, if training is selected and organised properly, it should be more than off-set by the value added. Some thought should be given to recouping some or all of this cost, if things do not go according to plan, as discussed in **Chapter 1**.

One example of this is where training is organised for a group of lawyers within the firm but, at the eleventh hour, four of the delegates cancel out of the 12 who were scheduled to attend. The cost of organising the training may already be committed. If the total cost of the course is £2,400, by way of example, the cost per head if everyone had attended would have been £200. With only eight people attending, the cost per head increases to £300. It would not seem fair to re-charge £300 to those who attended as they did nothing wrong. However, to encourage full attendance, which leads to greater cost-efficiency, and arguably better training if four is below the optimum number for the session, those who cancelled at the last minute could be charged an additional fine of 100 per cent of the course cost, which would be an additional £200 per head. In this situation the training department would incur a cost of £2,400 in organising the course but would raise re-charges of £3,200, making a 'profit' of £800. While there is no real profit to the firm, it reduces the apparent cost of training and penalises those with the lack of commitment to training, as well as incentivising their practice areas to commit to training.

Another situation where the firm's investment in training can be lost is where the firm has paid for the training of staff who then leave the firm (see **4.1**) another challenge to the case for training. There are some firms which quite deliberately do not train solicitors but look to recruit good people on qualification who have trained at top firms, by paying a salary premium. To discourage other firms from benefiting from your investment in training the individual to qualification, consideration could be given to including in a trainee's employment contract the right to re-claim the cost of training should the trainee or lawyer leave within a certain period, say within two years of qualification. The firm may, of course, decide not to enforce its right to re-claim. Equally, if the employee leaves to join a competitor, the firm might ask the new firm to re-pay to the firm the cost of training. Another approach in relation to trainee solicitors would be to provide trainees with a loan from the firm to pay their LPC fees (and course fees for the Common Professional Exam/Graduate Diploma in Law (CPE/GDL), if appropriate), with an agreement between the firm and the trainee that the loan will be written off once the trainee has stayed for an agreed period post-qualification. Whether a firm decides to enforce the agreement will depend on the risk of people leaving soon after they have received the training. There is also the risk that imposing these types of conditions might reduce the chances of recruiting good people. However, at the time of being recruited, an employee is likely to be more interested in getting good training and experience than in restrictions on his or her leaving at some later point. Although this sort of arrangement is not normal practice in law firms, it is something that has been tried in the accountancy profession. While there is more demand for traineeships than there are traineeships available, an employee is perhaps more likely to accept such conditions. This too could change, however, if the SRA ceases to prescribe pathways to qualification as a solicitor (see **Chapter 6**). Even if a traineeship was no longer required, though, and more routes to qualification were made available, there would still be a finite number of places for solicitors available in the profession. So, all that may change in the future is the point of unemployment – which moves from pre-qualification to qualification. In any case, given the investment many firms make in recruiting and training their trainees, particularly where firms have sponsored their trainees on the LPC, and even CPE/GDL, some way of recouping the firm's investment if the trainee leaves within two years of qualifying is certainly worth considering.

PART B

Qualification as a solicitor in England and Wales

Part B explains how education and training for solicitors is regulated in England and Wales. This may sound dry as dust and not particularly relevant to running your business – but it is relevant. The regulatory framework which this Part explains imposes a number of compulsory requirements on firms, as well as on a firm's lawyers individually, in terms of training and development. For instance, every solicitor with a practising certificate is required to meet Continuing Professional Development (CPD) requirements, and if a firm employs trainees there are a whole raft of supervisory and other requirements that go with that as well. Firms can waste a lot of money by not understanding just what is involved, what is required, and what in fact will satisfy the regulatory requirements.

Even for firms that have been familiar with these requirements, the Solicitors Regulation Authority's (SRA) reforms to legal education and training since the Legal Education and Training Review (LETR) mean that there is much that is new – in fact very little of the regulatory framework has not been the subject of change in the years since the report of the LETR.

Apart from regulatory sanctions, not understanding the compulsory requirements carries reputational risk if the firm is perceived externally as not taking its responsibilities for training and developing its staff seriously – not good for recruitment or retention. However, there may also be an impact on the firm's professional indemnity cover – and premiums – on the basis that failing to comply with its regulatory responsibilities to train and develop its staff means that the firm is not managing its risk properly. So, knowing and understanding the regulatory obligations is a case of being better safe than sorry.

For some readers, this may all be known and familiar. However, in order to cater for those readers for whom it is not, Part B explains:

- the relevant bodies involved in regulating legal education and training (**Chapter 5**);
- the reforms to the regulatory framework (**Chapter 6**);
- the routes to qualification (**Chapters 7, 8, 9** and **11**) and exemptions available (**Chapter 10**);
- the academic and vocational stages (**Chapters 12, 13, 14, 15** and **16**);
- qualification and admission (**Chapters 17, 18** and **19**);
- post-qualification requirements (**Chapters 20** and **21**).

SECTION B1

Regulation of legal education and training

This section sets out:

- the regulatory bodies with responsibility for the education and training of solicitors in England and Wales, and the underpinning regulations (**Chapter 5**);
- the reforms to legal education and training of solicitors in England and Wales which have been introduced by the SRA since 2004 which saw the report of the LETR (**Chapter 6**).

CHAPTER 5

Regulatory authority

5.1	Introduction	5.4	Solicitors Regulation Authority
5.2	The Legal Services Board		
5.3	The Law Society of England and Wales		

5.1 INTRODUCTION

The regulation of legal education and training in England and Wales is the responsibility of the Solicitors Regulation Authority (SRA), overseen by the Legal Services Board (LSB). However, because of the Legal Services Act (LSA 2007), the position of the Law Society of England and Wales (Law Society) also needs to be understood. This chapter explains the role of each of the bodies with regulatory authority and, in relation to the SRA, its regulatory approach, training strategy, policy making and operations responsibilities, and the training regulations for which the SRA is responsible.

5.2 THE LEGAL SERVICES BOARD

The LSB is an oversight regulator and oversees the front-line regulatory bodies for the legal profession.

The LSB was created by LSA 2007 and came into existence on 1 January 2009 with an overriding mandate to ensure that 'regulation in the legal services sector is carried out in the public interest, and that the interests of consumers are placed at the heart of the system'.[1]

---

[1] LSB website, 'About Us'.

5.3 THE LAW SOCIETY OF ENGLAND AND WALES

The Law Society is the Approved Regulator under LSA 2007 for solicitors in England and Wales. However, the Law Society discharges its regulatory functions through the SRA in line with the requirements of LSA 2007 that regulatory and representative functions should be separated.

Following delegation of its regulatory powers to the SRA the Law Society remains the independent professional body for solicitors, its stated purpose being to 'represent and support [its] members, promoting the highest professional standards and the rule of law'.

5.4 SOLICITORS REGULATION AUTHORITY

The SRA, as the independent regulatory body of the Law Society, deals with all regulatory and disciplinary matters, and sets, monitors and enforces standards for solicitors across England and Wales. The SRA, specifically, has responsibility for education, training and development both leading up to (with one exception) and following qualification as a solicitor.

5.4.1 Regulatory approach

To quote from the SRA's Corporate Strategy 2014/15 to 2016/17:

> 2.1 We regulate the conduct of solicitors and law firms to protect consumers and to support the rule of law and the administration of justice.
> 2.2 We are a part of the Law Society, the professional body for solicitors, but have full operational independence and all our regulatory decisions are made independently in the public interest.
> 2.3 We work within a statutory framework for regulation provided by the Solicitors Act 1974, the Administration of Justice Act 1985 and, primarily, by the Legal Services Act 2007. We also work within a framework provided by internal governance rules which guarantee our independence from the Law Society and also by formal guidance provided by the Legal Services Board, the oversight body for all legal service regulators.[2]

The SRA must adhere to best regulatory practice and the better regulation principles set out in LSA 2007, s.28(3)(a) that 'regulatory activities should be transparent, accountable, proportionate, consistent and targeted only at cases in which action is needed'.

It is also guided by the objectives set down in LSA 2007 to:

---

[2] SRA, Corporate Strategy 2014/15 to 2016/17, 20 November 2014.

- protect and promote the public interest;
- support the constitutional principle of the rule of law;
- improve access to justice;
- protect and promote the interests of consumers;
- promote competition in the provision of services;
- encourage an independent, strong, diverse and effective legal profession; and
- increase public understanding of the citizens' legal rights and duties.[3]

The SRA requires those it regulates to:

- Act with independence and integrity
- Maintain proper standards of work
- Act in the best interests of clients
- Comply with their duty to the court to act with independence and integrity
- Keep client affairs confidential[4]

Comment

What is important to know about the SRA's regulatory ambit and approach is that:

- the SRA changed its focus from individual-based to entity-based regulation in 2011. This means that its primary regulatory concern is the entity, and all who are owners of and employees within an entity;
- as a Licensing Authority for Alternative Business Structures (ABSs) under LSA 2007, the SRA does not only regulate individual solicitors and solicitor-owned firms, but also ABSs which include owners or managers who do not belong to one of the legal professions and which may employ qualified lawyers regulated by other Approved Regulators;
- the SRA introduced principles-based and outcomes-focused regulation in 2011, with a corresponding Code of Conduct comprising over-arching mandatory principles, supported by mandatory outcomes and non-mandatory indicative behaviours which are contained in the SRA Handbook.

The SRA sets standards for solicitors in order to give the public full confidence in the solicitors' profession. To that end, among the SRA responsibilities are those of:

- setting the standards for qualifying as a solicitor;
- monitoring the performance of organisations that provide legal training;
- drafting the rules of professional conduct, particularly to make sure they protect the interests of clients; and
- setting requirements for solicitors' Continuing Professional Development.[5]

---

[3] SRA, Corporate Strategy 2014/15 to 2016/17, 20 November 2014, para.2.7.
[4] SRA, Corporate Strategy 2014/15 to 2016/17, 20 November 2014, para.2.5.
[5] SRA website, 'What We Do'.

5.4.2 Training strategy

In response to government pressure to remove unnecessary regulation and reduce the burden on businesses, the SRA commenced an initiative in 2013 to identify and remove unnecessary regulation. It launched a programme of regulatory reform in May 2014, which included removal of perceived unnecessary regulation of legal education and training (see **Chapter 6**). This has been evidenced in one of the four strategic objectives for its Corporate Strategy 2014/15 to 2016/17, namely to 'work with solicitors and firms to raise standards and uphold core professional principles.'[6] To this end, the SRA is focusing on '[modernising] the systems for educating, admitting, training and developing solicitors so that they are fit for the current and future challenges posed by modern society, consumer needs and the needs of a rapidly developing and changing legal services market.'[7]

This is in line with another of the SRA's strategic objectives, to 'reform our regulation to enable growth and innovation in the market and to strike the right balance between reducing regulatory burdens and ensuring consumer protection'. The SRA has therefore been focusing on measures to:

- remove unnecessary regulatory barriers and restrictions and enable increased competition, innovation and growth to better serve the consumers of legal services;
- reduce unnecessary regulatory burdens and cost on regulated firms;
- maintain robust, proportionate and transparent systems to ensure the protection of those consumers that require regulatory protection;
- ensure that regulation is properly targeted and proportionate for all solicitors and regulated businesses, particularly small businesses; and
- ensure that our regulation remains relevant in a legal services market with multiple regulators and where legal services will increasingly be combined with the delivery of other professional services.[8]

Comment

What this has resulted in is a new set of training regulations in, and reform of, nearly every stage and component of the legal education and training framework. Very little is as it was before the LETR, and for some aspects of legal education and training the new regime and the old are co-existing for a period.

5.4.3 Policy and decision making

The SRA Board delegates work on education and training to the SRA Policy Committee. This committee was created in February 2016 as a merger of the

---

[6] SRA, Corporate Strategy 2014/15 to 2016/17, 20 November 2014, para.1.1.
[7] SRA, Corporate Strategy 2014/15 to 2016/17, 20 November 2014, p.8.
[8] SRA, Corporate Strategy 2014/15 to 2016/17, 20 November 2014, para.4.2.

previous Education and Training Committee (ETC) with the Standards Committee. The Policy Committee advises the SRA Board (the SRA's governing body) on matters relating to pre-admission and post-admission training of solicitors. The Policy Committee will make recommendations regarding education and training to the SRA Board, which are then for the Board to approve. In certain cases, further approval will be required from external bodies, such as approval from the LSB for regulation changes or, in the case of Legal Apprenticeships (see **Chapter 11**), from the Department for Business, Innovation and Skills.

The Policy Committee is chaired by a member of the SRA Board, although the committee's actual membership comprises solicitor and lay members.

5.4.4 Day-to-day operations

In terms of day-to-day operations, education and training comes under the auspices of the SRA's Regulation and Education Unit, which is headed by the Director of Education and Training and overseen by the Executive Director, Policy.

5.4.5 The training regulations

The education and training requirements for qualification and admission as a solicitor are set out in the SRA Training Regulations 2014 – Qualification and Provider Regulations ('Qualification and Provider Regulations'), which came into effect on 1 July 2014.

The Qualification and Provider Regulations regulate any individual seeking to be admitted as a solicitor and any organisation providing, or intending to provide, recognised training or the Qualifying Law Degree (QLD), Common Professional Examination (CPE) or Graduate Diploma in Law (GDL), Exempting Law Degree (ELD), Legal Practice Course (LPC) or Professional Skills Course (PSC). The Qualification and Provider Regulations do not apply to those seeking admission under the SRA Qualified Lawyer Transfer Scheme Regulations 2011.

The Continuing Professional Development (CPD) requirements for solicitors are governed by the SRA Training Regulations 2011 Part 3 – CPD Regulations ('CPD Regulations'). The CPD Regulations and the Qualification and Provider Regulations ('the Solicitor Training Regulations') are based on outcomes, in line with the SRA's outcomes-focused approach to regulation, and are part of the SRA Handbook.

Comment

LSA 2007, which is responsible for the regulatory framework that is described in this book, is to be the subject of review before the end of the current Parliament in 2020. This was announced by the Lord Chancellor on 15 July 2015, who while not wishing to pre-empt the outcome of the review, described the current position as having 'a danger of regulators falling over each other's feet'.

CHAPTER 6

Reform of legal education and training

6.1	Introduction	6.4	Consultations
6.2	The Legal Education and Training Review	6.5	Proposed consultations and reforms
		6.6	The SRA Training Regulations
6.3	Reforms		

6.1 INTRODUCTION

Since 2004, legal education and training of solicitors has undergone extensive reform by the Solicitors Regulation Authority (SRA) (the regulatory body for solicitors in England and Wales – see **5.4**), affecting nearly all parts of the qualification framework in England and Wales. At the date of publication, further reforms are to come. Given the extent of the reforms and the short period within which they have been produced, organisations can be confused as to what has changed and why. In order to provide context for the chapters on the different aspects of the qualification framework, and to explain for those who are used to the pre-reform position what has changed and why, and what is likely to change and when, this chapter therefore explains:

- the background to the reforms;
- changes in terminology arising from the reforms;
- transitional arrangements;
- the various consultations and proposals, and their status;
- the status of the various training regulations; and
- future and proposed reforms.

6.2 THE LEGAL EDUCATION AND TRAINING REVIEW

The legal education and training of solicitors, barristers and Chartered Legal Executives underwent extensive review between June 2011 and October 2013, when the SRA, Bar Standards Board (BSB) and ILEX Professional Standards

(IPS)[1] commissioned a fundamental review of the education and training requirements of the legal profession in the light of the Legal Services Act 2007, largely at the behest of the Legal Services Board.[2] The review was called 'The Legal Education and Training Review' or LETR.

The LETR was conducted by an independent research team, the UKCLE Research Consortium ('the Research Team'), managed by a Review Executive comprising the Chief Executive Officers of the SRA, BSB and IPS. The Review Executive, in turn, was supported by a Consultation Steering Panel which provided advice and information to it and to the Research Team as and when required.

To quote the LETR:

> The primary objective of the Review was to ensure that England and Wales has a legal education and training system that advances the regulatory objectives contained in the Legal Services Act 2007, and particularly the need to protect and promote the interests of consumers and to ensure an independent, strong, diverse and effective legal profession. It examined regulated and non-regulated legal services.[3]

The required outcomes of the LETR were to identify 'the scope for deregulation of existing training requirements and whether there was a case for bringing aspects of the non-regulated sector within a scheme of regulation'.[4]

The LETR was conducted in four phases, as described below, with briefing and discussion papers also produced in relation to the various phases:

- **First phase**: A literature review and analysis of the literature and past research on the system of legal education and training in England and Wales and internationally, as well as a comparative study of other sectors and professions.
- **Second phase**: 'Contextual analysis', which involved analysing 'the impacts of contextual changes on individuals and entities and defined the range of legal and broader emerging professional roles, as well as the skills, knowledge and experience necessary to provide high quality and competitive services in the legal services market of the future'.[5]
- **Third phase**: Research into the legal services sector workforce to identify 'potential future structural change and its implications for future education and training needs'.[6] This resulted in LETR Briefing Paper 2/2012: Future Workforce Demand in the Legal Services Sector, 25 September 2012.
- **Fourth and final phase**: Preparation of a final report with final recommendations 'on the main challenges and changes that will influence the shape of the

---

[1] Now re-named CILEx Regulation.
[2] The then Chief Executive of the LSB called for an assessment of the fitness of education and training in equipping the legal workforce of the future in England and Wales when giving the annual Lord Upjohn lecture in 2010 – Press Release, 4 March 2014.
[3] LETR website, 'What is LETR?'
[4] LETR website, 'What is LETR?'
[5] LETR website, 'What is LETR?'
[6] LETR website, 'What is LETR?'

future legal services sector and determine the legal services education and training system(s) necessary to underpin that structure'.[7]

> **Comment**
>
> The commissioning regulators would probably regard their activities in response to the final report also as part of LETR, and the work carried out by the Resource Team merely as the 'research phase'. However, as LETR tends to be understood within the profession as referring to the work of the Research Team resulting in the final report, that is the meaning of 'LETR' which is used in this book.

In all, the Research Team published the following Discussion Papers, Briefing Papers and Research Updates, the abstracts for which have been used to summarise the purpose and content of each.

Briefing Paper 1/2011. Competence	Purpose: • To provide understanding of the basic strengths and weaknesses of competence-based models in evaluating possible ways forward for the regulation of legal education and training Content: • A guide to the notion of competence and the way it is used in competence-based systems of learning • An outline of the key issues concerning competence and the use of competencies • A caution against the assumption that competence-based approaches are largely accepted and unproblematic
Discussion Paper 01/2011. Project Scope, Research Questions and Assumptions	Purpose: • To provide an overview for members of the Consultation Steering Panel of the Research Team's approach, research questions and proposed methodology Content – introduced a number of assumptions: • Recommendations for change must, so far as possible, be evidenced-based • The focus of the Review is on assuring competence to deliver legal services • The Review is shaped by the new regulatory context • The Review is sector-wide in its scope

---

[7] LETR website, 'What is LETR?'

Discussion Paper 02/2011. Equality, Diversity and Social Mobility	Purpose: • To offer a general map of the sector in terms of its demographic composition, drawing primarily on the literature reviewed as part of Phase 1 of LETR Content: • Explores ways in which existing education and training practices might constitute initial and continuing barriers to access, and therefore a constraint on diversity and social mobility
Discussion Paper 01/2012. Key Issues I: Call for Evidence	Purpose: • To provide a brief description of context for the Review, focusing particularly on the current regulatory framework, and discussing emerging issues from work undertaken to date Content: • Describes key strengths and weaknesses of the current system • Seeks to establish a relatively high-level consensus on what needs to change
Briefing Paper 1/2012. Knowledge, Skills and Attitudes Required for Practice at Present	Purpose: • To identify a range of knowledge, skills and attitudes for paralegal practice, and for professional practice at point of qualification and post-qualification • Presentation of a set of broad taxonomies for each of these 'levels' (broadly defined) • Identification of a range of generic skills, knowledge, behaviours and attitudes that may be missing from the existing frameworks and regulatory structure
Briefing Paper 2/2012. Future Workforce Demand in the Legal Services Sector	External report – produced by Warwick Institute of Employment Research: Purpose: • To examine changing pattern of legal employment through employment projections for the legal services sector in England and Wales, based primarily on official statistics Content: • Summary highlighting main quantitative findings from study and speculating on implications for future of legal services education and training

	• Fuller technical report setting out a baseline of quantitative information about the changing workforce over the decade to 2020, and identifying some gaps in and limits of existing data on the legal services workforce
Briefing Paper 3/2012. Provocations and Perspectives	Paper by external consultant, Richard Susskind

Purpose:

• To explore issues and challenges facing the LETR, including what is changing, what the purposes of education and training should be, and the considerable impact of IT on the delivery of both legal services and legal education and training

Content – Paper highlights the following needs:

• To develop a new generation of 'hybrid professionals'

• To create opportunities for students to study current and future trends in legal services, and to develop new skills, such as risk and project management

• To address key training problems for the profession as clients become less willing to subsidise training, and traditional trainee work becomes less available as a consequence of outsourcing, etc.

• To develop tools and cultures that support just-in-time rather than just-in-case learning

• To ensure that all law students have the opportunity to develop a 'thick understanding' of law, its theory, history, structure and impact on society

• To reduce the missed opportunities for research, collaboration and training that arise from existing gaps between academics and practitioners

• To create a formal structure that will facilitate the systematic appraisal of the education and training system and training needs every three to five years |
| Discussion Paper 02/2012. Key Issues II: Developing the Detail* | Purpose:

• To identify short-term future trends in the delivery of legal services and consider their implications for legal services education and training (LSET)

• To summarise responses to Discussion Paper 01/2012, relate them to findings emerging from the Research Team's fieldwork and identify key issues for the Review

• To offer some initial indications of solutions under consideration, and to highlight important aspects of the relatively high-level, structural work the Research Team is undertaking on the frameworks, standards and tools for regulating LSET

• To seek further information, evidence and views from |

	stakeholders on a range of specific questions raised by the Research Team's work to date, and on the future direction of LSET
Research Update 12/01. Contextual Analysis: Progress and Headline Findings*	Purpose: • To describe methodology and core areas of work conducted as stage 2 ('contextual analysis') of the LETR research phase • To highlight interim findings from work with both regulated and unregulated sectors Content: • Sets out what the LETR Research Team has done, how the team has done it, and outlines work remaining
Research Update 12/02. Workforce Development: Progress and Headline Findings	Purpose: • To describe core areas of work conducted as part of stage 3 ('workforce development' and future training needs) of LETR research phase Content: Findings concerning – • knowledge, skills and attributes required for practice; role of technology and future forms of practice; paralegal and 'technician' roles within the sector and barriers to entry • legal developments in Wales and implications for LETR
Briefing Paper 4/2012. Symposium Report	Content: • Keynote papers and summaries of parallel and workshop sessions from LETR Symposium held in July 2012

*No longer available on LETR website because superseded by the final report of the Research Team.

The Research Team reported its findings in June 2013 in the 'Legal Education and Training Review final research report' ('LETR Report'), which also presented a number of prioritised actions and recommendations for future regulation of legal education and training. The status of the Report and its recommendations, however, was advisory only and the commissioning regulators were not bound to accept the Report or adopt the recommendations. Consequently, each regulator has responded to the LETR Report individually and has taken forward its own initiatives following on from the Report, independently of the other regulators. The responses of the LSB and SRA have been as follows.

6.2.1 The LSB's response to the LETR

Following the publication of the LETR Report, the LSB issued a consultation in September 2013 on a draft guidance for regulators on education and training. In March 2014, the LSB published its guidance, 'Guidance on Regulatory Arrangements for Education and Training Issued under Section 162 of the Legal Services Act 2007' ('LSB Guidance'), which set out the principles it expected Approved Regulators to take account of in undertaking their own review in the light of the evidence and recommendations in the LETR Report and in what timeframe. Although only 'guidance', the LSB warned that 'Any approved regulator that departs from our guidance must justify doing so with explicit reference to the regulatory objectives and better regulation principles supporting such departure'.[8] The main themes of the LSB guidance were outcomes and flexibility: it expected regulators to have in place regulatory arrangements for education and training that delivered the following outcomes:

- education and training requirements focus on what an individual must know, understand and be able to do at the point of authorisation;
- providers of education and training have the flexibility to determine how to deliver training, education and experience that meet the outcomes required;
- standards are set that find the right balance between what is required at the point of authorisation and what can be fulfilled through ongoing competency requirements;
- regulators successfully balance obligations for education and training between the individual and the entity both at the point of entry and on an ongoing basis;
- regulators place no inappropriate direct or indirect restrictions on the numbers entering the profession.

6.2.2 The SRA's response to the LETR

The SRA, for its own part, published a policy statement, 'Training for Tomorrow – Ensuring the lawyers of today have the skills for tomorrow' ('Policy Statement') in October 2013, which set out its proposals 'for radical reform'[9] of the regulatory framework for the legal education and training of solicitors in England and Wales, and which in fact pre-empted the LSB's Guidance and the principles contained in it. To quote the SRA:

---

[8] LSB, 'Guidance on Regulatory Arrangements for Education and Training Issued under Section 162 of the Legal Services Act 2007', Version 1, 4 March 2014, p.1.
[9] SRA, 'Training for Tomorrow: Regulation Review', 25 April 2014, p.1.

REGULATION OF LEGAL EDUCATION AND TRAINING

> Those proposals have been informed by recognition that for too long we have been doing too little to assure appropriate standards and have instead been overly preoccupied with detailed educational design and inputs. We intend to move our attention from prescribing the educational 'how' and to focus instead on assuring standards of competence against a framework which is fit for modern legal practice.[10]

What this approach revolved around was, firstly, a desire to remove regulation as part of the so-called 'Red Tape Initiative' which the SRA was undertaking more widely to 'remove layers of regulation which neither assure quality nor enable excellence',[11] and secondly, to build a framework based on flexibility rather than prescription. These initiatives were given the collective name, 'Training for Tomorrow' (T4T), and a T4T section was set up on the SRA website,[12] where the various reforms and their status are detailed.

Comment

Firms should check the T4T website regularly to find out about the status of reforms. The T4T team has a T4T blog[13] as well as webinars to keep organisations and individual solicitors informed, and it is also possible to subscribe to T4T email alerts in relation to the T4T programme of legal education and training reform.

6.3 REFORMS

6.3.1 Summary of SRA reforms and reforms to be consulted upon

Following the LETR Report and the Policy Statement, the SRA introduced a number of reforms to the legal education and training framework. The extent of these reforms, together with those which have already been put in place since 2010, and those reforms still to be consulted upon, is illustrated in the following table (proposed reforms are indicated by italics).

---

[10] SRA, 'Training for Tomorrow: Regulation Review', 25 April 2014, p.1.
[11] SRA, 'Training for Tomorrow: Regulation Review', 25 April 2014, p.1.
[12] SRA website, 'About Us: Training for Tomorrow'.
[13] SRA website, 'About Us: Training for Tomorrow'.

REFORM OF LEGAL EDUCATION AND TRAINING

Qualification	Reform
Academic stage	
• Qualifying Law Degree (QLD) • Common Professional Examination (CPE)/Graduate Diploma in Law (GDL) • Exempting Law Degree (ELD)	Introduction of whole or partial exemption for Equivalent Means* (see **Chapter 10**) *Entry requirements for proposed centralised Solicitor Qualification Examination (SQE) may not require or recognise the QLD or CPE/GDL (see **6.5.1**)*
Vocational stage	
Legal Practice Course (LPC)	Introduction of partial exemption for BVC/BPTC graduates* (see **Chapter 10**)
	Introduction of whole or partial exemption for Equivalent Means* (see **6.4.1**)
	*Entry requirements for proposed SQE may not require or recognise the LPC (see **6.5.1**)*
Period of Recognised Training (PRT)	Removal of Training Contract requirement and introduction of a Period of Recognised Training* (see **6.4.1**)
	Removal of reference to contentious and non-contentious experience* (see **6.4.1**)
	Introduction of whole or partial exemption for Equivalent Means* (see **6.4.1**)
	*Entry requirements for proposed SQE may not require PRT and may require other forms of work-based experience (see **6.5.1**)*
Professional Skills Course (PSC)	Removal of requirement of when PSC must be completed* (see **6.4.1**)
	Introduction of whole or partial exemption for Equivalent Means* (see **6.4.1**)
	*Entry requirements for proposed SQE may not require PSC (see **6.5.1**)*
Sign-off	Replacement of Guidelines on the Assessment of Character and Suitability (2008) with SRA Suitability Test 2011* (see **Chapter 18**)
	*Competence Statement to replace Day One Outcomes as standard to be met for admission (see **Chapter 10**)*
Admission	*Introduction of Solicitor Apprenticeships as satisfying education and training requirements for admission under Qualification and Provider Regulations (see **Chapter 11**)*
Post-qualification	
Continuing Professional Development (CPD)	Removal of requirements for authorisation of CPD providers, and of requirement to attend accredited courses* (see **6.4.2**)

Qualification	Reform
	Introduction of option to adopt a Continuing Competence approach into the CPD regime as alternative to annual minimum hours requirement** (see **6.4.2**)
	Introduction of Competence Statement to be used with Continuing Competence approach** (see **6.4.4**)
	Replacement of CPD regime and 16 hours' requirement with Continuing Competence approach from 1 November 2016 for all solicitors (see **6.4.2**)
Management training	Removal of requirement to undertake Management Course Stage 1** (see **6.4.3**)

*Reforms introduced pre- or during 2014.
**Reforms introduced during 2015/16.

6.3.2 Transitional arrangements

For some of these reforms, parallel systems are in place:

- Until 31 October 2016, solicitors may meet the CPD requirements under the SRA Training Regulations 2011 Part 3 – CPD Regulations ('CPD Regulations') either by adhering to the 16-hour annual requirement or by adopting the Continuing Competence approach (see **20.9**).
- Trainees who started their Training Contract on or before 30 June 2014 are subject to the SRA Training Regulations 2011 Part 2 – Training Provider Regulations ('2011 Training Provider Regulations'), while trainees who undertake a PRT under a contract of employment from 1 July 2014 are subject to the SRA Training Regulations 2014 – Qualification and Provider Regulations ('Qualification and Provider Regulations'), although trainees under the 2011 Training Provider Regulations may opt to be governed by the Qualification and Provider Regulations (see **5.4.5**).

6.3.3 Status of future and proposed SRA reforms as at date of publication

Reforms which are due to be introduced after the date of publication are:

- replacement of the current CPD scheme with a Continuing Competence scheme from 1 November 2016 (see **Chapter 20**); and
- introduction of Solicitor Apprenticeships from September 2016 (see **Chapter 11**).

Reforms which have been proposed but not decided upon are:

- introduction of a centralised Solicitors Qualification Examination (SQE).

Reforms which will be consulted upon in 2016 are:

- entry requirements for the SQE, including pre-qualification work experience and workplace assessment (see **6.4.6**); and
- regulation changes in relation to the SQE.

6.3.4 Terminology

With the reforms has come a wealth of new terminology.

Stage	Pre-reform terminology	Post-reform terminology
Academic		QLD/CPE/GDL
	QLD provider CPD provider GDL provider	Approved Education Provider
Vocational		LPC
	LPC provider	Authorised Education Provider
	Training Contract	Period of Recognised Training
	Training Establishment	Authorised Training Provider
	Trainee Solicitor	
	Training Principal	
	PSC	
	PSC provider	Authorised Education Provider

6.4 CONSULTATIONS

The reforms which have been introduced by the SRA have all been the subject of consultations based on specific consultation documents. The details of each consultation, and the specific proposals relating to legal education and training consulted upon, as well as the respective status of each, are as follows.

6.4.1 SRA consultation: 'Training for Tomorrow: Regulation Review'[14]

Date consultation opened: 6 December 2013
Date consultation closed: 25 February 2014
Number of responses: 41
SRA response: 'Regulations Review: Removing Unnecessary Regulations and Simplifying Processes', 28 April 2014

---

[14] SRA, 'Training for Tomorrow: Regulation Review', 25 April 2014

6.4.1.1 Proposals and status

Proposal	Note/comment	Status of proposal
1. Remove complex and inflexible exemption arrangements: To introduce the concept of 'Equivalent Means', creating greater flexibility within the current routes to qualification by enabling the SRA to recognise equivalent education and training	To expand permitted exceptions and exemptions to recognise that knowledge and skills outcomes (and the standard at which they must be achieved) may have been achieved by an individual through assessed learning and work-based learning See **Chapter 10** (Equivalent Means), **Chapter 12** (QLD), **Chapter 13** (Conversion courses), **Chapter 14** (LPC), **Chapter 15** (PRT) and **Chapter 16** (PSC)	Adopted
2. To remove the requirement for certificate of completion of academic stage to be issued by SRA: To remove the necessity for students to apply to the SRA for a certificate to confirm that they have completed the academic stage of training	The certificate was necessary to confirm that a student had completed the academic stage of training, in order to enrol on the LPC See **Chapter 14** (LPC)	Adopted
3. Remove duplicated arrangements for CPE and LPC: To remove requirements which duplicate the regulatory requirements placed on higher education institutions (HEIs) by the Quality Assurance Agency (QAA)	To remove requirements for a student with an overseas degree or non-standard qualifications to apply to the SRA for a certificate of academic standing before being eligible to enrol on the CPE; to apply to the SRA for partial or full exemption from the CPD; to complete the CPE with one provider See **Chapter 13** (Conversion courses) and **Chapter 14** (LPC)	Adopted
4. Clarify the regulatory requirements for training: To remove the requirement for training to take place under the terms of a contract specified by SRA	Introduce concept of a 'period of recognised training' and place regulatory focus on defining and assuring the standard and quality of training, rather than specifying the employment rights and obligations between trainee and Training Provider See **Chapter 15** (PRT)	Adopted

Proposal	Note/comment	Status of proposal
5. Clarify the regulatory requirements for training: To remove the restrictions on the number of trainees a firm may train, and how many practising certificates a Training Principal must have in order to hold that role	SRA believed no data to support assumption that quality of training and supervision is assured by these requirements. Replace requirements on training establishments and supervisors with new concept of an 'Authorised Training Provider'. More appropriate to look more holistically at a Training Provider's resources and infrastructure See **Chapter 15** (PRT)	Adopted
6. Re-phrase requirement for trainees to experience a breadth of legal practice: To remove the requirement for development of skills in 'contentious' and 'non-contentious work', and amend the wording of the three areas of law requirements to 'at least three distinct areas of English law and practice'	Also, Training Provider does not need to apply to SRA to terminate training; SRA no longer to participate, either directly or by appointing a conciliator, in the resolution of disputes between Training Providers and trainees; no longer specify when PSC must be completed See **Chapter 15** (PRT)	Adopted
7. Remove the requirement for student enrolment: To remove the requirement in Part 3 of the Qualification and Training Regulations to have student enrolment in place before commencing a Legal Practice Course and serving under a Training Contract	Replace with requirement for disclosure of any character or suitability issue to be assessed by SRA prior to commencing a Period of Recognised Training See **Chapter 14** (LPC)	Adopted

6.4.2 Training for Tomorrow: A New Approach to Continuing Competence[15]

Date consultation opened: 5 February 2014
Date consultation closed: 2 April 2014
Comment: This was committed to in the Policy Statement
Number of responses: 64
SRA response: Consultation Response – Training for Tomorrow: A New Approach to Continuing Competence, 23 May 2014

---

[15] SRA, 'Consultation Response – Training for Tomorrow: A New Approach to Continuing Competence'.

6.4.2.1 Proposals and status

Proposal	Note/comment	Status of proposal
1. Approach to Continuing Competence Option 1: A shift from procedural compliance to competence	SRA preferred option: Remove the prescriptive requirement for solicitors to undertake CPD through specific regulations. Rely instead on existing provisions in the SRA Handbook and Code of Conduct requiring regulated entities and individuals to deliver competent legal services and train and supervise their staff. For regulated entities and individuals to decide how these outcomes are achieved. Implicit in the requirement to deliver competent legal services is an obligation to reflect on whether the quality of practice is good enough, identify areas for development and ensure appropriate development activity is undertaken See **Chapter 20** (CPD)	Adopted – but implementation delayed until 1 November 2016 to allow firms to adapt. Will also develop a 'toolkit' and a statement of competence to set out what a competent solicitor should be able to do. 16% of respondents preferred Option 1
2. Approach to Continuing Competence Option 2: Regulations requiring solicitors to plan and reflect on their development	Retain a mandatory requirement for solicitors to undertake CPD but address some of the weaknesses of the current approach by requiring solicitors to identify and document their training needs in a development plan, to implement that plan and to evaluate its effectiveness on a documented annual cycle	Rejected. 9% of respondents preferred Option 2
3. Approach to Continuing Competence Option 3: Retain a minimum hours scheme with some modifications	Retain a mandatory requirement for solicitors to undertake CPD but address some of the weaknesses of the current scheme by requiring the CPD to relate to the individual's current or anticipated area of practice and allow a wider range of activities to count, recognising the value of on-the-job learning. This could be supported by the use of targeted education	Rejected, although over 50% of respondents preferred Option 3

Proposal	Note/comment	Status of proposal
	and training as a regulatory tool where specific risks have been identified or for remedial purposes where after the event regulation has been ineffective	
4. How should the SRA monitor Continuing Competence?	Possible approaches: (i) require a nominated individual within a regulated entity to take responsibility for the competence of legal services and/or compliance with CPD requirements and for reporting material breaches to the SRA (ii) requirement for all entities to nominate an individual to take responsibility for compliance with the SRA's education and training-related requirements. This could be the Compliance Officer for Legal Practice (COLP) or another person, *or* require entities to have in place a specific individual with responsibility for education and training matters but reporting to the SRA only in the event of the need for targeted supervision or enforcement activity by the SRA (iii) If a prescribed CPD Scheme retained (as under Options 2 and 3), require all regulated entities to make an annual declaration to the SRA that the solicitors employed by them had complied with the CPD requirement	No conclusion. SRA noted this question 'did not generate as much debate and engagement from respondents as the previous questions and that there was an 'even split' of views as to the preferred approach[16]

---

[16] SRA, 'Consultation Response – Training for Tomorrow: A New Approach to Continuing Competence', p.9.

6.4.3 Red Tape Initiative – Phase 3: Changes to the SRA's Education and Training Regulations[17]

Date consultation opened: September 2014
Date consultation closed: 17 November 2014
Comments: Changes proposed in consultation arose as a consequence of recent changes made to education and training regulations in relation to student enrolment and CPD, and the need to make other education and training requirements consistent with those changes
Number of responses: 23
SRA response: SRA Analysis of responses and SRA response: 'Education and Training Regulations Review: Red Tape 3', 8 January 2015

6.4.3.1 Proposals and status

Proposal	Note/comment	Status of proposal
1. Include the Welsh language in education and training	To recognise Welsh language skills in the outcomes prefacing the SRA's education and training regulations as an alternative to English language skills for solicitors practising in Wales	Approved
2. Remove the requirement for a lawyer who is qualified in jurisdiction outside the UK to obtain a certificate of eligibility to undertake QLTS Assessment	To remove requirements for qualified lawyers overseas to have a certificate issued by the SRA confirming their eligibility to sit the Qualified Lawyers Transfer Scheme (QLTS) Assessment and, in removing the requirement, to remove regulation which relates to a requirement to undertake a separate English language test for non-EEA international applicants and remove the restriction on the number of assessment attempts permitted in a 5-year period See **Chapter 9** (QLTS routes)	Approved
3. Remove the requirement on individual solicitors to undertake Management Course Stage 1	See **Chapter 20** (CPD)	Approved

---

[17] SRA, 'Red Tape Initiative – Phase 3: Changes to the SRA's Education and Training Regulations', 8 January 2015.

REFORM OF LEGAL EDUCATION AND TRAINING

6.4.4 SRA consultation 'Training for Tomorrow – A Competence Statement for Solicitors'[18]

Date consultation opened: October 2014
Date consultation closed: 12 January 2015
Comments: The proposal for a Competence Statement for solicitors arose out of the commitment in the SRA's Policy Statement, 'Training for Tomorrow', to define solicitors' standards more rigorously through the development of a Competence Statement for solicitors, as part of its programme of reform
Number of responses: 72
SRA response: 'A Competence Statement for Solicitors – SRA Response to the Consultation', March 2015

6.4.4.1 Proposals and status

Proposal	Note/comment	SRA's conclusion
Part One: Developing the Competence Statement		
*See **Chapter 20** (CPD)*		
Consultation question 1: Does the competence statement reflect what you would expect a competent solicitor to be able to do?		Yes
Consultation question 2: Are there any additional competencies which should be included?		No
Consultation question 3: Have we struck the right balance in the Statement of Legal Knowledge between the broad qualification consumers tell us they understand by the title solicitor and the degree of focus which comes in time with practice in a particular area?	• SRA did not believe it appropriate to include a statement that the standard required for practice is 'high' • Re: the concern that all solicitors would be required to maintain knowledge of all areas set out in the Competence Statement – this is not the SRA's intention; rather, solicitors are required to know areas of law which are relevant, even if outside their particular practice area. Therefore addition to A4C made and to footnotes	Some amendments made to proposed Competence Statement but without further opportunity for consultation on amendments. To support solicitors in moving to the new Continuing Competence approach, the SRA to issue online resources (including a toolkit)

---

[18] SRA, 'Training for Tomorrow: A Competence Statement for Solicitors'.

Proposal	Note/comment	SRA's conclusion
	• Re: criticisms of the structure and drafting of the Competence Statement – amendments made, including a note that the Competence Statement should be read holistically, and some amendments to structure	
Part Two: Using the Competence Statement to assure competence at admission		
*See **Chapter 21** (Competence Statement)*		
Consultation question 4: Do you think that the Threshold Standard articulates the standard at which you would expect a newly qualified solicitor to work?		Yes
Consultation question 5: Do you think that the Statement of Legal Knowledge reflects in broad terms the legal knowledge that all solicitors should be required to demonstrate they have prior to qualification?		Yes
Part Three: Using the Competence Statement to define Continuing Competence		
*See **Chapter 20** (CPD)*		
Consultation question 6: Do you think that the Competence Statement will be a useful tool to help entities and individuals comply with Principle 5 in the Handbook and ensure their continuing competence?		Yes
Consultation question 7: Are you aware of any impacts, either positive or negative, which might flow from using the Competence Statement as a tool to assist entities and individuals with complying with Principle 5 in the Handbook and ensuring their continuing competence?		

6.4.5 'Regulatory Reform Programme – Improving Regulation: proportionate and targeted measures'

Date consultation opened: April 2015
Date consultation closed: 11 June 2015
Comments: This consultation arose from the SRA's support for the development of new apprenticeship routes to qualification, as stated in its position statement, 'Training for Tomorrow'. The consultation contains other proposals not relevant to 'Training for Tomorrow', however
Number of responses: Not known at date of publication
SRA response: Not available at date of publication; however, the SRA Board at its September 2015 meeting approved the proposals in relation to Legal Apprenticeships. However, the SRA had not, as at date of publication, produced a formal consultation response

6.4.5.1 Proposals and status

Proposal	Note/comment	Status of proposal
Consultation question 18: Do you agree with our proposal to enable qualification as a solicitor through the Apprenticeship route?	Proposal would involve 'minor changes' to reg.2 of the SRA Qualification and Provider Training Regulations 2014 to permit qualification through the English or Welsh apprenticeship pathways. Qualification would require apprentices to demonstrate that they have met the requirements set out in the assessment plan for the Trailblazer Apprenticeship or in the apprenticeship framework for the Welsh apprentice SRA Handbook Glossary would also be amended to include definitions of 'Apprenticeship', 'The Apprenticeship Standard for a Solicitor (England)' and 'The Level 7 Higher Apprenticeship in Legal Practice (Wales)' in the SRA Handbook Glossary See **Chapter 11** (Legal Apprenticeships)	Approved by SRA Board, September 2015. Rule change made in 1 November 2015 re-issue of SRA Handbook

6.4.6 'Training for Tomorrow: Assessing Competence'

Date consultation opened: December 2015
Date consultation closed: 4 March 2016
Comments: Having published the Competence Statement, the next stage in the SRA's programme of reform is 'to develop a new assessment framework, aligned to the Competence Statement, which will enable us to assess in a consistent, rigorous and fair manner that intending solicitors can demonstrate the competencies set out in the Competence Statement'.[19] This arises from the SRA's concerns about consistency, highlighted in the LETR report, and the SRA's perception that there is a need to enable a more flexible range of pathways to qualification to emerge.[20] The proposals in this consultation therefore address 'how best to assess the competence of intending solicitors'.[21]
Number of responses: Not known at date of publication
SRA response: Not available at date of publication

6.4.6.1 Proposals and status

Proposal	Note/comment	Status of proposal
1. Do you agree that the introduction of the SQE, a common professional assessment for all intending solicitors, best meets the objectives set out in paragraph 10?	Proposal is based on Option 3 in the SRA's consultation on the Competence Statement (see **6.4.4**) to develop a centralised assessment of competence that all candidates are required to undertake prior to qualification, aligned to the Statement of Solicitor Competence, Statement of Legal Knowledge and Threshold Standard.[22] The proposed assessment would be called the Solicitors Qualifying Examination (SQE)	Pending

---

[19] Transitional arrangements published on the SRA website.
[20] SRA website – Questions and Answers [CPD position statement], 28 October 2014.
[21] SRA Consultation 'Training for Tomorrow: Assessing Competence', 7 December 2015, p.4.
[22] SRA Consultation 'Training for Tomorrow: Assessing Competence', 7 December 2015, p.8.

Proposal	Note/comment	Status of proposal

2. Do you agree that the proposed model assessment for the SQE described in paragraphs 38 to 45 and in Annex 5 will provide an effective test of the competencies needed to be a solicitor?	Proposed assessment model would consist of two assessment components:
	Part 1: Functioning Legal Knowledge Assessments:
	• Assessing sufficient knowledge to practise effectively
	• Computer-based modularised assessments
	• Including unflagged ethical questions
	• Part 1 to be passed before attempting Part 2
	Part 2: Practical Legal Skills Assessments
	• Assessing competence in:
	  – interviewing and advising
	  – advocacy/oral presentation
	  – negotiation
	  – writing
	  – drafting
	  – legal research
	• Standardised practical legal tasks using simulation
	• Live role plays with standardised clients to assess oral skills
	• Computer-based assessment of written skills using applied tasks and case studies
	• Assessment of each skill twice in two different practice contexts
	• Including unflagged ethical questions
	• Modularised assessments able to be taken separately[23]
		Pending

---

[23] SRA Consultation 'Training for Tomorrow: Assessing Competence', 7 December 2015, p.17.

Proposal	Note/comment	Status of proposal
3. Do you agree that all intending solicitors, including solicitor apprentices and lawyers qualified in another jurisdiction, should be required to pass the SQE to qualify and that there should be no exemptions beyond those required by EU legislation, or as part of transitional arrangements?	SRA has concluded that it should not grant an exemption from the SQE if the intending solicitor has done a law degree because the Competence Statement assesses different competencies to those examined on the law degree,[24] and SRA has concerns about variability in academic standards on law degrees	Pending
4. With which of the stated options do you agree and why: (a) offering a choice of 5 assessment contexts in Part 2, those aligned to the reserved activities, with the addition of the law of organisations? (b) offering a broader number of contexts for the Part 2 assessment for candidates to choose from? (c) focusing the Part 2 assessment on the reserved activities but recognising the different legal areas in which these apply?	Part 2 Practical Legal Skills Assessments would be based on reserved activities (probate, property, criminal and civil litigation) and law of organisations (business law and practice) 'because it is a major practice area for solicitors'.[25] However, SRA recognises that 'not all firms can offer experience in all five practice areas',[26] so its preferred proposal is that 'candidates take three out of five contexts, with at least one being contentious and one non-contentious'.[27] However, it is offering two further alternative models b) and c) because some firms and employers might have difficulty providing experience for even three of these assessment contexts	Pending

---

[24] SRA Consultation 'Training for Tomorrow: Assessing Competence', 7 December 2015, p.19.
[25] SRA Consultation 'Training for Tomorrow: Assessing Competence', 7 December 2015, p.19.
[26] SRA Consultation 'Training for Tomorrow: Assessing Competence', 7 December 2015, p.19.
[27] SRA Consultation 'Training for Tomorrow: Assessing Competence', 7 December 2015, p.19.

Proposal	Note/comment	Status of proposal
5. Do you agree that the standard for qualification as a solicitor, which will be assessed through the SQE, should be set at least at graduate level or equivalent?	SRA has chosen not to benchmark the SQE on to the level descriptors in the Framework for Higher Education Qualifications (FHEQ), which is used for the law degree and LPC because it says that the FHEQ is designed for use in a different context and purpose. Instead, the standard for Part 2 assessment will be 'comparable to the level trainee solicitors currently reach by point of qualification, therefore higher than the current LPC standard'[28] SRA would produce its own Assessment Framework document during 2016	Pending
6. Do you agree that we should continue to require some form of pre-qualification workplace experience?	SRA has taken expert advice that 'pre-qualification workplace experience has an important role to play in developing the competence of intending solicitors' and 'in assuring both the credibility of the new approach to qualification and of the solicitor brand'.[29] SRA is therefore likely to continue to require some form of workplace experience. The question is whether this should be the PRT, which SRA sees as a significant barrier to qualification for some[30] Q6–12 are intended to elicit early views for further work SRA will be doing and consulting on during 2016	Pending
7. Do you consider it necessary for the SRA to specify a minimum time period of pre-qualification workplace experience for candidates?		Pending

---

[28] SRA Consultation 'Training for Tomorrow: Assessing Competence', 7 December 2015, p.21.
[29] SRA Consultation 'Training for Tomorrow: assessing competence' 7 December 2015, p.23.
[30] SRA Consultation 'Training for Tomorrow: assessing competence' 7 December 2015, p.24.

Proposal	Note/comment	Status of proposal
8. Should the SRA specify the competencies to be met during pre-qualification workplace experience instead of specifying a minimum time period?		Pending
9. Do you agree that we should recognise a wider range of pre-qualification workplace experience, including experience obtained during a degree programme, or with a range of employers?		Pending
10. Do you consider that including an element of workplace assessment will enhance the quality of the qualification process and that this justifies the additional cost and regulatory burden?		Pending
11. If you are an employer, do you feel you would have the expertise to enable you to assess trainee solicitors' competencies, not capable of assessment in Part 1 and Part 2, to a specified performance standard?		Pending
12. If we were to introduce workplace assessment, would a toolkit of guidance and resources be sufficient to support you to assess to the required standard? What other support might be required?		Pending

REFORM OF LEGAL EDUCATION AND TRAINING

Proposal	Note/comment	Status of proposal
13. Do you consider that the prescription or regulation of training pathways, or the specification of entry requirements for the SQE, are needed in order to: (a) support the credibility of the assessment? (b) and/or protect consumers of legal services and students at least for a transitional period?	In the Training for Tomorrow position paper in 2013, SRA said it would consider the extent to which it needed to prescribe content and structure of the stages to qualification. In relation to requiring a law degree, SRA believes that a degree is not an essential requirement and can see no regulatory justification because it says the profession has never required all solicitors to have a degree, quoting the five-year articles route previously and the CILEx route. Q14 about the law degree is intended to elicit early views for further work SRA will be doing and consulting on formally during 2016	Pending
14. Do you agree that not all solicitors should be required to hold a degree?		Pending
15. Do you agree that we should provide candidates with information about their individual and comparative performance on the SQE?	Although SRA does not believe that its proposal for the SQE would discriminate against particular groups of candidates, it is concerned at differences in pass rates for the GDL and LPC based on ethnicity, gender and disability status, and is considering providing candidates with details of their individual performance on the SQE, as objective evidence of their quality and suitability to be a solicitor. However, this would mean designing the assessment to rank candidates according to a score, rather than on a pass/fail basis, which has various risks.[31] Qs 15 and 16 are intended to provide early views for further work SRA will be doing and consulting on during 2016	Pending
16. What information do you think it would be helpful for us to publish about: (a) overall candidate performance on the SQE? (b) training provider performance?		Pending

---

[31] SRA Consultation 'Training for Tomorrow: Assessing Competence', 7 December 2015, p.31.

Proposal	Note/comment	Status of proposal
17. Do you foresee any additional electronic data interchange (EDI) impacts, whether positive or negative, from our proposal to introduce the SQE?	This is to do with whether the SQE would increase the cost of qualification	Pending
18. Do you have any comments on these transitional arrangements?	SRA published the principles which would underpin its approach to transition for the domestic routes to qualification in July 2015 (see **6.5.1**)	Pending
19. What challenges do you foresee in having a cut-off date of 2025/26?		Pending
20. Do you consider that this development timetable is feasible?	SRA has set out a timetable of a programme of work leading to the possible introduction of the SQE	Pending

Comment

It might appear curious that all proposals made by the SRA in all the consultations which have closed have been adopted. When the reports of the individual consultations are considered, however, it is clear that this is not because no contrary views, opinions or issues were raised by respondents; rather, the SRA takes the approach that consultations are not voting exercises but an opportunity for respondents to raise issues or concerns which the SRA can then consider, so that it can ensure that it has itself considered all the issues and, if not, possibly to amend or refine its proposals. Although the proposed introduction of the new Continuing Competence regime in place of the CPD regime was postponed in order to allow time for the necessary cultural change to take place within the professions, generally the SRA's response to concerns is either to produce a 'toolkit' or other information and guidance. What the SRA's consultations appear to be, in fact, are presentations of proposals the SRA has decided upon after due consideration and research but about which it is required to consult in accordance with best regulatory practice and the SRA's policy on consultation set out in its 'Our Approach to Consultation'. To be fair to the SRA, the reality is that the level of responses to consultations is consistently low and generally from institutions, some of which suffer from a 'they would say that, wouldn't they' perception. That should not discourage organisations and individuals responding to consultations: on the contrary. Perhaps higher levels of responses might have more influence with the SRA. Further, organisations and individuals need to provide perspectives on issues which the SRA as a regulator may not possess.

6.5 PROPOSED CONSULTATIONS AND REFORMS

6.5.1 Entry requirements for the Solicitors Qualification Examination (SQE) and pre-qualification work experience

If the SRA decides to introduce the SQE following the 'Training for Tomorrow: Assessing Competence' consultation (see **6.4.6**), then the next step will be to consult on what, if any, entry requirements there should be for the SQE.

In its 'Training for Tomorrow: A Competence Statement for Solicitors' consultation (see **6.4.4**), the SRA identified three possible approaches, which might also have various combinations. These were that the SRA would:

- continue to prescribe specific pathways to qualification (such as the QLD/CPE + LPC + recognised period of training), subject to their being matched against the Competence Statement, and which would be taught and assessed by authorised trainers and providers;
- permit education and training providers to design and assess their own programmes, provided the programmes are matched to the Competence Statement;
- develop centralised assessment of competence that all candidates are required to undertake prior to qualification.[32] Candidates might be able to take the assessment regardless of the education and training pathway which they have followed. This approach could also include specifying pre-requisites such as satisfactory completion of a period of practical experience or of an authorised pathway.

The SRA has opted for the third approach, which is the basis for the 'Training for Tomorrow: Assessing Competence' consultation, and now needs to decide whether or not it will continue to require completion of academic and vocational stages of education and training, and of the QLD, CPE/GDL, LPC, PRT and PSC specifically. It stated in the 'Training for Tomorrow: Assessing Competence' consultation document that the three options given above 'are not mutually exclusive: we could require candidates to have met particular entry requirements, such as specified qualifications, before they take the centralised assessment, or to have completed a period of recognised training prior to qualification'.[33] However, it has also said already that pre-qualification work-based experience is likely to be required,[34] as well as possible workplace assessment, but that a law degree 'is not an essential pre-requisite for safe practice as a solicitor and we can see no regulatory justification for requiring all solicitors to be graduates'.[35]

---

[32] www.sra.org.uk/sra/policy/training-for-tomorrow/Resources/transitional-arrangements-qanda.page.
[33] SRA Consultation 'Training for Tomorrow: Assessing Competence', 7 December 2015, p.9.
[34] SRA Consultation 'Training for Tomorrow: Assessing Competence', 7 December 2015, p.23.
[35] SRA Consultation 'Training for Tomorrow: Assessing Competence', 7 December 2015, p.28.

The SRA intends to issue a consultation on specific proposals for entry requirements for the SQE and pre-qualification work experience in 2016, if it decides to introduce the SQE, and will make its decision on entry requirements and pre-qualification workplace experience and/or assessment at the end of 2016. A further consultation on regulation changes would take place in early 2017, with a view to new regulations coming into effect in 2018, and admission under the existing regulations ceasing at the end of the academic year 2025/26.[36]

The SRA intends to publish full transitional arrangements once the consultation on entry requirements has been completed and decided upon. Until then, all that is known are the principles upon which the SRA will base transition arrangements for the domestic routes to qualification.[37] These are that:

- candidates would not have to repeat a stage of training they have already completed;
- those part-way through a QLD or CPE/GDL would be able to complete those qualifications and complete the academic stage of training but would then have to transfer to the new regulations. So, they would be exempt from the corresponding part of Part 1 of the SQE but would be required to pass the remaining parts of Part 1 and Part 2;
- those partway through the LPC, PSC, PRT or ELD could either complete the vocational stage and qualify under the existing assessment requirements, or transfer to the new regulations.[38]

Those principles would also apply to candidates qualifying through Equivalent Means. However, no transitional requirements would be required for:

- candidates on the Solicitor Apprenticeship route, for which they are required to pass centralised assessments; or
- QLTS candidates, as the QLTS would be merged into the SQE.

6.5.2 Timetable for proposed reform activity

The timetable for proposed and future legal education reform known at the date of publication is set out in the following table.[39]

---

[36] SRA Consultation 'Training for Tomorrow: Assessing Competence', 7 December 2015, pp.33–4.
[37] SRA Consultation 'Training for Tomorrow: Assessing Competence', 7 December 2015, p.33.
[38] SRA Consultation 'Training for Tomorrow: Assessing Competence', 7 December 2015, p.33.
[39] Based on timetable included in SRA Consultation 'Training for Tomorrow: Assessing Competence', 7 December 2015, p.35.

REFORM OF LEGAL EDUCATION AND TRAINING

Date anticipated	Reform	Action
June 2016	SQE	Publication of SRA's response to the SQE consultation, and decision by SRA as to introduction of SQE
Summer 2016	SQE	If the SQE is being introduced, publication of second SRA consultation on entry requirements for the SQE and pre-qualification workplace experience/assessment
Sept 2016	Legal Apprenticeship	Commencement of Apprenticeship programme leading to qualification as a solicitor
1 Nov 2016	CPD	Introduction of Continuing Competence approach for all solicitors in place of CPD
End 2016	SQE	Publication of SRA's response its consultation on entry requirements for the SQE, and decision by SRA as to point of entry requirements/regulation of pathways and on place of pre-qualification workplace experience or assessment
End 2016	SQE	If the SQE is being introduced, publication by SRA of a draft Assessment Framework document for the SQE
End 2016	SQE	If the SQE is being introduced, commencement by SRA of a tender process to procure an assessment organisation to run the SQE
Early 2017	SQE	If the SQE is being introduced, publication by SRA of a third consultation on changes to regulations, including transitional regulations, to the extent that these have not been covered in the consultation on entry requirements for the SQE
Mid-2017	SQE	If the SQE is being introduced, appointment by SRA of the assessment organisation to deliver the SQE
During 2017 and 2018	SQE Legal Apprenticeship	If the SQE is being introduced, development and testing of the SQE. Piloting of apprenticeship centralised assessment, subject to introduction of SQE
2018	Legal Apprenticeship	Earliest that centralised assessment for Legal Apprenticeship leading to qualification as a solicitor will be available, although subject to introduction of SQE
Not before start of the academic year 2018/19	SQE	Commencement of the SQE, if it is to be introduced

6.6 THE SRA TRAINING REGULATIONS

Because of the reforms arising out of the consultations described above, a new set of training regulations was produced in 2014, the SRA Training Regulations 2014 – Qualification and Provider Regulations, which came into effect on 1 July 2014. These replaced the SRA Training Regulations 2011 Part 1 – Qualification Regulations ('2011 Qualification Regulations'), and Part 2 – Training Provider Regulations 2011 ('2011 Training Provider Regulations') and the Monitoring of Courses Regulations 1991. However, because of the transitional arrangements with CPD and Training Contracts, previous regulations continue to apply. The position, which is therefore somewhat confusing, is summarised in the following table.

Name of Regulations	Status	From	Comment
SRA Training Regulations 2011 Part 1 – Qualification Regulations	Replaced by: SRA Training Regulations 2014 – Qualification and Provider Regulations	1 July 2014	However, the 2011 Qualification Regulations still apply to Training Contracts entered before 30 June 2014
SRA Training Regulations 2011 Part 2 – Training Provider Regulations	Replaced by: SRA Training Regulations 2014 – Qualification and Provider Regulations	1 July 2014	However, the 2011 Training Provider Regulations still apply to Training Contracts entered before 30 June 2014
SRA Training Regulations 2011 Part 3 – CPD Regulations	Current until 31 October 2016		Will be repealed and replaced from 1 November 2016
Monitoring of Courses Regulations 1991	SRA Training Regulations 2014 – Qualification and Provider Regulations	1 July 2014	However, the Monitoring of Courses Regulations 1991 still apply to Training Contracts entered before 30 June 2014
SRA Training Regulations 2014 – Qualification and Provider Regulations	Current		

> **Comment**
>
> If the SQE is introduced (see **6.4.6**), and depending on the entry requirements which the SRA decides upon, the Training Regulations will need to be amended if not replaced. According to the timetable set out in the 'Training for Tomorrow: Assessing Competence' consultation document, this would be during 2018.

SECTION B2

Routes to qualification

There are various ways to qualify as a solicitor in England and Wales, and not all require a law degree, as one might assume. Here, the routes are described so that the components can then be understood as steps along a particular pathway. In essence, all routes comprise an academic stage of education and training, as well as a vocational stage.

The routes to qualification as a solicitor of England and Wales can be divided into the domestic routes to qualification, which are covered in:

- **Chapter 7** (Domestic routes);
- **Chapter 11** (Legal Apprenticeships)

and re-qualification routes for those who are already qualified, which are covered in:

- **Chapter 8** (European Directive routes);
- **Chapter 9** (Qualified Lawyers Transfer Scheme routes).

Available exemptions from the domestic route to qualification are covered in:

- **Chapter 10** (Equivalent Means).

OPTIONS OTHER THAN RE-QUALIFICATION

With regard to re-qualification, it is important to say that there is actually no requirement for a lawyer who is already qualified in a jurisdiction other than England and Wales to re-qualify as a solicitor in order to provide legal services in England and Wales as an 'Authorised Person' under the Legal Services Act (LSA) 2007. Under LSA 2007, Authorised Persons include not only solicitors but also barristers, Chartered Legal Executives, patent attorneys, trade mark attorneys, notaries, licensed conveyancers, Costs lawyer, Registered European Lawyers, Registered Foreign Lawyers and, subject to conditions, Exempt European Lawyers (although he or she may be obliged to register as a registered European lawyer – see **8.2** below).

The reasons, traditionally, why a qualified lawyer would seek to re-qualify as a solicitor in England and Wales are many and varied, and include:

- having the right to carry on reserved legal activities, namely the exercise of rights of audience, the conduct of litigation, reserved instrument activities, probate activities and the administration of oaths, under LSA 2007, s.12;
- being able to become a partner, or more correctly, manager, in a firm regulated by the Solicitors Regulation Authority (SRA), or other career development (although registered non-UK lawyers and Exempt European Lawyers may become partners);
- reasons of perceived status.

The reality is that subject to meeting requirements for supervision, anyone, whether qualified or not, may undertake Reserved and Regulated Areas of Legal Practice under LSA 2007 if authorised by an Approved Regulator under LSA 2007. If the individual is not authorised by the SRA, then that person may only practise in reserved areas under the supervision of an Authorised Person under LSA 2007.

Under LSA 2007, non-lawyers, let alone non-solicitors, are able to become managers – 'partners' – in an Alternative Business Structure (ABS). The status that the qualification of solicitor might hold for someone is a subjective one and may be outweighed by opportunities created by LSA 2007 to practise and pursue a career path in non-traditional business structures which does not require the time or cost commitment of the traditional domestic pathways.

RE-QUALIFICATION ROUTES

For lawyers who are already qualified in jurisdictions other than England and Wales, or as a non-solicitor Authorised Person under LSA 2007, and who wish to re-qualify as a solicitor of England and Wales, the possible routes for re-qualification are either:

- Route 1: the Qualified Lawyers Transfer Scheme Regulations 2011 (QLTSR) and under European Directive 2013/55/EU[1] (the Recognition of Professional Qualifications Directive) and European Directive 98/5/EC (the Establishment Directive);
- Route 2: under the QLTSR if qualification under the Recognition of Professional Qualifications or Establishment Directives is not available; or
- Route 3: by way of one of the domestic routes.

Which of these routes is applicable to the particular lawyer will be determined by nationality and the jurisdiction in which the lawyer qualified:

- If the lawyer qualified in, and is a national of, a European Union (EU) member state or Iceland, Liechtenstein, Norway or Switzerland, with one of the professional titles recognised in the European Communities (Lawyer's Practice) Regulations 2000, SI 2000/1119 then Route 1 is applicable.

---

[1] Directive 2013/44/EU amends the previous Recognition of Professional Qualifications Directive 2005/36/EC.

- If not, but the lawyer qualified in a jurisdiction which comes within the 'list of jurisdictions and is eligible under the QLTSR',[2] then Route 2 is applicable.
- If neither of the above, the lawyer's only choice is to follow one of the domestic routes to qualification outlined above or to consider exemption from some or all of the requirements by way of Equivalent Means

Routes to qualification may change in the future, if the SRA introduces its proposed centralised Solicitors Qualification Examination (SQE), depending on the entry requirements it imposes for an SQE (see **6.4.6**, **6.5** and **Chapter 17**).

---

[2] SRA, 'Completing the Application to Transfer under the Qualified Lawyers Transfer Regulations 1990'.

CHAPTER 7

Domestic routes

7.1	Introduction	7.4	Non-degree routes
7.2	The law degree route	7.5	Equivalent Means
7.3	The non-law graduate route	7.6	Proposed changes

7.1 INTRODUCTION

The domestic routes to qualification permitted under the Solicitors Regulation Authority (SRA) Training Regulations 2014 – Qualification and Provider Regulations ('Qualification and Provider Regulations') have traditionally required a law degree, or a non-law degree followed by a 'conversion course'. However, from September 2016, when Legal Apprenticeships are introduced, a non-graduate route will also be available.

This chapter explains the three domestic routes to qualification as a solicitor that are now, or soon to be, available:

- the law degree route;
- the non-law degree route; and
- the non-degree route.

7.2 THE LAW DEGREE ROUTE

The traditional route to qualification is the law degree route, which involves completion of a law degree which is recognised by the SRA as a Qualifying Law Degree (QLD) (see **Chapter 12**), followed by the Legal Practice Course (LPC), a two-year Period of Recognised Training (PRT)[1] and the Professional Skills Course

---

[1] At present the two-year period may be reduced under the time-to-count regime if the trainee has had relevant experience in legal practice in a non-qualified position. A maximum of six months may be deducted on the basis of at least 12 months' experience (see **Chapter 15**). Alternatively, the requirement may be satisfied under Equivalent Means (see **Chapter 10**).

(PSC) (see **Chapter 16**). Depending on the type of QLD, the average time this route would take, assuming there were no gaps between the different stages, would be six years from starting the QLD.

7.3 THE NON-LAW GRADUATE ROUTE

There is an alternative route for individuals who do not have a QLD but who have a non-law honours degree. This route requires a non-law graduate to undertake and pass a conversion course – the Common Professional Examination (CPE) or Graduate Diploma in Law (GDL) (it is known as both) (see **Chapter 13**). This route merges into the QLD route at the point of commencement of the LPC, and also requires completion of a two-year PRT and PSC in the same way as the QLD route. Depending on the type of undergraduate non-law degree, the average time this route would take, assuming there were no gaps between the different stages, would be seven years from starting the non-law degree, or four years from starting the CPE/GDL.

Although called the 'non-law graduate' route, the route is also open to graduates with a non-QLD law degree.

7.4 NON-DEGREE ROUTES

Traditionally, the non-degree route to qualification as a solicitor has been via the Chartered Legal Executive route (see **Chapter 24**). However, in November 2015 the SRA Board 'agreed to amend the rules to allow qualification as a solicitor through an apprenticeship route'.[2]

7.4.1 Chartered Legal Executive route

A Chartered Legal Executive who wishes to qualify as a solicitor is exempted from the requirement to do the CPE/GDL (which, ordinarily, a person without a QLD would be required to do). In terms of the vocational stage requirements, a Chartered Legal Executive would be required only to undertake and pass the LPC, and undertake the Compulsory Core subjects of the PSC before being admitted. A Chartered Legal Executive would also be exempted from the requirement to do a PRT, given the work-based experience required in order to achieve the Chartered Legal Executive qualification.

---

[2] SRA, Minutes of the SRA Board meeting held on 9 September 2015, Public.

7.4.2 Legal Apprenticeship route

Reg.2.1(a)(ii) of the Qualification and Provider Regulations now provides for admission as a solicitor by completing a Legal Apprenticeship, as an alternative to completing the academic and vocational stages of training[3] in order to satisfy the SRA's education and training requirements for admission as a solicitor.

A legal apprentice who follows the Solicitor Apprenticeship Standard (see **Chapter 11**) may already have achieved the Paralegal Apprenticeship Standard or Chartered Legal Executive Standard, or may have obtained a QLD or done the CPE/GDL or LPC (any of which may entitle the legal apprentice to exemptions from the training requirements under the Solicitor Apprenticeship Standard). If not, the recommended minimum entry requirements are:

- five GCSEs, which include mathematics and English, and which are all at grade C or above, or their equivalent;
- three A-levels (or equivalent) at grade C as a minimum;

as well as:

- relevant employer-led work experience; and/or
- Level 3 Advanced Apprenticeship in a relevant occupation such as Legal Services, Professional Services or Providing Financial Services (possible exemptions).[4]

The Solicitor Apprenticeship Standard is based on the SRA's Statement of Solicitor Competence (see **21.1**), and final achievement of the required competencies is tested through a centralised assessment (see **Chapter 11**), leading to admission as a solicitor, provided that the SRA's Suitability Test (see **Chapter 18**) is also satisfied.

Legal Apprenticeships will be available from September 2016, although the SRA centralised assessment, which provides the 'endpoint' assessment, is not expected to be available until 2018 at the earliest.

7.5 EQUIVALENT MEANS

It is important to note that exemptions from some or all of the academic and vocational stage requirements on the domestic routes to qualification may be available on the basis of prior learning (assessed or work-based) under the SRA's Equivalent Means policy (see **Chapter 10**).

How the routes compare in terms of the time involved is shown in the following table.

---

[3] Qualification and Provider Regulations, reg.2.1(a)(i).
[4] 'Apprenticeship standard: solicitor (ready for delivery)', which can be found at **www.gov.uk/ government/collections/apprenticeship-standards**.

Years	Law degree route	Non-law degree route	Non-degree routes	
			CILEx route	Legal Apprenticeship route
1	QLD	Non-law honours degree	Qualifying employment + CILEx examinations	Legal Apprenticeship + Centralised Assessment Part 1 and Part 2
2				
3				
4	LPC	CPE		
5	PRT + PSC	LPC		
6		PRT + PSC	LPC + PSC	
7	Admission		Admission	Admission*
8		Admission		

*Based on six years to complete apprenticeship.

7.6 PROPOSED CHANGES

Should the SRA decide to introduce a centralised Solicitors Qualifying Examination (SQE) as proposed in its consultation document, 'Training for Tomorrow: Assessing Competence' (see **6.4.6**), anyone wishing to qualify as a solicitor would be required to undertake and successfully pass the SQE in order to qualify. Whether and how the components of the existing qualification pathway – QLD, CPE/GDL, LPC, PRT, PSC – would fit with the SQE, and whether the SRA would set entry requirements for the SQE (it may not), would be the subject of a separate consultation during 2016. What the SRA has already indicated, however, is that it believes that:

- the QLD should not justify exemption from the SQE and
- pre-qualification work-based experience would be likely to be required.

The SRA's decision on whether to introduce the SQE is due in June 2016 (see **6.5**), and the decision on entry requirements would be made at the end of 2016. Introduction of the SQE would not be before the start of the 2018/19 academic year, with new regulations coming into effect during 2018. This would mean the cut-off date for admission under the existing regulations would be the end of the 2025/26 academic year.

CHAPTER 8

European directive routes

8.1	Introduction	8.4	Partially qualified European lawyers
8.2	Registered European Lawyer status	8.5	Foreign lawyer status
8.3	Recognition of Professional Qualifications Directive		

8.1 INTRODUCTION

An EU-qualified lawyer may only provide legal services in the UK:

- under his or her home professional title if he or she is registered with the Solicitors Regulation Authority (SRA) as a Registered European Lawyer (REL); or
- by re-qualifying as a solicitor of England and Wales under European Directive 89/48/EEC[1] ('Recognition of Professional Qualifications Directive').

This chapter explains:

- what is required for registration as an REL;
- the requirements for re-qualification under the Directive;
- the position of partially qualified EU lawyers;
- the position of 'foreign' lawyers.

8.2 REGISTERED EUROPEAN LAWYER STATUS

If a lawyer who is both qualified in, and a national of, an Establishment Directive state wishes to provide legal services on a permanent basis in England and Wales under his or her home professional title, then the lawyer must apply for registration with the SRA under the European Communities (Lawyer's Practice) Regulations 2000, reg.17 as an REL. An REL is subject to the SRA's Code of Conduct in the

---

[1] Previously 2005/36/EC.

same way as a solicitor admitted in England and Wales. RELs are also able to practise the same reserved areas as solicitors, subject to some additional professional requirements, such as working in conjunction with a locally qualified lawyer for court work, and subject to restrictions on probate and conveyancing work, where the lawyer is qualified in a jurisdiction where these activities are reserved to the notarial profession. RELs are also authorised by the SRA to undertake reserved work in relation to immigration tribunal proceedings.

Lawyers of Establishment Directive states who work for a firm regulated by the SRA but who are based entirely outside England and Wales are classified as 'Exempt European Lawyers', and are exempt from registration and from direct regulation by the SRA (although they will be subject to the SRA Code of Conduct to the extent that the firm they work for is subject to the Code). Registered status is not concerned with qualification in England and Wales, but with entitlement to practise in England and Wales, and is analogous to the obligation on English and Welsh solicitors to have a practising certificate if they provide reserved legal activities or hold themselves out as solicitors.

8.3 RECOGNITION OF PROFESSIONAL QUALIFICATIONS DIRECTIVE

A lawyer who is a national of an EU member state and is qualified as a lawyer in an EU member state may re-qualify as a solicitor in England and Wales by way of an aptitude test under the Recognition of Professional Qualifications Directive. The European lawyer may, however, be able to apply for exemption from the aptitude test under the Establishment Directive.

8.3.1 Aptitude test

Under the Recognition of Professional Qualifications Directive, the SRA must recognise the qualifications of an EU national who is qualified as a lawyer in an EU member state and must consider those qualifications, as well as the experience of the individual, in order to allow the European lawyer to re-qualify as a solicitor. The European Communities (Recognition of Professional Qualifications) Regulations 2007, SI 2007/2781 implement the Recognition of Professional Qualifications Directive in the UK, and permit UK regulators, such as the SRA, to require the EU national applying to re-qualify to sit an aptitude test, defined in the Regulations as: 'a test of the applicant's professional knowledge conducted by the competent authority with the aim of assessing the ability of the applicant to pursue that profession in the United Kingdom'. Scotland and Northern Ireland both have set aptitude tests. However, the SRA takes a different approach by considering applications under the Recognition of Professional Qualifications Directive on the basis of jurisdiction and on an individual application basis. This means the SRA will require the applicant to take a set of exams on the basis of the SRA's assessment of the differences in qualification between that jurisdiction and England and Wales, which it requires of all applicants from that jurisdiction. The applicant can, however, seek individual exemption from the standard set of exams for that jurisdiction on the basis of relevant qualifications and experience. The particular aspects required to be covered in an aptitude test will comprise components from the Qualified Lawyers' Transfer Test, described below. If the applicant passes the bespoke test, he or she will be eligible to apply for admission.

8.3.2 Exemption from aptitude test

If the applicant is an REL, he or she is still subject to the requirements of the Recognition of Professional Qualifications Directive and the requirement of passing an aptitude test in order to re-qualify as a solicitor in England and Wales. However, under the European Communities (Lawyer's Practice) Regulations 2000, an REL may apply to the SRA to be exempted from the aptitude test requirement where he or she has been registered as an REL in England and Wales for at least three years and either:

- has practised for at least three years under his or her home professional title in England and Wales;[2] or
- has practised the law of England and Wales under his or her home title in England and Wales for less than three years, but has practised in England and Wales under his or her home title for at least three years.[3] In this case, the REL would have to prove to the SRA that his or her knowledge and experience of the law of England and Wales is equivalent to having practised the law of England and Wales for at least three years. This might be able to be established if the REL has undertaken further academic studies in English law, such as an LLM, or even Continuing Professional Development (CPD) courses in English law.

The SRA is not bound to grant an exemption even if one of these conditions is met, if it considers the applicant would be unfit to practise as a solicitor.[4]

A summary of the directives and UK enactments is given in the following table.

---

[2] European Communities (Lawyer's Practice) Regulations 2000, reg.29(2).
[3] European Communities (Lawyer's Practice) Regulations 2000, reg.29(3).
[4] European Communities (Lawyer's Practice) Regulations 2000, reg.30(3).

Directive no.	Directive name	UK enactment	Purpose
EU-qualified lawyers			
2005/36/EC	Recognition of Professional Qualifications Directive (repealed and replaced by Directive 89/48/EEC)	European Communities (Recognition of Professional Qualifications) Regulations 2007	
98/5/EC	Establishment Directive	European Communities (Lawyer's Practice) Regulations 2000	Facilitate practice of the profession of lawyer on a permanent basis in a member state other than that in which the qualification was obtained
22 March 1977	Services of Lawyers	European Communities (Services of Lawyers) Order 1978, SI 1978/1910	Enable, under certain conditions, lawyers qualified in other (non-UK) member states to provide services in the UK which could otherwise only be provided by advocates, barristers or solicitors
		Regulatory Arrangements (Changes to Regulation of Entities Owned or Managed by Registered European Lawyers) Rules 2014	
Non-EU qualified lawyers			
		Registered Foreign Lawyers Order 2009, SI 2009/1589	
		Courts and Legal Services Act 1990	

8.4 PARTIALLY QUALIFIED EUROPEAN LAWYERS

The decision of the European Court of Justice (ECJ) in the *Morgenbesser* case[5] concerns applications from EU nationals to qualify as lawyers in another EU

---

[5] *Morgenbesser* v. *Consiglio dell'Ordine degli Avvocati di Genova* (Case C-313/01), 13 November 2003.

member state, who have not completed the requirements for qualification in their home state. The ECJ decision requires the competent authority for the legal profession in an EU member state, such as the SRA in England and Wales, when faced with such an application, not to treat the applicant as ineligible to qualify in England and Wales, but to consider the extent to which the applicant's qualifications and experience to date satisfy the domestic route to qualification, whether partly or fully. This means that the SRA could, for instance, require the applicant to complete the Legal Practice Course (LPC), or to undertake a Period of Recognised Training (PRT) if that was the relevant experience missing.

> **Comment**
>
> What the decision does not say is that anyone who applies to the SRA must be allowed to qualify – on the contrary: what the decision states is that a competent authority is entitled to set its own standards and requirements for admission. However, what the authority must do is measure an applicant against those standards and requirements on a case-by-case basis, and then determine whether and to what extent the applicant needs to complete part/s of or all of the domestic route.

The SRA has recognised the *Morgenbesser* decision in its provisions for Equivalent Means (see **Chapter 10**).

8.5 FOREIGN LAWYER STATUS

A lawyer who is not a solicitor or barrister of England and Wales but who is a member of a regulated legal profession outside England and Wales, and is entitled to practise as a member of that legal profession, is a 'foreign lawyer'. There is no requirement on a foreign lawyer who is practising under his or her home professional title to re-qualify as a solicitor of England and Wales. In fact, if the foreign lawyer does not wish to enter into partnership with solicitors of England and Wales and/or RELs – or to be a manager of a recognised body – there is no obligation even to register as a Registered Foreign Lawyer (RFL).

If a foreign lawyer does wish to enter into partnership or become a manager of a recognised body as described above, however, he or she is required to apply to the SRA to be registered as an RFL, under the Courts and Legal Services Act 1990, s.89, supplemented by Sch.14 of the Act.

Comment

Registration as an RFL would only be necessary in a law firm which was not an Alternative Business Structure, but would not be necessary in a firm that was. However, the foreign lawyer would have to apply for authorisation as an 'Authorised Person', in order to become a 'Manager' under LSA 2007 in a recognised body under the Administration of Justice Act 1985, s.9, which is more onerous than RFL registration. Registered status is not concerned with qualification in England and Wales but with entitlement to partnership and the ensuing obligations.

CHAPTER 9

Qualified Lawyers Transfer Scheme routes

9.1	Introduction	9.6	Application for the QLTS
9.2	The scheme	9.7	Appeals
9.3	Requirements	9.8	Admission and qualification
9.4	Variations in requirements	9.9	Proposed changes
9.5	The QLTS Assessment		

9.1 INTRODUCTION

Qualified lawyers from another jurisdiction have a route to qualification under the Solicitors Regulation Authority (SRA) Qualified Lawyers Transfer Scheme Regulations 2011 (QLTSR), without having to complete the full education and training requirements currently specified in the SRA Training Regulations 2014 – Qualification and Provider Regulations ('Qualification and Provider Regulations'). Instead, the Qualified Lawyers Transfer Scheme (QLTS) involves sitting prescribed assessments but without any course or study requirements.

This chapter explains:

- the features and requirements of the QLTS;
- the variations in requirements depending on jurisdiction;
- the assessments involved in the QLTS;
- how to apply for the QLTS;
- the rights of appeal that are available;
- the requirements for, and obligations following, admission and qualification as a solicitor through the QLTS.

9.2 THE SCHEME

Whereas the Common Professional Exam (CPE) (or Graduate Diploma in Law (GDL)) is a conversion test for non-law graduates to 'convert' to law, the QLTS is effectively a conversion test for non-English and Welsh qualified lawyers to re-qualify as solicitors in England and Wales.

9.3 REQUIREMENTS

9.3.1 General

The requirements for and features of the scheme are summarised in the table below.

Eligibility	A candidate for qualification under the QLTS ('Candidate') is required by the QLTSR to: • be a qualified lawyer in a recognised jurisdiction • have followed the 'full route to qualification' in that jurisdiction • be entitled to practise as a qualified lawyer of that recognised jurisdiction, and • be of the character and suitability to be admitted as a solicitor (reg.2.1) See **9.3.2** Experience of working in England and Wales not required, although an advantage
Pre-requisites	• Ensure that qualification and jurisdiction are listed in the SRA's list of recognised jurisdictions and qualified lawyers • Apply to home jurisdiction regulator for confirmation that he or she is admitted in his or her home jurisdiction and has no outstanding disciplinary matters on his or her record • Apply to the SRA using the appropriate QLTS form *Note: Certificate of eligibility and English language requirements removed from 1 April 2015*
Exemptions	If a Candidate has previously taken and passed the Legal Practice Course (LPC), he or she may apply for an exemption from Part 1 of the QLTS Assessment, which is the multiple choice test (MCT) (reg.3.4)
Timing	The QLTS Assessment is run twice a year and takes place in London
Assessment provider	The QLTS Assessment is run by Kaplan QLTS as the sole Authorised Assessment Provider appointed by the SRA
Assessment content	The QLTS Assessment is in two parts: • MCT • Objective Structured Clinical Examination (OSCE)

Assessment requirements	• Candidates must pass the MCT before permitted to sit the OSCE • Candidates are required to sign a declaration acknowledging that the content of the QLTS Assessment is confidential, and that they will not disclose or discuss any of the content with anyone else Requirements differ for: • EU nationals • fully qualified barristers of England and Wales, non-solicitor LSA 2007 qualified lawyers • lawyers from another UK jurisdiction (i.e. Scotland, Northern Ireland but also Republic of Ireland) See **9.4**
Preparation required	No mandatory preparation required for the QLTS Assessment; rather, it is for each Candidate to determine how, and the extent to which, he or she needs to prepare by assessing his or her experience, knowledge and skills against the Day One Outcomes and the indicative content, which form the syllabus for the QLTS Assessment See **9.3.3**
Pass mark	For the MCT, the pass mark is determined by a Standard Setting Panel convened by the SRA based on the Angoff method supplemented by statistical test equations, as appropriate For the OSCE, the Candidate must pass the OSCE overall. The pass mark is set using the borderline regression method The standard required is of a newly qualified solicitor in England and Wales
Grades	n/a
Number of attempts permitted	No limit on the number of attempts See **9.3.4**
Results available	Guidance as to results is provided on the Kaplan QLTS Results page on its website one to two weeks before the relevant assessment. Results are sent to Candidates by email
Period of validity	No requirement to complete the QLTS within a specified period
Cost	The fees for 2016 are: MCT: £565 + VAT OSCE: £2,925 + VAT
Eligibility for admission	Candidate must have passed both the MCT and the OSCE (see **9.8**)
Monitored/regulated by:	The SRA is required to validate and authorise the provision of the QLTS Assessment by the Authorised Assessment Provider (reg.3.1(b)) and to monitor the Authorised Assessment Provider's provision of the QLTS Assessment

| **Relevant regulations** | SRA Qualified Lawyer Transfer Scheme Regulations 2011 |

9.3.2 Eligibility

9.3.2.1 *Qualified lawyer in a recognised jurisdiction*

The SRA defines 'qualified lawyer' as either:

> (i) a lawyer whose qualification we have determined:
>   (A) gives the lawyer rights of audience;
>   (B) makes the lawyer an officer of the court in the recognised jurisdiction; and
>   (C) has been awarded as a result of a generalist (non-specialist) legal education and training; or
> (ii) any other lawyer to whom we determine Directive 2005/36/EC on the recognition of professional qualifications applies.[1]

The SRA defines 'recognised jurisdiction' as a jurisdiction where the SRA has determined that:

> (i) to become a qualified lawyer applicants have completed specific education and training at a level that is at least equivalent to that of an English/Welsh H-Level (e.g. Bachelor's) degree;
> (ii) members of the qualified lawyer's profession are bound by an ethical code that requires them to act without conflicts of interest and to respect their client's interests and confidentiality; and
> (iii) members of the qualified lawyer's profession are subject to disciplinary sanctions for breach of their ethical code, including the removal of the right to practise, and
> all European jurisdictions to which Directive 2005/36/EC on the recognition of professional qualifications apply are 'recognised jurisdictions' for the purposes of the QLTSR.[2]

Jurisdictions will be recognised as eligible for the scheme if:

- the professional qualification of the jurisdiction requires education and training equivalent at least to that of a Bachelor's degree from an English or Welsh university;
- they have an ethical code which binds the members of the jurisdiction's legal profession and which requires the profession to respect the client's interest and confidentiality while not allowing conflicts of interest;

---

[1] SRA, 'Key Features of the New Transfer Scheme', 22 May 2015.
[2] SRA, 'Key Features of the New Transfer Scheme', 22 May 2015.

- they subject members of the profession to disciplinary sanctions, which could include removal of a lawyer's right to practise if the ethical code is breached.

Lawyers who apply for admission pursuant to the Recognition of Professional Qualifications Directive 89/48/EEC[3] (or any implementing legislation) or the Establishment Directive 98/5/EC (or any implementing legislation) are deemed to have followed the full route to qualification (reg.2.2). Under reg.5.1, if the QLTS candidate seeks to establish eligibility pursuant to the Establishment Directive or implementing legislation, then the candidate must prove to the SRA that he or she has met the requirements of the Establishment Directive and implementing legislation and, in particular:

- the nationality requirements set out in the legislation;
- the SRA's registration requirements; and either:
  - 'effectively and regularly pursued for a period of at least three years a professional activity in the UK in the law of the UK including Community Law in accordance with article 10.1 of the Establishment Directive';[4] or
  - 'effectively and regularly pursued a professional activity in the UK for a period of at least three years where [the candidate's] professional activity in the law of the UK has been for a period of less than three years, under the conditions set out in article 10.3 of the Establishment Directive'.[5]

Previously, the SRA would issue a certificate of eligibility upon being satisfied of an individual's eligibility for admission under the QLTSR. However, from 1 April 2015 the SRA removed the requirement for QLTS candidates to obtain a certificate of eligibility in order to sit the QLTS Assessment.

Comment

Removal of the requirement to obtain a certificate of eligibility does not remove the requirement for the individual to satisfy the Character and Suitability Test as a requirement for admission, however.

TRANSITIONAL ARRANGEMENTS

QLTS candidates who held Certificates of Eligibility as at 1 April 2015:

- are no longer restricted as to the number of attempts permitted at the QLTS Assessment or the time period within which they must pass the QLTS Assessment;
- are still subject to the same exemptions granted under the certificate;

---

[3] Previously 2005/36/EC.
[4] QLTSR, reg.5(c).
[5] QLTSR, reg.5(d).

- are not able to obtain a refund from the SRA for the fee for obtaining a certificate of eligibility;
- have an ongoing obligation to meet the SRA's Suitability Test 2011 requirements;
- may 'bank' their MCT pass if they have passed the MCT but failed the QLTS overall, and will be permitted to re-commence the QLTS by taking the OSCE;
- if they are transitional candidates who have passed the MCT and either the old OSCE or the old Technical Legal Skills Test (TLST) (but not both) will be allowed to exhaust their entitlement to three attempts during the five-year validity period of their certificate of eligibility by sitting either OSCE Part 1 or OSCE Part 2 alone. However, if the candidate is still unsuccessful, he or she will be required to sit the OSCE as a whole, although he or she will not be required to re-take the MCT.

In terms of the individual candidate, as opposed to the jurisdiction in which he or she qualified, the candidate would also need to:

- satisfy the SRA's requirements as to character and suitability; and
- have the right to practise in the jurisdiction in which he or she qualified, having followed the full route to qualification in that jurisdiction.

9.3.2.2 Full route to qualification

A QLTS candidate is recognised as having completed a full route to qualification if he or she has not qualified by way of a shortened or fast-track route, for example a route which does not assess all the same outcomes, subjects or practices in the law of that jurisdiction prior to qualification as a domestic lawyer of the other jurisdiction.

The SRA has a list of recognised jurisdictions. Because the list is subject to review, it is not reproduced here but the latest version can be found on the SRA website.

Comment

In theory, under reg.4.1 the SRA is required to review the lists of recognised jurisdictions and qualified lawyers every five years at least and, in fact, 'whenever written evidence is received which suggests the need for a jurisdiction or qualification to be reviewed' (QLTSR, reg.4.1).

If either an individual's qualification or jurisdiction is not recognised by the SRA, then the SRA advises the individual to contact his or her home bar or law society to ask whether it has applied to the SRA for recognition If it has not, the bar or law society should be asked by the candidate to email the SRA for a survey. The SRA would then check whether, according to the survey response, the qualification and/or jurisdiction met the SRA's regulatory requirements for recognition. The SRA advises that this process can take some months.

The fact that an individual's qualification or jurisdiction is not recognised by the SRA, so that the individual is therefore ineligible for the QLTS, is not able to be appealed by the individual concerned.[6]

The previous scheme, the Qualified Lawyers Transfer Test (QTTT), which was replaced by the current QLTS in 2009, had an experience requirement, which is not present under the current scheme, although it is recognised by the SRA that it would be difficult for a candidate to pass the QLTS Assessment if he or she did not have experience of practice in England and Wales. This is the purpose of the OSCE: to use practical exercises as an objective way of assessing a candidate's ability to practise in England and Wales.

9.3.2.3 English language ability

Previously, one of the requirements of eligibility for the QLTS was that a candidate had to meet the SRA's English language requirements. Unless these requirements were deemed to be satisfied (in the case of EEA and Swiss applicants), they could be satisfied by the candidate studying on a degree taught in English, or sitting an English language test, such as the International English Language Testing System (IELTS). However, from 1 April 2015 the English language requirement was removed, and instead the SRA relies on the QLTS Assessment as evidence of the required English language ability. The SRA therefore recommends that QLTS candidates ensure that their standard of English for writing, speaking, reading and listening is appropriate for the assessment.[7]

The SRA advises QLTS candidates to ensure they have the appropriate visa to enter the UK. The timing of the QLTS Assessment is such that a candidate who passes the MCT at the first attempt should be able to book on the next sitting of the OSCE and, conceivably, could be admitted as a solicitor within a year, provided the candidate passes the OSCE at the first attempt also, and has no character and suitability issues.

9.3.3 Preparation

Sample questions may be made available by the Authorised Assessment Provider on its website. Although the Authorised Assessment Provider is not permitted by the SRA to provide any preparatory courses (as was the case under the previous QLTT scheme), some courses are offered by other training providers by way of face-to-face or distance learning for the MCT and OSCE. The SRA does not validate or assure the quality of these courses.

Although QLTS candidates are no longer required to obtain a certificate of eligibility from the SRA, they are required to undergo an identity check when they present for the QLTS Assessment, and identity will also be checked at admission.

---

[6] QLTSR, reg.4.2.
[7] SRA website, 'Qualified Lawyers Transfer Scheme (QLTS) Update', 14 April 2015.

9.3.4 Number of attempts

The limit of three attempts during the five-year validity of the certificate of eligibility was removed as from 1 April 2015, following the SRA's Red Tape 3 consultation, 'Changes to the SRA's Education and Training Regulations' (see **6.4.3**).

9.4 VARIATIONS IN REQUIREMENTS

The transfer process is not available for partially qualified lawyers. If the individual is not fully qualified in his or her home jurisdiction, he or she may not sit the QLTS but needs to follow the domestic route to qualification described in **Chapter 7**, as appropriate, in order to be admitted as a solicitor of England and Wales, or he or she may apply to the SRA to assess the equivalence of his or her qualifications, following the judgment in *Morgenbesser*[8] (see **Chapter 8**).

Regulation 3.3 permits the SRA to determine which parts, if any, of the QLTS Assessment a lawyer applying for admission pursuant to EC Directive 2005/36/EC or a UK-qualified lawyer will need to pass. If a Candidate has passed the LPC, he or she is eligible under reg.3.4 for an exemption from Part 1 of the QLTS Assessment, namely the MCT (however, this exemption must be applied for). Otherwise, 'international lawyers' must pass all parts of the QLTS Assessment.[9]

9.4.1 EEA lawyers

Registered European Lawyers (RELs) who meet the criteria of the Establishment Directive 98/5/EC may apply directly for admission (see **Chapter 8**).

EEA lawyers who are not RELs will be individually assessed against the Day One Outcomes. If they have met the Day One Outcomes through prior learning and experience, they will not be required to take the QLTS Assessment. However, if they have not, then they may need to sit one or more parts of the QLTS Assessment.

An EU/EEA lawyer applying by way of a QLTS1 application form will need to provide evidence of how he or she has met the following outcomes in the context of the law and practice of England and Wales:

> A1 Knowledge of the jurisdiction, authority and procedures of the legal institutions and professions that initiate, develop, interpret and apply the law of England and Wales and the European Union
> A2 Knowledge of applicable constitutional law and judicial review processes
> A3 Knowledge of the rules of professional conduct, including the Solicitors' Accounts Rules
> A4 Knowledge of the regulatory and fiscal frameworks within which business,

---

[8] *Morgenbesser* v. *Consiglio dell'Ordine degli avvocati di Genova* (Case C-313/01), 13 November 2003.
[9] Reg.3.2.

legal and financial services transactions are conducted
- A5 Understanding of contract law
- A6 Understanding of Torts
- A7 Understanding of criminal law
- A8 Understanding of property law
- A9 Understanding of Equitable rights and obligations
- A10 Understanding of Human Rights
- A11 Understanding of the laws applicable to business structures and the concept of legal personality
- C1 The ability to establish business structures and transfer businesses
- C2 The ability to seek resolution of civil and criminal matters
- C3 The ability to establish and transfer proprietary rights and interests
- C4 The ability to obtain a grant of probate and administer an estate

9.4.2 Republic of Ireland qualified lawyers

9.4.2.1 Republic of Ireland qualified solicitors

The SRA has determined that the only area of substantial difference between the Day One Outcomes and the qualification process for Irish solicitors is the law and practice of land law or property law.[10] For that reason, solicitors admitted by the Law Society of Ireland who are eligible under the Recognition of Professional Qualifications Directive 2005/36 in terms of nationality, and who have completed the qualification process to become a solicitor of Ireland, may qualify as a solicitor of England and Wales either by:

- completing the land/property elements of each part of the QLTS Assessment (which will mean being assessed on probate as well as property in the OSCE because the probate element is 'inextricably linked');[11] or
- completing the Law Society of Ireland's English Property Law module, which, once passed and the SRA has been so informed, entitles the Candidate to apply for admission using an AD1 form (see **9.8**).

A Republic of Ireland qualified solicitor applying by way of a QLTS1 application form will need to provide evidence of how he or she has met the following outcomes in the context of the law and practice of England and Wales:

- A8 Understanding of property law
- C3 The ability to establish and transfer proprietary rights and interests
- C4 The ability to obtain a grant of probate and administer an estate

---

[10] SRA website, 'Qualified Lawyers Transfer Scheme'.
[11] SRA website, 'Qualified Lawyers Transfer Scheme'.

9.4.2.2 Republic of Ireland qualified barristers

Barristers qualified in the Republic of Ireland may re-qualify as a solicitor of England and Wales by using the assessment table for EU applicants.

9.4.3 UK qualified lawyers

9.4.3.1 Scottish qualified solicitors

The SRA has benchmarked the Scottish solicitor qualification against the Day One Outcomes, so that Scottish solicitors are automatically exempt from some areas. An application from a Scottish qualified solicitor will be assessed individually against the Day One Outcomes. If the Scottish solicitor has met the Day One Outcomes through prior learning and experience, he or she will not be required to take the QLTS Assessment. If not, then he or she may need to sit one or both parts of the QLTS Assessment.

A Scottish qualified solicitor applying by way of a QLTS1 application form will need to provide evidence of how he or she has met the following outcomes in the context of the law and practice of England and Wales:

> A1 Knowledge of the jurisdiction, authority and procedures of the legal institutions and professions that initiate, develop, interpret and apply the law of England and Wales and the European Union
> A3 Knowledge of the rules of professional conduct, including the Solicitors' Accounts Rules
> A5 Understanding of contract law
> A7 Understanding of criminal law
> A8 Understanding of property law
> A9 Understanding of equitable rights and obligations

9.4.3.2 Northern Irish qualified solicitors

Solicitors who have passed a Qualifying Law Degree (QLD) (see **7.2**) and have been admitted as a solicitor by the Law Society of Northern Ireland are not required to pass any part of the QLTS Assessment, but may apply for admission using an AD1 form (see **9.8**). This is because the SRA has determined that there are no areas of substantial difference between Northern Ireland and England and Wales in terms of law and practice.

9.4.3.3 Northern Irish qualified barristers

Barristers qualified in Northern Ireland may apply under the QLTS by using the assessment table for EU applicants.

9.5 THE QLTS ASSESSMENT

The QLTS Assessment is in two parts:

- the Multiple Choice Test (MCT); and
- the Objective Structured Clinical Examination (OSCE).

OSCEs are well known in medical and dental education. Because the aim of the QLTS is to ensure that a lawyer qualified in another jurisdiction has met the standard of knowledge and skill required of a newly qualified solicitor of England and Wales, the QLTS Assessment tests the SRA's Day One Outcomes. The Day One Outcomes represent the outcomes a solicitor who qualifies via the domestic route is expected to have achieved at the point of admission as a solicitor.

> **Comment**
>
> The assessment against Day One Outcomes will be replaced at some point by assessment against the Competence Statement (see **Chapter 21**).

9.5.1 Day One Outcomes

The Day One Outcomes are set out below without the indicative content. The indicative content for each of these outcomes can be found in the Qualified Lawyers Transfer Scheme Outcomes on the SRA website.

> **Day One Outcome A – Core knowledge and understanding of the law applied in England and Wales**
>
> A1 Knowledge of the jurisdiction, authority and procedures of the legal institutions and professions that initiate, develop, interpret and apply the law of England and Wales and the European Union
> A2 Knowledge of applicable constitutional law and judicial review processes
> A3 Knowledge of the rules of professional conduct, including the SRA Accounts Rules
> A4 Knowledge of the regulatory and fiscal frameworks within which business, legal and financial services transactions are conducted
> A5 Understanding of contract law
> A6 Understanding of torts
> A7 Understanding of criminal law
> A8 Understanding of property law
> A9 Understanding of equitable rights and obligations
>
> **Day One Outcome B – Intellectual, analytical and problem-solving skills**
>
> B1 Ability to review, consolidate, extend and apply knowledge and understanding
> B2 Ability to frame appropriate questions to identify clients' problems and objectives, and to obtain relevant information

B3 Ability to evaluate information, arguments, assumptions and concepts
B4 Ability to identify a range of solutions
B5 Ability to evaluate the merits and risks of solutions
B6 Ability to communicate information, ideas, problems and […] solutions to clients, colleagues and other professionals
B7 Ability to initiate and progress projects

Day One Outcome C – Transactional and dispute resolution skills

C1 Ability to establish business structures and transfer businesses
C2 Ability to seek resolution of civil and criminal matters
C3 Ability to establish and transfer proprietary rights and interests
C4 Ability to obtain a grant of probate and administer an estate
C5 Ability to draft legal documentation to facilitate the above transactions and matters
C6 Ability to plan and progress transactions and matters expeditiously and with propriety

Day One Outcome D – Legal, professional and client relationship knowledge and skills

D1 Knowledge of the legal services market
D2 Knowledge of commercial factors affecting legal practice
D3 Ability to undertake factual and legal research using paper and electronic media
D4 Knowledge to use technology to store, retrieve and analyse information
D5 Knowledge to communicate effectively, orally and in writing, with clients, colleagues and other professionals
D6 Ability to advocate a case on behalf of a client
D7 Ability to exercise solicitors' rights of audience
D8 Ability to recognise clients' financial, commercial and personal priorities and constraints
D9 Ability to exercise effective client relationship management skills
D10 Ability to act appropriately if a client is dissatisfied with advice or services provided

Day One Outcome E – Personal development and work management skills

E1 Ability to recognise personal and professional strengths and weaknesses
E2 Ability to identify the limits of personal knowledge and skills
E3 Ability to develop strategies to enhance professional performance
E4 Ability to manage personal workload
E5 Ability to employ risk management skills
E6 Ability to manage efficiently, effectively and concurrently a number of client matters
E7 Ability to work effectively as a team-member

Day One Outcome F – Professional values, behaviours, attitudes and ethics

F1 Knowledge of the values and principles upon which the rules of professional conduct have been developed
F2 Ability to behave professionally and with integrity
F3 Ability to identify issues of culture, disability and diversity
F4 Ability to respond appropriately and effectively to the above issues in dealings with clients, colleagues and others from a range of social, economic and ethnic backgrounds
F5 Ability to recognise and resolve ethical dilemmas

The MCT and OSCE each test different parts of the Day One Outcomes, as set out in the following table.

QLTS Assessment	Day One Outcomes	Length of Assessment
MCT	Part A Day One Outcomes	6 hours
OSCE	Parts C, D and F Day One Outcomes	6 days
	Part 1: Interviewing and advising, and oral presentations/advocacy	3 consecutive days
	Part 2: Legal writing, legal drafting, legal research	3 consecutive days

Candidates are not tested on Parts B and E of the Day One Outcomes because the SRA assumes these of all qualified lawyers.

9.5.2 The MCT

The MCT tests knowledge by way of multiple choice questions, samples of which are made available on the Authorised Assessment Provider's website.

9.5.3 The OSCE

Whereas the MCT tests knowledge, the OSCE tests practical application of knowledge and skills. Candidates are examined in the practice areas of:

- business;
- property and probate;
- civil and criminal litigation.

The OSCE is split into two parts, usually taken on separate days. It involves the candidate undertaking exercises – or 'stations' – in relation to the three practice areas. Part 1 of the OSCE involves:

- a client interview and completion of an attendance note or case analysis; and
- advocacy or an oral presentation.

Part 2 of the OSCE involves:

- legal research;
- legal writing;
- legal drafting.

9.5.4 Transitional provisions

Prior to January 2014, the QLTS consisted of three tests: the MCT, a Technical Legal Skills Test (TLST) and the OSCE. From January 2014, the TLST and OSCE were combined into a single – or 'combined' – OSCE. The position for Candidates who may not have completed each component prior to January 2014 is summarised in the table below.

Before Jan 2014			After Jan 2014
MCT	TLST	OSCE	
Passed	Not taken	Not taken	Sit combined OSCE, Parts 1 and 2. Fee payable for new OSCE
Passed	Not passed	Not passed	Sit combined OSCE, Parts 1 and 2. Fee payable for new OSCE
Passed	Not passed	Passed	Sit new OSCE Part 2 only. Fee payable for old TLST only
Passed	Passed	Not passed	Sit new OSCE Part 1 only. Fee payable for old OSCE only

9.6 APPLICATION FOR THE QLTS

It is not just a case of completing the required application form in order to undertake the QLTS: a candidate must also demonstrate that he or she is of good standing.

9.6.1 Certificate of Good Standing

A candidate must obtain a Certificate of Good Standing from his or her home bar. If a candidate is qualified in more than one jurisdiction, then he or she must submit an original Certificate of Good Standing from each of those jurisdictions.

All Certificates of Good Standing must have been issued no more than three months prior to the candidate's QLTS application.

The SRA reserves the right under reg.8.5 to require:

- such evidence as the SRA considers necessary to support an application;
- facts relevant to a candidate's application to be accompanied by statutory declaration;
- the candidate to attend an interview.

9.6.2 Application forms

Only once the SRA has received confirmation of the candidate's good standing from the applicant's home bar can he or she book a place on the QLTS Assessment with the Authorised Assessment Provider.

ROUTES TO QUALIFICATION

There are two application forms, depending on the candidate's nationality and jurisdiction in which he or she qualified: the QLTS1 form and the QLTS2 form. These forms are not generally available, and a potential QLTS candidate has to submit an initial application enquiry to the SRA in order to obtain the appropriate application form.

Type of lawyer		Relevant form
UK-qualified lawyer		QLTS1 form
EEA or Swiss national	Qualified lawyer	QLTS1 form
	Not qualified as a lawyer	Application to SRA under *Morgenbesser* to assess equivalence of qualifications
Other	Qualification on recognised list	QLTS2 form
	Qualification not on recognised list	Contact home bar or law society

The SRA may contact a candidate if more information is required to support the candidate's application, or may refer the application to an SRA assessor.[12]

9.7 APPEALS

There are various rights of appeal available under the QLTSR against decisions by the SRA in relation to a candidate's eligibility or application. Notification is deemed to have been given in the following circumstances according to the guidance note to reg.6:

- on the date on which the communication is delivered to or left at the candidate's last notified address or if it is sent electronically to the candidate's last notified email address or fax number;
- in the case of candidates in the EEA or Switzerland, seven days after the communication has been sent by post or document exchange to the candidate's last notified contact address;
- in the case of candidates outside the EEA or Switzerland, 14 days after the communication has been sent by post or document exchange to the candidate's last notified contact address.

Under reg.8.6, a candidate who has failed one or more assessment of the QLTS parts may not apply to the SRA for a review of a decision by the Authorised Assessment Provider.

---

[12] SRA website, 'FAQs about the Qualified Lawyers Transfer Scheme'.

9.8 ADMISSION AND QUALIFICATION

9.8.1 Application for admission

Even if a candidate passes the QLTS Assessment, he or she will not be entitled to be admitted as a solicitor unless the candidate:

- holds the correct professional qualification in a recognised jurisdiction;
- satisfies the SRA's requirements as to character and suitability.

The SRA therefore recommends[13] that candidates should make these checks before 'embarking on the QLTS Assessment'.

When the QLTS candidate does apply for admission, the candidate will also be asked whether he or she wishes to take part in an admission ceremony at the Law Society, participation in which is voluntary.

9.8.2 Character and suitability requirements

Once a QLTS candidate has passed both the MCT and CSCE, he or she may apply for admission by completing the appropriate admissions application form, and paying the requisite fee.

QLTS candidates who have lived in the UK are required to complete an applicant screening. The SRA may also require similar vetting checks in other countries where the candidate has worked to be submitted as well. Irrespective, all QLTS candidates who apply for admission are subject to the SRA Suitability Test (see **Chapter 18**) and, if the SRA uncovers issues of character and suitability, the SRA may prevent the candidate from being admitted.

The SRA therefore recommends that, if a candidate is aware of anything which might prevent him or her from meeting the SRA character and suitability requirements, he or she apply to the SRA for an early check on a character and suitability issue. Such a check may take up to six months, however, for the SRA to assess the application.

9.8.3 Continuing Professional Development obligations

Solicitors who qualify by taking the QLTS are required to attend the Financial and Business Skills module of the Professional Skills Course (PSC) (but not the Financial and Business Skills exam), and the Client Care and Professional Standards module of the PSC during their first Continuing Professional Development (CPD) year. The hours for these can be counted against the CPD hour requirement, if they are complying with the CPD requirements under reg.3.1(a) (see **Chapter 20**). However, there are a number of exceptions to this requirement, namely:

---

[13] SRA website, 'Qualified Lawyers Transfer Scheme (QLTS) Update', 14 April 2015.

- solicitors who undertook the Legal Practice Course (LPC) and PSC prior to admission;
- solicitors who sat the Professional Conduct and Accounts heads of the QLTT;
- solicitors transferring from Scotland via the QLTT.

Once a QLTS candidate has been admitted as a solicitor, he or she is required to renew his or her practising certificate each year, in the same way as solicitors who have qualified via the domestic qualification route. If the candidate does not take out a practising certificate but remains on the roll of solicitors, he or she is required to use the title 'non-practising solicitor'.

9.9 PROPOSED CHANGES

Should the SRA decide to introduce a centralised Solicitors Qualifying Examination (SQE) as proposed in its consultation document, 'Training for Tomorrow: Assessing Competence' (see **6.4.6**), anyone wishing to qualify as a solicitor would be required to undertake and successfully pass the SQE in order to qualify as a solicitor in England and Wales, whether as a domestic or overseas-qualified candidate. In other words, the SQE would replace the QLTS. The entry requirements for the SQE (and there may not be any) would be the subject of a separate consultation during 2016. However, the SRA has already indicated that pre-qualification work-based experience would be likely to be required.

The SRA's decision on whether to introduce the SQE is due in June 2016 (see **6.5**), and the decision on entry requirements would be made at the end of 2016. Introduction of the SQE would not be before the start of the 2018/19 academic year. The transitional arrangements proposed by the SRA for QLTS candidates would be that:

- candidates who had successfully completed the MCT component of the QLTS would be able to complete their qualification by taking Part 2 of the SQE;
- candidates who had attempted but not successfully completed either the MCT or the OSCE component of the QLTS would be required to take Part 1 or Part 2 of the SQE instead.[14]

---

[14] SRA Consultation 'Training for Tomorrow: Assessing Competence', 7 December 2015, p.33.

CHAPTER 10

Equivalent Means

10.1	Introduction	10.4	Exemptions
10.2	What is meant by 'Equivalent Means'	10.5	Applying for exemptions
		10.6	Proposed changes
10.3	Eligibility		

10.1 INTRODUCTION

This chapter could just as easily have been called 'Exemptions from education and training requirements', because that is what the Equivalent Means policy, introduced by the Solicitors Regulation Authority (SRA) in 2014 (see **6.4.1**), is all about. Exemptions have been permitted to parts of the Legal Practice Course (LPC) since September 2010. However, under Equivalent Means, exemptions have been extended to all parts of the legal education and training framework, namely:

- the Qualifying Law Degree (QLD) (see **Chapter 12**);
- the LPC (see **Chapter 14**);
- the Period of Recognised Training (PRT) (see **Chapter 15**);
- the Professional Skills Course (PSC) (see **Chapter 16**).

Under reg.2.2 of the SRA Training Regulations 2014 – Qualification and Provider Regulations ('Qualification and Provider Regulations'), the SRA may admit someone as a solicitor if he or she has completed the academic stage and/or vocational stage by Equivalent Means.

This chapter explains:

- what is meant by the term 'Equivalent Means';
- the eligibility requirements for exemptions under Equivalent Means;
- the exemptions available under Equivalent Means, and the requirements for these exemptions;
- how to apply for an exemption under Equivalent Means.

10.2 WHAT IS MEANT BY 'EQUIVALENT MEANS'

Under the Equivalent Means policy, the SRA will recognise prior learning as a basis for granting exemption from all or part of the legal education and training framework. The prior learning can be assessed learning or work-based learning. But to satisfy the requirements, it must have achieved the same knowledge and skills (and at the same level) as are required for the stage, or the part of the stage, from which exemption is being sought.

This means that the SRA looks for indications that:

- the level, standard, volume and content of the prior learning achieved is equivalent to all or part of a particular stage of educational training; and
- there is relevant, sufficient and adequate evidence of the achievement of that prior learning.

10.3 ELIGIBILITY

To be eligible to apply for an exemption under Equivalent Means, an individual must:

- have undertaken assessed learning in the law of England and Wales at or equivalent to level 4 or above of the Framework Qualification for Higher Education; and/or
- have undertaken relevant work-based learning; and/or
- be an EU, EEA or Swiss national who is partially qualified in another EU/EEA country.

Lawyers qualified in a jurisdiction outside England and Wales or as a barrister of England and Wales are not eligible to claim exemption under the Qualification and Provider Regulations on the basis of Equivalent Means, but must seek admission by way of the SRA Qualified Lawyers Transfer Scheme Regulations 2011 (QLTSR) (see **Chapter 9**).

There are various types of prior learning which can be recognised, which are summarised in the following table.

Type of prior learning recognised	Description of prior learning	Comment
Prior assessed or certificated learning	Learning undertaken in an HE or FE institution which has led to an academic award	Must have led to a qualification, e.g. Bachelors degree, or an award, e.g. higher education diploma Note: If award obtained outside UK, awarding body must be recognised by UK NARIC[1]
Accreditation of Prior Learning (APL)	Prior learning or experience	Application should be made to provider in accordance with provider's policies at same time as applying for the course For provider to assess whether or not entitled to credit for prior learning Note: If exemption is based on a non-UK award, awarding body must be recognised by UK NARIC
Prior experiential learning/Work-based learning	Prior work-based experience	Evidence of having had the experience of doing something is not sufficient; needs to be evidence that learning and outcomes have been achieved
Morgenbesser	EU/EEA/Swiss national who is partially qualified in another EU/EEA member state	Equivalence of professional qualifications are assessed against Day One Outcomes

Although exemptions from the vocational stage (LPC and PSC) are available (see **10.4.4** and **10.4.6**), they are not permitted on the basis of learning gained during the academic stage. This is because of the 'progressive element to the standard at which the knowledge and skills that [the SRA requires] are achieved.'[2] A further reason is that the knowledge and skills acquired during the vocational stage 'are acquired at a higher level than that obtained during the academic stage'.

---

[1] UK NARIC provides 'advice, guidance and expert opinion on international qualifications and how they compare to UK qualifications' (SRA, Equivalent Means Information Pack, 'Key Principles', 5 June 2015).
[2] SRA, Equivalent Means Information Pack, 'Key Principles', 5 June 2015.

10.4 EXEMPTIONS

10.4.1 Block exemptions

The exemptions that are available under Equivalent Means are not just from specific parts of the academic or vocational stages, but also according to the prior qualifications of the individual. A summary table of the exemptions available under Equivalent Means is provided at the end of this section.

Chartered Legal Executives are exempted automatically from the requirement to undertake a PRT or the Electives on the PSC, provided they meet the requirements for the block exemption (see **Chapter 24**).

10.4.2 Partially qualified EU/EEA/Swiss nationals

As explained in **Chapter 8**, EU, EEA or Swiss nationals who are partially qualified in another EU/EEA member state may apply to the SRA to have the equivalence of their professional qualifications assessed against the Day One Outcomes. Depending on the results of this assessment, the SRA may determine that the individual should undertake further assessment or training in order to meet the Day One Outcomes.

To apply for assessment by the SRA of equivalence of professional qualifications, the 'Equivalent Means – *Morgenbesser*' form needs to be completed, and details and evidence provided of the applicant's knowledge and skills so that the SRA can evaluate the extent to which the Day One Outcomes have been met. Included in the evidence that is required is evidence of the individual's qualifications and experience, with English translations where necessary.

10.4.3 Mature applicants

Although not an exemption as such, the SRA may recognise work experience and the general education of an individual who wishes to be eligible to commence the Common Professional Examination (CPE)/Graduate Diploma in Law (GDL) but who does not have the normally required underlying degree. The SRA does not define 'mature applicants' in age terms but will consider whether the individual has:

- considerable experience or has shown exceptional ability in an academic, professional, business or administrative level; and
- achieved a sufficient standard of general education,

to determine whether the individual is eligible to commence the CPE/GDL.

Examples of 'considerable experience' or 'exceptional ability' include 'several years of experience as a teacher, police officer, doctor' or similar at middle-management level or above. A sufficient standard of general education would normally be A-level passes sufficient to be admitted to a full-time degree programme.[3] What is also required is 'a good command of both spoken and written English' for admission on to the CPE.

To apply for eligibility to commence the CPE, the 'Equivalent Means – Eligibility to Commence the CPE for Non-Graduates' form needs to be completed.

10.4.4 Exemptions from the Legal Practice Course

10.4.4.1 General

An individual may claim exemption from:

- all of both Stage 1 and Stage 2;
- all of either Stage 1 or Stage 2; or
- parts of either Stage 1 and Stage 2

of the LPC (see **Chapter 14**).

Application should be made to the SRA using the 'Equivalent Means – Legal Practice Course' form for the first two exemptions, and to the LPC provider for the third exemption, which will be assessed against the provider's own policy on APL.

10.4.4.2 BVC and BPTC graduates

Graduates of either the Bar Vocational Course (BVC) or Bar Professional Training Course (BPTC) who have successfully completed the BVC/BPTC not more than five years prior to enrolling on the LPC may apply for exemption from attendance and assessment for some parts of Stage 1 or Stage 2 of the LPC. Exemptions are granted by the LPC provider rather than by the SRA. However, a provider is not obliged to grant an exemption, particularly if the nature of the academic award they make for the LPC does not permit this. The SRA therefore recommends that a BVC/BPTC graduate checks with his or her preferred LPC provider before enrolling on the course. The LPC provider will also decide whether the BVC/BPTC graduate may study the LPC over less time or at a reduced fee.

Type of graduate	Exemptions from
BVC graduates	• Stage 1 – Litigation, advocacy, drafting, practical legal research • Stage 2 – Two of the Vocational Electives
BPTC graduates	• Stage 1 – Litigation, advocacy, drafting • Stage 2 – Two of the Vocational Electives

---

[3] SRA, Equivalent Means Information Pack, 'Mature Applicants', 5 June 2015.

10.4.5 Exemption from the PRT

For the SRA to recognise prior work-based learning, it will assess what the applicant has done against the requirements for the PRT, having regard to the requirements under the Qualification and Provider Regulations, reg.12 in relation to:

- effective supervision of trainees by those with the necessary skills and experience to provide relevant learning and development opportunities and personal support to enable the trainee to meet the Practical Skills Standards;
- the provision of practical experience in at least three distinct areas of English and Welsh law and practice;
- provision of appropriate training to ensure the trainee knows the requirements of the SRA Principles and is able to comply with them; and
- regular review and appraisal of the trainee's performance and development in respect of the Practice Skills Standards and SRA Principles, and of the trainee's record of training.

The SRA will therefore expect evidence:

- that the applicant has worked alongside a solicitor;
- of the legal nature of the work the applicant has undertaken;
- of the level of supervision, feedback and appraisals the individual has received, and the interaction the individual has had with clients 'or similar'.[4] What the SRA is looking for is 'a clear alignment between the work [the applicant] has done and the work which would be done by a trainee'.[5] However, if the applicant at any time during the period of work-based learning would not have been able to meet the SRA's character and suitability requirements, then the SRA may not recognise the period of prior work-based learning, irrespective of whether it satisfies the other Equivalent Means requirements (see **9.8.2**).

10.4.6 Exemption from Professional Skills Course

The prior experience and/or training which an individual relies on to be granted an exemption from the PSC (see **Chapter 16**) must cover the same ground as the PSC Written Standards.

---

[4] SRA, Equivalent Means Information Pack, 'Key Principles', 5 June 2015.
[5] SRA, Equivalent Means Information Pack, 'Key Principles', 5 June 2015, p.3.

10.4.7 Summary of exemptions

Full or partial	Type of Equivalent Means applicable	Available from	Exemption available from	Outcomes specified in
Exemption from Qualifying Law Degree (QLD)				
Full		University provider		Joint Statement
Partial	APL	University provider	Assessment in one or more subjects	
Exemption from CPE				
Full	Individual qualifications or experience	SRA	If he or she has passed corresponding subjects within a degree programme, and been awarded the degree	Joint Statement
	Block exemption	SRA	For a Chartered Legal Executive or graduate of CILEx, if he or she has passed corresponding papers in the Level six membership examinations	
	Individual qualifications or experience	CPE provider	If he or she has passed corresponding subjects within a degree programme, and been awarded the degree *Note: Must apply for partial exemption when applying to CPE provider to enrol on CPE*	
	APL	CPE provider	Assessment in one or more subjects	
	Block exemption	CPE provider	For a Chartered Legal Executive or graduate of CILEx, if he or she has passed corresponding papers in the Level six membership examinations	

ROUTES TO QUALIFICATION

			Exemption from LPC	
Full – all of both Stage 1 and Stage 2	Individual qualifications or experience	SRA	Make application on 'Equivalent Means – Legal Practice Course' form	Legal Practice Course Outcomes
Partial – all of Stage 1 or Stage 2	Individual qualifications or experience	SRA	Make application on 'Equivalent Means – Legal Practice Course' form	
Partial – some of either Stage 1 or Stage 2	APL	LPC provider	Assessment in one or more subjects but not from all or either Stage 1 or 2; only from some part of either or both stages *Note: No exemption based on learning gained during academic stage (i.e. QLD or CPE)*	
			Exemption from PRT	
	Prior experiential learning	SRA	Clear alignment between work done and work which would be done by a trainee *Note: SRA may not recognise if character and suitability issues*	
Full	Block exemption	Automatic exemption	Chartered Legal Executive who has: • satisfied requirements of academic stage through study or exemptions granted • completed LPC, and • been engaged as Chartered Legal Executive in the practice of law	Practice Skills Standards
Full	Block exemption	SRA	Assistant Justices' Clerk (AJC) who has: • completed academic stage • completed LPC • completed core modules of PSC, and	

EQUIVALENT MEANS

			• before attending LPC, served for at least 5 years out of the last 10 years in the Magistrates' Courts Service as an AJC	
Exemption from PSC				
Partial – one or more of the core elements	Prior experiential learning	SRA	*Note: No exemption based on learning gained during academic stage (i.e. QLD or CPE) or from the core elements of the PSC based on completion of the LPC*	PSC Written Standards
Partial – one or more of the core elements	APL	SRA		
Partial: from Electives	Courses in recognised topics/ subjects	SRA	• Shortened Accounts course – Law Society Finals or pre-1997 LPC • Higher Rights of Audience Qualification courses • Human Rights Act courses *Note: No requirement to sit assessments in these courses for exemption*	Deemed Electives
Partial: from Electives	Block exemption	Automatic exemption	Chartered Legal Executive who has: • satisfied requirements of academic stage through study or exemptions granted • completed LPC, and • been engaged as Chartered Legal Executive in the practice of law	PSC Written Standards

Partial: from Electives	Block exemption	Automatic exemption	AJC who has: • completed academic stage • completed LPC • completed core modules of PSC, and • before attending LPC, seved for at least 5 years out of the last 10 years in the Magistrates' Courts Service as an AJC	PSC Written Standards

10.5 APPLYING FOR EXEMPTIONS

Applications for exemptions (other than block exemptions (see **10.4.1**)) and exemptions required to be made to the training provider) must be made to the SRA, using the prescribed forms. The different forms, together with the fees payable for each (correct at the time of publication), are summarised in the following table.

Exemption from:	Form	Fee
CPE	Equivalent Means – Common Professional Examination	£55
	Equivalent Means – Eligibility to Commence the CPE for Non-Graduates	£35
LPC	Equivalent Means – Legal Practice Course	£600
PRT	Equivalent Means – Period of Recognised Training	£600
PSC	Equivalent Means – Professional Skills Course (not CILEx)	£210
Any stage	Equivalent Means – *Morgenbesser*	£600

If more than one exemption is being applied for, the individual is recommended to contact the SRA.

The SRA requires applications to contain 'the necessary details and evidence of [the applicant's] knowledge and skills to enable [the SRA] to evaluate whether or not [the applicant] has met the outcomes claimed'.[6] The evidence provided must objectively verify the knowledge and skills that the applicant is claiming, such as certificates or transcripts of academic qualifications or records of supervised training verified by the applicant's supervisor. Unless the evidence provided is 'relevant, sufficient and adequate'[7] the SRA will not assess the application.

---

[6] SRA, Equivalent Means Information Pack, 'Making an Application', 5 June 2015.
[7] SRA, Equivalent Means Information Pack, 'Key Principles', 5 June 2015.

For experiential learning, the SRA requires details of:

1. the duration of your work experience and the number of hours worked (e.g. per week)
2. the level of employment and how much responsibility you held
3. the nature of work undertaken relevant to the outcomes claimed
4. the jurisdiction to which your experience relates, and
5. details of how you were supervised, if at all.[8]

These must be supported with references from employers which:

1. corroborate the work experience evidence provided
2. is written by a named person who could be contacted for verification if necessary; and
3. is written for the purpose of this application.[9]

Having assessed the application, the SRA will decide whether to grant the exemption or to require the applicant to undertake further assessment or training.

10.6 PROPOSED CHANGES

Should the SRA decide to introduce a centralised Solicitors Qualifying Examination (SQE) as proposed in its consultation document, 'Training for Tomorrow: Assessing competence' (see **6.4.6**), anyone wishing to qualify as a solicitor would be required to undertake and successfully pass the SQE in order to qualify as a solicitor in England and Wales, whether as a domestic or overseas-qualified candidate.

The SRA's decision on whether to introduce the SQE is due in June 2016 (see **6.5**), although actual introduction of the SQE would not be before the start of the 2018/19 academic year, with new regulations coming into effect during 2018. This would mean the cut-off date for admission under the existing regulations would be the end of the 2025/26 academic year, in order to enable candidates who had already commenced the QLE, CPE/GDL, LPC, PRT or PSC to complete and not have to repeat a stage of training. This would also apply to candidates qualifying through Equivalent Means. The example given by the SRA in the consultation document is that 'those who have completed a QLD and the LPC, but not yet a PRT, would have the choice of completing their vocational training stage using the Equivalent Means mechanism and qualifying under the existing system or transferring to the new regulations.[10]

---

[8] SRA, Equivalent Means Information Pack, 5 June 2015.
[9] SRA, Equivalent Means Information Pack, 5 June 2015.
[10] SRA Consultation 'Training for Tomorrow: Assessing Competence', 7 December 2015, p.33.

CHAPTER 11

Legal Apprenticeships

11.1   Introduction
11.2   Background
11.3   The apprenticeship standards in law
11.4   The Solicitor Apprenticeship
11.5   Proposed changes

11.1 INTRODUCTION

Legal Apprenticeships are a relatively new phenomenon in the profession and, following the rule change[1] in November 2015 of the SRA Training Regulations 2014 – Qualification and Provider Regulations (Qualification and Provider Regulations), will provide a new, non-degree route to qualification as a solicitor (see **Chapter 7**) from September 2016.

For firms and other employers, Legal Apprenticeships offer a funded way to train future practitioners, using the general apprenticeship concept of on-the-job training and nationally recognised qualifications,[2] which in this case will be qualifications as solicitor, Chartered Legal Executive or paralegal.[3]

This chapter explains:

- the background to the introduction of Legal Apprenticeships;
- what Legal Apprenticeships are;
- the features of and requirements for the Solicitor Apprenticeship, particularly:

    – the training and assessment requirements
    – the apprenticeship standards
    – the assessment plan for solicitors
    – the roles and responsibilities of employers and training providers;

---

[1] Amendment of reg.2.1(a) of the SRA Training Regulations 2014 – Qualification and Provider Regulations, as well as the introduction of a new reg.2.5 to the Regulations.
[2] CILEx Level 4 Legal Services Apprenticeship Qualifications.
[3] SRA, T4T Blog, 'A new route into the profession' by Sophie Crookson, Policy Officer – Stakeholder Engagement, 7 October 2015.

- funding and the responsibilities which go with government contributions;
- proposed changes.

11.2 BACKGROUND

The Legal Apprenticeship is a slightly unfamiliar animal to solicitors unless they have had some experience – or memory – of the old five-year articles route. Consequently, an explanation of why and how Legal Apprenticeships have been introduced may be helpful.

The National Apprenticeship Service is a government initiative by the Department for Business, Innovation and Skills (BIS), the Department for Education (DfE) and the Skills Funding Agency. The initiative's aim is 'to raise our nation's skills'.[4] Practically speaking, apprenticeships are intended to create career opportunities for young people, and school leavers in particular, who may not wish or be able to pursue higher education pathways into employment.

A government-commissioned review published in November 2012, the Richard Review of Apprenticeships (Richard Review), considered what an apprenticeship should be and how apprenticeships could meet changing economic needs. The Richard Review recommended redefining apprenticeships to focus with greater rigour on the outcome of an apprenticeship and to use industry standards as the basis of an apprenticeship. The idea was to assure endpoint standards while providing flexibility for employers and training providers as to how the endpoint standards would be reached, rather than imposing a 'one size fits all' approach.

The government's response to this was to launch the Trailblazers scheme – a 'new approach to apprenticeships in England, designed to make apprenticeships better aligned to the requirements of employers'.[5] Trailblazer Apprenticeships do not have a predefined training programme; rather, each sector has developed its own apprenticeship standards to identify the competencies that need to be achieved at the end of the apprenticeship, and it is then for each employer to develop appropriate training and assessment suited to their particular business need, to 'enable flexibility and innovation in the delivery of the training programme and the integration of "on-and-off-the-job" learning and assessment'.[6]

The legal sector was included in the second phase of the Trailblazers Apprenticeship initiative, and a number of law firms participated to develop the apprenticeship standards in law, with a commitment by the SRA to develop a Legal Apprenticeship programme which could, 'for the first time lead to qualification as a solicitor'.[7] To this end, the SRA published a consultation paper, 'Regulatory Reform Programme

---

[4] 'The Future of Apprenticeships in England: Next Steps from the Richard Review', March 2013, p.4.
[5] SRA, Regulatory Reform Programme – Improving regulation: proportionate and targeted measures, 16 April 2015, para.67.
[6] BIS, 'Apprenticeship standard leading to qualification as a solicitor – Assessment Plan', p.3.
[7] SRA news release, 'SRA signs up for Trailblazers apprenticeship scheme', 4 March 2014.

– Improving regulation: proportionate and targeted measures' (see **6.4.5**), in April 2015, to consult on a proposal to enable qualification as a solicitor through an apprenticeship route.

Although the SRA did not publish a response to the consultation, the SRA Board 'agreed to amend the rules to allow qualification as a solicitor through an apprenticeship route'[8] at its September 2015 meeting.

11.3 THE APPRENTICESHIP STANDARDS IN LAW

As Legal Apprenticeships under the Trailblazers scheme will not in fact commence until September 2016, what is known of the detail is somewhat limited. The centralised assessment has yet to be developed, and although funding arrangements for 2015/16 have been agreed (based on the employer paying one third of training costs and the government funding two thirds), from April 2017 apprenticeship funding will be subject to the rules relating to the Apprenticeship Levy – a fund that businesses with a pay bill of £3 million or more will have to contribute to.

The earliest that the centralised assessment will be available is 2018, according to the SRA. Nonetheless, the SRA hopes that Legal Apprenticeships 'will appeal to talented young people who are looking for an alternative to the traditional graduate route to qualification'.[9]

Three apprenticeship standards in law have been approved by BIS:

- Apprenticeship standard: paralegal ('Paralegal Apprenticeship');
- Apprenticeship standard: Chartered Legal Executive (Chartered Legal Executive Apprenticeship); and
- Apprenticeship standard: solicitor ('Solicitor Apprenticeship').

This chapter focuses on the Solicitor Apprenticeship but, because of the interrelationship between the three standards (a Paralegal Apprenticeship can lead on to a Chartered Legal Executive Apprenticeship or to a Solicitor Apprenticeship; a Chartered Legal Executive Apprenticeship can also lead on to a Solicitor Apprenticeship), the requirements for each are summarised in the following table, based on the information provided on the BIS website.

---

[8] Solicitors Regulation Authority, minutes of the SRA Board meeting held on 9 September 2015 – Public.
[9] SRA, T4T Blog, 'A new route into the profession' by Sophie Crookson, Policy Officer – Stakeholder Engagement, 7 October 2015.

Apprenticeship standard	Paralegal[10]	Chartered Legal Executive[11]	Solicitor[12]
Level	Level 3 Apprenticeship	Level 6 Apprenticeship	Level 7 Apprenticeship
Duration	24 months	Approx. five years	Five to six years
Entry requirements	GCSE Maths and English – grade C above (or equivalent) Two A-levels (or equivalent) – minimum grade C	No formal entry requirements but four GCSEs at grade C or above recommended (including English Language or Literature) or equivalent qualifications	As specified by individual employers in terms of previous qualifications or other criteria Recommended minimum entry requirements: • five GCSEs, including Maths and English at grade C or above (or equivalent) • three A-levels (or equivalent) at minimum grade C and/or: • relevant employer-led work experience • Level 3 Advanced Apprenticeship in a relevant occupation such as Legal Services, Professional Services, Providing Financial Services (possible exemptions) • Paralegal apprenticeship (possible exemptions) • Chartered Legal Executive apprenticeship

---

[10] BIS website – Further education and skills (**www.gov.uk/topic/further-education-skills**) – guidance – Apprenticeship standard: Paralegal (ready for delivery).
[11] BIS website – Further education and skills (**www.gov.uk/topic/further-education-skills**) – guidance – Apprenticeship standard: Chartered Legal Executive (ready for delivery).
[12] BIS website – Further education and skills (**www.gov.uk/topic/further-education-skills**) – guidance – Apprenticeship standard: Chartered Legal Executive (ready for delivery).

Apprenticeship standard	Paralegal[10]	Chartered Legal Executive[11]	Solicitor[12]
			(possible exemptions) • law degree (not necessarily a QLD) or CPE/GDL or LPC (possible exemptions)
Qualification awarded	CILEx Level 3 Diploma in Providing Legal Services	• CILEx Level 3 Professional Diploma in Law and Practice • CILEx Level 6 Professional Higher Diploma in Law and Practice	Achievement of the standard set out in the SRA's Statement of Solicitor Competence (see **21.2**) *and* the apprenticeship assessment plan (see **11.4.4**) *and* meeting SRA's character and suitability requirements (see **Chapter 18**) will lead to qualification as a solicitor

In addition to the information provided in the table above, each apprenticeship standard, which can be found on both the BIS and SRA websites, also sets out:

- the occupational profile;
- the requirements in order to successfully meet the apprenticeship standard; and
- the assessment plan.

11.4 THE SOLICITOR APPRENTICESHIP

A Solicitor Apprenticeship is expected to take five to six years and, rather than just examinations at the end, there will be continuous assessment throughout the apprenticeship, with training obligations on the employer.

11.4.1 Training and assessment obligations

At first sight, the Solicitor Apprenticeship might look somewhat like the Period of Recognised Training (PRT), with the firm or employer having similar supervision and training obligations to those for a trainee solicitor. However, the Solicitor Apprenticeship includes assessment obligations as well as training obligations, and the apprentice's performance is subject to assessment against the apprenticeship standard throughout each year of the five to six years of the apprenticeship.

A further difference is that, with the PRT, the training is done on the job, and although trainee solicitors are required to undertake the Professional Skills Course (PSC) during the PRT, all or some (such as the Elective elements) of this can be done in-house. With the Solicitor Apprenticeship, however, the idea is that the training and assessment is handed to a training provider, which the firm or employer contracts to deliver the required training and assessment under a training programme for the particular apprentice, and the training provider also has responsibility for ensuring that the solicitor apprentice reaches the standard specified in the solicitor apprenticeship standard. It is towards the cost of this training and assessment supplied by a training provider for which government funding is available (see **11.4.6**). A firm or employer could do the required training in-house but government funding would not be available for the in-house component.[13]

It is for the firm or employer and its lead provider to determine what training and assessment is required for the particular apprentice – all that is prescribed is that the apprentice must be able to demonstrate the competencies in the solicitor apprentice standard in order to complete the apprenticeship successfully, which will be determined by successfully completing an external endpoint assessment.

In addition to on-the-job learning with the firm or employer, the training provider will deliver off-the-job training (i.e. training delivered away from the firm or employer) in accordance with the training programme that has been designed for the individual apprentice. Training delivered solely by distance learning is not eligible for funding.[14]

11.4.2 Training and assessment responsibility

In order to obtain government funding for the training and assessment costs of the apprenticeship, the firm or employer needs to select the education and training provider(s) to deliver the training and assessment. The firm or employer must also appoint a lead provider, who will coordinate the training programme and be responsible for applying for and receiving payments of funding on behalf of the firm or employer. The lead provider must be listed on the Skills Funding Agency's register of training organisations and must hold a funding agreement with the Skills Funding Agency for delivering apprenticeships during the relevant academic year. The lead provider may contract with other training providers to provide the required training and assessment.

---

[13] Skills Funding Agency, 'Trailblazer Apprenticeship Funding 2014 to 2015 Requirements for Employers', p.9.
[14] Skills Funding Agency, 'Trailblazer Apprenticeship Funding 2014 to 2015 Requirements for Employers', p.7.

11.4.3 Apprenticeship standard

The reason the Solicitor Apprenticeship is able to lead to qualification as a solicitor is because the relevant apprenticeship standard has been based on, and is in fact the same as, the SRA's Statement for Solicitor Competence, Threshold Standard and Statement of Legal Knowledge ('Competence Statement') (see **Chapter 21**). Admission as a solicitor will be subject to successfully completing the required assessments, and satisfying the SRA's character and suitability requirements.

11.4.4 Assessment plan

A solicitor apprentice will be required to demonstrate the competencies in the apprenticeship standard/Competence Statement at the level described in the Threshold Statement in order to complete the apprenticeship.[15]

How achievement of the competencies will be measured is set out in the BIS's 'Apprenticeship standard leading to qualification as a solicitor – Assessment Plan' (BIS Assessment Plan), which applies to all Trailblazer assessments. This requires:

- on-programme assessment;
- work-based assessment; and
- an SRA centralised assessment.

On-programme assessment takes place in each year of the apprenticeship and is to test an apprentice's progress in achieving the skills and knowledge competencies set out in the apprenticeship standard. For the Solicitor Apprenticeship, the on-programme assessment is Part 1 of the SRA centralised assessment (see below).

The purpose of the work-based assessment is to 'ensure the development and on-programme assessment of the knowledge, skills and behavioural elements of the apprenticeship standard in the context of the particular practice areas in which apprentices are employed'.[16] It is formative in nature and should provide an employer with the opportunity to check the apprentice's progress over the five or six years of the Solicitor Apprenticeship. How work-based assessment takes place is not prescribed – it is for the employer or training provider to decide. However, the training provider, or the firm or employer, has to be able to certify that the apprentice has satisfactorily completed the work-based assessment to the Threshold Standard of competence in order to be eligible to sit Part 2 of the SRA centralised assessment.

The SRA centralised assessment is a very similar idea to the proposed Solicitors Qualification Examination (SQE) (see **6.5**). It is intended to be an assessment in two parts:

- Part 1 – Functioning Knowledge Tests (this is the in-programme assessment); and
- Part 2 – Standardised Practical Legal Examination.

---

[15] BIS, 'Apprenticeship standard leading to qualification as a solicitor – Assessment Plan', p.1.
[16] BIS, 'Apprenticeship standard leading to qualification as a solicitor – Assessment Plan', p.1.

In order to complete any Trailblazer Apprenticeship, the apprentice must take an endpoint assessment. This 'allows the skills, knowledge and behaviours detailed in the standard to be assessed in an integrated way at the end of the apprenticeship'.[17] For the Solicitor Apprenticeship, only Part 2 of the centralised assessment constitutes the 'endpoint' assessment (to avoid an apprentice having to take both Parts 1 and 2 in the last six months of the apprenticeship).

There are no exemptions from the centralised assessment, and candidates are assessed on a competent/non-competent basis only. An apprentice is also required to pass both parts.[18]

The earliest the centralised assessment will be introduced by the SRA, however, will be 2018. So, a solicitor apprentice who starts a Solicitor Apprenticeship in academic year 2016/17, for example, will not be able to sit Part 1 of the centralised assessment until 2018 at the earliest. Once the centralised assessment has been introduced, Part 1 may be sat at any time during the apprenticeship, bearing in mind the requirements under the current assessment plan that Part 1 must be passed before Part 2 can be attempted, and that Part 2 must be passed within the last six months of the apprenticeship.[19]

What each part of the assessment will cover, and how, is set out in the BIS Assessment Plan, but until the centralised assessment is developed and piloted changes may be made to the assessment structure, so the current BIS Assessment Plan may not represent the final version.

11.4.5 Roles and responsibilities of the employer

The current roles and responsibilities for employers of any Trailblazer apprentice, including a solicitor apprentice, are set out in the Skills Funding Agency's 'Trailblazer Apprenticeship Funding 2014 to 2015 Requirements for Employers'. At the time of publication, the latest version was Version 2, which had been last updated in March 2015. The requirements may be subject to furtherer amendment 'as Trailblazer Apprenticeships progress', to quote the Skills Funding Agency.

As requirements currently stand, what a firm or employer needs to do if taking on a solicitor apprentice is similar to what is required in offering a PRT to a trainee solicitor (see **Chapter 15**):

- decide previous qualifications or other requirements for selection;
- recruit the solicitor apprentice;
- enter a contract of apprenticeship, which like the PRT (see **15.7.3**) may only be terminated in certain circumstances;
- pay the solicitor apprentice the national minimum wage from the second year of the apprenticeship for their age;

---

[17] Skills Funding Agency, 'Trailblazer Apprenticeship Funding 2014 to 2015 Requirements for Employers', p.7.
[18] BIS, 'Apprenticeship standard leading to qualification as a solicitor – Assessment Plan', p.7.
[19] BIS, 'Apprenticeship standard leading to qualification as a solicitor – Assessment Plan', p.1.

- permit the solicitor apprentice paid time-off to attend 'off-the-job' training;
- provide on-the-job experience which will help the apprentice acquire the necessary competencies; and
- provide the apprentice with the support and resources that he or she needs to complete the apprenticeship.

Where the Solicitor Apprenticeship differs from the PRT is that:

- The apprentice must meet the eligibility criteria for a Solicitor Apprenticeship and must 'be able to achieve the apprenticeship within the time that they have available'.[20] In fact, a firm or employer is required to confirm at the start of the apprenticeship that the apprentice will be able to achieve the Solicitor Apprenticeship within five to six years.
- If the apprentice is progressing from another Legal Apprenticeship (i.e. Paralegal or Chartered Legal Executive), the firm or employer must be sure the apprentice has completed that apprenticeship first.
- Under the contract of employment, the apprentice must be employed for at least 30 hours a week, and for the full duration of the apprenticeship.
- If the solicitor apprentice is under 19 years of age or in the first year of the apprenticeship, it is the apprentice minimum wage which must be paid as a minimum.
- Time spent on 'off-the-job' training must be included in the apprentice's usual hours of work.
- The weekly contracted number of hours that the apprentice will be at work, including training time and 'off-the-job' training time, must be agreed by the firm or employer with its lead provider – and the apprentice. Study periods also need to be agreed.

In terms of practicalities, an employer who is considering taking on a solicitor (or paralegal or Chartered Legal Executive) apprentice, should familiarise themselves with the Solicitor Apprenticeship standard and the funding that is available as soon as possible.

Having decided to take on a solicitor apprentice, the firm or employer is then required, during the apprenticeship, to:

- ensure the apprentice is undertaking real work, which is also productive. The Occupational Profile in the BIS's 'Apprenticeship standard for a solicitor' sets out that:

    'This role has responsibility for providing legal advice to clients through:
    - acting ethically, with professionalism and judgement;
    - progressing legal matters and transactions;

---

[20] Skills Funding Agency, 'Trailblazer Apprenticeship Funding 2014 to 2015 Requirements for Employers', p.5.

- applying legal knowledge and commercial judgement to produce solutions which meet clients' needs and address their commercial or personal circumstances;
- deploying the full range of legal skills – research, interviewing and advising, advocacy, negotiation, drafting, communicating orally and in writing;
- establishing and maintaining effective and professional relationships with clients and other people; and
- managing themselves and their own work effectively.'

- provide the apprentice with a range of experience and opportunities that will help the apprentice develop the skills, knowledge and behaviours in the apprenticeship standard, and the training provider should work with the firm or employer to help with this;
- confirm with the training provider, once the apprentice has completed the endpoint assessment, that the apprentice has achieved the apprenticeship standard.[21]

11.4.6 Funding

There is an adage that you do not get something for nothing, and so it is with apprenticeship funding: a firm or employer which takes on a solicitor apprentice will be required to make a cash contribution towards the costs of training and assessing their apprentice. In turn, the government will provide funding to the firm or employer, up to a maximum cap set for the Solicitor Apprenticeship standard.[22] The term BIS uses for this is 'co-payment'.

At the time of publication, the position on funding is as follows:

- for the 2015/16 academic year, the government pays for all training costs of apprentices who are 18 years old or younger when they sign up to the apprenticeship, and 50 per cent of training costs for apprentices aged 19–24;
- for the 2016/17 academic year, the government pays two thirds and the employer pays one third (so, for every £1 an employer pays for training, the government pays £2);
- for the 2017/18 academic year, the Apprenticeship Levy, announced by the government in 2015, will be in force from April 2017.

Funding of the Solicitor Apprenticeship, which begins in September 2016, is, however, subject to a cap of £18,000 under Core Government Contribution Cap 5. This effectively equates to a £27,000 apprenticeship, of which, in 2016/17, the government will pay two thirds.

Funding may be subject to change, depending on government policy and budgets at the time.

---

[21] National Apprenticeship Service, 'Apprentices – Apprenticeship Standards', p.1.
[22] Skills Funding Agency, 'Trailblazer Apprenticeship Funding 2014 to 2015 Requirements for Employers', p.8.

11.4.7 Complying with the funding requirements

There is another adage relevant to apprenticeship funding, which is: what is given can also be taken away. If a firm or employer, or its training provider, does not comply with the funding requirements and rules then, as far as the training provider is concerned, it will be in breach of its funding agreement with the Skills Funding Agency, and action will lie against it according to that agreement. For the firm or employer, the Skills Funding Agency has a right to recover any government funding from the lead provider, which will then recover the funding from the firm or employer.

11.5 PROPOSED CHANGES

Should the SRA decide to introduce a centralised Solicitors Qualifying Examination (SQE) as proposed in its consultation document, 'Training for Tomorrow: Assessing competence' (see **6.4.6**), anyone wishing to qualify as a solicitor would be required to undertake and successfully pass the SQE in order to qualify as a solicitor in England and Wales. The SQE would be aligned to the Competence Statement (see **Chapter 21**).

What this would mean for those intending to qualify via the Legal Apprenticeship route if the SQE is introduced is that the SRA centralised assessment for Solicitor Apprentices would be subsumed into the SQE, and no transitional provisions would be required.[23] So, the in-programme assessment would be Part 1 of the SQE, and the endpoint assessment would be Part 2 of the SQE. It would just depend on timing (the SRA has said that the SQE would not be introduced before the start of academic year 2018/19) as to whether a separate Solicitor Apprenticeship centralised assessment is in fact introduced, or whether Solicitor Apprenticeships would be assessed by the SQE from the start.

The SRA's decision on whether to introduce the SQE is due to be made in June 2016.

---

[23] SRA Consultation 'Training for Tomorrow: Assessing Competence', 7 December 2015, p.33.

SECTION B3

The academic stage requirements

The Solicitors Regulation Authority (SRA) will regard the academic stage as satisfied if an individual has:

- graduated with a Qualifying Law Degree (QLD) (**Chapter 12**);
- passed, or been exempted from, the Common Professional Exam (CPE) or Graduate Diploma in Law (GDL) (**Chapter 13**).

Exemptions from the academic stage requirements may also be available under the SRA's Equivalent Means policy (see **Chapter 10**).

CHAPTER 12

Qualifying Law Degree

12.1 Introduction
12.2 The degree
12.3 Requirements

12.4 Exempting Law Degree
12.5 Proposed changes

12.1 INTRODUCTION

If a student wishes to qualify and be admitted into the legal profession, then the law degree he or she obtains must be either a Qualifying Law Degree (QLD) or one which meets the requirements for recognition by the Solicitors Regulation Authority (SRA) as a QLD.

This chapter explains the requirements for a QLD, and also the Exempting Law Degree.

12.2 THE DEGREE

For a law degree to be a QLD it must:

- be awarded either by a university in the UK or Republic of Ireland, or by an institution in England or Wales which, although not a university, has degree awarding powers;[1]
- meet the SRA standards in terms of the course of study and learning resources;
- include study of the 'Foundations of Legal Knowledge'; and
- require assessments regarded by the SRA as appropriate, to be passed in the Foundations of Legal Knowledge subjects.

It is not a case of enrolling on a QLD as such, but completing a law degree which satisfies the requirements for a QLD. The SRA maintains a list on its website of providers offering QLD programmes.

---

[1] SRA Training Regulations 2014 – Qualification and Provider Regulations.

12.3 REQUIREMENTS

12.3.1 General

The requirements for a QLD are summarised in the table below.

Eligibility	Eligibility depends on entry requirements of the particular provider
Pre-requisites	Depends on type of law degree which is to be studied, and provider's own requirements
Exemptions	May be available under Equivalent Means policy (see **12.3.5**)
Duration	Varies according to type of law degree programme (see **12.3.2**)
Timing	Law degree follows the academic year calendar of the particular provider. Normally studies commence in late September or early October
Course provider	Approved Education Provider, approved by the SRA. The SRA maintains a register of Approved Education Providers. As with any other degree, a law degree may only be offered by institutions with degree-awarding powers conferred by the Privy Council ('providers')
Compulsory content	The Joint Statement (see **12.3.2**) prescribes the knowledge and general transferable skills required for a QLD. Foundations of Legal Knowledge: • public law, including constitutional law, administrative law and human rights • law of the European Union • criminal law • obligations including contract, restitution and tort • property law • equity and the law of trusts
Pass mark	40%, although condonation of marks of at least 35% is possible (see **12.3.3**)
Grades	Grades are awarded by particular provider for particular type of degree. Usual grades for Honours degrees are 1st class, 2nd class Upper (2:1), 2nd class Lower (2:2) and 3rd class; 'Pass' or 'Fail' for Ordinary degrees
Number of attempts permitted	SRA prescribes maximum of three attempts at each Foundation of Legal Knowledge subject, but subject to provider's own regulations, e.g. provider may only permit one re-sit
Results available	Depends upon particular provider. Usually following exam board in June/July
Period of validity	No limit on period of validity for degree (see **12.3.4**)
Cost	Tuition fees charged by particular university. Currently capped at £9,000 per annum
Quality control	Internal quality assurance procedures Quality Assurance Agency (QAA) monitoring (see **12.3.6**)

THE ACADEMIC STAGE REQUIREMENTS

Monitored/ regulated by	Approved Education Providers must comply with QAA Quality Code, and self-certify to the SRA that they have complied with the Joint Statement (see **12.3.7**)
Relevant regulations	Qualification and Provider Regulations

12.3.2 Content

The content of a QLD must comply with the requirements set out in what is known as the 'Joint Statement' (A Joint Statement issued by the Law Society and the General Council of the Bar on the Completion of the Initial or Academic Stage of Training by Obtaining an Undergraduate Degree), which is available on the SRA website.

The Knowledge and General Transferable Skills which the Joint Statement requires to be taught on a QLD are as follows:[2]

A. Knowledge

Students should have acquired:

i. Knowledge and understanding of the fundamental doctrines and principles which underpin the law of England and Wales particularly in the Foundations of Legal Knowledge;
ii. A basic knowledge of the sources of that law, and how it is made and developed; of the institutions within which that law is administered and the personnel who practise law;
iii. The ability to demonstrate knowledge and understanding of a wide range of legal concepts, values, principles and rules of English law and to explain the relationship between them in a number of particular areas;
iv. The intellectual and practical skills needed to research and analyse the law from primary resources on specific matters; and to apply the findings of such work to the solution of legal problems; and
v. The ability to communicate these, both orally and in writing, appropriately to the needs of a variety of audiences.

B. General Transferable Skills

Students should be able:

i. To apply knowledge to complex situations;
ii. To recognise potential alternative conclusions for particular situations, and provide supporting reasons for them;
iii. To select key relevant issues for research and to formulate them with clarity;
iv. To use standard paper and electronic resources to produce up-to-date information;
v. To make a personal and reasoned judgement based on an informed understanding of standard arguments in the area of law in question;
vi. To use the English language and legal terminology with care and accuracy;
vii. To conduct efficient searches of websites to locate relevant information; to exchange documents by email and manage information exchanges by email;
viii. To produce word-processed text and to present it in an appropriate form.

---

[2] Joint Statement, Schedule One.

In addition, students are expected to have received training in legal research.

> **Comment**
>
> Something which firms are often surprised by is the absence of company law or business law from the Foundations of Legal Knowledge, a subject which is required for law degrees in other jurisdictions.[3] The academic bodies justify the exclusion on the basis that the law degree is a liberal arts degree, and to require company law to be studied would be to make the degree vocational in nature, which cannot be justified on the basis that at least half of law graduates do not enter the profession.
>
> The result is that Business Law and Practice, including company law, is taught on the Legal Practice Course (LPC).

Various types of law degree may be a QLD:

- three- or four-year full-time law degrees;
- four- to six-year part-time law degrees;
- accelerated two-year full-time degrees;
- joint and mixed honours degrees, where law is studied with another discipline such as a language;
- senior status (often two-year) degrees for degree graduates in non-law disciplines; or
- Exempting Law Degrees

What the Joint Statement requires for a QLD is that the degree must include 'the study of legal subjects for the equivalent of not less than two years out of a three-year or four-year course of study'[4] and that the Foundations of Legal Knowledge are covered in 'not less than one and a half years' study'.[5] This means that the remainder of the two years must involve 'study of legal subjects',[6] broadly interpreted, which can be subjects other than the Foundations of Legal Knowledge.

The Joint Statement also requires that the 'course of study will normally be spread over the full duration of the degree course' and that 'some study of legal subjects will be expected to take place in the final year of the degree course'.

How the different types of law degree compare in terms of length is shown in the following table.

---

[3] In Australia, the 'Priestley 11' requires study of criminal law, torts, contracts, property, equity (including trusts), administrative law, constitutional law, civil procedure, evidence, corporations or company law, legal ethics and professional responsibility. In Scotland, an Exempting Scottish Law Degree must include study of public law and the legal system, conveyances, Scots private law, evidence, Scots criminal law, tax affairs, European Community law, Scots commercial law.
[4] Joint Statement, para.2(iv).
[5] Joint Statement, para.2(v).
[6] Joint Statement, para.2(v).

THE ACADEMIC STAGE REQUIREMENTS

Type of degree	Minimum period for degree	Maximum period for degree	Minimum period of study of legal subjects	Time required for Foundations of Legal Knowledge
Full-time law degree	3 years	4 years	2 years	1.5 years
Part-time law degree	4 years	6 years	2 years	1.5 years
Joint honours and mixed degrees full-time	3 years	4 years	Half degree	Half degree
Senior status law degree, full-time	2 years	3 years	4 years	1.5 years
Senior status law degree, part-time	3 years	5 years	2 years	1.5 years
Exempting Law Degree	4 years	5 years	2 years[7]	1.5 years

12.3.3 Pass mark

The Joint Statement does not specify a pass mark but leaves this to the external examiners for the particular degree programme. The SRA, however, specifies a pass mark of 40 per cent, irrespective of what the provider itself may require.[8] So, if a provider set its pass mark at 30 per cent, a student 'passing' the degree by achieving more than 30 per cent but less than 40 per cent would not have met the SRA's requirements for satisfaction of the academic stage. Having said that, the vast majority of undergraduate degrees do have 40 per cent specified as the pass mark with the possibility of limited condonation of marks above 30 per cent, depending on the institution.

> **Comment**
>
> The pass mark for the QLD, although usual for undergraduate degrees generally in the UK, can cause some surprise in other jurisdictions which require a pass mark of at least 50 per cent. This surprise would be the greater if it were also realised that the SRA has the discretion, in exceptional circumstances admittedly, to 'condone' a 'marginal' failure of between 35 per cent and 40 per cent[9] in one of the Foundations of Legal Knowledge.

---

[7] There is also a requirement to meet the LPC Outcomes within the ELD programme which is likely to add another year for a course that contains both Stage 1 and Stage 2 of the LPC.
[8] SRA, 'Completing the Academic Stage of Training: Guidance for Providers of Recognised Law Programmes – Education and Training Unit', 26 February 2008.
[9] SRA, 'Completing the Academic Stage of Training: Guidance for Providers of Recognised Law Programme – Education and Training Unit', 26 February 2008, para.2.9.

12.3.4 Period of validity

Degrees are for life, as they say. So, there is no issue of the law degree obtained only being valid for a limited period of time. However, there may be time limits in relation to other study or qualifications, for which a law degree needs to have been obtained.

12.3.5 Exemptions

Prior certified or experiential learning may entitle an individual to exemption from assessment in some subjects on the QLD, under the SRA's Equivalent Means policy (see **Chapter 10**). Applications for credit for prior learning are made to the Approved Education Provider and must comply with the provider's policies and procedures for Accreditation of Prior Learning.[10]

Exemption from study of any of the Foundations of Legal Knowledge subjects is permitted where the student has passed examinations in the subject in other recognised courses, such as CILEx Professional Higher Diploma in Law (PHDL) Level 6 (see **Chapter 24**) or the Council for Licensed Conveyancers (see **Chapter 25**).

12.3.6 Quality control

Irrespective of whether the law degree programme is recognised as a QLD, it is subject to strict internal quality control by reason of the fact that the provider institution has been granted degree-awarding powers by the Privy Council, and is subject to Quality Assurance Agency (QAA) recommendations and requirements.

12.3.7 Monitoring/regulation

Until December 2013 the academic stage of qualification for both solicitors and barristers[11] was subject to joint oversight by both the SRA and the Bar Standards Board (BSB) under the auspices of the Joint Academic Stage Board (JASB). The JASB was a joint committee of the BSB and the SRA, and had responsibility for setting and implementing policies for the academic stage of training for qualification as a solicitor or as a barrister.

The distinction between oversight and regulation is important. The SRA has had responsibility delegated to it by the Law Society under the Courts and Legal Services Act 1990 and the Solicitors Act 1974 for setting the requirements for qualification as a solicitor, but it does not regulate the law degree: rather, the SRA

---

[10] SRA website, 'FAQs for Students'.
[11] The academic stage for both professions comprises a QLD or the Common Professional Examination (CPE), also known as the Graduate Diploma in Law (GDL) (see **Chapter 13**).

merely specifies what it will recognise for the purpose of entry to the profession. At present,[12] this is a QLD.

The JASB was disbanded at the end of 2013 and the position since then has been that:

- QLDs continue to be required to meet the SRA's and BSB's requirements for satisfying the academic stage of training for entry to either profession contained in the Joint Statement.
- The SRA and BSB continue to approve providers of QLDs and the CPE/GDL (see **Chapter 13**) jointly but this is based on a process of self-certification by providers, supported by documents evidencing compliance with the Joint Statement and QAA standards and quality assurance requirements. This is in place of the inspection which used to take place under the JASB.
- The SRA acts as the administrator for itself and the BSB in relation to approval of the QLD and CPE/GDL, and monitors the self-certification documents.
- The law degree, whether a QLD or not, in the same way as other degree programmes, is subject to the relevant QAA standards which the QAA sets for all Higher Education degree programmes.[13] Law degree programmes are subject to the 'QAA Benchmark Standards for Law Degrees in England, Wales and Northern Ireland', and may therefore be subject to QAA Institutional Review (previously known as an Institutional Audit), which an institution can expect to take place about every six years.[14] The QAA may look at samples of periodic review by the institution itself, which could include the periodic review of the law department, but not necessarily. Apart from this, there is no monitoring of law degrees as such.[15]

Comment

A new, revised QAA Subject Benchmark Statement for Law was published in August 2015, which was reviewed:

'to acknowledge the wider attributes expected of a graduate in terms of quality of mind, including intellectual abilities, legal knowledge and understanding, and self-management and academic integrity. It now comprises one single version for employers, the general public and law schools. Language tone, style and structure have been updated to reflect contemporary issues in teaching, learning and assessment, and employability skills have been included. Finally, [the QAA has] clarified [its] use of the term "awareness" in regard to the study of ethics to mean "the quality or state of being informed, cognisant, conscious, sensible".'[16]

---

[12] See proposals for removing specification of pathways to qualification in **Chapter 6**.
[13] 'The Framework for Higher Education Qualifications in England, Wales and Northern Ireland' (FHEQ).
[14] See QAA, 'Institutional Review of Higher Education Institutions in England and Northern Ireland: Operational Description', March 2011.
[15] The same applies to the CPE/GDL.
[16] QAA website, Newsroom, 'QAA publishes revised Subject Benchmark Statements', 3 August 2015.

12.4 EXEMPTING LAW DEGREE

An Exempting Law Degree (ELD) is a degree programme which satisfies the academic stage requirements and also incorporates the Legal Practice Course (LPC) (see **Chapter 14**), so that both are undertaken at the same time.

The programme has to meet the requirements of the Joint Statement, as well as the outcomes for the LPC. Because of the combination of programmes involved, the law degree will be subject to the same monitoring as the QLD (see **12.3.7**), and to the SRA's requirements of authorisation and validation for the LPC component.

12.5 PROPOSED CHANGES

Should the SRA decide to introduce a centralised Solicitors Qualifying Examination (SQE) as proposed in its consultation document, 'Training for Tomorrow: Assessing competence' (see **6.4.6**) anyone wishing to qualify as a solicitor would be required to undertake and successfully pass the SQE in order to qualify as a solicitor in England and Wales. Whether and how the components of the existing qualification pathway, such as the QLD, would fit with the SQE, and whether the SRA would set entry requirements for the SQE (it may not), would be the subject of a separate consultation during 2016. What the SRA has already indicated, however, is that it believes that the QLD should not justify exemption from the SQE.

The SRA's decision on whether to introduce the SQE is due in June 2016 (see **6.5**), and the decision on entry requirements would be made at the end of 2016. Introduction of the SQE would not be before the start of the 2018/19 academic year and, under the transitional arrangements proposed by the SRA, those partway through a QLD would be able to complete the qualification and complete the academic stage of training – in other words, they would be exempt from the corresponding part of Part 1 of the SQE – but would be required to pass the remaining parts of Part 1 and Part 2.[17]

---

[17] SRA Consultation 'Training for Tomorrow: Assessing Competence', 7 December 2015, p.33.

CHAPTER 13

Conversion course

13.1 Introduction
13.2 The course
13.3 Requirements
13.4 Integrated Course
13.5 Proposed changes

13.1 INTRODUCTION

Non-law graduates and certain other non-graduates may qualify as a solicitor by way of a non-law degree or 'conversion course' route. This involves passing the Common Professional Examination course (CPE) or completing a Graduate Diploma in Law (GDL).

This chapter explains:

- what the CPE is and how it relates to the GDL;
- what the features and requirements are for the CPE and GDL;
- delivery of the CPE or GDL in an Integrated Course.

13.2 THE COURSE

The Solicitors Regulation Authority (SRA) describes the CPE as an 'intense course built around the core curriculum and assessment requirements of a QLD. It is specifically designed for graduates, whether or not in the UK, and for individuals who have acquired career experience or vocational qualifications that the SRA considers to be equivalent to an undergraduate degree'.[1]

Because providers are permitted to embed the CPE within their academic award frameworks, many providers refer to the CPE as the 'GDL'. The GDL is defined in the SRA Training Regulations 2014 – Qualification and Provider Regulations ('Qualification and Provider Regulations') as:

---

[1] SRA website, 'FAQs for Students'.

CONVERSION COURSE

a graduate diploma in law or second degree awarded by:
(i) a university in the United Kingdom or the Republic of Ireland;
(ii) an institution in England and Wales empowered by the Privy Council to award degrees;
(iii) a polytechnic or college authorised to award the degrees of the Council of National Academic Awards before its dissolution on 31 March 1993;
(iv) the College of Law;
(v) an overseas university or college approved by the SRA.

Being of such standard as the SRA determines and following a course of study which is acceptable to the SRA and which includes:
(a) the study of the Foundations of Legal Knowledge: and
(b) the passing of appropriate set in those foundations.

Both the CPE and GDL are recognised in the same way as the Qualifying Law Degree (QLD) for satisfaction of the academic stage.

Although the Qualification and Provider Regulations distinguish a GDL from the CPE, to all practical purposes there is no difference, and the terms 'GDL' and 'CPE' are used interchangeably. To use the SRA's words, 'the CPE is the professional qualification and the GDL is the academic award'.

> **Comment**
>
> It is for the provider to choose the name of the academic award, although 'GDL' is the most usual.

13.3 REQUIREMENTS

13.3.1 General

The general requirements for, and features of, the Common Professional Exam/ Graduate Diploma in Law (CPE/GDL) are summarised in the table below.

Eligibility	Applicant must demonstrate to CPE/GDL Provider that the applicant:
	• holds a non-QLD law degree from a UK or ROI university
	• holds a degree in a subject other than law from a UK/ROI university
	• is an overseas graduate who has studied any subject for a minimum of 3 years full-time
	• holds other academic or vocational qualifications that the SRA recognises under Equivalent Means (See **13.3.2**)

THE ACADEMIC STAGE REQUIREMENTS

Exemptions	Full or partial exemptions available for assessed learning or work-based learning Equivalent Means. Partial exemptions from subjects granted by Approved Education Provider subject to own policies; full exemptions may only be granted by the SRA by way of an Equivalent Means application
	Block exemptions for: • Chartered Legal Executives • Assistant justices' clerks
Duration	Full-time: minimum 1 year and maximum 3 years Part-time: minimum 2 years and maximum 4 years Application for an extension of time due to exceptional circumstances should be made to the CPE/GDL Provider
Timing	Full-time CPE/GDL normally commences in September and must be at least 36 weeks in length[2] Final exams usually take place around June (see **13.3.4**)
Course provider	Approved Education Provider, approved by the SRA. The SRA maintains a register of Approved Education Providers (see **13.3.3**)
Compulsory content	Foundations of Legal Knowledge and one other area of legal study (see **Chapter 12**)
Pass mark	40% with possible compensation for one subject at 35% or more
Grades	Distinction: generally over 70%
	Commendation: between 60% and 69%, provided all subjects passed at first attempt and no subjects compensated
	Pass: at least 40%
	(see **13.3.5**)
Number of attempts permitted	Three at each Foundations of Legal Knowledge subject permitted If a student fails any subject three times, he or she is required to re-take the full CPE/GDL course
Results available	Following the Approved Education Provider's exam board in June/July
Period of validity	7 years unless extended by SRA
Cost	From £3,500
Quality control	Internal quality assurance processes; Quality Assurance Agency (QAA) monitoring, if applicable
Monitored/regulated by	Approved Education Providers must comply with QAA Quality Code, and self-certify to the SRA that they have complied with the Joint Statement (see **12.3.7**) New CPE/GDL courses initially validated for 3 years, then

---

[2] Excluding vacation periods but including examination weeks.

	re-validation usually for 5 years unless concerns identified
Relevant regulations	Qualification and Provider Regulations

13.3.2 Eligibility

It is possible to be eligible for the CPE/GDL as a non-graduate if the student falls into one of the categories of mature student and can demonstrate at least 10 years of experience at middle management level or of holding academic or vocational qualifications which the SRA regards as equivalent to a degree. A mature student must also have a good command of spoken and written English.

It is also possible to do the CPE/GDL as a law graduate where the law graduate has failed one or more of the Foundations of Legal Knowledge subjects, with the result that he or she has achieved a law degree, but not a law degree recognised as a QLD (see **Chapter 12**).

13.3.3 Providers

An Approved Education Provider ('CPE/GDL Provider') does not need to have degree-awarding powers to deliver the CPE/GDL.

A list of CPE/GDL Providers is available on the SRA website.[3]

13.3.4 Timing

If a student fails a Foundation of Legal Knowledge subject three times, the student must re-take the full CPE/GDL to satisfy the requirements for completion of the academic stage. The CPE/GDL does not need to be re-taken at the same CPE/GDL Provider. However, in the situation of having to re-take the CPE/GDL, credit will not be granted for subjects which have been passed previously.

There is no limit on the number of times a student may undertake the CPE/GDL.

13.3.5 Grades

The SRA specifies that if a student achieves the averages set out in the summary table overall in the assessments, and has passed all the assessments at the first attempt and without compensation of any subject, the specified grades must be awarded. However, a CPE/GDL Provider has a discretion, within certain parameters[4] (the requirements of passing at the first attempt and no subject being compensated must still be met, however) and subject to the provider's exam board considering the award is not inappropriate, to award the same grades without the specified overall averages having been achieved.

---

[3] See SRA website, 'Students: CPE/GDL Course Providers'.
[4] SRA, Academic Stage Handbook July 2014, pp.39–40.

THE ACADEMIC STAGE REQUIREMENTS

> **Comment**
>
> What employers should therefore enquire into are a candidate's overall averages in order to ascertain the basis for the grade.

13.4 INTEGRATED COURSE

The CPE/GDL may also be studied on an Integrated Course. An Integrated Course will also include the LPC, so on completion the student would have satisfied the academic stage requirements, and would be eligible to undertake the period of recognised training (PRT) in the vocational stage.

As with an ELD, an Integrated Course would need to meet the requirements of the Joint Statement, as well as the outcomes for the LPC.

Many of these courses are offered by providers as 'LLB' programmes of study.

> **Comment**
>
> Although Integrated Courses were previously provided for under the SRA's Training Regulations, the Qualification and Provider Regulations refer only to the Exempting Law Degree (ELD) (see **12.4**), even though Integrated Courses are still referred to in the SRA Academic Handbook. As the SRA no longer specifies the order in which the various stages – academic and vocational – need to be taken, study on an Integrated Course would probably be recognised by the SRA under Equivalent Means (see **Chapter 10**).

13.5 PROPOSED CHANGES

Should the SRA decide to introduce a centralised Solicitors Qualifying Examination (SQE) as proposed in its consultation document, 'Training for Tomorrow: Assessing Competence' (see **6.4.6**) anyone wishing to qualify as a solicitor would be required to undertake and successfully pass the SQE in order to qualify as a solicitor in England and Wales. The SRA's decision on whether to introduce the SQE is due in June 2016 (see **6.5**), and whether and how the CPE/GDL would fit with the SQE, and whether the SRA would set entry requirements for the SQE (it may not), would be decided at the end of 2016, following consultation. Introduction of the SQE itself would not be before the start of the 2018/19 academic year and, under the transitional arrangements proposed by the SRA, those partway through a CPE/GDL would be able to complete the qualification and complete the academic stage of training – in other words, they would be exempt from the corresponding part of Part 1 of the SQE – but would be required to pass the remaining parts of Part 1 and Part 2.[5]

---

[5] SRA Consultation 'Training for Tomorrow: Assessing Competence', 7 December 2015, p.33.

SECTION B4

The vocational stage requirements

The vocational stage is the second stage of training for qualification as a solicitor, and comprises:

- the Legal Practice Course (**Chapter 14**);
- the Period of Recognised Training (PRT), previously the Training Contract (**Chapter 15**); and
- the Professional Skills Course (**Chapter 16**)

each of which needs to be completed in order to be eligible for admission.

CHAPTER 14

Legal Practice Course

14.1 Introduction	14.5 Course structure
14.2 The course	14.6 Course assessment
14.3 Requirements	14.7 Quality assurance
14.4 LPC outcomes	14.8 Proposed changes

14.1 INTRODUCTION

The Legal Practice Course (LPC) acts as a bridge between the academic stage (see **Section B3**) and the Period of Recognised Training (PRT) (see **Chapter 15**), by introducing would-be solicitors to the practical knowledge and skills they will require for practice.

Although the LPC is normally provided by external LPC providers, firms which employ trainee solicitors as Authorised Training Providers need to know about the LPC for two particular reasons:

- Firms which sponsor future trainees on the LPC are making an investment and need to know how they can use the LPC to ensure they make a return on that investment. Most firms do not (see **Chapter 1** and **Chapter 29**).
- All Authorised Training Providers, whether they have sponsored their future trainees or not, need to understand what the trainee they employ will have done on the LPC, in order to understand what they can expect the trainee to be able to do when he or she commences the PRT. This informs the training which the firm will then need to provide to fulfil its obligations under the Solicitors Regulation Authority (SRA) Training Regulations 2014 – Qualification and Provider Regulations ('Qualification and Provider Regulations'), reg.11. Reg.11 requires that an Authorised Training Provider is able to provide training to enable the trainee to meet the SRA's Practice Skills Standards (see **15.11.4**).

This chapter therefore explains what the LPC is, the requirements for the LPC, the Outcomes that students need to achieve, the LPC structure, assessment on the LPC and quality assurance of the LPC.

14.2 THE COURSE

The LPC is a postgraduate professional course which builds on the academic stage in order to prepare the student for the work-based learning he or she will do during the PRT. At the same time, the LPC introduces the student to the practical knowledge and skills he or she will require for practising as a solicitor.

Traditionally, the LPC has been a year-long course. However, accelerated LPCs of usually seven months' duration are also available. Accelerated LPCs are very intensive, and those currently offered tend to be geared for City or commercial practice.

The LPC may also be undertaken as a part of an Exempting Law Degree (ELD) (see **12.4**) or Integrated Course (see **13.4**).

Although successful completion of the LPC is a requirement for admission as a solicitor, a student on the LPC may commence the PRT before he or she has completed the LPC by studying the LPC part-time.

> **Comment**
>
> However, to commence a PRT, a student must meet the SRA's requirements of character and suitability, which would not be a requirement for enrolling on the LPC only.

14.3 REQUIREMENTS

14.3.1 General

The general requirements for, and features of, the LPC are summarised in the table below.

Eligibility	Successful completion of academic stage (unless part of an Exempting Law Degree or Integrated Course) and satisfaction of LPC provider's requirements
Pre-requisites	Student must satisfy LPC provider that he or she has met academic requirements for admission (see **14.3.2**)
Exemptions	• Exemptions from certain elements of LPC may be permitted to BPTC graduates, at LPC provider's discretion • Full or partial exemptions may be available by way of Equivalent Means based on prior experience and professional qualifications which are similar to LPC outcomes and acquired at requisite standard (see **Chapter 10**)
Duration	Minimum 1,100 notional learning hours (NLHs) for Stage 1, and 330 NLHs for Stage 2 Actual LPC duration: usually September–May, but will vary for accelerated LPCs

Timing	Generally, the LPC starts in September but also January for accelerated LPCs Stage 1: September unless an accelerated LPC Stage 2: For most providers March but will vary, especially for accelerated LPCs (see **14.3.3**)
Course provider	Authorised by SRA as Authorised Education Provider. A list of authorised providers is available on the SRA website

Compulsory content	• Core Practice Areas:
	  – Business Law and Practice (including Business Accounts and Revenue)
	  – Property Law and Practice
	  – Litigation (Civil and Criminal)
	• Professional Conduct and Regulation
	• Wills and Administration of Estates
	• Course Skills:
	  – Practical Legal Research
	  – Writing and Drafting
	  – Interviewing and Advising
	  – Advocacy
	• Electives – depending on provider (student to select two)

Pass mark	50%. Condonations are not permitted
Grades	None – marks only (although provider may award own grades) Skills: Competent/Not yet competent (see **14.3.5**)
Number of attempts permitted	Three. A student is permitted three attempts at each subject
Results available	After exam board, usually July, but will vary for Accelerated LPCs
Period of validity	5 years. A student is permitted three attempts at each subject. Both stages must be completed successfully within 5 years of the student's first attempt at an assessment (see **14.3.4**)
Cost	£7,400–£14,076 for Stages 1 and 2[1] – separate fees for one stage only or separate Electives
Quality control	Quality assurance for the LPC is based on: • the authorisation and validation process for the provider. Both authorisation and validation are paper-based exercises and do not involve a visit to the provider unless evidence that the quality or standard of a course is at risk

---

[1] For 2015/16 courses.

	• Annual Course Monitoring Report • external examiners
Monitored/regulated by	SRA. An LPC must also be validated by SRA
Relevant regulations	Qualification and Provider Regulations

14.3.2 Prerequisites

Although a Certificate of Enrolment from the SRA used to be required to be obtained prior to enrolling on the LPC as evidence that the student had satisfactorily completed the academic stage, this requirement was removed in 2014 (see **6.4.1**). Responsibility now lies with the LPC provider to confirm eligibility.

14.3.3 Timing and duration

Because of the flexibility given to LPC providers in the way they design their courses, with only minimum requirements for notional learning hours and face-to-face teaching hours, it is up to the LPC provider to determine how long the course actually lasts, thus the advent of accelerated courses of only seven months. The length of a particular LPC will therefore depend on the particular LPC provider.

14.3.4 Period of validity

If a student is not able to pass all exams and assessments successfully within five years, in exceptional circumstances the student may apply to the SRA for an extension.

14.3.5 Grades and transcripts

Providers are required to produce a transcript in a form prescribed by the SRA, which sets out a student's actual mark for each subject, as well as the number of attempts it has taken the student to pass, and for each stage that a student has undertaken with that provider.

LPC providers are free to award grades but, in that case, the LPC provider would issue its own certificate showing the grades achieved, in addition to the SRA-prescribed transcript. Further, where a student studies the Vocational Electives at different providers, each provider must provide a transcript in the prescribed form for the particular Vocational Elective studied there.

> **Comment**
>
> A firm looking for evidence of a student's successful completion of the LPC should therefore expect to see at least two transcripts: one for Stage 1 and one for Stage 2 (even

> if both stages are completed at the same provider), as well as a transcript for any Vocational Electives studied at a different provider.
>
> Firms should also be aware that there is no central record kept by the SRA of where students do the different stages and Vocational Electives. So, it is not possible for a firm to know whether the student has had previous unsuccessful attempts at different providers before passing, unless the student chooses to disclose this him- or herself.

14.4 LPC OUTCOMES

The content of the LPC is based on the LPC outcomes, which detail the requirements for the LPC and the knowledge which a student should have on successful completion of the LPC. To quote the SRA, the LPC outcomes represent 'what a successful student should, under appropriate supervision, be able to do on conclusion of the Course'.[2]

The intention of the SRA is that the LPC should be flexible, so that aspiring solicitors and employers are able to choose the LPC which best suits their practice needs. The flexibility in the LPC exists in:

- the use of learning outcomes for each subject;
- the course being split into two severable stages;
- the use of irreducible minimums in the components of the curriculum.

Consequently, the LPC outcomes represent an irreducible minimum, rather than a complete prescription as to what a provider should teach in each subject. Outcomes are also required for each Elective subject offered, and an LPC provider is required to produce outcomes for the Elective subjects that provider offers as part of its validation application.

The standard by which the LPC is judged by the SRA is that it should enable the diligent and capable student (a sort of 'man on the Clapham omnibus' concept) studying on the course to demonstrate the specified outcomes by the end of the course.

14.5 COURSE STRUCTURE

The LPC is divided into two stages:

- Stage 1 – the Core Practice Areas, pervasive subjects and Course Skills; and
- Stage 2 – three Vocational Elective subjects.

The two stages are intended to be severable, although a provider can design the course so that the delivery of Stage 1 and Stage 2 is combined. However, a provider

---

[2] SRA, Legal Practice Course Information Pack, 1 July 2014, p.2.

would need to satisfy the SRA as to its rationale for combining the two stages, and that the requirements for both stages are met.

Dividing the LPC into severable stages means students may take a break between the stages, should they so wish. They may also study the stages with different providers, rather than doing the whole course with one provider. In fact, each of the Vocational Electives can be studied at different providers.

If a student does take time out between stages or between Electives, then the student needs to ensure that he or she successfully completes both stages within five years from his or her first attempt at his or her first assessment.

Comment

This means that a firm has the option of recruiting a trainee who has completed both stages of the LPC, or a 'trainee' who has only completed Stage 1 and has yet to complete Stage 2. There are considerations around this which are discussed in **Chapter 29**.

Outcomes are also specified for Wills and Administration of Estates, Solicitors' Accounts, Business Accounts and Taxation, which are expected to be taught pervasively.

Comment

The fact that the Outcomes represent an irreducible minimum is significant because it allows providers more flexibility in designing their own curriculum.

What the SRA does require is that Stage 1 in the new LPC has a minimum of 1,100 notional learning hours ('notional learning hours' being a concept of the time involved in preparing for sessions and revising for exams, as well as attending the actual session, rather than the amount of time of actual teaching). Of these notional learning hours, there must be a minimum of 110 hours of face-to-face teaching – not e-learning or virtual learning, but actual classroom teaching which involves interaction between the tutor and students, and between the students themselves.

The reason for this flexibility is to provide students and firms with a choice of LPCs which will better meet their practice needs. Because of the 'headroom' in the curriculum (17 per cent, as described below), firms can work with providers to customise the LPC, perhaps by weighting the Core Practice Areas, developing more relevant Vocational Electives, and so on. The flexibility in the LPC is such that there is the possibility for a firm to have a wholly customised LPC – and in fact a firm could apply for authorisation and validation to run the LPC in-house (see **Chapter 29**). This flexibility is also intended to enable providers to design LPCs in the way they think would be most effective.

14.5.1 Stage 1

Of the minimum 1,100 notional learning hours and 110 hours of face-to-face teaching for Stage 1:

THE VOCATIONAL STAGE REQUIREMENTS

- at least 60 per cent (i.e. 66 hours of face-to-face teaching) must cover the three Core Practice Areas, each of which must have a minimum of 15 per cent (or 16.5 hours of face-to-face teaching);
- at least 15 per cent (i.e. 16.5 hours of face-to-face teaching) must be devoted to the Course Skills; and
- at least 8 per cent (i.e. 8.8 hours of face-to-face teaching) to professional conduct and regulation (PCR).

If a Provider chose only to meet the minimum requirements, there would still be a further 17 per cent of the curriculum (i.e. 18.7 hours of face-to-face teaching) at the Provider's discretion. In fact, if the Provider allocates the minimum 15 per cent to each of Business Law and Practice (BLP), Property Law and Practice (PLP) and Litigation (Civil and Criminal), there would be a further 15 per cent (or 16.5 hours of face-to-face teaching) of the Core Practice Area curriculum available as well. This is probably best illustrated by the following diagram.

Figure 14.1 – Stage 1 curriculum: minimum % requirements

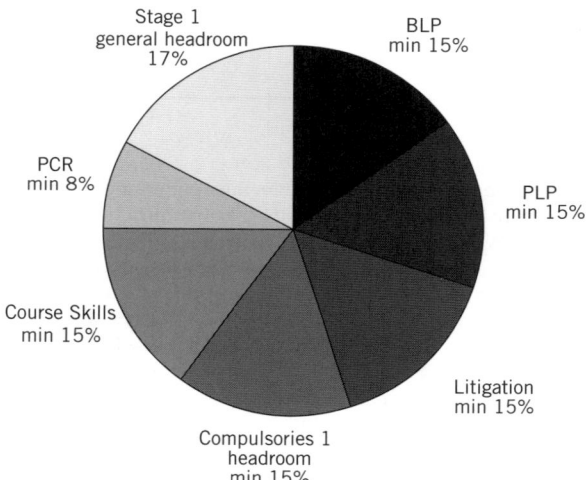

14.5.2 Stage 2

For Stage 2, the requirement is for a minimum of 100 notional learning hours per Vocational Elective, of which there must be a minimum of 10 hours of face-to-face teaching.

Students are required to study three Vocational Electives, which must be selected from at least two different Elective groups (each Vocational Elective offered by a provider must belong to one of the SRA's prescribed subject groups for Electives. This is intended to prevent students doing the same Vocational Elective at different providers).

14.6 COURSE ASSESSMENT

The assessment requirements for the LPC are summarised in the table below.

Stage 1	Subject	Assessment requirements
Core Practice Areas	Business Law and Practice (including Business Accounts and Revenue)	Formal, supervised, written examinations by end of Stage 1
	Property Law and Practice	
	Litigation (Civil and Criminal)	
Other required subjects	Professional Conduct and Regulation (including Solicitors' Accounts)	Discrete assessment by end of Stage 1 and 5% of each of Core Practice Area assessments (separate supervised assessment for Solicitors' Accounts at end of Stage 1)
	Wills and Administration of Estates	Assessed (no requirement as to how) by end of Stage 1
	Taxation	Assessed (no requirement as to how) at end of Stage 1
Course Skills		Assessed under supervised conditions by end of Stage 1. May be combined with Core Practice Area assessments or other Course Skills assessments
	Practical Legal Research	No specific requirement
	Writing and Drafting	No specific requirement
	Interviewing and Advising	Assessed as a whole or in separate parts of interviewing and of advising
	Advocacy	Assessment in context of either Civil or Criminal Litigation or both

Because Stages 1 and 2 are severable, the Outcomes for the Core Practice Areas, Professional Conduct and Regulation, Wills and Administration of Estates, Business Accounts and Course Skills must all be assessed by the end of Stage 1, and before students may commence Stage 2 (students who fail one of the Stage 1 assessments may still commence Stage 2 but will need to pass the re-sit successfully in order to complete the course).

LPC providers are able to devise their own assessment strategy, which has to be approved as part of the validation process for the course (see below). This means that LPC providers have flexibility in how they might approach assessments and may, for instance, combine a Course Skill assessment with a Core Practice Area assessment, such as assessing drafting in the Property Law and Practice assessment to make the assessment more practice-based; or by combining it with another Course Skill assessment (for instance, Writing could be assessed with Practical Legal Research).

14.7 QUALITY ASSURANCE

Quality assurance for the LPC is based on the authorisation and validation process for the Provider. Both authorisation and validation are paper-based exercises and do not involve a visit to the Provider. The SRA states, however, that 'it will arrange visits to Providers from time to time to ensure that it has an understanding of, and an insight into, the range of courses on offer'. Visits will also inform 're-authorisation decisions'. The SRA will also visit an LPC Provider if it has evidence that the standard or quality of the course is at risk.

Once a Provider has been authorised and its course validated, ongoing quality assurance is achieved by way of external examiners. External examiners produce an evaluative annual report for the SRA, as does the Provider, which submits an Annual Course Monitoring Report. The only time there would be a monitoring visit to a Provider would be if a concern were to arise, say, from an external examiner report, and the SRA believed that the concern raised justified a visit.

Providers are required to publish a minimum set of factual information about the course to assist students (and firms) in making an informed decision as to which course they wish to do.

> **Comment**
>
> Although this may be a requirement, it has never been consistently done, or 'policed' by the SRA. Originally there was an enhanced external examiner regime, with the external examiners appointed by the SRA. This was so that the Provider could not influence the choice of external examiner, and the external examiners acted as independent and impartial advisers to the SRA. External examiners for a particular Provider were also overseen by an institutional lead external examiner for that Provider. The authorisation and validation process for a Provider and the enhanced external examiner regime were the SRA's justification for dispensing with its previous monitoring regime of monitoring visits and grading Providers. However, institutional lead external examiners have been dispensed with, and at the time of publication external examiners had ceased being appointed by the SRA; it is left to the Provider to appoint them.

14.8 PROPOSED CHANGES

Should the SRA decide to introduce a centralised Solicitors Qualifying Examination (SQE) as proposed in its consultation document, 'Training for Tomorrow:

Assessing competence' (see **6.4.6**) anyone wishing to qualify as a solicitor would be required to undertake and successfully pass the SQE in order to qualify as a solicitor in England and Wales. Whether and how the components of the existing qualification pathway, such as the LPC, would fit with the SQE, and whether the SRA would set entry requirements for the SQE (it may not), would be the subject of a separate consultation during 2016.

The SRA's decision on whether to introduce the SQE is due in June 2016 (see **6.5**), and the decision on entry requirements would be made at the end of 2016. Introduction of the SQE would not be before the start of the 2018/19 academic year and, under the transitional arrangements proposed by the SRA, those partway through the LPC, GLD, PRT or PSC could either complete the vocational stage and qualify under the existing assessment requirements, or transfer to the new regulations.[3]

---

[3] SRA Consultation 'Training for Tomorrow: Assessing Competence', 7 December 2015, p.33.

CHAPTER 15

Period of Recognised Training

15.1	Introduction	15.9	Notification requirements
15.2	Governing regulations	15.10	Support requirements
15.3	The PRT and the Training Contract	15.11	Training requirements
15.4	Exemption from the PRT	15.12	Supervision, review and appraisal requirements
15.5	Authorisation as a Training Provider		
15.6	Training Principal	15.13	Monitoring
15.7	Employing trainees under the PRT	15.14	Summary of responsibilities
15.8	Eligibility to commence a PRT	15.15	Proposed changes

15.1 INTRODUCTION

The Period of Recognised Training (PRT) is a period of work-based learning, which is intended:

> to give trainees supervised experience in legal practice through which they can refine and develop their professional skills. It is the final stage of the process of qualification as a solicitor. Trainee solicitors gain practical experience in a legal environment such as a solicitor's firm, a local authority or an in-house legal department.[1]

The PRT was introduced on 1 July 2014, prior to which the vocational stage requirement was for completion of a two-year Training Contract in a form prescribed by the Solicitors Regulation Authority (SRA). Since then the two regimes – training contract and PRT – have co-existed, although trainees employed from 1 July 2014 are required to undertake a PRT rather than a training contract.

Although there are relatively few pre-1 July 2014 training contracts still in place, the transitional arrangements for training contracts are explained and, for those more familiar with the training contract than the PRT, the similarities and differences between the two regimes, including terminology, are explained.

---

[1] SRA, Authorised Training Provider Information Pack, 18 August 2014, p.1.

Otherwise, the chapter focuses on the requirements of the PRT as firms need to understand them, in terms of

- obtaining authorisation as a Training Provider;
- employing trainees under the PRT regime;
- the eligibility requirements for a trainee to commence the PRT;
- the procedural requirements to commence the PRT;
- the support requirements during the PRT;
- the training requirements during the PRT;
- the supervision, review and appraisal requirements during the PRT;
- monitoring by the SRA.

To further assist firms, the responsibilities of the Training Provider, Training Principal and trainee are also summarised at the end of the chapter.

15.2 GOVERNING REGULATIONS

All PRTs which commenced on or after 1 July 2014 are governed by the SRA Training Regulations 2014 – Qualification and Provider Regulations ('Qualification and Provider Regulations'), which are supplemented, in line with the SRA's principles-based approach to regulation, by non-mandatory guidance from the SRA, such as the Training Provider Information Pack,[2] the Trainee Information Pack[3] and the FAQs for training providers[4] and trainees.[5]

Rather prosaically, the Qualification and Provider Regulations specify the purpose of the PRT as enabling the individual to meet the Practice Skills Standards and comply with the mandatory Principles set out in the SRA Handbook.[6]

15.3 THE PRT AND THE TRAINING CONTRACT

15.3.1 Transitional arrangements

Trainees employed on or after 1 July 2014 are subject to the PRT regime under the Qualification and Provider Regulations.

Trainees who were employed under a training contract on or before 30 June 2014 have the option of agreeing to be bound by the new Qualification and Provider Regulations. However, if this option is not taken, the Training Contract remains subject to the Training Contract regime under the SRA Training Regulations 2011 Part 2 –Training Provider Regulations ('2011 Training Provider Regulations'). This situation is a transitional arrangement only, and trainees under a PRT do not have an equivalent option to be bound by the 2011 Training Provider Regulations.

---

[2] SRA, 'Authorised Training Provider Information Pack', updated 18 August 2014.
[3] SRA, 'Trainee Information Pack', 4 July 2014.
[4] SRA, 'FAQs for training providers'.
[5] SRA, 'FAQs for trainees'.
[6] Qualification and Provider Regulations, reg.5.2.

15.3.2 Terminology

The following provides a glossary of the terminology under both regimes:

PRT regime	Training Contract regime
Recognised Training or Period of Recognised Training	Training Contract
Training agreement	Training Contract
Authorised Education Provider (in relation to the Professional Skills Course (PSC))	PSC provider
Trainee solicitor	Trainee solicitor
Training Principal	Training Principal
Authorised Training Provider or Training Provider	Training Establishment
Supervisor	Trainee Supervisor

15.3.3 Comparison of PRT regime requirements and Training Contract regime requirements

	PRT regime	Training Contract regime
Governing regulations	SRA Training Regulations 2014 – Qualification and Provider Regulations ('Qualification and Provider Regulations')	SRA Training Regulations 2011 Part 2 – Training Provider Regulations ('2011 Training Provider Regulations')
Ambit of regulations	• Trainees employed on or after 1 July 2014 • Trainees employed under a training contract on or before 30 June 2014 who have adopted the Qualification and Provider Regulations	Trainees employed under a training contract on or before 30 June 2014
Employer	Authorised Training Provider: • All Training Establishments authorised as at 1 July 2014 • Organisations whose application for authorisation as a Training Provider has been approved by the SRA	Authorised Training Establishment

Basis of employment	Contract of employment, terms agreed between employer and trainee as employee	SRA-specified training contract
Duration of contract	2 years full-time (pro rata reductions for part-time)	2 years full-time (pro rata reductions for part-time)
Reduction of time requirement	Maximum reduction by Training Provider of six months for relevant work-based experience (adjusted pro rata for part-time trainees)	Maximum reduction by Training Establishment of six months for relevant work-based experience under time-to-count policy (adjusted pro rata for part-time trainees)
Exemptions	• Block exemptions for Chartered Legal Executives and justices' clerks • Under Equivalent Means policy – application to SRA	Block exemptions for Chartered Legal Executives and justices' clerks
Requirements as to number of trainees	No limitations	No limitations since 2014. Previously, limit of 2 trainees per partner and non-partner solicitor qualified for at least 5 years
Firm's contact for SRA	Training Principal	Training Principal
Eligibility requirements for Training Principal	• Solicitor of England and Wales holding a practising certificate or a practising barrister; and • Competent to meet the requirements of the Qualification and Provider Regulations	• Solicitor with a current practising certificate; • Has held four consecutive practising certificates prior to the current one; and • Is a partner or of partner equivalent status Required to undertake such training as SRA prescribes.
Training required	Exposure to three different areas of English and Welsh law and practice	Practical experience in at least three distinct areas of English law, as well as opportunity to develop skills in contentious and non-contentious work
Salary to be paid to trainee	Main hourly rate of national minimum wage	Main hourly rate of national minimum wage
Notification requirements	Notify SRA using prescribed form	Register training contract with SRA

THE VOCATIONAL STAGE REQUIREMENTS

Absence during training contracts	Subject to terms of employment contract	Certain absences allowed up to a maximum of four months. Extension required if longer. Prescribed form.
Termination	• By mutual agreement between trainee and Training Provider • Failure of trainee to pass academic stage or LPC if a condition of employment • Unacceptable conduct of trainee • Trainee incapacitated or incapable of being trained • Training Provider has closed or fundamentally changed business	• By mutual agreement between trainee and Training Establishment • Under a cancellation clause • By application to SRA by either trainee or Training Establishment
Disputes	Training Provider to resolve with trainee, SRA will not intervene	May be referred to SRA to resolve or terminate training contract
Monitoring	SRA monitoring regime	SRA monitoring regime

Comment

What is different about the Qualification and Provider Regulations and the regime they create for the PRT is not just in terms of content but also in terms of regulatory approach; whereas the 2011 Training Provider Regulations were based on prescription of what was permissible, the Qualification and Provider Regulations are permissive. In other words, unless the Regulations specifically prohibit or exclude, everything else is permissible.

'Training Providers' which have previously been 'Training Establishments' under the 2011 Training Provider Regulations, will be used to a range of requirements being specified which are not mentioned in the Qualification and Provider Regulations or in the accompanying guidance documents. The regime under the Qualification and Provider Regulations therefore has required a change of mindset.

A word of caution, however: just because something is not explicitly stated does not mean it is not required; rather, it may be implicit because of something else. For example, although the Qualification and Provider Regulations require experience of practice in three distinct areas of English and Welsh law and practice, one might think that there is no longer a requirement for trainees to have experience of both contentious and non-contentious practice. This would be a mistake, since to meet the Practice Skills Standards requires a trainee to have experience of contentious as well as non-contentious work.

15.4 EXEMPTION FROM THE PRT

Exemption from the requirement to undertake the PRT in order to satisfy the vocational stage requirement for admission as a solicitor may be available under the SRA's Equivalent Means policy (see **10.4.5**).

Reductions in the training period may also be available (see **15.7.7**) for prior work experience.

15.5 AUTHORISATION AS A TRAINING PROVIDER

15.5.1 Requirements for authorisation

Under the Qualification and Provider Regulations, only an Authorised Training Provider ('Training Provider') may provide recognised training to trainee solicitors, and confirmation of authorisation needs to have been received before that training may commence. Authorisation applies to the registered office, head office(s) and all branch offices, so a firm which, for example, has more than one office does not need to make a separate application for each office.

A Training Provider can be an organisation, body, firm, company, in-house practice or individual, provided it is able to meet the requirements for authorisation as set out in the Qualification and Provider Regulations; it does not have to be a firm of solicitors.[7]

If an organisation was authorised as a Training Establishment under the 2011 Training Provider Regulations, it obtained automatic authorisation as a Training Provider regulated by the Qualification and Provider Regulations from 1 July 2014 for trainees employed by the organisation on or after 1 July 2014.

If an organisation was not already authorised as a Training Establishment as at 1 July 2014, it needs to apply to be authorised as a Training Provider, by completing the prescribed application form and paying the prescribed fee[8] at the same time as submitting the completed application.

Comment

The SRA advises that any organisation which is thinking of employing trainees should be sure that it is able to provide the breadth of experience and supervision required by the Qualification and Provider Regulations, and should be aware that it may be monitored by the SRA to ensure that the training it provides to its trainees is of an appropriate quality and standard. So, if an organisation is considering employing trainees for the first time, it should make sure that it understands what will be involved, and has the resources necessary to provide the required supervision and training (see **15.7**).

---

[7] SRA Handbook, Version 15, Glossary, 'Authorised Training Provider' entry.
[8] £100 at the date of publication.

THE VOCATIONAL STAGE REQUIREMENTS

15.5.2 Applying for authorisation

The 'Application for Authorisation as a Training Provider' form requires:

- the organisation's details, including the 'Organisation SRA ID' (Section 1);
- confirmation and details of how the organisation will meet the training requirements (see **15.11**) (Section 2);
- details of the Training Principal (see **15.6**) (Section 3);
- a declaration made by a 'Manager' (in the Legal Services Act 2007 sense) in the organisation.

15.5.3 Grant of authorisation

Once the SRA has considered an application for authorisation as a Training Provider, it will either:

- grant authorisation without conditions;
- grant authorisation with conditions; or
- refuse to grant authorisation.

Authorisation, if granted, will be for such period as the SRA considers appropriate (reg.11.3). According to SRA guidelines, however, authorisation once granted lasts for the lifetime of the organisation, although the SRA reserves the right to revoke authorisation if it has serious concerns about the quality of the training being provided.

Comment

The way concerns would normally come to the SRA's attention would be through monitoring of the Training Provider (see **15.13**) or from a complaint received from a trainee or an application from a Training Provider to opt-out of or waive a requirement/s.

15.5.4 Sanctions

Under reg.16, if a Training Provider fails to comply with the Qualification and Provider Regulations or the SRA's requirements, the SRA may:

- revoke the organisation's authorised status;
- grant continued authorisation subject to conditions;
- refuse to recognise any training received by the trainee as a PRT.

If a trainee fails to comply with the Qualification and Provider Regulations or the SRA's requirements, the SRA may refuse to recognise any training received by the trainee as a PRT.[9]

---

[9] Qualification and Provider Regulations, reg.16.2.

15.6 TRAINING PRINCIPAL

In order to be able to provide recognised training once an organisation has been authorised as a Training Provider, the organisation is required by reg.10.2(b) to appoint a 'Training Principal' and notify the SRA of the appointment using the 'Application for Authorisation as a Training Provider' form.

For a Training Provider which was already authorised as Training Establishment as at 1 July 2014, and which became authorised as from that date as a Training Provider under the Qualification and Provider Regulations, its appointed Training Principal continues automatically as well.

> **Comment**
>
> There may be a temptation to appoint a Training Principal in name only on the basis that many of the responsibilities of the Training Principal can be delegated. However, some caution is necessary: the Authorised Training Provider Information Pack expands on this requirement under the Qualification and Provider Regulations by describing the Training Principal as someone 'who agrees to take a central role in the training provision'.
>
> Although the Information Pack provides non-mandatory guidance, the SRA would expect the Training Principal to take a central role in the training provision,[10] and were the Training Principal not to do so, the Training Provider would need to demonstrate how the requirements under the Qualification and Provider Regulations were being met by a Training Principal who was not centrally involved.

Under reg.13, a Training Principal must:

- be a solicitor of England and Wales who holds a current practising certificate (unless exempt from holding a practising certificate under the Solicitors Act 1974, s.68) or a practising barrister; and
- be competent to meet the requirements of the Qualification and Provider Regulations (reg.13.1(a) and (b)).

According to the SRA's 'Becoming a Training Provider Q&A',[11] the nomination of a Training Principal does not require approval by the SRA; rather, responsibility is on the Training Provider to ensure that the nominated Training Principal is appropriate. The SRA would only involve itself if the nominated individual had a condition on his or her practising certificate which related to the training of trainees.[12]

If a Training Provider changes its Training Principal, then the Training Provider is required by reg.12.4 to notify the SRA by completing a 'Declaration of a New Training Principal' online.[13] The online form needs to be completed by a manager

---

[10] SRA, Authorised Training Provider Information Pack, 18 August 2014, p.2.
[11] SRA, 'FAQs for Training Providers'.
[12] SRA, 'Becoming a Training Provider Q&A', p.2.
[13] SRA, 'FAQs for Training Providers', p.3.

of the Training Provider, who is required in the preamble to the form to 'read the [Qualification and Provider Regulations] and the related guidance prior to completing the form'. At the same time, the Training Provider needs to formally end the role of the previous Training Principal, which the SRA suggests be done through the organisation's 'mySRA' profile. In addition to providing the relevant information regarding the Training Provider and nominated new Training Principal, the manager who is completing the declaration must declare that:

- he or she has read, understood and agreed to Part 1 of the Qualification and Provider Regulations; and
- he or she will ensure that the nominated Training Principal will comply with reg.13.1 of the Qualification and Provider Regulations.

Comment

The SRA advises that, for a Training Principal to fulfil his or her responsibilities, the Training Principal needs to fully understand the training requirements in the Qualification and Provider Regulations. So, it is advisable for a Training Principal to ensure that he or she has read and understands the Qualification and Provider Regulations when nominated.

The Training Principal acts as the main liaison with the SRA about the Training Provider's trainees, and is expected to advise the SRA of any changes which are relevant to the training that is required to be provided to the trainees.[14]

The responsibilities of the Training Principal are to:

- ensure that the training provided meets the requirements of reg.12 (reg.13.1(c)), namely, to provide the trainee with training which:
  - is supervised by solicitors and others with the necessary skills and experience to provide effective supervision, so that the trainee has the learning and development opportunities and personal support which will enable the trainee to meet the Practice Skills Standards;
  - provides practical experience in at least three distinct areas of English and Welsh law and practice;
  - ensures the trainee knows, and is able to comply with, the requirements of the Principles contained in the SRA Handbook; and
  - includes regular review and appraisal of the trainee's performance and development in relation to the Practice Skills Standards and the Principles, as well as regular review of the trainee's training record;
- ensure that the trainee maintains a record of training which meets the requirements of reg.14 (reg.13.1(d)) (see **15.12.4**) to:

---

[14] SRA, Authorised Training Provider Information Pack, 18 August 2014, p.2.

PERIOD OF RECOGNISED TRAINING

- – contain details of the work performed;
- – record how the trainee has acquired, applied and developed his or her skills by reference to the Practice Skills Standards and the SRA Principles;
- – record the trainee's reflections on his or her performance and development plans; and
- – be verified by the individual/s who supervise the trainee;
- ensure that any person involved in the training and supervision of a trainee has adequate legal knowledge and experience in the practice area he or she is supervising, and the skills to provide effective supervision (reg.13.1(e)) (see **15.12**);
- certify to the SRA that the trainee:
  - – has completed the required training (reg.5.5), using the prescribed admission form AD1;
  - – is of the proper character and suitability to be admitted as a solicitor; and
  - – has completed the PRT.

All the above responsibilities are able to be delegated by the Training Principal but, if this happens, the trainee needs to be informed of the delegation.[15]

Comment

The Training Principal has a pivotal role in relation to the firm's trainees, as well as being the conduit between the Training Provider and the SRA. However, there is little prescription beyond that as to what exactly the Training Principal must do. Many of the responsibilities may be delegated, but if they are the Training Principal must still ensure that the responsibilities are met.

The SRA's Trainee Information Pack advises the trainee 'to talk with your training principal and supervisor to understand how your learning during this time will be structured and supported'.[16]

The trainee is also told that 'if you have any queries or problems relating to your training, you should discuss these with your training principal in the first instance. However, if the issue remains unresolved you may contact [the SRA] for advice'.[17] So, there is a pastoral aspect to the Training Principal role as well.

---

[15] SRA, Authorised Training Provider Information Pack, 18 August 2014, p.2.
[16] SRA, Trainee Information Pack, 4 July 2014, p.1.
[17] SRA, Trainee Information Pack, 4 July 2014, p.1.

15.7 EMPLOYING TRAINEES UNDER THE PRT

15.7.1 Recruitment practices

Although the SRA does not prescribe how a Training Provider should make offers of training to prospective trainees, it identifies good practice as sending an offer letter to a successful candidate as soon as possible following the organisation's decision to recruit.[18]

The SRA also recommends that organisations adopt and operate good recruitment practices and procedures which adhere to the requirement of the Code of Conduct.[19]

> **Comment**
>
> The SRA previously supported the Voluntary Code to Good Practice in the recruitment of trainee solicitors. However, it withdrew from the Voluntary Code from 1 April 2015, leaving it to universities and recruiting organisations to decide whether or not to adhere to the practices agreed under the Voluntary Code in terms of dates and processes by which individual employers and employees may make recruitment choices. The reason given by the SRA at the time for withdrawing was that it did not feel that its regulatory role was to be involved in deciding the dates and processes by which individual employers and employees made recruitment choices.[20]

Although firms were previously limited under the 2011 Training Provider Regulations as to the number of trainees they could recruit, the SRA no longer imposes a limit on the number of trainees a Training Provider may employ;[21] rather, a Training Provider may employ as many trainees as it feels appropriate, subject to being able to meet the requirements of the Qualification and Provider Regulations.

15.7.2 Employment contract

A PRT is viewed as a contract of apprenticeship for employment law purposes.[22] This means that the contract of employment is subject to an implied term that the Training Provider will educate and train the apprentice in the practical and other skills needed to practise the trade or profession for which he or she is being trained.[23] Under an apprenticeship, a trainee also has enhanced protections, of which the SRA advises Training Providers to be aware.

---

[18] SRA, Authorised Training Provider Information Pack, 18 August 2014, p.3.
[19] SRA, Authorised Training Provider Information Pack, 18 August 2014, p.3.
[20] SRA news release, 6 March 2014, 'SRA and the Voluntary Code'.
[21] SRA Consultancy, 'Training for Tomorrow: Regulation Review', 6 December 2013 (see **6.4.1**).
[22] SRA, Authorised Training Provider Information Pack, 18 August 2014, p.3, and SRA, Trainee Information Pack, 4 July 2014, p.1.
[23] SRA, 'Regulations Review: Removing Unnecessary Regulations and Simplifying Processes', 28 April 2014, p.5.

> **Comment**
>
> This was not so much of a problem under the training contract regime, which was based on standard form training contracts prescribed by the SRA. Under the PRT regime, each Training Provider will use its own contract of employment.

In terms of general employment law, a Training Provider needs to provide a trainee with the terms and conditions of employment, covering such things as:

- place of work
- working hours
- starting salary
- supervisory arrangements
- length of training
- learning elements.

The SRA suggests that those terms should be provided to the trainee when he or she starts work or soon thereafter.[24]

Holiday and sickness leave is a matter for agreement between the trainee and Training Provider, and will be subject to the Working Time Regulations 1998[25] (unless otherwise agreed by the trainee and Training Provider).

15.7.3 Termination of training

As an apprenticeship, if a Training Provider wishes to terminate the contract of employment before the end of the training period, the SRA's guidance states that it may only do so where:

- the Training Provider and the trainee agree to the termination;
- the training is conditional upon the trainee passing any of the academic stages of qualification or the Legal Practice Course (LPC), and the trainee does not pass;
- there is serious misconduct and the SRA regards the trainee's conduct as unacceptable;[26]
- the trainee is so incapacitated that he or she is incapable of being trained. In this case, the trainee would have to be incapable of meeting the Practice Skills Standards, in the SRA's judgment; or
- the Training Provider has closed its business or has fundamentally changed to the extent that it is not possible to train the trainee properly.[27]

---

[24] SRA, Authorised Training Provider Information Pack, 18 August 2014, p.3.
[25] Working Time Regulations 1998, SI 1998/1833.
[26] SRA, Authorised Training Provider Information Pack, 18 August 2014, p.3.
[27] SRA, Authorised Training Provider Information Pack, 18 August 2014, p.6.

THE VOCATIONAL STAGE REQUIREMENTS

The SRA also advises that unfair dismissal could lead to a claim for compensation by the trainee for loss of earnings and loss of prospects attaching to the qualified position the apprenticeship was intended to lead to.[28]

15.7.4 Disputes

Because training is subject to the Qualification and Provider Regulations, a trainee is entitled to report any breach by its Training Provider of the training requirements under the Regulations and, as an apprentice, may have 'recourse to the courts'.[29] The SRA will not participate in the resolution of disputes between a Training Provider and its trainee, either directly or by appointing a conciliator.[30]

15.7.5 Salary

Until 1 August 2014, the SRA required Authorised Training Providers (and Training Establishments for training contracts under the 2011 Training Provider Regulations) to pay trainees a regulatory minimum salary. From 1 August 2014, the SRA changed this to a requirement to pay at least the single hourly rate of the national minimum wage specified in the National Minimum Wage Regulations 1999, SI 1999/584.[31]

Comment

The removal of the regulatory minimum salary has been controversial. According to the Law Society,[32] whereas firms were required to pay trainees at least £18,590 if they were working in central London and £16,650 outside London, under the national minimum wage, this has dropped to £11,830.

In response to concerns of the Junior Lawyers Division of the Law Society, the Law Society made a recommendation to the profession in November 2015 that, as a matter of good practice, Authorised Training Providers should pay their trainees a minimum salary based on a 35-hour week living wage of £9.40 per hour in London (and £8.25 per hour outside London), plus an average yearly Legal Practice Course re-payment of £3,168. This would provide a recommended minimum salary of £20,276 for trainees working in London and £18,183 for trainees working outside London,[33] which the Law Society will review in November each year.

This is a recommendation only and not a regulatory requirement.

---

[28] SRA, Authorised Training Provider Information Pack, 18 August 2014, p.4.
[29] SRA, Authorised Training Provider Information Pack, 18 August 2014, p.4.
[30] SRA, 'FAQs for Training Providers', p.2.
[31] Qualification and Provider Regulations, reg.11.
[32] Law Society website, 'Recommended minimum salary for trainee solicitors', 11 November 2015.
[33] Law Society website, 'Recommended minimum salary for trainee solicitors', 11 November 2015.

15.7.6 Length of training period

In line with the requirements of reg.5.2, a full-time training period ('full-time' meaning working five days per week) 'shall normally be not less than two years if undertaken full-time or pro rata if part-time'. In the Authorised Training Provider Information Pack, two years is also counted as 730 calendar days or 522 working days.

If a trainee works part-time, then the period is increased proportionately. For example, a trainee working four days per week would be required to undertake a training period of two years and six months (or 913 calendar days), whereas a trainee who worked three days per week would be required to undertake a training period of three years and four months (or 1,216 calendar days).

The SRA also permits trainees to undertake training while they are studying on the Qualifying Law Degree (QLD), Common Professional Examination (CPE)/ Graduate Diploma in Law (GDL) or LPC, with the training period being extended in the way described above if they are working part-time.[34]

15.7.7 Reduction of training period

Under reg.12.3, a Training Provider may recognise relevant – and equivalent – prior experience which a trainee may have obtained through working in a legal environment before starting training under a PRT. The Training Provider may take this time into account to reduce the period of training ('relevant work-based experience') 'on a like-for-like basis' by a maximum of six months (or 183 calendar days). This is adjusted pro rata for trainees who work part-time.

According to the SRA guidance,[35] a trainee who worked, say, two and a half days per week for six months, would have his or her training period reduced by three months.

A Training Provider is not obliged to recognise relevant work-based experience, and it is entirely at its discretion whether to grant a reduction in the training period. The SRA advises that when considering whether to recognise previous experience, the experience needs to have:

1. been gained in the previous three years
2. been in English and Welsh law and practice, and in one or more areas of law
3. enabled the acquisition of one or more of the Practice Skills Standards and/or the Principles, and
4. been adequately supervised and appraised.[36]

---

[34] SRA, Authorised Training Provider Information Pack, 18 August 2014, p.3.
[35] SRA, Authorised Training Provider Information Pack, 18 August 2014.
[36] SRA, Authorised Training Provider Information Pack, 18 August 2014, p.4

THE VOCATIONAL STAGE REQUIREMENTS

The SRA also advises a Training Provider to take account of the following when considering relevant work-based experience for a trainee who completed a 'sandwich placement' during the academic stage:

1. the placement should normally have been at level 3 of the national qualifications framework or above
2. the placement should have been for at least three months
3. whether the placement was with a Training Provider
4. whether the trainee was paid a reasonable salary during the placement, taking account of the national minimum wage and the SRA minimum salary for trainees
5. whether the trainee satisfactorily completed the placement and was awarded the academic stage of qualification.[37]

As a practical matter, it is advisable that the Training Principal retains copies of the documentation in support of the application in case the Training Provider receives a monitoring visit from the SRA (see **15.13**). A trainee should also keep copies, and the Trainee Information Pack in fact says that 'It is important that you keep copies of any supporting documentation as part of your training record, as we and/or your training principal may request to see them at any time'.[38]

Comment

There are arguments for and against granting a reduction to the training period: the argument in favour is probably more from the point of view of the trainee who wishes to qualify as soon as possible; equally, a firm will be in favour if it means being able to charge the trainee out as a qualified solicitor sooner, or if the trainee needs rights of audience for the work he or she is required to do, or his or her work involves carrying out reserved activities.

However, against this is the argument that having trainees spend two years working in different practice areas of the organisation means that they will have a greater knowledge and understanding of the organisation and its practice, which goes to easier collaboration and co-operation, as well as greater ability to cross-sell the firm's services. There is also an argument that working as a paralegal, even though the paralegal may be carrying out equivalent tasks to a trainee, is not working at the level of a trainee who is subject to professional conduct rules. Equally, although a paralegal may be supervised, this may not be to the same level as required for the supervision of trainees, and therefore the actual experience is not equivalent, particularly if the role the paralegal was performing was not one which was intended to lead to qualification. In the end, it will come down to the particular application.

---

[37] SRA, Authorised Training Provider Information Pack, 18 August 2014, p.4.
[38] SRA, Trainee Information Pack, 4 July 2014, p.9.

15.8 ELIGIBILITY TO COMMENCE A PRT

15.8.1 Determining eligibility

A PRT is not allowed to commence until the SRA has determined that the trainee is eligible to do so. In order to be eligible to commence a PRT, a trainee must meet the SRA's character and suitability requirements (see **Chapter 18**). The way eligibility is determined is as follows: before commencing a PRT, the trainee must either –

- confirm that he or she has no character or suitability issues which require consideration by the SRA; or
- disclose any issues as to character and suitability for assessment by the SRA. The SRA advises that assessing character and suitability issues may take up to six months, during which time a trainee is not eligible to commence training.

Comment

The way this is actually done is as follows:

- If the trainee has no character or suitability issues, then the trainee will effectively declare this to the SRA by completing the relevant section in the 'Notification of a Period of Recognised Training' form. This is the form which the Training Provider must complete and submit to notify the SRA in advance of the training starting (see **15.14.1**).
- If, however, the trainee does have issues as to character and suitability, he or she must complete and submit an 'Eligibility to Commence a Period of Recognised Training' form: there is no fee for submitting this form. The form also requires the trainee to read the Qualification and Provider Regulations and Student Information Pack. Although disclosure must be made before the trainee commences a PRT, the obligation is in fact to disclose any issue which may cause the trainee not to meet the outcomes of the SRA Suitability Test 2011 once the trainee has been made an offer of employment as a trainee solicitor.

If a trainee does disclose an issue, this will not necessarily mean that the trainee may not train: the SRA states that it 'may permit [the trainee] to train, or require [the Authorised Training Provider] to suspend [the trainee's] training pending an assessment of the issue disclosed to us'.[39] Once the SRA has made its assessment, it may, under reg.6.7:

- apply conditions; or
- refuse to recognise training.[40]

---

[39] SRA, 'FAQs for Trainees', p.3.
[40] SRA, 'FAQs for Trainees', p.3.

15.8.2 Ongoing obligation

A trainee is also required to notify the SRA during the PRT of 'any matters that may affect their ability to meet the outcomes of [the SRA's] Suitability Test' (see **Chapter 18**). This is an ongoing obligation and failure to do so may result in:

- the trainee's eligibility to train being revoked; or
- the training itself being terminated; and/or
- the trainee's application for admission as a solicitor being refused at the end of the training period.

In fact the SRA may treat a trainee's failure to disclose an issue of character or suitability to the SRA as *prima facie* evidence of dishonest behaviour.[41]

Comment

If an issue as to character and suitability does arise once the PRT has commenced, the SRA also advises the trainee to inform his or her Training Principal. The practical impact of disclosing an issue of character and suitability during the training period is that the SRA may (or may not) suspend the period of training until it has determined whether the trainee does in fact satisfy the SRA Suitability Test outcomes. If the SRA does suspend the training, then it will notify the Training Principal of the suspension, which is why it is wiser for the trainee to let the Training Principal know in advance, as the Training Principal will find out anyway if the training is suspended.

It is also worth saying that although the SRA does strive to resolve character and suitability issues as quickly as possible, depending on the particular case, it can take a long time to resolve. Planning on a 'glass half empty' basis (rather than a 'glass half full' basis) is therefore probably wiser.

15.8.3 Subsequent applications

If a trainee fails to meet the outcomes of the Suitability Test but there is then 'a material change in circumstances', the trainee may make a new application to undertake a PRT, and is permitted to make three further applications for eligibility to commence training, but at least 12 months from the decision on the previous application.

If the SRA were to decide, on a new application, that the trainee was eligible to commence a PRT, the SRA may recognise training that the trainee had undertaken prior to the issue of character and suitability arising, which would then count towards the period of training.

---

[41] SRA, 'FAQs for Trainees', p.3.

PERIOD OF RECOGNISED TRAINING

15.9 NOTIFICATION REQUIREMENTS

A Training Provider is required to notify the SRA of a trainee who is to commence a PRT with the Training Provider. To do this, a Training Provider needs to complete and submit a 'Notification of a Period of Recognised Training' form, together with payment of the requisite fee.

> **Comment**
>
> The notes on the 'Notification of a Period of Recognised Training' form state that the SRA '[aims] to make an assessment of [the] application within 30 days'. However, if the SRA finds the application to be incomplete or it requires further information, it will contact the applicant to request that information. The 30 days run from receipt of all necessary information. What is important to understand is that the PRT cannot commence – or will not be recognised for the purposes of counting towards the PRT – until the SRA has determined the eligibility of each trainee included in the notification form.

The 'Notification of a Period of Recognised Training' form consists of the following five sections:

Section 1. Organisation Details: this merely requires details of the Training Provider to be entered, including the SRA ID, as well as the number of trainees being registered on the application.

Section 2. Training Provider Declaration: The declaration is to the effect that the signatory will 'agree to notify the SRA of any issue/s under the SRA Suitability Test 2011 that arise during the PRT for each individual notified on this notification'. The signatory must either be the Training Principal or the 'Authorised Signatory'.

Section 3. Trainee Details: According to the guidance notes to the form, this section must be completed by the Authorised Signatory or Training Principal. The section requires the personal details of each trainee who is included in the Notification to be inserted, including his or her SRA ID and starting salary.

> **Comment**
>
> The 'Notification of a Period of Recognised Training' form can be used for more than one trainee, in which case 'Section 3. Trainee Details' can be photocopied for each trainee or, if completed online, a continuation form for each additional trainee can be completed and submitted online.

The guidance notes to the form reiterate the requirement for Training Providers to pay a trainee '(exclusive of any benefits) no less than the main hourly rate of the

National Minimum Wage specified in Regulation 11 of the national minimum wage Regulations 1999'[42] (see **15.7.5**).

If the trainee is working at an office which is different to the address provided in Section 1, then the address of that office also needs to be provided. The other information which needs to be inserted in Section 3 in respect of each individual trainee is the 'Start' and 'End' date of the PRT. If the Training Provider has agreed to recognise previous relevant work-based experience, then the amount of time that is being recognised (up to a maximum of six months – see **15.7.7**) should be deducted from the actual end date, so that this is an 'adjusted' date in fact rather than a putative date.

Similarly, if the trainee is undertaking the PRT on a part-time basis, then the end date must be adjusted accordingly (see **15.7.6**).

The other information required in this section is whether the trainee will be working full-time or part-time, and also the number of hours, on average, per week that the trainee will be working.

Section 4. Trainee Declaration: The declaration covers 'Previous applications' and 'Character and Suitability'. As with Section 3, Section 4 also needs to be completed by each individual trainee. In practical terms, this means photocopying the section for the number of trainees included in the Notification.

Under 'Previous applications', the trainee must declare whether he or she has previously applied for enrolment as a student of the SRA or for eligibility to commence a PRT, and if so whether his or her most recent application had been granted or refused, and if granted whether the trainee has any further matters to declare that may affect his or her suitability to be admitted as a solicitor. If the trainee declares that he or she does have further matters to declare, he or she will be contacted by the SRA for further details.

Under 'Character and Suitability', the trainee must declare whether he or she has any issues which may affect his or her ability to meet the requirements of the SRA Suitability Test 2011. A trainee in answering 'No' is satisfying the requirement, expressed in the Authorised Training Provider Information Pack[43] to confirm to the SRA that he or she has no character and suitability issues which require the SRA's consideration.

Comment

The notes on the form state that 'There is no requirement to advise the SRA of any character and suitability matters on which a decision has already been made' under reg.34.1 of the Provider Regulations 2011 or reg.6 of the Qualification and Provider

---

[42] SRA, 'Notification of a Period of Recognised Training', Version 5, 30 June 2015, p.6.
[43] SRA, Authorised Training Provider Information Pack, 18 August 2014, p.2.

> Regulations. The 2011 Regulations would relate to a trainee who commenced a training contract prior to 1 July 2014.

If the trainee declares that he or she does have an issue to declare, then he or she is required to complete and return an 'Eligibility to Commence a Period of Recognised Training' form (see **15.3**).

> **Comment**
>
> This means that the trainee will have to allow time for the SRA to consider the application, and the trainee may not commence the training period, in the same way had the trainee completed an 'Eligibility to Commence a Period of Recognised Training' form when the trainee was offered a PRT (see **15.8**).

Even if the trainee has no character and suitability issues to declare, he or she, in making the declaration:

- agrees to notify the SRA should any issue/s arise under the SRA Suitability Test 2011 during the PRT;
- understands that he or she has an ongoing obligation to notify the SRA should any such issues arise;
- understands that if he or she fails to disclose such issues, the failure to disclose will be treated as *prima facie* evidence of dishonesty.

The SRA also states in the guidance notes to Section 4 that the information provided by the trainee in this section 'will be verified with third parties as part of the application process'.

> **Comment**
>
> The guidance notes to the form require the trainee when completing Section 4 to have read the SRA Suitability Test 2011, presumably before making the declaration. Given the consequences of failing to disclose character and suitability issues (i.e. *prima facie* evidence of dishonesty), it is as well that trainees are provided with a copy of the SRA Suitability Test 2011 or directed to it in the SRA Handbook or on the SRA website as soon as possible following recruitment.
>
> Due to an error in the guidance notes on the form, the notes on completing the declarations in respect of character and suitability appear under 'Section 3. Trainee Details', rather than 'Section 4. Trainee Declaration'.[44]

Section 5. Returning the form: This section provides the post, DX and email options for returning the completed form. The fee needs either to be sent with the application in the post or DX, or paid by bank transfer.

---

[44] SRA, 'Notification of a Period of Recognised Training', Version 5, 30 June 2015, p.6.

15.10 SUPPORT REQUIREMENTS

15.10.1 Support arrangements

The SRA expects, but does not require, that a Training Provider has adequate support arrangements in place which include:

- a desk for the trainee's own work;
- appropriate secretarial support;
- access to library and relevant research facilities to support the training the trainee is required to undertake.

Comment

On the basis of the permissive approach taken by the SRA under the Qualification and Provider Regulations regime, the requirement for the trainee to be provided with a desk would be met by 'hot desking', given the move by some organisations to open plan offices and hot desking policies – provided the arrangements enable the trainee to gain the required experience and develop the required skills.

15.10.2 Induction

A Training Provider is expected, but not required, to provide an induction for trainees. The SRA regards it as good practice to provide an induction at the beginning of the training period, even if the trainee has worked for the Training Provider previously, since the purpose of an induction is 'as an opportunity to clarify the roles and responsibilities of those who will be involved in the trainee's training, to familiarise the trainee with office procedures, to introduce fellow staff members and to explain the nature of the work that they will undertake'.[45]

The SRA does not prescribe the format or length of the induction and, in fact, the Authorised Training Provider Information Pack says that a Training Provider is free to organise the induction as best suits the organisation. However, the SRA suggests that the induction could cover:

---

[45] SRA, Authorised Training Provider Information Pack, 18 August 2014, p.5.

- an introduction to your organisation, the training scheme, the Practice Skills Standards and your expectations of the trainee
- how the training will be organised
- the form of the training record that you want the trainee to keep, how and when it is to be completed, and when it will be reviewed
- arrangements for supervision, performance review and formal appraisals
- your office procedures, including pastoral care, office hours, holidays, health and safety
- any other relevant matters, such as your IT and office equipment and systems for time-recording and billing, library and research facilities; secretarial and administrative support [46]

Comment

Whenever a promotion takes place and a person 'steps up' to a new role, some sort of preparation for what will be expected of them in their new role is sensible. This equally applies to trainees, who are not only stepping up but usually stepping into a new environment – of which they may have little or no knowledge and comprehension (subject to any engagement they have had with the firm before starting the training contract, either through vacation placements or through interaction with the firm during the LPC (see **29.4**)). Therefore, to have an induction for trainees joining the firm would be sensible practice in any case, not least because the induction can be used to support the firm's business objectives by enabling new trainees to function effectively within the firm as soon as possible.

If the Training Provider uses the SRA's suggestions for content, then the following might also be considered:

- A session on 'IT and office equipment'. This could include training on using the telephone, photocopier, printer – whatever equipment the trainee would be expected to use. Although trainees may be from the Y generation and beyond and be completely at home with computers, they may never have worked in an office before, so may not have had to use the particular types of equipment available in the firm (which may even seem 'prehistoric' . . .). In any case, this sort of training is best delivered through hands-on demonstrations, supplemented by brief user notes that the trainee can refer to afterwards.
- A session on library and research facilities. This should cover whatever knowledge management (KM) systems for capturing and retrieving information are used in the firm, in addition to the firm's library services, and online as well as hard copy sources. Where the firm has subscriptions to online services, it may be possible to have the online provider come in and give a demonstration of the services where the numbers justify it; alternatively, someone in the firm who is proficient in using the service could also do this. The point is to make sure that the trainee is able to use all the resources the firm has invested in, and which the trainee will be expected to use.
- In the 'introduction to your organisation' session, consider including talks on all the firm's practice areas, so that all trainees start with an understanding of what it is the firm does, irrespective of where they do their 'seats'. After all, trainees might only do seats in three practice areas during the PRT. The reason for giving talks on the firm's different areas of practice is not just to give the trainee information about

---

[46] SRA, Authorised Training Provider Information Pack, 18 August 2014, p.5.

the organisation the trainee is joining, but to assist the socialisation process of the trainee to become part of the firm: it is important knowledge that will help a trainee know who in the firm has expert knowledge they can refer to if they need to (risk management), and also to cross-sell the firm's expertise should the opportunity arise either in the trainee's work with clients or when networking. The sooner the trainee has this awareness and the sense of belonging to the firm as a whole, the better.

Although it is no longer compulsory for the Training Principal to ensure that there are suitable pastoral arrangements for trainees (although it is recommended in the SRA's suggestions for what the induction could cover and is implicit (see **15.6**)), it would be best practice to ensure that there are suitable pastoral care arrangements. What trainees need to know is that there is a named person they can contact if they have a problem or an issue arises. For many trainees, arriving in the firm is going to be extremely daunting, so the human element can be very important. People who could be the contact for pastoral care include:

- the Training Principal, subject to his or her work commitments and availability;
- the person who deals with graduate recruitment and whom trainees may already know; or
- someone with HR skills to whom trainees can address concerns but, it will depend on who is appropriate in the organisation.

What is also important is to have systems which provide effective channels of communication so that any issues or concerns which are raised can be escalated to the appropriate person (the Training Principal in particular) and dealt with promptly and to the satisfaction of all.

Other areas a Training Provider might consider covering in its trainee induction could include:

- risk management and compliance;
- introduction to marketing (including cross-selling);
- finance, and how time-recording contributes to the firm's overall profitability;
- how to work with secretaries;
- how to use equipment and software in the firm to produce their work;
- talks by fee earners on what is expected of trainees;
- talks by other trainees on their experience of being a trainee.

It may go without saying but it is important to say it anyway: trainees should be introduced to a range of people through the induction process, from partners to secretaries and business support staff. In fact, as trainees they are likely to have more contact with, and rely on, secretaries and business support staff than partners.

A word of caution, however: there is a limit to how much trainees are going to be able to take in, particularly in the first days – and weeks – of joining the organisation. Being bombarded with information will not necessarily guarantee the easing into the organisation and practice that the induction is intended to achieve. The SRA recommends that the induction take place 'at the beginning of the training contract'; it does not say on the first day, although when and how it is held should be determined by how much there is for trainees to take in. The answer may be to run the main sessions over the first few days, and then to follow up or introduce other topics over a longer period of, say, a few weeks. This means that trainees have a chance to settle in and familiarise themselves, so that what they are being told starts to have some context. In fact, when trainees are starting to ask 'how', 'where', 'why', it is usually a good indication that they are ready for the next phase of their induction.

PERIOD OF RECOGNISED TRAINING

> Just as training does not need to be delivered in formal training sessions only, nor does the induction have to be done in a formal way, particularly if the number of trainees does not justify it. If the firm only has one or two trainees, the induction proper can be given one-to-one or even by way of pre-recorded webinar (which is more resource-efficient). The trainee can then be given a few weeks to shadow, familiarise, read files and so on. Another way of making trainees familiar with office procedures, information resources and so on, is to give trainees a project/s to do during the first two weeks. Projects can also be used to make an assessment of the trainee in terms of his or her literacy, numeracy, initiative and personal organisation skills, to give a few examples – a diagnostic, in other words.

15.10.3 Other obligations on Authorised Training Providers

According to reg.10.2(e), a Training Provider is required to pay the fees and expenses for its trainees' first attempt at the PSC. The Authorised Training Provider Information Pack puts the requirement as one of paying reasonable expenses but with no 'regulatory requirement ... to allow time-off for study of the PSC'.[47] However, the SRA does recommend that a Training Provider 'consider[s] whether to offer paid study leave at the outset of training, and advise[s] the trainee accordingly'.[48]

15.11 TRAINING REQUIREMENTS

15.11.1 Structure of training

The SRA permits training to be organised either by way of:

- the trainee spending a specified period (usually about six months) in at least three distinct departments or 'seats'; or
- the training working in various areas of law on a day-to-day basis, according to the work which is available

provided that the Training Provider ensures that:

- the trainee spends sufficient time in each area in order to be trained properly in that area. The SRA anticipates that at least three months (or equivalent) would normally be required to achieve this;
- the trainee is guided and tutored in professional conduct, ethics and client care;
- the level and complexity of the trainee's work is increased gradually during the training period.

---

[47] SRA, Authorised Training Provider Information Pack, 18 August 2014, p.8.
[48] SRA, Authorised Training Provider Information Pack, 18 August 2014, p.8.

THE VOCATIONAL STAGE REQUIREMENTS

> **Comment**
>
> It would be wrong to say that the only way a trainee can receive the training he or she needs during the PRT is by moving between different areas of practice in seats of whatever length. In-house legal departments, for example, which may not have different practice groups so the training remains in one 'seat', can achieve the necessary mix of work by balancing work allocation.

15.11.2 Responsibility

The Qualification and Provider Regulations specify that an individual must complete a PRT before the individual will be admitted as a solicitor by the SRA (reg.5.1). The SRA therefore needs to be satisfied that the training a trainee is receiving or has received is adequate. Specific requirements for the training which a Training Provider must provide are set out in reg.12 of the Qualification and Provider Regulations:

> 12.1 An authorised training provider must provide a trainee with training which:
> - (a) is supervised by solicitors and other individuals who have the necessary skills and experience to provide effective supervision, to ensure that the trainee has relevant learning and development opportunities and personal support to enable the trainee to meet the Practice Skills Standards;
> - (b) provides practical experience in at least three distinct areas of English and Welsh law and practice;
> - (c) provides appropriate training to ensure that the trainee knows the requirements of the Principles and is able to comply with them; and
> - (d) includes regular review and appraisal of the trainee's performance and development in respect of the Practice Skills Standards and the Principles, and the trainee's record of training.

A Training Provider may delegate many of its responsibilities to the Training Principal or Supervisors. However, the Training Provider retains responsibility to ensure that these delegated responsibilities are carried out.

Although the Qualification and Provider Regulations do not specify that a trainee must be provided with experience in contentious as well as non-contentious work, which was required by the 2011 Training Provider Regulations, this is still necessary if the trainee is to meet the Practice Skills Standards, since these 'include requirements relating to contentious, or dispute-based, matters, such as skills in advocacy and dispute resolution, as well as requirements relating to all matters whether contentious or not, such as case management and client care'.[49]

---

[49] Closed consultation, 'Training for Tomorrow: Regulation Review', 25 April 2014, p.7.

PERIOD OF RECOGNISED TRAINING

15.11.3 Practical experience of law

Reg.12 requires a trainee to gain practical experience in at least three distinct areas of English and Welsh law and practice. The SRA does not prescribe those areas, but suggests that they may include, although are not limited to:

Administrative and Public Law	Immigration Law
Agricultural Law	Insolvency and Bankruptcy
Aviation Law	Insurance
Banking Law	International Law (non-EC)
Business Affairs	Landlord and Tenant – Residential
Chancery	Libel and Defamation
Children Law	Liquor Licensing/Gaming
Insurance and Reinsurance	Maritime/Shipping/Admiralty
Civil Liberties/Human Rights	Media
Commercial Law	Mediation – Civil/Commercial
Commercial Property	Mediation – Family
Company Law	Medical Negligence
Computer and IT Law	Mental Health
Construction/Civil Engineering	Mergers and Acquisitions
Consumer Problems	Military Law
Conveyancing – Residential	Neighbour Disputes
Corporate Finance	Pension Law
Crime – General, Motoring, Juvenile	Personal Injury
Debt and Money Advice	Planning Law
Education Law	Professional Negligence
Employment	Taxation
Energy and Natural Resources	Transport – Road and Rail
Environmental Law	Travel and Tourism
European Community Law	Trusts
Family	Welfare Benefits
Financial and Investment Services	Wills and Probate
Fraud	

15.11.4 Practice Skills development

Regulation 12 also requires trainees to be provided with opportunities to develop the practice skills set out in the following Practice Skills Standards.

Apart from setting the level of competence expected in the skill and the required outcomes, the Standards also provide the tasks which should be given to trainees to enable them to develop the skills.

THE VOCATIONAL STAGE REQUIREMENTS

SRA PRACTICE SKILLS STANDARDS[50]

Advocacy and oral presentation

On completing the training period, trainee solicitors should be competent to exercise the rights of audience available to solicitors on admission.

Their experience will enable them to understand

1. the communication skills of the advocate
2. the techniques and tactics of examination, cross-examination and re-examination
3. the need to act in accordance with the ethics, etiquette and conventions of the professional advocate.

The tasks trainees perform must enable them to grasp the principal skills required to prepare, conduct and present a case:

1. identifying the client's goals
2. identifying and analysing relevant factual and legal issues, and relating them to one another
3. summarising the strengths and weaknesses of the case
4. planning how to present the case
5. outlining the facts in simple narrative form
6. formulating a coherent submission based on the facts, general principles and legal authority in a structured, concise and persuasive manner.

The following activities are likely to foster these skills:

1. helping to advise on pre-trial procedures
2. helping to prepare cases before trial
3. with one or more lawyers, attending the magistrates' courts to observe trials, bail applications, pleas of mitigation or committal, and observing submissions in chambers, examination, cross examination and re-examination in open court
4. observing proceedings in family cases, industrial tribunals, planning tribunals or other tribunals or forms of dispute resolution
5. as training progresses, and under appropriate supervision, conducting interim applications before a Master or District Judge
6. becoming involved in presentations for clients or in preparing or delivering in-house training.

Case and transaction management

Trainee solicitors must begin to acquire skills in managing and running a case or transaction.

Trainees must be given work to enable them to understand the importance of:

1. producing a schedule for a case/transaction, broken up – where necessary – into phases
2. planning out phases of work to include time, cost and risk management
3. developing techniques to diarise, follow up and revisit matters at the appropriate time
4. keeping accurate records and attendance notes
5. effectively managing files

---

[50] SRA, Authorised Training Provider Information Pack, 18 August 2014.

6. regularly and fully reporting back to clients
7. co-ordinating teams to review progress and revise options
8. bringing matters to a timely, client-satisfactory conclusion
9. wrapping up the matter, closing the file, and recovering costs and disbursements.

To develop these skills trainees should work on larger cases or transactions as members of a team, or they should be given smaller transactions to run themselves, under close supervision.

Client care and practice support

To enable trainees to work effectively in an efficient practice, they must develop the skills required to manage time, effort and resources.

They should be given work that will enable them to

1. prioritise tasks
2. set and meet deadlines
3. review and report progress on matters
4. balance immediate and long-term objectives
5. keep appropriate records
6. understand the processes of setting fees and billing clients.

Activities that will help them to achieve this include

1. planning work by the use of their diaries
2. using email, word-processing, scheduling and organisational systems regularly and appropriately
3. working effectively with support staff
4. recording expenses and disbursements and obtaining reimbursement
5. opening and closing files
6. understanding the processes of setting fees and billing clients.

Trainees should develop good working habits, and supervisors should check this regularly.

Communication skills

Trainees should understand the need to refine their communication skills so that they can present oral and written communication in a way that achieves its purpose and is appropriate to the recipient.

They should be given work that will help them to

1. select appropriate methods of communication
2. express ideas concisely, clearly and logically
3. use appropriate language
4. use correct grammar, syntax and punctuation
5. pay attention to detail by proof-reading, checking the format and numbering of documents, cross-referencing and using consistent terminology
6. listen actively and speak effectively.

Trainees can develop these skills by

1. drafting letters, internal notes and memos
2. reporting to clients and others by telephone
3. taking notes in meetings
4. dictating notes and letters.

The importance of keeping clients regularly informed of the progress of a matter and the client care outcomes in Chapter 1 of the SRA Code of Conduct should be emphasised to trainees. Trainees should be given regular advice, guidance and feedback on their performance.

Dispute resolution

Trainees should become familiar with contentious work and gain a full understanding of the skills and practice of resolving disputes, including settling, mediation and adjudication, in a fair, cost-effective and timely way that meets client needs.

Trainees should be given opportunities to observe and/or assist in resolving disputes so that they will understand the need to

1. take careful instructions
2. identify the client's purpose and advise on the possible outcomes and costs
3. thoroughly research the parties' liabilities
4. gather evidence from witnesses or elsewhere
5. consider all the options for resolving a dispute
6. meet deadlines and keep clients informed of progress
7. draft or prepare papers to assist in resolving a contentious matter
8. control information central to the dispute throughout the proceeding
9. represent the client and the client's interests through meetings, conferences and hearings
10. ensure that settlements and judgments are secure and enforceable.

Trainees can develop these skills by attending tribunal hearings or alternative dispute resolution meetings, observing proceedings and assisting with the preparation of cases.

Supervisors should explain how the work the trainee undertakes fits into the strategies pursued in a case and into the context of litigation as a whole. Trainees should be given feedback on work they have done and should be offered a perspective on the significance of their work to the case as a whole.

Drafting

Trainees should recognise the need for and be able to produce documents that are clear, precise and achieve their purpose.

They should be given work that enables them to

1. maintain a standard of care that protects client interests and meets client objectives
2. address all relevant and factual legal issues
3. identify relevant options
4. demonstrate a critical use of standard forms and precedents
5. draft documents that
   a. are consistent and coherent
   b. are clear and precise
   c. meet any requirements of form and style.

Trainees can develop these skills by drafting

1. witness statements and affidavits
2. corporate resolutions
3. wills and trust deeds

4. statements of case
5. transfer of property documents
6. leases
7. instructions to counsel
8. contracts.

The complexity of trainees' work should be increased incrementally, and they should be given opportunities to amend drafts of documents received from the other side and to practise using standard forms and precedents.

Interviewing and advising

Trainees should understand the importance of identifying the client's goals along with the need to take accurate instructions.

They should be given opportunities to observe and to conduct interviews with clients, experts, witnesses and others.

They should be given work that helps them understand the need to

1. prepare for an interview
2. allow clients or professional advisers to explain their concerns
3. identify the client's goals and priorities
4. use appropriate questioning techniques
5. determine what further information is required
6. identify possible courses of action and their consequences
7. help the client decide the best course of action
8. agree the action to be taken
9. accurately record the interview, confirming the instructions and the action that needs to be taken
10. establish a professional relationship with the client, and deal with any ethical problems that may arise.

Trainees can develop these skills by observing and taking notes of meetings and interviews, whether face to face or on the telephone.

The purpose of a meeting should be explained to the trainee, and the conduct of the meeting should be reviewed with them afterwards. Where a trainee is conducting an interview, the supervisor should carefully monitor any advice given by the trainee during the meeting, and give guidance and feedback on the trainee's performance after the meeting.

Legal research

Trainees should learn to find solutions by investigating the factual and legal issues, analysing problems and communicating the results of their research.

They should be given work that makes use of traditional and computerised research tools and sources, business information and other relevant sources.

Trainees could be required to

1. research specific legal issues and factual, historical or commercial matters
2. prepare for client interviews
3. analyse corporate searches
4. investigate title to property and other relevant searches
5. review title documents and clients' papers
6. assist with due diligence enquiries.

The person allocating the work should give the trainee
1. background information on the context and purpose of the research
2. clear instructions
3. defined tasks
4. information about any limitations to be imposed on their research
5. guidance on where to begin.

Trainees must also be given guidance and feedback on their performance.

Negotiation

Trainees should understand the processes involved in contentious and non-contentious negotiations, and appreciate the importance to the client of reaching agreement or resolving a dispute.

They should be given opportunities to observe negotiations conducted by experienced practitioners and/or to conduct negotiations under close supervision. They should be given work that will help them understand the process of negotiation including:

1. identifying the central issues and explaining them to the client
2. assessing the bargaining-positions of each party
3. planning a negotiation
4. establishing an agenda at the start
5. listening actively
6. using appropriate questioning techniques
7. generating alternative solutions to resolve the issues
8. using an appropriate negotiating style
9. identifying the strategy and tactics used by the other side
10. documenting the agreement or settlement
11. explaining the benefits and disadvantages of the agreement or settlements.

Guidance should be given on the purpose of negotiation, and feedback should be provided on the outcome and on the trainee's performance.

15.11.5 Secondments

If a Training Provider is not able to provide training in all areas of the Practice Skills Standards or in three distinct areas of English and Welsh law and practice, reg.12.2 provides that the requirements may be satisfied by the Training Provider arranging a secondment of the trainee so that he or she can gain the necessary training and experience.

Comment

Although reg.12.2 says 'may', the Authorised Training Provider Information Pack puts this in more mandatory language, even though (as guidance) the guidance itself is non-mandatory. According to the Information Pack, a Training Provider 'must' arrange for a trainee to be seconded in these circumstances. So, the position would appear to be that a Training Provider has no choice but to arrange a secondment for the trainee if the

> Training Provider itself is not able to provide the trainee with the training that is required under the Qualification and Provider Regulations.

Secondments of trainees, for whatever purpose, do not need to be approved by the SRA, although the Training Provider will continue to be responsible for ensuring that, while on secondment, the trainee will be:

- adequately supervised;
- appraised regularly;
- provided with training in English and Welsh law and practice.

The SRA also recognises that the reason a Training Provider may second a trainee will not simply be for reasons of meeting the experience requirement; it can also be for the purpose of providing the trainee with additional experience or to gain an in-depth knowledge of a client or of the work of another of the firm's offices.[51]

Comment

Although the SRA acknowledges the possibility of secondment to a client, there are other options as well if a Training Provider is not able to provide the necessary training and opportunities.

One possibility is to second the trainee to another Training Provider or to a client with an in-house team, which can offer the necessary experience. As this may mean sending a trainee to a competitor law firm, there may be some anxiety about doing this, particularly if the firm has sponsored the trainee on the LPC and possibly even the CPE. If the trainee were to jump ship to the competitor after the investment the organisation has made in the trainee's training and development to that point would be rather unfortunate to say the least (although see **4.6.4** for possible financial redress). However, the problem is probably more illusory than real.

An alternative to secondment is to set up some sort of consortium between like-minded or local firms with similar problems in providing the required experience for trainees. Consortia can be used for other training (such as the PSC), and have economies of scale which outweigh the risks. If firms do wish to set up a consortium, they may agree the arrangements between themselves without needing to seek approval from the SRA.

Another solution for satisfying the experience requirements is to send trainees on a training course – for example on litigation, which is a common problem for small, specialist non-contentious practices. The Training Provider does not need to apply to the SRA to approve its trainee/s attending the course. However, the Training Principal has the responsibility of ensuring the trainee is able to meet the practical experience requirements in order to be able to sign-off the trainee at the end of the training period (see **15.6**).

---

[51] SRA, Trainee Information Pack, 4 July 2014, p.2.

THE VOCATIONAL STAGE REQUIREMENTS

15.12 SUPERVISION, REVIEW AND APPRAISAL REQUIREMENTS

15.12.1 Supervision requirements

The responsibilities of a Supervisor are not able to be delegated since, by definition, the Supervisor should be supervising the trainee personally. However, it may be that a trainee will have a number of Supervisors, either over the training period or conceivably at the same time. All Supervisors must:

- meet the requirements to be a Supervisor;
- comply with the supervision and training requirements;
- carry out the required reviews and appraisals.

> **Comment**
>
> Although it is not a requirement, the SRA suggests that Training Providers allow Supervisors time and resources to undertake the supervisory role. One way of evidencing that this takes place is to have trainee supervision – or supervision generally – included as an activity recognised by the firm's time-recording system, with its own code, if that is not already the case. It is worth noting that time spent in supervision can be counted for CPD to meet the minimum hours requirement under the existing CPD Scheme (see **Chapter 20**).

Anyone who supervises a trainee is required to have the appropriate legal knowledge and experience in the practice area he or she is supervising, as well as having the skills to perform the supervisory role effectively.

A Supervisor may also be required by the Training Provider 'to demonstrate in some way a sound understanding both of the training requirements and of all that is expected of them as supervisors', according to the SRA's guidance.

> **Comment**
>
> It is unclear how this should be demonstrated – probably a lack of complaints from trainees would be a positive indicator – but it could possibly be incorporated in the Trainee Supervisor's own appraisal or performance review. Ultimately, the Training Provider needs to be satisfied about this (see **15.12.3**). A Supervisor needs to be able to give guidance, advice and feedback to trainees on their performances. So when a Supervisor is considering his or her own training and development needs, it would be sensible to consider whether training in giving feedback or mentoring skills, for example, would be useful.

Although the SRA does not impose it as a requirement, it does recommend that the Training Provider:

- allows Supervisors adequate time and resources;

- requires Supervisors to demonstrate that they have 'a sound understanding of the training requirements and of all that is expected of them as supervisors'.[52]

> **Comment**
>
> The Training Provider is also responsible for ensuring the required supervision, feedback and appraisal of its trainees. Although the reality is that this responsibility is usually delegated to the Training Principal, who is responsible for ensuring that a trainee's Supervisor is doing what is required, the Training Provider needs to be able to ensure that it is taking place. What is sensible therefore is for the Training Provider to set up a reporting mechanism between Supervisors and the Training Principal, and the Training Principal and management, so as to avoid duplication but at the same time give comfort that supervision, feedback and appraisals are taking place.

For those who have not supervised a trainee before, providing training in supervising, giving feedback, mentoring and coaching, or even giving appraisals may be appropriate.

> **Comment**
>
> If the firm is adopting reg.3.1(a) of the SRA Training Regulations 2011 Part 3 – CPD Regulations ('CPD Regulations') prior to 1 November 2016 (see **20.2**), the training can count towards the 16-hour requirement.
>
> If the firm has adopted reg 3.1(b) (see **20.9**), then supervision training would be identified as a training need and evidence of the training need being satisfied.

What is fundamental is to provide each Supervisor in the organisation with a copy of the Practice Skills Standards and the relevant parts, if not all, of the Authorised Training Provider Information Pack.

> **Comment**
>
> Whether the Training Principal retains responsibility for ensuring Supervisors have the appropriate legal knowledge and experience, and supervisory skills, or delegates this to someone else in the organisation, consideration needs to be given to how best to ensure that Supervisors do have the necessary supervisory skills. One way of doing this is to hold a briefing session for all Supervisors when trainees are about to join the organisation. This provides an opportunity for experienced Supervisors to share best practice with those who may be less experienced.

---

[52] SRA, Authorised Training Provider Information Pack, 18 August 2014, p.7.

15.12.2 Supervision requirements

The SRA guidance states that a Supervisor is responsible for providing practical day-to-day training and for giving trainees appropriate opportunities to develop their legal skills and knowledge. This is predominantly through work allocation and supervising the work that the trainee does.

Although not mandatory, the SRA sets out 'typical' Supervisor responsibilities as:

1. allocate work and tasks of an appropriate level, gradually increasing the level and the complexity of the work over time, while encouraging the trainee to suggest solutions independently
2. provide a balance between substantive and procedural tasks that – as a whole – demands the use of a broad range of skills
3. provide clear instructions and ensure that they have been understood
4. offer advice and guidance on appropriate research methods and materials along with sufficient information and factual background about a case or matter
5. set a realistic time-scale for work to be completed and answer questions as they arise, within a supportive environment that does not deter the trainee from asking questions in the future
6. monitor the trainee's workload to ensure they have a sufficient but not excessive amount of work
7. help ensure that the trainee maintains an up-to-date training record that identifies the work they have performed and the skills they have deployed
8. review the training record regularly to ensure that an appropriate balance of work and skills is struck
9. give regular feedback to the trainee regarding their performance, recognising achievements and improvements, and constructively addressing areas that require further effort
10. conduct or participate in formal appraisals of the trainee
11. provide an environment that encourages the trainee to take responsibility for their own development.[53]

Comment

Although not replicated in the PRT guidance, the Training Contract regime guidance included sensible considerations for Supervisors, such as:

- providing an environment that encourages the trainee to ask for help, find solutions to problems and take responsibility for his or her own development;
- being clear on expectations, and ensuring that the trainee understands them;
- having an open-door policy;
- keeping an open mind;
- involving/including the trainee whenever possible;
- listening carefully;
- stretching the trainee but not 'pushing the trainee in at the deep end';
- being enthusiastic and making time for the trainees the Supervisor is supervising.

---

[53] SRA, Authorised Training Provider Information Pack, 18 August 2014, p.9.

Comment

The preamble to the Practice Skills Standards observes that trainees develop their practice skills through a mixture of:

- completing work and tasks by themselves;
- assisting others;
- observing experienced practitioners.

The best way of developing skills is in fact by observing, then practising the skill oneself, and then receiving feedback. So, in providing a trainee with this mix of activities, what is essential is that the trainee receives feedback as he or she practises a skill. The best way of doing this, and providing a role model, is by having the trainee sit in the same office as another solicitor, preferably the trainee's Supervisor if this is possible. The move to open-plan offices may help with this, or may not, if it means there is less privacy for feedback.

15.12.3 Review and appraisal requirements

Reg.12.5(b) requires the Training Provider to certify, at the end of the training period, that the trainee has completed training in accordance with reg.5. For the Training Provider to certify this, the SRA's guidance states that the Training Provider needs to be satisfied that the trainee:

- has received appropriate training; and
- has achieved the required skills.

The SRA expects that this responsibility will usually fall to the Training Principal, who will need to rely on documented, regular, informal reviews and formal performance appraisals which are required by reg.12.1(d), and the practical reality is that it will be a trainee's current Supervisor who should carry out regular reviews of a trainee's performance while under that Supervisor's supervision.

The review and appraisal expected by the SRA would consist of:

- daily feedback;
- informal weekly reviews of the trainee's training record;
- informal progress reviews;
- formal appraisals at least three times during the training period but preferably every six months.

The 'frequent' informal reviews of the trainee's training record should:

- review progress towards agreed objectives;
- deal with any difficulties close to the event;
- compare the breadth and depth of work being performed by the trainee with requirements of the Practice Skills Standards;
- address any professional conduct or ethics issues that may have arisen;
- discuss future training.

THE VOCATIONAL STAGE REQUIREMENTS

> **Comment**
>
> The reason it is important to go through the training record weekly, if possible, is so that the Supervisor can identify early on if the trainee is not getting an appropriate balance of work and skills. If gaps are identified, the Supervisor can then be on the alert to involve the trainee in appropriate work should the opportunity to gain the missing experience or skills arise. In other words, it aids better deployment of the trainee to meet the outcomes he or she will be expected to have achieved by the end of the training period in order to qualify and be admitted.
>
> What exactly the SRA means by 'informal' is not clear. If informal performance reviews are expected to contribute to the trainee being able to demonstrate achievement of the practice skills at the end of the training period (or not, as the case may be), documenting the discussions at informal reviews would be advisable. However, 'informal' may mean the review can be conducted by the Supervisor alone or outside the usual requirements for the conduct of appraisals within the Training Provider. Either way, keeping a record of what has been discussed and agreed is advisable.
>
> With regard to the requirement for formal appraisals, for which the SRA advises one in the first year, one in the second year and one at the end, but ideally every six months, the SRA provides no prescription or guidance as to who should conduct them. Common sense would dictate that the trainee's Supervisor – or main Supervisor if the trainee has had more than one – during a particular seat, for example, should be present.
>
> What the SRA's guidance does say is that the purpose of formal appraisals is 'to review the trainee's overall performance, assess the development of their skills, identify areas of strength and weakness, agree new objectives and plan future training'. As with any appraisal, if there has been proper supervision and informal engagement, an appraisal should not contain any surprises.

In addition to the Practice Skills, the SRA's sample appraisal document covers the following personal skills:

- working with others;
- initiative and motivation;
- personal organisation;
- innovation;
- flexibility;
- balancing quality and quantity of work;
- reliability;
- commercial awareness;
- self-development.

The SRA does not prescribe the format of the training record; however, the SRA website recommends that it include the elements in the sample form, which include the personal skills listed above, as well as:

- summary of achievement against objectives previously agreed;
- achievements against skills standards;
- summary of personal skills;
- legal knowledge;
- other achievements;

- overall performance summary;
- training needs identified at last appraisal;
- looking forward – objectives;
- training/development needs.

In terms of the three formal appraisals, the SRA advises that a trainee should receive one in the first year, one in the second year and one at the end of the training period. However, the SRA also recommends that trainees be appraised at least every six months.

The SRA expects appraisals to be carried out face-to-face, with the trainee being given the opportunity to ask questions and raise concerns. A record of the discussions should also be made and kept by those doing the appraisal.

> **Comment**
>
> The requirement for at least three appraisals should be regarded as an opportunity for the firm to exercise sensible performance management practice: if a trainee is not performing (as distinct from the trainee being incompetent, in which case they could not be signed off) and a firm does not wish to keep on the trainee on qualification, the firm needs to have evidence of the trainee's poor performance and the opportunities the firm has given to the trainee to improve, all of which can be evidenced through the appraisal meetings. To be fair to the trainee who is under-performing, it is only right that the trainee knows that there is an issue and is given an opportunity to improve as early as possible. It might be, however, that the trainee's under-performance is due to poor supervision or inadequate opportunities to gain experience, in which case the firm needs to know that too at the earliest opportunity, since poor supervision or inadequate opportunity to gain experience puts the firm in breach of its responsibilities under the Qualification and Provider Regulations.
>
> Even if a firm intends to keep the trainee on following qualification, given the firm's investment in the trainee (in terms of salary and time spent in supervising, let alone if the firm has paid for the LPC and even the CPE), it is in the firm's interest to bring the trainee up to the mark as soon as possible. So, the earlier any performance issues are spotted, the better for everyone. Thus, it is a sensible practice to have regular performance appraisals, which logically should be done at the end of each seat at the least.

15.12.4 The training record

Under reg.5.3 of the Qualification and Provider Regulations, a trainee is required to maintain a record of training in accordance with the requirements of reg.14. Regulation 14.1 specifies that the record of training:

(a) contains details of the work performed;
(b) records how the trainee has acquired, applied and developed their skills by reference to the Practice Skills Standards and the Principles;
(c) records the trainee's reflections on his or her performance and development plans; and
(d) is verified by the individual(s) supervising the trainee.

THE VOCATIONAL STAGE REQUIREMENTS

So, by the end of the training period, the record should evidence that the trainee has 'good' experience in at least three distinct practice areas and has met the Practice Skills Standards.

> **Comment**
>
> Although 'good' is not defined, the experience will need to be sufficient to equip the trainee with what is necessary 'to meet the Practice Skills Standards and comply with the Principles' according to reg.5.

The SRA does not prescribe the format of the training record but does recommend that the training record include:

- details of the work the trainee has performed;
- details of the skills the trainee has used in performing the work, which should align with the Practice Skills Standards;
- the trainee's observations and reflection on his or her performance;
- details of any other training or professional development;
- details of any professional conduct issues which may have arisen in performing the work.

> **Comment**
>
> Although the SRA guidance does not specify what 'frequent' means, the SRA Sample Training Record states that the training record should be completed weekly.
>
> This is probably sensible, but it can also be difficult to achieve in reality and when work is busy. Rather than an arbitrary weekly requirement, a trainee should be encouraged to enter information in his or her training record while it is fresh, although trainees can find this difficult to do simply because they are often busy doing their actual work. The problem is, though, that if they do not record the work they are doing close to the time they are doing it, they are likely to forget, which makes it more difficult to record later. The first time the trainee does a particular task, he or she is more likely to note it; the next time he or she does the same task again, it may have lost its novelty and seem less important to record. What can help the trainee in recording the work he or she does is to have regular meetings with his or her Supervisor at which the work the trainee has been doing is discussed – an incentive for keeping the training record up to date. As well as giving the trainee an opportunity to identify the actual work he or she has completed, the regular meeting is also a good opportunity for a trainee to reflect on what he or she has gained from the work, which is important for self-development. But it is easier said than done in a busy practice.

The SRA may ask to review the training record and use it as evidence that the trainee has met the required standards.[54] To assist Authorised Training Providers and trainees, the SRA provides a sample training record.

---

[54] SRA, Trainee Information Pack, 4 July 2014, p.9.

15.13 MONITORING

Reg.15 provides that the SRA may monitor the training provided by a Training Provider. Monitoring of Training Providers is carried out in much the same way as the monitoring of training contracts under the 2011 Training Provider Regulations, with the same purpose, namely, to ensure that a Training Provider is providing adequate training.

The SRA describes the purpose of the monitoring scheme, which focuses on the overall training provision, as identifying and recognising best practice, and providing guidance and advice where training improvements could be made.

Comment

Whereas monitoring of training contracts regulated by the 2011 Training Provider Regulations was an annual exercise with a set number of Training Establishments monitored each year, monitoring of the PRT under the Qualification and Provider Regulations adopts the same risk-based approach taken by the SRA in the SRA Handbook, which is based on entity-, outcomes- and principles-based regulation. What this means is that the SRA will select Training Providers and Training Establishments for monitoring where, for example:

- there is an application for a training regulation waiver;
- there has been a referral;
- a trainee is being required by his or her Training Provider to opt-out of the Working Time Regulations 1998; or
- some other concern has been identified.

15.13.1 Monitoring process

Monitoring is a two-stage process, comprising:

- completion of questionnaires;
- a monitoring visit.

The one does not guarantee the other. So, just because a Training Provider is sent and completes a questionnaire, it does not follow that the Training Provider will then receive a monitoring visit.

15.13.1.1 Questionnaires

When the SRA sends a questionnaire to the Training Principal of a Training Provider, it will also send a questionnaire to the Training Provider's trainee(s). Trainees are asked to provide a summary of their training record, giving details of the type of work they have been doing and the skills they have used.

THE VOCATIONAL STAGE REQUIREMENTS

> **Comment**
>
> It has to be said that completing the questionnaire is not something that can be done in five minutes. It requires some detail, and also some thought about just how the skills are able to be developed by the trainee in the firm. This may be the most difficult part for the Training Principal to complete as many of the skills are part and parcel of the everyday work any trainee or solicitor is likely to be involved in, and analysing them into 'tasks' may seem somewhat artificial and overly analytical. It perhaps helps to understand the purpose, which is so that the SRA can ensure that the trainee is being given work which will allow the trainee to develop the skills.

15.13.1.2 The monitoring visit

Having received the completed questionnaires and requested information, the SRA will decide whether to arrange a visit by an SRA monitor (monitors are solicitors who have been trained for the role).

If the SRA does decide to make a monitoring visit, the SRA will first contact the Training Provider to let it know that the organisation will be receiving a monitoring visit and to inform the organisation of the name of the intended monitor. This is to give the Training Provider the opportunity to raise a conflict of interest (for example, if the Training Principal or trainees know the named monitor).

Once the monitor has been confirmed, the SRA will send the monitor the completed questionnaires from the Training Provider, trainees and others, as appropriate. The completed questionnaires will form the basis of the meetings the monitor will hold during the monitoring visit.

It will then be the monitor who will contact the Training Provider directly to arrange the date and time of the visit, which the SRA expects to take place within the following three to four weeks.

To help the Training Provider plan for the visit, and 'to minimise disruption' before the visit, the monitor will also provide the Training Principal with details of:

- the visit format;
- approximately how long:
  - the visit is likely to last in total (this is normally around four to five hours, but depends on the number of trainees)
  - the meeting with the Training Principal will last
  - the meetings with the trainees will last;
- if there is more than one trainee:
  - the names of the trainees the monitor will talk to;
  - the order in which they will be seen;
- any other personnel involved in the training, such as Supervisors, with whom the monitor will wish to speak.

The Training Provider is required to make a room available for the monitor to use during the visit, for meetings and to review the documentation the Training Provider is required to make available on the day of the visit (see **15.7.7**).

15.13.2 Monitor's role

The monitor's job is to:

- assess the range and depth of the training provision;
- identify areas of good practice; and
- give guidance on areas that could be improved.

The visit itself will start with an initial meeting with the Training Principal, so that the monitor can gain an understanding of the background of the organisation and the way in which the training is arranged. The monitor will then interview the trainees, and then the Supervisors or other staff the monitor has requested to see.

During the visit the documentation that the monitor will wish to see and which the Training Provider will need to make available is:

- the offer letter, contract of employment or Training Contract (as applicable), training record and appraisal documents for each trainee;
- the training plans created by the Training Provider to timetable training for its trainees;
- the Training Provider's equal opportunities policy;
- granted exemptions based on Equivalent Means or time-to-count (TTC) (as appropriate) application forms.

At the end of the monitoring visit, the monitor will meet with the Training Principal to discuss the monitor's findings from the visit and any suggestions and/or recommendations the monitor has.

The monitor will not close the meeting until all the findings and recommendations have been agreed. That agreement is then documented in the monitor's report which is sent to the firm following the visit.

The monitor's 'findings' will be one of the following:

- 'No concerns': if all the required standards are being met or are exceeded;
- 'Suggestions for improvement': if the training requirements are being met but some improvements could be made, which the monitor will set out;
- 'Recommendations and follow-up action': this is where not all of the training requirements are being met, and the monitor has made recommendations to address the problems. The monitor will discuss an appropriate action plan and timescale with the training principal to implement the recommendations, which might include submitting documentation to the SRA;
- 'Follow-up visit': where not all of the requirements are being met, and the monitor considers a further visit should be made to check whether the monitor's recommendations have been implemented.[55]

---

[55] SRA, Training Trainee Solicitors – Guidelines on Monitoring of Training Contracts, 7 November 2013.

THE VOCATIONAL STAGE REQUIREMENTS

15.13.3 Monitor's report

Following the visit, the monitor will submit the report of the visit to the SRA. The report will summarise the monitor's discussions during the visit and provide an overview of the monitor's findings. A copy of the report is sent to the Training Principal, as well as to the trainees and anyone else who was interviewed by the monitor during the visit. The Training Provider is then asked to confirm that any recommendations will be implemented within two weeks of receipt of the report.

The report will detail the deadlines for the actual recommendations, some of which may be required to be implemented before the end of the PRT, such as secondments. If the Training Provider has been asked to provide evidence that any recommendations have been implemented, this would normally be submitted when the Training Provider sends in its confirmation. If a Training Provider does not implement the recommendations, a follow-up visit may be arranged and, if implementation of the recommendations still does not occur, the Training Provider may be referred for adjudication to determine whether it can retain its authorisation or whether its authorisation should be revoked.

The SRA encourages feedback from Training Providers on their experience of the monitoring process, and will send an evaluation form to the Training Provider at the same time as sending the report. The completed evaluation form should be sent to the Quality Assurance Team at the SRA.

15.14 SUMMARY OF RESPONSIBILITIES

15.14.1 Training Provider

The Training Provider's responsibilities are to:

- appoint a Training Principal;
- ensure the Training Principal understands the training requirements;
- notify the SRA if the Training Principal changes;
- pay trainees the minimum of the single hourly rate of the national minimum wage;
- provide training which:
  - is effectively supervised to have learning and development opportunities to meet the Practice Skills Standards;
  - provides practical experience in at least three distinct areas of English and Welsh law;
  - is appropriate to ensure trainees know and can comply with the Principles in the SRA Handbook;
  - includes regular review and appraisal of the trainee's performance, and regular review of the trainee's training record;

- certify to SRA that trainee is of proper character and suitability to be admitted, and has completed the recognised training;
- pay PSC fee and reasonable expenses for trainees' first attempt at PSC.

It is recommended that a Training Provider:

- has in place adequate support arrangements (desk, secretarial support, access to library and research facilities);
- provides an induction for trainee(s);
- allows Supervisors adequate time and resources, and requires Supervisors to demonstrate they understand the requirements for supervision.

15.14.2 Training Principal

The Training Principal's responsibilities are to:

- act as main liaison with the SRA about the Training Provider's trainees;
- ensure the training provided to trainees is in accordance with reg.12, i.e.:
  - effectively supervised to have learning and development opportunities to meet Practice Skills Standards;
  - provides practical experience in at least three distinct areas of English and Welsh law;
  - appropriate to ensure trainees know and can comply with the Principles in the SRA Handbook;
  - includes regular review and appraisal of the trainee's performance, and regular review of the trainee's training record;
- ensure the trainee maintains the training record;
- ensure Supervisors of trainees have adequate legal knowledge and experience in practice area, and have the skill for effective supervision;
- take on any of the responsibilities of the Training Provider which have been delegated to the Training Principal.

15.14.3 Trainee responsibilities

A trainee's responsibilities are to:

- understand and comply with the Qualification and Provider Regulations;
- be proactive and take responsibility for his or her own personal and professional development, and the direction of his or her training;
- notify the SRA that he or she intends to start a PRT and either confirm that he or she has no character and suitability issues, or disclose those issues at least six months before commencing the PRT;
- develop and apply the practice skills he or she will use as a qualified solicitor;
- report any matters during the PRT which affect his or her suitability to be admitted as a solicitor;

- if applying for a reduction of the term of PRT on the basis of prior relevant work-based experience under a time-to-count application, approach his or her Supervisor or Training Principal at his or her previous firm or organisation to certify that the experience gained there was equivalent. The trainee should also keep copies of supporting documentation as part of his or her training record;
- keep a record of the work he or she does, the skills he or she gains and reflection on what he or she has learnt.

15.15 PROPOSED CHANGES

Should the SRA decide to introduce a centralised Solicitors Qualifying Examination (SQE) as proposed in its consultation document, 'Training for Tomorrow: Assessing Competence' (see **6.4.6**), anyone wishing to qualify as a solicitor would be required to undertake and successfully pass the SQE in order to qualify as a solicitor in England and Wales. Whether and how the components of the existing qualification pathway, such as the PRT, would fit with the SQE, and whether the SRA would set entry requirements for the SQE (it may not), would be the subject of a separate consultation during 2016.

The SRA's decision on whether to introduce the SQE is due in June 2016 (see **6.5**), and the decision on entry requirements would be made at the end of 2016. Introduction of the SQE would not be before the start of the 2018/19 academic year and, under the transitional arrangements proposed by the SRA, those partway through the PRT could either complete the vocational stage and qualify under the existing assessment requirements, or transfer to the new regulations.[56] This is similar to the option given to trainees when the PRT was introduced in place of the Training Contract.

What the SRA has already indicated, however, is that it believes that pre-qualification work-based experience is likely to be an entry requirement for the SQE. The SRA agrees with the expert advice it has taken, that 'pre-qualification workplace experience has an important role to play in developing the competence of intending solicitors' and 'in assuring both the credibility of the new approach to qualification and of the solicitor brand'.[57] For these reasons, the SRA has said that it is therefore likely to continue to require some form of workplace experience. Whether or not it is workplace experience under a PRT is another matter, as the SRA sees the current requirement for a PRT as 'a significant barrier to qualification for some'.[58]

Another consideration is whether or not the SRA will 'seek to assess trainees' competence during the period of pre-qualification workplace experience'.[59] The reason why this could be required is because of the SRA's concern arising out of

---

[56] SRA Consultation 'Training for Tomorrow: Assessing Competence', 7 December 2015, p.33.
[57] SRA Consultation 'Training for Tomorrow: Assessing Competence', 7 December 2015, p.23.
[58] SRA Consultation 'Training for Tomorrow: Assessing Competence', 7 December 2015, p.24.
[59] SRA Consultation 'Training for Tomorrow: Assessing Competence', 7 December 2015, p.24.

expert advice it has received, that not all of the competencies in the Competence Statement can be assessed through the proposed SQE, in which case the SRA feels that those competencies must be assessed in some other way. Consequently, the SRA is also considering possible work-place assessment options, such as appraisals by Supervisors, or trainee portfolios, although each has issues as well. Options for workplace assessment will also be consulted upon during the summer of 2016.

CHAPTER 16

Professional Skills Course

16.1 The course
16.2 Governing regulations
16.3 Requirements
16.4 Course content
16.5 Authorisation as PSC Provider
16.6 Proposed changes

16.1 THE COURSE

The Professional Skills Course (PSC) is a course of instruction which the Solicitors Regulation Authority (SRA) requires all trainee solicitors to undertake as one of the requirements for completion of the vocational stage of training leading to qualification a solicitor. It is seen by the SRA as 'an integral part of the period of recognised training'.[1]

The significance of the PSC for firms is that, unlike the law degree, Common Professional Examination (CPE) or Graduate Diploma in Law (GDL), and Legal Practice Course (LPC), which are completed before a trainee starts in the firm, the PSC is undertaken during the Period of Recognised Training (PRT). Not only that, but firms as Authorised Training Providers have particular obligations in relation to the PSC. Further, firms may themselves obtain authorisation to deliver all or part of the PSC themselves. This chapter therefore explains:

- the general requirements of the course;
- the requirements for each of the different components of the course; and
- the requirements for, and responsibilities which follow, authorisation to provide the PSC.

The PSC may be delivered in-house or by external providers. Either way, it may only be delivered by a provider who has been authorised by the SRA as an Authorised Education Provider. A firm which is an Authorised Training Provider (see **15.5**) is also able to apply for authorisation as an Approved Education Provider to deliver the PSC in-house.

---

[1] SRA, Professional Skills Course Information Pack, 1 July 2014.

16.2 GOVERNING REGULATIONS

The PSC is governed by the SRA Training Regulations 2014 – Qualification and Provider Regulations ('Qualification and Provider Regulations').

The requirements for and features of the PSC are set out in the SRA's 'Professional Skills Course: Guidelines and Written Standards' ('PSC Guidelines'), and the SRA's Professional Skills Course Information Pack ('PSC Information Pack') provides non-mandatory guidance on the PSC structure, how to obtain authorisation as an Authorised Education Provider, and accreditation of courses.

> **Comment**
>
> The PSC Guidelines are not available on the SRA website but must be requested from the SRA.

16.3 REQUIREMENTS

16.3.1 General

The requirements for and features of the PSC are summarised in the table below.

Eligibility	All trainee solicitors must complete the PSC
Exemptions	• Equivalent Means (see **Chapter 10**) • Chartered Legal Executives from the Electives (see **Chapter 24**)
Course duration	No requirements
Timing	PSC must be completed before admission SRA recommends that a trainee: • has equivalent of 6 months' full-time experience before doing the Client Care and Professional Standards module • undertakes Elective subjects after completing the relevant area of Compulsory Core (see **16.3.3**)
Course provider	Must be an Authorised Education Provider. Authorised Training Providers may apply for authorisation to deliver all or part of the PSC as an Authorised Education Provider
Course content	The PSC covers three subject areas: • Financial and Business Skills • Advocacy and Communication Skills • Client Care and Professional Standards (see **16.4**)
Course structure	• Compulsory Core for each subject area

THE VOCATIONAL STAGE REQUIREMENTS

	• Electives • Pervasive elements (see **16.3.4**)
Responsibilities of Authorised Training Provider	Authorised Training Providers required to pay: • course fees • reasonable travel expenses for trainee's first attempt at PSC
Governing regulations	SRA Training Regulations 2014 – Qualification and Provider Regulations (see **16.2**)

16.3.2 Exemptions

Completion of the PSC is a requirement for completion of the vocational stage, which is a requirement for admission. Therefore, unless an individual is exempted from the PSC, it must be completed.

If a trainee can demonstrate that the knowledge and skills outcomes (and the standards at which they must be acquired) have been achieved through other assessed learning and supervised work-based learning, exemption from some of the modules of the PSC may be available under the SRA's Equivalent Means policy (see **Chapter 10**).

16.3.3 Timing

Normally, the PSC is undertaken during the PRT (see **15.8**). However, the SRA no longer specifies when the PSC must be completed (see **Chapter 6**), although SRA guidance advises that it is best completed during the PRT and that certain modules (Client Care and Professional Standards (see **16.4.1**)) are more effective if the trainee completes this modules after he or she has had the equivalent of six months' worth of training on a full-time basis. If, however, an individual is exempt from undertaking a PRT (see **Chapter 15**), then the PSC must be completed before admission.

Comment

The PSC does not tend to get good press from trainees. Part of the problem is that trainees see the Compulsory Core parts of the course as a repetition of what they have just done on the LPC – Financial Services, Accountancy, Advocacy, Professional Conduct and so on.

The reason for having the PSC is to ensure all trainees receive formal training in those areas which the SRA perceives are best taught once the trainee has some experience of practice. This approach has produced a 'one size fits all' solution, which tends to be perceived by firms as a bit of a straitjacket. To be fair, the straitjacket effect is mitigated by the fact that there is no prescription as to which Electives trainees have to do. However, some firms still see it as an unnecessary imposition because of the training the firm itself provides for its trainees and the fact that the firm must pay for each trainee's place on the PSC (even if the firm does not fund the LPC). The problem for the SRA as regulator is that not all firms do provide training for their trainees. If they did, the need for the PSC might possibly be removed. (This issue may be resolved by the SRA's proposals for a centralised Solicitor Qualification Examinations (SQE), and the entry requirements it decides upon for the SQE (see **6.5**).)

The two main issues for firms are really to do with timing

- When should a firm require its trainees to do the compulsory parts of the PSC?
- How and when should the firm deliver the Elective/optional elements of the PSC?

The PSC is intended to be undertaken throughout the two years of the PRT. However, because trainees will do different seats in a different order, many Training Providers, from a desire to maximise the benefit of the PSC to trainees and a desire to cut down on disruption to the firm's business in having trainees taken away from work at different times, 'front load' the PSC and require their trainees to do the compulsory parts of the PSC before or as they start their PRT.

16.3.4 Course structure

The SRA requires that the content of the course meets the intended aims and objectives and that it is:

- up to date; and
- supported by appropriate materials, which have to be clearly organised, well presented and comprehensive.

16.3.5 Responsibilities of a trainee's Authorised Training Provider

All Authorised Training Providers are required to pay the fees and reasonable travel expenses for their trainees' first attempt at the PSC.[2] There is no obligation on the Training Provider to pay for further attempts or to give trainees paid leave, whether for their first or a subsequent attempt.[3] Aside from this, responsibilities only arise if the Training Provider becomes authorised as an Education Provider to deliver the PSC.

16.4 COURSE CONTENT

16.4.1 Compulsory Core

For each of the three subject areas:

- Financial and Business Skills;
- Advocacy and Communication Skills; and
- Client Care and Professional Standards

---

[2] Qualification and Provider Regulations, reg.10.2(e).
[3] SRA, Trainee Information Pack, 4 July 2014.

THE VOCATIONAL STAGE REQUIREMENTS

there is a compulsory core element ('Compulsory Core') of face-to-face tuition, and an assessment requirement as set out in the following table.

Professional Skills Course – Compulsory Core

Subject area	Minimum number of hours of face-to-face tuition	Assessment requirement
Financial and Business Skills	18 hours	Element 1: no assessment Elements 2–6: $1\frac{1}{2}$ hour examination
Advocacy and Communication Skills	18 hours	Skills appraisal
Client Care and Professional Standards	12 hours	No assessment

'Face-to-face' tuition does not include time spent in preparing or completing work between tuition sessions, and any departure from the prescribed student/tutor ratios has to be approved by the SRA's Validation and Monitoring Team Manager.

The requirements for and features of each of the Compulsory Core subjects are summarised in more detail in the table in Annex 16A.

> **Comment**
>
> There is some overlap between the PSC and the LPC: the LPC covers Advocacy, FSMA 2000 and some aspects of Client Care, for instance. This overlap is, however, deliberate: the SRA feels that further training in these areas once trainees have some experience of practice is beneficial. The aim of the PSC, to use the SRA's words, is designed 'to build on the foundations laid by the [LPC] and to ensure that all trainees receive formal instruction in matters being studied once the trainee has some exposure to practice'.[4]

16.4.2 Electives

In addition to the compulsory modules, trainees are also required to complete 24 hours of Elective subjects.

The Elective subjects 'must have as their primary objective the development of a trainee's professional skills'.[5] Unlike the Compulsory Core, the Electives are not subject to prescribed Written Standards. What is required for the Electives is that a trainee undertakes the additional 24 hours of instruction in at least one of the areas of Financial and Business Skills, Advocacy and Communication Skills or Client Care and Professional Standards, ideally following completion of the Compulsory Cores in each of those subjects.

---

[4] SRA, PSC Information Pack, 1 July 2014, p.1.
[5] SRA, PSC Information Pack, 1 July 2014, p.2.

At least 12 hours of the total 24 hours must be undertaken by way of face-to-face delivery, and a maximum of 12 hours only of the total 24 hours may be undertaken by way of distance learning, provided that the distance learning is suitably supervised or assessed.

As to what an Elective should cover, this is left to the Training Provider and trainee to choose what is going to be most relevant for the particular needs of both, bearing in mind that the primary objective of the Electives is that the trainee develops, and has the opportunity to practise, his or her professional skills.

Consequently, there is scope for tailoring the PSC Electives to meet the trainee's, and the firm's, particular needs.

Although substantive law topics would not normally qualify as Electives for the PSC, the Electives may deal with topics under the headings of Financial and Business Skills, Advocacy and Communication Skills, and Client Care and Professional Standards, which are not covered in the Compulsory Core for each of these subjects (these headings are able to be interpreted more broadly for the purposes of the Electives). Nor does an Elective have to be confined to a single area: it can in fact cover something already covered in the Compulsory Core but in more detail or by looking at related topics. An Elective can also cover a topic which comes under one of the three subjects not covered in the relevant Compulsory Core. Consequently, there is scope for tailoring the PSC Electives to meet the trainee's, and the Training Provider's particular needs.

The SRA also specifies that the following courses, formerly called 'Special Electives', will also count as PSC Electives:

- the shortened Accounts Course for trainees who took the LSF or the pre-1997 LPC;
- the courses leading to the Higher Rights of Audience Qualification;
- the Human Rights Act.

If any of these courses happens to involve an assessment, the assessment does not need to be passed for the course to be recognised as a PSC Elective, the justification for this being that PSC Electives are not assessed.

Comment

The following list of possible Elective courses is provided in the SRA guidelines, for illustrative purposes.

Financial and Business Skills

- Drafting business documents
- Information technology as a business tool
- Terms of engagement: what to include and what to watch for
- Advanced business accounts
- Understanding group accounts
- Probate accounts
- Trust accounts

- Structured settlements
- Stock exchange matters
- Start of specialist diplomas (e.g. the local government diploma)

Advocacy and Communication Skills

- Advocacy in employment tribunals
- Advocacy in planning enquiries
- Mediation
- Alternative dispute resolution (ADR)
- Advising in the police station
- Information technology in litigation support
- Prosecution
- Negotiation skills (in any context)
- Interviewing skills (in any context)
- Drafting skills (in any context)

Client Care and Professional Standards

- Complaints avoidance and complaints handling
- Case and file management
- Information technology and case management
- Claims avoidance
- Self-management for solicitors

Electives for commercial litigators

- Litigation support and case management
- Drafting pleadings
- Negotiation skills
- ADR workshop
- Estimating litigation costs
- Selecting and instructing experts

Electives for corporate lawyers

- Understanding financial statements
- Interviewing and advising the in-house lawyer
- The international perspective
- Negotiating financial covenants
- Drafting agreements
- Terms of engagement: what to include and what to watch for

Electives for matrimonial practitioners

- Mediation
- Drafting pleadings
- Negotiation skills
- Family dispute resolution (FDR) workshop
- Estimating litigation costs
- Selecting and instructing experts

PROFESSIONAL SKILLS COURSE

Electives for conveyancers

- Case management
- Undertakings
- Negotiating leases
- Using and amending standard documentation
- Using information technology to maximise the management of the workload
- Conveyancing file management
- Proactive and profitable client care

Electives for criminal lawyers

- Selecting and instructing experts
- Dealing with ethical conflicts
- Drafting defence statements
- Principles of 'active defence'
- Assessing sentencing options
- Implications of franchising and criminal contracts

Electives for legal aid practitioners

- Implications of franchising and contracting
- Conditional fees
- Assessing and explaining the statutory charge
- Variation, discharge and revocation of legal aid orders
- Costs and taxation in legal aid care

The Electives should either:

- expand upon the content of the Compulsory Core, looking at some or all of the prescribed elements in more depth (e.g. Discrete Investment Business – Advising on Management would expand on Financial and Business Skills);
- develop from the content of the Compulsory Core into related topics (e.g. Interpretation of Business Accounts would develop the Element 1 Accounting and Financial Issues of the Financial and Business Skills Compulsory Core); or
- come under one or more of the three areas of the course but not be derived from the Compulsory Core (e.g. Negotiation of Financial Covenants would come under Financial and Business Skills but would not derive from any of the Elements in the PSC Written Standards).

Comment

If a firm provides tailored, in-house training for its trainees, it can 'piggy back' on its internal training to meet the PSC Elective requirements, authorised as an Authorised Education Provider to provide the PSC, particularly the Electives (see **16.4.2**). This is far more cost-effective than having to send trainees on external courses by authorised PSC Providers to satisfy the 24-hour Elective requirement. Delivering the Compulsory Core in-house is more problematic because of the assessment requirements.

THE VOCATIONAL STAGE REQUIREMENTS

	Summary – PSC Electives
Aims and objectives	Primary aim: 'to allow flexibility and to provide a PSC which is perceived to be (and is) more relevant to the needs of trainees, and their employers'.[6] This may involve 'a broad general training or (at the other extreme) provide the foundation for a high degree of specialisation'[7]
Assumed knowledge from the LPC	No requirement
Elements	No requirement. However, content is likely to fit within one of three categories: • 'more of the core', e.g. Discrete Investment Business – Advising on Management • 'move on from the core', e.g. Interpretation of Business Accounts, Pensions Management • 'under the heading', e.g. Negotiation Skills, Negotiation of Financial Covenants
Course criteria	Following completion of the relevant area of the Compulsory Core, undertake a minimum of 24 hours' tuition on Elective courses, which should fall within one or more of the prescribed three areas of the course: • Minimum face-to-face tuition: 12 hours' face-to-face • Permitted student/tutor ratio: 40:1 • However, because primarily concerned with enhancing trainee's professional skills, small group work with a ratio of 16:1 is encouraged • Length of sessions: Minimum of one hour face-to-face. Half-day (three hours) and full-day (six hours) tuition encouraged
Distance learning	• Maximum of 12 hours out of the 24 may be by way of distance learning provided the total number of 12 hours is not exceeded for the Electives overall • Providers required to 'devise appropriate distance learning materials'[8] • Distance learning must be 'suitably supervised and assessed'[9]
Tutor requirements	No requirements
Assessment	No requirements

---

[6] SRA, 'Professional Skills Course – Guidelines and Written Standards', p.19.
[7] SRA, 'Professional Skills Course – Guidelines and Written Standards', p.19.
[8] SRA, 'Professional Skills Course – Guidelines and Written Standards', p.19.
[9] SRA, 'Professional Skills Course – Guidelines and Written Standards', p.19.

16.4.3 Pervasive subjects

The SRA requires that both information technology and business/commercial awareness are treated as pervasive by PSC providers (as opposed to being taught explicitly), and are addressed throughout the Compulsory Core and Electives. The aim, according to the SRA, is that 'trainees should be able to demonstrate that they understand the importance of information technology and business/commercial awareness in their work' and that they should understand the applications of both 'across a range of professional activities'.[10]

16.5 AUTHORISATION AS PSC PROVIDER

Training Providers which were authorised to deliver the PSC as at 1 July 2014 under earlier training regulations continue to be authorised under the Qualification and Provider Regulations.

It is not just commercial or academic training organisations which can deliver the PSC – firms which are Authorised Training Providers under the Qualification and Provider Regulations may also apply for authorisation and, once authorised as an Authorised Education Provider, are able to self-accredit further PSC courses, and also appoint or replace tutors without having to make any further applications to the SRA, provided the SRA's requirements continue to be met. The advantage of this is that the firm may be able to satisfy the requirements of the PSC (particularly the Elective requirements) with training which is already delivered within the firm.

The authorisation process is relatively straightforward, depending on whether the authorisation being applied for is to deliver one or more of the Compulsory Cores (and there are additional requirements for Financial and Business Skills, and for Advocacy and Communication Skills) or the Electives, or both.

16.5.1 Types of authorisation

There are three types of authorisation which may be applied for:

- **Authorisation to provide Compulsory Core**. A firm can apply for authorisation to provide courses for one or more of the Compulsory Cores, and once authorised, will be automatically authorised to provide Electives within that subject area. So, if the firm is authorised to offer the Compulsory Core of, say, Financial and Business Skills, it would also be authorised to offer any Electives under Financial and Business Skills. It would not, however, be automatically authorised to offer Electives under, say, Advocacy and Communication Skills if it has not also been authorised to offer the Compulsory Core of Advocacy and Communication Skills.

---

[10] SRA, PSC Information Pack, 1 July 2014, p.3.

THE VOCATIONAL STAGE REQUIREMENTS

- **Authorisation to provide Compulsory Core in one subject area, and Electives in another subject area.** Alternatively, a firm can apply for authorisation to offer the Compulsory Core of one area, say, Financial and Business Skills, and the Electives of one or more of the other areas – namely, Advocacy and Communication Skills and/or Client Care and Professional Standards in this example.
- **Authorisation to provide Electives only.** A further alternative is to apply for authorisation to offer the Electives only, whether in one or more of the Compulsory Core areas. Although the firm would not be authorised to offer the Compulsory Core of that subject area, it would be authorised to offer further Elective subjects in the same subject area by self-accrediting. The SRA is entitled to ask to see a list of the titles of Elective courses which the firm has self-accredited, or to ask for more information about the Electives.

16.5.2 Requirements for authorisation

16.5.2.1 General requirements

The requirements for authorisation are summarised in the following table.

Timing for application	An application for authorisation must be submitted (see **16.5.2.3**) at least eight weeks in advance of the scheduled start date for the course, which includes copies of the course materials, tutor details and payment of the SRA's authorisation fee (see **16.5.2.4**)
Types of authorisation	1. To provide Compulsory Core instruction in one or more of the three subject areas 2. To provide Compulsory Core instruction in one, or more, of the three subject areas and to provide Electives in one or more of the other subject areas 3. To provide Electives only in one or more of the three subject areas
Course Director requirements	A firm needs to appoint a PSC Course Director (see **16.5.2.2**) and provide the SRA with the Course Director's details
Authorisation fee	Initial application: £125 + £450 per subject area applied for, either as a Compulsory Core or Elective subject/s in that area Subsequent application: £450 per subject area applied for, either as a Compulsory Core or Elective subject/s in that area (see **16.5.2.4**)
Period of authorisation	3 years initially 5 years if re-authorised
Additional requirements for	Application must be accompanied by: • details of the proposed examination arrangements (see

PROFESSIONAL SKILLS COURSE

authorisation to deliver Financial and Business Skills	**16.5.2.3)** • a draft examination paper and answers which will need to be approved by a Financial and Business Skills assessor • a curriculum vitae for the Moderator (see **16.5.2.3**)
Additional requirements for authorisation to deliver Advocacy and Communication Skills	Application needs to include a copy of the appraisal form that the firm proposes using
Additional requirements for authorisation to deliver Electives by distance learning	Application to set out how trainees will be supervised and assessed on the Elective

16.5.2.2 Course Director

The SRA does not specify who the Course Director should be but it would normally be the person who takes responsibility for managing the administration of the PSC and issuing confirmation of successful completion of the PSC.

16.5.2.3 Application

The following information is also required to be submitted with the application:

- copies of course materials;
- details of the tutors the firm proposes using;
- details of the proposed administrative arrangements the firm will have in place for recording attendance at face-to-face courses, to supervise or assess distance learning courses and to certify that accredited courses have been completed satisfactorily.

Comment

The SRA does not specify that the course materials to be included with the application should be those for the first PSC that the applicant proposes delivering. However, common sense would suggest that this should be the case. One clue is given in the Professional Skills Course Information Pack statement that 'Potential providers must demonstrate that all planned courses – those for which they seek accreditation, and those that they subsequently accredit themselves – meet [the guidelines in the PSC Information Pack] and the accreditation criteria'.[11]

---

[11] SRA, PSC Information Pack, 1 July 2014, p.3.

Where authorisation is sought for Financial and Business Skills, details of the proposed assessment requirements, a draft exam paper and answers, and the Moderator's curriculum vitae also need to be included.

Where authorisation for Advocacy and Communication Skills is sought, details of appraisal arrangements on the course, and a copy of the appraisal form which will be used also need to be included with the application.

16.5.2.4 Authorisation fee

The following examples illustrate how the authorisation fee is calculated:

- An application to provide the Compulsory Core of Financial and Business Skills would be: £125 + £450 = £575.
- An application to provide the Compulsory Core of Financial and Business Skills and also Client Care and Professional Standards would be: £125 + £450 + £450 = £1,025.
- An application to provide the Compulsory Core in Advocacy and Communication Skills and Electives in Client Care and Professional Standards would be: £125 + £450 + £450 = £1,025.
- An application to offer Electives within Advocacy and Communication Skills and in Client Care and Professional Standards would be: £125 + £450 + £450 = £1,025.
- An application to offer the Compulsory Core in Financial and Business Skills, as well as the Electives, however, would be: £125 + £450 = £575. There is no fee payable to run Electives in the same subject area for which a Training Provider is applying to run the Compulsory Core.

If, having obtained authorisation for one subject area, a firm later wishes to offer either the Compulsory Core or Electives in another subject area, it would need to make a further application. However, the fee would be £450 per subject area, without the initial fee of £125.

16.5.3 Authorisation process

Once an application for authorisation is received by the SRA, it is reviewed to check that it has all the necessary information and supporting documentation. If anything is missing, the firm applying will be asked to submit additional information or an amended application.

After the application has been checked, the SRA sends the course materials and programme submitted with the application to a PSC assessor to review. The PSC assessor submits a report on the course materials to the SRA, in which the PSC assessor may raise issues or concerns. If so, the firm will be asked to comment on and/or address these before authorisation will be granted.

16.5.4 Conditions of authorisation

A firm authorised as a PSC Provider is required to provide a PSC which will:

- build on the LPC to develop the trainee's professional skills
- be of clear benefit and value to the trainee and represent the start of a trainee's post-qualification development
- enable the tailoring of the course to reflect the range of environments in which trainees work and the increasing specialisation of practice
- be a dynamic course capable of developing to match the changing and diverse needs of the profession
- accommodate both well-developed trainee development programmes provided by many large employers for their own trainees, and public courses offered by local law societies and commercial providers.[12]

The conditions of authorisation are that the firm will:

- only self-accredit courses which are within their authorisation and which meet the Written Standards and other SRA criteria
- present, assess and supervise (where appropriate) accredited courses in accordance with the Written Standards and [the PSC Information Pack] (subject to any variations and additional guidance [issued by the SRA] from time to time)
- supply information to [the SRA] concerning the presentation, assessment or supervision of accredited courses as requested
- provide details of forthcoming courses as requested
- co-operate in the monitoring of accredited courses
- co-operate in the investigation of any complaint about the provider
- notify [the SRA] of any change of Course Director or person to whom the day to day responsibility has been delegated in the provider's address.[13]

16.5.5 Accreditation of courses

Once authorised, the firm may:

- self-accredit Electives it intends to offer, where the Elective is within the subject area for which the firm has been authorised, whether as Compulsory Core instruction or Elective instruction;
- vary or adapt the Compulsory Core courses for which the firm is authorised without the SRA's prior approval;
- appoint or replace tutors, provided that new/replacement tutors meet the criteria required by the SRA.

---

[12] SRA, PSC Information Pack, 1 July 2014, p.2.
[13] SRA, PSC Information Pack, 1 July 2014, p.3.

THE VOCATIONAL STAGE REQUIREMENTS

16.5.6 General responsibilities of authorisation

With these permissions go a number of responsibilities – general responsibilities irrespective of the area of authorisation. Most, if not all, of these responsibilities may be delegated. However, even if a responsibility has been delegated, the firm must ensure that the responsibility is carried out as required by the SRA. These responsibilities concern:

- tutors;
- venue and accommodation;
- administrative arrangements;
- evaluating and reviewing courses;
- informing and notifying the SRA;
- delivering courses in accordance with the PSC Written Standards;
- co-operating in SRA monitoring.

16.5.6.1 Tutors

The firm must:

- ensure that the qualifications and experience of tutors are appropriate to meet the criteria for tutors;
- ensure that all tutors are competent instructors, by carrying out observations of the tutor's teaching, reviewing feedback from delegates who have attended courses delivered by the tutor, or by written references;
- ensure that a tutor has up-to-date knowledge of the subject/s which he or she is to teach;

Comment

This could be done by using feedback from delegates on courses given by the proposed tutor, or from taking up references.

- review periodically whether a tutor continues to satisfy the relevant general and/or specific criteria;
- ensure that arrangements are made for the appropriate training of new tutors.

Comment

Although the firm must ensure that the qualifications and experience of tutors are 'appropriate', there is no guidance as to what would be 'appropriate' other than that the tutor either has experience in teaching students, trainees, solicitors or other professionals, or has attended a presentation skills, communication skills, 'train the trainer' or similar course. These requirements should be complied with as part of the recruitment or appointment process, at which time any training needs the tutor may have should be identified, and training provided before the tutor starts delivering any accredited PSC course.

16.5.6.2 Venue and accommodation

The firm must ensure that the venue and accommodation for delivery of the PSC meet the SRA's requirements.

16.5.6.3 Informing and notifying the SRA

The firm is required to provide the SRA with details of the accredited PSCs the firm is proposing to deliver. This information is normally provided either through the authorisation and re-authorisation processes or as part of the SRA's annual routine monitoring.

If there is a change to the PSC Course Director or the person to whom the PSC Course Director has delegated day-to-day responsibility for accredited PSCs, the firm must notify the SRA. In any case, this responsibility is likely to be delegated. However, the firm remains responsible for ensuring these things are done.

> **Comment**
>
> The SRA does not specify who this should be but it would normally be the person who takes responsibility for managing the administration of the PSC and issuing confirmation of successful completion of the course.

The firm must also supply the SRA with any information the SRA requests concerning the presentation, assessment or supervision of accredited courses.

16.5.6.4 Deliver courses in compliance with SRA requirements.

The firm is expected to ensure that the PSC course materials are kept up to date and that they continue to cover the PSC Written Standards, as well as meeting the authorisation criteria.

> **Comment**
>
> This is more likely to be a case of checking with the person to whom the task of looking after materials has been delegated, to ensure that it happens.

THE VOCATIONAL STAGE REQUIREMENTS

The firm also needs to ensure that the accredited PSCs delivered in the firm are presented, assessed and supervised in accordance with the PSC Written Standards and guidance to providers, such as the PSC Guidelines.

> **Comment**
>
> As the firm is relying on others to carry out the presenting, assessing and supervision, some means of follow-up by management, or a reporting structure, should be considered.

16.5.6.5 Co-operating in SRA monitoring

The firm is required to co-operate in the SRA's monitoring of its courses (see **16.5.10**), and in the investigation of any complaint about the firm. If the firm is to have a monitoring visit as part of its authorisation to deliver the PSC, it will be notified by the SRA at least two weeks before the monitoring visit, and will be required to submit the prescribed documentation. During the actual visit, the PSC Course Director, tutor and trainees are normally required to be available to meet with the monitor.

16.5.6.6 Administrative arrangements

The firm must ensure that there are appropriate and effective administrative arrangements and support for all courses. Specifically, this means ensuring that attendance at face-to-face courses is recorded, and that distance learning courses are supervised and assessed. There is no specification by the SRA as to supervision or assessment; instead, it is for the firm to determine and demonstrate these arrangements to the satisfaction of the SRA.

The firm also needs to certify satisfactory completion of accredited courses in a manner acceptable to the SRA, which can be by letter or certificate of satisfactory completion. (This is needed for sign-off by the Training Principal that a trainee has completed the required training, including the PSC – see **Chapter 17**.)

16.5.6.7 Evaluating and reviewing courses

The firm must put in place a system for evaluating and reviewing its accredited courses, which:

- enables feedback from trainees and their Supervisors to be obtained; and
- the feedback itself to be analysed and responded, to which includes copies of the course materials, tutor details and payment of the SRA's authorised fee.

16.5.7 Responsibilities if authorised to deliver Financial and Business Skills

16.5.7.1 Moderator

The 'Moderator', whom a firm must appoint if it wishes to deliver the Compulsory Core of Financial and Business Skills, is required to have:

- appropriate academic or professional qualifications. This requirement will be satisfied if the individual is either an academic or a solicitor;
- appropriate standing, expertise and experience. This requirement can be satisfied by the Moderator's:
  - present (or, if retired, last) post and place of work;
  - experience in professional practice, higher education, professional training or other teaching;
  - research, academic or professional activities in investment business; or
  - recent assessment experience.

A Moderator must also not be over-extended by other moderating or external examining duties. In other words, the firm would need to satisfy itself that the Moderator does not have too many other external examining appointments. Another thing the firm needs to check is that the Moderator does not have (or has not had) close involvement with the firm which could compromise the Moderator's objectivity.

Although so-called reciprocal arrangements between firms as authorised PSC providers to appoint Moderators is not allowed, if the firm is part of an authorised consortium to deliver the PSC, the consortium could use the one Moderator.

If the firm changes its Moderator, it has to notify the SRA of the change, and ensure that the new Moderator satisfies all the same criteria.

16.5.7.2 Examination arrangements

The examination arrangements need to cover:

- the arrangements for setting exam papers, and marking and moderating exam scripts;
- the exam venue and the invigilation arrangements;
- arrangements for disabled and special needs candidates;
- arrangements for an exam board (which has to consist of the Moderator and at least one practising solicitor) to consider the results and any extenuating circumstances;
- the appeal process;
- re-sits (two re-sits are permitted);
- the number of examinations per year (there has to be a minimum of two).

THE VOCATIONAL STAGE REQUIREMENTS

The firm must also:

- fulfil additional requirements for authorisation to deliver Financial and Business Skills, check draft examination papers to ensure that the questions are appropriate in terms of content, standard and coverage of the Written Standards;
- review marked scripts to ensure that the marking is consistent and of an appropriate standard;
- submit an annual report on the conduct and outcomes of the examinations to the examination board;
- keep all the exam papers and exam scripts[14] for two years after the course, in case the SRA wishes to see them.

16.5.8 Responsibilities if authorised to offer Elective courses

If the firm is authorised to offer PSC Elective courses, it has additional responsibilities to the general responsibilities outlined above. However, these are not as arduous as the additional responsibilities involved if the firm is authorised to deliver the Compulsory Cores. The additional responsibilities in relation to the Electives are to:

- provide details of accredited courses. Where a firm is authorised to offer Elective courses, it must provide the list of titles of Elective courses it has accredited as part of the monitoring process;
- supervise and assess distance learning. It is possible for Elective courses to be delivered wholly or partly by way of distance learning. Where distance-learning delivery is involved, the firm is required to 'develop and implement strategies to ensure adequate supervision [and] assessment';[15]
- retain and keep records. Where the course is delivered by distance learning, the firm is required to preserve all documentation forming part of the supervision or assessment process for a period of two years following completion of the course in case the SRA wishes to see this documentation.

The firm must also record in writing the details of supervision and assessment arrangements for distance learning courses which it self-accredits following authorisation, and have this record available in case the SRA wishes to see it.

---

[14] An 'exam paper' is the question paper, and the 'exam script' is the candidate's attempt at answering the exam paper, which is then marked.
[15] PSC Guidelines, p.21.

PROFESSIONAL SKILLS COURSE

16.5.9 Termination of authorisation

If a firm no longer wishes to be authorised, it can terminate its authorisation at any time by notifying the SRA in writing. The authorisation will be terminated once any course or assessment which is in the process of delivery at the date of termination has been completed.

The SRA can also terminate authorisation if:

- the SRA considers that allowing authorisation to continue would be detrimental to the interests of the profession or to the trainees undertaking courses accredited by the firm;
- there is evidence (whether from a monitoring report or otherwise) that the standard of teaching and/or administrative arrangements and support are below the standards acceptable to the SRA;
- the firm does not comply with the conditions of its authorisation; or
- the firm is dissolved, declared bankrupt, enters into administration, receivership or liquidation, or enters into an arrangement with its creditors.

16.5.10 Monitoring of authorisation

Once authorised, the SRA will request the firm to submit details of the PSCs it will be delivering in the coming year. The 'year' runs from the date of the letter from the SRA requesting this information.

> **Comment**
>
> Depending on when the letter is sent, it may be problematic for a firm to provide details of PSCs for the next year, if its training programme does not cover the full period requested. However, in that case the firm should just explain this to the SRA.

Each year the SRA selects particular Compulsory Core courses and/or Electives in a specific subject to monitor. This selection is partly random but not completely.

The SRA states that its aims in monitoring PSC providers and courses are to:

- provide the profession with confidence in the PSC;
- assess the quality of the course in terms of its administration, content, materials and teaching;
- ensure the Written Standards are met in the content;
- have open and honest discussion on the quality of the course;
- ensure consistent standards between providers of PSC courses;
- assist providers to improve their courses;
- review the course as a means of ensuring that it continues to meet its aims and objectives;
- review the Written Standards to ensure their relevance.[16]

---

[16] SRA PSC Guidelines, pp.34–35.

THE VOCATIONAL STAGE REQUIREMENTS

Monitoring is done by evaluating attendee feedback questionnaires and also by assessors sitting in on courses. The assessors used by the SRA tend to be solicitors or senior academics.

If a firm is going to be monitored, it will be contacted by the SRA about eight to ten weeks before the monitor intends to sit in. (Part of the reason that the firm will have been asked to submit details of its PSCs for the coming year is so that the SRA will know when courses are being run which it can select for monitoring.) Two weeks before the course, the firm will need to submit the following documentation to the SRA, which the SRA will then forward to the monitor:

- the complete programme for the particular course, giving a breakdown of the timing/content for each day and session;
- a complete set of up-to-date course materials for the course being observed;
- the curriculum vitae of the course tutor/s;
- the firm's details (although the SRA already has these via the application for authorisation, it requires a further set to give to the monitor);
- the venue details and map;
- a contact name of someone at the firm, in case of difficulties;
- any other information which the firm believes is relevant – which is a bit of a catch-all.

In terms of what happens when, the monitor should arrive just before the start of the course and should explain to the contact and to the tutor delivering the course what the format for the visit will be. The tutor should introduce the monitor to the attendees and explain that the monitor is there as an observer rather than a participant, although the monitor will be talking to the attendees and the tutor during the day to obtain their views on the course content, the level of the course, the administrative arrangements and the like. At the end of the day (or at the end of the course if it is not a whole day), the monitor is required to provide 'constructive feedback' to the tutor and/or course provider, and to discuss any concerns the monitor has, and agree any action which the monitor thinks is required.

The way the monitor assesses the course is against the following criteria:

- the general criteria for authorisation;
- the specific criteria for the relevant subject area;
- whether the aims and objectives of the course were met;
- whether the training venue was suitable in terms of:
  - size;
  - layout;
  - temperature;
  - lighting;
  - equipment;
  - noise;
  - special needs;
- whether the content was at the correct level for the trainees, factually correct and met the Written Standards;

PROFESSIONAL SKILLS COURSE

- whether handouts were available and, if so, whether they were:
  - relevant;
  - given at the most appropriate time;
  - used and presented effectively;
- whether the tutor's/tutors' knowledge of the subject was accurate, relevant and up-to-date and whether he or she was able to present, ask and answer questions effectively;
- whether the balance/structure of the course and teaching methods was appropriate;
- whether the topics were covered in the most appropriate order;
- whether the length of sessions was within the recommended criteria.

On the basis of these criteria, the monitor will assess the course as 'Satisfactory' if:

- the training took place in a supportive learning environment with all necessary equipment provided;
- the course met its objectives, and the requirements of the Written Standards were achieved;
- the sessions were well organised and taught by competent tutors who used suitable and well-presented teaching materials;
- the oral and written responses of the trainees were of an appropriate standard and displayed a sound grasp of the course content.

If not, the monitor will assess the course as 'Not satisfactory'.

The monitor will then submit his or her report to the SRA. The report should contain the issues which the monitor raised with the firm during the monitoring visit, as well as the monitor's overall assessment of the course. A copy of the report should then be sent to the firm.

16.6 PROPOSED CHANGES

Should the SRA decide to introduce a centralised Solicitors Qualifying Examination (SQE) as proposed in its consultation document, 'Training for Tomorrow: Assessing Competence' (see **6.4.6**), anyone wishing to qualify as a solicitor would be required to undertake and successfully pass the SQE in order to qualify as a solicitor in England and Wales. Whether and how the components of the existing qualification pathway, such as the PSC, would fit with the SQE would be the subject of a separate consultation during 2016. The SRA's decision on whether to introduce the SQE is due in June 2016 (see **6.5**). Introduction of the SQE would not be before the start of the 2018/19 academic year and, under the transitional arrangements proposed by the SRA, those partway through the PSC could either complete the vocational stage and qualify under the existing assessment requirements, or transfer to the new regulations.[17]

---

[17] SRA Consultation 'Training for Tomorrow: Assessing Competence', 7 December 2015, p.33.

ANNEX 16A SUMMARY OF THE REQUIREMENTS AND FEATURES OF THE COMPULSORY CORE SUBJECTS

	Requirements – Financial and Business Skills
Aims and objectives	On completion of this area of the Compulsory Core, trainees should: • have developed improved financial awareness • be able to undertake exempt regulated activities under the Financial Services and Markets Act 2000 (FSMA 2000), Part XX • be able to apply the rules of professional conduct relating to financial and accounting matters
Assumed knowledge from the LPC	Trainees who have undertaken the LPC prior to September 2001 will not have gained any understanding of FSMA 2000, the Solicitors' Financial Services (Scope) Rules 2001 ('Scope Rules') or the Solicitors' Financial Services (Conduct of Business) Rules 2001 ('Conduct of Business Rules'). However, as a consequence of completing the LPC trainees should have gained an understanding of: **Solicitors' accounts and the Solicitors' Accounts Rules 2011 (SAR)** This will have included: • the need to maintain separate office and client accounts • the obligations regarding payment into and drawing from client account • the need to record receipts and payments of office and client monies • transfers between client accounts and between client and office accounts • the obligation to prepare accounts in respect of clients' accounts • the power of the SRA to secure compliance with the SAR • the processes involved in recording transactions for the purposes of paying of VAT • the processes involved in recording abatements, bad debts and split money • the processes involved in preparing a statement for clients on completion of a matter • the need to pay interest to clients when appropriate • the distinction between interest earned in general deposit and designated deposit accounts and preparation of accounts as appropriate • the requirements in respect of the holding of trust monies

ANNEX 16A

	The principles of accounting and an awareness of the need to interpret business accounts to ensure clients are appropriately advised. This will have included: • an understanding of the need for accounts, the principles of bookkeeping, the terms used in accounts and basic accounting concepts and their uses • an understanding of the processes involved in recording transactions, familiarity with books used to record transactions and an understanding of how accounting data is used to prepare trial balances, profit and loss accounts and a balance sheet • an understanding of the need to make provision for depreciation and other year-end adjustments • the ability to analyse and interpret entries in the balance sheet and profit and loss accounts of a sole trader, partnership and limited company • an understanding of the nature of shareholders' funds and the need to account for taxation and the circumstances in which consolidated fund accounts are required
Elements	**Element 1 – Accounting and financial issues** Trainees should be able to identify accounting and financial issues in the areas of work in which they or the Training Provider are involved, and have an awareness of: • the potential need to involve other professionals (e.g. accountants, financial services specialists) when advising business and/or private clients • possible sources of financial information which can be utilised in advising business and/or private clients • the need to determine whether additional accounting and financial information is required (including in appropriate cases the possibility of employing investigative accounting techniques) to meet the client's needs • the financial regulatory environment in which clients' businesses operate and the need to identify the appropriate accounting regulatory regime applicable to a client's business **Element 2 – Introduction to the market place** Trainees should also be able to identify the main investment products on the market, distinguish their main features (e.g. long or short term, safe or speculative) and determine their suitability for different types of client Trainees should be able to identify the tax and other advantages or disadvantages of particular types of investment

THE VOCATIONAL STAGE REQUIREMENTS

Element 3 – The regulatory framework
Trainees should have an understanding of the implications of:
- FSMA 2000
- the Scope Rules
- the Conduct of Business Rules and
- any money laundering regulations (MLR)

Trainees should have an understanding of the role of the Financial Services Authority (FSA) and the role of the SRA as a Designated Professional Body (DPB)

Trainees should have an awareness of:
- what is regulated by the FSA
- the requirements for FSA authorisation
- the consequences of carrying out a 'regulated activity' without FSA authorisation
- the method of obtaining FSA authorisation

Trainees should also have an understanding of:
- what constitutes a 'regulated activity' and the principal exclusions in the FSMA 2000 (Regulated Activities) Order 2001, SI 2001/544 (RAO 2001)
- the exemption in FSMA 2000, Part XX for professional firms not conducting 'mainstream regulated activities' but carrying on 'exempt regulated activities'
- basic conditions which must be satisfied by firms wishing to undertake 'exempt regulated activities' (FSMA 2000, s.327 and FSMA 2000 (Professions) (Non-Exempt Activities) Order 2001, SI 2001/1227)

Trainees should be able to relate FSMA 2000, the Scope Rules and the Conduct of Business Rules to the areas of work in which they or the training establishment are involved

In the context of the regulatory structure set up by FSMA 2000 and the concepts underpinning it, trainees should have an understanding of:
- the distinction between tied and independent sectors (to be kept under review)
- the FSA and the major compliance obligations contained in the FSA Handbook
- the appropriate Law Society rules and guidance

Trainees should know what constitutes a financial promotion and the principal exemptions in the FSMA 2000 (Financial Promotion) Order 2001, SI 2001/1335

ANNEX 16A

Element 4 – The Scope Rules

Trainees should be able to identify the type of regulated activities which may be undertaken under the Scope Rules and be aware of the consequences of a breach of the Scope Rules

Trainees should be able to identify the steps needed to comply with the Scope Rules, the Conduct of Business Rules and the practice rules relevant to regulated activities under FSMA 2000

Trainees should have an understanding of the role of the solicitor in the financial services industry and should understand the implications of:

- the solicitor's independence
- the employment of investment specialists, the establishment within a practice of a specialist financial services department and the mechanisms for such an establishment
- the inter-relationships of financial services work with other areas of work in the Training Provider

Trainees should be able to identify the steps needed to comply with the Conduct of Business Rules for exempt regulated activities

Trainees should be able, under appropriate supervision, to maintain the required records and follow the firm's complaints procedure

Trainees should understand how the receipt of commission should be dealt with under Practice Rule 10 and the Scope Rules and should also understand the significance of the receipt of commission in connection with some of the exclusions in RAO 2001

Trainees should:

- have a good understanding of when an activity 'arises out of or is complementary to' a particular professional service to a particular client
- know who is able to act as an Authorised Person
- be able to identify the appropriate Authorised Person for use in any particular situation

Element 5 – Money laundering

Trainees should be able to apply the rules of professional conduct in connection with financial dealings and in particular should understand what constitutes money laundering and the steps necessary to comply with any MLR

Element 6 – Mortgage fraud

Trainees should be able to apply the rules of professional conduct in connection with financial dealings and understand the need to be alert to the possibility of mortgage fraud

THE VOCATIONAL STAGE REQUIREMENTS

Course criteria	• Minimum tuition: 18 hours face-to-face • Student/tutor ratio: 40:1. Small group work is encouraged, e.g. 16:1 • Length of sessions: Minimum of one hour face-to-face. Half-day (three hours) and full-day (six hours) tuition encouraged
Tutor requirements	Must have detailed knowledge of FSMA 2000, the Scope Rules and the Conduct of Business Rules, and understanding of a solicitor's role in giving investment advice
Assessment	Element 1 – no assessment requirement Elements 2–6 – 1.5 hour unseen open book written examination at a 'suitable venue' Overall pass mark: 60% Element 2 – not less than 33% Elements 3 and 4 – not less than 33% Remainder – Elements 2–6 as Training Provider considers appropriate Not more than 30% of marks may be attributed to multiple choice questions

ANNEX 16A

	Requirements – Advocacy and Communication Skills
Aims and objectives	On completion of this area of the Compulsory Core, trainees should be able to exercise the rights of audience available on admission in the civil and criminal courts
Assumed knowledge from the LPC	As a consequence of completing the LPC trainees should be able to: • interview a client • identify the client's goals • identify and analyse factual material • identify the legal context in which factual issues arise • relate the central legal and factual issues to each other • state in summary form the strengths and weaknesses of the case from each party's perspective • develop a case presentation strategy • outline the facts in simple narrative form • prepare in simple form the legal framework for the case • formulate a coherent submission based upon facts, general principles and legal authority in a structured, concise and persuasive manner • identify, analyse and assess the specific communication skills and techniques employed by the presenting advocate • demonstrate an understanding of the purpose, techniques and tactics of examination, cross-examination and re-examination to adduce, rebut and clarify evidence • demonstrate an understanding of the ethics, etiquette and conventions of advocacy Trainees should, in addition, be able to advise a client on the appropriate pre-trial procedures and proceedings, understand the crucial importance of preparation and the best way to undertake it, and assist in the preparation and conduct of pre-trial procedures and proceedings Trainees should be able to make an interlocutory application before a District Judge

THE VOCATIONAL STAGE REQUIREMENTS

Elements	**Element 1** Trainees should be able, in the context of a civil and a criminal case, to: • use language appropriate to the client, witness/es and triers of fact and law • listen, observe and interpret the behaviour of triers of fact and law, clients, witness/es and other advocates and be able to respond to this behaviour as appropriate • speak and question effectively and thereby competently use appropriate presentation skills to open and close a case • use a variety of questioning skills to conduct examination in chief, cross examination and re-examination • prepare and present a coherent submission based upon facts, general principles and legal authority in a structured, concise and persuasive manner • present a submission as a series of propositions based on the evidence • organise and present evidence in a coherent and organised form **Element 2** Trainees should be able to identify and act upon the ethical problems that arise in the course of a trial
Course criteria	• Minimum tuition: 18 hours face-to-face • Student/tutor ratio: 16.1 • Length of sessions: Minimum of one hour face-to-face. Half-day (three hours) and full-day (six hours) tuition encouraged
Tutor requirements	Must have relevant litigation experience, including advocacy experience gained through either appearing as an advocate or observing advocacy in court, and current knowledge of the procedural rules and evidence. As a rule of thumb, the tutor will need to have been in practice for at least three years
Assessment	No formal pass/fail assessment but an appraisal of the trainee's performance with a written appraisal of overall performance. The SRA does not prescribe criteria to be used for the appraisal

ANNEX 16A

	Requirements – Client Care and Professional Standards
Aims and objectives	On completion of this area of the Compulsory Core, trainees should be able to: • identify and understand the significance of client care, ethical and professional conduct issues and be able to respond in an appropriate way within the training context • apply appropriate professional standards • understand and apply business awareness • understand the need to work effectively with others • initiate and implement appropriate methods of personal work organisation, and • appreciate the importance of and take responsibility for their own personal and professional development
Assumed knowledge from the LPC	As a consequence of completing the LPC, trainees should be able to: • identify, understand and deal with aspects of client care, ethics and professional conduct which may arise while conducting matters covered within the LPC • understand the relevant practice rules and basic principles of the SAR • understand those areas of substantive law (e.g. negligence and fiduciary duties) and the practice rules which deal with the conduct of fee-earning work of a type which trainees are likely to encounter before admission • understand the relevant practice rules and basic principles regulating the organisation of the profession, obtaining work, client care and professional relations • appreciate the need for good personal organisation and an orderly approach to work Trainees should be able to identify and deal with issues concerning their ethical responsibilities to: • their clients • the court • other solicitors • other professionals • the SRA and other relevant bodies • their colleagues • themselves This area of the Compulsory Core comprises three elements: • Client Care and Communication Skills • Professional Standards, and • Work and Case Management

235

THE VOCATIONAL STAGE REQUIREMENTS

| Elements | **Element 1 – Client Care and Communication Skills**
• Communication both orally and in writing
• Interviewing skills
• Taking instructions
• Keeping clients informed
• Discussing costs
• Handling client expectations
• Dealing with difficult clients
• Avoiding complaints
• Identifying potential complaints
• Handling complaints

Element 2 – Professional Standards
• The Practice Rules
• Client confidentiality
• Conflicts of interest
• Undertakings
• Negligence warnings
• Discussing, advising and reporting on costs
• Contingency arrangements
• Retainers
• Letters of engagement
• Avoiding, identifying and handling complaints

Element 3 – Work and Case Management
• Time limits
• Time management
• Identifying and minimising risk
• The risk of professional liability
• Case file management | | |

ANNEX 16A

Course criteria	• Minimum tuition: 12 hours face-to-face • Module must not be completed until trainee has completed at least six months full-time of a PRT (or equivalent time part-time) • Essential material: 'The Guide to the Professional Conduct of Solicitors' • Other relevant materials: 'Keeping Clients: A Client Care Guide for Solicitors'; the Practice Management Standards • Use of case studies recommended • Student/tutor ratio: 20:1 • Length of sessions: No prescription
Tutor requirements	Must have thorough knowledge of the principles of professional conduct and experience in dealing with ethical issues. As a rule of thumb, the tutor will need to have been in practice for at least five years
Assessment	No formal pass/fail assessment but an appraisal of the trainee's performance with a written appraisal of overall performance. The SRA does not prescribe criteria to be used for the appraisal

237

SECTION B5

The requirements for qualification and admission

To become qualified as a solicitor, under the Solicitors Act 1974, s.1 an individual must first be admitted as a solicitor, entered on the roll of solicitors and hold a practising certificate.

This section explains the requirements for admission, which involve:

- completing the academic and vocational stage requirements of education and training (**Chapter 17**);
- meeting character and suitability requirements (**Chapter 18**); and
- complying with the procedural requirements for gaining admission (**Chapter 19**).

CHAPTER 17

Education and training requirements for admission

17.1 Introduction
17.2 Requirements
17.3 Rights of appeal against SRA decisions

17.4 Proposed changes

17.1 INTRODUCTION

This chapter explains how the education and training requirements for admission may be satisfied, following reforms by the Solicitors Regulation Authority (SRA) in 2014.

17.2 REQUIREMENTS

The SRA Training Regulations 2014 – Qualification and Provider Regulations ('Qualification and Provider Regulations'), following amendment in November 2014, now require either:

- completion of the academic stage and vocational stage in order to satisfy the education and training requirements for admission; or
- completion of an apprenticeship.[1]

17.2.1 Completion of the academic and vocational stages

The 'academic stage of training' is defined in the SRA Handbook Glossary as meaning:

---

[1] Qualification and Provider Regulations, reg.2.1.

the undertaking by an individual of the following programmes of study which satisfy the requirements of the Joint Statement:
(i) a QLD [Qualifying Law Degree, see **Chapter 12**];
(ii) a CPE [Common Professional Examination – also known as the Graduate Diploma in Law (GDL) – see **Chapter 13**]; or
(iii) an Exempting Law Degree [ELD, see **12.4**].

The 'vocational stage of training' is defined as meaning:

(i) the LPC [Legal Practice Course, see **Chapter 14**];
(ii) a required period of recognised training [PRT, see **Chapter 15**]; and
(iii) the PSC [Professional Skills Course, see **Chapter 16**].

A trainee will have completed the academic stage of training in order to commence the PRT, unless the trainee has completed the academic stage by way of Equivalent Means (see **Chapter 10**). The vocational stage is completed by:

- undertaking and passing the LPC, unless exempt or deemed to have satisfied it by Equivalent Means (see **Chapter 10**);
- undertaking a PRT in the way prescribed by the SRA; and
- completing the PSC.

The Qualification and Provider Regulations, reg.12.5(o) requires the Training Provider to certify, at the end of the training period, that the trainee has completed a PRT in accordance with reg.5. The Training Provider needs to be satisfied that the trainee has completed the PRT in order to meet the Practice Skills Standards and comply with the SRA Principles.

The SRA expects that this responsibility will usually fall to the Training Principal, who will need to rely on documented regular informal reviews and formal performance appraisals which are required by reg.12.1(d) (see **15.12**), and by the trainee's Supervisor verifying the trainee's training record, as required by reg.14.1(d).

For a trainee solicitor to be admitted as a solicitor, in addition to meeting the education and training requirements, the Training Provider must also certify that there are no issues which may affect the trainee's character and suitability, although the SRA anticipates that it would usually be the Training Principal who would make the certification.

17.2.2 Completion of an apprenticeship

Reg.2.5 of the Qualification and Provider Regulations provides that:

You will have completed an apprenticeship for the purposes of 2.1(a)(ii) if you have met the requirements set out in the assessment plan for the Apprenticeship

> Standard for a Solicitor (England) or set out in the Apprenticeship Framework specified in the Level 7 Higher Apprenticeship in Legal Practice (Wales), including successfully passing an assessment which is either conducted by the SRA or approved by the SRA as suitable for the purpose.

Legal Apprenticeships will be available from September 2016, although the proposed assessment will not be developed until 2018 at the earliest. So, detail of the assessment provided at the time of publication regarding the assessment may be subject to SRA amendments (see **Chapter 11**).

17.2.3 Other admission requirements

The Qualification and Provider Regulations, reg.2.1 also include as a condition that the individual must comply with the SRA Admission Regulations 2011 ('Admission Regulations').

Comment

This requirement is slightly misleading. The Admission Regulations, although governing the process for admitting people to the roll of solicitors, according to the Overview at the beginning, do not in fact impose any further requirements on a trainee applicant for admission, other than the requirements to have completed the vocational stage and to be of the required character and suitability for a solicitor. Rather, the Admission Regulations set out the rights of appeal against SRA decisions arising from character and suitability issues, and set out the requirements for an application for admission, issuing a certificate of satisfaction, cause for preventing admission following issue of a certificate of satisfaction, and review of such a decision; and issuing admission certificates.

17.3 RIGHTS OF APPEAL AGAINST SRA DECISIONS

17.3.1 Decision not to recognise period of authorised training

Reg.17.1 of the Qualification and Provider Regulations provides that if the SRA refuses to recognise a period of training under regs.5.5 or 16.2, the applicant may apply to the SRA in writing for a review of the decision within one month of receiving notification of it. If the SRA upholds its original decision on a review of that decision, reg.3.1 of the Admissions Regulations provides for the right of appeal to the High Court against a decision by the SRA on an application under reg.17.1 of the Qualification and Provider Regulations, for review of a refusal to recognise a period of training or eligibility to commence or continue recognised training.

17.3.2 Decision to refuse to issue certificate of satisfaction

The SRA may refuse to issue a certificate of satisfaction because an individual has failed to satisfy the requirement of either:

- compliance with the Qualification and Provider Regulations, Qualified Lawyers Transfer Regulations 2009 (QLTR) or SRA Qualified Lawyers Transfer Scheme Regulations 2011 (QLTSR); or
- character and suitability to be a solicitor[2]

in which case the SRA will notify the individual of the refusal and of the grounds for refusal. The SRA is required to notify within one month of the individual having complied with all reasonable requirements that the SRA has made in respect of the application for admission.[3] The individual may then apply to the SRA to review its decision, which the individual must do in writing and within one month of receiving the SRA's notification.[4]

If the SRA fails either to issue a certificate of satisfaction or to notify its refusal to do so within that time period, the application is deemed to have been refused and the refusal notified, so that the individual may then apply to the SRA to review its decision.

If the SRA upholds its decision to refuse issuing a certificate of satisfaction after reviewing its decision, the individual has a right of appeal to the High Court. Individuals whose eligibility has been established under QLTR, reg.4 or QLTSR, reg.2 pursuant to Directive 2005/36/EC or the Establishment Directive, have a right of appeal in these circumstances to the High Court under the European Communities (Recognition of Professional Qualifications) Regulations 2007, reg.36 or the European Communities (Lawyer's Practice) Regulations 2000, reg.35 respectively, within three months of notification (or deemed notification) of the SRA's refusal.

An appeal to the High Court must be brought within three months of the applicant receiving notification of the SRA's decision on the review.[5] On appeal, the High Court may:

- affirm the SRA's decision;
- direct the SRA to issue a certificate of eligibility; or
- make such recommendations to the SRA as the High Court thinks fit.[6]

17.4 PROPOSED CHANGES

The SRA issued a consultation document, 'Training for Tomorrow: Assessing Competence' (see **6.4.6**) in December 2015, proposing the introduction of a

---

[2] Admission Regulations, reg.6.1.
[3] Admission Regulations, reg.6.2.
[4] Admission Regulations, reg.6.3.
[5] Admission Regulations, reg.3.3.
[6] Admission Regulations, reg.3.4.

centralised assessment of competence called the Solicitors Qualifying Examination (SQE), aligned to the Statement of Solicitor Competence, Statement of Legal Knowledge and Threshold Standard (see **Chapter 21**).[7] Anyone wishing to qualify as a solicitor would be required to undertake and successfully pass the SQE in order to qualify.

The SRA believes this would 'provide a mechanism to assure solicitors' competence consistently and fairly'[8] because of the perceived inconsistency of performance standards both within and across the existing pathways to qualification.[9]

What the SRA proposes is a two-part assessment, as follows.

Part 1: Functioning Legal Knowledge Assessments

Assessment of the candidates' ability to draw on sufficient knowledge to practise effectively

Through computer-based objective testing, assessing the application of knowledge and legal processes

Unflagged ethical questions throughout

Modularised assessments which can be taken separately

Part 1 must be passed before attempting Part 2

Part 2: Practical Legal Skills Assessments

Assessment of the candidates' competence in the following six areas:
- interviewing and advising
- advocacy/oral presentation
- negotiation
- writing
- drafting
- legal research

Through standardised practical legal tasks, simulating the real demands of practice

Oral skills assessed through live role plays, involving standardised clients

Written skills assessed through computer-based applied tasks and case studies

Each skill area assessed twice, in two different practice contexts

Unflagged ethical questions throughout

Modularised assessments which can be taken separately[10]

The SRA has chosen not to benchmark the SQE on to the level descriptors in the Framework for Higher Education Qualifications (FHEQ), which is used for the law degree and LPC, because it says that the FHEQ is designed for use in a different context and purpose. Instead, the standard for the Part 2 assessment will be

---

[7] SRA Consultation 'Training for Tomorrow: Assessing Competence', 7 December 2015, p.8.
[8] SRA Consultation 'Training for Tomorrow: Assessing Competence', 7 December 2015, p.9.
[9] SRA Consultation 'Training for Tomorrow: Assessing Competence', 7 December 2015, p.10.
[10] SRA Consultation 'Training for Tomorrow: Assessing Competence', 7 December 2015, p.17.

'comparable to the level trainee solicitors currently reach by point of qualification, therefore higher than the current LPC standard'.[11]

Instead, the SRA would produce its own Assessment Framework document during 2016, setting out in relation to the SQE:

- breadth and depth of knowledge and skills to be assessed;
- level of difficulty of assessments;
- structure and design of assessments;
- standard setting and quality assurance processes;
- administrative arrangements;
- arrangements for candidates with particular requirements.

In the 'Training for Tomorrow' position paper in 2013, the SRA said it would consider the extent to which it needed to prescribe content and structure of the stages to qualification. Whether and how existing components of the qualification pathway (QLD, CPE/GDL, LPC, PRT, PSC) would fit with the SQE, and whether the SRA will in fact set entry requirements (it may not), will be the subject of a separate consultation during 2016.

Should the SQE be introduced, it would not be before the start of the academic year 2018/19. If changes to the requirements for qualification were to be introduced in relation to existing pathways and components, the SRA is planning that new regulations could come into effect during 2018, on the basis of which the cut-off date for admission under existing regulations would be the end of the academic year 2025/26. This would enable candidates who had already started on the QLD, CPE/GDL, LPC, PRT or PSC to complete, and not have to repeat, a stage of training they had already completed. The proposed transition provisions are set out at **6.4.6**.

The SRA is due to give its decision on the introduction of the SQE in June 2016.

---

[11] SRA Consultation 'Training for Tomorrow: Assessing Competence', 7 December 2015, p.21.

CHAPTER 18

Character and suitability requirements

18.1 Introduction
18.2 The test
18.3 DBS disclosures

18.4 Self-disclosures under the SRA Suitability Test 2011

18.1 INTRODUCTION

It is not enough to satisfy the education and training requirements set out in **Chapter 17** to be eligible for admission as a solicitor: a candidate for admission must also satisfy character and suitability requirements. Because the Solicitors Regulation Authority (SRA) is responsible for setting and maintaining standards for all solicitors practising in England and Wales, it has:

> a duty to consider the character and suitability of anyone who wishes to enter the profession, and must ensure that any individual admitted as a solicitor has, and maintains, the level of honesty, integrity and professionalism expected by the public and other stakeholders and professionals, and does not pose a risk to the public or the profession.[1]

This chapter explains the test of character and suitability that the SRA uses and what is required to meet the conditions of that test.

18.2 THE TEST

To maintain the reputation of the profession (and protect the public), the SRA assesses character and suitability issues against the criteria set out in the SRA Suitability Test 2011 ('Suitability Test').

---
[1] SRA website, 'FAQs for Students'.

CHARACTER AND SUITABILITY REQUIREMENTS

Character and suitability are assessed at various stages of the qualification process:

- before commencing a Period of Recognised Training (PRT); and
- at admission.

The SRA in its non-mandatory Guidance Note (i) to the SRA Admission Regulations 2011 ('Admission Regulations'), reg.6 states that it will satisfy itself as to an applicant's character and suitability to be a solicitor 'in a number of ways', which will include but will not be limited to:

- Disclosure and Barring Service (DBS) disclosures;
- self-disclosures by the applicant in accordance with the Suitability Test.

18.3 DBS DISCLOSURES

All applicants for admission to the roll of solicitors must complete a screening process which takes about eight weeks to complete. In terms of process, the SRA will send a trainee the forms and guidance some ten weeks prior to the end of the trainee's PRT. The form includes a declaration by the trainee to agree to the checks required by the SRA under the screening process. As well as completing the declaration, the trainee must at the same time pay to the SRA the £42 fee for the DBS Standard Criminal Record Check. Payment methods may be found on the SRA website.

The SRA requires three different checks:

- an online UK credit reference agency check with Experian

    This check will validate the trainee's name, address and other personal information supplied during the application process against third party databases.

- a Standard Criminal Record Check issued by the DBS

    The DBS will send the trainee a Standard Certificate which may or may not have 'disclosures'. If the certificate does have disclosures, then the SRA requires that it be provided with the original certificate. If, however, there are no disclosures on the certificate, then the SRA does not require the certificate. The 'disclosures' will include details of any current and spent convictions, police cautions, reprimands and final warnings held on the Police National Computer, except for protected convictions and protected cautions and other convictions or cautions which have been filtered out by virtue of the Rehabilitation of Offenders Act 1974 (Exceptions Order).

- criminal record checks from other non-UK countries where the trainee has lived for a period of six continuous months during the previous five years. The SRA requires that the check is not less than three months old, and where it is not in English it must be translated into English by an accepted translation body.

The SRA warns that the applicant should allow sufficient time to obtain the check prior to the applicant's preferred admission date.

18.4 SELF-DISCLOSURES UNDER THE SRA SUITABILITY TEST 2011

18.4.1 Disclosure requirements

In the Overview to the Suitability Test, the SRA states that it 'must ensure that any individual admitted as a solicitor has, and maintains, the level of honesty, integrity and the professionalism expected by the public and other stakeholders and professionals, and does not pose a risk to the public or the profession'.[2] It is these 'high standards' which the Suitability Test applies to 'all those seeking admission or restoration to the roll as a solicitor, as well as legally qualified and non-legally qualified applicants for roles in authorised bodies as authorised role holders'.[3]

The Suitability Test is intended to make clear to applicants what standard is required of an applicant's character, suitability, fitness and propriety,[4] and will be used by the SRA when it has to decide on character, suitability, fitness and propriety in respect of an application. Most importantly, the onus is on the applicant 'to discharge the burden of satisfying suitability under the Suitability Test'.[5]

Although disclosure is required for admission, the obligation to make disclosure of issues of character and suitability arise both before a trainee commences a PRT and during the PRT.[6] A student may also ask for an assessment of an issue before commencing the Legal Practice Course (LPC), if the student is concerned that the issue may cause him or her not to meet the requirements of the Suitability Test. However, there is no obligation to do so.

Comment

The risk of not raising an issue before commencing the LPC is that a student could pay a considerable amount of money for the LPC, and spend the time undertaking and passing the LPC, only to find that he or she does not meet the character and suitability requirements, either to commence a PRT or to be admitted as a solicitor. Consequently, it is better to be safe than sorry. It is also worth pointing out that issues which require disclosure apply equally to trainees at the start of and during the PRT, as at the point of applying for admission.

It is also worth stressing to trainees the seriousness of the disclosure obligation, and that it rests with them – particularly since removal by the SRA of the requirement for student enrolment (see **6.4.1.1**).

---

[2] SRA Suitability Test 2011, p.1.
[3] SRA Suitability Test 2011, p.1
[4] SRA Suitability Test 2011, p.1
[5] SRA Suitability Test 2011, p.1.
[6] SRA Training Regulations 2014 – Qualification and Provider Regulations, reg.6.1.

CHARACTER AND SUITABILITY REQUIREMENTS

The Suitability Test (which can be found on the SRA website) sets out what needs to be disclosed, and what the SRA's decision is likely to be. Issues that require disclosure (which equally apply to trainees at the start of and during the PRT, as at the point of applying for admission) are not necessarily confined to criminal offences or convictions but also include assessment offences, financial mismanagement, regulatory action or behaviour which demonstrates the applicant cannot be relied upon to discharge his or her regulatory duties as a solicitor. The following is a non-exhaustive list of what would require disclosure to the SRA, and which would result in the SRA refusing an application for admission unless there were exceptional circumstances:

- dishonest, violent or discriminatory behaviour;
- misuse of position to obtain pecuniary advantage;
- misuse of position of trust in relation to vulnerable people;
- plagiarism or cheating;
- mismanagement or dishonest management of finances;
- bankruptcy, individual voluntary arrangements (IVA) or a county court judgment;
- a serious disciplinary finding, sanction or action by a regulatory body;
- registration refused by a regulatory body;
- a rebuke, reprimand or warning by a regulatory body
- disqualification from being a charity trustee;
- disqualification as a company director;
- being manager or owner of a body corporate which has been wound up or put into administrative receivership;
- an offence under the Companies Act 2006.

In terms of disclosure, the SRA requires that all material information relating to an applicant's application must be disclosed, whether in the UK and/or overseas. Failure to disclose material information will be treated by the SRA as *prima facie* evidence of dishonest behaviour. This includes failure to disclose information about convictions and/or cautions for criminal offences which are not protected convictions or cautions, whether they are spent or unspent, where the applicant falls within the Rehabilitation of Offenders Act 1974 (Exceptions) Order 1975. However, protected convictions and protected cautions do not need to be disclosed, and failure to disclose those will not be considered as *prima facie* evidence of dishonesty by the SRA.

'Protected conviction' and 'protected caution' are defined in paras.(v) and (vi) of the guidance notes to Section 8 'Rehabilitation' of the Suitability Test.

18.4.2 Evidence requirements

Having made a disclosure, the SRA requires under s.7.1 that an applicant include the following evidence where relevant:

THE REQUIREMENTS FOR QUALIFICATION AND ADMISSION

- at least one independent report relating to the event(s), such as sentencing remarks following a criminal conviction;
- references from at least two independent professional people (of which one should preferably be from an employer or tutor) who know you well and are familiar with the matters being considered;
- evidence of any rehabilitation (e.g. probation reports, references from employers and/or tutors);
- documentary evidence in support of your case and where possible, an independent corroboration of your account of the event(s);
- your attitude towards the event(s);
- the extent to which you were aware of the rules and procedures governing the reference of material, or the use of group work or collaborative material;
- the extent to which you could reasonably have been expected to realise that the offence did not constitute legitimate academic practice;
- credit check information (in the relevant circumstances); and/or
- actions you have taken to clear any debts, satisfy any judgments and manage your finances.[7]

The SRA places the onus on the applicant to provide any evidence the applicant considers necessary and/or appropriate. However, the SRA will not limit itself to evidence provided by the applicant, and reserves the right to carry out its own investigation if it considers that the applicant has provided insufficient evidence. The SRA may also refuse the application if the applicant does not provide further evidence.

> **Comment**
>
> Although not cast as such in the Suitability Test itself, the evidence adduced by an applicant will also provide the basis for any exceptional circumstances which may change what would otherwise be a refusal by the SRA to a grant of admission. A factor which will be key in the SRA recognising exceptional circumstances will be evidence of rehabilitation.

18.4.3 Evidence of rehabilitation

The SRA also places the onus on the applicant to demonstrate successful rehabilitation, and will weigh the individual circumstances against the public interest and the need to safeguard members of the public and maintain the reputation of the profession.

Factors which the SRA will consider include:

- the provisions of the Rehabilitation of Offenders Act 1974 and the Rehabilitation of Offenders Act 1974 (Exceptions) Order 1975, and the fact that the

---

[7] SRA Suitability Test 2011, para.7.1.

conviction is spent, and the time that has passed since conviction, together with any other material circumstances;
- that the applicant has undergone a period of rehabilitation by way of a period of good behaviour, and that the applicant has taken steps to rehabilitate him- or herself of his or her own volition. However, a period of rehabilitation following the SRA's refusal of an application will not of itself give rise to automatic admission.

CHAPTER 19

Admission process

19.1	Introduction	19.3	Admission application
19.2	Issue of certificate of satisfaction	19.4	Practising certificate

19.1 INTRODUCTION

Having satisfied the Solicitors Regulation Authority's (SRA's) education and training requirements (see **Chapter 17**) and its Suitability Test (see **Chapter 18**), an individual may commence the process for admission as a solicitor.

Although admission as a solicitor is not technically part of the education and training process, it is the end result of that process: all pathways (whether domestic, EU directive-based or under the Qualified Lawyers Transfer Scheme (QLTS)), if successfully pursued, lead to admission as a solicitor. Therefore, this chapter explains the various steps involved, from issue of a certification of satisfaction to the actual application for admission, and the application for a practising certificate.

19.2 ISSUE OF CERTIFICATE OF SATISFACTION

Reg.6.1 of the SRA Admission Regulations 2011 ('Admission Regulations') specifies that, if the SRA is satisfied:

- that the applicant has complied with the SRA Training Regulations 2014 – Qualification and Provider Regulations ('Qualification and Provider Regulations'); and
- as to the applicant's character and suitability to be a solicitor

the SRA will issue the applicant with a certificate of satisfaction in accordance with the Solicitors Act 1974, s.3.1.

Once the certificate of satisfaction has been issued, the SRA is obliged to admit the individual as a solicitor 'within a reasonable period on a day [the SRA] determines'.[1]

Having said that, even though a certificate of satisfaction has been issued, it is still possible for the SRA to refuse to admit an individual 'if cause is shown in writing to [the SRA's] satisfaction' that the individual should not be admitted as a solicitor. If this happens, the SRA is obliged under reg.8.1 of the Admission Regulations to notify the individual of its decision in writing. The individual concerned may request the SRA to review its decision within one month of receiving notification of the decision and, if the SRA affirms its decision, the individual has a right of appeal to the High Court under the Admission Regulations, reg.8.3. It is open to the High Court to:

- affirm the SRA's decision;
- direct the SRA to admit the individual as a solicitor; or
- make such recommendations to the SRA as the High Court thinks fit.

If the individual concerned has been certified eligible pursuant to Directive 2005/36/EC or pursuant to the Establishment Directive, he or she has the right to appeal to the High Court under the European Communities (Recognition of Professional Qualifications) Regulations 2007, reg.36 or the European Communities (Lawyer's Practice) Regulations 2000, reg.35, as appropriate. That appeal may be against either the SRA's decision not to admit the individual as a solicitor under reg.8.1, or against the SRA's refusal to reverse that decision on a review under reg.8.2. In either case, it must be brought within three months of receipt of the SRA's notification of its decision on the review.

An individual may make up to three applications to the SRA to reverse its decision to refuse admission, but applications may only be made after intervals of not less than 12 months from the final determination as to the initial decision, or from the final determination of the previous application for review.

19.3 ADMISSION APPLICATION

There is no time requirement for applying for admission; rather, application can be made at any time after the requirements of the Qualification and Provider Regulations, the Qualified Lawyers Transfer Regulations 2009 (QLTR) or the Qualified Lawyers Transfer Scheme Regulations 2011 (QLTSR), as appropriate, have been complied with.[2]

The SRA requires the application for admission to be made in the prescribed form, AD1, and accompanied by the specified fee which is currently £100.[3]

---

[1] Admission Regulations, reg.7.1.
[2] Admission Regulations, reg 4.1.
[3] Admission Regulations, reg.5.1.

THE REQUIREMENTS FOR QUALIFICATION AND ADMISSION

For admission under the European Establishment Directive, Art.10, an applicant is required to complete form AD15, accompanied by payment of the fee, which is currently £500.

Both forms have accompanying guidance notes available on the SRA website.

19.4 PRACTISING CERTIFICATE

A solicitor is able to request his or her practising certificate to commence from the date of admission given in section 6 of the AD1 application form. Practising certificate fees vary from year to year but can be found on the SRA website.

Whether a practising certificate is in fact required for the work a solicitor does on qualification is outside the scope of this book but information on this can be obtained from the SRA.

SECTION B6

Post-qualification requirements

It is interesting that, once qualified, a solicitor has few further tests of competence. Until March 2015, the post-qualification requirements for solicitors to ensure competence and the protection of the public – apart from a solicitor's professional obligations under the Solicitors Regulation Authority (SRA) Handbook, such as Principle 5 – consisted of a one-off, compulsory seven hours of management training (Management Course Stage 1) and an annual requirement of 16 hours of Continuing Professional Development (CPD).

From 1 April 2015, the requirement for the Management Course Stage 1 was removed, and solicitors were provided with a further option for meeting their CPD obligations, which did not require a set number of hours, and which relies on identifying learning and training needs by reference to a Competence Statement.

The future is one of solicitors taking responsibility for identifying and meeting their own learning and development needs, with the overriding requirement of SRA Principle 5 to provide a proper standard of service to one's clients. Is that enough to assure competence, protect the public and maintain the quality of the profession? Time will tell.

This section explains:

- the current and proposed requirements for CPD (**Chapter 20**); and
- the Competence Statement, its components and its intended use (**Chapter 21**).

CHAPTER 20

Continuing Professional Development

20.1	Introduction	20.8	Minimum hours option – reg.3.1(a)
20.2	Governing regulations	20.9	Continuing Competence approach
20.3	Who is subject to the CPD scheme		option – reg.3.1(b)
20.4	CPD year	20.10	Confirmation of compliance with
20.5	CPD requirements		requirements
20.6	Waivers	20.11	Sanctions
20.7	Monitoring compliance with CPD requirements	20.12	Proposed changes
		20.13	Management Course Stages 1 and 2

20.1 INTRODUCTION

The Solicitors Regulation Authority (SRA) defines Continuing Professional Development (CPD) as 'the training requirement(s) set by [the SRA] to ensure solicitors and [Registered European Lawyers] maintain competence'. 'Competence' is about being able to comply with Principle 5 in the SRA Handbook to 'provide a proper standard of service to [one's] clients'.[1]

SRA reforms have introduced an alternative way of complying with CPD requirements, and a new regime will replace CPD entirely from 1 November 2016.

This chapter therefore explains the dual regime for meeting CPD requirements until 1 November 2016, and what is proposed from that date.

20.2 GOVERNING REGULATIONS

Until 31 October 2016 (see **20.12**), professional competence is assured by the CPD Scheme, which has been operating since 1985. The CPD Scheme is governed by the SRA Training Regulations 2011 Part 3 – CPD Regulations ('CPD Regulations') and prescribes a minimum number of hours of CPD activity to be undertaken annually.

---

[1] SRA Handbook, Version 15, Glossary, 'CPD' entry.

CONTINUING PROFESSIONAL DEVELOPMENT

The CPD Regulations were amended on 1 April 2015 and a new reg.3.1(b) inserted. This means that, until 1 November 2016, a solicitor or Registered European Lawyer (REL) has two options for satisfying the CPD requirement under reg.3, either by:

- completing a minimum of 16 hours per year, during each complete CPD year in legal practice or employment in England and Wales, under reg.3.1(a) (this is known as the 'minimum hours option' or 'reg.3.1(a) option'); or
- adopting a Continuing Competence approach under reg.3.1(b) by considering and undertaking the learning and development the solicitor or REL deems necessary to ensure his or her ongoing competence, and to ensure that he or she is in a position to provide a proper standard of service to his or her clients (known as 'the Continuing Competence approach' or 'reg.3.1(b) option').

20.3 WHO IS SUBJECT TO THE CPD SCHEME

Under the CPD Regulations[2] all solicitors admitted to the roll of solicitors, whether or not they hold a practising certificate, and all RELs are required to undertake CPD in accordance with the CPD Regulations, subject to suspension.

Registered Foreign Lawyers are not subject to the CPD Regulations, however, according to reg.2.3.

20.4 CPD YEAR

The CPD year runs from 1 November (the date for renewal of practising certificates or REL registration) to 31 October of the following year.

20.5 CPD REQUIREMENTS

The requirements relating to the CPD Scheme depend upon whether the solicitor or REL adopts reg.3.1(a) or 3.1(b).

The requirements of each approach are summarised in the following table.

---

[2] CPD Regulations, reg.2.2.

POST-QUALIFICATION REQUIREMENTS

	Reg.3.1(a) option (16 hours)	Reg.3.1(b) option (Continuing Competence)
Governing regulations	SRA Training Regulations 2011 Part 3 – CPD Regulations (see **20.2**)	
Subject to CPD requirements	All solicitors and RELs Not registered foreign lawyers (RFLs) (see **20.3**)	
CPD year	From 1 November to 31 October (see **20.4**)	
CPD requirement	• Undertake a minimum of 16 hours of CPD during each complete CPD year they are in practice or employment in England and Wales according to circumstances such as working part-time, first CPD year, returning from self-suspension of CPD requirements (see **20.8.1** and **20.8.2**) • Keep a record of CPD activities • Sign declaration confirming compliance when applying for renewal of practising certificate or REL registration	Solicitors required to: • reflect on their practice to identify their learning and development needs • plan how they will address their learning and development needs • address those learning and development needs • record the learning and development they undertake, and • evaluate whether the learning and development they have undertaken has addressed their learning and development needs See **20.9.1**
Carry-over of CPD hours	If a solicitor or REL accrues more than 16 hours in a CPD year, the additional hours may not be 'banked' against next year's CPD requirement[3] (see **20.8.1**)	Not applicable
Exemptions from CPD requirements	There are no exemptions from the CPD Scheme. Some waivers from monitoring only are permitted (see **20.6**)	
Reduction of CPD requirements	For: • New solicitors or RELs • Solicitors returning to practice following suspension of CPD requirements • Solicitors working part-time (See **20.8.2**)	Not applicable

---

[3] 2011 CPD Training Regulations, reg.3, Guidance note (i).

CONTINUING PROFESSIONAL DEVELOPMENT

	Reg.3.1(a) option (16 hours)	Reg.3.1(b) option (Continuing Competence)
Reduction for part-time working	Yes (see **20.8.2**)	Not applicable
Providers	No accreditation requirements (see **20.8.8**)	
Requirement to plan CPD	No requirement to plan but SRA encourages solicitors to do so (see **20.8.6**)	Requirement to reflect on one's practice and to identify individual learning and development needs, plan how to address those needs, and record those needs (see **20.9.4**)
Requirement to keep record of CPD	Reg.10.1 requires solicitors and RELs to keep a record of all the CPD training they undertake, and the number of hours they accrue (see **20.8.5**)	Requirement to record: • learning and development needs identified • how those needs will be addressed • activities undertaken to address learning and development needs • evaluation of effectiveness of activities undertaken (see **20.9.6**)
	Reg.10.3 requires a solicitor to keep his or her CPD training record for at least 6 years	
Consequences of failure to comply with CPD requirements	Could lead to disciplinary procedures against the solicitor or REL and/or delay in renewal of the solicitor's or REL's practising certificate If a solicitor or REL has not undertaken the full CPD requirement by the time he or she applies for his or her practising certificate, he or she may contact the SRA to apply for an extension (see **20.8.7**)	Failure to demonstrate that a solicitor or REL has reflected on quality of practice and addressed any learning and development needs may be an aggravating factor in disciplinary action the SRA may take (see **20.11**)
Monitoring by SRA of compliance with CPD requirements	Under reg.10.2 the SRA can request to see a solicitor's or REL's CPD training record at any time, and it must be produced on demand upon the request being made (see **20.7**)	

	Reg.3.1(a) option (16 hours)	**Reg.3.1(b) option (Continuing Competence)**
Responsibility for compliance with CPD requirements	Reg.8.2 provides that responsibility for meeting the CPD requirements falls on the individual solicitor or REL, and not on his or her employer	'Employers are responsible for delivering a proper standard of service to their clients and for training their staff to maintain a level of competence appropriate to their work and level of responsibility'[4]
Obligation on employer to fund CPD activities	An employer is not obliged to pay for CPD training or to allow time off to attend courses[5]	
Obligation on employer to allow time-off:	No (see above)	
Requirements for eligible CPD	Reg.8.1 specifies that, for a CPD activity to count towards the CPD requirements, it must be at an appropriate level and contribute to an individual's general professional skill and knowledge (see **20.8.4**)	CPD activities should be linked to solicitor's/REL's role and must meet obligations under SRA Principle 5 (see **20.9.1**)
Accreditation	From 1 November 2014, the requirement for solicitors to undertake accredited training as part of the CPD requirements was removed, and the SRA ceased to recognise accredited training (see **20.8.8**)	No requirement for accreditation

20.6 WAIVERS

Although there are no exemptions from the CPD Scheme, reg.17.1 provides that the following waivers apply in relation to the routine monitoring of CPD records for:

- solicitors or RELs in firms and organisations with Lexcel/Investors in People (IIP) accreditation;
- solicitors or RELs in firms holding a legal aid franchise;
- solicitors or RELs working in firms and organisations holding ISO 9000 accreditation.

---

[4] SRA, 'A New Approach to Continuing Competence (Toolkit)', p.11.
[5] SRA website, 'FAQs about Continuing Professional Development (CPD)'.

CONTINUING PROFESSIONAL DEVELOPMENT

Although there may be a waiver from monitoring, reg. 17.2 makes clear that there is no waiver of the number of CPD hours required to be completed, or the requirement to maintain one's personal CPD training record to plan one's CPD. However, in reg.17.3 the SRA reserves the right to waive in writing the provisions of regs.17.1 and 17.2, and to revoke the waivers granted by reg.17.1.

20.7 MONITORING COMPLIANCE WITH CPD REQUIREMENTS

The monitoring regime for CPD is not the same as monitoring of other SRA compulsorily-required courses. This is because the responsibility falls on the individual solicitor or REL to maintain a record of CPD activities, and to ensure that he or she complies with the annual CPD requirement. A solicitor or REL must sign a declaration when renewing his or her practising certificate or REL registration respectively, each year, to the effect that he or she has complied with the previous year's requirement (see **20.10**). What solicitors and RELs need to be aware of is that:

- it is the solicitor's or REL's responsibility to ensure that he or she complies with the CPD requirements, not his or her employer's responsibility to do so;
- even where the solicitor's or REL's employer looks after renewal of practising certificates or renewal of REL registration (e.g. by way of bulk renewal), each solicitor or REL in the firm must ensure that he or she has met his or her individual CPD requirement;
- the SRA has the right to check the training record of a solicitor or REL at any time.

20.8 MINIMUM HOURS OPTION – REG.3.1(A)

20.8.1 Requirements

Regulation 3.1(a) is an 'inputs-based' scheme and has the basic requirement that a solicitor or REL undertakes a minimum of 16 hours of CPD during each complete CPD year they are in practice or employment in England and Wales.

A solicitor or REL may not carry over hours to next year's CPD allocation. So, if a solicitor or REL accrues more than 16 hours in a CPD year, the additional hours may not be 'banked' against the next year's CPD requirement.[6] (This will only be relevant for the 2014/15 and 2015/16 CPD years because a new Continuing Competence Scheme will apply to all solicitors from 1 November 2016.)

---

[6] 2011 CPD Training Regulations, reg.3, Guidance note (i).

20.8.2 Calculation of the number of hours

The minimum 16-hour requirement will vary for a solicitor or REL, depending on whether:

- the solicitor or REL works part-time;
- the solicitor was recently admitted;
- the REL was recently registered;
- the REL has recently been admitted as a solicitor;
- the solicitor or REL has suspended his or her CPD requirements;
- the solicitor or REL has returned to work after having suspended his or her CPD requirements for a period.

Consequently, the number of hours of CPD that must be undertaken by a particular solicitor or REL should be calculated according to his or her circumstances.

20.8.2.1 Part-time

For solicitors who work part-time (fewer than 32 hours per week but more than two hours per week), the 16-hour requirement is adjusted on the basis of one hour of CPD for every two hours worked per week.[7] If the solicitor or REL works, on average, fewer than two hours per week, then he or she is permitted to suspend the CPD requirements.[8] Where the solicitor or REL works part hours, then the total from the calculation should be rounded up to the nearest whole hour.

The SRA recommends that a solicitor or REL who works part-time should keep a record of the hours worked so that he or she can calculate the average number of hours worked per week over the course of the CPD year.[9] SRA guidance recommends that if the solicitor or REL works a variable number of hours per week, then he or she should calculate the average number of hours worked per week during the CPD year, and then base the calculation of one hour of CPD per two hours worked on the average number of hours.[10]

20.8.2.2 New solicitors/RELs

For someone who is admitted before 1 November, or who becomes registered as an REL before 1 November, that 'year' (i.e. the period of time between qualification and 1 November) will not be counted as the first CPD year but as a type of transition. For this 'transitionary year', which will not be a full year by definition, the requirement is that the solicitor or REL undertakes one hour's CPD for each whole month from admission or from the date of initial registration as an REL, respectively, to the next 1 November.

---

[7] 2011 CPD Training Regulations, reg.7.1.
[8] 2011 CPD Training Regulations, reg.7.3.
[9] 2011 CPD Training Regulations, reg.7, Guidance note (ii).
[10] 2011 CPD Training Regulations, reg.7, Guidance note (iii).

CONTINUING PROFESSIONAL DEVELOPMENT

The newly admitted or registered period covers the first 12 months following the date of a solicitor's or REL's admission or registration, respectively.[11]

If, however, the solicitor's admission date or REL's date of initial registration is 1 November 2015, even though 1 November 2015 is a Sunday and the admission or initial registration is shifted to the following week, the solicitor or REL automatically enters his or her first full CPD year from 1 November, and therefore would be required to complete the full 16 hours of CPD during his or her first year of admission/registration.[12]

Although CPD cannot be 'banked' as such, if a solicitor or REL, having lodged his or her application for admission or registration, undertakes CPD before the solicitor's actual day of admission or REL's actual date of registration, the solicitor or REL can credit that number of hours against the first year requirement. A solicitor in these circumstances must have completed his or her Period of Recognised Training (PRT).

20.8.2.3 REL admitted as a solicitor

The CPD requirements apply as if the REL was a solicitor admitted on the date of his or her original registration as an REL. So, if REL registration and admission happen within the same CPD year, the solicitor will be subject to the CPD requirements for new solicitors detailed above under regs.3 and 5 and, if the solicitor works part-time, the CPD requirement will be reduced, as described above, for solicitors and RELs who work part-time

20.8.3 Suspension of CPD requirements

The CPD Regulations provide for self-suspension of CPD requirements.

The circumstances in which a solicitor or REL may suspend his or her CPD requirements are where the solicitor or REL:

- is not working in legal practice or employment;
- is retired from practice as a solicitor or REL;
- is working less than two hours per week on average in legal practice or employment.[13]

This also covers periods out of legal practice or employment because of illness, maternity/paternity leave, long-term illness and/or working abroad.

Although there is no obligation to notify the SRA[14] of a self-suspension, the dates of the start and end of the self-suspension should be entered in the CPD training record.

---

[11] 2011 CPD Training Regulations, reg.13.2, Guidance note (ii).
[12] 2011 CPD Training Regulations, reg.6, Guidance note (i).
[13] 2011 CPD Training Regulations, reg.12.2.
[14] 2011 CPD Training Regulations, reg.12.4.

According to the guidance notes to reg.12.1, the solicitor or REL cannot be in a role which requires the solicitor or REL to provide legal advice to:

- a member of the public;
- a company;
- an internal department;
- an officer or member of staff; or
- representative of the solicitor's or REL's firm

whether by way of paid or voluntary employment, and whether or not the solicitor or REL holds a practising certificate. This means that a retired solicitor would not be eligible to suspend his or her CPD requirements if he or she practises or undertakes legal work of any description, whether paid or unpaid, or is acting as a consultant, or undertakes pro bono or voluntary work of a legal nature.

If the solicitor or REL, having suspended his or her CPD requirements, undertakes any training which would otherwise have counted for CPD purposes, that training may not be counted towards CPD on the solicitor's or REL's return to legal practice or employment.[15]

In the case of a solicitor or REL who works part-time, then the CPD requirements are reduced pro rata on the basis of one hour of CPD for every two hours per week worked.

The guidance notes to reg.12.4 advise that a solicitor or REL considering suspending his or her CPD requirements should give consideration to:

- the length of time he or she will be out of practice or legal employment;
- the number of CPD hours ('amount of credit') already accrued during that CPD year (if the solicitor or REL has not completed all of his or her CPD requirements for the current CPD leading up to the suspension, he or she will also be required to make up any shortfall on returning to work, although the SRA may grant an extension of time in order to do this);[16]
- the availability of courses/access to training while out of practice;
- his or her financial circumstances and whether the solicitor or REL would be required to fund the training him- or herself.

Comment

This will be relevant for the 2014/15 and 2015/16 CPD years for reasons explained at **20.8.1**. For the 2016/17 CPD year, all solicitors will be subject to the Continuing Competence Scheme.

---

[15] 2011 CPD Training Regulations, reg.12.3.
[16] 2011 CPD Training Regulations, reg.13.4.

20.8.4 CPD activities

The non-mandatory guidance note to reg.8.1 deems the following activities to be 'CPD activities where they are relevant and beneficial to [the solicitor's] area of work and/or practice'.[17] These activities include:

(a) structured training, coaching or mentoring sessions;
(b) live or recorded webinars;
(c) writing on law or practice, for example law books, journals, publications for clients, client's own publications, newspapers and magazines, online or in print;
(d) structured work shadowing schemes with clear aims and objectives and requiring feedback or reflection on the activity;
(e) research which relates to legal topics or has relevance to the practice/organisation which results in some form of written document, precedent, memorandum, questionnaire/survey etc;
(f) study for or production of a dissertation counting towards a qualification recognised by the SRA;
(g) watching DVDs, webcasts, podcasts, television broadcasts or videotapes and/or listening to audio podcasts, radio broadcasts or audio tapes produced by learning and development providers;
(h) work towards the Qualification Credit Framework (QCF) awards relating to assessment, verification and/or quality assurance of competence-based assessment models (such as, for example, National Vocational Qualifications);
(i) participating in the development of specialist areas of law and practice by attending meetings of specialist committees and/or working parties of relevant professional or other competent bodies charged with such work;
(j) work towards the achievement of any National Vocational Qualifications in any business-related area and at any level;
(k) study towards professional qualifications.[18]

Comment

Reading on its own is not in the list of deemed CPD activities and, traditionally, has only counted for CPD purposes if it forms part of a recognised CPD activity.

Preparing and delivering any of the deemed CPD activities may also count 'where appropriate', in addition to attending the CPD event.

Comment

So, if a solicitor is delivering a structured training session, for example, the time he or she spends in preparing the session and then in delivering the session may be counted.

---

[17] 2011 CPD Training Regulations, reg.8.1, Guidance note (i).
[18] 2011 CPD Training Regulations, reg.8.1, Guidance note (i).

> However, the SRA Guidance Note (iii) to reg.8 says that the solicitor may also count the time of the session. This is in fact double-dipping if the solicitor has already counted the delivery time – since he or she is both delivering and attending at the same time.

20.8.5 CPD record

The SRA provides a template training record on its website,[19] as well as a completed example.[20] The date and course title need to be recorded, as well as the number of hours' CPD credit allocated and the provider's reference where it is an accredited course (although accreditation was dispensed with from 1 November 2014).

What needs to be entered in the CPD training record is the following:

- details of each CPD activity undertaken;
- the number of hours undertaken for each CPD activity;
- the start and finish dates of any period of suspension, and reasons for suspending (reg.10.4).[21]

If the solicitor or REL works part-time, then the details of the hours he or she works should also be entered in the CPD training record.[22]

20.8.6 Planning CPD

There is no regulatory requirement to plan one's CPD if a solicitor or REL is meeting the CPD requirement under reg.3.1(a). Even so, the SRA does encourage solicitors and RELs to 'adopt a planned approach to their CPD, by assessing their individual training needs and linking those to the objectives of the organisation in which they work',[23] on the basis that 'unplanned training and development activity is very unlikely to bring the maximum return on your investment in terms of time and money'.[24]

The SRA suggests identifying training needs by using a SWOT analysis (analysis of one's strengths, weaknesses, opportunities and threats) based on the individual's own profile and circumstances. To assist solicitors/RELs with assessing and planning, the SRA provides a completed example of a needs analysis and training and development plan,[25] as well as a blank version on its website.[26]

---

[19] SRA, CPD Training Record – blank form.
[20] SRA, CPD Training Record – completed example.
[21] 2011 CPD Training Regulations, reg.10, Guidance note (i).
[22] 2011 CPD Training Regulations, reg.7.4.
[23] SRA, CPD Requirements, 1 April 2015.
[24] SRA, Continuing Professional Development: Example Needs Analysis and Training and Development Plan – completed, Version 2.
[25] SRA, Continuing Professional Development: Example Needs Analysis and Training and Development Plan – completed, Version 2.
[26] SRA, Continuing Professional Development: Example Needs Analysis and Training and Development Plan – blank.

> **Comment**
>
> Training needs analysis and planning is covered in detail in **Chapter 3**.

20.8.7 Non-compliance

If a solicitor, for whatever reason – justified or unjustified – has not achieved the necessary CPD hours by the time 1 November comes around, he or she should contact the SRA. The SRA will want to know what CPD the solicitor or REL has in fact undertaken that year and the reason/s he or she has not complied with the full requirement. The SRA may then either grant an extension of time to make up the shortfall, or grant a concession to attend a specific course in the next CPD year. That said, if a solicitor or REL is a persistent non-complier, the SRA may not take quite such a supportive position and there may be a delay in renewal of the practising certificate or REL registration. Practising without a current practising certificate could constitute a breach of the Solicitors Act 1974, the Legal Services Act 2007, the Solicitors' Code of Conduct 2007 and the Solicitors' Indemnity Insurance Rules 1998, with possible penalties and sanctions imposed by the SRA's Fraud and Investigations Department.

> **Comment**
>
> To determine the extent to which this may be an actual problem, see **20.10** in relation to the declarations required for particular CPD years, in the transition to the new Continuing Competence regime from 1 November 2016.

20.8.8 Accreditation

From 1 November 2014 the requirement to undertake accredited training was removed and the SRA ceased to recognise accredited training. Prior to 1 November 2014, in order to provide or deliver accredited CPD, as defined under the CPD Regulations, a provider had to be authorised by the SRA as either an in-house or external CPD provider. This is no longer a requirement

> **Comment**
>
> Although the CPD Scheme and the requirement to undertake the appropriate number of CPD hours continues until 1 November 2016, the SRA no longer 'awards' CPD hours for webinars, workshops, consultation events, external events and other activities it organises. So, it is for the solicitor or REL to count the real time of the activity towards his or her CPD requirements.

20.9 CONTINUING COMPETENCE APPROACH OPTION – REG.3.1(B)

20.9.1 Requirements

Under reg.3.1(b), instead of meeting a minimum requirement of 16 hours of CPD activity per year, a solicitor or REL can determine what his or her own learning and development requirements are and, in meeting those requirements, will satisfy the CPD requirements under reg.3.1(b). The activities which the solicitor or REL undertakes to meet his or her learning and development needs should be linked to his or her role and should meet the obligation under Principle 5 of the SRA Handbook to provide a proper standard of service to clients.[27] A solicitor or REL should also agree his or her learning and development requirements with his or her employer.

> **Comment**
>
> From 1 November 2016 all solicitors and RELs will be required to adopt the Continuing Competence approach. The question for solicitors is whether they wish to do so before 1 November 2016. What is advised is that solicitors and RELs understand what is required by the Continuing Competence approach before deciding whether or not to adopt it ahead of 1 November 2016.

The Continuing Competence approach is based on compliance with Principle 5 in the SRA Code of Conduct 2011, and the requirement to provide a proper standard of service to one's clients. The notes to Principle 5 were amended from 1 April 2015 to include: '2.10 For a solicitor, meeting the competencies set out in the Competence Statement forms an integral part of the requirement to provide a proper standard of service.' The Continuing Competence approach requires solicitors and RELs to:

- reflect on their practice to identify their learning and development needs;
- plan how they will address their learning and development needs;
- address those learning and development needs;
- record the learning and development they undertake;
- evaluate whether the learning and development they have undertaken has addressed their learning and development needs; and
- make an annual declaration to confirm that they have done this.

> **Comment**
>
> The SRA described its new approach in the Q&A it published on its website on 28 October 2014 as permitting solicitors and RELs to address their identified learning and

---

[27] SRA website, 'FAQs about Continuing Professional Development (CPD)'.

CONTINUING PROFESSIONAL DEVELOPMENT

> development needs in a way that they saw as appropriate, and in a way that was also appropriate to their own client and business needs.[28]

In fact, under the Continuing Competence approach:

- any approach to learning and development is valid as long as a solicitor or REL can demonstrate it contributes to how a solicitor or REL remains competent to deliver a proper standard of service; and
- how a solicitor or REL accesses a learning and development activity that he or she believes is required is a matter for the solicitor or REL and his or her employer.

> **Comment**
>
> The requirements to consider and undertake learning and development as required by reg.3.1(b) mirror the approach to be taken under the Continuing Competence Scheme when it is introduced on 1 November 2016. However, it is possible that in the period until then while the regulations for the new scheme are being drafted, changes may be made. Until the regulations for the Continuing Competence Scheme from 1 November 2016 are made available, it is therefore not possible to know the full detail of that scheme, other than it will mirror the reg.3.1(b) approach.

The SRA has produced a toolkit, 'New Approach to Continuing Competence' ('SRA Toolkit'), which provides non-mandatory guidance on:

- ways to reflect on one's practice and identify training needs;
- the range of ways in which training needs might be addressed;
- how to record and reflect on training undertaken;
- tools that are available to assist with this process;
- examples of good practice.[29]

Having said that, the SRA also says that the toolkit is not intended to specify how much learning and development a solicitor should do, or the type of activity a solicitor should undertake, since this will depend on the individual solicitor's role, area of practice, clients' needs experience, and learning and development needs.

> **Comment**
>
> The point is that there are no generic requirements under the Continuing Competence approach and that everything really can only be determined by, and according to, the individual solicitor – for which reason the SRA also says that its suggestions may or may not be followed. That is fine except that, under the SRA's principles-based

---

[28] The Q&A is no longer available on the SRA website.
[29] SRA Position Statement, 'Moving Towards a New Approach to Continuing Competence: Information for the Continuing Professional Development (CPD) Year 2014/15', 15 October 2014.

> approach to regulation, if one does not follow non-mandatory guidance, one must be able to show that one has been able to achieve the required outcomes nonetheless.
>
> The SRA also recognises that firms and individuals may have their own existing systems or ideas as to how to ensure their solicitors' and RELs' competence, which by implication firms, individual solicitors and RELs are free to follow. (See **Part D**.)

The SRA Toolkit provides brief case studies of four different types of organisation:

- sole practitioner;
- small firm;
- large firm; and
- 'traditional' law firm

to help solicitors and RELs understand how the Continuing Competence approach works in different contexts.

20.9.2 Suspension of CPD requirements

Under the CPD Scheme, a solicitor may self-suspend from the CPD requirements if, for example, the solicitor is absent from practice on maternity leave. Under the Continuing Competence approach, there is no expectation that the solicitor on maternity leave would need to do training in the same way as under the CPD Scheme. Rather, on returning to work, the solicitor would need to identify any training needs and take appropriate steps to address them. The examples the SRA gives are of updating oneself on the law or brushing up one's skills.

20.9.3 Identify learning and development needs

The SRA's Competence Statement (see **Chapter 21**) is the tool which each solicitor and REL should use to identify whether he or she has learning and development needs.

To identify learning and development involves an element of reflection. The reflection that is required is summarised in the following table.

Definition of reflection

'[C]reating opportunities to step back from one's practice to consider:
- How you think you are performing
- What you think you have learned from your experience
- What you might do differently in the future'[30]

What to reflect on

One's technical skills, soft skills or knowledge in terms of:
- What are my strengths and weaknesses?

---

[30] SRA, Continuing Competence Toolkit, 'How to Reflect'.

- Could I have done that better? If so, what? (And how?)
- Was it related to knowledge, technical skills or 'soft' skills/behaviours? If so, what knowledge, skills or behaviours were lacking?
- In relation to that knowledge, or those skills or behaviours, how would I describe where I am now compared to where I need to be?
- What do I need to do to get to where I need to be?

How to reflect

Identify, in relation to something that is happening or has happened during your work, something that:

- you think you have done well
- you think you could have done better and which you know how to do better next time, or
- you think you could have done better but which you are not sure how to do better next time or that you cannot put right without some work on your own or some external help (note: in this example, you have identified a 'development need')

by

- using appraisal or performance development reviews
- using the SRA Competence Statement (see **Chapter 21**)
- monitoring changes in practice, law and regulation
- reviewing client feedback, client surveys or client complaints
- carrying out file and case reviews
- obtaining feedback from colleagues, managers or clients, whether formal or informal, on one's performance

When to reflect

Regularly, and dedicate an appropriate amount of time to doing so

How regularly?

Looking forward/back over a period of three, six or 12 months and reviewing both your development plan and development record to identify:

- where you think you are as against your development objectives and are you continuing to provide a proper standard of service?
- what you think you need to do to achieve and/or maintain your development objectives and ensure you continue to provide a proper standard of service

How to record reflection

The SRA has a template development plan on its website

This reflection can be at a 'transactional' level, by reflecting on the work that the solicitor is currently doing or has recently completed, or 'at a more general level', such as by considering one's work generally or a particular type of job that one does often.

POST-QUALIFICATION REQUIREMENTS

> **Comment**
>
> This drive to fit training to actual training need is to be commended. However, the problem is that these requirements could have the result of imposing an additional level of bureaucracy, which removing a CPD hours requirement was intended to avoid. In many firms the activities suggested by the SRA are already in place and being used. However, the difference with the Continuing Competence approach is that what was previously implicit, or a case of unconscious competence, becomes explicit and consciously recorded.

20.9.4 Planning learning and development

Having identified one's learning and development needs, the next step is to plan how one can address those needs. The planning that is required is summarised in the following table.

How to plan
- Record how you plan to address the learning and development needs you have identified from your reflection on your practice
- Identify and set priorities according to how urgent and important it is to address your learning and development needs to ensure that you continue to deliver a proper standard of service
- Review that plan regularly

How to record planning

Produce a development plan which captures:
- what you plan to do by way of addressing your learning and development needs over the coming three months/six months/12 months, and
- why you plan to do it (i.e. how important is the activity in meeting your identified learning and development need/s?)

> **Comment**
>
> The Toolkit is 'light' on how to plan one's learning and development needs, other than thinking about:
>
> - what you need to do;
> - why you need to do it;
> - when you need to do it;
> - how you will do it;
> - prioritising your learning and development needs.
>
> The Toolkit's example of what a development plan may include, namely to:
> 'keep up to date with the latest legal, procedural and practice developments by:
>
> - reviewing daily and weekly email updates on an ongoing basis

CONTINUING PROFESSIONAL DEVELOPMENT

- attending monthly team meetings to discuss developments
- attending the 'Legal Update' training sessions delivered by [. . .] twice a year',[31]

could be criticised as not only stating the obvious but turning what happens automatically (unconscious competence) into another layer of unnecessary bureaucracy, particularly if it has to be undertaken at arbitrarily set intervals.

20.9.5 Addressing learning and development needs

The SRA Toolkit states at the outset that:

- any approach to learning and development is valid as long as you can demonstrate it contributes to how you remain competent to deliver a proper standard of service;
- you can tailor learning and development to suit your learning style;
- it is important to turn your learning into doing something differently in your job.

The toolkit also provides a non-exhaustive and non-prescriptive list of various ways learning and development needs may be met.

Comment

The SRA includes:

- 'formal' training;
- in-house training;
- shared learning; and
- 'informal' training

by way of example. These are not mutually exclusive, however: formal training can consist of in-house training or training delivered externally, while shared learning can be effective in both formal and informal training settings.

By 'formal' training, the SRA means face-to-face or online training, whether externally or in-house (the SRA describes 'in-house' training as training which is delivered by individual solicitors, teams or departments within the firm).

Under 'informal' training, the SRA includes:

- Research, reading and discussion:
    - 'general', e.g. reading publications, case reviews, journals, articles, blogs from 'thought leaders', receiving email updates;
    - assigned reading and monthly update meetings;
    - 'targeted', e.g. on a question in a particular case.

---

[31] SRA Toolkit, 'Planning Your Learning and Development'.

- File reviews.
- Speaking to 'colleagues', i.e. people you work with, about a specific knowledge or skill gap.
- Speaking to 'peers', i.e. people external to your organisation to help address gaps or further learning and development.
- Networking, e.g. your own contacts on a one-to-one basis, local, regional or national groups or associations; learning and development networks.
- Observation, particularly for 'behavioural' or 'softer' skills, e.g. communication and relationships with others.
- Mentoring, either formal or informal.
- Coaching.
- Social media, e.g. by following blogs or Twitter accounts.

The SRA describes shared learning as sharing with one's colleagues what one has learnt at the formal training one has attended, and how it can be applied to a colleague's practice area, role, unit or department, e.g. by a formal presentation or informally by email; or proactively contacting a colleague who has attended training to find out what is relevant.

> **Comment**
>
> In the summary section of the SRA Toolkit, the SRA states that 'It is important to turn your learning into doing something differently in your job'.[32] This smacks of change for change's sake: if a solicitor is competent in what he or she does and how he or she does it, does he or she need to do something differently in his or her job?

20.9.6 Recording learning and development activity

Identifying learning and development needs, and then undertaking training to meet those needs is not enough; the SRA also requires solicitors and RELs under the new Continuing Competence approach to keep a record of the activity that they have undertaken to address their learning and development needs. To this end, the SRA recommends in the toolkit that solicitors and RELs keep a development record, which 'contains information that enables you to demonstrate that you have taken appropriate steps to maintain your competence and provide a proper standard of service',[33] such as:

- what you did;
- how it was related to ensuring your competence;
- what you learnt;
- when the activity was completed.

---

[32] SRA, 'A New Approach to Continuing Competence (Toolkit)', p.12.
[33] SRA, 'A New Approach to Continuing Competence (Toolkit)', p.10.

CONTINUING PROFESSIONAL DEVELOPMENT

The SRA does not prescribe how this should be done, since it recognises that there may be existing systems in the firm which a solicitor or REL can use or adapt. However, a template development record is available on the SRA website.

20.9.7 Evaluate the learning and development activity

The SRA believes that 'evaluating your learning and development activity will help you to identify any key points you can introduce into your practice or where further learning and development is required'.[34]

Although the SRA says that the effectiveness of learning and development activity can be evaluated 'by simply thinking about what you have learnt and considering whether it has met your identified need or whether you need to undertake further activity', the SRA actually also wants that evaluation recorded.

The reason for this is so that a solicitor can demonstrate that he or she is addressing his or her learning needs and has taken steps to ensure his or her ongoing competence.

Comment

It is questionable whether it follows that by demonstrating one has taken steps, one is therefore competent, particularly if the actual recording and evaluation becomes perfunctory. Competence is not proved by a training record.

As a general comment, all the components of the Continuing Competence approach in relation to learning and development needs (reflecting, identifying, planning, addressing, evaluating) are all things many solicitors do automatically – unconscious competence. Consequently, embracing the idea of identifying training needs, planning how to meet them, undertaking activity that will meet them, and evaluating how effective the activity was in meeting the need is to be welcomed. The problem is that, instead of a solicitor doing this automatically whenever it is needed, the Continuing Competence regime is regimenting what happens anyway, and with an added level of bureaucracy and additional administration. In so doing, it is adding a burden instead of removing one.

The other problem that follows from this is the extent to which the SRA enforces these requirements. The SRA maintains in the SRA Toolkit that the Continuing Competence approach 'is not a soft option to learning and development' and that 'if after you have reflected, you believe you are competent to provide a proper standard of service, then in principle you do not need to do any learning and development. However, you will need to demonstrate to us, if required, how you arrived at this conclusion'.

The words 'if required' are the key ones: how real in fact is the risk that the SRA will ask to see an individual solicitor's training and development record? The SRA's intention is not to have a formal monitoring procedure, such as by sampling a percentage of CPD records each year. The SRA would probably say that if a solicitor or REL makes the declaration required for practising certificate renewal, while not being able to demonstrate that he or she has ensured that he or she is competent in delivering services to clients, then that solicitor or REL has failed to comply with Principle 5 (and therefore put his or her professional reputation and career at risk).

---

[34] SRA Toolkit, 'Recording and Evaluating Your Learning and Development Activity'.

Be that as it may, if solicitors believe that there is no check on whether they are recording their reflections on the effectiveness of the chat they had next to the kettle with one of their colleagues on an abstruse point of law, they are unlikely to do so. If, however, a firm is not prepared to take the risk that the SRA may monitor and find that its solicitors have not been adhering to the spirit as well as the letter of the Continuing Competence approach, then requiring its solicitors to abide by the letter of the guidance will impose a significant administrative burden. It is also likely to lead to 'template compliance', where templates are developed for the required paperwork so that the analysis, reflection, planning and so on do not need to be undertaken.

Where the Continuing Competence approach will work best is in a firm which already has a culture of regular performance review (such as annual performance appraisals), on which personal development plans are based, which are reviewed at, say, the six-monthly mark to check progress and then at the annual appraisal meeting to review and identify training and development plans for the next period.

If the firm does not already have a culture of reflection, planning and evaluation, not having the processes just described will be the least of its problems.

What the Continuing Competence approach means for firms which do not already have planning and evaluation as part and parcel of their culture is not only a change in approach but significant behavioural change as well. And behavioural change does not happen overnight. So, if that is not the firm's culture, to 'opt-in' before 1 November 2016 could be a recipe for disaster. To put it another way: if your firm has problems in convincing the more senior solicitors, for example, of the need to attend training if for no better reason than to meet the CPD hour requirements, do you really think those same solicitors are going to embrace the Continuing Competence requirements of evidencing that they have reflected on their practice, and against the Competence Statement; that they have identified their training and development needs (would they even accept that they have any?); that they have considered how best to meet those needs, planned the training they are going to undertake to meet those needs, do the training (the fundamental problem they had in the first place) then record what training they have done and, even better, evaluated its effectiveness? Highly unlikely, to put it politely.

It was in recognition of the 'cultural' change that would be required in some firms (to use the SRA Board's words), or what is behavioural change in fact, that the introduction of the Continuing Competence approach when approved by the SRA Board and LSB in 2014 was then delayed until 1 November 2016 for full introduction.

One can gamble on the risk of being monitored by the SRA. However, while there is a risk, no matter how small, if compliance with the requirements of the Continuing Competence approach cannot be demonstrated and evidenced, there will be problems for the firm and its solicitors and RELs alike. So, unless a firm believes its culture chimes with that required for the Continuing Competence approach, and has the disciplines in place through its existing commitment to performance appraisal and training and development, it may be better to spend the time until 1 November 2016 working on changing the culture and putting in place the processes and procedures that will be needed to ensure that both the firm and its solicitors and RELs are able to comply with what is currently reg.3.1(b) and with Principle 5, if it has not started to do so already.

CONTINUING PROFESSIONAL DEVELOPMENT

20.9.8 Considerations for opting in to reg.3.1(b) (Continuing Competence approach) before 1 November 2016

20.9.8.1 Firms

The SRA issued a position statement on 15 October 2014, although not called a position statement but 'Moving Towards a New Approach to Continuing Competence: Information for the Continuing Professional Development (CPD) Year 2014/15', which sets out what the SRA expects from solicitors who choose to adopt the Continuing Competence approach under reg.3.1(b) to comply with their CPD obligations until 1 November 2016.

If a solicitor or REL decides to opt in to the Continuing Competence Scheme prior to 1 November 2016, he or she:

- may do so at any time up to 1 November 2016;
- does not need to advise the SRA that he or she has opted in;
- does not need to complete a pro rata portion of the CPD requirements prior to opting-in;
- will be required to make a declaration when applying for his or her 2016/17 practising certificate that he or she has reflected on his or her practice and addressed and identified learning and development needs.

The SRA expects that 'before deciding whether to adopt the new approach ... solicitors will discuss these changes with their employer, where appropriate, to ensure they can continue to deliver a proper standard of service'.[35]

> **Comment**
>
> The 'they' in the above sentence is somewhat confusing: is it to ensure that the solicitor can continue to deliver a proper standard of service, or that the employer organisation can? Actually, the confusion raises a more important point, which is that obligations under the Continuing Competence Scheme, unlike the CPD Scheme, fall on the organisation (under entity-based regulation) as well as on the individual. Consequently, the SRA expects 'that many employers may make an entity-wide decision about which permitted approach to adopt during the transitional period. Where [a firm does], [the SRA] would expect that the individual solicitor will comply with the preference of their employer'.[36]
>
> So, if a firm does not wish to opt in to the Continuing Competence Scheme prior to 1 November 2016, an individual solicitor in that firm would not be able to either – and vice versa.

---

[35] SRA Position Statement, 'Moving Towards a New Approach to Continuing Competence: Information for the Continuing Professional Development (CPD) Year 2014/15', 15 October 2014, p.1.

[36] SRA, 'Questions and Answers', 28 October 2014, 'I would like to move to the new approach from 1 April 2015, but my firm has said that it will continue with the current CPD Scheme until 1 November 2016. What can I do?'

> In fact, not only does the SRA not require solicitors/RELs who opt in after 1 April 2015 to pro rata their CPD requirements for the 2014/15 CPD year, according to the Q&A the SRA issued on 28 October 2014 on its website in relation to its CRD position statement, the SRA would not 'have any expectation that [a solicitor or REL] will undertake 16 hours of training activity'. In other words, solicitors or RELs who decide to opt in to the Continuing Competence Scheme on or after 1 April 2015 and before 1 November 2015 would be under no obligation to do any of the CPD hours for the period prior to opting in, although they would be required to ensure that they had complied with the Continuing Competence approach to ensure that they were adhering to Principle 5 of the SRA Handbook.
>
> The SRA will permit opt-in right up until 31 October 2016. This is interesting from a pragmatic perspective: why would someone opt in on, say, 31 October or even in the month before, if the new scheme is compulsory for all solicitors or RELs from 1 November? One could speculate that it may be because the individual has not completed the number of CPD hours under reg.3.1(a) by the end of October 2016 and, given the SRA's statement that 'we won't have any expectation that you will undertake 16 hours of training activity' if a solicitor/REL moves to the new approach after 1 April 2015, by opting in a solicitor or REL avoids the problem, because the SRA doesn't have any expectation, and the solicitor or REL does not have to declare that he or she has completed 16 hours of CPD during the 2015/16 CPD year, provided the solicitor or REL is not in breach of Principle 5.
>
> However, what the solicitor or REL in that situation would have to declare in order to renew his or her practising certificate from 1 November 2016 is that he or she has considered his or her learning and development needs and has taken measures to maintain competence for the 2014/15 practising year.
>
> So, if the individual in question has undertaken no training activity during the 2014/15 practising year, that individual will need to be able to demonstrate, if monitored by the SRA (another issue), that he or she had no learning development needs during 2014/15 that required addressing and that, notwithstanding this, he or she was able to maintain competence and provide a proper standard of service to clients in accordance with Principle 5.

20.9.8.2 In-house solicitors

In-house solicitors are in exactly the same position as solicitors and RELs in private practice and have the option to move to Continuing Competence prior to 1 November 2016. However, the SRA regulates the solicitor or REL and not his or her employer in an in-house situation.

> **Comment**
>
> The SRA in fact, in the Q&A it published on its website on 28 October 2014, stated that an in-house solicitor would not have to inform his or her employer about whether he or she has decided to 'move to the new approach', although the in-house solicitor 'would need to be honest about the basis upon which [he or she was] asking for training – i.e. in order to provide a proper standard of service, not in order to comply with a regulatory requirement to do 16 hours CPD per annum'. Unfortunately, the Q&A is no longer available on the SRA website.

> Presumably, the reason for requiring an in-house solicitor to disclose this to his or her employer is so that the employer is not misled into thinking that it must either allow its solicitor employee time to attend training in order to meet a regulatory requirement to undertake 16 hours of CPD activity per year. One would have thought that needing training in order to provide a proper standard of service would be a justifiable reason in its own right, since it underpins the 16-hour CPD requirement implicitly, if not explicitly. However, there is a risk that for the employer, it might raise the question of whether the solicitor employee was providing a proper standard of service previously!

20.10 CONFIRMATION OF COMPLIANCE WITH REQUIREMENTS

The date from which the CPD year runs, 1 November, is also the date for renewal of practising certificates and REL registration. To apply to renew a practising certificate or REL registration, reg.16.1 of the CPD Regulations requires a solicitor or REL to confirm that he or she has complied with the CPD requirements (i.e the requirements as the CPD Regulations apply to the solicitor's or REL's particular circumstances) during the previous, not the immediately preceding, CPD year.

> **Comment**
>
> Many solicitors, if asked, would probably say that they sign the declaration for their practising certificate in relation to the CPD year just gone – that is to say, if they were renewing their practising certificate for the 2016/17 Practising Certificate Year (PCY), they would be making their declaration in relation to the 2015/16 CPD year just finished. However, this is not correct: the declaration has always been for the previous CPD year – for the 2014/15 CPD year in the example above.

Because of the introduction of the Continuing Competence Scheme for all solicitors from 1 November 2016:

- For the 2016 Practising Certificate Renewal Exercise (PCRE), the CPD declaration will relate to PCY 2014/15, and solicitors and RELs who continued to adopt the minimum hours option under reg.3.1(a) will make the usual 16-hour declaration. Solicitors and RELs who adopted the Continuing Competence approach during the 2014/15 CPD year will make a new declaration that 'I have reflected on my practice and addressed and identified learning and development needs'.
- For the 2017 PCRE, the declaration will be altered so that solicitors will be making a declaration relating to the current (rather than previous) PCY, and all solicitors will make the new declaration in respect of the 2016/17 CPD – or rather Continuing Competence – year.

To put it another way:

CPD year	PCRE	Declaration if following reg.3.1(a)	Declaration if following reg.3.1(b)/Continuing Competence regime
2014/15	2017 (i.e. from 1/11/16)	Usual 16-hour declaration	'I have reflected on my practice and addressed and identified learning and development needs'
2015/16	n/a	No declaration required	No declaration required
2016/17	2018 (i.e. from 1/11/17)	n/a	'I have reflected on my practice and addressed and identified learning and development needs'

In other words, the 2015/16 year will not have a declaration of compliance required.

> **Comment**
>
> This is a bit like a leap year but in reverse: the 2015/16 CPD year effectively disappears. The reason given by the SRA for this unusual regulatory 'fix' is that it is in the interests of simplicity in moving to the new Continuing Competence regime. However, solicitors and RELs still have a professional duty to be complying with either reg.3.1(a) or reg.3.1(b) during the 2015/16 CPD year, even if they are not required to make a declaration about this.

> **Comment**
>
> On the basis that the SRA requires compliance with the CPD requirements in order to apply for a practising certificate on 1 November 2016 it will still be necessary to apply for an extension beyond 1 November 2016 if a solicitor or REL has not adopted the Continuing Competence approach under reg.3.1(b) and has not undertaken the full 16 hours required during the 2014/15 CPD year. This will not be necessary for the 2015/16 CPD year, for which the SRA will not require any declaration to be made.

Confirmation of compliance in order to renew one's practising certificate therefore varies according to if and when a solicitor or REL adopts reg.3.1(b) to satisfy his or her CPD requirements.

For solicitors and RELs who adopt the Continuing Competence approach in reg.3.1(b) before 1 November 2016, the declaration they will be asked to make:

- for the 2016 PCRE (for the practising year commencing on 1 November 2015) is that they have considered their learning and development needs and taken measures to maintain their competence for the 2014/15 practising year;
- for the 2017 PCRE (for the practising year commencing on 1 November 2016) is that they have considered their learning and development needs and taken measures to maintain their competence for the 2015/16 practising year.

For solicitors and RELs who 'move to the new approach' after 31 October 2015, the declaration they will be asked to make:

- for the 2016 PCRE (for the practising year commencing on 1 November 2015) is that they have met the current CPD requirements for the 2014/15 practising year; and
- for the 2017 PCRE (for the practising year commencing on 1 November 2016) is that they have considered their learning and development needs and taken measures to maintain their competence for the 2015/16 practising year.

Comment

From 1 November 2016 (i.e. the 2017 PCRE), the declaration of compliance with the CPD – or by then Continuing Competence – requirements will be in respect of the prospective 'CPD' year. This is the opposite of the previous CPD position, which is not only retrospective but in fact relates to the CPD year before the CPD year just ended. This appears inconsistent at first reading: for the CPD Scheme, a solicitor confirms his or her compliance with the CPD requirements for the past CPD year – retrospectively, in other words. This makes sense – to a point – for planning one's training and development needs but not for undertaking them, which at best can be aspirational rather than a confirmation of what has taken place. The reason it only makes sense to a point is because it seems to be based on an assumption that a solicitor or REL will have identified his or her training and development needs prior to the start of the next practising year. This may or may not be the case: the value of a scheme which is not prescriptive as to hours but based on individual need is that it enables the individual to identify training and development needs as and when they arise, which may be during the practising year rather than at the start of it.

The requirement to declare that one has considered one's learning and development needs and taken measures to maintain one's competence for the forthcoming practising year requires consideration.

Under the CPD Scheme what was implicit rather than explicit was that, by undertaking the required CPD year, one assured one's competence and compliance with Principle 5. One would have thought that this would be similar for the Continuing Competence Scheme, namely, that when renewing one's practising certificate for the next practising year one declared that one had considered one's training and development needs during the past practising year and undertaken the necessary training and development activities to ensure one's competence during that practising year. However, this is not what is being required: instead, the SRA requires a declaration on renewing one's practising certificate for the next practising year that one has already considered one's learning and development needs and taken measures to maintain one's competence for the next practising year. This aligns the meeting of training and development needs solely with a guarantee of competence. It does not seem to allow that having a training and development need may not mean that there is any compromise in one's competence. So, if in the next practising year one identifies a training and development need, does that mean that one's declaration of competence for that practising year is flawed? One would hope not. Equally, though, just because one makes a declaration at the point of renewing one's practising certificate that one is competent for the next practising year does not guarantee that that remains the position. There could be a new and important change in the law which, if a solicitor or REL does nothing about it, means that although he or she was competent at the time of making the declaration, he or she does not remain competent during the practising year.

The effectiveness of both reflection to identify learning and development needs, and evaluation of the effectiveness of the training activity undertaken to meet those learning and development needs, are only going to be as good as the self-awareness and self-honesty of the individual. Just because someone is a solicitor does not guarantee the necessary levels of self-awareness and self-honesty – particularly if an individual's development record is to be seen by others in the firm. There is a risk of not wanting to disclose need, if attempts to satisfy a learning and development need have been unsatisfactory. Unless there is a mandatory requirement for training in emotional intelligence, or a firm is able to assist individual solicitors with the necessary reflection, particularly through performance appraisal, mentoring and coaching, then merely writing down on a record that one has reflected and that 'everything seemed to be OK' is no greater guarantee of competence than was undertaking 16 hours of CPD each year.

20.11 SANCTIONS

The SRA expects solicitors to use the Competence Statement (see **Chapter 21**) to identify 'where there may be weaknesses in [their] work which may lead to the delivery of incompetent legal services'.

Where the SRA identifies incompetent legal services and decides to act, it 'will expect solicitors to be able to demonstrate that they have considered their learning and development needs and taken appropriate steps to address them'.[37]

Because of employers' responsibilities to deliver a proper standard of service to clients and train staff to monitor a level of competence appropriate to their work and level of responsibility, the SRA recommends that firms therefore consider the extent to which the recommendations in the toolkit align with the firm's current approach to learning and development so that the firm can continue to meet this obligation.

20.12 PROPOSED CHANGES

From 1 November 2016 the CPD Scheme will be replaced by a new scheme of Continuing Competence. The new Continuing Competence Scheme will be based

---

[37] SRA Toolkit, 'Reflecting on Your Practice: How to Identify Your Learning and Development Needs'.

CONTINUING PROFESSIONAL DEVELOPMENT

on an 'outputs' as opposed to an 'inputs' model, and will not specify the minimum number of hours of CPD activity that an individual solicitor is required to undertake.

At the time of publication, the proposed regulations and details of the new scheme had not been published.

> **Comment**
>
> The SRA's intention is that the CPD Regulations will be repealed from 1 November 2016[38] and removed from the SRA Handbook, which will itself then be amended to reflect the new Continuing Competence approach. Without the regulations for the new Continuing Competence Scheme, it is in fact not possible to know exactly what the requirements of the scheme will be. The intention is that it will mirror the Continuing Competence approach as introduced by new reg.3.1(b) in the CPD Regulations and described in the SRA Toolkit. However, it is conceivable that, until the regulations have been drafted, changes may be introduced and there may be differences to the previews provided by the SRA so far.

20.13 MANAGEMENT COURSE STAGES 1 AND 2

20.13.1 Removal of requirement for MCS1

Prior to 1 April 2015, the SRA required solicitors within their first three CPD years to complete a compulsory management course called Management Course Stage 1 (MCS1). There was also an optional course called Management Course Stage 2 (MCS2).

Following the SRA's consultation, 'Red Tape Initiative – Phase 3: Changes to the SRA's Education and Training Regulations' (see **6.4.3**), the SRA removed the regulatory requirement that solicitors undertake MCS1 within the first three years of qualification, with effect from 1 April 2015. The removal of the requirement to do MCS1 was in fact retrospective and applied to all solicitors whether they qualified before 1 April 2015 and at that date had not satisfied the requirement to undertake MCS1 within their first three CPD years, or after 1 April 2015.

> **Comment**
>
> So, a solicitor who qualified between 31 March 2012 and 31 March 2015, and who had not done MCS1 by 1 April 2015 effectively was given a get-out-of-jail-free card.

The SRA's reasons for doing this included recognition that as a generic course, MCS1 was unlikely to be meeting the needs of any solicitor, and that many firms

---

[38] SRA Principles 2011, Version 15, reg.18.1.

already provide their solicitors with the management skills they need to be competent. The SRA also believed that having a prescriptive requirement to do MCS1 was inconsistent with its new Continuing Competence approach.

It is still open for solicitors to undertake an MCS1 should they wish to and should the course still be offered; similarly MCS2. However, the compulsory requirement has gone.

Comment

Although removing the requirement to attend an MCS1 is probably generally welcomed, it would be unfortunate if firms and solicitors took this as a statement on the need for management training at all. Solicitors do need to develop and have management skills appropriate to their level of experience and role, and firms need to have solicitors who have the skills required to manage themselves, others, the client relationship, finances and the business. So, solicitors who qualified between 31 March 2012 and 31 March 2015 and feel aggrieved that they had done MCS1 by 1 April 2015 should look at it another way: all that the decision to dispense with the compulsory requirement to do MCS1 did was to acknowledge that a generic 'one size fits all' course is not the best way of developing management expertise. In other words, it is not the content *per se* of MCS1 that had been the problem, but the way it was universally imposed. So, at least those solicitors have had an introduction to what are in fact necessary management skills.

From a firm's perspective, whether there is a requirement to do MCS1 or not, a firm still needs its solicitors to be able to manage finance, manage client relationships, manage people, manage information and, ultimately, manage the firm. So, any temptation to toss management training on the bonfire, along with training programmes and training budgets, should be resisted, and instead consideration given to more effective ways of developing the management skills and expertise that MCS1 was intended to do but did not always achieve.

For firms which do not otherwise provide management training to its solicitors, the MCS1, although not perfect, did provide some introduction to management skills, and in the absence of anything else firms would do well to consider still providing training for their junior lawyers in the management skills covered in the MCS1, in the context of their own practice and business needs. Important areas to focus on are:

- managing finance;
- managing the firm;
- managing client relationships;
- managing information; and
- managing people.

Management training is discussed further in **31.3.4**.

20.13.2 Practice Framework Rules, rule 12: Person who must be 'qualified to supervise'

The removal of MCS1 has not affected the requirement under rule 12 of the Practice Framework Rules that solicitors in specified roles or practices must undertake at least 12 hours of management skills training in order to be 'qualified to supervise'.

CHAPTER 21

Competence Statement

21.1 Introduction
21.2 Statement of Solicitor Competence
21.3 Threshold Standard
21.4 Statement of Legal Knowledge
21.5 Proposed changes

21.1 INTRODUCTION

A Competence Statement for solicitors was introduced by the Solicitors Regulation Authority (SRA) on 1 April 2015 to set the standard for practice as a solicitor.

The Competence Statement consists of three parts:

- a Statement of Solicitor Competence;
- a Threshold Standard; and
- a Statement of Legal Knowledge

and is intended to define the standards expected of solicitors at the point of qualification and subsequently.

The SRA has taken a broad definition of competence namely, 'the ability to perform the roles and tasks required by one's job to the expected standard',[1] recognising:

> that requirements and expectations change depending on job role and context [and that] competence develops and that an individual may work competently at many different levels, either at different stages of their career, or indeed from one day to the next depending on the nature of their work.[2]

---

[1] SRA, Statement of Solicitor Competence.
[2] SRA, Statement of Solicitor Competence, p.1.

The notes to Principle 5 in the SRA Handbook were also amended on 1 April 2015 to include a new note: '2.10 For a solicitor, meeting the competencies set out in the Competence Statement forms an integral part of the requirement to provide a proper standard of service'.

The Competence Statement is therefore intended to be 'generic' in the sense that solicitors need to apply it to their particular role, level of experience and area of practice. The aim is that 'it will help them think through whether their work is good enough, and to identify where they need to do some training or other development work'.[3]

21.2 STATEMENT OF SOLICITOR COMPETENCE

The Statement of Solicitor Competence defines the continuing competencies that the SRA requires from all solicitors. The Statement of Solicitor Competence itself is set out at the end of this section.

The SRA does not intend that all solicitors should demonstrate every competency in the Statement of Solicitor Competence; rather, an individual solicitor will need to demonstrate the competencies appropriate to his or her particular role, level of experience and area of practice, and is required to provide a proper level of service to his or her clients. According to the SRA Toolkit, solicitors need to apply the Competence Statement to their practice and practice area in order to:

- identify the competencies that are relevant to what they do;
- identify and address their learning and development needs;
- continue to maintain their knowledge and skills in relation to what they do; and
- continue to maintain knowledge of relevant areas of law, even if they are outside the solicitor's particular practice area.

To quote the SRA:

> The competence statement is an integral part of our new approach to continuing competence. For a solicitor, meeting the competencies set out in the competence statement forms an integral part of the requirement to provide a proper standard of service in accordance with Principle 5 of the SRA Principles (2011).[4]

The SRA Toolkit states that to meet this requirement, a solicitor needs to:

---

[3] SRA website, T4T blog, 'A New Competence Statement for Solicitors', 1 April 2015.
[4] SRA, Statement of Solicitor Competence, 'About the Competence Statement'.

- Apply the Competence Statement to your practice and practice area to identify what is relevant
- Use the Competence Statement to identify and address your learning and development needs
- Continue to maintain your knowledge and skills in relation to your practice and practice area
- Continue to maintain knowledge of those areas of law which are relevant, even if outside your particular practice area.[5]

However, a solicitor is not required to maintain knowledge of law which has no bearing on his or her practice area.

The Competence Statement has two particular practical applications:

- to identify training and development needs under the Continuing Professional Development (CPD) Scheme; and
- to identify what intending solicitors will need to know and be able to do in order to be admitted.

21.2.1 How the Statement of Solicitor Competence should be used

Many firms already have their own competency framework or equivalent. The SRA's Statement of Solicitor Competence is not intended to replace those; rather, the SRA recommends that firms compare their own against the SRA's Competence Statement to identify any 'gaps' in their own competence framework, which they would then need to 'fill'. It is likely, however, that the competencies required by the SRA are present implicitly, if not explicitly, in firms' performance models or competence frameworks. It is really for firms which do not use a competency framework that the SRA's Statement of Solicitor Competence is intended, which those firms can then use for identifying training and development needs under the Continuing Competence approach.

Comment

For firms which do not already have or use a competency framework to underpin appraisals and career development, the way to look at it is that they have just saved themselves a whole lot of consultants' fees to produce one.

What firms and solicitors need to do is to familiarise themselves with the Statement of Solicitor Competence, and then ensure that each solicitor customises the competencies to what he or she does. This is essential if a firm or solicitor has adopted the Continuing Competence approach under reg.3.1(b) to satisfy the CPD requirements (see **Chapter 20**), as it is the Statement of Solicitor Competence against which a solicitor needs to measure the quality of his or her practice.

---

[5] SRA Toolkit, 'Resources'.

The SRA suggests that the Statement of Solicitor Competence may be used either 'as a starting point to develop something new' or 'aligned to existing approaches', and provides a non-exhaustive list of non-mandatory suggestions of ways in which the Statement of Solicitor Competence can be used by individual solicitors and by organisations which employ solicitors. The significance for organisations which employ solicitors and are therefore regulated by the SRA is that those organisations also have a regulatory obligation not only to deliver a proper standard of service to their clients but also to train their staff to maintain a level of competence appropriate to their work and level of responsibility, in accordance with Outcome 7.6 in the SRA Code of Conduct.

Individual solicitor	To reflect on one's practice and ensure ongoing competence by using it as a learning and development tool on a regular basis
Employer organisations	To identify organisational learning and development needs and develop plans to meet these needs by: • integrating Competence Statement into existing performance management systems • introducing a performance management system • integrating into existing competence frameworks • developing a competence framework

To assist, the SRA provides templates of both a development plan and a development record on its website, which are for guidance only and may be used or ignored.

Comment

The SRA Toolkit suggests that firms consider the Statement of Solicitor Competence and how it aligns with their own 'internal competence frameworks, performance development frameworks, appraisal systems and any structured organisational training plans' with a view to achieving an alignment between the two. In fact, the SRA suggests that 'Where gaps are identified, [employers] may wish to consider how [they] reflect the Competence Statement'.

This is not a regulatory requirement and a firm may feel that its own competence framework is superior to the SRA Competence Statement and appropriate for its employees and its business. Given that the SRA describes its Competence Statement as generic and to be applied to individual circumstances, there is no need to adopt the SRA Competence Statement in place of the firm's own; rather, what a firm needs to do is to ensure that the competencies contained in the SRA Competence Statement are present, either explicitly or implicitly, in its own internal competence framework. The reason why this has to be done is because of the amendment to the Guidance Note to Principle 5 which was made on 1 April 2015.

21.2.2 Allowance for disability

The Competence Statement is not absolute, and solicitors with disabilities 'are entitled to reasonable adjustments in the manner in which the competencies in the Competence Statement can be demonstrated'[6] in line with the SRA's Reasonable Adjustment Policy.

Statement of Solicitor Competence[7]

> Solicitors should be able to:
>
> **A Ethics, professionalism and judgement**
>
> A1 Act honestly and with integrity, in accordance with legal and regulatory requirements and the SRA Handbook and Code of Conduct, including
> a. Recognising ethical issues and exercising effective judgement in addressing them
> b. Understanding and applying the ethical concepts which govern their role and behaviour as a lawyer
> c. Identifying the relevant SRA principles and rules of professional conduct and following them
> d. Resisting pressure to condone, ignore or commit unethical behaviour
> e. Respecting diversity and acting fairly and inclusively
>
> A2 Maintain the level of competence and legal knowledge needed to practise effectively, taking into account changes in their role and/or practice context and developments in the law, including
> a. Taking responsibility for personal learning and development
> b. Reflecting on and learning from practice and learning from other people
> c. Accurately evaluating their strengths and limitations in relation to the demands of their work
> d. Maintaining an adequate and up-to-date understanding of relevant law, policy and practice
> e. Adapting practice to address developments in the delivery of legal services
>
> A3 Work within the limits of their competence and the supervision which they need, including
> a. Disclosing when work is beyond their personal capability
> b. Recognising when they have made mistakes or are experiencing difficulties and taking appropriate action
> c. Seeking and making effective use of feedback, guidance and support where needed
> d. Knowing when to seek expert advice
>
> A4 Draw on a sufficient detailed knowledge and understanding of their field(s) of work and role in order to practise effectively, including
> a. Identifying relevant legal principles
> b. Applying legal principles to factual issues, so as to produce a solution

---

[6] SRA, Statement of Solicitor Competence, p.1.
[7] **www.sra.org.uk/solicitors/competence-statement.page**.

which best addresses a client's needs and reflects the client's commercial or personal circumstances
  c. Spotting issues that are outside their expertise and taking appropriate action, using both an awareness of a broad base of legal knowledge[1] (insofar as relevant to their practice area) and detailed knowledge of their practice area

A5 Apply understanding, critical thinking and analysis to solve problems, including
  a. Assessing information to identify key issues and risks
  b. Recognising inconsistencies and gaps in information
  c. Evaluating the quality and reliability of information
  d. Using multiple sources of information to make effective judgements
  e. Reaching reasoned decisions supported by relevant evidence

B   Technical legal practice

B1 Obtain relevant facts, including
  a. Obtaining relevant information through effective use of questioning and active listening
  b. Finding, analysing and assessing documents to extract relevant information
  c. Recognising when additional information is needed
  d. Interpreting and evaluating information obtained
  e. Recording and presenting information accurately and clearly

B2 Undertake legal research, including
  a. Recognising when legal research is required
  b. Using appropriate methods and resources to undertake the research
  c. Identifying, finding and assessing the relevance of sources of law
  d. Interpreting, evaluating and applying the results of the research
  e. Recording and presenting the findings accurately and clearly

B3 Develop and advise on relevant options, strategies and solutions, including
  a. Understanding and assessing a client's commercial and personal circumstances, their needs, objectives, priorities and constraints
  b. Ensuring that advice is informed by appropriate legal and factual analysis and identifies the consequences of different options

B4 Draft documents which are legally effective and accurately reflect the client's instructions, including
  a. Being able to draft documents from scratch as well as making appropriate use of precedents
  b. Addressing all relevant legal and factual issues
  c. Complying with appropriate formalities
  d. Using clear, accurate and succinct language

B5 Undertake effective spoken and written advocacy,[2] including
  a. Preparing effectively by identifying and mastering relevant facts and legal principles
  b. Organising facts to support the argument or position
  c. Presenting a reasoned argument in a clear, logical, succinct and persuasive way
  d. Making appropriate reference to legal authority
  e. Complying with formalities
  f. Dealing with witnesses appropriately

g. Responding effectively to questions or opposing arguments
h. Identifying strengths and weaknesses from different parties' perspectives

B6 Negotiate solutions to clients' issues, including
   a. Identifying all parties' interests, objectives and limits
   b. Developing and formulating best options for meeting parties' objectives
   c. Presenting options for compromise persuasively
   d. Responding to options presented by the other side
   e. Developing compromises between options or parties

B7 Plan, manage and progress legal cases and transactions, including
   a. Applying relevant processes and procedures to progress the matter effectively
   b. Assessing, communicating and managing risk
   c. Bringing the transaction or case to a conclusion

C Working with other people

C1 Communicate clearly and effectively, orally and in writing, including
   a. Ensuring that communication achieves its intended objective
   b. Responding to and addressing individual characteristics effectively and sensitively
   c. Using the most appropriate method and style of communication for the situation and the recipient(s)
   d. Using clear, succinct and accurate language, avoiding unnecessary technical terms
   e. Using formalities appropriate to the context and purpose of the communication
   f. Maintaining the confidentiality and security of communications
   g. Imparting any difficult or unwelcome news clearly and sensitively

C2 Establish and maintain effective and professional relations with clients, including
   a. Treating clients with courtesy and respect
   b. Providing information in a way that clients can understand, taking into account their personal circumstances and any particular vulnerability
   c. Understanding and responding effectively to clients' particular needs, objectives, priorities and constraints
   d. Identifying and taking reasonable steps to meet the particular service needs of all clients, including those in vulnerable circumstances
   e. Identifying possible courses of action and their consequences and assisting clients in reaching a decision
   f. Managing clients' expectations regarding options, the range of possible outcomes, risk and timescales
   g. Agreeing the services that are being provided and a clear basis for charging
   h. Explaining the ethical framework within which the solicitor works
   i. Informing clients in a timely way of key facts and issues including risks, progress towards objectives, and costs
   j. Responding appropriately to clients' concerns and complaints

C3 Establish and maintain effective and professional relations with other people, including
   a. Treating others with courtesy and respect
   b. Delegating tasks when appropriate to do so

c. Supervising the work of others effectively
  d. Keeping colleagues informed of progress of work, including any risks or problems
  e. Acknowledging and engaging with others' expertise when appropriate
  f. Being supportive of colleagues and offering advice and assistance when required
  g. Being clear about expectations
  h. Identifying, selecting and, where appropriate, managing external experts or consultants

D   Managing themselves and their own work

D1 Initiate, plan, prioritise and manage work activities and projects to ensure that they are completed efficiently, on time and to an appropriate standard, both in relation to their own work and work that they lead or supervise, including
  a. Clarifying instructions so as to agree the scope and objectives of the work
  b. Taking into account the availability of resources in initiating work activities
  c. Meeting timescales, resource requirements and budgets
  d. Monitoring, and keeping other people informed of, progress
  e. Dealing effectively with unforeseen circumstances
  f. Paying appropriate attention to detail

D2 Keep, use and maintain accurate, complete and clear records, including
  a. Making effective use of information management systems (whether electronic or hard copy), including storing and retrieving information
  b. Complying with confidentiality, security, data protection and file retention and destruction requirements

D3 Apply good business practice, including
  a. Demonstrating an adequate understanding of the commercial, organisational and financial context in which they work and their role in it
  b. Understanding the contractual basis on which legal services are provided, including where appropriate how to calculate and manage costs and bill clients
  c. Applying the rules of professional conduct to accounting and financial matters
  d. Managing available resources and using them efficiently

Notes

1. Legal System of England and Wales, constitutional law and EU law (including human rights), contract law, torts, ethics, professional conduct and regulation, including money laundering and solicitors' accounts, criminal law and evidence, criminal litigation, civil litigation, property law, wills and administration of estates, trusts and equitable wrongs, law of and taxation, and other areas relevant to the solicitor's particular field of practice
2. Note this applies to advocacy both in and out of court.

21.3   THRESHOLD STANDARD

The Threshold Standard sets the level at which a solicitor at the point of qualification should be able to perform the competencies in the Statement of Solicitor

Competence. In other words, a solicitor on qualification is not expected to have the same level of knowledge and competence as a solicitor who is many years qualified.

Unlike the Statement of Solicitor Competence, which must be used by all solicitors and Registered European Lawyers (RELs) who adopt the Continuing Competence approach in reg.3.1(b) to fulfil their CPD obligations under the SRA Training Regulations 2011 Part 3 – CPD Regulations (CPD Regulations'), the Statement of Solicitor Competence and Threshold Standard are not yet being used for determining admission, and admission continues to be governed by the SRA Training Regulations 2014 – Qualification and Provider Regulations ('Qualification and Provider Regulations') until further notice.

The Threshold Standard sets out various levels for performing the competencies in the Competence Statement. The level at which a solicitor at the point of qualification should be able to perform the competencies is Level 3, which is set out below.

Level 3

Threshold Standard required at qualification.

Functioning knowledge

Identifies the legal principles relevant to the area of practice, and applies them appropriately and effectively to individual cases.

Standard of work

Acceptable standard achieved routinely for straightforward tasks. Complex tasks may lack refinement.

Autonomy

Achieves most tasks and able to progress legal matters using own judgement, recognising when support is needed.

Complexity

Able to deal with straightforward transactions, including occasional, unfamiliar tasks which present a range of problems and choices.

Perception of context

Understands the significance of individual actions in the context of the objectives of the transaction/strategy for the case.

Innovation and originality

Uses experience to check information provided and to form judgements about possible courses of action and ways forward.

21.4 STATEMENT OF LEGAL KNOWLEDGE

The Statement of Legal Knowledge specifies the knowledge that solicitors are required to demonstrate at the point of qualification, as well as the skills and knowledge which solicitors are intended to maintain throughout their practising career.

The Statement of Legal Knowledge may come as something of a shock. However, before allowing panic to set in, it is not expected that a solicitor will have all the knowledge outcomes; rather, the SRA states that it does not require solicitors to maintain knowledge of law that has no bearing on their practice area, although it does expect solicitors to maintain knowledge of areas of law which, although outside their particular practice area, are relevant – so-called 'peripheral' knowledge.

So, again, it is a case of identifying at the individual solicitor level what knowledge they would be expected to have for their particular practice area and at their level of experience.

> **Comment**
>
> What a firm can do is to identify the relevant, generic knowledge outcomes for each practice area, and levels of knowledge indicated according to levels of experience rather than for each individual solicitor in the firm, unless of course an individual solicitor has a 'unique' practice in the firm.

The SRA also does not expect solicitors to retain all knowledge that they are expected to have on qualification, for the rest of their careers.

> **Comment**
>
> Another use for the Statement of Legal Knowledge is to inform the training providers' curricula for the Qualifying Law Degree (QLD), Common Professional Examination/ Graduate Diploma in Law (CPE/GDL) and Legal Practice Course (LPC) – assuming, of course, that any or all of those continue to be required for admission (see **21.5**).

The Statement of Legal Knowledge is set out below.

1. **Ethics, professional conduct and regulation, including money laundering and solicitors' accounts**
   1a. The ethical concepts governing the solicitor's role and behaviour, including as expressed in the law, and the economic, social and cultural influences that can bias independent and ethical judgement
   1b. The SRA Principles
   1c. The Code of Conduct:
   - commitment to the rule of law and proper administration of justice

- duties and responsibilities owed to clients
- running the business
- interacting with the regulator
- duties to others

1d. Money laundering
1e. Financial services
1f. Solicitors' accounts
- identification of office/client money
- receipts into and payments out of office and client account/money
- payment of deposit interest
- accounting systems and internal controls
- recording transactions and preparation of financial statements
- regulatory controls

1g. Obligations to report relevant to a solicitor's practice

2. Wills and administration of estates

2a. Pre-grant practice
- validity, revocation and alteration of wills and codicils
- total and partial intestacy
- identification of property passing by will, intestacy or outside of the estate
- valuation of assets and liabilities and the taxable estate

2b. Application for a grant of representation
- the necessity for and main types of a grant
- the powers and duties of personal representatives and their protection
- the main types of oath for executors or administrators
- the prior submission of inheritance tax account to HMRC before grant is obtained and payment of tax shown due on account

2c. Post-grant practice
- collection and realisation of assets, and claims on the estate
- raising funds and the payment of all tax and debts
- pecuniary legacies, vesting of gifted property in the beneficiaries entitled and distribution of the residuary estate

3. Taxation

3a. Income tax
- who is chargeable (residence/domicile)
- what is chargeable (types of income/main reliefs and exemptions)
- how is charge levied (deduction at source/PAYE/self-assessment)
- outline of anti-avoidance provisions

3b. Capital gains tax
- who is chargeable (residence/domicile)
- what is chargeable (calculation of gains/allowable deductions/main reliefs and exemptions)
- how is charge levied (self-assessment/recovery through PAYE system/ agents)
- outline of anti-avoidance provisions

3c. Inheritance tax
Key principles
- basis of charge to tax (potentially exempt gifts/lifetime chargeable gifts/ transfers on death)
- main exemptions/reliefs

POST-QUALIFICATION REQUIREMENTS

- outline of anti-avoidance provisions (reservation of benefit regime, restrictions on deductibility of certain debts/encumbrances)
- person liable to make returns and payment

3d. Corporation tax
Key principles
- chargeability to corporation tax
- tax treatment of company distributions or deemed distributions to shareholders
- payment and collection of tax (self-assessment)
- outline of anti-avoidance legislation

3e. Value added tax
- key principles relating to scope, supply, input and output tax
- registration requirements and issue of VAT invoices
- returns/payment of VAT and record keeping

4. Law of organisations

4a. Business and organisational structures
4b. Legal personality and limited liability
4c. Procedures required to incorporate a company/form a partnership/LLP and the approvals and other steps required under companies and partnerships legislation to enable the entity to commence operating
4d. Corporate governance
- rights, duties and powers of directors and shareholders of companies
- procedures relating to company decision making and meetings
- minority shareholder protection rights

4e. Raising capital, including company borrowing
4f. Insolvency (corporate and personal insolvency)

5. Property

5a. Key concepts of real property
5b. The property legislation of 1925; registered and unregistered land; Land Registration Act 2002
5c. Estates and interests in land and their transfer: freeholds, leases, mortgages, easements; and rights over land: licences, tenancies at will
5d. The trust of land and co-ownership
5e. Adverse possession
5f. The landlord/tenant relationship; leasehold covenants; enfranchisement
5g. Real property and human rights
5h. Tax considerations relevant to property transactions

6. Torts

6a. Negligence:
- duty of care and breach of duty of care
- causation and remoteness of damage
- problematic areas, including pure economic loss and psychiatric illness damage

6b. Breach of statutory duty and product liability
6c. Nuisance, and the rule in *Rylands* v *Fletcher*
6d. Trespass to the person
6e. Defamation
6f. Vicarious liability
6g. Remedies, including damages and injunctions

6h. Defences, including consent and contributory negligence

7. Criminal law and evidence

7a. Elements of offences – *actus reus* and *mens rea*. Factors affecting culpability: e.g. insanity, automatism and intoxication. Capacity to commit offences
7b. Modes of liability: secondary participation, vicarious and corporate liability
7c. Specific offences: public order offences, fatal, non-fatal and sexual offences against the person, property offences
7d. Inchoate offences: assisting and encouraging crime, attempt and conspiracy
7e. Defences: self-defence, necessity, duress. Partial defences to murder: loss of control, diminished responsibility
7f. Evidence, including burden and standard of proof, bad character and hearsay
7g. The European Convention of Human Rights, particularly articles 5 and 6

8. Criminal litigation

8a. Criminal Procedure Rules, their overriding objective, and their application
8b. Pre-trial procedures, including plea before venue and allocation
8c. The role of the defendant's representative in police stations both as own client and as duty solicitor and the role of the defendant's solicitor at court under the duty solicitor scheme
8d. Custody, review and detention limits under PACE and the role of the custody officer
8e. Key steps for making an application for a representation order
8f. Key steps for making or contesting a bail application
8g. The trial process
8h. Sentencing
8i. Appeals

9. Contract law

9a. Formation, including offer and acceptance, consideration, intention to create legal relations, certainty
9b. Variation and promissory estoppel
9c. Privity of contract and rights of third parties
9d. Terms, including terms implied by common law and statute
9e. Interpretation of contracts
9f. Exemption clauses and unfair terms
9g. Vitiating factors: including mistake, misrepresentation, duress and undue influence
9h. Termination of contract for breach or frustration
9i. Remedies: damages, award of an agreed sum, specific performance, injunctions
9j. Restitution for unjust enrichment (especially in the context of termination of a contract)

10. Trusts and equitable wrongs

10a. Difference between legal and equitable interests
10b. Creation of express trusts
10c. Resulting trusts
10d. Constructive trusts
10e. Charitable and non-charitable purpose trusts
10f. Trustees: their appointment, removal, powers, duties and liabilities
10g. Fiduciary duties and remedies for breach of these duties

10h. Knowing receipt of trust property and dishonest assistance in breach of trust or fiduciary duty
10i. The rights, remedies and powers of beneficiaries, including proprietary remedies after tracing
10j. Equitable remedies: specific performance, injunctions, rescission, rectification and proprietary remedies

11. Constitutional law and EU law (including human rights)

11a. The basic institutions (the Crown and Parliament, central government, devolved institutions, EU institutions and the judiciary) and principles of the British Constitution
11b. The nature, status and procedure for passing primary and delegated legislation
11c. Government accountability (and in particular the relationship between the Government and Parliament)
11d. Parliamentary sovereignty
11e. Separation of powers (including judicial independence)
11f. The rule of law
11g. The place of EU law in the constitution
11h. Human Rights Act 1998 and key principles of anti-discrimination legislation
11i. Judicial control of the Executive, in particular the process and principles of judicial review

12. Legal system of England and Wales

12a. The main legal institutions (including the main legal professions)
12b. Sources of law:
- legislation
- case law
- European context

12c. Rules of interpretation
12d. Legal services
12e. Funding of legal services

13. Civil litigation

13a. Different options for dispute resolution: litigation, arbitration, mediation and other forms of alternative dispute resolution
13b. Funding
13c. Costs consequences, possible liability for costs and cost recoveries
13d. Preliminary considerations: limitation, jurisdiction and applicable law
13e. The Civil Procedure rules, including Practice Directions, Forms and Court Guides
13f. Pre-action steps, court structure and choice of court, issue, service, acknowledgment of service, judgments in default and summary judgment, drafting and service of statements of case, disclosure, part 36 and other settlement offers, interim applications and interim remedies, preparing for trial, settlement
13g. The court's case and costs management powers and duties
13h. Evidence: expert witnesses and witnesses of fact
13i. Key elements of trial procedure
13j. Methods of enforcement and enforcement procedures
13k. Rights of appeal and appeal procedures

21.5 PROPOSED CHANGES

The SRA issued a consultation document in December 2015, 'Training for Tomorrow: Assessing Competence' (see **6.4.6**), setting out a new assessment framework for admission. This would consist of a centralised assessment of competence, called the Solicitors Qualifying Examination (SQE), aligned to the Statement of Solicitor Competence, Statement of Legal Knowledge and Threshold Standard.[8] The SRA has therefore warned that the Competence Statement will be kept under review as the assessment framework is developed, should the proposal for the SQE be adopted (the SRA's decision is due in June 2016), and there may therefore be changes to the Statement of Solicitor Competence.

> **Comment**
>
> If the SQE is introduced, it would not be before the start of the academic year 2018/19, and until then the Competence Statement, in the collective sense, as published on 1 April 2015 should continue to be used for CPD by solicitors who have adopted reg.3.1(b) to satisfy the requirements of the CPD Regulations until 1 November 2016.

For the purposes of determining admission eligibility until then, admission continues to be based on the requirements in the Qualification and Provider Regulations.

If the SRA does decide to introduce the SQE, the SRA will consult on the entry requirements for the SQE at the end of 2016, which may require new regulations. According to the 'Training for Tomorrow: Assessing Competence' consultation document, if new regulations were introduced during 2018, admission based on the existing requirements in the Qualification and Provider Regulations would cease at the end of the academic year 2025/16.

---

[8] SRA Consultation 'Training for Tomorrow: Assessing Competence', 7 December 2015, p.8.

PART C

Other qualified lawyer qualification requirements

This section sets out the qualification requirements for:

- Barristers (**Chapter 23**)
- Chartered Legal Executives (**Chapter 24**)
- Licensed conveyancers (**Chapter 25**)
- Intellectual property practitioners – patent attorneys and trade mark attorneys (**Chapter 26**)
- Notaries (**Chapter 27**)
- Costs lawyers (**Chapter 28**)

Although the focus of this book is on solicitors, with the licensing of Alternative Business Structures a legal services provider which is licensed by the Solicitors Regulation Authority (SRA) may employ – or even have as an owner – non-solicitors. The potential that comes from being able to offer a wider range of services or provide a wider, or more specialist, range of expertise than that of just the solicitor, is attractive to many firms. To this end, it may help a firm which is considering employing, or has employed, a non-solicitor lawyer to understand:

- what the qualification brings to the business; and
- what ongoing costs, overheads or investment will be required to ensure the business continues to benefit from the individual's qualification.

If a firm is recruiting, say, a licensed conveyancer, it helps to know what level of expertise is assured by the qualification; equally, in recruiting a patent attorney, it is important to know what he or she is permitted to do under his or her qualification, and whether there are ongoing costs involved in maintaining the licensed conveyancer or patent attorney qualification, such as practising certificates or ongoing Continuing Professional Development (CPD) obligations.

It is also important to know what the regulatory standards of professional conduct are which the individual must adhere to, and how regulation by his or her own regulator will fit with regulation by the SRA.

Chapter 22 explains the context of non-solicitor lawyers employed by SRA-regulated/licensed firms, and provides comparisons of some of the important features of the various qualifications.

OTHER QUALIFIED LAWYER QUALIFICATION REQUIREMENTS

The remaining chapters summarise in respect of each qualification:

- what distinguishes the qualification from that of solicitors;
- what the qualification permits the lawyer to do, including reserved and regulated activities;
- how the qualification is regulated and represented, and by which body;
- the requirements for obtaining the qualification, including training and admission requirements;
- CPD and other ongoing training requirements;
- the costs involved, both in obtaining and maintaining the qualification;
- the professional conduct obligations.

Because qualification as a Chartered Legal Executive also provides a route to qualification as a solicitor, and Chartered Legal Executives often qualify while in employment in law firms, further detail is provided in **Chapter 24** on the requirements:

- for qualification as a Chartered Legal Executive; and
- for qualification as a solicitor.

Chapter 26 deals with both patent attorneys and trade mark attorneys under the generic title 'Intellectual property practitioners', because both share a common regulator.

The Sources sections at the end of **Chapters 23–28** in Part C provide the website links, should further information be required.

CHAPTER 22

Lawyers under the Legal Services Act 2007

22.1   Introduction

22.1 INTRODUCTION

Before the Legal Services Act 2007 (LSA 2007) word, the label of 'lawyer' conjured up pictures of solicitors or barristers. Nor was the term 'legal services provider' bandied around very much, if at all. Following LSA 2007, that has all changed, not least because LSA 2007 widened the ambit of the qualified lawyer. Those regulators listed in LSA 2007, Sch.4, Pt.1 as 'approved regulators' were given powers under s.20(6) to 'authorise persons to carry on an activity which is a reserved legal activity, in respect of which it is a relevant approved regulator'.

These Approved Regulators listed in Sch.4, Pt.1, and the 'Authorised Persons' they regulate are set out in the table below.

Existing Approved Regulator	Authorised Person
The Law Society	Solicitors
The General Council of the Bar	Barristers
The Master of the Faculties	Notaries
The Institute of Legal Executives	Chartered Legal Executives
The Council for Licensed Conveyancers	Licensed conveyancers
The Chartered Institute of Patent Attorneys	Patent attorneys
The Institute of Trade Mark Attorneys	Trade mark attorneys
The Association of Law Costs Draftsmen	Law costs draftsmen (re-named 'Costs lawyers')

Since the Act, six of the eight Approved Regulators have delegated their regulatory functions to an independent regulatory body, with the Approved Regulator retaining a representative role as is the case with the Law Society in respect of solicitors.

The Approved Regulators which have not delegated their regulatory functions are the Council of Licensed Conveyancers and the Master of the Faculties Office of the Archbishop of Canterbury, neither of which had a combined regulatory and representative function to begin with. The Chartered Institute of Patent Attorneys and the Institute of Trade Mark Attorneys, however, have adopted a common regulator.

The separation of regulatory and representative powers for each type of Authorised Person is illustrated in the following table.

	Approved Regulator	Independent regulatory body
Solicitor	The Law Society of England and Wales	Solicitors Regulation Authority (SRA)
Barrister	Bar Council	Bar Standards Board (BSB)
Chartered Legal Executive	Chartered Institute of Legal Executives (CILEx)	CILEx Regulation
Licensed conveyancer	Council for Licensed Conveyancers	
Patent attorney	Chartered Institute of Patent Attorneys	Intellectual Property Regulation Board
Trade mark attorney	Institute of Trade Mark Attorneys	
Costs lawyer	Association of Costs Lawyers	Costs Lawyer Standards Board
Notary	Master of the Faculties	

So, an Alternative Business Structure (ABS) which employs Authorised Persons under more than one of the Approved Regulators has in fact a choice as to the regulator by which it would prefer to be regulated.

For SRA-regulated firms and ABSs, the SRA's entity-based approach to regulation means that the firm or ABS must ensure that all the Authorised Persons it employs have met, and continue to meet, the requirements for their particular authorisation, and that they offer legal services within their authorisation, subject also to requirements for supervision, and that all receive the necessary training and development to assure their ongoing competence.

This places a considerable management, not to mention administrative, responsibility on a firm which employs non-solicitor qualified lawyers, as well as solicitors, which is why it is important for the firm to understand the extent of an individual lawyer's authorisation, and to be aware of the sanctions should the authorisation requirements fail to be met. For instance, a firm or ABS authorised/licensed by the

SRA would be in breach of Principle 7 to 'comply with your legal and regulatory obligations and deal with your regulators and ombudsmen in an open, timely and co-operative manner', and would risk breaching Principle 5 of the SRA Handbook to 'provide a proper standard of service to your clients' should it not ensure that its non-solicitor managers and employers were meeting the regulatory requirements for their qualification.

CHAPTER 23

Barristers

23.1	What is a barrister?	23.6	Ongoing CPD and other training obligations for barristers
23.2	What a barrister does and is permitted to do	23.7	Costs of maintaining the qualification
23.3	Regulation of barristers	23.8	Professional conduct requirements
23.4	The barrister qualification	23.9	Proposed changes
23.5	Maintaining qualification as a barrister	23.10	Source

23.1 WHAT IS A BARRISTER?

A practising barrister[1] holds a full qualification certificate and a current full practising certificate from the Bar Standards Board (BSB).

The General Council of the Bar ('Bar Council') describes barristers as lawyers who 'provide specialist legal advice and represent their clients in courts and tribunals'.[2] Barristers are referred work by solicitors or other professionals. However, members of the public are also able to instruct a barrister directly for advice or representation under what is called 'Public Access'.

A senior barrister may be made a Queen's Counsel as a mark of outstanding ability.

23.1.1 Self-employed barrister

The majority of barristers are self-employed and belong to a set of chambers, not as joint owners of the business as partners in a solicitors' firm, but as sole practitioners for the purpose of sharing overheads.

---

[1] A barrister may be unregistered and non-practising.
[2] Bar Council website, 'The Bar Council', 25 March 2015.

23.1.2 Employed barrister

Barristers may also be employed, as opposed to self-employed, and work in-house for an employer, and provide legal services for their employers only. They may be employed in specialist legal departments in industry and commerce, central or local government, or in a solicitors' firm, where they work only for the firm's clients.

It is also possible for a barrister to be both self-employed and employed.

23.2 WHAT A BARRISTER DOES AND IS PERMITTED TO DO

The Bar Council describes the typical work of a barrister as to:

- advise their clients on the law and the strength of their legal case. This often requires considerable amounts of legal research, followed by writing an 'opinion' for the client in which the barrister sets out their advice;
- hold 'conferences' with clients to discuss their case and give them legal advice;
- represent their clients in court. This can include presenting the case, cross-examining witnesses, summing up all relevant material and giving reasons why the court should support their client's case; and
- negotiate settlements with the other side.[3]

Barristers differ from solicitors in that a member of the public would usually go to a solicitor first with a legal problem, and a solicitor would refer work to a barrister if the solicitor felt that specialist advice were needed or if the client needed to be represented in court and the solicitor does not have the expertise or rights of audience.

A barrister is authorised to undertake the following reserved legal activities.

Exercise of a right of audience	Yes
Conduct of litigation	Yes – subject to application
Reserved instrument activities	Yes
Probate activities	Yes
Administration of oaths	Yes
Notarial activities	No

Unlike solicitors, a barrister has rights of audience in all proceedings in all courts of England and Wales.

Traditionally, solicitors had the conduct of litigation; not barristers. However, it is now possible for a barrister to extend his or her practising rights to the conduct of litigation and have this added to his or her practising certificate.

---
[3] Bar Council website, 'The Bar Council', 25 March 2015.

23.3 REGULATION OF BARRISTERS

The Bar Council is the Approved Regulator under the Legal Services Act 2007 (LSA 2007) for barristers in England and Wales. The Bar Council discharges its regulatory functions through the independent BSB in the same way the Law Society discharges its regulatory functions through the Solicitors Regulation Authority (SRA), in line with the requirements of LSA 2007 to separate regulatory and representative functions.

However, unlike the situation with solicitors, admission to the Bar is exclusively regulated by the Inns of Court: the Honourable Societies of Inner Temple, Gray's Inn, Lincoln's Inn and Middle Temple.

23.4 THE BARRISTER QUALIFICATION

To qualify as a barrister requires completion of three stages of training, as summarised in the table below.

Stage	Level of qualification achieved	Required course/training/ employment	Terminology
Academic stage		QLD/CPE	
Vocational stage	Pre-qualification	BCAT Inn membership BPTC	**Student**
	Admission	Call to the Bar	**Barrister-at-law**
Professional stage		Pupillage first six: non-practising period	**Pupil barrister**
	Provisional qualification	Pupillage second six: practising period Provisional practising certificate	**Pupil barrister**
	Qualification	Tenancy	**Tenant**

23.4.1 Academic stage

The academic stage requirements are the same as for solicitors, namely completion of a Qualifying Law Degree (QLD) (see **Chapter 12**) or the Common Professional Examination (CPE) (see **Chapter 13**). (The CILEx qualification is not recognised by the BSB as meeting academic stage requirements.)

23.4.2 Vocational stage

The vocational stage involves completion of the Bar Professional Training Course (BPTC), as well as membership of one of the Inns of Court and completion of a required number of qualifying sessions. It is following completion of the vocational stage that a barrister is eligible to be 'called' to the Bar.

The purpose of the BPTC is 'to ensure that students intending to become barristers acquire the skills, knowledge of procedure and evidence, attitudes and competence to prepare them, in particular, for the more specialised training in the twelve months of pupillage'.[4] The BPTC involves study of the following subjects:

- Knowledge areas:
    - civil litigation, evidence and remedies;
    - criminal litigation, evidence and sentencing;
    - professional ethics.
- Skills areas:
    - advocacy
    - opinion writing
    - drafting
    - conferencing
    - resolution of disputes out of court (including negotiation, mediation and arbitration).
- Options:
    - Two option subjects (depending on provider – student to select).

23.4.3 Professional stage

A barrister must complete a pupillage in order to obtain a full practising certificate and obtain tenancy in a set of barristers' chambers as a self-employed barrister, or go into practice as an employed barrister.

Pupillage is on-the-job training under the supervision of an experienced barrister or barristers, similar to but not the same as the Period of Recognised Training (PRT) for solicitors, and can be undertaken in barristers' chambers or in another organisation which has been approved by the BSB as an Approved Training Organisation (ATO). Pupillage is in two parts:

- A 'first six', also called the 'non-practising period', is six months during which pupils shadow their pupil supervisor and may not accept professional instructions except for noting briefs if permitted by their pupil supervisor. During this time, a pupil is required to complete an Advocacy Training Course.

---

[4] BSB website, 'Qualifying as a Barrister'.

- A 'second six', which is also called the 'practising period', is a further six months during which pupils can accept instructions on their own account under supervision and with permission. During the 'second six', a pupil is also required to complete a practice management course.

A barrister will also have completed a forensic accountancy course either during pupillage or within three years of starting to practise.

Any organisation may be authorised by the BSB as an ATO if it meets the BSB's requirements, and is required to pay pupils a minimum of £1,000 per month during each of the first six and second six.

23.4.4 Qualification and admission

A barrister is entitled to exercise rights of audience in the superior courts of England and Wales once called to the Bar.

A pupil barrister is issued with a provisional qualification certificate and a provisional practising certificate once the first six of pupillage has been completed. A full practising certificate is only issued at the end of the second six, which is also when a barrister is entitled to commence practice, and to enter into independent practice as a tenant (which means first obtaining tenancy in a set of chambers) or a squatter (where the barrister does not have tenancy but makes use of chambers' premises and pays rent, without belonging to the set of chambers. This is also known as a 'third six pupillage').

23.5 MAINTAINING QUALIFICATION AS A BARRISTER

A barrister is required to renew his or her practising certificate on an annual basis, which is called the Authorisation to Practise (ATP) process. This is done online through Barrister Connect, and the process requires a barrister to:

- update his or her insurance information;
- make a declaration of truth;
- verify Continuing Professional Development (CPD) requirements;
- declare the appropriate income band for the purposes of setting the appropriate fee;
- select optional fees;
- update any personal details;
- pay the appropriate fee.[5]

The requirements for maintaining qualification as a barrister are summarised in the table below.

---

[5] BSB, 'Authorisation to Practise (ATP) Process Guidance 2015'.

Practising certificate year	1 April to 31 March, inclusive
Process	Online or paper based
Fees payable	Practising certificate and other compulsory discretionary and optional fees (see **23.7**)
Consequence of failure to renew/pay	• If not renewed by 1 April: a barrister may incur a surcharge of 20% of the practising certificate fee (PCF) • If not renewed by 30 April: a barrister will not be listed on the BSB's Barristers' Register and will not be authorised to practise *Note: Offering legal services without a practising certificate is a criminal offence and a breach of the Code of Conduct*

23.6 ONGOING CPD AND OTHER TRAINING OBLIGATIONS FOR BARRISTERS

23.6.1 CPD requirements

All barristers are required to complete CPD in accordance with the requirements of the CPD Rules in the BSB Handbook, Pt.4.

The BSB defines CPD as:

> work undertaken over and above the normal commitments of barristers with a view to such work developing their skills, knowledge and professional standards in areas relevant to their present or proposed area of practice, and in order to keep themselves up to date and maintain the highest standards of professional practice.[6]

The requirements relating to CPD are summarised in the following table.

Authority	BSB Extensions and waivers: CPD Panel of the Qualifications Committee
Governing regulations	Continuing Professional Development Regulations
CPD hours	CPD hours spent in either seminars or lectures, added up and rounded down to the nearest half an hour and do not include registration, refreshment and lunch breaks *Note: Each course, seminar, lecture or other training event must be treated individually and not amalgamated with other CPD activities, with the total number rounded down*
CPD year	Calendar year (i.e. 1 January to 31 December)

---

[6] Bar Standards Board, 'Continuing Professional Development', February 2015.

OTHER QUALIFIED LAWYER QUALIFICATION REQUIREMENTS

'Accredited hours'	CPD hours accrued by undertaking attendance-based or online courses, conferences, lectures or seminars which are delivered by CPD providers accredited by the BSB
	The Inns are now also able to accredit their own CPD
Minimum CPD points required	New Practitioners' Programme: 45 hours of CPD over 3 years, including:
	• 9 hours of Advocacy Training
	• 3 hours of Ethics
	Established Practitioners' Programme: 12 hours of CPD per year
Carry-over of CPD points	Not permitted
Reduction of minimum CPD points requirement	• If admitted during CPD year, one CPD hour for each month or part month in practice
	• If maternity leave or other pro rata reduction in CPD hours if practising certificate suspended
Providers	Accredited providers. Non-accredited providers may be granted 'one-off' accreditation
Reduction for part-time working	No
Requirement to keep record of CPD	Requirement to maintain an up-to-date CPD record card, prescribed by BSB. CPD record card must be completed and signed, and kept for 6 years
Consequences of failure to comply with CPD requirements	Possible referral to the Professional Conduct Committee for breach of the BSB Handbook. The Committee may impose penalties for failure to comply or may require 'Corrective Action to regularise [the barrister's] CPD position'
Monitoring by BSB of compliance with CPD requirements	Random spot checks of barristers' CPD record cards
Responsibility for compliance with CPD requirements	Individual barrister
Obligation on employer to fund CPD activities	No
Obligation on employer to allow time-off for CPD activities	No
Requirements for eligible CPD	Whether accredited or unaccredited, CPD must be relevant to a barrister's present or proposed area/s of practice and must satisfy the BSB's CPD definition
Accreditation	New Practitioners' Programme: Training must be BSB-accredited
	Established Practitioners' Programme: 4 hours each year must be BSB-accredited

The calculation of CPD hours for the different types of CPD activities are set out in the BSB's 'Compliance with CPD Regulations – A General Guide to CPD'.

The amount and type of CPD required depends on the level of qualification of the barrister:

- barristers within the first three years of practice are subject to the 'New Practitioners' Programme';
- barristers more than three years qualified are subject to the 'Established Practitioners' Programme'.

23.6.1.1 New Practitioners' Programme

The New Practitioners' Programme (NPP) requires 45 hours of CPD to be undertaken during the three years from 1 January following commencement of practice, namely from commencement of tenancy, squatting, a third six or from the date of employment if in employed practice, subject to holding a practising certificate. A barrister is also able to start accruing CPD from the date he or she commenced practice, i.e. in the period from issue of a full qualification certificate, up to 1 January of the next CPD year.

For training to count as CPD under the NPP, the training must be undertaken with BSB-accredited CPD providers, and the BSB maintains a CPD courses database on its website, on which accredited CPD providers can list their courses.

If the training undertaken is not provided by a BSB-accredited trainer, it can only qualify for CPD under the NPP if the barrister submits an application to the BSB for 'one-off' CPD accreditation. The application fee is £45 per event and needs to be made at least two weeks before the event.

During the NPP, a barrister must also undertake specified advocacy training and ethics training. The specified ethics training is provided by the Inns and Circuits exclusively, while advocacy training is also offered by the Crown Prosecution Service and National Institute of Trial Advocacy (UK), in addition to the Inns and Circuits.

23.6.1.2 Established Practitioners' Programme

The Established Practitioners' Programme (EPP) applies to all practising barristers who have completed the first three years of practice. Although at least four hours must be accredited by the BSB, the remaining hours may be acquired through unaccredited CPD.

Unaccredited courses can include lectures and seminars given by solicitors' firms and do not require one-off accreditation. The only restriction is that they can only count for up to eight hours of the CPD requirement.

23.6.2 Monitoring and enforcement

The BSB has ceased the practice of requiring barristers to submit their CPD records to the BSB annually, and instead has instigated spot checks. If a barrister is selected for a spot check, he or she will need to provide evidence of completion of his or her CPD hours, in addition to his or her CPD record card. The BSB states that it is 'flexible about the types of evidence that can be submitted' and provides a non-exhaustive list of acceptable evidence.

If it is not possible to verify completion – for example, with online courses – the BSB will accept a barrister's declaration of completion.[7]

Any practising barrister who undertakes CPD through the EPP may be randomly selected for a spot check. However, barristers who have a recent history (since 1 January 2012) of having had enforcement action taken against them for a breach of the rules will automatically be assessed as high risk for the purposes of a CPD spot check.

Non-compliance with the CPD requirements, even if corrective action is undertaken, will also make a barrister likely to be subject to a spot check.

23.6.3 Extensions of time

The BSB does grant extensions of time to complete CPD requirements, specifically in cases of illness and bereavement, or if a barrister takes a break from practice, for example, for maternity leave. In the case of a barrister taking a break from practice though, the BSB advises the barrister to retain his or her practising certificate and complete his or her CPD notwithstanding the fact that he or she is absent from practice, and then if the barrister finds he or she is unable to meet the full CPD requirement, he or she can apply for a waiver on the basis of absence from practice. Alternatively, the BSB recommends the barrister to suspend his or her practising certificate for the period he or she is not practising, in which case the CPD requirement will be automatically reduced on a pro rata basis. Any reduced CPD requirement must have a third of the requirement satisfied through undertaking accredited CPD.

If a barrister has difficulty in meeting the CPD requirements, the BSB advises the barrister to contact the BSB's CPD Supervision Team 'immediately for advice and assistance'[8] – and, in any case, before he or she is selected for a spot check. The BSB advises that the Qualifications Committee is unlikely to consider retrospective extensions of time or waivers once a barrister has been selected for a spot check.

Applications for extensions and waivers of CPD requirements are made to the Qualifications Committee of the BSB, for which the prescribed form must be used and for which a fee is payable. Applications are considered by the Committee's CPD Panel and dealt with within eight weeks of receipt.

---

[7] BSB website, 'Qualifying as a Barrister'.
[8] BSB website, 'Qualifying as a Barrister'.

23.7 COSTS OF MAINTAINING THE QUALIFICATION

A barrister is required to renew his or her practising certificate each year, by 1 April. The fees payable include:

- a compulsory practising certificate fee (PCF);
- compulsory Legal Services Board (LSB) and Office of Legal Complaints (OLC) levels;
- Bar representation fee (BRF);
- an optional but recommended pro bono donation.

The PCF for employed barristers is based on the barrister's gross earnings for the tax year as shown on his or her P60, for example, subject to permitted deductions. Where the barrister is both employed and self-employed, the aggregate of employed earnings and gross fee income excluding VAT is the figure used. The actual fee payable is calculated on a scale based on income bands, as shown in the table below for the 2015/16 practising certificate year.[9]

Income bands (£)	0–30,000	30,001–60,000	60,001–90,000	90,001–150,000	150,001–240,000	240,001+
Compulsory:						
PCF	£100	£200	£400	£725	£1,100	£1,500
LSB/OLC levy	£9	£18	£36	£69	£105	£133
Discretionary fees:						
BRF (incl. VAT)	£100					
Pro bono donation	£30					

Payment may be made online or through debit/credit card and bank transfer. It is also possible for the employer to pay on behalf of an individual barrister or make a block payment for more than one barrister employed in the organisation, in which case a discount on a sliding scale according to the number of barristers employed is available. For five or more barristers, for instance, the discount is 2.5 per cent.

Even if a barrister delegates renewal and/or payment, he or she retains individual responsibility for ensuring renewal and payment is carried out as required. If a barrister renews online or delegates payment to his or her employer, the deadline is 13 March rather than 31 March.

---

[9] BSB website, '2015/16 Practising Certificate Fee for the Self-Employed Bar'.

23.8 PROFESSIONAL CONDUCT REQUIREMENTS

Barristers are subject to a Code of Conduct which is contained in the Bar Standards Board Handbook. The Handbook contains all the rules which govern practice, authorisation, qualification, conduct and disciplinary action in respect of barristers.

The Code of Conduct consists of Core Duties and Conduct Rules. The Core Duties are very similar to the Principles of the SRA's Code for solicitors. As with the SRA's Code of Conduct, the BSB Code is also based on outcomes but, unlike the SRA Code, the outcomes are supported by rules rather than non-mandatory guidance.

The Inns also have their own conduct rules through the Council of the Inns of Court (COIC), which administers the Bar Tribunal Board and the Adjudication Service. The COIC also issues Bench Training Orders, with which Inn members are required to comply. The Conduct Committee of an Inn only deals with the conduct of students and members of the Inn prior to the call to the Bar. Once called, conduct issues are referred to the BSB and dealt with in accordance with the BSB Code of Conduct.

Under LSA 2007, it is a criminal offence to practise as a barrister without a practising certificate. It is also an offence for a pupil to hold him- or herself out as a tenant or squatter before the grant of a full qualification certificate, which is a breach of the BSB's Code of Conduct, rule C19. Breaches of the Code are referred to the Professional Conduct Committee of the BSB.

Barristers have an ongoing duty to report all criminal convictions, except parking offences.

23.9 PROPOSED CHANGES

As with the SRA (see **Chapter 6**), the BSB is also reviewing its legal education and training framework following the LETR Report (see **6.2**), information about which can be found on the 'Future Bar Training' page of the BSB website, including the new Professional Statement, issued in October 2015, which describes the knowledge, skills and attributes that a newly qualified barrister should have when he or she is issued with a full practising certificate (see **23.4.4**).

23.10 SOURCE

- The Bar Standards Board: **www.barstandardsboard.org.uk**

CHAPTER 24

Chartered Legal Executives

24.1	What is a Chartered Legal Executive?	24.6	Ongoing CPD and other training obligations
24.2	What a Chartered Legal Executive does and is permitted to do	24.7	Costs of maintaining the qualification
24.3	Regulation of Chartered Legal Executives	24.8	Professional conduct requirements
24.4	The Chartered Legal Executive qualification	24.9	Requirements for a Chartered Legal Executive to qualify as a solicitor
24.5	Maintaining the Chartered Legal Executive qualification	24.10	Sources

24.1 WHAT IS A CHARTERED LEGAL EXECUTIVE?

A Chartered Legal Executive is a Fellow of the Chartered Institute of Legal Executives (CILEx) and holds a practising certificate issued by CILEx.

A Chartered Legal Executive is the equivalent of a solicitor in terms of the work he or she does, the main difference being that a legal executive may follow a non-degree route to qualification based on at least three years' experience of working under the supervision of a solicitor, Chartered Legal Executive, barrister or licensed conveyancer. This is not dissimilar to the previous 'five-year articles' route for solicitors. A further difference is that, whereas the solicitor's qualification produces a generalist, Chartered Legal Executives through the qualification process will usually specialise in only one area of practice, although increasingly this is also the case with solicitors.

24.2 WHAT A CHARTERED LEGAL EXECUTIVE DOES AND IS PERMITTED TO DO

A Chartered Legal Executive is able to:

- be self-employed or a locum, and provide legal services to solicitors and unreserved legal work to the public;
- be employed in private practice;
- become a partner in a firm of solicitors;
- obtain individual practice rights and become a CILEx litigator and legal executive advocate or CILEx conveyancing, immigration or probate practitioner (subject to training requirements);
- apply for judicial appointment as a district judge, deputy district judge or tribunal chair.

The reserved and regulated legal activities a Chartered Legal Executive is authorised to undertake are summarised in the following table.

Reserved or regulated legal activity	Right to undertake	Delivery requirements
Exercise of a right of audience	If qualified as: • CILEx litigator • Chartered Legal Executive advocate, or • associate prosecutor or if working under an Authorised Person	Via a regulated entity only
Conduct of litigation	If qualified as: • a CILEx litigator or • an associate prosecutor for criminal proceedings only or if working under an Authorised Person	Via a regulated entity only
Reserved instrument activities	Only if, or working under, an Authorised Person or having obtained individual practice rights	
Probate activities	If qualified as a CILEx probate practitioner or if working under an Authorised Person	Via a regulated entity only
Administration of oaths	If a Chartered Legal Executive	
Notarial activity	No	
Conveyancing	If qualified as a CILEx conveyancing practitioner or if working under an Authorised Person	Via a regulated entity only

Reserved or regulated legal activity	Right to undertake	Delivery requirements
Immigration	If qualified as a CILEx immigration practitioner or if working under an Authorised Person	Via a regulated entity only

Qualification as a CILEx probate practitioner or conveyancing practitioner is also open to non-members of CILEx.

A Chartered Legal Executive may also be licensed by the Bar Direct Committee of the Bar Council to instruct barristers directly.

24.3 REGULATION OF CHARTERED LEGAL EXECUTIVES

CILEx is the Approved Regulator under the Legal Services Act 2007 (LSA 2007) for Chartered Legal Executives. CILEx discharges its regulatory functions through the independent CILEx Regulation (formerly ILEX Professional Standards (IPS)), which is a subsidiary company of CILEx but with its own board of directors.

24.4 THE CHARTERED LEGAL EXECUTIVE QUALIFICATION

The CILEx qualification structure is equivalent to A-level and honours degree level, and originally intended for people such as school leavers, graduates, legal support staff, mature students or those with other commitments, who did not wish to pursue, or who were not eligible for, the Qualifying Law Degree (QLD) or non-law graduate routes (see **Chapter 7**).

The Chartered Legal Executive (Fellow) lawyer qualification consists of:

- completion of an academic stage;
- a period of Qualifying Employment;
- meeting Work-Based Learning outcomes.

The requirements for each stage will depend on the qualification route followed. The two routes are:

- qualification via CILEx Level 3 and 6 examinations ('non-law degree' route); and
- qualification via the fast-track graduate diploma for those with a law degree, LPC or Bar Professional Training Course (BPTC).

These are summarised in the following table.

	Non-law degree route	**Graduate fast-track route**
Academic stage	Stage 1: CILEx Level 3 Professional Diploma in Law and Practice Stage 2: CILEx Level 6 Professional Higher Diploma in Law and Practice	2 units from CILEx Level 6 Practice subjects, one of which relates to subjects studied on QLD or CPE, plus Client Care, a Professional Skills unit *Note: Graduates who have passed the LPC or BPTC are exempt from Academic Stage requirements*
	Graduate Member of CILEx	
Professional stage	• 3 years' Qualifying Employment, with the two years immediately prior to application being consecutive, and the final year at Graduate Member grade • Work-based learning logbook and portfolio	• 3 years' Qualifying Employment, with the two years immediately prior to application being consecutive, and the final year at Graduate Member grade • Work-based learning logbook and portfolio
	Chartered Legal Executive (Fellow)	

Exemptions may be available from Level 3 and/or Level 6 units where applicants can demonstrate that they have passed examinations in law and/or practice at a comparable standard and with substantially similar subject content. Examples of exemptions available are at Level 3 for A-level Law, where one or two exemptions may be available, and completion of the Legal Practice Course (LPC) or BPTC.

24.4.1 Non-law degree route

24.4.1.1 *Level 3 Professional Diploma in Law and Practice*

The Level 3 Professional Diploma in Law and Practice requires the study of 10 units in total, of which five are mandatory Law units and two are Professional Skills units. At least two units must be Practice units.

LEVEL 3 LAW UNITS

Mandatory:

- Unit 1 Introduction to Law and Practice
- Unit 2 Contract Law
- Unit 3 Criminal Law
- Unit 4 Land Law
- Unit 5 Law of Tort

Optional:
- Unit 6 Employment Law
- Unit 7 Family Law
- Unit 8 Law of Wills and Succession

LEVEL 3 PRACTICE UNITS

Minimum of two required:

- Unit 9 Civil Litigation
- Unit 10 Conveyancing
- Unit 11 Criminal Litigation
- Unit 12 The Practice of Family Law
- Unit 13 The Practice of Employment Law
- Unit 14 Probate Practice
- Unit 15 The Practice of Law for the Elderly Client
- Unit 18 The Practice of Child Care Law
- Unit 19 Residential and Commercial Leasehold Conveyancing

PROFESSIONAL SKILLS UNITS (MANDATORY)
- Unit 16 Client Care Skills
- Unit 17 Legal Research Skills

24.4.1.2 Level 6 Professional Higher Diploma in Law and Practice

The Level 6 Professional Higher Diploma in Law and Practice builds on the Level 3 Diploma by requiring 'candidates to demonstrate a broad and detailed understanding of the law in three specific areas. For one of these areas the candidate must also demonstrate a sound practical understanding of the legal practice that arises from the law'.

Study of two mandatory Professional Skills units – Client Care and Legal Research Skills – is also required. A total of six Level 6 units are studied: one Practice unit, three Law units and two Professional Skills units. The units are often studied on a free-standing basis by non-CILEx members.

Level 6 requires the study of the following:

LEVEL 6 LAW UNITS (THREE TO BE SELECTED, ONE LINKED TO A PRACTICE UNIT)

- Unit 1 Company and Partnership Law
- Unit 2 Contract Law
- Unit 3 Criminal Law
- Unit 4 Employment Law
- Unit 5 Equity and Trusts

- Unit 6 European Union Law
- Unit 7 Family Law
- Unit 8 Immigration Law
- Unit 9 Land Law
- Unit 10 Landlord and Tenant Law
- Unit 11 Planning Law
- Unit 12 Public Law
- Unit 13 Law of Tort
- Unit 14 Law of Wills and Succession

LEVEL 6 PRACTICE UNITS (ONE TO BE SELECTED, LINKED TO A LAW UNIT)
- Unit 15 Civil Litigation
- Unit 16 The Practice of Company and Partnership Law
- Unit 17 Conveyancing
- Unit 18 Criminal Litigation
- Unit 19 The Practice of Employment Law
- Unit 20 The Practice of Family Law
- Unit 21 Probate Practice

LEVEL 6 SKILLS UNITS (MANDATORY)
- Unit 22 Client Care
- Unit 23 Legal Research Skills

24.4.2 The Graduate Fast-Track Diploma

The Graduate Fast-Track Diploma (GFTD) is a pathway to qualification as a Chartered Legal Executive for QLD and Common Professional Examination/Graduate Diploma in Law (CPE/GDL) graduates (see **Section B3**) who have graduated within the last seven years.

The GFTD requires the study of the following:

LEVEL 6 LAW AND PRACTICE UNITS (TWO TO BE SELECTED AND ONE LINKED TO A LAW SUBJECT STUDIED ON THE QLD OR CPE/GDL)
- Unit 15 Civil Litigation
- Unit 16 The Practice of Company and Partnership Law
- Unit 17 Conveyancing
- Unit 18 Criminal Litigation
- Unit 19 The Practice of Employment Law
- Unit 20 The Practice of Family Law
- Unit 21 Probate Practice

LEVEL 6 SKILLS UNIT (MANDATORY)
- Unit 22 Client Care

Having completed the required units, a graduate is eligible to become a Graduate Member of CILEx and once he or she has completed three years of qualifying employment, one of which must be in the Graduate Member grade, he or she will be eligible to qualify as a Chartered Legal Executive (Fellow of CILEx (FCILEx)).

24.4.3 Qualifying Employment

Qualifying Employment is work that is wholly of a legal nature and undertaken for at least 20 hours per week. Guidance as to what CILEx Regulation will recognise as Qualifying Employment in terms of duties and responsibilities is available on the CILEx Regulation website.

Rule 6 of the CILEx Regulation Application for Fellowship Rules (Work Based Learning) defines 'qualifying employment' as:

- employment by an Authorised Person in private practice; or
- employment by an organisation, which is subject to supervision by an Authorised Person employed in duties of a legal nature by that organisation

where the work under the terms of employment:

- is for at least 20 hours per week; and
- is wholly of a legal nature.

Work is 'wholly of a legal nature' if it involves undertaking an activity that involves the application of the law or legal practice or procedure in areas such as:

- taking instructions;
- advising and making recommendations;
- drafting documents;
- undertaking legal research;
- corresponding with the parties to an action or transaction;
- making decisions in a legal matter based on legal principles or rule of law;
- representing in negotiations and submissions.

For the individual to be 'employed' means[1] that he or she is:

- employed under a contract of service and engaged on the employer's business for specified hours;
- a partner in any firm or an owner of a company; or
- at CILEx Regulation's discretion, is employed under a contract for services, whether as an independent contractor or through an intervening agent.

---

[1] CILEx Regulation Application for Fellowship Rules (Work Based Learning), rule 7.

Part-time employment and even unpaid work may be accepted as Qualifying Employment: the work must provide the opportunity for practical expertise to be developed.[2]

It is also possible to have CILEx Regulation assess a member's work, and provide a decision as to whether it qualifies as Qualifying Employment. There is a prescribed application form and a fee is payable.

The requirement is for a minimum of three years of Qualifying Employment, of which the two years immediately preceding the application for Fellowship must be served consecutively, and at least one year must be served as a Graduate Member of CILEx.

A break in the two years of continuous employment is permitted if the break is for a period of up to 12 months. This will not break the continuity of employment, although it will not be counted towards the two-year period.

Under the CILEx Regulation Application for Fellowship Rules (Work Based Learning), rule 4, attending the LPC or BPTC for up to 43 weeks will be treated as Qualifying Employment.

24.4.3.1 Application for Fellowship via Work-Based Learning

A Graduate Member is eligible to apply for Fellowship once he or she has completed the required qualifying employment, including the full year as a Graduate Member. CILEx recommends that applicants, regardless of the route taken to qualify, apply to have their Qualifying Employment assessed at an early stage to confirm eligibility to apply for Fellowship under the Work-Based Learning scheme (not all Graduate Members will have studied Level 6 CILEx exams). Members can start to think about collecting evidence the year prior to becoming a Graduate Member, on the basis that the evidence for the Work-Based Learning portfolio (see **24.4.4**) should not be more than two years old at the time of applying for Fellowship.

24.4.4 Work-Based Learning

The Work-Based Learning application comprises an application form, a portfolio of evidence, and log sheets which are completed by the applicant. The logbook sheets need to be signed by the member's supervisor and the supporting evidence redacted. CILEx Regulation provides examples of completed logbook sheets on its website.

In order to apply for Fellowship an applicant must, in addition to satisfying the Qualifying Employment requirements, demonstrate that he or she has met a series of Work-Based competencies, which are broken down into learning outcomes. Members provide evidence from their day-to-day work, to demonstrate that the outcomes have been met. The evidence can be collated during the last two years of

---

[2] CILEx Regulation Application for Fellowship Rules (Work Based Learning), rules 8 and 9.

their Qualifying Employment, and the application may be submitted once they have served all three years, including the year as a Graduate Member.[3] The Competencies cover:

1. Practical application of the law and legal practice
2. Communication skills
3. Client relations
4. Management of workload
5. Business awareness
6. Professional conduct
7. Self-awareness and development
8. Working with others

Rule 11[4] requires all learning outcomes to be met three times, except for those shaded in grey in the table of Work-Based Learning outcomes given at Rule 10,[5] which need to be met once.

To demonstrate that the Work-Based Learning outcomes have been met, a student or Graduate Member is required to complete a logbook and portfolio of evidence, and submit this for assessment to demonstrate that the learning outcomes have been met. The requirements as to how the logbook and evidence should be compiled and maintained, and how the various components of the application should be completed are explained in detail in the CILEx Regulation Work Based Learning Handbook, which is available on the CILEx Regulation website.

24.4.5 Qualification and admission

Once the academic requirements have been met and the necessary Qualifying Employment completed, application may be made for Fellowship of CILEx.

In addition to meeting the Work-Based Learning outcomes, the other requirements for admission as a Fellow under the Application for Fellowship Rules (Work Based Learning), rule 2 are that the applicant:

- has paid all subscription and other fees payable to CILEx;
- provides a Certificate of Fitness signed by an Authorised Person who supervises the applicant's work or employs the applicant. The certificate must confirm the nature of the work that the applicant does and that the applicant is competent to be a Fellow;
- accepts the obligations imposed upon him or her by the CILEx Charter and Bye Laws, and rules and regulations made by the CILEx Council.

What it is crucial for an applicant to demonstrate is that the work he or she does goes beyond legal administration, and in the final year of Qualifying Employment that the work he or she does is autonomous rather than directed, although it must still be

---

[3] CILEx Regulation, Work Based Learning: Handbook.
[4] CILEx Regulation Application for Fellowship Rules (Work Based Learning).
[5] CILEx Regulation Application for Fellowship Rules (Work Based Learning).

supervised. Examples that CILEx Regulation gives of the types of roles and tasks which would be appropriate at this level include:

- working on a caseload at an appropriate level;
- completing legal forms;
- dealing with client enquiries which involve the provision of advice on law and procedure.

If the applicant works in-house, similar tasks would be expected to be undertaken, albeit that the applicant's employer is in fact his or her client.

The CILEx Regulation Work Based Learning Handbook indicates that the following roles and tasks would not be regarded as Qualifying Employment:

- typing
- photocopying
- filing
- book-keeping duties
- document production
- Companies House returns
- file maintenance
- data entry
- office management
- dealing with complaints.

Although some administrative tasks may be undertaken in connection with legal tasks, for the work to be Qualifying Employment, the work that a member undertakes must be 'wholly of a legal nature' for at least 20 hours per week.

24.4.6 Other CILEx qualifications

A Chartered Legal Executive may also obtain the following qualifications from CILEx:

- CILEx Litigator and Chartered Legal Executive Advocate: this qualification grants rights to conduct litigation, including an award of advocacy or rights of audience in the practice area in which the Chartered Legal Executive works, the options being:
  - civil litigation;
  - criminal litigation;
  - family litigation.

- Chartered Legal Executive Advocate: this qualification grants advocacy rights in the practice area in which Chartered Legal Executive works, the options being:
  - civil litigation;
  - criminal litigation;

- family litigation.
- CILEx Immigration Practitioner: this qualification grants rights to provide immigration advice and services through a regulated entity.

CILEx also provides qualifications as:

- Associate Prosecutor for employees of the Criminal Prosecution Service;
- CILEx Probate Practitioner;
- CILEx Conveyancing Practitioner.

24.5 MAINTAINING THE CHARTERED LEGAL EXECUTIVE QUALIFICATION

A Chartered Legal Executive is required to renew his or her practising certificate on an annual basis by evidencing compliance with the Continuing Professional Development (CPD) requirements and paying the annual subscription fee.

24.6 ONGOING CPD AND OTHER TRAINING OBLIGATIONS

CPD is described by CILEx as 'the means by which individuals in our regulated community maintain, improve and broaden their knowledge and skills'.[6]

24.6.1 Summary of requirements

The CPD requirements for the various levels of CILEx membership are summarised in the table below.

Membership category	Annual CPD requirement
Student Member	None
Affiliate Member	None
Associate Member	Eight hours of CPD + additional professionalism element
Graduate Member	Nine CPD outcomes, including one in Professionalism
Chartered Legal Executive (Fellow)	Nine CPD outcomes, including one in Professionalism
Chartered Legal Executive Advocate	Same as for Fellows and must include a minimum of two outcomes related to advocacy skills each year

---

[6] CILEx Regulation website, 'Continuing Professional Development (CPD)'.

A new CPD Scheme was introduced from 1 October 2014, to replace the previous hours-based scheme with an outcomes-based scheme, which focuses on 'what has been achieved, or what benefit has been gained, relating to learned knowledge or skill'.[7]

The requirements for and features of the new CPD Scheme are summarised in the following table.

Authority	CILEx Regulation
Governing regulations	CPD Policy Statement, 23 February 2015
CPD requirement	• To complete required 'entries'. An 'entry' is an activity which is undertaken, and which is logged as an outcome on the a member's CPD record • To review learning and development needs at the start of the CPD year and identify at least five outcomes the individual would like to achieve
Exempt from CPD requirements	Student Members, Affiliate Members, non-practising members, members on maternity/paternity leave and retired members
CPD activities	CPD activities are not prescribed but can include: • courses • short workshops • one-to-one training or update sessions at work • journal articles • listening to podcasts • shadowing colleagues with particular expertise/knowledge • work appraisals A list of recognised activities is provided in the CPD Handbook
CPD year	1 October to 30 September
Minimum CPD entries required	Nine CPD entries each year, of which: • at least one outcome must relate to 'Professionalism' • five outcomes must be 'planned' at the start of the CPD year, and • up to four outcomes may be 'unplanned' *Note: It is possible for multiple entries to be logged from one activity on the basis of more than one thing being learnt*
Carry-over of CPD entries	Not permitted
Reduction of CPD requirements	Reductions available: • for Graduate Members of CILEx who have completed and submitted their Work-Based

---

[7] CILEx Regulation, CPD Policy Statement, 23 February 2015, p.3.

	Learning application, by application to CILEx Regulation, to reduce the requirement to five entries per CPD year for a maximum of two years • where an individual has been absent from employment for at least six months, he or she may be eligible for dispensation
Reduction for part-time working	No
Requirement to keep record of CPD	Yes. A record must be maintained of CPD activities, together with evidence of the activity undertaken, and an evaluation of it which includes how it met (or did not meet) the individual's training needs. The record must also differentiate between 'planned' and 'unplanned' outcomes, and the Professionalism outcome's must be logged in a discrete part of the training record
	CPD must be recorded using the 'myCILEX' CPD recording system, with records completed and logged by 30 September
	CPD records must be retained for at least two years from the end of each CPD year
Consequences of failure to comply with CPD requirements	If a member feels an extension will be required, they should apply for this in writing from CILEx Regulation no later than 31 August
	A false declaration regarding completion of CPD will be treated as misconduct
	Failure to comply with the CPD requirements by 30 September, subject of reduction, extension or dispensation granted, will result in practice rights of the Chartered Legal Executive being suspended from 1 January of the following calendar year. It may also result in a referral to the Professional Conduct Panel, which may reprimand or warn the member. The Panel may also refer cases to the Disciplinary Tribunal, which has additional powers, including the power to exclude a member from membership of CILEx
Monitoring of compliance with CPD requirements	CILEx Regulation does random sampling of CPD records
Responsibility for compliance with CPD requirements	Individual Chartered Legal Executive or CILEx practitioner
Obligation on employer to fund CPD activities	No
Obligation on employer to allow time-off for CPD activities	No
Requirements for eligible CPD	CILEx does not consider it appropriate to prescribe the specific content of required or desirable CPD

Accreditation	No requirements
Recognition of CPD activity under other regulators	Yes, provided all conditions of the CILEx scheme are satisfied. Evidence of the CPD activity may be required to be submitted to CILEx
Administrative responsibilities for Chartered Legal Executives and CILEx Practitioners	• Reflect, plan, act, evaluate • Log entries by 30 September each year

24.6.2 Planned and unplanned outcomes

The distinction between 'planned' and 'unplanned' activities is not to do with the type of activity but whether the outcome was consciously chosen by the individual, following his or her reflection on what would be necessary or beneficial for his or her development. If the CPD outcome results from prior reflection, it is 'planned' CPD; if it results from being directed to undertake the activity or is an unexpected learning opportunity, then it is 'unplanned' CPD.

What CILEx Regulation calls 'the CPD cycle for planned CPD' is a cycle of reflection, planning, acting and evaluating, which is not dissimilar to the SRA's Continuing Competence approach for solicitors. CILEx Regulation has a template for planning and evaluation, which Chartered Legal Executives can use, available on its website.

24.6.3 Professionalism

The CILEx CPD Policy Statement defines a Professionalism outcome as relating to:

> competence and confidence in the broad range of skills, knowledge and experience that are part of the quality service for consumers of legal services, but not focused on the law itself. The outcome must develop or refresh [a Chartered Legal Executive's] existing professional knowledge or skills. It covers areas other than law, legal principles and matters directly related to the content and procedures of the law.[8]

There is a list of suggested 'Professionalism activities' on the CILEx website.

24.6.4 Sampling of CPD records

CILEx Regulation samples 2.5 per cent of CILEx members across all grades of membership each year, selected randomly from its database. If a member is 'sampled' he or she will be emailed and asked to provide information about his or her CPD outcomes. This information needs to cover the individual's planning, activities undertaken and evaluation. For the Management outcome, individuals are

---

[8] CPD Policy Statement, p.4.

also required to provide 'additional documentation in support of what they have already entered on to their online logbook which demonstrates that they have undertaken a Professionalism outcome, and achieved an appropriate outcome, in accordance with the CPD planning cycle'.[9] Of those sampled, 10 per cent will be selected by CILEx Regulation for an in depth discussion about their CPD record.

Failure to comply with sampling requests is a matter of misconduct.

24.6.5 Dispensations

An application for a dispensation from the CPD requirements must be made by 30 September in the particular CPD year.

If a dispensation is granted, the individual has the choice of either completing his or her outstanding CPD from previous years, or undertaking a CILEx 'Return to Legal Work' scheme prior to or within two months of returning to legal work.

24.7 COSTS OF MAINTAINING THE QUALIFICATION

The annual subscription fees for the various levels of CILEx membership are set out in the table below.

Annual subscription fees for	Amount of fee
Student Member	£50
Affiliate Member	£119
Associate Member	£168
Graduate Member	£200
Fellow	£318.50
Fellow (dual qualified with Journal)	£99
Fellow (dual qualified without Journal)	£50

24.8 PROFESSIONAL CONDUCT REQUIREMENTS

Upon his or her graduation, a Chartered Legal Executive is required to recite an oath to discharge his or her duties and responsibilities diligently, protect his or her independence as a lawyer, uphold the rule of law, and act at all times with integrity, and justify the confidence and trust of his or her clients, the courts, the public and the profession.

All Chartered Legal Executives are subject to the Code of Conduct of CILEx ('CILEx Code'). According to CILEx Regulation, the Code 'sets out the principles to which CILEx members, CILEx practitioners and CILEx Authorised Entities must adhere in their conduct, practice and professional performance, and the outcomes they must meet'.[10]

---

[9] CPD Policy Statement, p.7.
[10] CILEx website, 'About CILEx'.

As with the SRA Code of Conduct, each core principle in the CILEx Code is supported by a series of outcomes, which all CILEx members – not just Chartered Legal Executives – are required to adhere to and meet. They are also supported by 'non-exhaustive' guidance, intended to help CILEx members understand what is expected of them. As with the SRA non-mandatory guidance, a departure from the guidance would need to be justified if a member's behaviour was called into question.

A breach of the Code of Conduct will result in misconduct action. If a finding of misconduct is made, CILEx Regulation can:

- issue a reprimand;
- issue a warning;
- place conditions on the practising certificate;
- seek undertakings;
- fine; or
- exclude from membership or authorisation.

An annual declaration as to character and suitability is required to be made and there is an ongoing obligation to report any matter affecting character and suitability as soon as the matter occurs. Non-compliance or failure to disclose may result in disciplinary action.

24.9 REQUIREMENTS FOR A CHARTERED LEGAL EXECUTIVE TO QUALIFY AS A SOLICITOR

Qualification as a Chartered Legal Executive is recognised by the SRA as meeting the academic stage requirements for qualification as a solicitor, as the Chartered Legal Executive qualification is set and assessed at honours degree level. Although a Chartered Legal Executive who wishes to qualify as a solicitor is required to do the Legal Practice Course (see **Chapter 14**), he or she is exempt from the requirement to complete a Period of Recognised Training because of the work-based experience requirements of the Chartered Legal Executive qualification. A Chartered Legal Executive must, however, complete the Compulsory Cores of the SRA's Professional Skills Course (PSC) (see **Chapter 16**) prior to admission as a solicitor.

However, CILEx also provides an arguably viable route to qualification for law graduates who have difficulty finding a training contract, for example, following graduation.

24.10 SOURCES

- CILEx: **www.cilex.org.uk**
- CILEx Regulation: **www.cilexregulation.org.uk**

CHAPTER 25

Licensed conveyancers

25.1	What is a licensed conveyancer?	25.6	Ongoing CPD and other training obligations
25.2	What a licensed conveyancer does and is permitted to do	25.7	Costs of maintaining the qualification
25.3	Regulation of licensed conveyancers	25.8	Professional conduct requirements
25.4	Requirements for qualifying as a licensed conveyancer	25.9	Source
25.5	Maintaining the qualification		

25.1 WHAT IS A LICENSED CONVEYANCER?

A licensed conveyancer holds a licence from the Council for Licensed Conveyancers (CLC).

The CLC describes licensed conveyancers as 'property lawyers who are trained and qualified in all aspects of the law dealing with property'. A licensed conveyancer may also be licensed to offer probate services.

A licensed conveyancer may work anywhere which does conveyancing, provided the licensed conveyancer is supervised by a 'Qualified Person'. Consequently, licensed conveyancers work in law firms, but also in legal departments in housing associations and local authorities, banks and building societies, as well as property development companies and the like. With a Manager Licensed Conveyancer licence from the CLC, a licensed conveyancer may establish and manage his or her own practice. With an Employed Licensed Conveyancer licence, a licensed conveyancer may only offer conveyancing services through his or her employer.

25.2 WHAT A LICENSED CONVEYANCER DOES AND IS PERMITTED TO DO

A licensed conveyancer has the same legal authority to act in relation to a conveyancing transaction as does a solicitor, and is authorised to undertake the following reserved activities.

Exercise of a right of audience	No
Conduct of litigation	No
Reserved instrument activities	Yes
Probate activities	Under Probate Licence
Administration of oaths	Yes
Notarial activities	No

A licensed conveyancer may also be authorised by the Council for Licensed Conveyancers as a probate practitioner. The Probate Practitioner licence is based on qualification in the law of succession, trusts law, aspects of property law relating to inheritance and administration of estates, and grants the right to undertake probate.

The CLC also has authority to grant a stand-alone probate qualification which leads to a licence as a CLC probate practitioner, without the requirement to qualify as a licensed conveyancer first.

25.3 REGULATION OF LICENSED CONVEYANCERS

The CLC is the Approved Regulator for licensed conveyancers under the Legal Services Act 2007 (LSA 2007). Unlike the position with solicitors (see **5.3**), the CLC has an exclusively regulatory function, and is not a representative body.

The CLC regulates both individual licensed conveyancers and entities, and was the first front-line regulator to be authorised by the Legal Services Board to license Alternative Business Structures (ABSs), and licensed the first ABS in 2011.

25.4 REQUIREMENTS FOR QUALIFYING AS A LICENSED CONVEYANCER

The qualification framework for licensed conveyancers consists of:

- an academic stage of assessed study; and
- a professional stage of supervised, on-the-job training (in conveyancing work).

25.4.1 Academic stage

The academic stage is satisfied by undertaking the CLC examinations following study of the CLC course. The examinations cover:

- Part 1 Foundation:
    - Introduction to Conveyancing
    - Introduction to Land Law and Legal Method
    - Law of Contract
    - Land Law

- Part 2 Final:
  - Accounts
  - Conveyancing Law and Practice
  - Landlord and Tenant

25.4.2 Professional stage

In addition to completing the CLC examinations, a chartered licensed conveyancer is also required to complete a period of qualifying employment called 'Practical Training', consisting of the equivalent of 1,200 chargeable hours under the supervision of a 'Qualified Person'.

25.4.3 Qualification and admission

A licensed conveyancer obtains a licence after satisfactorily completing the CLC exams and meeting the practical training requirements.

The first licence granted is as an Employed Licensed Conveyancer, which entitles the licensed conveyancer to offer conveyancing services through an employer.

25.5 MAINTAINING THE QUALIFICATION

A licensed conveyancer must renew his or her licence annually. For individual licensed conveyancers and probate practitioners, licences need to be renewed before the end of the current licence period. The licence period runs from 1 November to 31 October, inclusive.

This may be done online, including payment of the renewal fee.

25.6 ONGOING CPD AND OTHER TRAINING OBLIGATIONS

A licensed conveyancer must comply with the Continuing Professional Development (CPD) requirements which are stipulated in his or her individual licence. This will be not just the required number of CPD hours, but also the content of the training which must be completed.

The requirements relating to CPD are summarised in the table below.

Authority	CLC
Annual CPD requirement	Yes
CPD year	1 November to 31 October, inclusive

OTHER QUALIFIED LAWYER QUALIFICATION REQUIREMENTS

Minimum CPD points required	Conveyancing Licence: • Manager: 12 • Employed licensed conveyancer: 6 Probate Licence: • Manager: 12 + 4 • Employed licensed conveyancer: 6 + 2
Carry-over of CPD points	No
Reduction of minimum CPD points requirement	In exceptional circumstances at CLC's discretion
Reduction for part-time working	No
Requirement to keep record of CPD	Required to maintain CPD training record for both previous and current CLC year, with • evidence of attendance • certificate provided by CPD provider • training record counter-signed by employer if DVD/video or in-house CPD claimed
	If CPD completed online or by video/DVD or CD, certificate also required or evidence from provider to substantiate the CPD undertaken
	Record must be completed and signed by employer and submitted to CLC for annual renewal of licence
Consequences of failure to comply with CPD requirements	CLC operates an escalating system of sanctions, e.g. • CPD may not be accepted by CLC towards an individual's quota, or • CLC may issue licence subject to conditions
Monitoring by CLC of compliance with CPD requirements	Annual random selection of a proportion of licensed conveyancers to provide copy of training record and supporting evidence
Responsibility for compliance with CPD requirements	Individual licensed conveyancer
Obligation on employer to fund CPD activities	No. However, CLC-regulated entities must ensure their qualified staff meet the requirements, including CPD, for renewal of entity licence
Obligation on employer to allow time-off for CPD activities	No
Requirements for eligible CPD	CPD must relate to the services the licensed conveyancer is licensed to offer
	CPD courses must be provided by an accredited provider. No CPD activity by non-accredited providers is recognised
Accreditation	By CLC or other LSB-Approved Regulator, e.g. SRA
	List of accredited CPD course providers on CLC website

	Condition of accreditation that CPD provider provide evidence of training and, for online, video/DVD or CD, a certificate confirming: • name of licensed conveyancer • date CPD completed • number of CPD hours earned • subject covered by the training • course code, if applicable
Recognition of CPD activity under other regulators	Yes, for regulators authorised under the LSA 2007, e.g. SRA
Administrative responsibilities for licensed conveyancers	Maintain CPD training record and evidence of attendance and certificate/s in relation to online or CD/DVD CPD activities

25.7 COSTS OF MAINTAINING THE QUALIFICATION

	Licence fee
Individual licensed conveyancer	£400
Individual probate practitioner	£400 + £75
Licensed entities	Fee based on turnover according to bands

25.8 PROFESSIONAL CONDUCT REQUIREMENTS

25.8.1 CLC Handbook

The CLC has adopted an entity-based, outcomes-focused regulatory regime, which is underpinned by the CLC Handbook. The Handbook consists of:

- the Codes, which comprise flexible, higher-level principles, and set out the regulatory responsibilities of all individuals and firms which the CLC regulates;
- guidance to the Codes, which is non-mandatory and is intended to provide useful information to those regulated by the CLC, as well as example policies or procedures, depending on the Code;
- regulatory and enforcement policies, which outline the CLC's approach to regulation and its likely response if regulatory responsibilities are not met by individuals or entities;
- frameworks, which set out the CLC's operating parameters and the process to be followed.

Not all frameworks are included in the Handbook, however. The frameworks which are relevant to the Licensed Conveyancer qualification are

- the CLC Student Training Framework, which sets out the requirements for the award of a Practising Licence; and
- the Continuing Professional Development Framework, which sets out the CPD requirements to be complied with annually.

Although the CPD Framework is included in the Handbook, the CLC Student Training Framework is contained in the CLC Frameworks document.

The first of the Codes is the Code of Conduct, which applies to all services which a licensed conveyancer is permitted or authorised by the CLC to deliver. The Code sets out six Overriding Principles, with which a licensed conveyancer must comply, and 20 outcomes which a licensed conveyancer must deliver.

The other Codes in the Handbook support the Code of Conduct.

The CLC also has a Client Charter which sets out the outcomes which clients may expect from using a licensed conveyancer, and what clients can do if their expectations are not met.

A breach of the Code of Conduct could result in enforcement action, such as:

- the issue of a reprimand;
- the imposition of a penalty;
- the imposition of a condition on the licence, e.g. an individual has to attend and pay for a specific course outside his or her CPD requirements;
- the withdrawal of CLC approval;
- the disqualification of the individual;
- the suspension/revocation of the licence.

25.8.2 Fit and proper person

In order to apply for a first licence, an individual must satisfy the CLC that he or she is a fit and proper person to practise as a licensed conveyancer, and is required to obtain a Criminal Records Bureau disclosure. On being granted a licence, the individual has the obligation to notify the CLC of any changes to the information provided in order to be licensed, within seven days of becoming aware of a change. The Notification Code in the CLC Handbook sets out matters which require notification. Various factors will be taken into account by the CLC when applying the fit and proper test, and the way in which the CLC will make its assessment of those factors is set out in item 8.22 of the Licensed Body (ABS) Licensing Framework.

25.9 SOURCE

- Council for Licensed Conveyancers: **www.clc-uk.org**

CHAPTER 26

Intellectual property practitioners

26.1	What is an intellectual property practitioner?	26.6	Ongoing CPD or other training obligations for IP practitioners
26.2	What IP practitioners do and are permitted to do	26.7	Costs of maintaining the qualifications
26.3	Regulation of IP practitioners	26.8	Regulation of the professional conduct of IP practitioners
26.4	The qualifications	26.9	Sources
26.5	Maintaining the qualifications		

26.1 WHAT IS AN INTELLECTUAL PROPERTY PRACTITIONER?

A qualified patent attorney has met the examination and practice requirements to be entered on the Register of Patent Attorneys ('patent attorney'). A qualified trade mark attorney has met the examination and practice requirements to be entered on the Register of Trade Mark Attorneys ('trade mark attorney'). Both are intellectual property practitioners ('IP practitioners') and because they have a common regulator and common qualification requirements, they are treated together in this chapter. It is also possible for an IP practitioner to be registered on one or both registers.

26.2 WHAT IP PRACTITIONERS DO AND ARE PERMITTED TO DO

26.2.1 Patent attorney

A chartered patent attorney's particular expertise is in the field of intellectual property, and encompasses patents, industrial designs, design rights and related copyright areas, and trademarks.

It is not, however, necessary to be a patent attorney in order to represent clients in relation to patents or to be a trade mark attorney in order to act in relation to trade marks.

26.2.2 Trade mark attorney

A trade mark attorney carries out all the work associated with securing and protecting trademarks and other intellectual property rights both in the UK and abroad.

26.2.3 Reserved activities

Both patent attorneys and trade mark attorneys are authorised to carry on the reserved activities and regulated legal activities as indicated in the table below.

Reserved legal activity	Patent attorney	Trade mark attorney
Exercise of a right of audience	Yes, in lower courts	Yes, in lower courts
Conduct of litigation	Yes	Yes
Reserved instrument activities	Yes, where instruments relate to IP rights	Yes, where instruments relate to IP rights
Probate activities	No	No
Administration of oaths	Yes	Yes
Notarial activities	No	No

IP practitioners, upon being entered on the appropriate register, have the same rights as solicitors to conduct litigation and to act as advocates in the lower courts, including the Intellectual Property Enterprise Court (previously the Patents County Court). However, IP practitioners may extend their rights to conduct litigation and rights of audience in the Intellectual Property Enterprise Court, High Court and, for some appeals, before the Court of Appeal and Supreme Court (see **26.4.6**).

26.3 REGULATION OF IP PRACTITIONERS

The Chartered Institute of Patent Attorneys (CIPA) and the Institute of Trade Mark Attorneys (ITMA) are the Approved Regulators under the Legal Services Act 2007 (LSA 2007) for patent attorneys and trade mark attorneys, respectively. Using the powers granted to them under LSA 2007, both bodies have delegated their regulatory powers to IP Regulation ('IPReg'), which is an independent body.

Regulatory responsibilities and sources of regulatory authority for IP practitioners are summarised in the table below.

In terms of authorisation to carry out reserved legal activities, the bodies responsible are as follows.

INTELLECTUAL PROPERTY PRACTITIONERS

	Patent attorney	Trade mark attorney
Grant of litigation and audience rights	IPReg	
Extension of litigation and audience rights	Patent Regulation Board (PRB)	Trade Mark Regulation Board (TMRB)

26.4 THE QUALIFICATIONS

The qualification frameworks for both patent attorneys and trade mark attorneys consist of three stages of training which involves the following.

Stage of training	Required training	
	Patent attorney	Trade mark attorney
Academic stage	Qualifying Examinations	Postgraduate Certificate
Vocational stage	n/a	Practice Course
Professional stage	Practice Experience	

26.4.1 Requirements

The requirements are set out in the patent attorney and trade mark attorney Qualification and Registration Regulations 2009 and the Rules for the Examination and Admission of Individuals to the Registers of Patent and Trade Mark Attorneys 2011. A patent attorney, however, will normally have a degree in science, engineering, technology or a mathematics-based subject, as well as a legal qualification in Intellectual Property.

26.4.2 Academic stage for IP practitioners

26.4.2.1 Patent attorneys

The Qualifying Examinations for Patent Attorneys consist of:

Either	Or
Foundation Examinations in: • UK Patent Law • English Law • International Patent Law • Design and Copyright Law • Trade Mark Law	IPReg-accredited IP Certificate from: • Queen Mary University London; • Bournemouth University; or • Brunel University London
And	

> Final Examinations in:
> - Advanced IP Law and Practice
> - Drafting of Specifications
> - Amendment of Specifications
> - Infringement and Validity

26.4.2.2 Trade mark attorneys

For trade mark attorneys, the academic stage of training is satisfied by obtaining an IPReg-accredited IP postgraduate certificate from either Queen Mary University London or Bournemouth University, followed by completion of a Practice Course, which is currently the IPReg-accredited Professional Certificate in Trade Mark Practice offered by Nottingham Law School.

26.4.3 Professional experience

To be eligible to be entered on either register requires professional experience of at least two years' practice under professional supervision, as prescribed.

26.4.4 Competencies

IPReg has developed non-mandatory skills sets of competencies for trainee patent and trade mark attorneys.

26.4.5 Qualification and admission

The requirements for qualification and admission are set out in the Rules for the Examination and Admission of Individuals to the Registers of Patent and Trade Mark Attorneys 2010 (amended May 2014).

A patent attorney or trade mark attorney will only be admitted to the relevant register if they are of appropriate character and suitability.

26.4.6 Further rights to conduct litigation and rights of audience

A registered patent attorney or trade mark attorney may also apply for further rights to conduct litigation and rights of audience under one of the following certificates:

- the Intellectual Property Litigation Certificate
- the Higher Courts Litigation Certificate
- the Higher Courts Advocacy Certificate.

The rights are granted by the PRB of the CIPA or the TMRB of the ITMA, as appropriate, under the Rights to Conduct Litigation and Rights of Audience and Other Reserved Legal Activities Certification Rules 2012.[1]

26.5 MAINTAINING THE QUALIFICATIONS

26.5.1 Registration

Under the Patent Attorney and Trade Mark Attorney Qualification and Registration Regulations 2009, reg.11.1, registration must be renewed annually, on 31 December each year.

On annual renewal of registration, an attorney is also asked to make the following declaration:

> I can confirm that nothing has occurred in the last 12 months which would call into question my character and suitability to remain on the register of patent attorneys or trade mark attorneys.

If unable to make the declaration, the attorney will be required to provide information which IPReg requires to assess whether or not renewal of the attorney's registration should be refused.[2]

26.5.2 Litigation and advocacy certificates

If an attorney holds an Intellectual Property Litigation Certificate, Higher Courts Litigation Certificate or Higher Courts Advocacy Certificate, the certificate will be renewed annually as part of the general registration renewal process.

If the attorney ceases to be registered as an attorney, a litigation or advocacy certificate would be revoked automatically.

26.6 ONGOING CPD OR OTHER TRAINING OBLIGATIONS FOR IP PRACTITIONERS

26.6.1 Continuing Professional Development

The guidance notes to continuing professional development (CPD) on the IPReg website state that all practising patent attorneys and trade mark attorneys 'have a

---

[1] IPReg, Rights to Conduct Litigation and Rights of Audience and Other Reserved Legal Activities Certification Rules 2012.
[2] IPREG, 'Guidelines on the Assessment of Character and Suitability'.

OTHER QUALIFIED LAWYER QUALIFICATION REQUIREMENTS

professional obligation to ensure that they maintain their skills and knowledge at the necessary level to be able to provide a proper service to existing and potential clients'.

The CPD requirements are set out in the IPReg Continuing Professional Development Regulations 2013 and are summarised in the table below.

Authority	Continuing Professional Development Regulations
	Administered by the IPReg Education and Qualifications Committee
CPD year	1 January to 31 December, inclusive
Minimum CPD points required	16 hours of CPD annually
	If registered on both Patent and Trade Mark Registers: 16 hours, split between patent and trade mark CPD according to proportion of patent and trade mark work attorney does
Additional/specific CPD requirements	Attorneys with litigation or advocacy rights: expected to undertake relevant activities on a sufficiently regular basis to ensure their skills in that area are maintained
	Attorneys with higher rights: a minimum of 5 hours of CPD relating to the provision of advocacy services in the higher courts in each of the 5 full CPD years following grant of higher rights
Requirements for eligible CPD	CPD undertaken:
	• must be relevant to area/s of practice in which registered
	• should be at an appropriate level
	• should contribute to the attorney's general professional skill and knowledge and not just advance a fee-earning matter
Planning requirement	No – expectation that the attorney will plan an annual programme of CPD activities based on an objective assessment of training and development needs in relation to nature of his or her practice
Carry-over of CPD points	No
Reduction of minimum CPD points requirement	Newly qualified attorneys are not required to undertake CPD during the CPD year in which they qualify
Reduction for part-time working	No
Requirement to keep record of CPD	Yes
Consequences of failure to comply with CPD requirements	Non-compliance is referred to the Joint Disciplinary Panel and may result in removal from the

	relevant Register
Monitoring of compliance with CPD requirements	IPReg monitors compliance by annual random sampling of registrants, requiring details of CPD undertaken to meet CPD requirements
Responsibility for compliance with CPD requirements	Individual attorney – he or she must self-certify that CPD requirements are met when he or she renews registration each year
Recognition of CPD activity under other regulators	Yes – CPD undertaken to fulfil requirements of other regulators, e.g. SRA, may be counted provided it is relevant to the practice of a patent attorney or trade mark attorney

26.6.2 Other training obligations

Patent attorneys and trade mark attorneys are required to attend and pass a basic litigation skills course, either:

- prior to qualification; or
- within three years from the end of the calendar year when first entered on the relevant register

unless they have already:

- obtained an IPReg Higher Courts Litigation Certificate within three years of qualifying;
- acquired a right to conduct civil litigation by qualifying as a solicitor or barrister; or
- successfully completed the Bar Professional Training Course (BPTC) or Legal Practice Course (LPC).

26.7 COSTS OF MAINTAINING THE QUALIFICATIONS

Practice fees for 2014/15 were as follows.

Practice fee types	Single register (i.e patent attorney or trade mark attorney) fee	Both registers (patent attorney and trade mark attorney) fee
Attorney solely undertaking corporate work	£154	£248
Attorney in private practice	£187	£308
Attorney not in active practice	£140	£225
Sole trader not employing other attorneys or other professionals	£308	£440

Practice fee types	Single register (i.e. patent attorney or trade mark attorney) fee	Both registers (patent attorney and trade mark attorney) fee
Sole trader employing others:		
Base fee	£308	£440
Plus for each employed registered attorney	£61	£61
And each employed other professional providing legal services	£248	£248

The administration fee for issue of the Higher Courts Litigation and Higher Courts Advocacy Certificates is £100.

Late payment of fees incurs a late payment charge of 50 per cent of the fee that was due, up to a maximum of £125.

26.8 REGULATION OF THE PROFESSIONAL CONDUCT OF IP PRACTITIONERS

26.8.1 Character and suitability

IPReg has the role of ensuring that registered trade mark attorneys and patent attorneys 'have the level of honesty, integrity and professional conduct expected by the public and other stakeholders, as well as other members of the profession, and do not pose a risk to the public or the profession'.[3]

Character and suitability issues are considered at the point of admission and a patent attorney or trade mark attorney must answer questions as to character and suitability (see **9.8.2**) in the Statutory Declaration required for entry in the Register of Patent Attorneys or Trade Mark Attorneys. IPReg may verify any information provided by an applicant and will regard failure to disclose information as evidence that the applicant may not be of acceptable character and suitability.

26.8.2 Code of Conduct

Patent attorneys and trade mark attorneys are required to comply with IPReg's Code of Conduct 2015. IP practitioners who either undertake litigation or represent clients in court are also bound by the Litigator's Code of Conduct.

---

[3] IPReg website, 'Admission'.

Advocates who have further rights to conduct litigation and rights of audience are also required to comply with the Special Rules of Professional Conduct applicable to Regulated Persons Conducting Litigation or Exercising a Right of Audience before the Courts.[4]

26.9 SOURCES

26.9.1 Websites

- Intellectual Property Regulation Board (IPReg) (regulatory body for patent and trade mark attorneys): **http://ipreg.org.uk**
- Chartered Institute of Patent Attorneys (CIPA): **www.cipa.org.uk**
- Patent Examination Board (PEB): **www.cipa.org.uk/patent-examination-board**
- The Institute of Trade Mark Attorneys (ITMA): **www.itma.org.uk**

---

[4] IPReg, Special Rules of Professional Conduct Applicable to Regulated Persons Conducting Litigation or Exercising a Right of Audience before the Courts.

CHAPTER 27

Costs lawyers

27.1 What is a costs lawyer?
27.2 What a costs lawyer does and is permitted to do
27.3 Regulation of costs lawyers
27.4 The qualification
27.5 Maintaining the qualification
27.6 Ongoing CPD or other training obligations
27.7 Costs of maintaining the qualification
27.8 Professional conduct requirements
27.9 Sources

27.1 WHAT IS A COSTS LAWYER?

Costs lawyers specialise in the law relating to legal costs and are qualified following a three-year academic course. Costs lawyers may apply to be authorised and regulated by the Costs Lawyer Standards Board (CLSB), which issues annual practising certificates. Costs lawyers are not to be confused with law costs draftsmen or costs draftsmen, who may not hold any legal qualification, and who are not qualified or regulated by the CLSB.

27.2 WHAT A COSTS LAWYER DOES AND IS PERMITTED TO DO

The term 'legal costs' is defined in guidance by the CLSB as 'the remuneration of legal representatives (e.g. solicitors and barristers) which are controlled by statute or common law'. Areas of legal costs in which costs lawyers may become involved are:

- costs payable 'between the parties';
- solicitor and 'own client' costs;
- publicly-funded (legal aid) costs.

The work of a costs lawyer includes:

- Advice on the charging and recovery of legal fees and disbursements.
- Advice on litigation funding.

- Costs budgeting.
- Preparing schedules of costs.
- Preparing bills of costs for provisional/detailed assessment by the court.
- Preparing points of dispute and replies.
- Attending court as an advocate on detailed assessment hearings.
- Arrangement of and attendance at Alternative Dispute Resolution (ADR).
- Acting as an expert witness on legal costs matters.
- The administration of oaths.[1]

A costs lawyer with a practising certificate issued by the CLSB is authorised under the Legal Services Act 2007 (LSA 2007) to undertake the following reserved and regulated legal activities.

Exercise of a right of audience	Yes
Conduct of litigation	Yes
Reserved instrument activities	No
Probate activities	No
Administration of oaths	Yes
Notarial activities	No

Costs lawyers may, when matters relate only to costs, conduct proceedings and represent clients in any court or tribunal, including criminal courts and courts martial, the Supreme Court or the Privy Council where:

- the proceedings are at first instance; or
- the proceedings include an appeal below the level of the Court of Appeal or Upper Tribunal, are on a first appeal (other than in the Court of Appeal) and the appeal itself relates to costs; or
- the proceedings do not fall within either of the categories above, but the costs lawyer's instructions are limited to dealing with the costs of the proceedings; or
- the court or tribunal grants permission for the costs lawyer to conduct proceedings or to represent a client (or both).[2]

Where proceedings relate to other matters in addition to costs, then a costs lawyer's rights apply only to those parts of the proceedings (if any) that:

- relate solely to costs; or
- when they relate to other issues, solely those issues that are not in dispute.

The Costs Lawyer Code of Conduct defines 'relates to costs' as meaning that it:

---

[1] CLSB website, 'Home'.
[2] CLSB, Code of Conduct: Costs Lawyers, 26 March 2014, pp.1–2.

relates to payments for legal representation, including payments in respect of pro bono representation under s194 of the LSA and/or to payments made for bringing or defending any proceedings, but only if and to the extent that those monies are not damages. For the avoidance of doubt, this includes:

- costs between opposing parties including costs management and budgeting;
- solicitor and client costs but not if and to the extent that issues of negligence arise when a lawyer competent to deal with allegations of negligence ought to be instructed instead;
- legal aid, criminal costs, wasted costs or costs against third parties.[3]

27.3 REGULATION OF COSTS LAWYERS

The Association of Costs Lawyers (ACL) is an Approved Regulator under LSA 2007, but discharges its regulatory functions through the independent CLSB in the same way that the Law Society discharges its regulatory functions through the Solicitors Regulation Authority (SRA). The ACL is now solely the representative body for the costs lawyer profession, membership of which is voluntary and affords the costs lawyer no authorised rights.

27.4 THE QUALIFICATION

The qualification framework for a costs lawyer involves undertaking two stages of training:

- an academic stage; and
- a professional stage.

The academic stage requires completion of a three-year course leading to a qualification at Level 6 of the Qualifications and Credit Framework (QCF), covering:

- The foundation of costs practice
- Entitlement and recovery
- Costs management and specialisms.

The professional stage comprises three years of supervised qualifying experience consisting of relevant work experience in costs law and practice. This can be achieved before, during or after the academic stage, and need not be continuous.

A costs lawyer will have been issued with a certificate of qualification after completing the costs lawyer qualification and required qualifying experience, and may then apply for a practising certificate, which authorises the costs lawyer to undertake reserved legal activities.

---

[3] CLSB, Code of Conduct: Costs Lawyers, 26 March 2014, p.2.

27.5 MAINTAINING THE QUALIFICATION

A costs lawyer must renew his or her practising certificate annually, the practising certificate year running from 1 January to 31 December.

27.6 ONGOING CPD OR OTHER TRAINING OBLIGATIONS

To practise as an authorised and regulated costs lawyer, the Costs Lawyer Practising Rules require that a costs lawyer complies with annual Continuing Professional Development (CPD) requirements. Compliance is subject to random audit by the CLSB.

Principle 4 of the Code of Conduct provides under para.4.4 that a costs lawyer 'must keep [his or her] professional knowledge up to date by undertaking relevant training in accordance with current Practising Rules'.

The requirements relating to CPD are summarised in the table below.

Authority	Training and CPD Rules
CPD year	1 January to 31 December, inclusive
Minimum CPD points required	12 CPD points
Carry-over of CPD points	Not permitted
Reduction of minimum CPD points requirement	• If authorised by CLSB during a CPD year: 1 point for each month authorised in that year • If on maternity leave, paternity leave or on sick leave for more than 1 continuous month: 1 point for each full month worked
Reduction for part-time working	No
Requirement for costs lawyer to keep record of CPD	Yes. CLSB issues an annual CPD record sheet for a costs lawyer to use; however, CLSB will accept a record of CPD in any other format provided it is signed and dated
Consequences of failure to comply with CPD requirements	Disciplinary rules will be applied
Monitoring by CLSB of compliance with CPD requirements	• Self-declaration by costs lawyer on annual renewal of practising certificate, and • Random audit by CLSB of CPD records
Responsibility for compliance with CPD requirements	Individual costs lawyer
Obligation on employer to fund CPD activities	No
Obligation on employer to allow time-off for CPD	No

OTHER QUALIFIED LAWYER QUALIFICATION REQUIREMENTS

	activities
Requirements for eligible CPD	• A minimum of 6 CPD points from accredited activities • Balance may be from non-accredited activities CPD activities are expected to relate to an individual costs lawyer's current role or future role
Recognition of CPD activity under other regulators	Yes, reciprocal arrangements with: • Law Society/SRA • Bar Council/BSB • CILEx

27.7 COSTS OF MAINTAINING THE QUALIFICATION

The costs of maintaining the costs lawyer qualification are summarised in the table below.

Annual renewal of practising certificate fee (2016)	£250 (no VAT)
Cost of CPD courses	Responsibility of individual costs lawyer

27.8 PROFESSIONAL CONDUCT REQUIREMENTS

Once authorised, a costs lawyer has an ongoing obligation to notify the CLSB in the event of any matter which arises 'which might reasonably be expected to be disclosed as affecting their fitness to act as a costs lawyer', in addition to specific matters such as being committed to prison, being charged with or convicted of an indictable offence, being made the subject of disciplinary proceedings, being made subject to a bankruptcy order, and any change of practising address.

27.9 SOURCES

27.9.1 Websites

- Costs Lawyer Standards Board (CLSB): **www.clsb.info**
- Association of Costs Lawyers (ACL): **www.associationofcostslawyers.co.uk**

CHAPTER 28

Notaries

28.1	What is a notary?	28.6	Ongoing CPD or other training obligations
28.2	What a notary does and is permitted to do	28.7	Costs of maintaining the qualification
28.3	Regulation of notaries	28.8	Professional conduct requirements
28.4	The Notary qualification	28.9	Sources
28.5	Maintaining the qualification		

28.1 WHAT IS A NOTARY?

A qualified notary holds a Faculty and Practising Certificate, and is admitted to the Roll of Notaries ('notary').

A notary's functions include preparing and executing legal documents for use abroad, attesting the authenticity of deeds and writing, and protesting bills of exchange.

There are two types of notaries:

- General notary
- Scrivener notary.

28.2 WHAT A NOTARY DOES AND IS PERMITTED TO DO

28.2.1 Notary

All notaries, apart from scrivener notaries and those working in notary firms, are sole practitioners. Although most notaries (apart from scrivener notaries) also practise as solicitors, a notary even if employed by a firm of solicitors, will be self-employed as a notary.

Notaries authenticate and certify signatures and documents for use abroad but also for domestic transactions and documents.

353

28.2.2 Scrivener notary

A scrivener notary has passed the advanced notarial practice and legal translation exams set by the Worshipful Company of Scriveners. Scrivener notaries will have knowledge of civil law and two languages other than English. Scrivener notaries' work is usually international and they will often work for a year in a law firm in mainland Europe. Some also do commercial property work, including conveyancing, and private client work, including wills, probate and administration of estates.

Scrivener notaries do and are permitted to do the same work as general notaries, but may also do more specialised work because of their language skills and advanced knowledge of civil law jurisdictions, which a general notary might not be competent to undertake.

28.2.3 Reserved activities

A notary is authorised to undertake reserved legal activities, as indicated in the following table.

Exercise of a right of audience	No
Conduct of litigation	No
Reserved instrument activities	Yes
Probate activities	Yes
Administration of oaths	Yes
Notarial activities	Yes

28.3 REGULATION OF NOTARIES

The Master of the Court of Faculties of the Archbishop of Canterbury (the Registry of the Court of Faculties is commonly called the 'Faculty Office') is the Approved Regulator under the Legal Services Act 2007 (LSA 2007) for notaries in England and Wales. The Master has authority to make rules for the regulation of the notarial profession.

Although the Master, acting through the Faculty Office, regulates notaries (and the 'Faculty' appointing a notary is issued in the name of the Archbishop), a notary is a secular lawyer and is not otherwise associated with the Archbishop of Canterbury or the Church of England.

The Faculty Office is responsible for the governance of notaries, and the Registrar of the Faculty Office oversees the training and qualification of notaries.

The Master:

- makes the Qualification Rules and appoints the Qualifications Board;
- makes and enforces the Practice and Disciplinary Rules;

- supervises the award of the Faculty and the issue of annual practising certificates.

Scrivener notaries are members of the Worshipful Company of Scriveners, which as noted at **28.2.2** is responsible for setting the additional examinations; however, they are otherwise regulated by the Master of the Court of Faculties in the same manner as a general notary.

Notaries in England and Wales also have two membership organisations, membership of which is voluntary:

- the Notaries Society; and
- the Society of Scrivener Notaries.

Both organisations have representative functions only and are separate from the Faculty Office.

28.4 THE NOTARY QUALIFICATION

To qualify and be admitted as a notary involves obtaining qualifications prescribed by the Notaries (Qualification) Rules 2013. The qualification framework consists of two stages of training, as set out below.

Academic stage	Law degree/CPE (or equivalent)
Professional stage	Notarial Practice Course

28.4.1 Professional stage

The professional stage involves passing the Notarial Practice Course or Postgraduate Diploma in Notarial Practice in:

- Roman Law (as an introduction to civil law systems);
- Private International Law; and
- Notarial Practice

followed by attending an Office Practice Course covering:

- practical aspects of preparing notarial acts, including the function of a newly qualified notary's supervisor and the use of other resources;
- application in practice of the Notaries Practice Rules;
- consular legislation and apostilles;
- record keeping, with particular reference to notarial acts in the public form, and accounts;
- client care and handling complaints;
- Conduct and Discipline Rules.

28.4.2 Admission to Roll of Notaries

Having attended the Office Practice Course, the student is able to apply to the Faculty Office for admission to the Roll of Notaries. This is done by petitioning the Court of Faculties for a 'Faculty'. A notary is granted authority to practise under a Faculty.

28.4.3 Qualification as a Scrivener notary

A scrivener notary will have first qualified and been admitted as a general notary before passing examinations set by the Worshipful Company of Scriveners in advanced notarial law and practice, the laws of a foreign jurisdiction relevant to notarial practice in England and Wales, a main foreign language and a subsidiary foreign language, followed by a two-year training period with a scrivener notary, six months of which have been undertaken overseas in the offices of a notary or other lawyer.

28.4.4 Period of practice under supervision

Following admission as a notary, a notary's practice is required to be supervised by another notary for two years. If the notary is practising conveyancing or probate as a notary, the required period for supervision is three years following admission.

There are specific requirements under the Notaries (Post-Admission) Rules 2009, rules 4 and 5, which deal with the actual working and supervisory arrangements.

28.5 MAINTAINING THE QUALIFICATION

Notaries are required to renew their practicing certificate annually, the practising certificate year running from 1 November to 31 October. The Faculty Office sends out a paper application for renewal in mid-September each year. The completed renewal form must be returned to the Faculty Office with the notary's completed Continuing Professional Education record and evidence of their professional indemnity and fidelity insurance cover.

28.6 ONGOING CPD OR OTHER TRAINING OBLIGATIONS

28.6.1 During period of supervision

During the period of supervision, a notary is also required to attend Post-Admission Education (PAE), which involves attending compulsory day courses or seminars on notarial practice.

A notary is required[1] during the supervised period to attend the training as indicated in the following table.

Type of practice	One day each year of PAE in:
General notarial practice	• Bills of Exchange • Notarial Practice • Professional Conduct
Conveyancing work	Conveyancing
Probate work	Probate

All courses must be approved by the Master and should be for a full day. Following a course or seminar, a notary is required to make a report on it to his or her supervisor.

28.6.2 Following period of supervision

Under the Notaries (Continuing Professional Education) Regulations 2010, notaries are required to comply with Continuing Professional Education requirements on an annual basis.

The Continuing Professional Education requirements are summarised in the table below.

Authority	The Master of the Faculties
Governing regulations	Notaries (Continuing Professional Education) Regulations 2010[2]
CPE period	1 November to 31 October inclusive
CPE credit points	One credit point = One hour of Continuing Professional Education Coffee and lunch breaks may not be counted
CPE requirements	All notaries, except if during period of supervision, are required to do six credit points each year, of which at least three are through accredited activity, in: • notarial practice, for all notaries • conveyancing, for notaries who do conveyancing work as a notary • probate, for notaries who do probate work as a notary 50% of Continuing Professional Education activities must be accredited by the Faculty Office (i.e. at least three hours)

---

[1] Notaries (Post-Admission) Rules 2011, rule 6.
[2] Faculty Office of the Archbishop of Canterbury Notaries (Continuing Professional Education) Regulations 2010 Application for Accreditation of an Activity Form.

	Accredited activities must be either physical attendance at a lecture or seminar, or participation in a course which is partly or wholly-distance-learning and involves written assessment[3]
	List of accredited activities kept on Faculty website. Non-accredited activities must be completed at an appropriate level and contribute to the notary's professional skill and knowledge in the relevant Continuing Professional Education requirements (i.e. general notarial, conveyancing or probate practice), and not merely advance a fee-earning matter
Carry-over of Continuing Professional Education points	Not permitted
Reduction of minimum Continuing Professional Education points requirement	Not normally. Would be at the Master's discretion to grant a full or partial waiver, for example, where a notary's practice has been suspended, whether voluntarily or otherwise, but the notary's practising certificate may also be suspended
Reduction for part-time working	No
Requirement to keep record of Continuing Professional Education	Yes, in prescribed form – Notaries (Continuing Professional Education) Regulations 2010, Sch.2. Must be submitted to the Registrar when applying for practising certificate renewal
	The Faculty Office sends out new Continuing Professional Education record sheets with practising certificate renewal forms
Consequences of failure to comply with Continuing Professional Education requirements	Faculty Office will not issue a practising certificate until Continuing Professional Education is completed. If the notary has not completed the annual requirement by 31 October for good reason accepted by the Master, the practising certificate may be issued subject to Continuing Professional Education being completed by end of that calendar year, i.e. by 31 December
Monitoring by Faculty Office of compliance with Continuing Professional Education requirements	Annual submission of Continuing Professional Education record to the Master. Faculty Office also carries out spot checks
Responsibility for compliance with Continuing Professional Education requirements	Individual notary
Obligation on employer to fund Continuing Professional	No

---

[3] The Faculty Office website, 'Notaries: Continuing Professional Education'.

Education activities	
Obligation on employer to allow time off for Continuing Professional Education activities	No
Requirements for eligible Continuing Professional Education	Non-accredited Continuing Professional Education activities must be completed at an appropriate level and contribute to a notary's professional skill and knowledge in the basic and special Continuing Professional Education requirements, and not merely advance a fee-earning matter
	Points may only be claimed if the Continuing Professional Education activity is completed
Accreditation	Accreditation is granted by the Master. Requirements for accreditation are that the course:
	• must be relevant to the subject matter of the Continuing Professional Education requirements • must have written learning objectives and a form of written assessment to evaluate notary's achievement of the objectives, e.g. a questionnaire • if delivered by distance learning, must involve assessment by dissertation or written assessment
	To obtain accreditation, an application must be submitted to the Faculty Office using the application form.[4] In addition, the application for accreditation should be accompanied by the provider's literature or a summary of the written objectives of the course, lecture or programme
Recognition of Continuing Professional Education activity under other regulators	Continuing Professional Education requirements for notaries are independent of any requirements by another professional body of which the notary is a member. However, to avoid duplication:
	• the notary may apply for an activity accredited by another professional body to be accredited by the Master (normally, if the activity is already approved by another regulator, the Master will grant accreditation) • an activity may be part of the non-accredited Continuing Professional Education component

The types of non-accredited Continuing Professional Education activities are set out in the Notaries (Continuing Professional Education) Regulations 2010, Sch.1.[5]

---

[4] Faculty Office of the Archbishop of Canterbury Notaries (Continuing Professional Education) Regulations 2010 Application for Accreditation of an Activity Form.
[5] CILEx website, 'About CILEx'.

Even if a Continuing Professional Education activity is not accredited, the provider may apply to the Master to have the training activity accredited. Providers of accredited Continuing Professional Education activities are required to provide a certificate which contains:

- the name of the person providing the accredited activity;
- the name of the notary who completed the activity;
- the date the activity was completed;
- a brief description of the activity;
- confirmation that the activity was accredited by the Master;
- the basic or special requirement in which the activity is accredited;
- the number of credit points awarded.

28.7 COSTS OF MAINTAINING THE QUALIFICATION

The costs of maintaining the notary qualification are set out in the following table.

Annual practising certificate fee	£450*
Annual contribution to the Contingency Fund	£80*

* For the 2015/16 practising certification year, but subject to variation.

28.8 PROFESSIONAL CONDUCT REQUIREMENTS

Notaries are bound by similar practice and accounting rules to those for solicitors. They are subject to the Notaries (Conduct and Discipline) Rules 2015 and it is the Faculty Office which exercises a disciplinary function over notaries, including scrivener notaries, in England and Wales.

28.9 SOURCES

28.9.1 General information and websites

- The Faculty Office: **www.facultyoffice.org.uk**
- The Notaries Society: **www.thenotariessociety.org.uk**
- The Society of Scrivener Notaries: **www.scrivener-notaries.org.uk**

PART D

Meeting training needs within the business

Let it be said at the start that there is no prescription as to what a firm should do by way of training – apart from what might be prescribed by the Solicitors Regulation Authority (SRA) as a regulator. What will be right for one firm will not be right for another. What a firm needs to do, therefore, is to identify what its training needs are according to its business needs, and then decide what is the best way of meeting those training needs (discussed in **Chapter 3**).

The reason the SRA prescribes training for the solicitors' profession in England and Wales is to assure the competence of a single profession to the public. This does not necessarily take account of the incredible diversity in the types of legal practices within that single profession. Therefore, the guiding principle for firms should be that the training it invests in should meet the training needs which arise out of the firm's business strategy and objectives. As firms will necessarily have different business strategies and objectives, it is not surprising that one firm's solution will be different from another firm's. Just because one firm has a special programme which another firm does not, does not mean the training in the former is better than the training in the latter: it is about the effectiveness of training, and whether the training is furthering the firm's business objectives. So, the focus should not be on what firms do and do not do, but on whether the training in which a firm is investing is in fact the training in which the firm needs to invest in line with its training strategy and business objectives.

Part D therefore covers the training which a firm might consider for delivering its training strategy. In looking at the training a firm may provide, the different forms of training are discussed in the context of whether the attendees are trainees, new qualifiers, senior assistants (more than three years' qualified) or partners.

Because this book is concerned with firms knowing how to make the most of their investment in training – and doing so – this section starts with recruitment of trainees and their time on the Legal Practice Course (LPC), since this ties in with the training of trainees once they are in the firm.

It is also important to remember that solicitors do not practise in isolation and, no matter how knowledgeable or skilled, the effectiveness of their performance will be enhanced or diminished by the effectiveness (or not) of support from other employees in the firm – those in business support roles. Consequently, to train the lawyers but not to train non-lawyer employees, if the non-lawyer employees have training needs also, is not only misguided in that it risks limiting the effectiveness of the training investment in the first place, it is also in breach of a firm's responsibility under the SRA Code of Conduct to train all individuals in the firm to maintain a level of competence appropriate to their work and level of responsibility.[1] Training for non-lawyer employees is therefore covered in **Chapter 33**. For firms which either have international offices or a number of overseas qualified lawyers, there are other challenges in meeting training needs which are covered in **Chapter 34**.

Training for clients is also a consideration for many firms. Clients may demand more than just legal services; they want 'added value' which can include help in training their own lawyers. Not doing this or worse, doing it badly, can be detrimental to the client relationship. Training for clients is discussed in **Chapter 35**.

There is no expectation that a firm must do everything covered in these chapters. Rather, it is for a firm to consider what sort of training will be appropriate in delivering its training strategy.

---

[1] SRA, Code of Conduct 2011, Version 15.

CHAPTER 29

Pre-period of recognised training

29.1	Introduction	29.3	Sponsoring on the CPE/GDL and/or LPC
29.2	Recruiting during the academic stage	29.4	During the CPE/GDL and/or LPC

29.1 INTRODUCTION

Although this is not strictly training delivered within the firm, if a firm recruits its future trainees during the academic stage (see **Section B3**) and then sponsors them on the Legal Practice Course (LPC) (see **Chapter 14**) and even on the Common Professional Examination/Graduate Diploma in Law (CPE/GDL) (see **Chapter 13**) if they are non-law graduates, the firm is making a substantial investment in the training of these individuals before they even reach the firm as trainees to undertake their Period of Recognised Training (PRT) (see **Chapter 15**). The firm will quite rightly expect that the trainees in whom it has made this investment will be competent for the firm's purposes when they arrive to start the PRT. Consequently, a firm will want to ensure that it is making the most of the investment even at this early stage.

29.2 RECRUITING DURING THE ACADEMIC STAGE

Firms also make an investment in the actual recruitment process which they use to select their future trainees. Firms that recruit students in the penultimate year of their undergraduate degree programme, be it law or a non-law degree, are usually looking for the student to start as a trainee in the firm some years hence. The issue for firms recruiting at this stage is that the potential candidates, particularly non-law students, are untried and untested in much of the knowledge and many of the skills they will need for practice: they have not yet done the LPC and, if they are non-law students, they will not have done the CPE/GDL – in other words they will not have studied law yet!

29.2.1 Law students

The law student in his or her penultimate year will not, by definition, have completed the degree, but will have completed a full year's worth of law studies and usually be part-way through the second year. In terms of acquiring intellectual knowledge, the student will not have studied all the Foundations of Legal Knowledge (see **Chapter 12**).

What then can a firm rely on to decide whether this individual will, by the time he or she starts the PRT, have the necessary aptitude for practice? Studying law in the academic stage, whether on a law degree or CPE/GDL, is predominantly about acquiring knowledge (see **Section B3**). There are some skills which the student will acquire during the academic stage but the usefulness of these for practice will be somewhat limited, and will by no means provide the whole gamut of the skills that will in fact be required for practice.

For example, research will be one skill which students are required to develop on the law degree and also the LPC. However, even that may not be what it seems: there is certainly more legal source material is available online through reputable legal publishers. The internet has enabled easier short-cuts for legal research – although not necessarily more accurate ones, and students may or may not be able to evaluate the quality and reliability of the results of a Google search. Firms would be shocked to know that some students finish law degrees and the CPE/GDL without having read a case report, and having never read a statute or set of regulations as a whole – only excerpts of legislation included in handouts or student manuals.

Then there are writing skills: one assumes writing skills must be developed on a law degree, and they are. However, they are academic writing skills rather than writing as a communication skill. Many Qualifying Law Degree (QLD) providers do try to focus on writing appropriately but without the context of the practice this can be difficult.

29.2.2 Non-law students

One of the attractions of non-law students is, perversely, that they have studied something other than law – hopefully something intellectually challenging, which provides them with a breadth of knowledge, as well as maturity (they will be at least three years older than the average undergraduate law student when they start their law studies, by reason of having done a non-law undergraduate degree). However, with the non-law student, upon what can a firm base its decision to recruit? The firm does not have the comfort that the student has at least passed some exams in law and has had to do research and writing in the legal context. Admittedly, non-law students may be studying disciplines that develop equivalent analytical and other intellectual skills, and which are easily transposed to law. However, comparing potential non-law candidates is like comparing apples with bananas because of the different degrees they will have done. What a firm should be looking for in these candidates is evidence of transferable skills, as well as some evidence that they will actually take to law – something of a gamble if the non-law student has had no experience of law or practice at the time he or she is interviewed. (He or she may only just have decided that converting to law may be a good idea if job prospects for his or her original degree are looking bleak.) The CPE/GDL is effectively learning in a year what law students learn in three or more years on a QLD, for which, to put this in context, the Joint Statement (see **Chapter 12**) requires a minimum of two years of legal study of the Foundations of Legal Knowledge on a QLD.[1]

29.2.3 Assessing potential

Consequently, at the point of interview it is very difficult, if not impossible, for firms to make an assessment of a potential trainee's skills, be they law degree or non-law degree candidates. And the other issue for firms, of course, is how little students may understand or know about practice.

What firms tend to rely on in their selection process, therefore, is intellectual ability – usually based on A-level results mostly, as an indicator that the individual has the intellectual ability to develop the necessary further knowledge and skills at a later date. In addition, there is the (possibly unfair) expectation that this further development will be delivered by the LPC, so that trainees are 'fully formed' by the time they arrive at the firm.

The reality is that firms can be disappointed in the finished product. Ask firms what they think of the general standard of trainees' research, writing and drafting skills, and you are opening up a reservoir of frustration at what firms see as deficiencies in these skills – and these are skills (well, certainly, research and writing) which students should already have been developing at the academic stage. The problem for the LPC, which often gets the blame for students being deficient in these skills, is that although the LPC can do much in turning students' attention and focus toward practice, the reality is that in the short period of the LPC, the course is not going to be able to make up for what may be fundamental weaknesses or problems in literacy, writing ability and research skills. The sad truth is that, if a student has these weaknesses by the time he or she reaches the LPC, it is probably too late.

If the firm recruits someone in, say, their penultimate year of a law degree, and the individual ends up going on the LPC with deficient writing and research skills which may scrape through the LPC (the LPC only grades the Course Skills as 'Competent' or 'Not yet competent' (see **Chapter 14**), these skills are unlikely to be up to the standard required by the firm for practice. What this will mean is that further training – paid for by the firm – may be required: and this is after the firm has paid for the LPC and even possibly the CPE/GDL.

What then can a firm do to minimise this risk when it is recruiting? Testing actual as opposed to predicted intellectual ability is certainly one way. This can be done by

---

[1] The 'Joint Statement issued by the Law Society and General Council of the Bar on the Completion of the Initial or Academic Stage of Training by Obtaining an Undergraduate Degree'.

reasoning tests or Myers-Briggs, for example. Another technique is to put candidates into a discussion group situation so that they can be observed not just for evidence of intellectual skill, but also for evidence of maturity and personality as well. It may also be worth including some testing of research skills and literacy. The problem is that testing at this point does have its limitations: testing will only test the capability of the individual at that point in time – not capability at the time of starting the PRT. The reason this is an issue is because of the desire of firms to recruit the best people. Firms risk missing good candidates who, at the time they are interviewed, may not be able to demonstrate their potential capability in any meaningful or empirical way, given that the interview may be two or three years in advance of commencement of the PRT. However, the same student given time and the opportunity for development, may become a first-class candidate – not everyone matures at the same rate after all – but he or she will have missed the boat for a firm which recruits that far in advance.

29.3 SPONSORING ON THE CPE/GDL AND/OR LPC

Not all firms sponsor their future trainees on the LPC, not least because they may not recruit their trainees until after they have completed the LPC. Equally, a firm may prefer only to sponsor someone who is a known quantity, and in whom the firm is prepared to make an investment, such as a paralegal or someone the firm has had on a vacation placement. This is possibly truer for smaller firms, who might sponsor a paralegal employed by the firm to study on the LPC part-time while working as a paralegal part-time.

The firms which recruit students in their penultimate year of undergraduate study are likely to be the larger firms which can plan their resourcing needs. They are also more likely to pay the students' LPC course fees, and sometimes a living allowance as well. If the student is doing a degree other than law and will need to 'convert' by way of the CPE/GDL, the firm may also pay their CPE/GDL fees and possibly a living allowance for the CPE/GDL year. Depending on the firm, the choice of which LPC (and CPE/GDL) the student attends may be dictated by the firm and not left to the student.

29.3.1 Choosing an LPC

29.3.1.1 Differentiating between providers

Because LPCs are not graded and there is no publicly available information about performance of individual LPC providers, the only way firms and students are able to differentiate between courses is by looking at the information about the course which LPC providers themselves make available. The Solicitors Regulation Authority (SRA) requires LPC providers to provide the following:

- evidence of their Qualifying Law Degree/CPE.
- the different LPCs it provides, e.g. full and part-time (future and previous), Stages 1 and/or 2.
- key features of its different courses, e.g. where there is an emphasis on particular types of practice.
- the maximum number of students in the different types of teaching and learning sessions.
- the maximum number of students it will recruit onto each course.
- entry requirements.
- the Provider's policy on the accreditation of prior learning, e.g. will students who have studied Stage 1 with another provider be accepted onto Stage 2 of the provider's course.
- any academic qualification that will be awarded to successful students.
- the learning resources available to support the course, including library and IT provision.
- the student:teaching staff ratio.
- the percentage of teaching staff who are qualified as solicitors or barristers.
- the percentage of teaching staff with higher level teaching qualifications.
- fees.
- pastoral support, including dedicated careers guidance staff.[2]

Otherwise, there is only the provider's advertising blurb on its own website, and the views of careers publications or student comment via social media.

What is important for a firm selecting a provider is to ensure that the culture of the provider is a 'fit' with the culture of the firm. Ideally, a firm considering whether to recommend a particular provider, or even to require its trainees to go to a particular provider, should get to know the provider by having those responsible in the firm – be it the graduate recruitment manager or recruitment partner – visit the provider and spend time talking to students, watching teaching, looking at class sizes, learning about the structure of the course, and so on. Obviously, this is a time commitment – but the cost of the LPC course fee for each trainee is also a commitment.

29.3.1.2 Beauty parades

Alternatively, or in addition, if a firm is considering sending all its future trainees to one provider under an exclusive arrangement, the firm might decide to put a number of providers through a 'beauty parade' process. As an exercise in itself, this can be instructive for a firm, just by being on the other side of the beauty parade process for a change – viewing rather than parading. However, what the beauty parade of potential LPC providers does is to provide an opportunity to question providers and compare what they do, and what they are prepared to offer. If a firm does decide to carry out a beauty parade, then it is important to give the providers involved a very clear and detailed brief about what it is the firm is looking for. Important things the firm should find out from providers include:

---

[2] SRA, 'Information for Providers of Legal Practice Courses', 1 July 2014.

- What will the provider do by way of reporting on students' progress on the course?
- What is the staff/student ratio?
- Who are the teaching staff? What are their areas of expertise? How recently have they been in practice?
- What requirements does the provider impose in terms of student attendance and punctuality on the course?

One thing to look for in the providers' presentations, apart from the information they give, is how closely the provider has adhered to the brief and the firm's specific needs. If a provider has not kept to the brief or has just ignored it, it is a possible indication of the level of personal service and customisation the firm is likely to receive generally from that provider. It should also be said that size is not everything: it is true that the provider needs to have the resources to deliver what it says it can deliver, but that applies both to large and small providers. What is most important is that the firm feels that the provider can deliver what it is that the firm is looking for on the LPC.

29.3.1.3 Negotiating with providers

One thing to bear in mind when you are negotiating with a provider is that very few providers recruit to their capacity. So, there are very few LPC providers who would not be pleased to have guaranteed student numbers and fee income. Therefore, firms should not be afraid to negotiate, as a provider may be prepared to offer a discounted fee rate for a guaranteed number of students coming through.

29.3.1.4 Consortia

One might think that negotiating will only work for big City firms, and that smaller firms are unlikely to have enough bargaining power, particularly if the firm does not take many trainees each year. This may or may not be the case. However, another option for firms of any size really, but particularly smaller firms, is to consider forming a consortium with similar-sized firms with similar practices, or possibly in the same geographical area. There are obviously issues which would need to be ironed out between the firms, but it can be a very cost-effective way to put a firm's trainees through the LPC (it can also be used for other sorts of training such as the Professional Skills Course (PSC), Management Course Stage 1 and Continuing Professional Development (CPD) (see **Chapter 31**).

29.3.2 Exclusive tie-ups

The advantages for a firm in having all its future trainees attend one provider for the LPC are many, particularly if the firm has had involvement in tailoring the course for its business needs. Access by the firm to the trainees when they are students is also easier if they are all at one provider, and it means that the firm is able to have more contact with the students throughout the period of the LPC, thereby starting the necessary socialisation and assimilation into the firm sooner than would otherwise be possible.

29.3.2.1 Reasons for exclusive tie-ups

The reasons for and against exclusive arrangements with one provider include:

REASONS FOR

- Certainty in knowing that they have all covered the same areas in the same way – the level playing field idea – so that the firm knows what it is getting on day one of the PRT, namely, consistency.
- The convenience of having all the firm's future trainees in one place, making it easier to stay in touch with them during the LPC year
- Cost savings if the provider offers a discounted fee.
- Being able to require its future trainees to do certain Electives which may not be available at every provider.
- The trainees arrive in the firm knowing each other.
- It makes customisation of the course easier, for instance, by incorporating firm-specific documents or by teaching firm-specific procedures.

REASONS AGAINST

- The firm may tend to recruit trainees once they have completed the LPC because it does not know its staffing requirements that far ahead.
- Recognition that students may have personal reasons for wishing to study on the LPC at a particular provider – freedom of choice and/or not being able to afford to study on an LPC away from home, even where the firm is sponsoring.
- Not wishing students to start specialising too soon, but preferring a more broad-based approach.

29.3.2.2 Alternative solution

Short of specifying where the trainee needs to do the LPC, what a firm may do is require that trainees do certain Electives or Electives of a certain type – such as private client or corporate commercial – but leave the actual choice of provider to the trainee. LPC Electives are allocated to 'Elective Groups' and students are required to choose Electives from at least two of these different groups. Consequently, a firm which does not want to prescribe which LPC its trainees need to attend could require that the three Vocational Electives should be taken from certain Elective Groups (see **Chapter 14**).

29.3.2.3 Teaching in exclusive groups

If the firm has entered into an exclusive tie-up with an LPC provider and sends all its future trainees to that provider, then the firm will need to decide how it wishes its trainees to be taught, that is to say in a firm-specific group or in 'mixed' groups. Some firms do require their future trainees to be taught together and separately from other students on the course. This may help with their socialisation in the firm. The firm may also feel that teaching in groups of mixed ability is less effective, and the firm after all is paying for its trainees to be developed on the course in the way that the firm needs. (Whether this is 'streaming' by another name is a separate issue and has its own controversies.) However, there is a potential trap here: good advice on keeping pets says that, if you want to buy a puppy, never buy two as they will bond with each other and not with you. Same is true of trainees: if trainees have a year as a group on the LPC, they will have bonded with each other before they reach the doors of the firm on day one of the PRT. The confidence from being part of such an established group may interfere with the integration the firm then wants to achieve with the trainees as individuals. Having to deal with such a problem is by no means unknown among firms which have tried the exclusive group approach.

Puppies aside, the trainees themselves may not like the exclusive group approach and may feel as if they are in a type of boot camp – that it is too restricted or rarefied always being with the same people all the time, and can also lead to a competitive environment. There is also a more general issue, which is that lawyers will meet and need to deal with a whole range of people in their practising life – not only clients but also colleagues and other employees within the firm. If all the trainee is used to dealing with is his or her own 'type' – and that is not to say that firms recruit clones, but they will be of a similar intellectual capability – this may not help prepare the trainee for working in the firm. An advantage of having a firm's trainees taught as part of the course's general population is that they will have to learn to deal with, gain co-operation from, and work together with all sorts of people with different abilities. They will also make contacts which will stand them – and the firm – in good stead further down the line – networking is, after all, a necessary skill in the modern-day lawyer's armoury. This is not to say that the firm's future trainees should never be taught or brought together as a group before starting in the firm: there is a lot to be gained from early socialisation and induction. However, it is better for the firm if it is the firm which leads the process and has control of the socialisation and integration.

The possibility of having the trainees taught as a group for the Electives subjects, for example, or if the firm is part of a consortium taught in groups comprising other consortium firms' trainees, should not be excluded, provided that the firm is aware of the potential problems in doing so and has evaluated the benefits as outweighing the potential disadvantages.

29.4 DURING THE CPE/GDL AND/OR LPC

29.4.1 Practical steps during the CPE/GDL and/or LPC

Whatever a firm does decide to do, there are some practical steps a firm should consider taking to help ensure that the trainee will be best prepared by the time he or she starts the PRT. These steps include the following:

1. Check with the particular CPE/GDL provider as to the provider's approach to teaching research and writing skills. Are students required to read case reports, for instance, or to search primary sources?
2. Similarly, check with the particular LPC provider as to its approach in teaching the Course Skills. Ask the provider about the extent of reliance on manuals (which merely summarise the law and provide extracts of relevant legislation), as opposed to using actual primary source material. Are LPC students trained in using both electronic and hard copy sources?
3. Engage with the CPE/GDL or LPC provider during the course so that the firm can follow students' performance.
4. Work with LPC providers in particular to shape the course in order to ensure the right level of skill is being taught (the LPC has considerable flexibility for curriculum design and for adding additional material and emphasis as is explained in **Chapter 14**).
5. Use the student transcript (see **Chapter 14**) to check a student's marks in these Course Skills, and also the number of attempts it took the student to pass. A firm might consider having a 'first attempt only' condition to their offer of employment. This would certainly focus a student's attention to take the course seriously if his or her PRT hung in the balance.
6. Require students to undertake the firm's own test in research and writing at the end of the LPC as a condition of the offer of employment.

Even by taking these steps, there is still a risk that trainees may not be at the necessary standard when they start in the firm, and that the trainee may use the firm's knowledge management (KM) systems as a crutch and in so doing, avoid having to improving his or her own skills. Therefore, dealing with the problem sooner rather than later is required.

29.4.2 Contact with the firm during the course

Irrespective of whether a firm requires all its trainees to go to the same LPC provider, if a firm is sponsoring its students through the LPC (and the same applies to the CPE/GDL), then one way of looking after its investment is to ensure its sponsored students are performing on the course as the firm requires (e.g. passing all assessments at the first attempt and achieving better than a pass in terms of grades) and achieving the standards the firm both needs and expects.

29.4.2.1 Progress reports

It is remarkable the number of firms which sponsor students on the LPC and then do not bother to check students' progress during the course. Apart from the obvious concern to make sure the firm has not wasted its money, it can also provide early indicators of unprofessional attitudes or difficulties which may occur once the trainee is in practice. LPC providers will not necessarily alert firms to student under-performance or behavioural concerns unless the provider has the express consent of the student to do so – or the firm has required this information as a condition of the PRT offer.

Many providers have attendance and punctuality requirements and each student will have a personal tutor. Obtaining a status report on a trainee's attendance and punctuality, as well as on performance in early assessments, can be of help to firms to identify potential problems. It is not necessarily about using this information to withdraw PRT offers. For many students, making the transition from the academic stage to the vocational can be very difficult even for the brighter students, some of whom may see the LPC as an irritation – a delay on their way to their real goal, which is starting in the firm as a trainee. The sorts of interventions described which a firm can take to obtain a progress report of the student's attitudes and performance can be a very effective way of focusing the student on the course and providing the necessary incentive for the student to take the course (and the firm's investment in paying the fees) seriously. It would be wrong to think that students with a First, for example, in their underlying degree do not have this sort of problem – they can too. How much worse to lose a potentially very good recruit because he or she has failed to make the transition and/or has failed to perform to his or her full potential out of impatience with study. Although the standard transcripts for the LPC show how many attempts it took a student to be successful in a subject, it is a bit late to wait for the transcript to be issued in order to identify a problem, particularly one which it may have been possible to rectify if the problem had been identified earlier and an intervention made sooner.

29.4.2.2 Help desks and surgeries

If the firm has the resources, a good practice is to have someone from the firm's graduate recruitment team visit the provider every couple of weeks and be there for, say, a couple of hours to man a help desk or surgery for the firm's trainees. The firm's 'rep' can identify problems, speak to the course director, to the tutors to get progress reports and to students to see if there are any concerns. This is obviously dependent on resources, and is made easier if all the firm's trainees are at one provider. However, even if they are not, a visit even every couple of months to the various providers – again subject to having the resources to do this – can prove enormously beneficial in letting the firm's trainees know that they are not invisible and therefore need to apply themselves, and also in dealing with problems before it is too late. This is something a firm should check with the provider, namely that the

PRE-PERIOD OF RECOGNISED TRAINING

provider will keep the firm up to date about its trainees, as part of the firm's due diligence before agreeing to an exclusive tie-up or prior to including a provider on its recommended list.

29.4.2.3 Firm-focused activities and events

Aside from checking on students' progress, firms can also use the LPC as the time to start the familiarisation and socialisation process with the firm. Some firms bring the trainees into the firm at different times during the course – some monthly, others on, say, six or seven occasions during the course. The trainees can be given talks about the firm and its different practice areas – the idea is to instil in them that with the LPC, their PRT with the firm has all but started. Alternatively (or additionally for that matter), the firm may give their students some additional exercises to be undertaken by them during the course, such as research and drafting which are more tied to the firm's practice. These could require the students to come into the firm and use the firm's library or other information resources in order to complete the exercise, if that was felt to be desirable. Firms which have adopted this approach of regular contact with their students have tended to notice a difference in their trainees' attitudes to the LPC at the start of their professional career, as opposed to an attitude that the LPC is their last year of freedom. The latter attitude is less likely to provide the firm with best value for its investment.

Finding time for these types of events and activities in the LPC calendar should not be difficult if discussed with the provider well in advance of the course starting. The firm should specify what it would like to do with its trainees while they are on the course, so that the provider has a chance to incorporate these activities into the timetable. Waiting until the course has started to ask the provider to build in meeting times, for instance, is a logistical nightmare for provider and students alike. Another idea might be to meet with the trainees the day before they start the LPC, perhaps with a lunch, so that they start as the firm means them to continue – namely, focused on the firm they will be moving into following the LPC.

29.4.3 About the Legal Practice Course

The LPC is discussed in detail in **Chapter 14**.

29.4.3.1 Severability

The LPC is run in severable stages so that students are able to break their studies or change to another provider should they wish to. The question is why would they and, more importantly for firms, why would the firm wish them to? No reason has to be provided for stopping after Stage 1 of the LPC and, given that there is a five-year 'use-by date' (five years counted from the date of the first attempt at an assessment), there is nothing to prevent a student finishing Stage 1 and then lounging on a beach in Goa for the next three years and 11 months).[3] With all going well and no re-sits required, the student jumps on a plane to Goa following completion of exams at the end of February in Year 1, returns to start Stage 2 in March of Year 5, completing assessments in June – and still has until February of Year 6 to deal with any re-sits, having been away from study (and possibly legal updates) for one month short of four years. This is obviously not likely to be a preferred path and is an extreme example, but firms need to understand that the opportunity is there.

29.4.3.2 Employability

The risk for the student who decides to complete only Stage 1 first, is whether he or she is likely to find employment, particularly if the student wants to commence a PRT. The reason for this potential difficulty is that firms may either not wish to have someone who is 'half-baked' so to speak, rather than 'fully cooked', or that firms may not be able to deal with a mix of trainees, some of whom have completed the whole course and others who have not – a potential administrative and training nightmare. If firms are not willing to recruit Stage 1 trainees, then the student who has stopped after Stage 1 may feel rather misguided if he or she is then not able to find employment to fund the remainder of his or her studies.

29.4.3.3 Completing Stage 2

Another concern for firms, particularly smaller firms but by no means only small firms, is the issue of how and when the Stage 1 trainee would complete Stage 2. Would it mean the trainee would have to take time out of work for each Elective subject – potentially one month per Elective subject? Would it mean the Stage 1 trainee doing Stage 2 part-time in his or her own time, which means having to add study on to what may be an already heavy workload? And, not to put too fine a point on it, who would pay: the firm or the trainee? If the Stage 1 trainee has done the LPC this way because of financial difficulties in supporting him- or herself through Stage 2, then requiring the trainee to fund Stage 2 course fees would seem to be perverse.

Where the firm already has part-time employees studying on the LPC part-time, then accommodating someone studying Stage 2 of the LPC while working may not be that difficult. Equally, it may be easier for trainees in in-house legal departments, and the in-house legal departments themselves might prefer this route since it would enable them to require the trainee to study an appropriate Elective at an appropriate time.

---

[3] If the student's first attempt at an assessment was in the February of Year 1, he or she would have until February of Year 6 to complete Stage 2.

29.4.3.4 To tailor or not to tailor?

SPECTRUM OF CHOICE

Firms which have exclusive links with LPC providers should have input into what and how their future trainees are to be taught, so that the finished product is what the firm needs for its business. It is not the case, however, that only those firms have the opportunity for tailoring the LPC. There is a wide spectrum of possible involvement – from the situation of not specifying either the LPC or the Electives that a trainee has to do, to providing a list of recommended providers or Electives, to an exclusive tie-up with a provider or a bespoke course for the firm, right through to the other end of the spectrum where a firm applies to be accredited and validated to run the LPC itself by way of a collaborative arrangement (discussed further below). It has to be said that this last extreme has not as yet been taken up by firms, and may not be (although in certain circumstances, discussed below, it could be considered). However, the point is that the possibility is there. Generally, most firms have tended to sit at the other end of the spectrum: either not specifying the provider, or at most specifying the provider and/or Electives. Obviously, the smaller the provider, the smaller the likelihood that the provider will be able to offer a number of variations of the LPC to suit a range of firms. That does not mean the firms are really only left with a choice of the larger providers – not at all; it just means that a firm needs to do its homework to identify which course is the best match for the firm's own particular culture and business needs, irrespective of the size of the provider.

BREADTH OR DEPTH?

Many firms are not attracted by the idea of customising the LPC to a particular focus: they prefer the LPC to produce graduates of sufficient breadth of knowledge and skills that the firm can then deploy where and when the firm requires. The firm will do any customising itself once its trainees have joined the firm. An important by-product of the breadth approach is that it produces greater 'peripheral vision', so that trainees have sufficient knowledge to have alarm bells ring even if they may not know the answer – they just know that they need to bring in someone who does know the answer. One of the greatest dangers to a firm's business is its lawyers not knowing there is a problem in the first place. This is why well-developed peripheral vision is so important.

However, even if the firm's preference is for a broad curriculum, the firm should not overlook the possibility of using the flexibilities that exist in the LPC curriculum to its advantage: for example, to incorporate the firm's standard documents (there is no harm in students becoming familiar with the key documentation used in different practice groups in the firm, whether in the Core Practice Areas or Electives as soon as possible), or to enhance the teaching of certain key skills such as research, writing and drafting.

PROVIDER EXPERTISE

Another concern firms may have about customising the LPC is not only whether the provider has the resources to deliver the customisation, but also whether the provider's teaching staff have the capability to deliver a course which has been customised to a firm's practice needs. Although LPC providers have policies to keep their teaching staff in touch with practice, the reality is that it is very difficult for teaching staff to return to practice in any meaningful way to 'refresh' their experience in practice. That is one reason that providers are keen to have involvement by firms and to have feedback from firms, in order to ensure that the course delivers what firms need. However, the reality is that if teaching staff are not able to return to practice on a regular basis, even though they may keep in contact with practitioners (and most do), there may be limitations on how effectively they will be able to teach a curriculum which has been customised. A more basic issue is whether there is the practice expertise among the teaching staff to teach a particular subject in the first place. If, for instance, a firm wishes to have an immigration Elective or a corporate finance Elective, it is important that the provider has the expertise within the team to teach the Elective. If the provider does not have the expertise, then the training would be better provided either within or by the firm (see **29.4.3.6**).

USING THE 'HEADROOM' IN THE CURRICULUM

One way of using the 'headroom' in the curriculum, if the firm does not want to make the LPC overly-specialised, is to incorporate client care elements. Clients, as well as partners, could be used to talk to students about client service and to understand the skills that are involved. Teaching client service without the input of clients or partners is not likely to be effective, particularly if students have had little or no experience of firms or practice up until then. In fact, how effective this can really be until the students are trainees in the firm is moot. However, as a way of introducing the concept of client care and the firm's own culture or policy, it can be useful. There is an inherent weakness in vocational courses, which is that although vocational courses such as the LPC try to emulate real life or practice, they do so outside practice and out of context. Although the LPC can introduce students to the concepts of practice, it is only when students become trainees and actually start to practise that what they have learnt on the LPC is put into context and the penny drops.

29.4.3.5 *Maximising performance on the LPC*

What a firm wishes to avoid is paying twice: paying for its trainees to attend the LPC and then investing in training in the firm that duplicates what they have been taught on the LPC. Whether the firm has wasted its investment will depend on why training is being duplicated. It may be because the firm is not aware of what its trainees have done on the LPC and runs training for its trainees without taking into account what they have been taught on the LPC. In this case, the firm is definitely wasting its money (fee-earner time of both trainer and trainees if the training is being done in-house).

Alternatively, the training may be needed because the trainees' knowledge and/or skills are not what they should be when the trainees start in the firm. This may be because the trainees did not apply themselves while they were on the LPC. As mentioned earlier, Course Skills on the LPC are marked only as 'Competent' or 'Not yet competent', and only a 'Competent' is required to pass (i.e. 50 per cent or over). The reasons trainees may not have applied themselves are many, but one reason could be that the firm simply has not kept in touch with the trainees during the course (see **29.4.2**). Students who do not have an offer of a PRT have the impetus to perform as well as possible. However, if the PRT offer is already 'in the bag', subject to the firm requiring a minimum grade such as a 'Commendation' or that all assessments are passed at the first attempt, along with meeting any attendance requirements, where is the pressure to do more than the minimum required? If the firm is prepared to engage with its trainees while they are on the course, and make it clear the assumed knowledge they will be expected to have when they start in the firm and that they will not be spoon-fed by going over what they have already covered on the LPC, then students are more likely to perform on the LPC. What that means for the firm is that it is less likely to need to waste money duplicating what has been covered on the LPC. Other inducements can also be used, such as financial incentives (a bonus if the trainee achieves a mark of more than 70 per cent, for example, or linking seat allocations during the PRT to performance on the LPC).

If, however, the reason trainees' knowledge and/or skills are not what they should be when they join the firm is that the LPC itself has not delivered, then the firm needs to see whether it did its due diligence well enough in the first place, but in any case should take this up with the LPC provider.

29.4.3.6 *Collaborative arrangements*

If a firm is paying for top-up training which would not have been needed had students applied themselves fully on the LPC, the firm could always consider obtaining authorisation and validation to offer the LPC itself and avoid duplicating what trainees have done on the LPC in training in the firm. This is likely to be unfeasible for most firms, unless perhaps a firm was prepared to invest in an 'academy'-type training function.

What would be more feasible is for the firm to have a collaborative arrangement with an Authorised Education Provider – LPC provider. Provided it does not involve itself in the setting or marking of assessments, a firm would not need to obtain authorisation itself.

The SRA does requires authorisation of collaborative provisions but it is a method of delivering the LPC which the SRA encourages.

The SRA defines 'collaborative provision' as provision of the LPC which involves 'delivery and/or assessment of aspects of the course by more than one organisation'.[4] This means that a firm may 'collaborate' with an authorised provider to deliver the LPC. Depending on which part/s of the LPC the firm wishes to deliver itself will determine whether or not the firm will also need to seek authorisation and validation. In summary:

Firm delivers	SRA requirements
Any part of the LPC except assessment	Firm to arrange this in partnership with an authorised LPC provider
	Responsibilities of authorised LPC provider: • seek SRA validation of the jointly-delivered course • accountable to the SRA for all aspects of the course • setting and marking assessments
Setting and/or marking LPC assessments	Apply for authorisation as an LPC provider and validation of course/s

A firm which is involved in the delivery of the LPC by way of:

- design, internal approval and review activities;
- preparation of course materials; and
- lecturers delivering aspects of course

does not constitute a collaborative arrangement, and the authorised LPC provider would manage and be responsible for the course overall, including the quality of the input from the firm.

The SRA's requirements for collaborative arrangements are that:

- Responsibilities between the partners are clear and documented
- Students will be able to understand and access information about the respective responsibilities of the partners, e.g. with regard to the receipt and investigation of complaints
- Assessment will be the responsibility of the provider authorised by the SRA
- There is effective communication between those involved with the delivery of the course both within and between each of the partner organisations
- The course will provide a coherent learning experience for students.[5]

The SRA will also require to see a copy of a binding agreement between the partners, and additional information about the partner organisation if that organisation is not applying for authorisation. This is all set out in the Legal Practice Course Information Pack.

---

[4] SRA, Legal Practice Course Information Pack, 1 July 2014, p.13.
[5] SRA, Legal Practice Course Information Pack, 1 July 2014, p.14.

CHAPTER 30

Trainee solicitors

30.1 Introduction
30.2 Understanding the firm as an organisation and the trainee's role
30.3 Legal technical knowledge for the particular practice area
30.4 Peripheral knowledge
30.5 Business awareness
30.6 Management skills

30.1 INTRODUCTION

Firms may think that the training they need to provide to trainees during the Period of Recognised Training (PRT) is that required by the Solicitors Regulation Authority (SRA). This would be a mistake.

The SRA's requirements for the PRT as set out in the SRA Training Regulations 2014 – Qualification and Provider Regulations ('Qualification and Provider Regulations'), reg.12.1 merely tell a firm that a trainee needs:

- to be supervised by people with the necessary skills and experience to provide effective supervision;
- to have learning and development opportunities and personal support to meet the Practice Skills Standards;
- to have practical experience in at least three distinct areas of law and practice;
- to have training so that he or she knows the requirements of the SRA Principles and are able to comply with the Principles;
- to have reviews and appraisals of his or her performance and development of the Practice Skills Standards, and knowledge and compliance with the SRA Principles.

These requirements generally can be satisfied by a firm:

- providing those who supervise trainees with supervision and feedback skills training;
- providing coaching/mentoring support to trainees;
- providing trainees with seats in at least three practice areas during the PRT;

- delivering a training session on the SRA Principles;
- conducting performance reviews and appraisals.

What it does not say is what actual training trainees should be provided with during the PRT, other than training which will enable them to develop the practice skills set out in the SRA Practice Skills Standards, which are:

- advocacy and oral presentations;
- case and transaction management;
- client care and practice support;
- communication skills;
- dispute resolution;
- drafting;
- interviewing and advising;
- legal research; and
- negotiation.

Many of these skills will have been taught on the Legal Practice Course (LPC) (Advocacy, Legal Writing and Drafting, Interviewing and Advising, and Legal Research), and some will be further delivered in the Professional Skills Course (PSC) (such as in the Compulsory Core of Advocacy and Communication Skills, and Client Care and Professional Standards).

What training then does a firm actually need to provide in addition? This is not just to ensure that the trainee will meet the standards required by the SRA for qualification, but also that a firm's trainees will be competent to be deployed profitably in the firm as soon as possible. This is actually what the real concern is for firms. To this end, trainees need to develop as soon as possible:

- understanding of the firm as an organisation and what is expected of them;
- the knowledge and skills which are required to perform effectively at their level in the particular practice areas they work in during the PRT;
- peripheral knowledge of related areas;
- business awareness of the firm's and clients' businesses; and
- management skills appropriate to the firm's work and practice.

30.2 UNDERSTANDING THE FIRM AS AN ORGANISATION AND THE TRAINEE'S ROLE

30.2.1 Induction

The best way of providing trainees at the start of the PRT with an understanding of the firm, its structure, its business and what is expected of the trainee is by way of an induction. If the firm has sponsored its trainees on the LPC and engaged with them while on the course, then some of this understanding may already have been developed. However, this would only possibly alter the content of the induction.

The SRA does not require Authorised Training Providers to provide an induction for trainees although it does regard it as good practice, even if the trainee has worked for the Training Provider previously, since the purpose of an induction is 'an opportunity to clarify the roles and responsibilities of those who will be involved in the trainee's training, to familiarise the trainee with office procedures, to introduce fellow staff members and to explain the nature of the work that they will undertake'.[1]

The SRA does not prescribe the format or length of the induction and it is for the Authorised Training Provider to organise the induction as best suits the firm. However, the SRA suggests that the induction could cover:

- an introduction to your organisation, the training scheme, the Practice Skills Standards and your expectations of the trainee
- how the training will be organised
- the form of the training record that you want the trainee to keep, how and when it is to be completed, and when it will be reviewed
- arrangements for supervision, performance review and formal appraisals
- your office procedures, including pastoral care, office hours, holidays, health and safety
- any other relevant matters, such as your IT and office equipment and systems for time-recording and billing, library and research facilities, secretarial and administrative support.[2]

If a firm decides to use the SRA's suggestions for content, then it might also consider the following suggestions:

- A session on IT and office equipment could include training on using the telephone, photocopier, printer – whatever equipment the trainee would be expected to use. Although trainees may be from the generation which is completely at home with computers, they may never have worked in an office before, so may not have had to use the particular types of equipment available in the firm (some of which may even seem prehistoric to them . . .). In any case, this sort of training is best done through hands-on demonstrations, supplemented by brief user notes that the trainee can refer to afterwards.
- A session on library and research facilities should cover whatever knowledge management (KM) systems for capturing and retrieving information are used in the firm, in addition to the firm's library services and online as well as hard copy sources. Where the firm has subscriptions to online services, it may be possible to have the online provider come in and give a demonstration of the services where the numbers justify it; alternatively, someone in the firm who is proficient in using the service could also do this. The point is to make sure that the trainee is able to use all the resources the firm has invested in, and which the trainee will be expected to use.

---

[1] SRA, Authorised Training Provider Information Pack, 18 August 2014, p.5.
[2] SRA, Authorised Training Provider Information Pack, 18 August 2014, p.5.

- In the 'introduction to your organisation' session, consider including talks on all the firm's practice areas, so that all trainees start with an understanding of what it is the firm does, irrespective of where they do their 'seats'. After all, trainees might only do seats in three practice areas during the traineeship. The reason for giving talks on the firm's different areas of practice is not just to give the trainee information about the firm the trainee is joining, but to assist the socialisation process of the trainee to become part of the firm: it is important knowledge that will help a trainee know who in the firm has expert knowledge to whom he or she can refer if he or she needs to (risk management), but also to cross-sell the firm's expertise should the opportunity arise either in the trainee's work with clients or when networking. The sooner the trainee has this awareness and the sense of belonging to the firm as a whole, the better.

Other areas a Training Provider might consider covering in its trainee induction could include:

- risk management and compliance;
- introduction to marketing (including cross-selling);
- finance and how an individual's time-recording contributes to the firm's overall profitability;
- how to work with their secretary;
- how to use equipment and software in the firm to produce their own work;
- talks by fee earners on what is expected of trainees;
- talks by other trainees on their experience of being a trainee.

It may go without saying but it is important to say it anyway: trainees should be introduced to a range of people through the induction process, from partners to secretaries and business support staff. In fact, as trainees they are likely to have more contact with and rely on secretaries and business support staff than partners.

A word of caution, however: there is a limit to how much trainees are going to be able to take in, particularly in the first days – and weeks – of joining the firm. Being bombarded with information will not necessarily guarantee the easing into the firm and practice that the induction is intended to achieve. When the induction is held, and how it is delivered, should be determined by how much there is for trainees to take in. The answer may be to run the main sessions over the first few days of trainees joining the firm, and then to follow up or introduce other topics over a longer period of, say, a few weeks. This means that trainees have a chance to settle in and familiarise themselves, so that what they are being told starts to have some context. In fact, when trainees are starting to ask 'how', 'where' and 'why' it is usually a good indication that they are ready for the next phase of their induction.

In the same way that you do not need a formal training session to train someone, a firm does not need to have a formal induction if the number of trainees does not justify it. If the firm only has one or two trainees, the induction proper can be given one-to-one or even by way of pre-recorded webinar (which can be resource-efficient). The trainee can then be given a few weeks to shadow, familiarise, read files and so on.

Another way of making trainees familiar with office procedures, information resources and so on, is to give trainees a project or projects to do during the first few weeks. Projects can also be used to assess the trainee's literacy, numeracy, initiative and personal organisation skills, to give a few examples – a diagnostic, in other words.

30.2.2 Role models

The most valuable training that occurs is on the job, from observing and learning from an experienced practitioner. The role model approach to learning and developing is underrated, although firms are increasingly putting in place coaching and mentoring in the firm.

For the trainee, the role model is extremely valuable. Practising law is not just about knowledge and skills; it is also about behaviours – values and attitudes. These may be capable of being described but they are not easily acquired out of context. Once a trainee starts in practice, it will be the observable behaviours of the trainee's supervisor and others with whom the trainee works who will shape and form the trainee's values and behaviours – for better or worse!

The whole concept of professionalism depends very much on the development of these appropriate values and behaviours. For many trainees, up until their interview with a firm – or vacation placement – they may have had little exposure to the legal profession and practice, other than perhaps what they have seen on TV. Many will turn up on day one of the PRT with no real idea of what legal practice is all about. They will have done the LPC – and passed – but this will not necessarily have given them an understanding of what practice is all about. How the trainee learns as a member of the firm is through observable behaviour: how to behave in the firm; how to gain the co-operation of secretaries and business support staff; how to behave with senior members of the firm; how to organise themselves; and so on.

It is therefore very important that those in the firm who supervise trainees are aware of the importance of acting as an effective role model and of being able to coach and mentor.

30.3 LEGAL TECHNICAL KNOWLEDGE FOR THE PARTICULAR PRACTICE AREA

In order to be able to do the work a trainee in a particular practice area is expected to do, the trainee is going to require some knowledge and understanding of the legal and practice framework for the area. Depending on the practice area, the trainee may have acquired at least some of this knowledge, or understanding at least, from the law degree or Common Professional Exam/Graduate Diploma in Law (CPE/

GDL) and LPC. However, that knowledge or understanding will have been acquired theoretically and may also have been acquired some time before.

Ten weeks of an Elective on the LPC does not create a specialist. However, it does serve to introduce an area of practice. What trainees tend to find is that, if they have done an Elective relevant to the practice area they are in, they find it easier to find their feet. It does not mean that if the trainee has not done an Elective that is relevant the trainee will not succeed in the seat, just that the learning curve will be steeper.

Depending on the practice area, the law and regulation that is relevant may be completely new. Without that knowledge and understanding, however, it is going to be difficult for the trainee to work effectively.

For this reason, some sort of introduction into the practice area in terms of the relevant laws and regulation, types of transactions, key documentation, reference and KM sources at the start of the seat is very important.

The problem is if the practice area does not have the critical mass to justify running an introductory session for, say, one trainee. Some might be of the view that the trainees the firm employs are capable, intelligent individuals who should be able to find their way. Another version of this is the 'I was dropped in the deep end and survived' justification. The 'dropping in the deep end' scenario is actually a good analogy to use to explain why equipping trainees at the start of their seat is so important.

If someone is dropped in the deep end of a swimming pool without having been shown how to swim, then the likelihood is that they will drown, unless they manage to work out how to stay afloat. There will have been a lot of energy expended and anxiety caused, however, in the attempt to avoid drowning and work out how to float. How much simpler it is if the person is given some basic information about how to stay afloat and warned of what he or she will experience beforehand. The likelihood is that he or she will be swimming in the pool a lot sooner, and developing his or her style and strength more quickly, without the need for a lifeguard always to be on hand.

The analogy is not perfect but the point being made is valid: a trainee will acquire competence much more quickly if he or she is given the wherewithal to do the work. If there is not the resource to give a dedicated introduction each time a new trainee starts in the practice area, then a simple intervention is to have a manual for the practice area which sets out all the necessary information for the trainee to be able to help him- or herself. If the practice area has a dedicated Professional Support Lawyer or other KM support, this is something which they could produce.

If a practice group is concerned about keeping the manual up to date, then it could make it the responsibility of each trainee to update the manual before he or she rotates to his or her next seat, thereby making a virtue out of necessity, and helping the trainee consolidate his or her knowledge and understanding at the same time.

30.3.1 Generic training needs

As a general rule of thumb, the sorts of things that trainees tend to need help with (or those supervising them feel they need help with) when they start the PRT or a new seat include:

- prioritising and managing their work;
- proof-reading and marking up documents;
- preparing bibles of documents;
- managing closing or completion meetings;
- dealing with clients (and overcoming the fear factor);
- drafting board minutes and other secondary documentation;
- extracting information from documents for due diligence;
- presenting research.

30.3.2 Required seat

An approach some firms take to ensure all their trainees have a common foundation of knowledge is to require all trainees to do a seat in a particular practice area, such as property, or corporate or private client. If that is the main focus of the firm's practice, and the number of trainees which the firm recruits and size of the particular practice group make it feasible, this is one way of providing common training to all the firm's trainees.

30.4 PERIPHERAL KNOWLEDGE

In any area of practice, there is going to be knowledge of related areas that will be relevant. It will be this 'peripheral knowledge' that is the mark of a good lawyer, who can identify issues and know when to seek others' expertise. For most lawyers, peripheral vision develops as one practises over time. However, being able to develop peripheral vision sooner is desirable if competence is what the firm wants its lawyers to achieve.

For trainees, having experience of at least two other practice areas may develop peripheral knowledge, depending on their relevance to the area of practice the trainee qualifies into. However, other ways of developing peripheral knowledge in trainees is by requiring trainees to attend training in other practice areas during the PRT. That way they are also meeting the lawyers in other practice areas, whom they may need to work with or seek advice from in the future.

30.5 BUSINESS AWARENESS

The trainee needs to be aware of the firm as a business, irrespective of what sort of firm it is, and of the need to time record, bill and work efficiently. This can be taught as part of the induction. Depending on the work of the firm and the particular practice areas in which the trainee sits, there may be awareness of industry sectors, the City or financial centres or other business contexts that the trainee will also need.

Business awareness can be acquired in many ways: training sessions to explain the business context; simply observing and learning on the job; participating in business games; joining special interest groups in the firm or externally; or simply reading relevant industry journals and publications.

30.6 MANAGEMENT SKILLS

If a firm believes that leaving it until a partner is appointed or elected managing or senior partner to be trained in management skills is too late, then it is wise to consider more structured development of management expertise. Although trainees may not be about to run the firm, they can start acquiring management skills which will provide the basis for the managers of the future. At trainee level, the management they need to know about and be able to do is essentially managing themselves, their work, their deadlines and the people whose support they will need. Management skills are not mentioned in the SRA's Practice Skills Outcomes but they are very important to the firm in having its trainees acquire the competency needed for the business as soon as possible.

CHAPTER 31

Qualified solicitors

31.1 Introduction	31.3 Training for qualified solicitors
31.2 Training for newly qualified solicitors	31.4 Training for senior assistants and leading to partnership

31.1 INTRODUCTION

It is important to distinguish between solicitors who have just qualified – 'new qualifiers' – and solicitors who have been qualified for at least two years or more. The experience of being a trainee one day and qualified the next can be akin to the stabiliser wheels being removed from one's first bike, and being told 'off you go'! That is when new qualifiers realise just how sheltered they have been as trainees. However, a properly managed transition should avoid any sudden shock, and allow the new qualifier to find his or her balance and start 'cycling'.

31.2 TRAINING FOR NEWLY QUALIFIED SOLICITORS

31.2.1 Induction

Qualifying is a 'step-up' in the same way as starting the Period of Recognised Training (PRT) or becoming a partner. Therefore, some sort of induction into the world of qualification and what is now expected of the new qualifier can help the transition so that the new qualifier understands, firstly, what it is to become a solicitor and, secondly, what it is to be a solicitor in that particular firm.

Not all firms provide formal inductions for new qualifiers, not least because the number of new qualifiers may not be felt to justify it. However, a chat with the head of the practice area into which the new qualifier has qualified is sensible, especially if the new qualifier is going to have an individual financial target set.

Where new qualifiers can find the biggest change is in having to take responsibility for their own files, and dealing with billing and monthly targets. So, whether it is an induction proper with a formal session, or merely an informal chat, the following areas might be worth covering, according to the size, type and practice of the firm:

- risk management procedures in the firm;
- client care policy and procedures;
- the role of the marketing department/manager, what he or she does and the importance of marketing;
- billing and billing targets, and costs control;
- the role of the Human Resources (HR) department and what the new qualifier needs to know and do when managing staff;
- Continuing Professional Development (CPD) requirements[1] and personal development;
- career structure and development pathways, including appraisals, salary structure, etc.;
- the firm's case management system even if they have had to use it as trainees.

There is a rite of passage in making the transition to becoming professionally qualified which can and should be marked, if for no other reason than to encourage a professional approach and taking responsibility. Encouraging new qualifiers to attend their admission ceremony is a way of emphasising this. However, there are other reasons for marking the rite of passage: building loyalty to the firm and encouraging future commitment. If nothing else, a lunch for the sole new qualifier with a partner, or a lunch or dinner for all new qualifiers, is a way of marking the occasion. The importance of social events in helping to build relationships should never be underestimated.

What a firm does not want is for the new qualifier to become disenchanted and leave before the firm has had the chance to recoup the investment it has made in the new qualifier's training up until then (trainee salary for two years, Professional Skills Course (PSC) fees and time out to do the PSC, and possibly Legal Practice Course (LPC) and Common Professional Examination/Graduate Diploma in Law (CPE/GDL) fees, and a living allowance…). The reality is that for many, the first six months after qualifying are going to be the most challenging in their career, and likely to be when their confidence dips.

Providing them with the tools to survive, and with support, can go a long way to alleviating any terror the new qualifier may feel, and help him or her to settle down into his or her new role as a practitioner. Training in 'lifestyle management' could also be considered, so that the new qualifier is able to manage work without undue detriment to his or her health and well-being.

---

[1] The 16-hour requirement for all solicitors will be removed from 1 November 2016 and replaced with a Continuing Competence regime. See **Chapter 20**.

31.2.2 Generic training

As discussed in **Chapter 30**, even if a firm sends all its trainees to one LPC provider, they still may have followed different routes to qualification: law degree, non-law degree or Chartered Legal Executive routes. If the trainees came from different LPCs, then there will have been even more differences in their experience. So, by the time trainees start their PRT in the firm, their levels of knowledge and aptitude may be quite variable. The firm may not have wished to address this unevenness in the prior learning of its trainees for the simple reason that it may not keep on all its trainees at qualification. Therefore, it would be wasting money to provide additional training to address this unevenness during the PRT.

However, for those trainees who do qualify into the firm, the firm has made a commitment by keeping them on, and now may be the time that the firm wishes to ensure that all its new qualifiers have the same or equivalent levels of knowledge and skills (see below). Although they may have been in the firm for two years as trainees, the combination of seats they will have done – not to mention the different seat supervisors – means that they may have had uneven development even within the firm. Whether this is a problem which needs to be addressed can only be decided by the firm. Depending on the size of the problem, and the resources available in the firm, investing in some form of generic training for all new qualifiers may or may not be justified. A firm may take a pragmatic approach that, as new qualifiers qualify into different practice areas, they will not all be doing the same work and therefore do not all need the same training, and that what is more important is training in the specific practice area.

If the firm has a large number of trainees, then the case for generic training may be stronger. A commercial practice, for example, may feel it is important to ensure that all of the firm's new qualifiers have an adequate grasp of fundamental concepts such as:

- contract law;
- execution of documents;
- boilerplate clauses;
- commercial awareness, etc. and that this is a worthwhile investment;
- professional privilege.

In some cases, addressing the unevenness can simply be a matter of refresher training, or even self-study of what the firm may specify as required knowledge and expertise for all qualified lawyers in the firm. An extension of this idea is to require trainees to have a viva-type interview as a precursor to being offered a seat in a particular practice area, during which their level of knowledge and understanding for that practice area is tested.

Alternatively, a formal training programme for all new qualifiers in the firm could be considered, which could cover the sort of topics listed above. Again, this will depend on whether there is a problem which needs to be addressed and how big the problem is.

Where a special programme cannot be justified, or is not felt to be necessary, time spent by the new qualifier with someone in the firm, talking over some of the fundamental concepts, can be of use – it does not always have to be about formal training sessions (see **Chapter 36**).

31.2.3 Practice area-specific training

Another practical need for training arises from the simple fact that it may conceivably be 18 months since the trainee was in the practice area or department into which he or she has now qualified. So, a practice area-specific refresher may also be of help. Again, this is going to depend on what training the new qualifier received as a trainee, the ability of the new qualifier and what is feasible in terms of resource.

Where there are not the numbers to justify a dedicated practice area-specific training for new qualifiers – or a sole new qualifier – but there is a need for some form of development, other ways of approaching this which could be considered include:

- a rolling training programme for those up to two years' qualified (0–2 years' post-qualification experience), subject to there being a sufficient number of people within that band;
- encouraging or requiring new qualifiers to attend specialist courses, or to study for professional qualifications or accreditation in certain practice areas, since these qualifications often carry credibility with clients.

This is not advice to send new qualifiers on external programmes; by the point of qualification, what is important is that they have been inculcated into the way the firm practises, which is not achieved with a generic approach. What is probably of most importance is to ensure that the new qualifiers are thoroughly acquainted with the main documents and procedures of the practice area. A good way of doing this is through negotiation exercises based on a key document, with the new qualifier having to negotiate the document on the basis of a fact scenario, either with another new qualifier or more senior member of the practice area if this has not already been done during his or her time as a trainee. Equally, just having a partner turn the pages of key documents with new qualifiers over a couple of lunchtime sessions can be valuable. It goes back to the best means of delivering the training to achieve the training objectives (see **Part E**).

A more lateral approach can be to ask a 'friendly' client to allow the new qualifier to do work for the client, under supervision of course, on the basis of a reduced fee, in order to give the new qualifier experience sooner. However, with downward pressure on fees, clients may not be keen to pay to train their lawyers.

31.2.4 Skills training

The pyramid diagram in **Chapter 1** illustrates that it is at the more junior levels of trainee and new qualifier that the greatest investment in training is likely to be needed for both legal technical and skills training.

However, given the transition from trainee to new qualifier, some firms prefer to focus on legal technical knowledge at this stage rather than skills, and to rely on the skills taught on the LPC and during the PRT and PSC.

One study[2] identified the range of skills that students could develop through studying law which would be needed for practice as the skills to:

- communicate effectively in writing;
- communicate effectively verbally;
- present complex arguments in appropriate language;
- analyse information effectively;
- think critically;
- evaluate and synthesise information;
- identify and analyse key issues;
- find practical solutions to problems;
- make effective use of time and resources;
- work effectively with others;
- contribute effectively to group tasks;
- work effectively on own initiative;
- cope with new situations;
- reflect on own performance;
- take constructive feedback/criticism;
- give constructive feedback/criticism;
- make use of IT tools/packages;
- use IT to support one's studies (i.e. legal databases and websites);
- understand and interpret numerical data and present it in assignments/reports.

This study was based on law students, rather than trainees or junior lawyers, so there are also skills not mentioned which are necessary for practice. However, as a starting point, it is useful to consider the skills needed against the possible training which could help develop such skills. This is particularly relevant when carrying out a training needs analysis (see **Chapter 3**) and in performance appraisals.

31.3 TRAINING FOR QUALIFIED SOLICITORS

Whereas training for new qualifiers may focus more on technical knowledge rather than skills, training for assistants as they gain post-qualification experience veers the other way. Legal technical expertise is developed through on-the-job training.

---

[2] Bell and Johnstone (1998) 'General Transferable Skills in the Law Curriculum'.

As solicitors increase in their level of responsibility, so too does the risk to the firm if their knowledge and ability is not on a par with or appropriate to that level of responsibility. Consequently, it is important to ensure the match between competence and responsibility. Training needs to be risk-based, in other words.

31.3.1 Generic training or CPD

Another point to bear in mind is that if a firm is paying to send its people on external courses, it should make the most of that investment and ensure that the benefits of the external course are brought back into the firm, be it into the firm's knowledge management (KM) systems (e.g. by simply uploading the handout) or in the improvement of the knowledge or understanding of other members of the firm by 'cascading' the information from the person who attended to those who did not. This could be done by the person who attended giving an internal seminar on what was covered at the external course, or by producing a practice note.

It is also questionable whether it is justifiable to send more than one person on the same external course. When it may be justified to have more than one person attend is where one of the objectives of attending the particular external course or seminar is not just training but marketing, networking or client relationship management or building. However, in that case it is arguable that the course fees should come out of the marketing budget, rather than the training budget.

To send a number of people to the same external course and not have anything from the course fed back into the firm – not even the handout – is a wasted investment.

31.3.2 Practice area-based training

Once members of a practice area have moved beyond the new qualifier stage and are familiar with the practice area's transactions, documentation and procedures, then the main training needs will be in relation to understanding and dealing with changes in the law, changes to practice, and so on. If the practice area develops a new precedent to use, then training on the new precedent is important.

Equally, as an assistant takes on responsibility for files and staff, then he or she also needs compliance training, such as anti-money laundering and health and safety, although this sort of training is usually compulsory for all lawyers in the firm.

31.3.2.1 Peripheral vision

As assistants become more senior, enhanced peripheral vision becomes more important – an 'alarm bell' sounding system – which enables them to identify when issues arise which may require the input of expert advice. This peripheral vision can be developed by cross-discipline training, and hopefully the peripheral vision will already have started developing by their having undertaken different seats during the traineeship. It may also be helpful to have junior solicitors attend training sessions, such as seminars, which are given by other related practice areas. This also builds relationships between practice areas within the firm, which can have benefits for more effective working and co-operation as well.

31.3.2.2 On-the-job training

The most valuable training for junior lawyers is the on-the-job training. This is partly 'learning the hard way', but balanced out by good supervision and feedback. On-the-job training is most effective if it reinforces what an individual does well – good practice – and identifies 'bad' practice that needs to be changed or avoided. The secret is feedback by the individual's supervisor, and the opportunity for reflection by the individual being supervised. Even the most conscientious of lawyers will admit that, with the best intentions, it is not always easy to provide feedback at the time. Transactions move very fast; client expectations are for very short turnarounds and sometimes there is not enough time in the day. If it is possible, though, coaching and mentoring should be encouraged. It is a shame to lose good people because of an underlying problem that may have been resolvable had it been detected. It is another reason that a formal appraisal process is so important – so that junior lawyers (in fact everyone for that matter) can receive feedback on their performance annually at the very least.

31.3.2.3 Post-transaction reviews

Another way of developing people on the job, which overcomes the problem of lack of time during the transaction and the problem of having to wait for the annual appraisal, is to conduct a post-transaction review – or post-mortem – by those who have been involved with the deal/transaction/case after it has been completed or closed.

At its most basic, the post-transaction review should consider:

- what went well;
- what didn't go well;
- what should be done next time;
- what shouldn't be done next time;
- comments on any precedents used – typos, suggestions for improvements, amendments to reflect changes in market practice, etc..
- documents which were used which should/could be made into useful precedents;
- any letters of advice or research which could be added to the firm's know-how system.

Apart from the obvious benefit of learning from the experience (i.e. what went well, what didn't go well, etc.), a post-transaction review is a means of:

- capturing know-how from the deal/transaction/case;
- team building; and
- encouraging buy-in and commitment to a common enterprise.

The reasons post-transaction reviews do not always take place include:

- a culture that fee earning is all that matters and anything that cannot be time-recorded or charged to the client is a waste of time or unnecessary;
- one deal ends and another is about to start – or more usually has already started – so there is no time;
- reluctance of the more senior lawyers (partners or senior assistants) to having what is effectively a 360 degree appraisal, and having any problems in the transaction made visible and able to be commented upon by those junior to them. These attitudes are unfortunate, as post-transaction review meetings can also provide other benefits for business development, as they may present an opportunity to spot post-transaction 'selling' opportunities: if the client has just bought a business, for instance, does the client need transitional IT services, advice on data protection, and so on?

There is rarely any time to do anything at the end of a deal other than to get the bill out. However, if a firm wants a workforce which is competent and maintains its competence – and in so doing reduces the firm's exposure to negligence claims – then the firm needs to develop the culture that makes this happen (see **Part A**).

31.3.3 Practice Skills training

The LPC will have introduced assistants to various practitioner skills in the Course Skills subjects of Legal Writing and Drafting, Practical Legal Research, Advocacy and Interviewing, and Advising. The PSC will have continued this development with further advocacy training, and the introduction of client care and communication skills, and work and case management skills. However, a criticism of the LPC is that, although its purpose is to prepare students for practice, by definition it is teaching students outside practice. Similarly, if the compulsory modules of the PSC have been front-loaded before the start of the PRT, they too will have been studied outside practice.

What further skills training is going to be needed for assistants post-qualification (in addition to the skills which they should have been developing on the job since qualifying) will depend very much on the individual assistant's performance appraisal, and reflection on and identification of their learning and development needs, which a Continuing Competence approach requires (see **Chapter 20**). The areas where skills training is often needed are:

- personal organisation;
- case/transaction management;
- drafting;
- team membership;

- negotiation;
- dealing with difficult people;
- presentations;
- marketing and networking;
- appraisals as appraisee;
- assertiveness.

As qualified solicitors become more senior, the areas of skills training which may additionally be required include:

- team leadership;
- beauty parades;
- business development;
- giving appraisals;
- mentoring and coaching;
- interviewing for recruitment;
- project management.

Training in many of these skills can be by way of generic courses, although particular exceptions of negotiation and project management are best done in the context of the particular type of work. For example:

- negotiation is not just about hammering the table – it is about knowing and understanding the parameters beyond which the client's interest will not be served;
- project management is not just about to-do lists, but about resourcing and pricing, which will depend on the particular project.

Consequently, training in these skills is usually best done in-house and within the particular practice area. Even within the firm, there will be differences in approach across practice areas, and different types of transactions and cases.

It is probably stating the obvious to say that all the different parts of a firm's business need to work together. However, this is also a consideration when it comes to training: if the firm is running training in business development, for instance, then it would be as well to involve the person in charge of business development in the firm. This prevents the training being merely theoretical, and takes forward the firm's business development strategy.

Similarly, training in interviewing for recruitment could usefully have input from HR – and so on. Just because it is training for lawyers does not mean that there are not valuable contributions to be made to the training by others within the firm, and which will provide lawyers with an insight not otherwise available to them.

31.3.4 Management training

The requirement for lawyers to have management skills increases – and expands – as a solicitor advances in seniority.

Solicitors are no longer required by the Solicitors Regulation Authority (SRA) to attend the compulsory Management Course Stage 1 (MCS1) for management training.[3] This means there is no actual requirement for solicitors to have management training; only the requirements under the SRA Code of Conduct, and Principle 5 in particular.

The SRA's reasons for removing the requirement for MCS1 included recognition that as a generic course, MCS1 was unlikely to be meeting the needs of any solicitor, and that many firms already provide their solicitors with the management skills they need to be competent. The SRA also believed that having a prescriptive requirement to do MCS1 was inconsistent with its new Continuing Competence approach (see **Chapter 20**).

Comment

Although removing this requirement is probably generally welcomed, it would be unfortunate if firms and solicitors took this as a statement on the need for management training at all. Solicitors do need to develop and have management skills appropriate to their level of experience and role, and firms need to have solicitors who have the skills required to manage themselves, others, the client relationship, finances and the business. So, solicitors who qualified between 31 March 2012 and 31 March 2015 and feel aggrieved that they had done MCS1 by 1 April 2015 should look at it another way: rather, all the SRA's decision to dispense with the compulsory requirement does is acknowledge that a generic 'one size fits all' course is not the best way of developing management expertise.

From the firm's perspective, whether there is a requirement to do MCS1 or not, firms still need their solicitors to be able to manage finance, manage client relationships, manage people, manage information and ultimately manage the firm. So, any temptation to toss management training onto the bonfire, along with training programmes and training budgets, because of the introduction of the Continuing Competence option to meet CPD requirements (see **Chapter 20**) should be resisted, and instead firms should give consideration to more effective ways of developing the management skills and expertise that MCS1 was intended to do but did not always achieve.

For firms which do not otherwise provide management training to their solicitors, the MCS1 curriculum does give a basis that firms can use to consider appropriate training in:

- managing finance;
- managing the firm;
- managing client relationships;
- managing information;
- managing people.

Management training is discussed further at **20.13**.

---

[3] Prior to 1 April 2015, solicitors were required to undertake MCS1 within three years of qualification.

These are the areas that many firms would want their solicitors to be able to do anyway. Many, especially larger firms, may indeed cover these areas in their own training programmes.

In order to be a lawyer with a successful practice, it is not just a case of having technical legal knowledge, but being able to manage one's practice and to win clients and work. This is so whether the lawyer is a sole practitioner or a partner in a larger international law firm. It means understanding one's practice as a business and it is the areas of:

- financial management
- management and strategy of the firm as a business, including preparation of business plans
- development and management of client relationships, and
- management of people

which have generally been under-developed in law firms.

Imposing good disciplines early on can add significantly to a firm's bottom line. So, there is an argument for starting to develop these skills from trainee and junior assistant level (as discussed in **Chapter 30**), as well as for those aspiring to partnership, and to those who have achieved partnership status.

PROJECTS

Therefore, ensuring its lawyers have the necessary management skills should be very important to a firm. Developing management skills need not be confined to training programmes. Another way is by using projects.

There may, for instance, be real management issues within the firm which need addressing. One way of creating assistant buy-in – as well as resolving a management issue – is to give a group of assistants a topic to discuss and problem-solve. They could be required to involve relevant business support departments, such as IT, Marketing, KM, and then to give a presentation of their ideas. This exercise has the additional advantage of involving other skills such as team work, work management, research, presentation, and business and management skills, to name a few.

Some firms have developed management training programmes that are akin to MBA programmes, although the advantages of this sophistication may not be easy to justify. The balance to be achieved is keeping senior assistants engaged in the business (which MBA-type programmes are designed to do) and even letting them know they have prospects, but not 'skilling them up' with the tools so that they will want to go elsewhere. An MBA programme may not be necessary, but certainly the sorts of areas that lawyers should be knowledgeable about and have their skills developed in include:

- billing (including negotiating bills);
- the firm's financial cycle;
- people management;

- personal organisation;
- project management and pricing;
- client relationship building;
- key client account managing;
- media;
- beauty parades and pitches;
- knowledge management.

31.3.5 Business awareness training

All lawyers in the firm need to understand the firm as a business and how they contribute to that business, particularly in terms of fee earning, but also through other activities (even training ...). This is one aspect of business awareness and knowledge; the other is an understanding of the commercial environment and marketplace/s in which the firm's clients operate. Some might classify business awareness training under management training. Understanding the firm as a business certainly can be included in management training. However, understanding a client's business is more externally-facing.

This sort of business awareness can range from a general understanding of the City and how it operates, to an industry-specific focus. What training is needed will really depend on the type of business of the particular firm, and the clients for which it works. As a rule of thumb, firms engaged in corporate/commercial work, be they located in the City of London or elsewhere, should ensure that all their lawyers involved in this sort of work – or acting for corporate/commercial clients – should have a basic understanding of the City and its institutions, the workings of business and the movement of money.

If one wanted to finesse this further, those involved in corporate/commercial work which involves financing in any way, be it equity or debt, should also have an understanding of financial institutions, how they operate and how they are regulated. To be fair, anyone coming off the LPC and PSC will have been trained in the Financial Services and Markets Act 2000 (FSMA 2000). However, this will have been on a rule-teaching and learning basis. What is usually still needed is an understanding of the implications of FSMA 2000 in practice.

Again, the LPC will have covered business accounts, so lawyers should be able to read and draw up a simple balance sheet and profit and loss account. Whether this will be enough, however, when they are doing private equity, debt financing, or mergers and acquisitions work, for example, is another matter. More advanced training may be called for (for example, on applicable accounting principles, discounted cashflows and internal ratio of return formulae).

A very good way of acquiring business awareness is through secondments – either to financial institutions, for example, or on secondment to a client. These sorts of secondments also have the added benefit of strengthening the client relationship and channelling workflow towards the firm – provided the person seconded is competent. The risk if he or she is competent, though, is that the client may wish to keep him or her permanently – a real test of the client relationship in those circumstances! Mini-secondments offer another (perhaps less risky) approach.

31.4 TRAINING FOR SENIOR ASSISTANTS AND LEADING TO PARTNERSHIP

Whether training is provided for senior assistants in preparation for partnership is a difficult one, particularly if not all candidates will be offered partnership. Again, it is very much a question of resources and priorities.

Some firms will have a development programme for their lawyers in line with a competency framework and linked to performance appraisal (see **3.3**). Other firms will not have formal training programmes, but will use a formal assessment centre for those whom the firm considers are ready for partnership. Other firms may have a combination of the two.

A key attribute senior associates need to demonstrate at this stage of their career is their ability to attract and retain clients and to build client relationships. Without these skills, a solicitor's career prospects in private practice will be limited. If a firm is considering training for its senior lawyers with a view to partnership, areas it might consider are:

- client relationship management;
- marketing;
- project management;
- people/team management.

The more senior a solicitor becomes the greater the requirement for him or her to take a lead in these areas.

As a starting point, training for senior assistants should be based on the individual's appraisals over the years, and the training needs identified in those appraisals.

Projects are an alternative way for more senior assistants who are looking for partnership to develop these skills. This can have a number of benefits:

- an assistant's success in carrying out the project, and the way in which he or she carries it out, can assist with the partner selection process;
- it gives the assistant experience or exposure to management, so that when promoted to partner he or she has had experience of more than just fee earning;
- it can take forward the firm's strategy or business objectives if the project is based on something that is needed in the firm – a publicity plan or a networking plan, for instance.

Training for senior assistants and new partners can benefit from being undertaken in-house rather than by external courses, as the training can be designed to provide the skills that are required for a senior assistant or new partner to take forward the firm's business, which is not as easy to achieve with generic training. That is not to say that the training cannot be delivered by external trainers or experts, particularly as partners within the firm may not have the expertise in non-law skills areas, but the context should be that of the firm's business.

At this point in a solicitor's career, he or she should also have access to coaching and mentoring. Firms can make the mistake of seeing coaching as only necessary for remedial cases, whereas the reality is that effective and timely coaching and mentoring can help develop a senior assistant's potential and can help a senior assistant focus on what is important, both to his or her career and for the client relationship. Its importance should therefore not be under-estimated. Given that the individual's future career path will be determined by senior members of the firm, external trainers may be considered for providing this coaching and mentoring.

CHAPTER 32

Partners

32.1 Introduction
32.2 New partners
32.3 Partners generally
32.4 Re-deployment of partners
32.5 Partner relocation

32.1 INTRODUCTION

Although the legal technical training needs of partners are likely to be far fewer than for trainee solicitors or junior assistants, that is not to say that partners have no training needs. Particular milestones in a partner's career which trigger training needs in particular are:

- becoming a partner;
- being re-deployed;
- taking on a management role;
- being relocated.

These training needs are all covered in this chapter. What is also discussed is the contribution that partners can – and should – make to protect and enhance the firm's intellectual capital.

32.2 NEW PARTNERS

In the same way that starting as a trainee or qualifying are 'steps up', so too is becoming a partner.

The transition to partnership requires new partners to understand:

- how people will perceive them in their new role; and
- what will be expected of them, particularly in terms of taking forward the firm's business, its strategic direction and the like.

Some form of induction is therefore advisable and it is probably one time where the fact that there are few new partners is irrelevant in justifying whether a formal induction should be held.

Areas which should be covered in a partner induction, depending on what training the partner has already had before becoming a partner, include:

- law firm management;
- building client relationships;
- billing and fee practices;
- networking;
- profile raising;
- project management;
- leadership;
- diversity and equal opportunities;
- team building;
- managing difficult situations.

A talk by the firm's senior or managing partner is a good way to 'kick-off' the induction. If there is only one new partner, this can be done on a one-to-one basis. However, whichever way it is done, a welcome to the partnership is very important.

If formal sessions are to be given, these could be run as a one-day or two-day programme, or even in blocks over a period of time to give the new partner the chance to absorb all the information, and the new role and its responsibilities. (Although the risk in doing it in a protracted format is that the new partner may have difficulty finding the time to attend subsequent sessions.) If the new partner has not previously supervised trainees, training in the requirements for trainee supervision is appropriate, if this is one of the responsibilities the new partner will be taking on (see **15.12**).

32.3 PARTNERS GENERALLY

There is a belief by some partners that having achieved partnership status, they have 'arrived', so to speak; that they are perfectly formed and no further training or development is needed. One hopes that keeping up to date with the law is implicit in this particular credo. Perhaps if an individual has developed along the path to partnership in a firm which has trained and developed him or her at each stage as described in **Chapters 29–31**, his or her knowledge, skills and expertise may indeed be par excellence. Does that mean that nothing further is needed apart from keeping up to date with the law and practice?

There are two types of training which a firm should consider for its partners for the benefit of the firm, both of which are concerned with assisting and encouraging partners to pass down their knowledge, skills and expertise to others in the firm.

Intellectual capital is mentioned a lot in this book – it is a firm's main asset: the knowledge, skills and expertise of the people in whom the firm has invested. If a partner has developed high levels of knowledge, skills and expertise, it is important that this is not lost to the detriment of the firm. So, it needs to be captured. This capturing can be done in many ways, such as:

- the writing of practice notes;
- the drafting of standard forms or precedent documents; and
- training of others in the firm.

The problem with law firm culture is that it is very much one of fee earning: anything that is not fee earning is difficult to justify.

There is also the additional push in law firms for 'youth' as opposed to 'age', with partners in middle-age sometimes feeling as Dickens' Scrooge, with the curtains on his bed being torn down before the body is cold. In some ways the drive for youth is quite sensible: a partner, say, in his or her fifties has probably been practising for some 25 years, working long hours under considerable stress. What is not sensible is if, instead of utilising the wealth of experience and expertise the partner has accumulated, he or she is effectively put on the scrap heap – made into a consultant to be eased out after a few years with a golden whatever. A firm which has this culture of actively turning off its 'older' (aka middle-aged) partners will have to re-invent the wheel unnecessarily to build up the knowledge, skills and expertise possessed by the retiree. The problem is that the financial structure of law firms, where fee earning is linked to bonus entitlements, militates against partners moving into non-fee earning roles, such as training, unless the firm management is particularly enlightened. This is unfortunate, as there is an important role for the more senior partners not only in training and guiding young lawyers, but also in providing a mentoring role. For this to work effectively, however, it must be supported by the firm's career and remuneration structure. Unfortunately, the trend for a lot of 'senior' partners is to cling on to their client relationships and the day-to-day work in the belief that this will protect them from the cull, rather than demonstrating their value to the firm in being able to develop others. It is something for partners and management to ponder.

The firm that is able to resist this culture of ageism, and which values its intellectual capital, will encourage its senior lawyers, particularly partners, to pass on their knowledge, skills and expertise in the ways suggested. Interestingly, there is usually no issue with a senior partner spending more of his or her time in a management, client relationship building or marketing role; it just seems to be training or knowledge management that does not have the kudos, or the acceptable face.

If a firm does wish to involve its partners in training, then it would be well advised to make available 'train the trainer' training (see **Chapter 38**). Just because partners might think they know everything, does not mean they can teach it.

32.3.1 Partners in management roles

Management training has been discussed generally in **20.13** and **31.3.4**. Where partners are appointed to the firm's management board or to the position of managing partner or similar, then quite specific training needs arise. Traditionally, promotion to these positions in firms is a case of promoting the competent to positions for which they are not competent. Partners who have excelled in their practice in the firm, who have become of a sufficiently high level of seniority or, let us be honest, popular, often find themselves elevated to management positions. Usually the partner will have managed his or her practice successfully financially, so is not without some financial acumen. However, depending on the partner's generation, he or she may not have been exposed to any formal management training as part of his or her legal education and training. The objective, therefore, is to ensure that partners moving into management positions (and this includes non-solicitor 'Managers' under the Legal Services Act 2007) are provided with the training they need to carry out their management role. The range of options is broad. Often, however, the focus is on doing a quasi- (or full) MBA, but it need not be: a lot of money can be spent on short courses provided by pre-eminent business schools, when what would be more useful is focused one-to-one training, supported by coaching over a longer period of time. One myth to de-bunk is that management skills are extraneous to a solicitor's skills set – a 'back of the envelope' job and nothing more.

32.4 RE-DEPLOYMENT OF PARTNERS

Another area for training which may be required for partners is where a partner needs to be re-deployed from one area of practice to another. This may or may not be recession-driven; sometimes it is part of the firm's strategic plan to develop a particular specialist area or industry sector connected with a client relationship. A capable partner may be regarded as able to make the transition, not least because of his or her business-building ability. In this case, training in the new area needs to be considered. However, depending on how close the new area is to the individual's existing expertise, it may be that he or she already possesses sufficient peripheral knowledge to equip him or her for the move. Even if that is not the case, a trainee-level or junior assistant-level training course may not be appropriate, since the partner's level of knowledge and skills, which have been acquired over years of practice, place the partner at a different level to a trainee or junior assistant, even if it is a new area for the partner. This may be a situation where a coaching approach might be more useful, and/or access to appropriate online learning.

32.5 PARTNER RELOCATION

Where a partner is relocated to another of the firm's offices, particularly if overseas, some induction (in the non-formal induction sense) into the office, the type of work, client base, market, as well as the jurisdiction, may be desirable, not to mention an introduction to the particular culture and practice style of the office, as appropriate.

CHAPTER 33

Training for non-lawyer employees

33.1 Introduction
33.2 SRA Code of Conduct and entity-based regulation
33.3 Benefits of training
33.4 Induction
33.5 Types of training
33.6 Projects

33.1 INTRODUCTION

A firm is the sum total of all its employees – not just its lawyers. An assumption that a lawyer's performance is entirely down to his or her innate ability is completely mistaken. No matter how clever the lawyer, what makes the lawyer effective and able to deliver a high quality service to the client is the support and assistance of others – not only other lawyers in the firm, but in particular non-lawyer members of the firm – paralegals, business support staff, and most importantly secretaries, to name a few. If a firm wishes to make the most of its investment in employing non-lawyer professional and other business support staff, then encouraging and enabling them to maximise their potential is the logical thing to do – and consistent with a firm's business objective of being successful.

33.2 SRA CODE OF CONDUCT AND ENTITY-BASED REGULATION

However, there is also a regulatory imperative to this: Solicitors Regulation Authority (SRA) Principle 5 and the obligation on a firm to provide a competent service to its clients, and the expectation under entity-based regulation that a firm will train all its staff to understand their responsibilities under the SRA Code of Conduct.

33.3 BENEFITS OF TRAINING

There are important side benefits, however, of training all members of the firm:

- Investing in training someone to realise his or her potential creates loyalty; making someone better at what they do alleviates stress if the person is struggling. Many non-lawyer professionals are considerably under-utilised in firms in terms of the contribution they could make if allowed to.
- Alleviating stress leads to a healthier workforce with less time off on sick leave.
- Including people in a culture of training and development, particularly where the training and development goes hand-in-hand with the firm's business objectives, creates a more homogenous community, which means lower staff turnover, higher morale, greater dedication and fewer staffing issues.

So, the firm which feels that investing in training for its non-lawyer staff cannot be justified should think again. It does not mean that staff are going to be taken away from their job unnecessarily – the same principle applies as for training for lawyers: the only training a firm should invest in is training which furthers its business objectives through the development of its staff, in line with those business objectives. If the training does its job, the investment will have been worthwhile.

33.4 INDUCTION

The one type of training that should be common across all staff is training which introduces new staff to the firm, its culture, its objectives and its collective values, and also which sets out what will be expected of employees in their respective roles within the firm. This can be done by way of an induction when staff join. If time away from their job is a real issue, then using e-learning, audio or audio-visual delivery may be a way of achieving this more conveniently.

33.5 TYPES OF TRAINING

In the same way that a solicitor in a supervisory role needs to have team leadership and people management skills, so too do those in business support departments and those leading teams.

The very fact that it is called a department signifies that there is likely to be more than one person involved, in which case someone is going to be leading and supervising. If the person in that role does not have the skills to run the department, then the firm's business can suffer.

In addition to a new joiner induction, other training which business support staff might need includes:

- training to enable the individual to do the role, if this is required;
- training to ensure the individual does the role as expected in the firm;
- training to enable the individual to progress to a more senior role, if a career path exists;

- training which is identified through the individual's performance appraisal and which forms his or her personal development plan, or which is remedial;
- training which ensures the individual understands and complies with absolute obligations of confidentiality in relation to both the firm and its clients.

So, the different types of training which might be considered for non-lawyer employees, should a need be identified, include:

- IT skills;
- anti-money laundering procedures;
- diversity and equal opportunities;
- health and safety;
- presentation skills (a good idea for trainee inductions is to have a senior secretary talk to the trainees about how to work with their secretaries, for instance, or someone from the finance department to talk about how to fill out time sheets. Anyone who is required to give a presentation should have access to presentation skills training);
- supervisory training;
- writing skills (if required to write reports);
- team building;
- managing difficult situations;
- client care (a good idea for secretaries who have client contact or switchboard responsibilities, or even library or information services staff if they deal with clients);
- communication skills;
- confidentiality and professional conduct requirements;
- overview of what the practice group does, if the individual is dedicated to a particular practice group, including jargon-busting.

33.6 PROJECTS

In the same way that projects can be used for developing management skills in lawyers, so too can projects be used for developing non-lawyer employees. In fact, involving business support staff in projects assistants may be undertaking for their business or management skills development can be beneficial, both in terms of building rapport between the fee earning and business support parts of the firm, and for engaging the non-lawyer population of the business, whose commitment is as necessary as that of the lawyer population in achieving the firm's business objectives.

CHAPTER 34

Overseas offices and overseas qualified lawyers

34.1   Introduction
34.2   Overseas qualified lawyers
34.3   Overseas offices

34.1   INTRODUCTION

In addition to solicitors qualified in England and Wales, a firm may also employ lawyers who are qualified in a jurisdiction other than England and Wales.
   They may be employed:

- to practise the law of England and Wales, which if they have not re-qualified as a solicitor of England and Wales must be under the supervision of a qualified solicitor of England and Wales if the overseas qualified lawyer is practising reserved areas (see **8.2**);
- as fee earners practising the law of England and Wales;
- as fee earners practising as lawyers under their home jurisdiction (i.e. not practising the law of England and Wales), and who will need to continue to comply with any Continuing Professional Development (CPD) and/or re-registration requirements of their home jurisdiction; or
- in an office outside England and Wales, either practising the law of England and Wales (under the appropriate supervision referred to above) or practising the law of their local or their home jurisdiction.

34.2   OVERSEAS QUALIFIED LAWYERS

Whether individual training programmes are needed for each of the above types of overseas qualified lawyer is moot. What can be said is that a firm should consider providing training to ensure that its overseas qualified lawyers who are doing the work of a solicitor know and understand the law of England and Wales in the particular area of practice. For lawyers coming from non-common law jurisdictions, this includes an understanding of the common law legal system. An EU lawyer who has been admitted under the Establishment Directive (see **Chapter 8**) has not been required to study the law of England and Wales, although the presumption is that by having worked in England and Wales for three years under supervision the lawyer will have acquired the necessary knowledge and understanding. A non-EU lawyer who has been admitted under the Qualified Lawyers' Transfer Scheme Regulations 2011 (QLTSR) (see **Chapter 9**) will have been required to demonstrate knowledge of the law of England and Wales, and competence as a practitioner according to the standards required of solicitors of England and Wales.

All overseas qualified lawyers who join the firm should be given an induction in the same way as all new joiners receive an induction into the firm. It may also be helpful, depending on the jurisdiction from which the lawyer comes, and also the lawyers' own familiarity with the law of England and Wales, to include an introduction to the English legal system and practice, and even some de-mystification of English culture as well as of practice.

Where the non-UK lawyer is practising his or her home law in the firm, in addition to the induction it will also be necessary to provide an explanation of the firm's policies on client care, client service, risk management and other matters under the Solicitors Regulation Authority (SRA) Code of Conduct (the SRA's regulatory reach applies to all members and employees of the firm, whether or not a solicitor with entity-based regulation), even if further legal or technical training may not be seen as being necessary.

34.3 OVERSEAS OFFICES

For firms with offices outside the UK, the issue is more complex. New joiners need to be inducted into the particular office, but also into the firm as a global entity. The difficulty with the latter is that how this is best done will depend on how cohesive a global entity the firm in fact is.

34.3.1 London nucleus with satellite offices

Some firms may have grown from a London nucleus with satellite offices elsewhere, staffed by partners and assistants on secondment. In this case, it is easier to establish a 'firm' culture, since the firm started from the one parent. As part of this, it is easier to have a homogenous approach to training across the firm, with equivalent training across all offices in order to ensure equivalent levels of expertise and performance. However, this homogeneity requires commitment by all offices.

Other firms may have grown from a London nucleus but by creating associations with existing, independent legal practices in different jurisdictions, or even through mergers with those practices. In this situation, the idea of one ethos is more difficult, and in fact more fraught. Local practices will be loath to lose their identity, or indeed to feel dictated to, which may make them feel subordinate to the UK parent and therefore resent a centralist approach.

There may also be cultural differences in approaches to training, particularly where a jurisdiction is able to train its junior lawyers on a one-to-one basis. Rather than imposing a 'one size fits all' training solution, it would be better in this situation to consider which areas require a completely standard approach to training across the firm, and those areas where a degree of local practice is not only acceptable but to be encouraged.

What should be the determining factor is which approach is going to be most likely to develop both the client relationship and the expertise of the local lawyers. If there is too much centralisation, a firm runs the risk of disenfranchising the lawyers in other offices if they feel that every relevant decision is made at 'head office'. This has to be balanced, however, against the risk that having too much decentralisation, without sufficient quality control, can damage the firm's brand. The point is that a firm needs to be sensitive to the issues, and to understand the nuances: just because someone takes a different approach does not mean that it is wrong, just that it is different! Understanding the differences is likely to be more effective than a paternalistic approach of 'they don't know what's good for them'. If the firm wants to present itself internationally as a seamless service, it has to be able to address these issues sensitively.

A firm can have a single but diverse culture but what it wants to avoid is acting and presenting as a heterogeneous group of independent offices and practices. How successful a firm will be in avoiding this will to a large extent be influenced by how successful the firm is in understanding and accommodating both legal and cultural differences within the firm.

34.3.2 Non-UK nucleus with UK satellite

Alternatively, the firm may have grown from a nucleus in another jurisdiction, such as the USA, building up a UK practice as an important but not dominant part of the firm, and possibly with offices in other jurisdictions as well. This is really a case of the UK office being in the shoes of the non-UK office in the other two examples in **34.3.1**. This scenario may be made more fraught if the dominant jurisdiction is one which has an entirely different legal education and training culture. For example, the US legal education system, although state-based, does not have any equivalent to the Common Professional Exam/Graduate Diploma in Law (CPE/GDL), Legal Practice Course (LPC), Period of Recognised Training (PRT) or Professional Skills Course (PSC). A US parent may therefore have difficulty understanding the requirements for lawyers in England and Wales.

An additional difference is that US law firms do not traditionally have an equivalent training culture, mainly because US lawyers do a law degree and then qualify to practise by sitting and passing the state bar exam. US lawyers then start in a firm as fully qualified lawyers.

In the 'London nucleus with satellites' scenario, it is easier to have firm-wide (i.e. global) training, particularly where the lawyers in the offices are predominantly solicitors qualified in England and Wales.

In the 'equal association or mergers' example, this will be less easy, and individual cultural and other differences and approaches may arise.

In trying to determine how to approach training in these scenarios the firm should adhere to the basic principle: is there a training need arising out of a business need to be addressed, and if so what is the most effective (in all senses) way of addressing it? In other words, the analysis should be exactly the same as described in **3.4** and the same considerations apply to what is the best way of delivering the training to meet the training needs (see **Chapter 37**).

34.3.3   Logistical issues

Where delivering training for overseas qualified lawyers can be different to general considerations for training design and delivery (see **Part E**) is in the logistical problems of having people in different geographical locations. Bringing people together in one place therefore has financial considerations. There are various possibilities to help get around this problem.

34.3.3.1   Mobile trainer

On the basis that it is cheaper to pay for one airfare and one hotel room, a firm could send the trainer to the people who need to be trained. If the firm uses an external trainer, the trainer's fees would need to be added to the cost of training, but it should still be more cost-effective to do it this way: the trainer's travel and accommodation expenses really represent a premium for delivering that training.

34.3.3.2   Mobile attendees

Alternatively the firm can bring together those to be trained to a particular office (preferably an office that is cheaper and easier to get to for the majority). The travel and accommodation costs for each attendee can be justified on the basis that there is an additional advantage to be had flowing from the training which is the bonding of individuals from different offices, promoting greater cohesion within the firm, and creating more effective working relationships between offices because people actually know each other. This can help lawyers from different countries to understand different approaches to practice in different jurisdictions, which then helps the lawyers in an international firm to work more effectively together – it is always easier to work with a lawyer you have met before and know. Working better together means better service for the client.

Bringing people together for training can also provide an opportunity to set up an informal network within the firm. A word of caution, however: having assistants in different offices know each other and communicate is not going to aid further integration of the firm's overall practice if the partners themselves have not bonded and established personal relationships. Consider, therefore, whether the expense might also be justified in bringing partners from different offices together.

34.3.3.3 Secondment

If the real objective is to achieve integration of the firm's offices by developing personal relations, then this can also be achieved through secondments. Probably the optimum secondment length is at least three months. However, if three months is not possible a mini-secondment – even two weeks in another office – might be possible. Two weeks is not going to achieve the same benefits as a longer secondment. However, if the objective is to have the firm's lawyers meet each other, and time away is a problem, then the two-week option might be better than nothing – the lawyer will not be lost to his or her 'home' office (assistants have after all been known to take a two-week holiday even if not often ...); for the host office, it does not have the burden of having to find work for the secondee over an extended period, but it is long enough for the secondee to meet and get to know people in the office and vice versa, and to socialise.

34.3.3.4 Use technology

Webinars – whether synchronous or asynchronous – are a good and relatively cost-effective way of delivering training to the many in different geographical locations. Even if the investment to produce webinars is not feasible, simply video-recording seminars or training sessions and uploading them on the firm's intranet can help. Where the outcome is appropriate, e-learning modules can be used. An e-learning module is particularly useful if the firm wishes to have a firm-wide induction or introduction to the firm for all people joining the firm in all offices; a pre-recorded webinar can be a good way of overcoming the problem of different time zones. If time zones are not an issue, and the firm has the facilities, the induction could be delivered to other offices by video conference. In fact, video conferencing can be used to deliver other training as well, which avoids the problem of travel and accommodation costs. The only limitation is that video conferencing may not be effective for interactive sessions, and if there are technical problems the effectiveness of the training can be impaired. However, in the absence of anything else video conferencing can deliver something.

34.3.3.5 Piggy-back

This involves using other things that are happening in the firm which require people to travel to other offices – for example, a partner's meeting or a firm AGM. This other event could be used to 'piggy-back' training onto it. If people are travelling anyway, the travel and accommodation will have been paid for or covered under another budget and it is only the cost of the training itself which would need to come out of the training budget. This could involve not only those attending the training, but also those delivering it.

34.3.3.6 Central 'academy'

Another option is to set up a central academy or training institution for all lawyers within the firm. This is definitely only an option for firms which have the resources (i.e. deep pockets) to do this. In addition to the travel and accommodation expenses of those attending, the firm also has the cost of setting up and running the training institution on a full-time basis. As admirable as the idea sounds, there are limitations:

- Not only would the firm need to take a homogenous approach to training as a whole, it would also have to decide what training, level of training and training content would apply to all lawyers in the firm.
- By definition, if there is a (separate) training institution, it is outside the practice areas of the firm and is going to consist of dedicated training professionals or lawyers who, although having practised previously, are no longer practising. In other words, there is the risk that the training will be divorced from practice. This can to a greater or lesser extent be overcome by using partners for the training. However, that then has logistical issues and means time away, particularly if the partner concerned has to travel to deliver the training. However, if participating in the central academy is regarded as part and parcel of a partner's role in the firm, and performance measurement and bonus allocation reflect this, then it is possible for this initiative to be an effective way of training in an international firm.

CHAPTER 35

Clients

35.1 Introduction
35.2 Issues to consider
35.3 Types of training
35.4 Practical arrangements

35.1 INTRODUCTION

In what is an increasingly challenging market for lawyers in which to win work, the balance of power has swung very much in favour of the client, and it is the client who dictates what is required from the lawyers that he or she is prepared to use. As part of this it is not uncommon that a client will ask for access to a firm's know-how or information resources. Even less uncommon is the request from a client to attend the firm's training.

35.2 ISSUES TO CONSIDER

A client's in-house legal department may not have the critical mass to justify running its own training programme, so it may be reliant on expensive external courses, which are likely to be generic rather than bespoke. Consequently, if the client is able to access the training that a firm runs for its own lawyers, it will provide a real benefit to the client. There is also the rationale that if the training is already being run, what difference do extra people sitting in on the training session make? In theory, the answer is no difference, but there can be other problems. If a firm approaches its marketing seriously, it will teach all its lawyers (and business support staff) that the firm is on show, not just when the client is at the firm in a meeting, but at all times and in all ways the firm is visible. Consequently, a training session's objectives can be hijacked from meeting the firm's training needs if its purpose becomes that of client-relationship management as well. The most obvious impact of this is on the content of the session – a firm will not be able to use examples of transactions of other clients for confidentiality reasons, so any 'tribal team' teaching is lost. Attendees may be inhibited from asking 'stupid' questions (or the firm may hope so!). However, this then compromises achievement of the learning objectives, and the investment in the training is jeopardised. A firm might argue that if in having the client attend the training it builds or strengthens the client relationship, then the loss of the training investment will be compensated by the strengthened client relationship. That may be so, but if a firm knows that its training investment could be compromised, why not consider ways of achieving both objectives and avoid any waste at all?

35.3 TYPES OF TRAINING

The sort of training that generally tends to be given to clients, either exclusively or inclusively, is in the form of:

- internal seminars;
- practice area-specific training;
- bespoke training for the client individually, possible given at the client's offices;
- public seminars.

35.3.1 Internal seminars

Internal seminars have the problems outlined above. If, however, the training objective of the seminar is purely to give information (see **36.2.2.1**) and some other way is offered to attendees of asking 'stupid' questions following the session when clients are not present rather than during it when they are, then this can work. In fact, 'hay may be made while the sun shines', and a number of clients could be invited to attend. A collateral advantage may be achieved if the client is impressed by the firm's appearance of altruism and/or the impressiveness of its client base. It may, however, have the reverse effect because a client feels just one of many. So, it is important to be careful about how it is done. If a firm does have more than one client attending, then it should ensure a relationship partner or someone with whom the client has worked is there to 'meet and greet' and look after the client throughout.

35.3.2 Practice area-specific training

Practice area-specific training has all the same warnings as seminars and is probably more difficult to adapt to meet both client relationship and training objectives, since the practice area-specific training that is being run is less likely to be generic and more likely to be for the necessary development of those, particularly junior lawyers, in the practice area. The inability to ask questions that those attending from the practice area need to ask becomes more of an issue with this sort of training.

35.3.3 Bespoke training

One way of dealing with these competing objectives is to offer to deliver training to the client in-house (i.e. in the client's 'house' rather than the firm's). There are obviously issues of time out of the office – duplicating time already committed to delivering the training within the firm. However, if the client relationship is seen as sufficiently important, then this perhaps should be put down as a client relationship cost. The advantages of taking the training to the client are that it gives the firm an entrée to the client and possibly other people in the firm; it can also provide an opportunity to introduce other, particularly more junior, members of the firm who could 'team teach' the session and in so doing can display their credentials to the client while providing something that is bespoke for the client.

35.3.4 Public seminars

A firm can, of course, offer 'public' seminars for clients: 'public' in the sense that the seminar is specifically externally facing, i.e. specifically for clients (usually more than one), as opposed to internal training, and therefore has marketing rather than training as its prime objective. This can be useful where there is a new legal development which is of interest to clients generally. If the firm is prompt off the mark – and has done its homework on the legal development and actually has some expertise and understanding about it – it can be a very effective marketing initiative. However, it has to be run well and to a professional training standard, particularly if clients are charged to attend, as suggested in **Chapter 4**. However, even if clients are not charged to attend, the firm which wishes to impress clients with its technical competence will need to ensure its event management professionalism is equally good.

There is a warning for both in-house seminars to which more than one client is invited and to 'public'-type seminars for clients, which is that both carry the risk of detracting from the potential development of the client relationship if the client feels merely one of many. Clients know that a firm has other clients but that does not change the human desire to feel special and valued.

A better approach, therefore, might be to have a training event which involves a number of people from the one client. This can do a lot to cement the relationship with the client, and it can be a good idea to involve lawyers from the client in the presentations, by encouraging them to give their perspectives. Similarly, in internal seminars where clients are invited to attend, it is good if the client can actively participate, rather than just being talked at by their lawyers.

35.4 PRACTICAL ARRANGEMENTS

If a firm intends either to include clients in training or to deliver training to clients, it is important to remember that the firm is on display, This starts with the security staff the client sees on entering the building, the staff who share the lift with the client to the meeting room floor, and the firm's website – everything and everyone is on show. This also includes the practical arrangements for training: the room being used for the seminar must be appropriate, well set out and comfortable, with (drinkable) coffee provided, and those attending from the firm should be advised in advance that clients will be present. It is also important that the speaker or trainer is aware there will be a client/clients in the room. If appropriate, the speaker or trainer might welcome the client by name – though check with the client whether he or she prefers to remain incognito or not, as he or she may be embarrassed and that is not what you want to achieve; thus the reason for having the relationship partner looking after the client. It can also provide a good opportunity of introducing the client to other people in the firm – cross-selling other services, for instance – by having partners or assistants from relevant practice areas attend who could be introduced to the client. If a firm or practice area has a regular seminar programme, it could even think ahead with some strategic planning, and identify seminars which it would be appropriate to invite particular clients to attend.

PART E

Delivering the training programme

Ask a lawyer whether they have had any experience of training and they will usually tell you about the seminars they have given or conferences they have spoken at. For many, lectures and seminars are the sum total of what training means. This is not only unfortunate, it is also wrong. There are many ways to deliver training depending on what the training is intended to achieve, who needs to achieve it and by when it needs to be achieved. The firm's goal should be to achieve effective training. This means, quite simply, being clear about the objectives the training needs to achieve, and then identifying the best way of delivering it to achieve those objectives. A seminar or lecture may be the best way – or it may not.

Part E is intended to be of use to fee earners, as well as training professionals. For the training professional, this section is intended to give assistance in converting a firm's training needs into an effective training session – training design, in other words.

For the fee earner, it is intended to provide help if a fee earner has to design training or deliver a training session – or both. (The assumption here is that the training professional, by definition, will not need help in delivering training!)

The intention is not to make fee earners into professional trainers – merely to assist them to become more effective in the training they deliver. Training which is delivered by the firm's lawyers, particularly partners and senior assistants, is incredibly valuable – more so than training delivered by external trainers. The reason for this is that the training is being given by true – and respected – experts in the field, who are passing on their knowledge and experience (preserving the firm's intellectual capital), as well as reinforcing the firm's values and culture. And, of course, they know their way around the firm's precedent documents and what is best practice. To deliver an effective training session, however, also requires a number of skills which a lawyer may feel he or she does not possess or to an appropriate standard: presentation, facilitation, feedback and coaching skills. However, when one steps back and analyses what a lawyer does in other roles he or she may have in the firm, these are the same skills as are required for those roles, particularly those which involve supervision, whether formal (e.g. supervising trainees) or informal (e.g. supervising lawyers working for them). So, a fee earner who needs to be convinced of the relevance of 'train the trainer' training should have it explained that these are valuable and transferable skills and will assist a fee earner in his or her role.

This section is not intended to spout training theory but gives a layman's synopsis of the key points, to provide an easy reference for other laymen who may have to design or deliver training in a law firm environment.

For the lawyer, **Chapter 36** explains how to design training, while **Chapter 37** provides practical tips on how to deliver a training session.

For those involved in running training within the firm, **Chapter 38** covers how to organise and run the training, and **Chapter 39** discusses how to evaluate training to provide the information and data necessary for evaluating the return on the firm's investment in training discussed in **Part A**.

CHAPTER 36

How to design training

36.1 Introduction
36.2 Forms of training
36.3 E-learning

36.1 INTRODUCTION

As already mentioned in the Introduction to Part E, training is not achieved through seminars alone. In fact, the most effective way to train and develop lawyers is through on-the-job training. Wherever possible, this is the best way for lawyers to learn. According to the 70:20:10 Learning and Development model,[1] 70 per cent of learning and development comes from on-the-job experiences – working on tasks and problems; about 20 per cent from feedback and working around good and bad examples; and 10 per cent from courses and reading. However, to use the swimming analogy from **30.3**, someone who is dropped in at the deep end of a swimming pool is going to be more likely to stay afloat and not drown if he or she has been given some instruction on how to swim first. His or her swimming will improve all the more with practice and coaching.

Consequently, effective on-the-job training involves: coaching and mentoring, shadowing, observation and reflection, and being given constructive and timely feedback. The problem is that one-to-one training is not always possible because of gearing levels and the speed of practice and client expectation, thanks to technology in particular.

Where firms have a number of people to train, training them together achieves economies of scale, such as in a formal training session. However, this is not the only option, which this chapter attempts to explain.

---
[1] Lombardo and Eichinger, *The Career Architect Development Planner*, Lominger, 1996.

36.2 FORMS OF TRAINING

There are in fact many forms that training can take and be extremely effective. It just takes a bit of thought and organisation. Not all training needs to be expensive and one of the most cost-effective but also valuable types of training is that provided by the firm's own lawyers.

Broadly, training divides into:

- formal training; and
- informal training.

Formal training includes 'seminars', which tend to be lectures, possibly with questions from the audience at the end of or during the session. It tends to be used in law firms in the form of a talk by an expert to a group, but usually without any group interaction other than questions the trainer may allow to be asked.

There are also workshops, which are 'small group teaching' and allow for greater interaction.

Informal training, however, covers a vast array of possibilities:

- self-learning – reading, audio and/or video training programmes, distance learning or e-learning modules;
- learning through participation in group projects, simulations or business/ management games;
- on-the-job – coaching, mentoring and shadowing;
- experiential – secondments, rotations, pro bono activities.

The Continuing Competence Toolkit which the Solicitors Regulation Authority (SRA) published in 2015 to support the Continuing Competence option for satisfying Continuing Professional Development (CPD) requirements (see **Chapter 20**) provides a useful resource for firms in considering – and understanding – the various means of informal training. The 'informal ways' the SRA recommends for solicitors to address their learning and development needs include:

- research, reading and discussion:
    - 'general' research, reading and discussion;
    - assigned reading and monthly update meetings;
    - 'targeted' research, reading and discussion;
- file reviews;
- colleagues;
- peers;
- networking;
- learning and development networks;
- observation.

36.2.1 Learning outcomes

In deciding which form of training is most appropriate, the first thing to do is to consider what it is that the training is intended to achieve – the learning outcomes, in other words. This involves a little bit of theory, but not too much.

The main types of learning outcomes are:

- verbal knowledge;
- intellectual application;
- cognitive strategies;
- attitudes;
- motor skills

and variations thereof. A simpler classification, using the reasons a firm is investing in the training, would be:

- to develop knowledge;
- to develop intellectual ability in using and applying knowledge;
- to develop a skill;
- to change attitudes or behaviour.

36.2.1.1 Knowledge

If the desired learning outcome is to develop knowledge, evidence that the outcome has been achieved would be that following the training the trainee is able to state, write or use that knowledge. In terms of the legal technical knowledge, this could be knowledge of the law or of practice and procedure, for example.

36.2.1.2 Intellectual application

Intellectual application as a learning outcome is really a combination of the ability to apply knowledge (intellectual skills) by way of problem-solving (cognitive strategies) – or just plain lateral thinking. Although knowledge is important, the ability to apply it is what is most important to lawyers.

36.2.1.3 Skills

'Intellectual application' conceivably covers the skills one needs in order to practise. However, a distinction, justified or not, has grown in legal training between knowledge and skills, with skills training often being divorced from the legal knowledge. For this reason, skills are treated here as a separate learning outcome, although, as will be discussed later in this chapter, the separation of the two is not always sensible.

36.2.1.4 Attitudes and values

A learning outcome of attitudes and values is exactly what it says on the tin – imparting attitudes and values, and in the legal context includes ethical behaviour, honesty and professionalism, as well as the firm's own values.

There is some argument about whether so-called affective behaviour (attitudes and values) can in fact be taught, but for these purposes we will assume that it can be learnt.

Working out which of these objectives needs to be achieved through training is the first step in designing the training session. The next step is to decide on the particular training method which should be used to achieve the learning outcome.

36.2.2 Training methods

If you decide that you need a training session to learn about, say, the Legal Services Act 2007 (in other words, knowledge is the desired outcome), merely stating that as the objective – knowledge of the Legal Services Act 2007 – is not much use. Are you seriously intending to cover the whole of the Legal Services Act in the session? Will those who attend be expected to come out of the session knowing everything about the Act? What is it in fact that you want those who attend to be able to do following the training? If it is to understand, say, a particular section, then that is the training objective. You need to be very clear about the focus of the training and what, realistically, attendees will be expected to obtain from the training. Only if this has been identified is it possible to decide what will be the best method for delivering the training.

The options for training delivery effectively break down into:

- in session;
- on-the-job; or
- online.

It is not always as clear cut as that, as more than one method of delivery may be appropriate. However, the classification is useful for present purposes. Which training method is selected within these choices of delivery will depend on a number of factors, such as:

- how many people need the training;
- when they need it by;
- what resources there are available to deliver the training;
- whether there are any time and cost constraints;
- how difficult the topic is likely to be for those attending, and whether they need some prior knowledge or assumed level of skill, for instance;
- whether they are likely to need feedback;
- whether they should be provided with an opportunity to try something for themselves;
- whether they will need one or more follow-on sessions for consolidation.

The choice of training delivery will particularly depend on which learning outcome it is that the training needs to achieve.

36.2.2.1 Desired learning outcome: knowledge

If the desired learning outcome is knowledge, then from the trainer's perspective the trainer needs to provide the information that will develop knowledge. In that case, a seminar can be effective (although see **35.3.1**), particularly where there is a large number of people needing the training. The particular benefit of a seminar is that it is an efficient way of delivering information to a large group of people; the only real limitations are the extent to which the audience can hear what the trainer says and can see what the trainer puts up on the screen/white board/flip chart, etc.

Delivering knowledge as a learning outcome could also be achieved through an e-learning module or simply by reading. The advantages of e-learning or reading are that either can be done in the learner's own time (self-study), when and where it is most convenient and is therefore likely to be more effective (called 'just in case' learning).

Using e-learning is only cost-effective if the technology has already been invested in, is in place, and the resourcing and expertise required are available within the firm. If not, then commercial online modules or audio and/or video training products may be easier and also more efficient. Also, unless you are able to offer an online tutor service, chat room or Wiki, then the face-to-face seminar offers what e-learning may not offer if it is not synchronised or real-time delivery, which is the opportunity for engagement by the audience so that they can ask questions and have their questions answered there and then. The reason this is important is that receiving an immediate response to a question reinforces learning. There is also an efficiency in face-to-face sessions in that the question asked by one person may be the question someone else might want to ask and have answered (even if they did not realise this before the question was asked), which allows people to learn from each other. This can also be achieved with an online tutor and/or chat room. Further, the answer given by a trainer or another attendee may prompt other questions which gives the opportunity for clarification and more effective understanding. It is therefore important in the seminar scenario, whether live or online, to factor in time for questions.

It will often be the case that someone will not be able to attend the seminar on the day, and inviting attendees to submit questions in advance can assist the trainer in spreading the learning from the seminar as widely as possible. Equally, if there are more questions than time allows during the seminar, it can be helpful for the trainer to email responses to questions not able to be covered in the session afterwards and copy in all attendees.

36.2.2.2 Desired learning outcome: intellectual application

A learning outcome of intellectual application is about more than just acquiring knowledge and skills; it is about being able to apply that knowledge and those skills to situations which the individual may not have come across before – cognitive ability, by another name. Developing intellectual application is not something that can be done passively – by just sitting and listening. Rather, it requires activity and engagement on the part of the individual. Consequently, seminars are not necessarily the best method of delivery. If a formal training session is to be used, it really needs to be a small group session, such as a workshop, which involves activities to develop intellectual application (see **36.2.3**). Outside formal sessions interactive e-learning modules are possible, as are any of the forms of group learning: assignments, projects, business games or simulation generally.

A learning tool which is much under-utilised by firms is pro bono work. It is better than simulation since real clients and their problems are involved. However, because pro bono clinics are open to real people with real problems, it is difficult to specify particular learning outcomes, as it will depend on who attends with what problem on the day. What pro bono clients do provide is the opportunity to practise the skills of interviewing and advising, research, writing and drafting, in a controlled environment provided that the pro bono work is properly supervised. Equally, intellectual application can be developed on the job by just 'doing', and then receiving feedback.

36.2.2.3 Desired learning outcome: skills

If the objective of the training is to develop skills, such as drafting or negotiation, then the training is more effective if delivered by way of a small group session – workshops – rather than the large group seminar model.

The received wisdom on how to teach skills effectively, is firstly to demonstrate the skill, then allow the learner to practise the skill, and lastly to provide feedback to the learner on his or her practice of the skill. This is not easily done on an individual basis in a large group session, particularly if attendees are seated in theatre-style (see **38.2.5**). A seminar could be used to explain the principles of a skill, and perhaps to provide a demonstration of the skill, such as by showing a video of good and bad examples. Those attending may even be able to practise the skill in the session – depending on how the room is set up, of course. However, it is unlikely that one-to-one feedback from the trainer on each individual's attempt would be possible, and the feedback which the trainer would therefore provide would have to be generic.

An even better way of developing a skill is through mentoring and coaching on the job. Mentoring is where someone who is outside the mentee's supervisory relationships takes an interest in guiding and supporting the mentee's development. This can be through regular meetings or discussions in which the mentor can take on a counselling or coaching role. Counselling is directed at personal issues which may be affecting performance, whereas coaching is focused on improving performance and is a continuous process, rather than just a one-off.

There is also no reason why achieving, say, a skills outcome cannot be achieved through a combination of formal training session plus mentoring. What is important is that, if coaching is to be used within the firm, it needs to start at the top – with partners themselves also being coached.

Where the aim is to develop management or practice skills, thinking out of the box can be very effective, such as by using assignments or projects. These can involve practical tasks which involve the participants relating their skills and knowledge to an actual problem in the firm. Projects in this way can be used not only to develop skills, but also to develop a greater engagement with the firm, its strategy and its business, for instance. If the objective is to create greater commercial awareness, business or management games could be used. Simulation through exercises which involve replicating practice is also very effective.

Firms have a reputation for adopting a 'drop them in at the deep end' approach to talent management – see who sinks or swims. Although not particularly nurturing, it is true that putting someone into a new situation presents them with a new experience and the opportunity to learn new skills and develop new insights. This happens each time a trainee changes seats – job rotation by another name. Another way of achieving this experiential development more gently than the 'drop them in at the deep end' approach is to use secondments as a way of developing knowledge and skills. This could be secondment with a client, which means the individual learns about the client and its business, or it could be secondment to a different office of the firm, which allows the individual to develop knowledge and understanding of other parts of the firm's business and to meet other members of the firm. All this helps a firm to operate as a single entity, to achieve co-operation within the organisation and make more of opportunities for cross-selling, because its members have a better understanding of what expertise resides within the firm.

36.2.2.4 Desired learning outcome: attitudes and values

If the learning objective is to develop or change attitudes or values, coaching and mentoring can play an important role, as can shadowing where the individual being trained sits alongside or follows and observes someone more senior, who acts as a role model. The importance of role models in developing ethical behaviour and values cannot be underestimated, not to mention in developing good practice habits.

36.2.3 Training activities

One of the challenges in designing and delivering training is to keep those being trained engaged. This has to do with learning styles – the theory that people learn in different ways: some are visual learners, others are auditory learners, kinaesthetic learners, verbal, logical, social, solitary… or observers, thinkers, deciders or doers… There is as much debate about the classification of learning styles as there are theories themselves. What is important, and this does seem to be agreed upon, is that if different learning activities are incorporated into a session most types of learners will be served. So, having a trainer talk for the whole time in a formal training session is unlikely to be effective, particularly as received wisdom has it that an audience's attention flags after 10 to 15 minutes. However, incorporating activities can achieve and maintain engagement, irrespective of whether the training is intended to achieve knowledge, intellectual application, skills or attitudes and behaviour, and can assist in delivering the learning outcome by creating interaction in the training session. These activities can be:

- **Simple exercises**: which involve solving a problem.
- **Case studies**: using a fact-based scenario which the participants analyse, discuss and, one hopes, resolve. Case studies can be used for group discussion or in what are called 'buzz groups' or 'break-out groups'. The fact scenario can be fictitious or even based on something that has actually happened in the firm, which can very effective for achieving buy-in to the firm.
- **Group discussion**: where a topic is set for discussion and the tutor acts as facilitator rather than lecturer, to encourage attendees to exchange their ideas and experience. This can take the form of a brain-storming session, i.e. unstructured, or it can be facilitated along specific lines.
- **Role play**: this involves simulating a particular role, based on a particular fact scenario.
- **Demonstration**: as has been explained in **36.2.2.3** above, skills are taught through a process of demonstration, practice and feedback. Practice of the skill can be done through role play, preceded by a demonstration, which can also be used to engender group discussion.

Where break-out groups are used in a training session, it is important that the trainer circulates among the groups during the exercise or discussion, to make sure that the attendees understand what they are supposed to be doing and that the discussion has not gone off-topic. It also helps the trainer in gathering points for generic feedback or for discussion in the plenary later.

When setting these activities, a trainer needs to make sure that the attendees know what is involved, what they are expected to do or produce, and how long they have to do it, as well as what the activity is intended to achieve.

It is also important in interactive sessions, as it is with coaching, that feedback is given by the tutor or coach.

Even in seminars – or perhaps particularly in seminars – some sort of interaction is necessary if the attendees' attention is to be maintained. This can be as simple as throwing a question to the attendees generally, even asking them to discuss the question with the person next to them. A question posed in this way can serve to consolidate understanding of what has been covered so far, or to lead into the next part of the seminar. The point is that just changing activity refreshes concentration.

36.2.4 Feedback

36.2.4.1 Individual feedback

The most valuable feedback comes from personalised comments. One-to-one feedback may be given during a training session where, for example, the trainer circulates around group activities or role plays, observes individual performances and then feeds back to each individual personally. Individual feedback can also be given in a later individual session, particularly if feeding back in a group session could be embarrassing or intimidating for the recipient. Feedback can also be given by written comments on the individual's performance.

36.2.4.2 Generic feedback

If one-to-one feedback is not possible, for instance because of the number of people being trained, then generic feedback can still be valuable. This is feedback which is generally applicable, for example, on the sorts of problems which are likely to arise – or have been observed to arise – from trying to practise a skill. Giving generic feedback means that everyone attending benefits; similarly, if the trainer provides feedback on some of the problems the trainer may have noticed from walking around the room, observing learners' attempts – when individual issues will be picked up as well.

36.2.4.3 Peer feedback

A further form of feedback is peer feedback – feedback from other attendees on each other's performance. This sort of feedback will only be useful if it is constructive and objective, as there is a risk that colleagues, especially if of different seniority or experience, may be loath to criticise another colleague's attempt, no matter how constructively. However, those who have been on the Legal Practice Course (LPC) are likely to have had experience of peer feedback and should be used to giving and receiving it.

The type and degree of feedback that is necessary to achieve the training's objectives will have an impact on the form of training, but also on the actual training venue and accommodation. For example, the training room must be large enough to give the trainer access to walk around break-out groups in order then to deliver individual or generic feedback.

36.2.5 Timing

Having decided what the session should achieve and what it should contain, the next step is to work out a timed programme so as to decide whether the amount of content to be covered needs to be done in more than one session or with, say, post-session follow-ups or one-to-one sessions.

There is a tension between the need to give sufficient time to training and at the same time, particularly when it is fee earners who are being trained, trying to minimise the time away from fee-earning work. The reality is that if insufficient time is allowed for the training it will not achieve the training objective, and if the training objectives are not achieved it will have been a wasted investment.

Pressure on costs can also have an adverse impact on the length of training. The example was given at **1.5** of a firm deciding that its assistants needed to develop better drafting skills, but only being prepared to pay for an hour and a half's session; nothing is more guaranteed to be a waste of both time and money. What the firm in this example is failing to do is to fit the solution to the particular problem: how big is the problem that training is needed to address, and how urgently does it need to be addressed? In this example, is it the case that the proposed attendees have deficient drafting skills, or is it a 'just in case' reason for training – out of abundant caution? If it is the former, then the objectives are not going to be achieved in an hour and a half's session, or even a full-day session for that matter. In sport, along with natural ability goes practice – and a lot of it – to achieve excellence. The same is true for developing skills as lawyers: if you want someone to develop a skill, be it in tennis or drafting, it needs to be practised. The moral of the story is to be realistic about what needs to be achieved, and then allocate the appropriate time to achieve it. For drafting skills, this may involve a series of sessions which consolidate the learning from the previous session/s, and/or with subsequent feedback sessions, perhaps even with post-session assignments set.

36.2.5.1 When to hold training

A perennial issue is when to hold training. For fee earners, there is never a right time if there is fee-earning work to be done. This is actually a symptom of the way training can become divorced from practice in firms (see **1.2.2**) when it is forgotten that training is a way of meeting the needs of the business. How can this issue be resolved? If it is a full-day course, the training could be arranged to allow those attending to go to their desk in the morning and clear their emails. The risk, though, is that people will become distracted by work that has come in overnight. One solution is to start the training earlier – before business hours, which means that attendees should in the room where the training is taking place before business begins, and they are also likely to be at their freshest. Obviously, there are 'owls' and 'larks', but generally people are likely to be less distracted with an early start. The quid pro quo for starting early is to finish early. The average full-day training session comprises about six hours of training plus breaks. A session which starts at, say, 8.45 am could finish at 4.30 pm, which frees attendees to return to their desks during business hours.

A session which is a half-day or an hour-long seminar may mean less time away from the desk. However, the challenge of prising attendees away from their desks if the training is during the day can be greater, and there is a related problem of an attendee's supervisor not allowing them to attend because of work needing to be done. A pragmatic approach is again to have training first thing in the morning, so it is over by lunchtime at the latest (still with breaks, of course, for the reasons given at **36.2.5.2**). If you think about it, this way a seminar which finishes at, say, 10 am or 10.30 am is really just making the fee earner late to start work, which could happen on any other day because of problems on the tube, or traffic on the ring-road or having to go to a dentist's appointment first thing. What starting training first thing in the morning does do is allow the fee earner to carry on with his or her work, uninterrupted, once the training session is finished. Starting earlier and finishing earlier is also likely to be appreciated by the person for whom the attendee is working. As a supervisor, there is nothing worse than getting to 5 pm with things still to be done, and an assistant or trainee announcing they are off to training or a seminar. This is even truer for firms with offices in North America, whose US West Coast offices, for instance, will just be coming live about then. So, the moral is to look at how a firm tends to work, and try to work with that rather than fight against it.

36.2.5.2 Breaks

Having sorted out whether a half-day, full day, several days or a session followed by further coaching is needed, appropriate breaks need to be factored in. If there is a lot to cover, resist the temptation to cram it all into one session without proper breaks. People cannot concentrate for long periods, which means cramming learning into long sessions without any breaks is likely to result in a waste of time, effort and money in running the training at all.

As a rule of thumb, breaks should be built in at intervals of an hour and a half or two hours maximum. Breaks do not need to be long – 15 minutes is enough time for people to take a comfort break, stand up and stretch, get coffee or whatever, and basically re-boot their intellectual faculties. If it is an all-day session, working through lunch should be resisted, for the same reasons that attendees need a break. Coffee breaks and a lunch break also provide more informal opportunities for attendees to get to know each other if they are from different practice groups or different offices.

36.2.5.3 Time for questions

In calculating the time needed for a training session, time for questions needs to be factored in. If it is a seminar, it is important that those attending are able to ask questions – the reason for holding live training is so that attendees have the opportunity to have their questions answered there and then. Otherwise, a webinar which people can watch in their own time might serve the purpose just as well (see **36.3.1**) – or just reading an article on the topic.

36.3 E-LEARNING

E-learning is just another method of delivering training. Without a proper understanding of what e-learning is able to deliver and what it involves, it is possible to waste a lot of money and not achieve the solution you are looking for. Used wisely, however, it can be very effective.

36.3.1 What is e-learning?

What in fact is e-learning? It is the delivery of training electronically – over a computer or even over the telephone. It is just another mode of delivering training. The choice of e-learning over face-to-face training should be made based on exactly the same training needs analysis (see **3.4**), training design and resourcing (see **Chapter 4**) as for any other training in the firm. If e-learning is to be outsourced, the same considerations discussed in relation to trainers apply. It is all about the most effective mode of delivering training to achieve the particular learning outcome.

Originally e-learning was about distance learning with no real-time interaction between 'attendee' and 'trainer'. However, with advances in technology and the sophistication in all of us as users of technology, e-learning has undergone a quantum leap in terms of what it can be used for, how it can be delivered and the benefits it can deliver to users. An e-learning session or module may therefore be synchronous or asynchronous. If it is synchronous, it is 'live' and virtually (in the technology sense) face-to-face, if video conferencing or technologies such as Skype are used.

Asynchronous learning is recorded and can be accessed at any time, when the learner has the time and the inclination to learn. Initial efforts in this area were largely text or PowerPoint slides online, where the learner could 'click and reveal' more information – essentially reading online. Audio can be added to make the content being delivered more engaging and memorable. Many firms also stream video globally. External e-learning providers use Flash technology and professional voice-over actors to create courses that simulate the real life of lawyers and are very effective in delivering quality training to a global audience. Studies show that tuition which combines seeing, hearing and interacting on-screen is the most effective, as different parts of the brain are brought to bear that engage learners regardless of their learning style.

Synchronous training, on the other hand, occurs in real time, with a trainer (who needs a modicum of IT skills) online at the same time as the learners. This is often referred to as a virtual classroom, where learners can react using audio or video (the latter if each has a webcam on his or her PC) by uploading documents or slides that everyone can mark up or comment on, and which can be recorded for later use (thus becoming afterwards part of a firm's asynchronous curriculum).

The benefits of e-learning arise when it is the right solution to the right problem. It can range from a distance learning module delivered over the computer – simply reading something and then submitting electronic answers to questions on what has

HOW TO DESIGN TRAINING

been read – to an interactive, live webinar (seminar being given over the internet in real time). There are also i-tutorials and web-casting. The particular e-learning solution will depend on:

- whether you are watching (video)/listening (audio) or doing both (audio visual);
- whether it is static or interactive;
- whether it is live or real time (synchronous) or not (asynchronous);
- whether it is accessed by DVD, video-conferencing or conference call, or over an intranet or the internet.

The point is that there is no magic about e-learning just because it is delivered electronically, and it is important to go through the analysis set out in **3.4** in order to determine whether it is the appropriate method of training delivery to use. What e-learning can do is to save time and money by not requiring everyone who may need the training to turn up in a classroom at a particular time on a particular day. Instead, it enables people to do training when it is convenient to them, in their own time and when they need it – anytime, any how, anywhere, as it is also known. It means that individuals can learn at their own pace, going over things again if they do not understand the first time; consolidating what they have learnt and refreshing when they need to.

If the e-learning solution is just a module on a computer, there is not the face-to-face interaction with the trainer that there is with in-session and on-the-job training, and therefore no opportunity for feedback, asking questions and having them answered. However, even if the technology is there to run real-time training, not everyone likes to learn that way. To be fair (to e-learning), this is likely to be more of a generational problem than anything else. However, although those who have come through school and university over the past 10 years have been exposed increasingly to e-learning in modular-style study, and Generation Y and the Millennials have little difficulty in adapting to an e-learning environment, e-learning delivery is not always the preferred way of learning. So, it is not just those who have been used to face-to-face education and training who do not always embrace e-learning delivery. What makes the difference is if the e-learning delivery meets a training need that would not otherwise be met, or meets it in a more convenient way.

36.3.2 Uses

There are certain training needs that e-learning is very good at meeting and should be considered quite seriously if a firm has those needs. These generally relate to the following scenarios.

36.3.2.1 Inductions

Where there is training which has a knowledge-learning outcome, but the numbers do not justify running the training, e-learning may provide a solution. Inductions are

DELIVERING THE TRAINING PROGRAMME

good examples: where there may be only one person joining the firm, and although it is important that he or she is introduced to the firm, its procedures, values, culture, etc. it is not possible to justify someone's time to give the new joiner a formal induction session. In that case, an e-learning induction module is worth its weight in gold. Extending the logic, it can be very valuable in firms with a number of offices, particularly if the offices are overseas, which creates even greater logistical difficulties for training, not to mention the expense of having to send someone to each office to deliver inductions for new joiners.

36.3.2.2 Assumed knowledge

Where there is a certain level of assumed knowledge required for a training session, an e-learning module can enable the potential attendee to acquire the requisite knowledge and/or to self-test or to do a test which someone else can look at, in order to decide whether he or she is at the appropriate level to attend the training.

36.3.2.3 Consolidation

An e-learning module can also be used where there is a need to consolidate what has been covered in a training session, either as an end in itself or with a view to attending a further session that will require a certain level of knowledge or ability.

36.3.2.4 Compliance training

Where training just has to be done for compliance reasons (such as anti-money laundering training) and is about providing information or acquiring knowledge, e-learning can be used to deliver the training and can also include a test to check whether learning has been achieved.

36.3.2.5 Just in time and refresher training

'Just in time' training is where someone needs training because a sudden need has arisen. This could be because the individual has been required to do work in a new area, or in an area he or she has not covered for some time and so requires a refresher. Provided the learning outcomes (usually knowledge as opposed to intellectual ability, skills or values and attitudes – see **36.2.1**) can be met through using e-learning, it is a very effective way of having training available as and when it is needed. A use related to this is refresher training, when training which has already been undertaken may need to be freshened up for a particular situation.

36.3.2.6 IT training

E-learning can also be very useful as a means of delivering IT training. For example, it can simulate the software the lawyer needs to use as a way of moving people up the learning curve more quickly. IT skills can often grow rusty through lack of use, and it is helpful to have courses available when the lawyers need to use an online application. Some firms have online courses on how to bill time, access client and other databases, conduct legal research, number or amend agreements, and much more.

36.3.3 Delivery

The options for delivering e-learning are:

- audio (and possibly visual) delivery supported by PowerPoint, or in real time so that questions can be 'asked' of the speaker ('asked' by way of email, video conferencing or conference call);
- static text underpinned by multiple choice questions (MCQs) to test comprehension.

Platforms for delivering e-learning include: the telephone, the computer (via DVD or intranet), iPods and mobile phones. PowerPoint slides can be synced with audio track; you can dial into a commercial provider to participate in a live session, while looking at the PowerPoint slides on your computer, and with the opportunity to email questions in for answer; there is the webinar, allowing you to watch and/or listen to the trainer live on your computer and ask real-time questions, or just download everything to your iPod, iPad, iPhone or equivalent device.

36.3.4 Sourcing e-learning

If a firm wants to use e-learning, the big issue is whether to do it yourself (DIY) or to outsource it. Outsourcing means either buying someone else's 'off the shelf' module, which is likely to be generic, or sourcing your own customised module, which carries cost implications.

If a firm wants to be able to create and make available its own e-learning modules, then it needs to have:

- the technology;
- the platform; and
- the support.

These all cost money, particularly if you want to do the design, production and delivery yourself. This may be entirely justified, depending on your particular training needs. However, it is a trap for the unwary if it is not justified, and a lot of money can (and has been) wasted by investing in e-learning naïvely. Having said that, DIY is now a lot easier than it ever has been before. At its simplest, e-learning can consist of videoing the seminars run in the firm. These can be available on DVD for people to borrow, or streamed on the firm's intranet – even made available via the internet to the firm's clients.

For internal purposes a welcome by the firm's senior partner could be video-recorded for all new joiners to watch by way of induction, for instance. It is not a great leap to take the video, to synchronise it with PowerPoint slides and make this available for people to watch in their own time, as and when they need to. Alternatively, instead of making a recording, you could arrange a live webcast (although this depends on people in the firm being able to dial in to watch it) – a synchronous webinar, as opposed to the asynchronous recorded seminar. Both asynchronous and synchronous seminars could be particularly useful for delivering seminars to clients, although a synchronous webinar, with the partner who is delivering available to answer questions at the time, could add significant value to the client.

If you cannot justify the investment in e-learning, that does not mean that e-learning is lost to you; what it is likely to mean is that you are left with what is available 'off the shelf'. For some things, particularly regulatory or generic-type training, this is not a problem. In fact, to a large extent there are common training needs across even the largest firms. However, if the training is intended to achieve specialisation or to impart valuable knowledge within the firm, it is not likely that a generic module will be the best fit. A firm should ask itself, though, whether a customised solution really is needed. If buying 'off the shelf' can deliver the necessary training objectives, it is likely to be more cost-effective than going the bespoke way. Some e-learning providers also offer a subscription system which gives discounts for members and for bulk-buying.

36.3.5 Accommodation and resources

Just as with in-session training, there are the physical considerations of accommodation and resources that will be needed to deliver e-learning. Many of the same considerations discussed in **38.2** apply to e-learning. The risk of interruption is one particular issue that does not disappear if a person is doing an e-learning module. In fact, the risk of interruption is greater if lawyers are sitting at their computers at their desks – in full sight of supervisors and colleagues, within reach of telephone calls and emails – so these possibilities need to be countered as well.

36.3.6 Learning management systems

One of the spin-offs of the e-learning initiative is the learning management system (LMS). LMSs were initially designed to track classroom registrations and had to be adapted for e-learning purposes. The LMS is a computer-based record system, which has functionality for recording who has attended what training – and more. It is a convenient management tool for producing statistics about what training has been run and what training people have attended – particularly useful for Continuing Professional Development (CPD) purposes, although this will not be for much longer once the SRA introduces the Continuing Competence regime from 1

November 2016 (see **Chapter 20**). Traditionally, the cost of buying and implementing an LMS has been prohibitive for most firms. However, many e-learning providers offer an LMS as part of the product/service the firm pays for. Some firms use LMSs which enable assistants to register for courses themselves, taking a lot of the administrative burden away from the operational responsibilities of organising training (see **Chapter 38**).

Many firms initially made the mistake of investing in systems that offered, paradoxically, too much functionality and were not fit for purpose. Many were not integrated with the firm's Human Resources and other performance management software. The better way to begin is to produce learning content and then think about how this can best be stored and tracked. Along with more slimmed-down LMSs sold by training providers, there is also a wide variety of open-source LMS software (Moodle being the most prominent) which are free and often provide enough functionality to get a firm started. Properly used, LMSs can integrate performance management objectives, competencies and job roles, so as to be able to provide tailored development plans for lawyers following their attendance at an off-site assessment centre or their appraisal meeting.

CHAPTER 37

How to deliver training

37.1 Introduction	37.4 Questioning skills
37.2 Presentation skills	37.5 Feedback skills
37.3 Facilitation skills	37.6 Managing skills

37.1 INTRODUCTION

So, you have been asked to deliver a training session. The first thing you need to know is that you do not need to be a trained teacher or trainer in order to train – not least because, as discussed in **Chapter 15**, training does not necessarily have to be delivered in a classroom-type environment.

Even where it is a formal training session you do not need any teaching qualifications. What you do need to have are:

- knowledge of the subject area;
- the credentials within the firm to achieve credibility;
- presentation skills;
- facilitation skills;
- questioning skills;
- feedback skills;
- managing skills relating to managing time, questions, interruptions and participation

– and good preparation!

The advantage of using someone within the firm to deliver training is not just that he or she will have the necessary credentials for the topic, he or she is also able to use work-related examples – 'war stories' – where appropriate, which can give the training session greater relevance and interest.

Presentation and facilitation skills are required of most lawyers, who in the course of their work have to perform in meetings or give presentations to clients. Knowledge of their subject area is what clients take as a given, and specialist knowledge is what clients believe they are paying for. Feedback skills are necessary for any lawyer who is in a supervisory role, or who has others working for or with him or her. When you look at it like this, you realise there is no real magic about being able to deliver training, and it is not that different from what a lawyer is required to do anyway. They are transferable skills.

As the trainer, you need to be clear about what your role in the particular training session is meant to be: facilitator, tutor or lecturer. The main features of each requirement are set out below.

37.2 PRESENTATION SKILLS

When talking about effective teaching and learning, the importance of presentation skills cannot be emphasised enough. If you are considering giving any training and are concerned about your presentation skills, 'do not pass go' as the Monopoly board says: do not go straight to the training room, but go direct to a training session yourself on presentation skills.

As a general refresher, good presentation skills consist of a number of components:

- good preparation and knowledge of the topic;
- clarity of speech – volume, enunciation, speed of delivery;
- absence of verbal mannerisms and distractions, i.e. no 'you know' or 'umm' after every phrase;
- a professional and non-distracting appearance;
- visual engagement with each part of the audience or each participant;
- confidence in delivery;
- effective use of PowerPoint and other learning aids – not allowing PowerPoint to dominate (see **38.2.2.1**);
- talking, not reading from a script;
- openness to questions – honesty if you don't know the answer, acknowledgement of a good question and absence of defensiveness

37.3 FACILITATION SKILLS

This is possibly a very broad generalisation but lawyers do not necessarily make good facilitators, because they tend to be both opinionated and articulate – necessary tools of the professional lawyer, but not necessarily of the professional trainer. What helps to understand the role of facilitator is to stand in the shoes of those being 'facilitated'. There is much truth in the claim that people tend to learn best by trying something themselves – learning from experience and through reflection. A parent will tell a child not to touch something because it is hot but it is only when the child touches it that he or she learns not to touch it again. The fact is that we do not really change all that much as we grow older: we still tend to learn the hard way. The reason for having training is to avoid having to burn yourself in order to learn not to touch things that are hot, by giving the opportunity for reflection on cause and effect and on the pain that burning your hand would have caused you. Reflection is, in fact, the most important tool, rather than the stimulus of feeling the heat. If we had the mental capacity of a goldfish, we would just keep touching whatever was hot and not learn from the experience because we would lack the ability to reflect and learn that it is hot and remember this in the future.

Fortunately, the good news is that we are not goldfish and our attention span should be sufficient to reflect and learn. In the case of skills teaching, the opportunity for reflection is particularly valuable. The point for the trainer is that reflection is helped by facilitation – not by being lectured or being told the answer.

To facilitate, the trainer moves away from leading and talking, and places the focus entirely on the attendees. As a general rule, if you are supposed to be facilitating and you hear yourself talking, it is likely you have stopped facilitating. An exception is when you need to explain at the start of a session what the attendees are expected to do during the session. In addition, you may need to intervene to keep the session on track in order that the learning objectives of the session can be achieved, such as when the discussion has gone completely off-piste. Straying from the topic is not necessarily a bad thing, though. However, if the direction of the detour and the time remaining for the session mean that the session's objectives are not going to be achieved, you as the facilitator need to bring things back on track. Equally, if among the attendees one attendee is dominating the discussion and/or not allowing other attendees to get a word in edgeways, then the session is unlikely to achieve the learning objectives for all attendees. It may also be that one attendee is happy to sit on the sidelines and not participate at all, in which case that attendee may need to be encouraged to contribute. The trick is to intervene briefly: you can simply remind the attendees of what they should be doing or how much time is left, or ask one of the attendees for their thoughts to bring them into the discussion – but no more than that. The golden rules are:

- leave the discussion to the attendees – do not take part;
- do not lead; and
- if you like to be in control, learn to let go and fight any urge to correct what is being said.

Even when leading the training rather than facilitating, it is important to remember what is explained above, namely that people learn best when they work things out for themselves. For instance, after attendees have been involved in break-out groups, the session may have a plenary (namely, discussion by the whole group), which the trainer leads in order to pull together the threads of the discussions of the various groups. Even then, it is important for the trainer to resist dominating, so that the attendees can arrive at conclusions themselves.

37.4 QUESTIONING SKILLS

Good questioning techniques, both in asking and answering questions, can assist you in avoiding 'trainer domination'.

37.4.1 Asking questions

These techniques are taught in Interviewing and Advising on the Legal Practice Course (LPC). As a refresher, remember that when you are asking questions it is better to use 'open' rather than 'closed' questions, since open questions will encourage greater thought on the part of the person/s being asked. Open questions do not suggest a 'yes/no' answer or a specific response, as closed questions do. If you ask an open question which does require thought, do not be put off by the ensuing silence and be tempted to jump in and give the answer yourself, as you do need to give people time to think before they respond.

Having said that, if the question is difficult, and if after what you judge is a reasonable time no one has attempted to answer it, you could re-phrase the question or ask another question which might help understanding.

37.4.2 Being asked a question

When, on the other hand, you are asked a question, it is good practice to repeat the question to make sure all attendees have heard it, and even to re-phrase the question to make sure that you yourself have understood (this reassures the person who has asked the question). Where the question you have been asked is seeking information which the attendees are unlikely to know, then giving a direct answer is appropriate. However, you can also try to encourage attendees to work out the answer for themselves if they have the necessary information but are not used to applying it or working with it. This is particularly important if the training is aiming to develop intellectual application. A technique you can use is to re-direct the question to all attendees, or to turn the question back to the person who asked it, either by asking them what they think the answer is or by asking a question which will help lead them to the answer.

The important thing about questions in a training session is to make it clear that questions are welcome. It may be that you would prefer questions to be saved for the end, particularly in a session where there is limited time. If that is the case, make this clear at the beginning of the session. However, the risk you run in keeping questions to the end is that if you say something that an attendee does not understand and the attendee is not able to ask you about it until the end, you may not have that attendee's attention for the rest of the session, and there is a risk that they will not understand what follows. For this reason, it is sensible to keep an eye on the body language of the attendees (a sigh, puzzled expression, whispering to the person next to them, for example) so that you know if something does need explaining or clarifying sooner rather than later, which again is an argument for taking questions as they arise.

DELIVERING THE TRAINING PROGRAMME

There can be two particular problems for a trainer with questions:

- the attendee you have encouraged to answer the question who then gives the wrong answer; and
- the question you are asked to which you don't know the answer!

37.4.2.1 Wrong answer

In the case of the wrong answer being given, you do not want to embarrass the attendee in front of the other attendees, harm his or her confidence or inhibit his or her participation in the remainder of the session. Techniques which you can use to avoid this include:

- giving the attendee the opportunity to think about the answer again (asking them 'are you sure?');
- relating the answer to what has been discussed previously ('how does that relate to what you said/X said/the feedback?', etc.);
- asking the attendee a more basic question to help him or her reach the correct answer.

37.4.2.2 Wrong question!

In the case of the question to which you don't know the answer, there is nothing for it but to be honest – or to adopt diversionary tactics and throw open the question to the other attendees. You could even ask the questioner what he or she thinks the answer might/should/could be. If diversionary tactics fail, then honesty is the best policy. If it is a good question, say so, and offer to discuss it with the particular attendee outside the session, or to email an answer to all attendees afterwards – but make sure you do. If it is a question which is completely left-field, say so, and bring the discussion back on track. There is no disgrace in not knowing something you cannot be expected to know and which is not on the topic.

37.5 FEEDBACK SKILLS

If you are providing feedback, it must relate to the criteria which have been established in the session as constituting good or effective practice of the skill, and it should be constructive. If, for example, the session has explained that good writing consists of clarity of expression, the feedback should relate to the criteria: for example, 'good clarity but there are some grammatical mistakes'. Just saying the participant's attempt was 'good' or 'bad' is not going to be useful, since it is not going to consolidate what the individual did, and did well, so that he or she knows what it is he or she should keep doing; or which aspect he or she is not so good at and needs to work on. Equally, a subjective comment is not helpful either – unless of course it relates to a criterion which is subjective in itself, e.g. 'made me feel comfortable'.

If the attendee is to benefit from the feedback, it is important that he or she understands the reason for what is being said, and that it helps him or her understand how to improve.

Peer feedback is feedback which is given not by the trainer but by other attendees. Apart from helping the individual who receives the feedback, peer feedback also helps the person who gives the feedback to improve his or her own understanding, since he or she has to understand the criteria and then be able to evaluate someone else's performance by applying the criteria (intellectual application in other words). What is important is that attendees have objective criteria on which to base their feedback. This saves the person giving the feedback as much embarrassment as the person receiving it – being able to refer to objective requirements or criteria de-personalises something that is otherwise potentially very personal, particularly between peers.

37.6 MANAGING SKILLS

Just as you would manage a client meeting, you should manage the training session you are delivering. In addition to good presentation skills discussed in **37.2**, this means:

- preparing thoroughly and being completely familiar with the session structure, content and materials;
- being punctual. In fact, as part of being prepared, you should turn up about 15 minutes in advance to make sure everything is set up properly and to give yourself time to get sorted;
- presenting the content in a logical order;
- dealing with questions honestly and confidently;
- keeping an eye on the time and being able to finish on time

– all things you would do in preparing for and running a client meeting.

Interruptions are an eventuality more likely to occur – or at least with greater potential for disrupting your calm and concentration – in the training session than in a client meeting. No matter whether there is a sign on the door saying 'No interruptions', it is the interruptions which can arise in the training room that are the problem, and can disrupt the effectiveness of both the teaching and learning. Interruptions can happen in many different ways:

- **The dreaded mobile phone**: the trainer should ask at the beginning of the session that everyone makes sure that their mobile and Blackberry is turned off, and not just turned to silent mode.

- **A phone ringing in the room**: switchboard or whoever is responsible for answering the phone and putting calls through in the firm can be asked not to do so during the session and only during the breaks. Even better is to ask switchboard to write messages to have available either during a break or at the end of the session.
- **Late arrivals**: there is not really much that can be done about late arrivals. However, if it is known, for instance, that there are transport or traffic problems, it would be sensible to delay the start of the session until most people are there. The situation can be explained to those already present. Attendees can be asked whether, in the circumstances, they would be prepared to cut short the coffee break/lunch or to finish late, for example.
- **Early departures**: again, there is not much to be done about this. Having people turn off their mobile phones and Blackberries does reduce the risk; it is then only if someone knows at the start of the session that he or she is going to leave early that the problem will arise. The trouble is, if attendees are asked at the start whether anyone has to leave early, it implicitly signals that early departures are expected/tolerated.
- **Technology going wrong or the trainer not knowing how to use the technology**: even if a trainer is competent in using audio-visual equipment (see **38.2.2.3**), it is always sensible to take the precaution of having someone expert on hand or on call should he or she have a problem. If the trainer has to use a piece of equipment he or she has not used before, he or she should be encouraged to practise using it beforehand. If that is not possible, the trainer should arrive early and be shown how to use the equipment before the session.
- **Flagging** (also known as nodding off): The problem is that hot stuffy rooms do not assist learning, and if it is a long session attention is bound to flag. So, it is important to ensure that the training room is as well ventilated as possible and that the temperature is controlled.
- **Calls of nature**: this is why it is important to have regular scheduled breaks in the programme (see **36.2.5.2**).

CHAPTER 38

How to organise and run training

38.1	Introduction	38.4	Recording training information
38.2	Developing the training in the training programme	38.5	Collecting and collating feedback from training
38.3	Organising the training session	38.6	SRA administration requirements

38.1 INTRODUCTION

Having developed the firm's training strategy, and from that a training programme, the training programme needs to be delivered through effective and efficient administration and support. It is easy for lawyers to be dismissive of management and administration and think it is something that can be done in a matter of minutes. This is probably because good administration is not usually visible: good administration avoids problems and anticipates and deals with the unexpected. If the firm is going to get the most out of its investment in training, its training function has to be effective at the operational level of delivering the training required by the training programme. This involves:

- organising the training;
- recording training information;
- collecting and collating feedback from training;
- complying with Solicitors Regulation Authority (SRA) requirements, e.g. for authorisation.

38.2 DEVELOPING THE TRAINING IN THE TRAINING PROGRAMME

Chapter 36 talks about how to design a training session from the perspective of the trainer, particularly when the trainer is a fee earner. That is really about content and structure. However, to deliver the session once designed involves a number of very practical considerations:

DELIVERING THE TRAINING PROGRAMME

- the trainer;
- the resources needed;
- the training venue or accommodation;
- the room set-up.

38.2.1 Trainer

The biggest decision, certainly in monetary terms, is in deciding whether to use the firm's own lawyers or the firm's training or Human Resources (HR) personnel to deliver the training, or whether to outsource it and use an external trainer/s. There are advantages and disadvantages for each.

38.2.1.1 Do-it-yourself

The advantages of having training delivered by lawyers in the firm is that, certainly in training on legal technical topics, they have credibility; they know the firm and its culture, and they can explain and promulgate the firm's practices and procedures. Most importantly, they are enhancing the firm's intellectual capital. In financial terms, depending on the firm's approach to the financial management of training (see **Chapter 4**), this will either be cost saving by not having to pay for an external trainer, or a cost from the loss of fee-earning time.

The disadvantages are that firstly, lawyers in the firm may not be trained as trainers, and the training they deliver may therefore not be as effective as it might otherwise be. Secondly, there is the danger that client work will prevent the trainer from turning up or turning up on time.

The former can be mitigated by providing 'train the trainer' training and providing guidance on how to train (see **Chapter 37**). Equally, if the training being delivered is part of a firm-wide training programme which is repeated, say, annually, developing tutor guides and accompanying PowerPoint slides for sessions means that whoever is going to deliver the training session has those tools to guide them.

The problem of the internal trainer not turning up is more problematic. However, the risk here can be mitigated by good administration which 'manages' the trainer. This involves:

- selecting a date for the training in consultation with the trainer;
- keeping in touch with the trainer in the lead-up to the date of the training;
- sending (gentle) reminders closer to the time;
- offering assistance in preparing for the session; and
- as a last resort, arranging for a substitute to be in reserve should the worst happen.

It should be said that this becomes less of an ordeal if the session has been run before and a tutor guide and accompanying slides have been produced (see **38.2.2.2**), which make it easier for someone else to come in at short notice and deliver the training.

38.2.1.2 Outsourcing

The advantages of outsourcing training and using an external trainer are the converse of the disadvantages of DIY – namely, external trainers are paid to turn up and deliver, and they are professionals at delivering training. The downside of using external trainers is that they cost money. They usually charge on a day or half-day basis, although some may charge for the number of attendees (what difference this makes to the session if there are neither too few nor too many attendees in the room is difficult to see). There is also the credibility risk: if the external trainer is not known to the attendees, and particularly if the trainer is not a lawyer, this may create an obstacle to the effectiveness of the training. Just as there are ways of minimising the possible disadvantages of the DIY approach, so there are interventions which can be used to mitigate the potential downside of using external trainers. The first way to minimise potential problems is to be very thorough in choosing the trainer in the first place.

SELECTING AN EXTERNAL TRAINER

As with any selection process, one starts with a list of potential trainers or training organisations with a view to interviewing those who seem most suitable after initial enquiry. Finding possible suitable trainers can be done simply by searching the internet. However, to separate the wheat from the chaff, it can help to:

- talk to training managers in other firms;
- use training networks and organisations for recommendations for trainers;
- talk to Professional Support Lawyer networking groups, particularly when looking for a trainer for something that is not mainstream.

It is simply due diligence.

PREPARING A BRIEF

Provided that the specific training needs (see **Chapter 3**) have been identified, a brief based on these should be prepared, which sets out:

- the objective in outsourcing the training;
- the learning objectives of the training itself;
- who the training is aimed at;
- how many people require the training and with what priority;

- how the training is to be delivered, i.e. on-site/off-site, timing, co-taught with internal trainer or not, etc.;
- what the budget is, if it is appropriate to give this information at this stage.

You may or may not wish to specify training methods but may wish the prospective trainer to address this.

ASSESSING AN EXTERNAL TRAINER

When you have drawn up a shortlist of potential suitable trainers or training organisations, those on the shortlist should be invited to submit a proposal based on the specific brief. What a proposal should do is:

- demonstrate an understanding of the firm's particular training needs; and
- be customised to those needs and to the training objectives.

If what you receive is merely an 'off the shelf' proposal, you know the degree to which the training organisation may – or may not – be prepared to meet the firm's specific needs and objectives.

Meeting the trainer should be part of the selection process. However, where the trainer who will actually deliver the training is part of a training organisation, it may be that the meeting will be with representatives of the training organisation's management or business development team, and may not include the trainer. If that is the case, due diligence needs to be carried out around the following areas:

- whether the training organisation has any experience of training lawyers, and if not which industry it does have experience of training. How comparable is that experience to the needs of the firm? Similarly, does the training organisation have any specific experience of professional partnerships if it has not had experience of training lawyers? Again, the comparability of this experience to training for law firms and to the needs of the firm will have to be determined;
- how the training organisation quantifies or measures the effectiveness of its training;
- who the training provider sees as its key competitors, and how it differs from its competitors in strengths and weaknesses;
- the training organisation's approach to training generally, and to training design, content and methodology specifically;
- whether the training organisation can provide references;
- what the training organisation's fee structure is;
- what the training organisation's areas of expertise and specialisms are, and what relevant experience its trainers have for delivering in the areas needed;
- what limitations the training organisation or its trainer may have.

A firm's key concern is to ensure that the training organisation does understand – and also wants to understand – the firm's business, and is in fact interested in meeting the firm's particular needs rather than merely providing an 'off the shelf' solution.

If it is not possible to meet the trainer, it is important to find out who the trainer will be and to ask for his or her CV or biography.

In terms of the training itself, you want to understand from the training organisation:

- the training methods that will be used and whether they will be appropriate to achieve your learning outcomes;
- for skills training, how skills will be practised and feedback given; and
- the format the training will take if this has not been specified already.

It is important that you feel there is a fit with the training organisation, as the credibility of not only the trainer, but of the firm's training itself, will depend to a large extent on the effectiveness of the delivery of the training by that training organisation. This means you need to be confident that the trainer understands the context in which you want the training to be done, and what it is that the training needs to deliver.

The next thing is to find out what the training organisation has that is 'off the shelf' which might nonetheless meet the firm's needs. It may be that a firm's training needs – or some of them at least – may be met by generic training courses which the training organisation already offers. Bespoke training is not always necessary to meet a firm's specific needs and objectives. In fact, the training needs of firms are more generic than they might like to think. Where generic will do, there is no point in spending money on unnecessary customising or tailoring.

If, however, there is no suitable content and/or the firm's training needs are not suitable for a generic solution, the firm needs to be very clear about:

- just how bespoke the training organisation is going to make the training – will it just be a case of changing the name of the firm on the title slide of the PowerPoint presentation?;
- how and by whom the training will be designed and the extent to which the firm will be involved; should the training, for example, be based on the firm's own standard forms or precedent documents? At the least the firm should sign-off on the design well before the training is delivered, and the training should only be delivered if it meets with the firm's approval; and
- the cost.

Once training materials have been produced by the training organisation, these should be checked ahead of the session, and the first time the training is run it is a good idea to sit in on the session. This is to check whether the training does in fact achieve the training objectives and that it is delivered in the way that has been agreed and to the standard you expect. If sitting in on the session is not going to be appropriate, then it is very important to obtain feedback from the attendees at the session. Bear in mind that giving a good show is not necessarily delivering good training. So, the trainer who puts on an excellent show may not in fact have achieved the training objectives of taking forward the knowledge, expertise or skills of the attendees, even though the feedback is glowing.

You also need to be aware that external training organisations work in a number of different ways:

- some employ their trainers, who are usually also involved in training design;
- others do not employ their trainers but have a 'stable' of trainers and practitioners they call upon to deliver particular types of training. The determining factor here can be subject area expertise rather than excellence at training, which is why it is important to find out about the actual trainer. The advantage of the stable approach is that the training organisation is more likely to be able to offer a wider range of training;
- as a sole trainer who specialises in a particular area or areas. Sole trainers are usually very expert in their area, but will not have the resources or support of the larger training organisations;
- some are Continuing Professional Development (CPD) departments within university law schools which might use their own staff or others from their university stable. It will depend on the particular CPD department as to its ability in understanding the needs of practice and to deliver. Universities may do this as part of their knowledge transfer initiatives.

COST AND NEGOTIATION

Irrespective of how the training organisation is structured, if you need to do a lot of training or training over a long period, do not be afraid to negotiate with the trainer or training organisation, as appropriate, as to cost.

How a training organisation charges needs to be considered. For example, beware the training organisation which charges per person when the training is being run purely for your firm (i.e. your lawyers are the only attendees), particularly if the training is being delivered in-house for you. Provided there are not too many or too few attendees in the room, it should be irrelevant how many attend. So, attempting to charge per person could be seen as profiteering. Similarly, beware the training organisation which wishes to charge development time – this is difficult to justify if the course is 'off the shelf' or if the customisation consists of just changing the name. Only if the training that is being commissioned is genuinely bespoke is a charge for development time acceptable. Once a training organisation has developed a bespoke course for a firm, it is then able to sell the same course to other firms, unless it is a term of the agreement that the training organisation may not do so because the training course is owned by the firm. If, however, the training organisation is able to use the course (but make sure this does not include using your standard forms or precedents) this is a justification for negotiating the fee down further – or even for the firm to take a profit share, if it were so minded.

Some training organisations encourage 'tie-ups' or subscriptions. These allow a firm to select courses from the training organisation's portfolio at preferential rates, usually discounted, which makes the training more cost-effective for the firm. The downside is that often the firm is choosing 'a dish off the menu', rather than having input into how the dish is made and ingredients used, and so may not end up with the course that it wants. The problem is greater when the training organisation acts more as a middle man, sourcing its trainers from its stable for particular courses, rather than employing its own trainers. The stable approach often uses lawyers in practice, but not always. While the lawyers may have the benefit of being cutting edge and up to date with practice they may not, however, be as good as trainers. Conversely, an experienced trainer may not be as close to practice as one might wish. By definition, the more experienced and full-time the trainer, the greater his or her likely distance from full-time practice.

BARRISTERS

An alternative is to use barristers. A number of chambers have a portfolio of talks they are willing to give to firms, and usually for free. This is in the barrister's interest as it is a way of establishing his or her credentials in the hope of securing future instructions.

38.2.2 Resources

The resources needed for delivering training are a bit of a mixed bag: from handouts to accommodation, and much in between.

38.2.2.1 Training materials

Training materials may seem obvious but are easy to overlook. In order to decide what training materials will be needed, consider the following questions:

1. Is there anything attendees need to know beforehand (putting aside administrative and housekeeping instructions)? If so, you can either send attendees an email referring them to the relevant internet link or firm precedent, for example, or attach a copy of whatever they need to read or think about.
2. Are there going to be exercises during the session? If there are going to be case studies, discussions or break-out groups, you will need to provide copies of the fact scenarios, questions and so on for each attendee. To preserve the Amazon rain forests, instructions in the session could simply be put on a PowerPoint slide or written on a flip chart for attendees to read in the session. However, in that case time will need to be allowed for attendees to write the instructions down, particularly if there are a lot of instructions or if the instructions are complex, and the room set-up will also need to allow everyone to see the screen or flip chart.

3. Also, if case studies, discussions or break-out groups are going to be used, will delegates be required to report back in plenary on the results of their group discussions? Reporting back can be done orally or each group may write up its results on a flip-chart sheet. If flip charts or white boards are to be used, special marker pens will also be needed – and either a white board eraser or cleaning cloth. Practical but true.
4. If there are exercises, will model answers or hints/tips be provided either during the session or afterwards? After the session, the answers can be sent by email, leaving it to the attendees to print out if and when they wish to. If provided during the session, these will need to be printed and copied.
5. Will attendees need to refer to any materials or sources during the session? If, for example, a particular statute is being considered, do copies need to be available in the room? If it is a practitioner text that everyone in a practice area should have their own copy of, then the instructions that are sent out for the session (see **38.3**) should remind people that they need to bring this with them. Extracts of legislation and similar can also be displayed on a PowerPoint slide or from a website, provided there is a computer in the room with internet access and connected to a projector, and provided all attendees can see the screen.
6. Is PowerPoint being used? If so, at its simplest attendees can be given copies of the PowerPoint slides. If these are printed as a handout, limit it to three slides to a page, with room for notes.

38.2.2.2 Tutor instructions or guides

Other materials which should be considered, especially where the training is likely to be run again and possibly by someone else, are tutor instructions or even a tutor guide, which avoids re-inventing the wheel the next time the training has to be done. It also is a way of encouraging and assisting fee earners who are new to giving training and who may therefore be under-confident. Another advantage, of course, is that it is a means of ensuring consistency and quality in the delivery of the training – stopping the more lugubrious fee earner from going off-piste and off-script. It also means that if a trainer has to pull out from doing the training it is easier for someone else to step in.

38.2.2.3 Audio-visual and other equipment

Technology is both a wonderful and a dangerous thing in training: used properly, it can enhance the training experience; used indiscriminately, it can obscure the benefits of training entirely. The latter tends to occur where the technology leads rather than the training. Putting aside e-learning as a method of delivery, which is discussed at **36.3**, the question to be considered is whether delivering effective training can be enhanced by the use of audio-visual and other aids. People learn in many and varied ways, as has been discussed earlier. However, a digital screen or an electric current is not what necessarily makes people learn, and 'chalk and talk' can be an effective training method.

The sorts of aids which can be considered include (and each is discussed in more detail below):

- PowerPoint slides (+ computer + screen + projector);
- digital camera;
- video/DVD recorder and/or player (+ screen + projector);
- computer with internet connection (+ projector);
- Smart Board;
- visualiser;
- white board (+ marker pens – and wipes/eraser);
- flip chart (+ stand + marker pens);
- microphone.

POWERPOINT

Most people these days are able to use PowerPoint. However, its convenience has also led to its abuse. The offences which are daily perpetrated with PowerPoint range from putting the whole talk on the slides (too much information), to too much 'whiz bang' – non-stop visuals which can be extremely distracting. The aim of PowerPoint is to assist listeners/learners by having the slides act as a type of learner's Sat Nav, to help them find their way through what is being delivered orally – not to provide a transcript on the screen.

In an ideal world, a trainer should not need to use PowerPoint because the presentation is so clear that the listener is able to follow and absorb just by listening. However, without casting aspersions on the trainer, in complex talks and sessions some visual navigation is useful. The point is that if the listener is concentrating on reading the close text on the slide, he or she will not be concentrating on what the trainer is saying. In fact, the attendees might just as well have been given a handout and left to read it for themselves, for the amount of attention that they will be paying to the trainer.

The remaining slides should consist of key words only – certainly not chunks of the transcript. If a quote is being used, if appropriate, put the whole quote on the slide. However, if it is a long quote and difficult to read from the screen, it is better either to read out the quote or to put relevant points from the quote on the screen, or the whole quote but with key words or phrases emboldened. Alternatively, include the quote in full in the handout.

DIGITAL CAMERA

Any video camera can be used – even a mobile phone. If the session is a skills training session, filming delegates can be useful for feedback, as well as for the attendees' attempts at review and reflection.

For skills training, one way of demonstrating a skill is to play a video of pre-recorded good (or bad for that matter) practice, and then have the attendees themselves identify the good (or bad) points in the performance.

Recording training sessions can also be useful if the firm has offices in different geographical locations, particularly overseas. DVDs of, say, seminars which have been recorded in one office can be used as the basis for a training session in another office: watching the video, then discussing the issues. If there is a partner or senior assistant in the office with the relevant expertise, he or she could act as a facilitator for questions from attendees after watching the video. These sessions are also available commercially, particularly for legal updates and compulsory training, such as anti-money laundering or health and safety.

COMPUTER WITH INTERNET CONNECTION

Depending on the session, it might be helpful to be able to connect to a website on the internet or to access an electronic service during the training. The computer will need to be connected to a projector so that what is being accessed can be projected onto the projector screen, unless of course there is an integrated system in the room which does all this automatically.

SMART BOARD

A Smart Board is basically a white board that thinks for itself. It is usually touch-sensitive and interactive. A PowerPoint presentation can be projected onto it, and special markers can be used if the trainer wishes to mark up the text on the board. If a Smart Board is not available, the same result can be achieved with just a white board or flip chart and a PowerPoint presentation.

VISUALISER

A visualiser is a bit like an overhead projector that projects normal sheets of paper onto the screen; the sheets do not have to be transparent. Visualisers come into their own if the training session is about writing or drafting skills, for instance, as attendees' efforts can be displayed by placing them on the visualiser for everyone's benefit.

Equally, if there is something that comes up during the session that it would be useful for everyone to see, such as a page in a textbook or a section of legislation, this can be displayed on the visualiser.

WHITE BOARD

On the principle that not everything has to have an electric current in order to be useful, the white board is a shiny white version of the blackboard. Instead of writing with chalk, however, special marker pens are used and the writing can then be wiped off by a special eraser. White boards are very helpful for writing up calculations or recording points made by attendees, drawing diagrams, and so on.

FLIP CHART

If the room being used for training doubles as a meeting or conference room, it may not have a white board on the wall. In that case, it is worth a firm investing in a flip chart and stand, which can be easily stored and brought out for training sessions when required. The flip chart works on the same principle as the white board – 'chalk and talk', basically. The sheets can also be kept if they contain anything that can be fed into a future session. The only ongoing expense is replacing the paper and marker pens.

If the training is being delivered to clients, the paper can be printed with the firm's logo for brand reinforcement.

Flip charts are also very useful for group work: if attendees are feeding back or making a presentation, they can write key points up on the sheets. If a number of sheets need to be displayed at the same time, and there is no way of clipping them on a white board in the room, use Blue-Tack to fix them to the walls.

MICROPHONE

Although using a microphone may look professional, and you would assume helps ensure that everyone can hear what is being said in a large room, it is a trap for the unwary: people can hold it too close so that the sound is distorted, or hold it too far away so that it is of no use whatsoever – or a bit of both, particularly if it is a hand-held mike. Shouts from the back of the room of 'speak up' or 'too loud' are not the sort of interruptions which help aid a speaker's confidence or train of thought. The best idea is to use a microphone only if someone sitting in the back row of the training room would not be able to hear a trainer with a reasonably clear speaking voice at the front of the room.

If the trainer needs to use a microphone then note the following:

- Make sure the trainer practises using it ahead of the session – and with someone else in the room to tell him or her whether it is booming or if the trainer cannot be heard.
- Use a lapel mike rather than a hand-held one. A hand-held mike makes it difficult to turn pages if the trainer is using notes, and is too susceptible to inadvertent movement (i.e. moving it too close or too far away). However, if a lapel mike is used, the trainer should be reminded to unclip it before trying to leave the room. Otherwise, there will be an undignified moment as the trainer is yanked back by the mike cord. A wireless mike is therefore preferable.
- If the room requires a microphone and the trainer is going to take questions from the floor, be aware that both the trainer and other attendees may have difficulty hearing the questions. If possible, have a roaming wireless mike that can be given to a person asking a question. It helps to have someone else in the room who can locate the person wanting to ask a question and take the

microphone to them (*à la Question Time*). If it is not possible to use a roaming mike, then when someone asks a question the trainer should move forward so that they can hear the question, then repeat the question for the benefit of everyone before answering it. There is nothing worse than hearing the answer, 'no' or 'yes' but not knowing what 'no' or 'yes' applies to.

38.2.3 Support

Quite simply, it is also important to consider who needs to be at the training session to make sure everything happens as it should and when it should. This may be a training manager or administrator. However, it is also sensible to have someone on hand or on call who can help with any IT or audio-visual equipment difficulties.

Where the session is being given by an external trainer, it may be that having a partner sit in or co-teach can help the effectiveness of the session and deal with any credibility issues from having, say, a non-lawyer trainer. An experienced trainer, either external or internal, can also give confidence and support to a fee earner (and that includes partners) who may not be experienced in giving training.

Whoever it is that needs to be involved, his or her availability should be checked well in advance and a reminder sent to them just before the session (see **38.3**).

38.2.4 Venue and accommodation

38.2.4.1 Internal or external venue?

The first decision is whether to hold the training session at an external venue or in the firm. If attendees have to go out of the office to attend the training, there is less chance of them being pulled off the training by senior members in the firm. There is still the hazard of mobile phones and Blackberries, however (see **37.6**). Depending on where the venue is, there may be some resistance because of the time taken in getting there and back. The advantage of going off-site is that you avoid the interruptions that are likely to happen in the office, which in theory should enable attendees to concentrate better. The downside is that there is likely to be a cost involved in hiring the venue – although this is not always the case, and by doing a bit of investigating alternatives to expensive training venues may be found. For example, some Legal Practice Course (LPC) providers, universities/law schools will allow firms to use their teaching accommodation, especially out of term time or in the evenings, usually for a lower cost. There are also purpose-built conference centres around, as well as hotels which are usually competitive in their pricing. It may even be a chance to curry favour with a client by paying to use their facilities.

Another reason for using an external venue is that it may be better set up for training, with access to more sophisticated audio-visual equipment than is available in the firm. Having said that, having IT support available will be even more important if it is technology that is not used in the firm and with which the trainer is not familiar.

The main advantage of holding the training in-house is that there is no room-hire fee (depending, of course, on whether the firm uses an internal profit centre charging model (see **Chapter 4**)) and there are no issues of travelling to and from the venue. However, it also means that attendees are within reach of those in the firm who may wish to pull them off the training (which might be entirely justified, it has to be said, but not always). If the training is to be held in the firm, consideration needs to be given to whether it is an appropriate physical environment for the training (the same applies when looking at external training venues).

38.2.4.2 Refreshments

It does help to have coffee on arrival and at breaks, and water in the room throughout. If it is an all-day training session, the budget will dictate whether lunch is provided or not. Just a couple of considerations: if one of the objectives is to get the attendees to get to know each other better, then coffee and lunch in the room or a room nearby encourages informal chatting and networking. If people have to go out to get lunch or coffee, their interaction is likely to be limited to the formal parts of the course and they are more likely to come in late.

38.2.4.3 Soundproofing

If training is taking place in the firm, it can be difficult to find a room which is soundproof. However, simple interventions can help: a note sent around the firm before the training, warning that the training will be taking place and asking people to be considerate with regard to noise and/or a sign in the corridor where the training is taking place and/or a sign on the actual door of the room.

38.2.5 Room set-up

The size of the room is important: it needs to be big enough to fit the number of delegates comfortably and in the most appropriate room set-up. The traditional choice of room set-ups are as follows:

- Theatre style: rows of chairs all facing the front. This is fine for seminars (although may be difficult if delegates are expected to take notes) but not much else.
- Classroom style: similar to theatre style, except with desks as well as chairs – writing surfaces for attendees, in other words.
- Cabaret style: groups of people (usually four to six) seated at separate tables in the room in clusters. This set up is good for workshop sessions and break-out activities such as case studies and role plays.
- Boardroom style: everyone is seated around a large rectangular table with no obvious 'front'. This set-up is good for discussions.

- U-shape: tables set-up in a U-shape with chairs on the outside of the U so that attendees can see each other. There can be a separate table for the trainer in the gap, if needed.
- Conference or hollow square style: a variation of the boardroom style set-up is to have tables forming a hollow square or rectangle. This has the same virtue of no obvious 'front' – although wherever the trainer sits will usually end up being the 'front'. The format usually allows for a larger number of attendees, subject to the size of the room itself, of course. However, it usually means attendees are at a greater distance from each other than if seated around a conference table, and the discussion may be less intimate.
- Perpendicular style: this set-up has the trainer at the front of the room and two rows of tables perpendicular to the front, with attendees sitting on the outside of each of the rows so that they are facing each other. The set-up allows the trainer to move around easily to look at attendees' work.

If the trainer is going to be walking around to check what attendees are doing and to give feedback (see **37.5**), the room needs to be large enough to let the trainer get round the chairs and tables. There is nothing more embarrassing than trying to squeeze around tables and have to flatten yourself against the wall. It is also important to check that the room is large enough for attendees in a wheelchair or with other access or specific needs.

Figure 38.1 – Room set-up

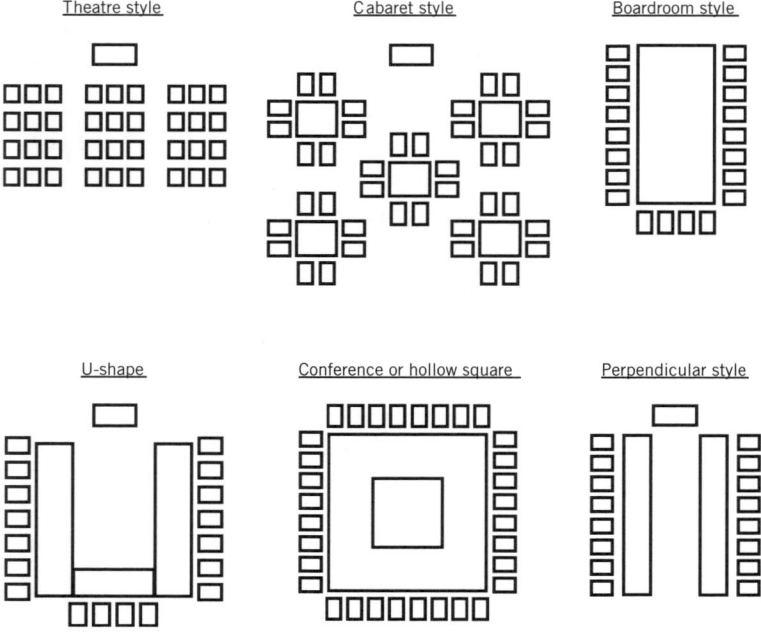

38.3 ORGANISING THE TRAINING SESSION

The basic steps involved are:

1. Preparation
2. Checking
3. Follow-up

38.3.1 Preparation

38.3.1.1 Managing attendee expectations

At its simplest, effective organisation of training should ensure that:

- attendees know what training they have to attend;
- where and when the training is taking place;
- attendees are given sufficient notice so that they can attend; and
- they are given reminders so that they do attend.

Quite simply, in a fee-earning environment there has to be good reason as to why time should be taken away from fee earning – there must be some benefit to be had which justifies the lawyer's loss of fee-earning time, and the additional pressure from having been away from his or her desk for the period. If those attending the training have any of this resistance, then the effectiveness of the training can be compromised and the firm will waste its investment: the individual will either not be as competent or as knowledgeable as he or she needs to be, or the firm is going to have to invest in further training.

How training is organised can go some way to dealing with initial resistance by making it very clear to the fee earners invited to attend:

- what the training is about, why it is felt to be necessary and what it is expected to achieve;
- why the training is being delivered in the particular way which has been decided upon, e.g. for training delivered by way of small group sessions, the emphasis should be that it provides an opportunity for one-to-one feedback, even if it might appear a classroom-like environment – appealing to the inner ambition to succeed, which most lawyers have;
- who is delivering the training and his or her credentials. At the same time, ensure that the trainer understands the legal practice environment: an external trainer who comes in and starts talking about the 'company's customers' immediately risks losing credibility, which he or she is unlikely to win back;
- that the training is for the benefit of those attending and that performance is confidential between the participant and trainer and is not being used to measure performance – unless of course it is, in which case this should be made clear;

DELIVERING THE TRAINING PROGRAMME

- how the training is going to be consolidated, e.g. by post-session voluntary/compulsory exercises, a follow-up session, etc.;
- that their feedback is important and will be used to review whether the training has been effective or not;
- whether further sessions may be required, etc.

All this information should be provided well ahead of the session – ideally at the alert stage or confirmation of attendance stage. Leaving clarification of these points until the session itself wastes time by having to break down resistance at the start of the session – time which could be better spent achieving the training objectives of the session. There may also be more no-shows.

38.3.2 Checking and on the day

You may think that having confirmed the date with both trainer and trainees and booked the room, there is nothing more to do but wait for the day. This is risky. Checking and following up arrangements minimises the risk of any slip. So, make sure you send a reminder to the trainer a week before the training date, and check whether the deadlines set out earlier have been met.

38.3.3 Follow-up

Just because the training has gone well does not mean resting on one's laurels. The fact that it has gone well needs to be evidenced so that its value can be demonstrated (see **4.5**). That means collating the feedback, following up any actions which have been promised to either the trainer or trainees, providing the trainer with feedback, and ensuring that all necessary information about the training is provided to those with responsibility for reviewing training.

This is best illustrated by a scenario.

Scenario

Let us assume that you are new to the training department and are arranging a training session which is going to be delivered by Partner X as the trainer – a very busy individual who is doing this out of the goodness of his heart (the same principles apply if the trainer is someone external, it should be said). So, Partner X's co-operation in giving the training is not an issue (if it is, see **1.6**). Assuming the date for the training has not been sorted, you need to find out from X's secretary, or directly from X, when he would be available to give the training. Bear in mind the discussion about optimal times for training, as discussed at **36.2.5.1**.

A sensible precaution before agreeing the date with Partner X is also to check with the practice area secretaries or practice area head as to whether there would be any issues with the proposed dates. It could be that the practice area head is planning an away day that day; or there is a big deal closing or trial starting, or assistants may have already booked holidays. The point with busy people is to bother them as little as possible and avoid having to go back to them to change what has just been agreed. Not because they are busy and important, but because if they think of themselves that way they may be less co-operative. Not always, but it is a risk. Consequently, it is also sensible to make sure the particular training venue is available on the proposed date and make a provisional booking to avoid it being booked by someone else in the time it takes you to confirm the date with Partner X.

Then, send a memo to assistants to tell them about the training either confirming the date, in which case make sure you are giving a reasonable amount of notice, or giving a choice of dates, asking people to indicate their availability, or give no options. If you do give a choice of dates, there is a risk that numbers may be evenly split, or only a few are able to go to any of the dates. However, if you do not give a choice of dates, there is the risk that the date will clash with something unforeseen or out of your control (such as booked holiday). One thing that you need to accept is that it does not matter how much notice you give – you will still not be able to guarantee that you will be able to prise people away from their desks on the day. You can try saying in the memo confirming the date that their practice area head has confirmed their availability – if that is true.

If lunch is going to be provided, you should also ask for any special dietary requirements.

If full details of the session are not yet available, attendees should be told that further details will be sent out and when – and diarise this. Attendees should also be asked to reply by a certain date.

If you gave a choice of dates, collate responses for date preferences as you receive them. If the deadline has passed and some responses are missing, follow up directly with individuals who have not responded. If you are dealing with a chronic training non-attender, you can take the 'stick' approach by reporting back to the practice area head, for example.

Once all availability is known, select the date. Then confirm the room booking, the date with Partner X and the date with those attending, also telling the attendees where the training will be held and again confirm the time.

Work out a timeline for yourself, working back from the date of the training session so that you know the deadline for:

- printing any handouts;
- sending the PowerPoint presentation to the IT department;
- ordering coffee and tea/lunch, etc.; and
- sending reminders.

Then diarise the dates.

When you confirm the date with Partner X, it might be an idea to offer assistance should he need any, but do also let him know when his PowerPoint slides/handouts, etc. will be needed by.

Then:

- prepare an attendance list and feedback form;
- arrange for any copying of the handout/s to be done. If the handout is very bulky, and you have the service, arrange for the copying to be delivered to the training room, if possible;
- send Partner X a list of who will be attending and ask him to arrive 15 minutes early in order to set up and check that everything is in order (this is likely to turn out to be five minutes in advance, which should be OK, but if you say five minutes in the first place you may end up with him arriving either right on time or late).

DELIVERING THE TRAINING PROGRAMME

On the day

On the day of the training, it is sensible to go to the training venue yourself in advance, if it is possible, to check that:

- everything is set up correctly (e.g. no-one will be sitting with their back to the screen);
- everything works (i.e. PC, projector, lights, etc.);
- the presentation is loaded if it has been sent in advance; and
- everything is there that should be there (e.g. writing pads, pens, etc. if these have been requested).

Half an hour before the session is due to start, return to the training venue to check everything is as you left it earlier and that anything due to arrive since has arrived, particularly any catering – tea, coffee, lunch, etc. If you can, try and be in the room 15 minutes before the start time so that you can welcome Partner X and do whatever needs to be done to help him set up. Offering to get Partner X a cup of coffee/water, etc. while he gets sorted can be very welcoming, if you do not mind doing this. It is not a case of being menial, but 'handling' the trainer in case he has nerves or is stressed. It also makes a good impression (start as you mean the training to continue) if you are able to.

Welcome the attendees as they arrive and check off their names. If Partner X does not know all the attendees, he might appreciate you discreetly drawing a seating plan for him to show who is sitting where.

With luck, everyone will have arrived ready for the planned start time. If you know there has been a problem affecting a number of the attendees, such as train problems or a meeting overrunning, then liaise with Partner X to see whether he would prefer to wait, rather than to have his flow interrupted by latecomers.

When everyone is ready to start, you should:

- make any housekeeping announcements – health and safety, no planned fire drill that day, etc.;
- say how long the session will be, when refreshments/lunch will be served, etc.;
- then introduce Partner X and thank him for giving the session.

Depending on what else you have on, you may wish to sit in on the session, particularly if it is the first time the training session has been run, or it is the first time that Partner X has given the session. This should be cleared with Partner X in advance, as if it is the first time for him he may feel hampered by someone sitting in. Similarly, depending on the subject matter of the session, someone else sitting in may hinder discussion. However, if it is appropriate and Partner X is happy, then sit in and use the opportunity to note anything that could be improved in the future, any points that arise which may need action, including anything that might be useful for the firm's knowledge management (KM) systems, and generally how you think the session went. If you are not going to sit in, make sure you give the attendees the feedback forms and ask them to complete the forms at the end of the session, if you want to do this on hard copy rather than online. The problem with hard copy is you have to decide how to get the completed forms. Having feedback completed online is a possible solution, except that return rates might be lower, as you are relying on attendees to do this once they return to their desk. At the end of the session, thank Partner X if you have been sitting in. Hand out the feedback forms if you are doing it this way, and ask attendees to complete them before they leave, or say that you will email the feedback form to them – and do.

After the session

After the session collate the feedback and convert it into a short report (see **Chapter 39**) for whomever has responsibility for training. Write to Partner X to thank him for giving the training (a good investment if you wish him to do it again), and provide him either with the feedback report or a summary (particularly politic if there are any comments which are overly personal or unhelpfully negative). If anything came out of the session which requires following up, do the follow-up and report back to the attendees, if this is what was promised.

38.3.4 What can go wrong – fire-fighting tips

As Robert Burns so aptly put it: 'the best laid plans of mice and men often go awry'. And so too does training. Proof of competence, somewhat ironically, is not so much in being able to do things properly, but being able to deal with things when they go wrong – and to put them right. What this means for running training successfully is not just that training is administered well in the sense that things happen how and when they are meant to happen, but also that the unforeseen is dealt with and with minimal disruption to the training itself, and therefore with minimal impact on the effectiveness of the training.

The following scenarios are examples of what can go wrong, and possible steps or interventions that can be taken to prevent or minimise the problem. These are not the only solutions by any means, but for someone new to running training in a firm they provide a starting point.

Scenario 1: The trainer calls in sick/is stuck on the tube, etc.

If the trainer is prevented at the last minute from giving the training, the best insurance is to have a back-up arranged or a stand-in ready, particularly if it is a session that is only being run once or if there are clients attending. If a stand-in has not been arranged and it is not going to be possible to run the training, then the important thing is to let the attendees know as soon as possible, particularly if they are travelling to the training specifically. Consequently, it is a sensible precaution always to ask for the mobile phone numbers of all attendees. Have the numbers loaded on your own mobile phone, in case you get a call from the trainer when you are not on site.

If the training has to be cancelled, do not forget to cancel the room and the catering, explaining why. You will also need to liaise with the trainer as soon as you can, either to re-arrange the training or to make some other arrangements, e.g. for distributing materials.

Scenario 2: The trainer is late

If the training is due to start at say, 9 am, and everyone is in the room but there is no trainer, the first step is to try to call him or her. Obvious – until you realise that you do not have the trainer's number. So, make sure that you have got the trainer's mobile number ahead of the training. Then you can ring to find out where he or she is, and when he or she is likely to arrive. Equally, always give the trainer, especially if it is an external trainer, a contact mobile number of whomever is going to be in the room and looking after the training session, so that the trainer knows whom to call if he or she falls ill or has another problem which prevents him or her from coming. If the contact number that you give to the trainer is for someone else, or even the switchboard, make sure you have 'cascade' arrangements in place so that the call reaches the appropriate person. The important thing is to let the attendees know why the training has not started and explain the reason (so they do not have an impression that the trainer is just slack – this goes to the credibility and effectiveness of the training when it ultimately happens). If it is going to be, say, another 10 minutes, then explain that that is the situation, and offer more coffee; if it is an internal training session, you might usefully be able to use the slot to make an announcement, or perhaps get feedback on another training session. If it is likely to be longer than 10 minutes – and don't forget that the trainer is going to have to de-stress, assuming he or she has been racing to get there, set up and catch breath, so that is likely to add another 10 minutes on anyway – ask attendees whether they are happy to wait. Where it is a training session of a couple of hours or more, it may be possible to make up the time with some re-scheduling of coffee and lunch breaks (people grabbing sandwiches and training over lunch, for example – not ideal but sometimes the best solution). Where the session is scheduled for just an hour, then it probably will not be worth going ahead, and you will need to look at re-scheduling. You should also make sure that you have given the trainer the correct address to come to, ideally with directions of how to get there, a map and the name of the person to ask for when he or she arrives, if it is an external trainer. What you do not want to happen is to go to reception later and find the trainer sitting there, not having known where to go or who to ask for – even worse if the trainer has been sitting in the reception of the company next door, having been given the wrong address ...

Scenario 3: The trainer is late and there are clients in the room

If clients are present for training, it is even more important to let everyone know what is happening, and to check that the clients are happy to wait for the trainer to arrive.

Scenario 4: The technology doesn't work

For example, the trainer cannot load the PowerPoint from his or her memory stick on to the computer in the room or the projector doesn't work – etc. It is always sensible to arrange for someone from the IT department (if you are so fortunate as to have one) or even a 'techy' trainee who knows how to do these things, on hand. It is actually sensible to have anyone involved in the training function trained up in how to do these things and to be able to do basic troubleshooting at least. The other way of avoiding the problem is to have the trainer email the PowerPoint slides to you in advance.

Scenario 5: The trainer goes over the time

The trainer goes well over the time, and the troops are getting increasingly restless: it is difficult if you have never used the trainer before to know whether you can trust his or her time-keeping abilities. However, you really cannot take the risk. And, if you have had prior experience of someone not keeping to time, then you are on notice and must take action.

So, what action do you take? Make it clear to the trainer in the preparation leading up to the session what the timings of the session are to be and emphasise that these must be adhered to. What can often cause it all to go awry are questions the trainer receives from the attendees. You can be tactful and say, even if the trainer is being bombarded with interesting questions and stimulating discussion, that unfortunately the session cannot run over 'because (some) attendees have a (client) meeting to go to/the room is booked for a meeting/another training session', etc. If the trainer is a serial offender, you really need to have someone sit in who is prepared to 'call time' as you do in debates. To help with the time-keeping, you can offer to let the trainer know when it is half an hour/10 minutes from the end, depending how long or short the session is to be. Then, when you introduce the trainer and make your housekeeping announcements, you can also tell the attendees what the timings will be; say there will be time for questions, but only X amount of time, and that if attendees are not able to ask their question in the session the trainer is happy to stay behind (check with the trainer first, of course) to answer any individual questions. If, having taken all these precautions, the trainer still pays no heed to your 10-minute call but proceeds to carry on over the finish time, you have no option but to wait for the trainer to catch breath, then stand up and say to everyone: thank you [name of trainer], this has been so interesting, but unfortunately we have run over our time and as you know the room is booked, etc. I am sure everyone would like to show their appreciation [cue: clapping], and if anyone has a question they have not been able to ask, [name of trainer] is happy to talk to you outside the training room.' You will probably receive looks of heartfelt gratitude from the attendees as they leave.

Scenario 6: Attendees walk out during the session

This is the opposite problem in some ways to Scenario 4, and will usually happen because the attendee has something else to go to or has just seen an email on his or her Blackberry or mobile, or may just think the training is a waste of time. The problem is that the reason for having to leave can be quite genuine, but it still has an impact on the session flow; on the trainer's pride if he or she was not aware the attendee had to leave early; on the other attendees who, if they don't know why the attendee has left, may think it is because the session is no good, which may influence their own perception. One person leaving, especially if the trainer is not as effective as one would wish, can start the 'rats leaving a sinking ship' syndrome, and end up with Schubert's *Surprise Symphony* and one lone violinist left on the stage – the trainer. The dilemma you have is whether to ask at the beginning if anyone has to leave, or not: if you do, it may send a message to the attendees that it is acceptable to leave early; if you do not, you will not know whether someone knows that they have to leave until they get up and go. The best way to manage this is through the preparation leading up to the session and in the pre-session correspondence with attendees, in which you say that the session is for X hours' duration and attendees are expected to stay until the end, both in order to obtain the CPD (although this will only work if the firm has not adopted the Continuing Competence approach to satisfy CPD requirements, and then only up until 31 October 2016, at which time the 16-hour requirement will cease (see **Chapter 20**)) and also out of courtesy to the trainer (although it will be the former reason which is likely to be of most effect). You could, in the correspondence say that where anyone finds he or she may not be able to stay for the whole duration he or she needs to let you know in advance.

If, notwithstanding these precautions someone does get up and leave, try to speak to them as soon as possible. You could follow them out of the training room if you happen to be sitting near the door and won't cause further disruption – although be aware that coming back into the room may also disrupt – and ask the attendee outside why he or she is leaving. If it is a genuine reason, say that attendees had been asked to advise you of this beforehand. If it is a

DELIVERING THE TRAINING PROGRAMME

case of an email on the phone or Blackberry, there is not much you can say other than that he or she was supposed to have mobile phones and Blackberries turned off, not just turned to silent mode. If it is not a genuine reason, you may or may not feel able to address this yourself with the attendee, i.e. lack of commitment, rudeness to trainer and other attendees, etc. If you don't feel that this is something you should deal with you could refer it to the attendee's supervisor. If the offender is a partner, you should refer it to your line manager and/or the firm's training partner to take up.

Scenario 7: Materials do not turn up

Where the in-session training materials do not turn up, this could be because you had not given clear instructions to the person responsible for doing the copying/collation/delivery. If the trainer says he or she will bring the materials with him or her there is always a risk that he or she will turn up having forgotten them or even having left them in a taxi. So, it is a good precaution to ask the trainer to send the materials to you electronically ahead of the session and offer to have the copying done in the firm (saying it is to save the trainer having to carry it all is a tactful way) and avoid the risk entirely – subject to the internal copying and delivery taking place.

Scenario 8: The trainer forgets the PowerPoint slides

Always ask the trainer to email the slides to you ahead of the session on the pretext that you can have the slides already loaded and ready to go (see Scenario 4 above re: technology not working). You can also say that you will have the slides copied as a handout, if that is what will be used in the session (see Scenario 7).

Scenario 9: There is no feedback/attendance sheet

If there is no attendance or feedback sheet or you have forgotten to bring one or the other with you to the session, there are a couple of possible fixes: if it is a longish session and there is going to be a break, and the training is either being done in the firm or close by, then it may be possible to go back to your office during the break to retrieve the form. If it is a short session with no breaks, you could ask attendees to write and sign their names on a sheet of paper (always carry paper with you is the moral of the story – and pens, Blu-Tack, white board marker pens, etc.) which you can then use as evidence of attendance (required for CPD purposes until 31 October 2016 (see **Chapter 20**). The better action is prevention, however, by making sure you have a pack of things you need to take to the session and that the copied feedback forms are in the pack. Remember – it is all about preparation.

Scenario 10: Attendees do not turn up

Attendees not turning up is a perennial problem for anyone who organises and runs training. If attendance at training is looked at in appraisal meetings, this can provide an incentive for people to attend (see **1.6.1**). If the reason the attendee has not turned up is because of some urgent client work, then there is not much you can say or do – fee earning is after all the business of the firm. However, it will not always be urgent client work that pulls an attendee off training: it may just be that the person for whom they are doing the work is a training agnostic who believes that the attendee's time is better spent at his or her desk (and therefore at the agnostic's service). Equally, the attendee may be similarly agnostic. Techniques for dealing with possible non-attendance include obtaining individual attendees' mobile phone numbers so that you can call them if they do not turn up. (However, be prepared to find that the agnostic will probably have his or her phone turned off.) If you are not able to contact the attendee to find out what is going on, then you could follow up with him or her as soon as possible after the training session, which by this stage he or she will have missed, to find out why he or she did not attend. Not following up gives the recalcitrant attendee the message that it did not matter that he or she did not attend and/or that his or her absence was not noticed (see suggested actions in Scenario 6). Dealing with the agnostic is more difficult. The best way may be to re-charge against the relevant practice area budget for the training which he or she did not attend and/or without a good and/or prior excuse (see **Chapter 4**) and where he or she was not able to arrange for someone else to attend in his or her place.

Scenario 11: The internal trainer is dire

If the problem is an internal trainer who turns out to be dire, then some particular tact and diplomacy will be required (although tact and diplomacy should already be in any training administrator's armoury). Having a practice of providing all trainers with copies of feedback is an arm's length way of letting a trainer know how he or she performed. However, that with nothing more is not likely to be constructive. If the feedback is negative and comes down to the trainer's own performance (as opposed to some other irritant – a hot room, the coffee being cold, the projector not working, etc.), it is good practice to give the feedback results to the trainer yourself (as opposed to putting them in the internal mail or emailing them). You can say to the trainer that you found the feedback a bit surprising, and ask the trainer how he or she felt the session had gone. You may find that the trainer may already be aware that there were issues, in which case a discussion about what would help the trainer, such as some further training or coaching, follows more easily. If the trainer has an attitude of everyone is out of step except him or her, then suggest that it might be helpful if you sit in on the next session the trainer gives to see if there is a problem. However, the trainer who sees nothing wrong with his or her performance is unlikely to be receptive to any feedback which does less than praise. In those circumstances, if it is possible, it might be better to cut your losses and find someone else to do the training in the future.

Scenario 12: The external trainer is dire

Where it is an external trainer who turns out to be dire, the same principles of tact and diplomacy as well as constructive discussion apply, particularly if you have paid for the inferior performance. You could send the trainer copies of the feedback and also your observations if you happened to sit in. Again, you should give the trainer the opportunity to give his or her views on the session and what the possible problem/s could have been. If the trainer is receptive to the feedback and has reflected on the session, then you can try to work with the trainer to overcome the problems. If, however, the trainer takes a similar attitude to the internal trainer who regards him- or herself as nothing less than perfect, then you are probably hitting your head against a brick wall and either you need to ask the training organisation to replace the trainer with someone more suitable or, if that is not possible, to

DELIVERING THE TRAINING PROGRAMME

sack the trainer/training organisation and go back to the drawing board (see **Chapter 36**) – after having obtained a refund or substantial reduction on the fee.

Scenario 13: The attendees do not co-operate

Attendees not co-operating can happen if attendees resent having to do the training in the first place. This may be because they have commitment issues with training. Ways of overcoming resistance to training include explaining the purpose of the training and why they are attending. If attendees still do not co-operate in the session, then there is nothing for it but to take it up with their managers as a conduct issue. Rudeness and lack of co-operation with someone who is giving his or her time and expertise to help attendees, whether he or she is in-house or external, is inexcusable and falls well short of appropriate professional conduct and, one would hope, the standards of conduct expected in the firm.

The problem generally when things go wrong is the panic that ensues as a result, usually because it means troubleshooting on the spot with limited time, and concern about the impact on those who are present. Unfortunately, it is not possible to anticipate every possible eventuality. However, you can develop a body of know-how which informs your administration. The way to do this is to review how things went on a regular basis. This is not just reviewing the success of the particular training session in meeting its training objectives (see **36.2.1**), but also reviewing how successful the administration was, i.e. were there any problems? If so, could they have been avoided and, if so, how? It is then important to make the necessary tweaks to your processes so that the same problem at least can be avoided in the future. You can also use feedback forms, by including questions about the training accommodation, catering administration and so on, as a way of obtaining another perspective (see **39.2**).

38.4 RECORDING TRAINING INFORMATION

38.4.1 SRA requirements

If a firm has obtained authorisation from the SRA to deliver the Professional Skills Course (PSC), then the firm will have various responsibilities imposed upon it which, if delegated, are likely to fall into the operational side of training. These responsibilities range from recording attendance and retaining records; obtaining, retaining and reviewing feedback; retaining details of courses delivered, together with course programmes and timings; keeping copies of course materials; and keeping details of tutors, including CVs. The specific obligations are set out in detail in **Chapter 16** in relation to the PSC. The reasons for the responsibilities of keeping and retaining records are primarily concerned with monitoring by the SRA and it is therefore important to be able to locate the necessary information should the firm receive a monitoring visit or a request from the SRA. Centralised record keeping will be an effective way of being able to find things, but not necessarily a practical one, depending on how training in the firm is organised: if, for instance, individual practice areas are largely responsible for the PSC Electives they run, then the record keeping is best done at the local level – provided that it is in fact done. The key for the person who is the firm's contact with the SRA and for ensuring compliance with the firm's authorisation conditions is to ensure that the necessary information is being collected and retained, and that it can be found when it is needed. This means good lines of communication with practice areas in this example, and ensuring effective delegation to the practice areas of these responsibilities.

38.4.2 Other reasons

Putting aside authorisation as an in-house PSC provider, there are other reasons for recording training information. As explained in **Chapter 20**, every solicitor is responsible for keeping a record of his or her training for CPD purposes. Some firms, nonetheless, will keep a central record as well, to ensure that no-one fails to comply, since this has implications for renewal of an individual's practising certificate or Registered European Lawyer registration. However, other reasons for wanting to record training information have nothing to do with CPD, and everything to do with being able to review training and its effectiveness within the firm.

- Whether feedback is obtained from feedback forms or in more informal ways (see **39.2**), that information needs to be captured and recorded. In the case of feedback forms, it is a case of entering the data into the learning management system (LMS). If the firm uses an LMS (see **36.3.6**), information can be more easily collated if attendees complete the feedback form electronically. Even if the data has to be entered manually, however, an LMS may be able to produce the necessary key performance indicator (KPI) reports, which can save a lot of time and effort compared to doing this manually.
- Details of the formal training sessions which take place need to be recorded in terms of date, time, topic and trainer, to make a comparison with the training that should have taken place under the training programme. This may point to the effectiveness of the training function in making sure training sessions take place; the reliability of the trainers in honouring their training commitment; and/or the commitment of attendees in actually turning up.
- Details of attendance at the training sessions should be recorded so that they are then available for appraisals.
- Individual training needs can be identified either through the appraisal process or discussion with the individual's manager or supervisor.

38.5 COLLECTING AND COLLATING FEEDBACK FROM TRAINING

38.5.1 SRA requirements

Again, if the firm is authorised to deliver the PSC in-house, it will be required to have systems in place for obtaining feedback and keeping copies of that feedback, as well as reviewing feedback on an annual basis. The firm is also required to carry out a periodic review of tutor performance. Details of the obligations arising from the various authorisations are provided in **Chapter 16**.

The methods for obtaining feedback from training are discussed in **Chapter 39**. It may seem a fine point, but there is a difference between imposing the method and obtaining a result. At the operational level, the responsibility is:

- to ensure the feedback forms, if used, are completed and returned; and
- to obtain information from appraisals.

38.5.2 Completed feedback forms

By far the best way of achieving a high level of return of completed feedback forms is to have attendees complete the form at the end of the training session and before they leave the room where the training has taken place. There is an argument, however, that feedback provided 'under duress' (attendees not being allowed to leave the room until they have completed their form even though they might need to be somewhere else) may affect the quality of the feedback provided (if the attendee is frustrated at not being able to leave the room, he or she may take out his or her frustrations on the training and mark it down accordingly, not because the training actually merited the lower score). A way around this is to send out the feedback forms by email or give a link to a template form for attendees to complete on their computers. The problem is that the longer the time since the training session, the less the chance of having the feedback form completed and returned. The fewer the number of completed feedback forms, the less reliable the data obtained from them, since they may not constitute a representative sample (there is an argument that it is usually those with an axe to grind who will make the effort, although this is not always true; sometimes, the fact that the session was good is enough to inspire someone to feed this back). Probably, the better way comes down on the side of quantity over quality – if in fact quality suffers because there is compulsion – and it is better to have attendees complete the forms at the end of the session before they leave.

If you do allow attendees to complete feedback forms in their own time, then you may need to follow up to ensure that you do get a decent representative sample. It is not just for internal evaluation purposes that this is important: the trainer is likely to want to know how attendees rated his or her performance. So, gentle email reminders are recommended. Don't leave it too long after the training session – a couple of days maximum. Alternatively, if you have the time – and the nerve – you can appear at the attendee's door and pleasantly ask if they have had a chance to complete the form; perhaps suggest that if they would like to do it now (no feedback form should take more than a few minutes), you could take it with you and save them the bother of having to return it, or you could show them where to find the electronic version on the intranet. If the feedback form is able to be completed online, then it may be a case of using inducements to get attendees to complete the form, or of using the 'stick' by recording failure to complete feedback forms as part of the training and performance information available for the individual's appraisal, or reporting non-cooperation to the practice area head. This is perhaps a bit draconian, but it depends on how difficult it is for you to obtain the level of feedback you need, and what sort of culture you are up against.

If the firm uses an LMS, then this may help as it makes it easier to identify who has not completed and returned feedback, and may allow automatic reminders to be sent.

If the firm does not use formal feedback forms, but uses informal means such as focus groups, then it will be important to minute the discussions of those groups and to keep these on record.

38.5.3 Appraisal reports

Reports of appraisal meetings tend to be confidential, which makes it difficult for someone in the training department, for instance, to look at the appraisal report to see whether any learning and development needs have been identified and whether learning and development needs identified previously have been met. This will depend on the practice in the firm as to whether it will be possible. Alternatively, if the firm uses personal development plans (PDPs), training needs may be easier to identify. PDPs also serve the purpose of focusing both the appraiser's and appraisee's attention on the appraisee's development needs and objectives. If the firm does not use PDPs, then part of the instructions to appraisers should be to record the training or development needs and to send these to the training department when the appraisal report has been finalised. It may be that someone from the training department or HR may have sat in on the appraisal, in which case it should be relatively straightforward to obtain this information. If, however, you are relying on the appraiser to obtain the information, you may need to follow him or her up (more commonly known as chasing), either by email or a visit, to make sure you obtain this information.

38.6 SRA ADMINISTRATION REQUIREMENTS

38.6.1 Period of Recognised Training

The SRA does not impose administrative arrangements *per se* on an Authorised Training Provider. However, if the Authorised Training Provider is to comply with its obligations, effective and efficient administrative systems are necessary.

For instance, trainee appraisals are expected to be carried out at the required intervals. Even though the Training Principal and trainee have their own responsibilities, it is a sensible precaution to have someone in the training department diarise any deadlines and carry out any 'following up' that is needed.

If the firm is to receive a monitoring visit, then a range of information will need to be available – from trainee offer letters to appraisal documents, training programmes, time-to-count applications and decisions (see **15.13.1.2**). Therefore, ensuring that this information is in order and kept so that it is able to be accessed easily, can make the difference between a stressful and a less stressful visit.

38.6.2 Professional Skills Course

Even if the firm is not authorised to run the PSC itself, it is still going to need to maintain records of who has done what and when, and where appropriate whether successfully or not, as this information is going to be needed when the time comes for the Training Principal to decide whether to sign off the trainee (a prerequisite to sign-off is successful completion of all parts of the PSC (see **Chapter 16**). Ideally, the record-keeping system should enable any shortfall in the PSC hour requirements (particularly the 24 hours of Elective subjects) during the lead-up to the end of the Period of Recognised Training (PRT) to be flagged so that the trainee has the opportunity to complete the PSC requirements in time.

If the firm is authorised to deliver the PSC in-house then it will, as part of its authorisation, be required to have in place appropriate administrative arrangements. These are detailed at **16.5**. In summary, they include:

- keeping attendance records;
- obtaining and keeping feedback from attendees;
- liaising with the SRA and giving required notifications;
- retaining, in addition to attendance records and feedback, course materials, tutor information CVs, course details and, depending on the authorisation, examination papers and scripts, and trainees' advocacy performance appraisals, as required;
- ensuring appropriate training venues and accommodation;
- ensuring compliance with authorisation requirements such as tutor reviews and submission of annual reports to the SRA;
- keeping records of trainee results and providing evidence of successful completion for sign-off.

As discussed in relation to record keeping (see **38.4.1**), if some of this information is retained at practice area level, it is important that the necessary administrative functions are carried out by or within the practice areas, so that the necessary information can be found easily when it is required.

CHAPTER 39

How to evaluate training

39.1	Introduction	39.3	Performance feedback
39.2	Feedback about the training		

39.1 INTRODUCTION

If the firm is to evaluate the effectiveness of its training, it needs to employ various means of measuring its effectiveness. At its simplest, this can be the ubiquitous feedback form or 'happy sheet' that attendees are asked to complete at the end of a training session. This will give an idea of how the attendees found the training session – depending on how effective the feedback form is in eliciting the necessary information – but it will only provide part of the picture. The fact that the attendees enjoyed the session is not necessarily conclusive that the training achieved the desired learning outcomes. Consequently, the feedback form alone is not going to be enough for a proper analysis. That is not to say that feedback forms do not have a place – they do, but they are just not the complete answer. Obtaining the feedback you need to determine the effectiveness of training involves feedback not just from the attendees, but also from others who are able to confirm whether the intended learning outcomes have been achieved.

What you want to be able to assess in terms of a specific training session is:

- how effective the session was in terms of training delivery;
- how effective the session was in terms of achieving the desired learning outcomes;
- how effective the session was in terms of achieving knowledge or skill transfer for each of the attendees;
- whether long-term behavioural change was achieved, if in fact that was an objective.

The first two bullet points are about the session itself; the second two are about the attendee's subsequent performance on the job, which needs to be looked at on a short-term, medium-term and long-term basis.

39.2 FEEDBACK ABOUT THE TRAINING

39.2.1 Feedback forms

39.2.1.1 Completion

The feedback form provides immediate feedback from the attendees on what they thought of the training session they have attended – provided the feedback form is given to attendees at the time, and ideally required to be completed straight after the training, preferably before they leave the training room. Having said that, with so much done online using electronic feedback forms does make sense – provided they are completed. If the training was delivered as an e-learning module, the feedback form can be incorporated in the module at the end. The point is to have immediacy in obtaining feedback, before memories fade, as well as obtaining as high a level of response as possible. Received wisdom indicates that the longer the period since the training, the lower the likely response rate. And the lower the response rate, the less representative the results.

39.2.1.2 Design

How well the feedback form is drafted will determine the value of the information provided in the form. A form which merely asks whether the attendees enjoyed the session or how they would rate it – in the absence of anything else – is fairly meaningless. The attendees may have enjoyed the session because it was a few hours away from their desk/the phone/their supervising partner, or because the trainer was an engaging performer. This sort of form is therefore not going to give an indication of how beneficial the training was, and is not going to help in deciding whether the training did in fact achieve its objectives. If you do want the attendees' opinions on whether the training achieved its objectives, then the form should:

- state what the objectives of the training session were; and then
- ask if the attendee felt that those objectives had been achieved in the session.

If you are putting together a feedback form yourself, the important things to be aware of are to be logical and consistent in the drafting, and to match the scoring system to the question. For instance, using a choice of 'Poor, Fair, Average, Good, Very Good or Excellent' is no use if the question is asking 'Do you agree?' For the 'Do you agree?' questions, the answer instructions should be 'Indicate which most closely represents your opinion, with 1 indicating least agreement and 6 indicating most'. Even using a scale of 'Poor … Excellent' can assist your analysis by giving each choice a numerical value – with the least value for 'Poor' and the highest value for 'Excellent'. Whichever scale you use (e.g. 1–3 or 1–10), provided you use the same scale for all other questions in the form, it is possible to calculate an overall satisfaction rating. The following tables illustrate the correct way of using a rating

HOW TO EVALUATE TRAINING

system, followed by an incorrect way. The tables are completed with numerical values entered as illustration only and would not necessarily appear on the form.

CORRECT:

	Were the objectives achieved?				
	Strongly agree	Agree	Don't know	Disagree	Strongly disagree
Numerical value	5	4	3	2	1
	How did you rate the trainer?				
	Excellent	Very Good	Good	Fair	Poor
Numerical value	5	4	3	2	1

INCORRECT:

	Were the objectives achieved?				
	Strongly agree	Agree	Don't know	Disagree	Strongly disagree
Numerical value	1	2	3	4	5
	How did you rate the trainer?				
	Excellent	Very Good	Good	Fair	Poor
Numerical value	1	2	3	4	5

Feedback forms often ask as the first question: 'What were your objectives in attending the training session?' The reason for asking this should not be that no learning objectives have been identified for the training. The question is justified when the aim is to find out how each attendee thought the training could be helpful to him or her – although if the training needs analysis has been done properly, this should already have been identified, not to mention the reason each attendee is on the course in the first place.

39.2.1.3 External courses

Where the attendee attends an external course, it is likely that he or she will complete a feedback form at the time, and which will then be given to the external provider. It is important to know, however, whether the money the firm has spent on the external course was well spent. So, there needs to be a system for obtaining feedback on external courses, or to follow up with attendees after they have attended a course outside the firm.

39.2.1.4 Other uses

If you do use feedback forms, they can also be used to check the effectiveness of your training administration processes, and to provide feedback to an internal trainer to assist in his or her development, or to help an external trainer or training organisation improve its offering. If the feedback form is merely a set of boxes to be ticked, this will not necessarily give the trainer much information. So, verbal feedback (particularly if you have sat in on the training or have chatted with the attendees) can be given to the trainer as well. Feedback is also important in identifying problems if no-one from the training function was able to sit in. How else are you going to know that the room was too hot or lunch did not arrive, let alone whether the training was up to par, unless an attendee makes a complaint?

Feedback should also be used to inform training design, and used when reviewing training sessions before running them again.

39.2.2 Informal feedback

Feedback on the training session does not have to be obtained only by way of feedback forms – it can also be obtained through more informal means. There is nothing wrong with this, particularly since views on the training session itself are only part of the evaluation of the effectiveness of training. What is more important is to measure the desired knowledge or skill transfer, and long-term behavioural change if that is relevant. Consequently, a firm with limited resources may decide that applying those limited resources to the appraisal process would be more beneficial in measuring the effectiveness of training.

The practical issue with using feedback forms is that the information from the forms needs to be collected and collated. Apart from needing the time and resource to review the forms, the other issue is whether the responses will actually be considered. If someone makes a comment on the form, is it welcomed or ignored? If the latter, then issuing a feedback form or making it available online is pointless, and everyone's time should be saved. If you are running a lot of training and have large numbers of people attending, collecting and collating information from the feedback forms can create an enormous administrative burden. If the firm uses a learning management system (LMS), this may be able to be automated, depending on the system used. There are, however, investment costs and training issues if all staff are to use the LMS to get the full benefit from having it (see **Chapter 36**). It also means that the form itself has to be set up so that data can be captured.

The Solicitors Regulation Authority (SRA) provides a sample feedback form for Continuing Professional Development (CPD) courses on its website.

39.3 PERFORMANCE FEEDBACK

39.3.1 Pre-training

To maximise the effectiveness of attending training, an attendee should be aware of why he or she needs the training in the first place, and what it is intended to achieve. The attendee therefore needs to have some understanding of his or her existing level of knowledge and skill before undertaking the training. Ways of explaining this to a prospective attendee include using the attendee's appraisal, which should have raised short-, medium- and long-term learning and development needs, or through discussion with the attendee's manager or supervisor, in order to set learning and performance objectives. The attendee's level of knowledge or skill can also come out of these discussions, or if something more empirical is required the attendee could undertake an online pre-course test, be it a self-test or a marked test: it does not matter so long as the attendee achieves a realistic idea of his or her current level of performance.

39.3.2 Post-training

After the attendee has attended the training, the objective is to see whether the desired transfer of knowledge or skill, or change in behaviour, has taken place. There are a number of ways this can be done – none is absolutely conclusive since performance evaluation, no matter how objectified, necessarily involves a certain degree of subjectivity. However, techniques which can be used include:

- an online post-session test, in the same way that a pre-training test may have been used to identify the attendee's original level of knowledge and skill or technology, such as TurningPoint at the end of the session (TurningPoint produces data on the responses);
- a de-briefing meeting between the attendee and his or her manager or supervisor to talk through the training objectives which had been set and the extent to which they have been achieved;
- a questionnaire or survey, perhaps a while after the training session, which focuses on how the attendee feels his or her job performance has been enhanced, rather than what he or she thought of the training session *per se*;
- discussion at the attendee's appraisal meeting. This forum is important, as not every performance problem is a training problem;
- assessment or development centres at which the attendee's performance can be evaluated. These normally only take place at specific milestones in a person's career path in the firm, such as a senior assistant being considered for partnership. So, using the assessment or development centre may not be timely enough. However, if an attendee at the appropriate time goes through an assessment or development centre successfully, one could argue that the long-term objectives have been achieved, even though this finding may be a bit after the event;

DELIVERING THE TRAINING PROGRAMME

- structured interviews by someone in the training function or even someone external, interviewing all attendees and asking the same questions of each about the training;
- observation by the attendee's supervisor or manager, which feeds in to the mentoring and/or coaching of the attendee;
- self-assessment – this speaks for itself but has its own inherent weaknesses, depending on the ability of the individual attendee to self-reflect.

Being realistic, the most that is likely to happen in terms of performance evaluation until the next appraisal may be a few minutes' chat between the attendee and his or her manager over the kettle. However, if the training is of particular importance or is a pilot, then some of the techniques described above might be useful. Where the attendee's manager is able to have a discussion or chat with the attendee following a training session, there is the benefit of immediacy, as well as of the learning itself being reinforced – provided that the manager/supervisor is competent at feedback, mentoring and coaching, of course.

39.3.3 Medium-term review

Change does not tend to happen overnight. With training, there also needs to be time for reflection, perhaps about how attendees think they can incorporate what they have learnt into their daily work. Consequently, evaluation that is too short term may not be helpful or really indicative. For this reason it is also sensible to carry out a more medium-term review, possibly at the appraisal depending on when that occurs, to see whether the individual has been able to apply the learning in practice, and whether the necessary skill or knowledge transfer has been achieved, or attitudinal or behavioural change has been demonstrated. If the appraisal is not taking place any time soon, the training department could use a questionnaire, say, one, three or six months after the training to check the attendee's perception of the effectiveness of what was learnt, and the extent to which the attendee has been able to alter his or her performance with the benefit of the knowledge, skills or behavioural/attitudinal change. The only problems with doing this are:

- the response rate is likely to plummet the further away in time the review is from the training;
- you are relying on the attendee's self-evaluation of his or her performance, which depends on how realistic the attendee's perception of his or her own performance is. One way around this is to have the attendee's supervisor or manager sign the questionnaire which the attendee has completed before it is returned. This might concentrate the attendee's attention and make his or her evaluation of his or her performance more objective – and realistic. The simple act of going to his or her supervisor or manager to have it signed may also prompt a (possibly necessary) discussion about the attendee's performance and development needs. The risk with this approach is that it is perceived as

overly-bureaucratic, particularly if the attendee's supervisor or manager is required to sign the form.

39.3.4 Appraisals

Appraisals are vital for capturing information about whether training has achieved its objectives in terms of personal development. Unfortunately, not all firms make annual appraisals compulsory, although best practice would support an annual appraisal. Some might argue that if there is ongoing feedback throughout the year, the annual appraisal meeting is superfluous. This, in theory, is possibly true. However, if as is likely the ongoing feedback is a matter of a few snatched moments about the particular job just done, it does not provide the overview necessary for an overall appraisal of the individual and his or her performance generally, let alone for his or her career development. Career development and HR issues are not covered in this book, although it is recognised that training is necessarily intertwined with both. What is important from the training perspective is that the appraisal meeting, in looking at the individual's performance as a whole, is able to identify any issues with performance, attitudes or behaviour which may give rise to a training need or needs. The word 'may' is used advisedly: not all problems with performance, attitudes or behaviour can or should be addressed by training (see **3.4.2**), which is why the appraisal is so important, since it provides an opportunity to identify the cause of any knowledge or performance gap.

The training component of the appraisal meeting should:

- look at what training needs were identified at the last appraisal;
- consider the training the appraisee has done since then, and identify whether there has been any appreciable improvement in performance, or change in attitudes or behaviour (for the better);
- identify whether any further training is needed or appropriate;
- identify if there is still some outstanding training need and how this can be addressed;
- consider any further/new issues with performance, attitudes or behaviour which have been identified since the last appraisal;
- identify whether these are training needs or need other action;
- identify what the outcomes are that the training should deliver;
- set a review date before the next appraisal to review the effectiveness of the training undertaken, and to see whether the individual requires further support.

To capture this information, the appraiser needs to have details of the training the appraisee has done since the last appraisal (it goes without saying that the appraiser should have a copy of the notes of the previous appraisal meeting). In addition, it might also be helpful for the appraiser to have some sort of benchmarking information, such as training undertaken by the appraisee's peer group, to put the appraisee's performance into context and to ensure consistent and fair treatment.

Appraisals by their very nature are subjective. Although 'evidence' or 'data' can be used – billing targets met or not, training attended – it is not scientific, nor is it black and white. The appraisee, faced with negative feedback, may react in a completely human way and put it down to bias on the part of the appraiser. In fact, the more negative the feedback, the greater the likelihood of the appraisee's disbelief. What helps everyone – appraisee and appraiser alike – is if the appraisal is underpinned by:

- **Objective criteria**: A competency framework which sets out the knowledge, skills, attitudes and behaviours that should be demonstrated in certain roles and at different levels within the firm. This provides an objective underpinning for performance evaluation. Not all firms use competency frameworks, however, and there is an investment cost in developing them. What may help firms which do not have a competency framework in place is the SRA's Competence Statement (see **Chapter 21**), which can, and in fact will need to, be adapted by firms and by each of their lawyers. A competency framework helps the individual understand what is expected of him- or her (so that there is no surprise at the appraisal meeting if told that he or she is not meeting the necessary standard), and helps the appraiser to point to an objective basis for the feedback. It also means that the ambitious individual who is looking beyond the short term can understand how he or she needs to develop in order to achieve his or her career aspirations.
- **A personal development plan (PDP)**: A PDP which has been developed for the appraisee should combine career aspirations with realistic expectations, and means the appraiser's feedback is referable to something which has already been discussed. Again, not all firms use PDPs, which may be regarded as yet another level of bureaucracy. The reality is, though, that PDPs are an essential component of the Continuing Competence approach which the SRA has introduced as an option for meeting CPD requirements, and which will be compulsory for all solicitors from 1 November 2016 (see **Chapter 20**).

What is important is that the PDP is actually used as the basis of performance appraisals, and not just produced and then 'filed'.

If these obstacles have been negotiated successfully in the appraisal, a remaining danger is the appraiser approving training needs which are unrealistic and not deliverable. There are various ways of dealing with this by:

- ensuring appraisers have training in how to carry out an appraisal, so that the appraiser knows that he or she should be identifying the training need rather than deciding how that need should be met, which is best done by those with training responsibility and expertise. So, rather than the appraiser saying to Joe Bloggs who has just been appraised, 'Yes, an MBA would be a good idea to meet your training needs', the appraiser would confirm that Joe Bloggs would like to develop his management skills further, with a view to partnership (bearing in mind he has just qualified . . .). The training function can then respond to the particular development request and explains that Joe Bloggs will be put on the management course the firm runs for new qualifiers in the coming year, or that given that Joe Bloggs has only just worked out where to find the photocopier and that Joe's responsibilities are no different to those of his peers, it is a little early for Joe to be given special management training but this should be put down in Joe's PDP as an objective/aspiration etc. The point is that the appraiser should make no promises but say that he or she will speak to the training function and come back to the appraisee – and then do so.

- having someone from the training function sit in on appraisals (this may or may not be someone from HR, depending on how training is structured in the firm). Having someone with HR skills there is good practice in any case. If he or she is also knowledgeable about training, then it is a way of keeping aspirations in check, as well as ensuring that the particular issue is correctly identified as a training need.

Index

Academic stage of training
    barristers 23.4.1
    completion of 17.2.1
    costs lawyers 27.4
    definition 17.2.1
    intellectual property practitioners 26.4.2
    licensed conveyancers 25.4.1
    recruiting during 29.2
        assessing potential 29.2.3
        law students 29.2.1
        non-law students 29.2.2
    see also Common Professional Examination/Graduate Diploma in Law; Qualifying Law Degree

Accommodation *see* Venue and accommodation

Admission
    appeal against SRA decisions
        recognition of period of authorised training 17.3.1
        refusal to issue certificate of satisfaction 17.3.2
    character and suitability requirements *see* Character and suitability
    education and training requirements 17.1
    appeal against SRA decisions 17.3
    completion of academic and vocational stages 17.2.1
    completion of apprenticeship 17.2.2
    proposed changes 17.4
    process 19.1
        admission application 19.3
        issue of certificate of satisfaction 19.2
        practising certificate 19.4
    SRA Admission Regulations 17.2.3, 19.2

Ageism 32.3

Alternative Business Structures (ABSs) 22.1
    Approved Regulators 22.1
    Licensing Authority 5.4.1
    management responsibility 2.4
    training needs 2.1.3

Appeal against SRA decisions 17.3

Appraisal 3.6.3, 20.9.7
    competency framework 1.6.1.2, 3.3, 21.2.1, 31.4, 39.3.4
    evaluating training 39.3.4
    personal development plan (PDP) and 20.9.7, 38.5.3, 39.3.4
    reports 38.5.3
    SRA requirements 15.12.3
    trained appraisers 39.3.4

Apprenticeships *see* Legal Apprenticeships; Solicitor Apprenticeship

Articles
    five-year articles 1.2, 1.2.1, 11.2, 24.1

Association of Costs Lawyers (ACL) 27.3

Audio-visual equipment 38.2.2.3

Authorisation as PSC provider 16.5
    accreditation of courses 16.5.5
    conditions of authorisation 16.5.4
    Elective courses 16.5.8
    fee 16.5.2.4
    Financial and Business Skills
        examination arrangements 16.5.7.2
        moderator 16.5.7.1
        responsibilities 16.5.7
    general responsibilities 16.5.6
        administrative arrangements 16.5.6.6
        co-operation in SRA monitoring 16.5.6.5

INDEX

**Authorisation as PSC
provider** – *continued*
  general responsibilities – *continued*
    delivery in compliance with SRA requirements   16.5.6.4
    evaluating and reviewing courses   16.5.6.7
    information and notifying SRA   16.5.6.3
    tutors   16.5.6.1
    venue and accommodation   16.5.6.2
  monitoring of authorisation   16.5.10
  process   16.5.3
  requirements   16.5.2
    application   16.5.2.3
    authorisation fee   16.5.2.4
    Course Director   16.5.2.2
    general requirements   16.5.2.1
  termination   16.5.9
  types of   16.5.1

Bar Council   23.1, 23.3, 24.2
**Bar Professional Training
Course (BPTC)**   23.4.2
  exemption from LPC   10.4.4
Bar Standards Board (BSB)
23.1, 23.3, 23.6
  Handbook   23.8
  website   23.10
**Bar Vocational Course (BVC)
graduates**
  exemption from LPC   10.4.4
Barristers
  academic stage   23.4.1
  admission to the Bar   23.3, 23.4.4
  Approved Regulator   23.3
  Authorisation to Practice (ATP)   23.5
  Code of Conduct   23.8
  CPD requirements   23.6.1
    CPD records   23.6.2
    definition of CPD   23.6.1
    enforcement   23.6.2
    Established Practitioners' Programme (EPP)   23.6.1.2
    extensions of time   23.6.3
    monitoring   23.6.2
    New Practitioners' Programme (NPP)   23.6.1.1
  CPE/GDL   23.4.1
  definition   23.1
  employed barrister   23.1.2
  giving talks   38.2.1.2
  Inns of Court   23.3
  Northern Irish qualified   9.4.3.3
  offences   23.8
  practising certificate   23.1, 23.4.4, 23.5
    Authorisation to Practice (ATP) process   23.5
    extensions of time   23.6.3
    practising without   23.8
    renewal   23.7
  professional conduct requirements   23.8
  professional stage   23.4.3
  proposed changes   23.9
  Public Access   23.1
  pupillage   23.4.3
  qualification   23.4
    academic stage   23.4.1
    costs of maintaining   23.7
    maintaining   23.5
    professional stage   23.4.3
    qualification and admission   23.4.4
    vocational stage   23.4.2
  Qualifying Law Degree   23.4.1
  Queen's Counsel   23.1
  regulation of   23.3
  Republic of Ireland qualified   9.4.2.2
  reserved legal activities   23.2
  self-employed barrister   23.1.1
  squatters   23.4.4, 23.8
  tenants   23.4.4, 23.8
  typical work   23.2
  vocational stage   23.4.2
Break-out groups   36.2.3, 36.2.4.3, 36.2.3, 36.2.4.3, 37.3, 38.2.2.1
Budgeting for training *see* Financial management of training; Training budget
Business awareness training
1.3, 30.5, 31.3.5
Business strategy and objectives   2.3
  management responsibility   2.4
  understanding   3.2

Case studies   36.2.3, 38.2.2.1, 38.2.5
Case for training *see* Training investment
Certificate of Good Standing
9.6.1
Certificate of satisfaction
  issue of   17.2.3, 19.2
  refusal to issue   17.3.2

486

INDEX

Character and suitability
    admission requirements 18.1–18.4
    assessment 18.2
    Chartered Legal Executives 24.8
    DBS disclosures 18.3
    intellectual property practitioners 26.8.1
    PRT requirements 15.8, 15.9
    QLTS candidates 9.8.2
    self-disclosures
        disclosure requirements 18.4.1
        evidence of rehabilitation 18.4.3
        evidence requirements 18.4.2
    SRA requirements 15.8, 15.9
    Suitability Test 18.2
        self-disclosures under 18.4
Chartered Institute of Legal Executives (CILEx) 24.1, 24.3
    Code of Conduct 24.8
    website 24.10
Chartered Institute of Patent Attorneys (CIPA) 22.1, 26.3
Chartered Legal Executive 24.1
    admission 24.4.5
    Advocate 24.4.6, 24.6.1
    apprenticeships 7.4.2, 11.3
    Approved Regulator 24.3
    character and suitability 24.8
    CILEx Litigator and Chartered Legal Executive Advocate 24.4.6
    Code of Conduct 24.8
    CPD requirements 24.6.1
        dispensations 24.6.5
        planned and unplanned outcomes 24.6.2
        Professionalism 24.6.3
        sampling of CPD records 24.6.4
    CPE exemption 7.4.1
    Equivalent Means exemption 10.4.1
    Legal Practice Course 7.4.1
    permitted activities 24.2
    practising certificate 24.1
        renewal 24.5
    professional conduct requirements 24.8
    Professionalism 24.6.3
    PRT exemption 7.4.1
    PSC requirements 7.4.1
    qualification 24.4
        application for Fellowship via Work-based Learning 24.4.3.1
    costs of maintaining 24.7
    exemptions 24.4
    Graduate Fast-Track Diploma (GFTD) 24.4.2
    Level 3 Professional Diploma in Law and Practice 24.4.1.1
    Level 6 Professional Higher Diploma in Law and Practice 24.4.1.2
    maintaining 24.5
    non-law degree route 24.1, 24.4.1
    other CILEx qualifications 24.4.6
    qualification and admission 24.4.5
    Qualifying Employment 24.4.3
    Work-based Learning 24.4.3.1, 24.4.4
    qualifying as a solicitor 7.4.1, 24.9
    regulation of 24.3
    reserved/regulated legal activities 24.2
    solicitor compared 24.1
    work of 24.2
Chartered Legal Executive Advocate 24.4.6
    CPD requirements 24.6.1
CILEx Immigration Practitioner 24.4.6
CILEx Litigator and Chartered Legal Executive Advocate 24.4.6
Client training
    bespoke training 35.3.3
    charging for 4.6.2
    internal seminars 35.3.1
    issues to consider 35.2
    practical arrangements 35.4
    practice area-specific training 35.3.2
    public seminars 35.3.4
    training needs 35.1–35.4
    types of training 35.3
Coaching 1.6.1.4, 4.3, 31.4
    attitudes and values training 36.2.2.4
    on-the-job training 31.3.2.2
    partners 1.6.3, 32.3
    skills training 36.2.2.3
Commitment to training *see* Training investment
Common Professional Examination/Graduate Diploma in Law (CPE/GDL) 7.3, 9.2, 13.1

Common Professional Examination/Graduate Diploma in Law (CPE/GDL) – *continued*
  contact with firm during course 29.4.2
  firm-focused activities/events 29.4.2.3
  help desks 29.4.2.2
  progress reports 29.4.2.1
  surgeries 29.4.2.2
  the course 13.2
  eligibility 13.3.2
  exemptions
    Chartered Legal Executives 7.4.1
    Equivalent Means 10.4.3, 10.4.7
  firm-focused activities/events 29.4.2.3
  general requirements 13.3.1
  grades 13.3.5
  help desks 29.4.2.2
  Integrated Course 13.4
  mature applicants 10.4.3
  practical steps during 29.4.1
  progress reports 29.4.2.1
  proposed changes 13.5
  Providers 13.3.3
  requirements 13.3
  sponsoring on 29.3
  SQE and 13.5
  surgeries 29.4.2.2
  timing 13.3.4
Competence framework 1.6.1.2, 3.3, 21.2.1, 31.4, 39.3.4
Competence Statement 3.3, 20.9.3, 20.11, 21.1
  appraisals 39.3.4
  proposed changes 21.5
  SQE and 21.5
  SRA definition of competence 21.1
  Statement of Legal Knowledge 21.4
  Statement of Solicitor Competence 21.2
    allowance for disability 21.2.2
    Solicitor Apprenticeship Standard and 7.4.2
    uses 21.2.1
  Threshold Standard 21.3
  Training for Tomorrow: A Competence Statement for Solicitors 6.4.4, 6.5.1
  see also Statement of Solicitor Competence

Computer
  internet connection 38.2.2.3
  learning management system (LMS) 36.3.6, 38.4.2, 39.2.2
  see also e-learning
Consortia arrangements 4.6.1, 29.3.1.4
Continuing Competence approach 1.4.1, 3.3, 4.6.2, 20.9
  considerations for opting in to before 1 November 2016 20.9.8
    firms 20.9.8.1
    in-house solicitors 20.9.8.2
  learning and development
    addressing needs 20.9.5
    evaluating effectiveness 20.9.7
    identifying needs 20.9.3
    planning 20.9.4
    recording activity 20.9.6
  new Scheme 20.8.1, 20.12
  requirements 20.9.1
  SRA Toolkit 20.9.1, 20.9.4, 20.9.5, 20.9.6, 20.9.7, 20.11, 21.2, 21.2.1, 36.2
  suspension of CPD requirements 20.9.2
  Training for Tomorrow: A New Approach to Continuing Competence 6.4.2
Continuing Professional Development (CPD) 20.1
  barristers *see* Barristers
  Chartered Legal Executive *see* Chartered Legal Executive
  costs lawyers 27.6
  CPD records
    barristers 23.6.2
    Chartered Legal Executive 24.6.4
    minimum hours option 20.8.5
  CPD year 20.4
  definition 20.1
  governing Regulations 20.2
  intellectual property practitioners 26.6.1
  licensed conveyancer 25.6
  Management Course Stages 1 and 2 20.13
    removal of requirement for MCS 1 20.13.1
    training for 'qualified to supervise' 20.13.2
  minimum hours option
    accreditation 20.8.8
    calculation of hours 20.8.2

INDEX

CPD activities 20.8.4
CPD record 20.8.5
new solicitors 20.8.2.2
non-compliance 20.8.7
part-time work 20.8.2.1
planning CPD 20.8.6
REL admitted as solicitor 20.8.2.3
RELs 20.8.2.2
requirements 20.8.1
suspension of CPD requirements 20.8.3
monitoring regime 20.7
no CPD hour requirement 1.4.1
notary 28.6.2
persons subject to Scheme 20.3
proposed changes 20.12
QLTS candidates 9.8.3
qualified solicitors 31.3.1
Registered Foreign Lawyers 20.3
requirements 20.5
confirmation of compliance with 20.10
monitoring compliance 20.7
suspension of 20.8.3, 20.9 2
sanctions 20.11
SRA Training Regulations 5.4.5, 6.3.2, 20.2
waivers 20.6
Conversion course *see* Common Professional Examination/Graduate Diploma in Law
Costs Lawyer Standards Board (CLSB) 27.1, 27.3
Costs lawyers 27.1
academic stage 27.4
Approved Regulator 27.3
Code of Conduct 27.2, 27.8
conduct of proceedings 27.2
costs draftsmen distinguished 27.1
CPD requirements 27.6
definition of 'legal costs' 27.2
law costs draftsmen distinguished 27.1
permitted activities 27.2
practising certificate 27.4
renewal 27.5, 27.7
professional conduct requirements 27.8
professional stage 27.4
qualification 27.4
academic stage 27.4
costs of maintaining 27.7

CPD requirements 27.6
maintaining 27.5
other training obligations 27.6
professional stage 27.4
work experience 27.4
regulation of 27.3
reserved and regulated activities 27.2
websites 27.9.1
work of 27.2
Council for Licensed Conveyancers (CLC) 22.1, 25.1, 25.3
Handbook 25.8.1
website 25.9

DBS disclosures 18.3
Delivering training 37.1
'do-it-yourself' 38.2.1.1
e-learning 36.3.3
external trainers 4.4.2, 38.2.1.2
facilitation skills 37.1, 37.3
feedback skills 37.1, 37.5
internal trainers 4.4.2, 38.2.1.1
managing skills 37.6
organising *see* Organising the training session
outsourcing 4.4.2, 38.2.1.2
presentation skills 37.1, 37.2
questioning skills 37.4
resources *see* Resources
SRA administration requirements 38.6
support 38.2.3
venue *see* Venue and accommodation
Demonstrations 15.10.2, 36.2.3, 36.2.2.3, 38 2.2.3
Designing training 36.1
e-learning *see* e-learning
feedback *see* Feedback
forms of training *see* Forms of training
timing 36.2.5
breaks 36.2.5.2
time for questions 36.2.5.3
when to hold training 36.2.5.1
Digital camera 38.2.2.3
Do-it-yourself training 38.2.1.1
Domestic routes to qualification 7.1
Chartered Legal Executives 7.4.1
Equivalent Means *see* Equivalent Means

INDEX

Domestic routes to qualification – *continued*
  law degree 7.2
  non-degree 7.4, 7.5, 11.1
  non-law graduate 7.3
  proposed changes 7.6

e-learning 36.3
  accommodation 36.3.5
  advantages 36.2.2.1
  assumed knowledge 36.3.2.2
  asynchronous learning 36.3.1
  chat room 36.2.2.1
  compliance training 36.3.2.4
  consolidation 36.3.2.3
  cost-effectiveness 36.2.2.1
  delivery 36.3.3
  induction 36.3.2.1
  IT training 36.3.2.6
  'just in time' training 36.3.2.5
  learning management systems (LMS) 36.3.6, 38.4.2, 39.2.2
  meaning 36.3.1
  online tutor service 36.2.2.1
  overseas offices 34.3.3.4
  refresher training 36.3.2.5
  resources 36.3.5
  sourcing 36.3.4
  synchronous training 36.3.1
  uses 36.3.2
  video conferencing 34.3.3.4, 36.3.1, 36.3.3
  webinars *see* Webinars

Economic downturns 1.4.2

EEA lawyers
  Equivalent Means exemption 10.4.2
  QLTS Assessment 9.4.1

Effectiveness of training
  evaluating *see* Evaluating training

English language ability 9.3.2.3

Equivalent Means 7.5, 10.1
  eligibility 10.3
  exemptions 10.4
    applying for 10.5
    block exemptions 10.4.1
    from LPC 10.4.4, 10.4.7
    mature applicants 10.4.3
    partially qualified EU/EEA/Swiss nationals 10.4.2
    from PRT 10.4.5, 10.4.7, 15.4
    from PSC 10.4.6, 10.4.7, 16.3.2
    Qualifying Law Degree 12.3.5
    summary 10.4.7
  meaning of 10.2
  Morgenbesser decision 10.3, 10.4.2
  prior learning recognition 10.2, 10.3
  proposed changes 10.6
  SQE and 10.6

European directive routes to qualification 8.1
  Exempt European Lawyers 8.2
  foreign lawyer status 8.5
  Morgenbesser decision 8.4, 9.4
  partially qualified European lawyers 8.4
  recognition of Professional Qualifications Directive 8.3
    aptitude test 8.3.1
    aptitude test exemption 8.3.2
  Registered European Lawyer status 8.2
  Registered Foreign Lawyer (RFL) 8.5

Evaluating training 3.7, 39.1
  appraisals 39.3.4
  Continuing Competence approach 20.9.7
  feedback *see* Feedback
  metrics 3.7.1

Exempting Law Degree (ELD) 12.4, 13.4, 14.2

External trainers 4.4.2, 38.2.1.2
  assessing 38.2.1.2
  barristers 38.2.1.2
  brief 38.2.1.2
  cost and negotiation 38.2.1.2
  feedback 39.2.1.3
  selecting 38.2.1.2
  support 38.2.3

Facilitation skills 37.1, 37.3

Feedback
  about the training 36.2.4, 39.2
  analysing 3.7.3
  appraisals 38.5.3, 39.3.4
  capturing 3.7.2
  collecting and collating 38.5
  comparative analysis 3.7.3
  evaluating performance 3.7.3
  external courses 39.2.1.3
  feedback forms
    completion 38.5.2, 39.2.1.1
    design 39.2.1.2
    external courses 39.2.1.3
  feedback skills 37.1, 37.5

generic feedback   36.2.4.2
identifying trends   3.7.3
individual feedback   36.2.4.1
informal feedback   39.2.2
one-to-one   36.2.4.1
peer feedback   36.2.4.3, 37.5
performance feedback   39.3
   appraisals   39.3.4
   medium-term review   39.3.3
   post-training   39.3.2
   pre-training   39.3.1
room set-up and   38.2.5
SRA requirements   38.5.1
written comments   36.2.4.1
Financial management of training   4.1
   budgeting for training   4.3
   client training   4.6.2
   consortia arrangements   4.6.1
   financial planning   4.3
   financial structure for training   4.2
   loans for course fees   4.6.4
   maximising financial investment   4.6
   measuring investment in/return from training   4.5
   recouping costs of training   4.6.4
   savings on training   4.6.3
   service level agreement (SLA)   4.2
   trained staff leaving firm   4.1, 4.6.4
   training budget *see* Training budget
Firm-focused activities/events   29.4.2.3
Five-year articles   1.2, 1.2.1, 11.2, 24.1
Flip chart   38.2.2.3
Foreign lawyer status *see* Registered Foreign lawyer
Forms of training   36.2
   break-out groups   36.2.3, 36.2.4.3, 37.3, 38.2.2.1
   case studies   36.2.3, 38.2.2.1, 38.2.5
   demonstrations   15.10.2, 36.2.3, 36.2.2.3, 38.2.2.3
   e-learning *see* e-learning
   formal training   36.2
   group discussion   36.2.3, 38.2.2.1, 38.2.5
   informal training   36.2
   learning outcomes   36.2.1
      attitudes and values   36.2.1.4, 36.2.2.4
      intellectual application   36.2.1.2, 36.2.2.2

      knowledge   36.2.1.1, 36.2.2.1
      skills   36.2.1.3, 36.2.2.3
   training methods   36.2.2
   mentoring *see* Mentoring
   pro bono work   36.2.2.2
   role play   36.2.3, 36.2.4.1, 38.2.5
   shadowing   20.8.4, 23.4.3, 36.2.2.4
   training activities   36.2.3
General Council of the Bar
see Bar Council
Graduate Diploma in Law (GDL) *see* Common Professional Examination/Graduate Diploma in Law
Graduate Fast-Track Diploma (GFTD)   24.4.2
Group discussion   36.2.3, 38.2.2.1, 38.2.5

Help desks   29.4.2.2

Identity check   9.3.3
In-house legal departments
   training needs   2.1.2
Independent regulatory bodies   5.4, 22.1
Induction
   e-learning   36.3.2.1
   knowledge management and   15.10.2, 30.2.1
   newly qualified solicitors   31.2.1
   non-lawyer employees   33.4
   overseas qualified lawyers   34.2
   partners   32.2
   Period of Recognised Training   15.10.2
   trainee solicitors   30.2.1
Inns of Court   23.3
Institute of Trade Mark Attorneys (ITMA)   22.1, 26.3
Integrated Course   13.4, 14.2
Intellectual capital   2.6
   internal trainers   4.4.2, 32.3, 38.2.1.1
   partners and   32.1, 32.3
   profitability and   4.3
   see also Knowledge management
Intellectual property practitioners   26.1
   academic stage   26.4.2
   admission   26.4.5
   advocacy certificate   26.4.6, 26.5.2

INDEX

Intellectual property practitioners – *continued*
  Approved Regulators 26.3
  CPD requirements 26.6.1
  litigation certificate 26.4.6, 26.5.2
  patent attorney 26.2.1
  permitted activities 26.2
  professional conduct
    character and suitability 26.8.1
    Code of Conduct 26.8.2
    regulation of 26.8
  qualifications 26.4
    academic stage 26.4.2
    competencies 26.4.4
    costs of maintaining 26.7
    CPD requirements 26.6.1
    further rights to conduct litigation 26.4.6
    maintaining 26.5
    other training obligations 26.6.2
    professional experience 26.4.3
    qualification and admission 26.4.5
    requirements 26.4.1
    rights of audience 26.4.6
  Register of Patent Attorneys 26.1
  Register of Trade Mark Attorneys 26.1
  registration 26.5.1
  regulation 26.3
  reserved activities 26.2.3
  trade mark attorney 26.2.2
  work of 26.2
Internal trainers 4.4.2, 38.2.1.1
Internet connection 38.2.2.3
Interviewing skills 3.3, 31.3.3
Investment in training *see* Training investment
IT training 36.3.2.6

Joint Academic Stage Board (JASB) 12.3.7
'Just in time' training 36.3.2.5

Knowledge management (KM) 1.4.2, 1.5, 1.6.1.1
  benefits from external course 31.3.1
  induction and 15.10.2, 30.2.1
  interaction with training 1.2.2, 2.6
  trainees and 29.4.1
  see also Intellectual capital
Knowledge/performance gaps
  see Training needs analysis

Law degree 7.2
Law firms
  structure of training 2.2
  training needs 2.1.1
Law Society of England and Wales 5.1, 5.3
Lawyers under the Legal Services Act 2007 22.1
  Approved Regulators 5.3, 22.1
  see also Barristers; Chartered Legal Executive; Costs lawyers; Intellectual property practitioners; Licensed conveyancer; Notary
Learning management system (LMS) 36.3.6, 38.4.2, 39.2.2
Legal Apprenticeships 7.4.2, 11.1
  apprenticeship standards 7.4.2, 11.3, 11.4.3
  background 11.2
  Chartered Legal Executive Apprenticeships 7.4.2, 11.3
  completion of 17.2.2
  Paralegal Apprenticeships 7.4.2, 11.3
  proposed changes 11.5
  Solicitor Apprenticeship *see* Solicitor Apprenticeship
  SQE and 11.5
Legal Education and Training Review (LETR) 5.4.2, 6.2
  Briefing Papers 6.2
  Discussion Papers 6.2
  final research report (LETR Report) 6.2
  LSB's response 6.2.1
  objective 6.2
  phases 6.2
  required outcomes 6.2
  Research Updates 6.2
  SRA's response 6.2.2
Legal Practice Course (LPC) 7.2, 14.1
  assessment 14.6
  Authorised Training Providers 14.1
  breadth of knowledge 29.4.3.4
  Chartered Legal Executives 7.4.1
  collaborative arrangements 29.4.3.6
  completing stage 2 29.4.3.3
  contact with firm during course 29.4.2
    firm-focused activities/events 29.4.2.3
    help desks 29.4.2.2

492

progress reports 29.4.2.1
surgeries 29.4.2.2
the course 14.2
course assessment 14.6
course structure 14.5
  breadth of knowledge 29.4.3.4
  severability 29.4.3.1
  Stage 1 14.5.1
  Stage 2 14.5.2, 29.4.3.3
duration 14.3.3
employability and 29.4.3.2
exclusive tie-ups 29.3.2
  alternative solution 29.3.2.2
  reasons for/against 29.3.2.1
  tailoring the course 29.3.2, 29.4.3.4
  teaching in exclusive groups 29.3.2.3
Exempting Law Degree 12.4, 14.2
exemptions
  BVC/BPTC graduates 10.4.4.2
  Equivalent Means 10.4.4, 10.4.7
  general 10.4.4.1
firm-focused activities/events 29.4.2.3
general requirements 14.3
grades 14.3.5
help desks 29.4.2.2
Integrated Course 14.2
maximising performance on 29.4.3.5
outcomes 14.4
period of validity 14.3.4
practical steps during 29.4.1
prerequisites 14.3.2
progress reports 29.4.2.1
proposed changes 14.8
providers
  'beauty parades' 29.3.1.2
  choosing 29.3.1
  consortia 29.3.1.4
  differentiating between 29.3.1.1
  exclusive tie-ups 29.3.2, 29.4.3.4
  negotiating with 29.3.1.3
  teaching in exclusive groups 29.3.2.3
quality assurance 14.7
requirements 14.3
severability 29.4.3.1
sponsoring on 2.1.1, 29.3
  choosing an LPC 29.3.1
  exclusive tie-ups 29.3.2
SQE and 14.8
Stage 1 14.5.1
Stage 2 14.5.2, 29.4.3.3

surgeries 29.4.2.2
tailoring the course 29.3.2, 29.4.3.4
  provider expertise 29.4.3.4
  spectrum of choice 29.4.3.4
  using 'headroom' in the curriculum 29.4.3.4
timing 14.3.3
training investment 29.4.3
  choosing a provider 29.3.1
  contact with firm during course 29.4.2
  exclusive tie-ups 29.3.2
  practical steps during course 29.4.1
  sponsoring on LPC 29.3
transcripts 14.3.5
Legal Practise Course (LPC) 7.2
Legal Services Board (LSB) 5.1, 5.2
  response to LETR 6.2.1
Legal technical knowledge 1.3, 30.3
  see also Practice areas
Level 3 Professional Diploma in Law and Practice 24.4.1.1
Level 6 Professional Higher Diploma in Law and Practice 24.4.1.2
Licensed conveyancer 25.1
  academic stage 25.4.1
  admission 25.4.3
  Approved Regulator 25.3
  Code of Conduct 25.8.1
  CPD requirements 25.6
  definition 25.1
  Employed Licensed Conveyancer 25.1, 25.4.3
  Manager Licensed Conveyancer 25.1
  permitted activities 25.2
  probate services 25.1, 25.2
  professional conduct requirements 25.8
    CLC Handbook 25.8.1
    fit and proper person 25.8.2
  professional stage 25.4.2
  qualification 25.4
    academic stage 25.4.1
    costs of maintaining 25.7
    CPD requirements 25.6
    maintaining 25.5
    other training obligations 25.6
    Practical Training 25.4.2
    professional stage 25.4.2

Licensed conveyancer – *continued*
  qualification – *continued*
    qualification and admission 25.4.3
    regulation of 25.3
    reserved activities 25.2
    supervision 25.1, 25.4.2
    work of 25.2
    see also Council for Licensed Conveyancers

Management responsibility 2.4, 3.6.1.1
Management skills training 1.3
  projects 31.3.4
  qualified solicitors 31.3.4
  trainee solicitors 30.6
Managing the training session 37.6
Master of the Court of Faculties of the Archbishop of Canterbury 22.1, 28.3
Mentoring 1.6.1.4, 4.3, 31.4
  attitudes and values training 36.2.2.4
  on-the-job training 31.3.2.2
  partners 1.6.3, 32.3
  skills training 36.2.2.3
Metrics 3.7.1
Microphone 38.2.2.3
***Morgenbesser* case** 8.4
  Equivalent Means 10.3, 10.4.2
  Qualified Lawyers Transfer Scheme (QLTS) 9.4

National Apprenticeship Service 11.2
Newly qualified solicitors
  training needs *see* Training needs
Non-law graduates
  Chartered Legal Executive 24.1, 24.4.1
  PRT 7.3
  PSC 7.3
  recruiting 29.2.2
Non-lawyer employees
  training needs *see* Training needs
Northern Irish qualified lawyers
  barristers 9.4.3.3
  QLTS Assessment 9.4.3.2, 9.4.3.3
  solicitors 9.4.3.2
Notaries Society 28.3
Notary 28.1
  Approved Regulator 28.3
  CPD requirements 28.6.2
  definition 28.1
  functions 28.1
  permitted activities 28.2
  practising certificate 28.1, 28.3
    renewal 28.5, 28.7
  professional conduct requirements 28.8
  professional stage 28.4.1
  qualification 28.4
    admission to Roll of Notaries 28.4.2
    costs of maintaining 28.7
    CPD requirements 28.6.2
    maintaining 28.5
    period of practice under supervision 28.4.4
    Post-Admission Education (PAE) 28.6.1
    professional stage 28.4.1
    scrivener notary 28.4.3
  regulation of 28.3
  reserved activities 28.2.3
  scrivener notary 28.2.2
    qualification as 28.4.3
    work of 28.2.2
  sole practitioner 28.2.1
  websites 28.9.1
  work of 28.2

Organising the training session 38.3
  after the session 38.3.3
  attendee expectations 38.3.1
  checking 38.3.2
  on the day 38.3.2, 38.3.3
  fire-fighting tips 38.3.4
  follow-up 38.3.3
  preparation 38.3.1
  scenarios 38.3.4
Outsourcing training *see* External trainers
Overseas offices
  central 'academy' 34.3.3.6
  e-learning 34.3.3.4
  logistical issues 34.3.3
  London nucleus with satellite offices 34.3.1
  mobile attendees 34.3.3.2
  mobile trainer 34.3.3.1
  non-UK nucleus with UK satellite 34.3.2

'piggy-back' training 34.3 3.5
secondment 34.3.3.3
technology 34.3.3.4
training needs 34.1–34.3
video conferencing 34.3.3.4
webinars 34.3.3.4
Overseas qualified lawyers
training needs 34.1, 34.2
Ownership of training 2.3, 3.6.1.1
training budget 4.4.1

Paralegal Apprenticeships
7.4.2, 11.3
Partners
coaching role 1.6.3, 32.3
developing the right culture 1.6.3
intellectual capital and 32.1, 32.3
mentoring role 1.6.3, 32.3
training needs 1.3, 32.1
induction 32.2
new partners 32.2
partner relocation 32.5
partners generally 32.3
partners in management roles 32.3.1
re-deployment of partners 32.4
senior assistants preparing for partnership 31.4
Patent attorney *see* Intellectual property practitioners
Period of authorised training
SRA decision not to recognise 17.3.1
Period of Recognised Training (PRT) 1.3, 7.2, 15.1
administration requirements 38.6.1
appraisal requirements 15.12.3
character and suitability
determining eligibility 15.8.1
ongoing obligation 15.8.2
subsequent applications 15.8.3
trainee declaration 15.9
Chartered Legal Executive 7.4.1
eligibility to commence 15.8
employing trainees under 15.7
disputes 15.7.4
employment contract 15.7.2
length of training period 15.7.6
recruitment practices 15.7.1
reduction of training period 15.7.7
salary 15.7.5
termination of training 15.7.3

exemption 15.4
Chartered Legal Executive 7.4.1
Equivalent Means 10.4.5, 10.4.7, 15.4
fees and expenses 15.10.3
governing Regulations 15.2
induction 15.10.2
monitoring 15.13
monitoring process 15.13.1
monitoring visit 15.13.1.2
monitor's report 15.13.3
monitor's role 15.13.2
questionnaires 15.13.1.1
non-law graduates 7.3
notification requirements 15.9
practical experience of law 15.11.3
Practice Skills development 1.3, 15.11.4
proposed changes 15.15
recruitment practices 15.7.1
review and appraisal requirements 15.12.3
secondments 15.11.5
SQE and 15.15
SRA administration requirements 38.6.1
SRA Training Regulations 15.2, 15.3.1, 30.1
structure of training 15.11.1
study leave 15.10.3
summary of responsibilities 15.14
supervision requirements 15.12.1, 15.12.2
support requirements 15.10
fees and expenses 15.10.3
induction 15.10.2
study leave 15.10.3
support arrangements 15.10.1
terminology 15.3.2
trainee responsibilities 15.14.3
Training Contract
regime requirements compared 15.3.3
terminology 15.3.2
transitional arrangements 15.3.1
Training Principal 15.6
responsibilities 15.14.2
Training Provider authorisation 15.5
applying for 15.5.2
grant of 15.5.3
requirements for 15.5.1
sanctions 15.5.4

INDEX

Period of Recognised Training (PRT) – *continued*
   Training Provider responsibilities
     induction   15.10.2
     notification requirements   15.9
     summary   15.14.1
     support requirements   15.10
     training requirements   15.11.2
     training record   15.12.4
     training requirements
       practical experience of law   15.11.3
       Practice Skills development   1.3, 15.11.4
     responsibility   15.11.2
     secondments   15.11.5
     structure of training   15.11.1
     work-based experience   15.7.7
Peripheral knowledge/vision   29.4.3.4, 30.4, 31.3.2.1
Personal development plan (PDP)
   appraisal reports   20.9.7, 38.5.3, 39.3.4
   identifying training needs   3.4, 3.6.1, 3.7.1
Post-qualification requirements *see* Competence Statement; Continuing Professional Development
PowerPoint   3.7.3, 37.2, 38.2.2.3
Practice areas
   developing the right culture   1.6.2
   knowledge/performance gaps   3.4.1
   legal technical knowledge   1.3, 30.3
   specific training
     clients   35.3.2
     newly qualified solicitors   31.2.3
     qualified solicitors   31.3.2
     trainee solicitors   30.3
   training needs analysis   3.4.1
Practice Skills training   1.3
   PRT requirements   15.11.4
   qualified solicitors   31.3.3
   Standard   15.11.4
Practising certificate
   barristers   23.1, 23.4.4, 23.5
   Authorisation to Practice (ATP)
     process   23.5
   extensions of time   23.6.3
   practising without   23.8
   renewal   23.7
   Chartered Legal Executive   24.1, 24.5
   commencement date   19.4
   costs lawyers   27.4, 27.5, 27.7

CPD requirements   20.7, 20.8.7, 20.9.7
   declaration   20.7, 20.9.7, 20.9.8.1, 20.10
   notary   28.1, 28.3, 28.5, 28.7
   practising without   20.8.7
   renewal   9.8.3, 20.7, 20.9.7, 20.10, 23.5, 24.5, 27.5, 28.5, 38.4.2
Practising Certificate Renewal Exercise (PCRE)   20.10
Presentation skills   37.1, 37.2
Pro bono work   36.2.2.2
Professional conduct requirements
   barristers   23.8
   Chartered Legal Executive   24.8
   costs lawyers   27.8
   intellectual property practitioners   26.8
   licensed conveyancer   25.8
   notary   28.8
Professional Skills Course (PSC)   1.2.3, 7.2, 16.1
   administration requirements   38.6.2
   authorisation as provider *see* Authorisation as PSC provider
   Authorised Education Provider   16.1
   Chartered Legal Executives   7.4.1
   compulsory core
     authorisation to provide   16.5.1
     course content   16.4.1
     summary of requirements and features   Annex 16A
   course content   16.4
   course structure   16.3.4
   Electives
     authorisation to provide   16.5.8
     course content   4.6.3, 16.4.2
   exemptions   16.3.2
     Equivalent Means   10.4.6, 10.4.7, 16.3.2
   fees and expenses   16.3.5
   Financial and Business Skills module   9.8.3
   general requirements   16.3.1
   governing Regulations   16.2
   non-law graduates   7.3
   pervasive subjects   16.4.3
   QLTS candidates   9.8.3
   requirements   16.3
   SRA administration requirements   38.6.2
   SRA Training Regulations   16.2
   timing   16.3.3

INDEX

Training Provider responsibilities 16.3.5
Professional stage of training
   barristers 23.4.3
   costs lawyers 27.4
   licensed conveyancer 25.4.2
   notary 28.4.1
Progress reports 29.4.2.1
Projects
   management skills training 31.3.4
   non-lawyer employees 33.6

Qualification
   academic stage requirements *see* Academic stage
   admission requirements *see* Admission
   domestic routes 7.1
     Chartered Legal Executives 7.4.1
     Equivalent Means *see* Equivalent Means
     law degree 7.2, 7.5
     non-degree 7.4, 7.5, 11.1
     non-law graduate 7.3, 7.5
     proposed changes 7.6
   European directive routes 8.1
     Exempt European Lawyers 8.2
     foreign lawyer status 8.5
     Morgenbesser decision 8.4, 9.4
     partially qualified European lawyers 8.4
     recognition of Professional Qualifications Directive 8.3
     Registered European Lawyer status 8.2
   five-year articles route 1.2, 1.2.1, 11.2, 24.1
   Legal Apprenticeships *see* Legal Apprenticeships
   QLTS *see* Qualified Lawyers Transfer Scheme
   regulation of legal education and training
     reform of legal education and training 6.1–6.6
     regulatory authority 5.1–5.4
   vocational stage requirements *see* Vocational stage
Qualified Lawyers Transfer Scheme (QLTS) 9.1
   admission and qualification 9.8
     application for admission 9.8.1

     character and suitability requirements 9.8.2
     CPD obligations 9.8.3
   appeals 9.7
   application for 9.6
     appeals 9.7
     application forms 9.6.2
     Certificate of Good Standing 9.6.1
   assessments 9.5
     Day One Outcomes 9.5, 9.5.1
     Multiple Choice Test (MCT) 9.5.2
     Objective Structured Clinical Examination (OSCE) 9.5.3
     transitional provisions 9.3.2, 9.5.4
   Day One Outcomes 9.5, 9.5.1
     EEA lawyers 9.4.1
     Republic of Ireland qualified solicitors 9.4.2.1
     Scottish qualified solicitors 9.4.3.1
   EEA lawyers 9.4.1
   eligibility 9.3.2
     appeals 9.7
     English language ability 9.3.2.3
     full route to qualification 9.3.2.2
     qualified lawyer in a recognised jurisdiction 9.3.2.1
   general requirements 9.3.1
   identity check 9.3.3
   Morgenbesser decision 9.4
   non-EU lawyers 34.2
   Northern Irish qualified lawyers
     barristers 9.4.3.3
     solicitors 9.4.3.2
   number of attempts 9.3.4
   preparation 9.3.3
   proposed changes 9.9
   Republic of Ireland qualified lawyers
     barristers 9.4.2.2
     solicitors 9.4.2.1
   requirements 9.3
     variations in 9.4
   the scheme 9.2
   Scottish qualified solicitors 9.4.3.1
   SQE and 9.9
   UK qualified lawyers 9.4.3
Qualified solicitors
   training needs *see* Training needs
Qualifying Law Degree (QLD) 7.2, 12.1
   barristers 23.4.1
   content 12.3.2
   the degree 12.2

497

INDEX

Qualifying Law Degree (QLD) – *continued*
    Exempting Law Degree 12.4, 13.4, 14.2
    exemptions 10.4.7, 12.3.5
    general requirements 12.3.1
    monitoring/regulation 12.3.7
    pass mark 12.3.3
    period of validity 12.3.4
    proposed changes 12.5
    quality control 12.3.6
    requirements 12.3
    SQE and 12.5
    writing skills 29.2.1
Queen's Counsel 23.1
Questioning skills 37.4

Recording training information 38.4
    CPD records
      barristers 23.6.2
    Chartered Legal Executive 24.6.4
    minimum hours option 20.8.5
    learning management system (LMS) 36.3.6, 38.4.2, 39.2.2
    SRA requirements 38.4.1
Recruitment
    during academic stage 29.2
      assessing potential 29.2.3
      law students 29.2.1
      non-law students 29.2.2
    good practice 15.7.1
    interviewing skills 3.3, 31.3.3
    practices 15.7.1
    training as incentive 1.2.3
    training needs and 2.1.1
Red Tape Initiative 1.2.3, 6.2.2, 6.4.3, 9.3.4
Reform of legal education and training 6.1–6.6
Refresher training 36.3.2.5
Refreshments 38.2.4.2
Register of Patent Attorneys 26.1
Register of Trade Mark Attorneys 26.1
Registered European Lawyer (REL)
    aptitude test 8.3.2
    recognition of Professional Qualifications Directive 8.3.2
    status 8.2, 9.4.1

Registered Foreign Lawyer (RFL) 8.5, 20.3
Regulatory authority *see* Law Society of England and Wales; Legal Services Board; Solicitors Regulation Authority
Regulatory Reform Programme – Improving Regulation: proportionate and targeted measures 6.4.5, 11.2
Republic of Ireland qualified lawyers
    barristers 9.4.2.2
    QLTS Assessment 9.4.2
    solicitors 9.4.2.1
Research skills 29.2.1
Resources 38.2.2
    audio-visual equipment 38.2.2.3
    digital camera 38.2.2.3
    e-learning 36.3.6
    flip chart 38.2.2.3
    internet connection 38.2.2.3
    microphone 38.2.2.3
    PowerPoint 3.7.3, 37.2, 38.2.2.3
    Smart Board 38.2.2.3
    training materials 38.2.2.1
    tutor guides 38.2.2.2
    tutor instructions 38.2.2.2
    visualiser 38.2.2.3
    white board 38.2.2.3
Richard Review of Apprenticeships 11.2
Role models 1.2, 1.5, 15.12.2, 30.2.2, 36.2.2.4
Role play 36.2.3, 36.2.4.1, 36.2.3, 38.2.5
Room set-up 38.2.2.1, 38.2.5

Satellite model 2.2
Scottish qualified solicitors
    QLTS Assessment 9.4.3.1
Scrivener notary *see* Notary
Secondments
    overseas offices 34.3.3.3
    PRT 15.11.5
Service level agreement (SLA) 4.2
Shadowing 20.8.4, 23.4.3, 36.2.2.4
Smart Board 38.2.2.3

INDEX

Society of Scrivener Notaries
28.3
Solicitor Apprenticeship 7.4.2,
11.4
    apprenticeship standard 7.4.2, 11.4.3
    continuous assessment 11.4
    duration 11.4
    employer roles and responsibilities
      11.4.5
    funding 11.4.1, 11.4.6
      complying with funding
        requirements 11.4.7
    proposed changes 11.5
    SQE and 11.5
    training and assessment
      assessment plan 11.4.4
      obligations 11.4.1
      responsibility 11.4.2
    see also Legal Apprenticeships
Solicitors Qualification
Examination (SQE) 7.6, 9.9
    admission requirements and 17.4
    assessment framework 17.4
    Competence Statement and 21.5
    CPE/GDL and 13.5
    entry requirements 6.5.1
    Equivalent Means and 10.5
    Legal Apprenticeships and 11.5
    LPC and 14.8
    pre-qualification work experience
      6.5.1
    PRT and 15.15
    QLD and 12.5
    QLTS candidates and 9.9
    SRA Training Regulations 6.6
    transitional arrangements 9.9
Solicitors Regulation
Authority (SRA) 5.1, 5.4
    administration requirements 38.6
    appeal against decisions of 17.3
    character and suitability
      requirements 9.8.2, 15.8, 18.1–18.4
    Code of Conduct 1.2.3
      non-lawyer employees 33.2
    Continuing Competence *see*
      Continuing Competence
    day-to-day operations 5.4.4
    decision-making 5.4.3
    Handbook 5.4.5, 15.2, 15.4.1, 15.6,
      15.14.2, 17.2.1
      Principle 5 1.2, 1.2.3, 1.4.1, 3.3, 20.1,
        20.9.1, 21.1, 22.1

    legal education/training reforms 6.3
      to be consulted upon 6.3.1
      consultations 6.4
      pre-qualification work experience
        6.5.1
      proposed consultations and reforms
        6.5
      reforms to be consulted upon 6.3.1
      response to LETR 6.2.2
      SQE entry requirements 6.5.1
      status of future/proposed reforms
        6.3.3
      summary 6.3.1
      terminology 6.3.4
      timetable for proposed reform
        activity 6.5.2
      Training Regulations 6.6
      transitional arrangements 6.3.2
    Policy Committee 5.4.3
    QLTS *see* Qualified Lawyers
      Transfer Scheme
    Qualification and Provider
      Regulations 5.4.5
    Red Tape Initiative 1.2.3, 6.2.2, 6.4.3,
      9.3.4
    regulatory approach 5.4.1
    regulatory reform programme 5.4.2
    Regulatory Reform Programme –
      Improving Regulation:
      proportionate and targeted
      measures 6.4.5, 11.2
    Training Regulations *see* SRA
      Training Regulations
    training strategy 5.4.2
    Training for Tomorrow: A
      Competence Statement for
      Solicitors 6.4.4, 6.5.1
    Training for Tomorrow: A New
      Approach to Continuing
      Competence 6.4.2
    Training for Tomorrow: Assessing
      Competence 6.4.6, 7.6, 9.9, 10.6,
      11.5, 12.5, 13.5, 14.8, 15.5, 17.4, 21.5
    Training for Tomorrow: Regulation
      Review 6.2.2, 6.4.1
    Training for Tomorrow (T4T)
      website 2.5, 6.2.2
Soundproofing 38.2.4.3
Split training function 2.2
Sponsoring on the CPE/GDL
and/or LPC 2.1.1, 29.3
    choosing an LPC 29.3.1
    exclusive tie-ups 29.3.2

INDEX

SRA Training Regulations
5.4.5, 6.6, 11.1, 20.2
    admission requirements 17.2
    CPD and 5.4.5, 6.3.2, 20.2
    definition of GDL 13.2
    Equivalent Means 10.1
    PRTs 15.2, 15.3.1, 30.1
    PSC and 16.2
    SQE and 6.6
    transitional arrangements 6.3.2
Statement of Legal Knowledge 21.4
Statement of Solicitor Competence 21.2
    allowance for disability 21.2.2
    Solicitor Apprenticeship Standard and 7.4.2
    uses 21.2.1
    see also Competence Statement
Strategy *see* Business strategy and objectives; Training strategy
Structure of training 2.2
    satellite model 2.2
    split function 2.2
    training budget 4.4.1
Suitability *see* Character and suitability
Surgeries 29.4.2.2
SWOT analysis 3.5, 20.8.6

Technology 1.2.1, 34.3.3.4
    audio-visual equipment 38.2.2.3
    see also e-learning; Resources
Timing 36.2.5
    breaks 36.2.5.2
    time for questions 36.2.5.3
    when to hold training 36.2.5.1
Trade mark attorney *see* Intellectual property practitioners
'Train the trainer' training
1.6.3, 32.3, 38.2.1.1
Trainee solicitors
    training needs *see* Training needs
Training budget 1.4.2, 3.6.1.1, 4.3, 4.4
    benchmarking 4.4.5
    centralised budget 4.4.1
    cost per day per person attending 4.4.5.1
    cost per employee 4.4.5.1

    costs per training day delivered 4.4.5.1
    CPD hours per fee earner 4.4.5.1
    de-centralised budget 4.4.1
    direct costs 4.4.3
    expenses incurred 4.4.4
    external resourcing 4.4.2
    indirect costs 4.4.3
    internal resourcing 4.4.2
    measures of performance 4.4.5.1
    as percentage of annual fee income 4.4.5.1
    services provided 4.4.4
Training Contract *see* Period of Recognised Training
Training investment 1.1, 1.1–1.6
    case for training 1.2
    challenges to 1.4
    economic downturns and 1.4.2
    imperatives 1.2.3
    no CPD hour requirement and 1.4.1
    reality of legal practice 1.2.1
    training divorced from practice 1.2.2
    commitment to training 1.5
    lack of 1.6.1.3
    rewarding 1.6.1.1
    contact with firm during the CPE/GDL and/or LPC 29.4.2
    developing the right culture 1.6
    firm-wide 1.6.4
    management level 1.6.1
    partner level 1.6.3
    practice area level 1.6.2
    during the CPE/GDL and/or LPC 29.4
    Legal Practice Course 29.4.3
    choosing a provider 29.3.1
    contact with firm during 29.4.2
    exclusive tie-ups 29.3.2
    practical steps during 29.4.1
    sponsoring on 29.3
    management level 1.5, 1.6.1
    changing performance measurement 1.6.1.2
    developing the right culture at 1.6.1
    imposing responsibility 1.6.1.4
    punishing lack of commitment 1.6.1.3
    rewarding commitment 1.6.1.1

maximising the investment 1.5
practical steps during the CPE/GDL and/or LPC 29.4.1
pre-PRT 29.1–29.4
recruiting during academic stage 29.2
  assessing potential 29.2.3
  law students 29.2.1
  non-law students 29.2.2
sponsoring on the CPE/GDL and/or LPC 29.3
where investment needs to be made 1.3

Training materials 38.2.2.1
see also Resources

Training needs
Alternative Business Structures (ABSs) 2.1.3
analysis *see* Training needs analysis
business awareness training 1.3, 30.5, 31.3.5
clients 35.1
  bespoke training 35.3.3
  internal seminars 35.3.1
  issues to consider 35.2
  practical arrangements 35.4
  practice area-specific training 35.3.2
  public seminars 35.3.4
  types of training 35.3
CPD planning 20.8.6
identifying 3.4, 3.4.1, 3.6.1, 3.6.1.1, 3.7.1, 20.9.3
in-house legal departments 2.1.2
induction *see* Induction
law firms 2.1.1
management skills training 1.3
  projects 31.3.4
  qualified solicitors 31.3.4
  trainee solicitors 30.6
newly qualified solicitors 31.2
  generic training 31.2.2
  induction 31.2.1
  practice area-specific training 31.2.3
  skills training 31.2.4
non-lawyer employees 33.1
  benefits of training 33.3
  entity-based regulation 33.2
  induction 33.4
  projects 33.6
  SRA Code of Conduct 33.2
  types of training 33.5

overseas offices 34.1, 34.3
  central 'academy' 34.3.3.6
  e-learning 34.3.3.4
  logistical issues 34.3.3
  London nucleus with satellite offices 34.3.1
  mobile attendees 34.3.3.2
  mobile trainer 34.3.3.1
  non-UK nucleus with UK satellite 34.3.2
  piggy-back 34.3.3.5
  secondment 34.3.3.3
  technology 34.3.3.4
  video conferencing 34.3.3.4
  webinars 34.3.3.4
overseas qualified lawyers 34.1, 34.2
partners 1.3, 32.1
  induction 32.2
  new partners 32.2
  partner relocation 32.5
  partners generally 32.3
  partners in management roles 32.3.1
  re-deployment of partners 32.4
  senior assistants preparing for partnership 31.4
peripheral knowledge/vision 29.4.3.4, 30.4, 31.3.2.1
personal development plan (PDP) 3.4, 3.6.1, 3.7.1
practice area-specific training
  clients 35.3.2
  knowledge/performance gaps 3.4.1
  legal technical knowledge 1.3, 30.3
  newly qualified solicitors 31.2.3
  qualified solicitors 31.3.2
  trainee solicitors 30.3
Practice Skills training 1.3, 31.3.3
  PRT requirements 15.11.4
  qualified solicitors 31.3.3
  Standard 15.11.4
qualified solicitors 1.3, 31.3
  business awareness training 31.3.5
  CPD 31.3.1
  generic training 31.3.1
  management skills training 31.3.4
  newly qualified solicitors 31.2
  on-the-job training 31.3.2.2
  peripheral vision 31.3.2.1
  post-transaction reviews 31.3.2.3
  practice area-based training 31.3.2
  Practice Skills training 31.3.3
research skills 29.2.1
responsibility for identifying 3.6.1.1

INDEX

Training needs – *continued*
    senior assistants preparing for partnership 31.4
    trainee solicitors 1.3, 30.1
      business awareness 30.5
      generic training needs 30.3.1
      induction 30.2.1
      management skills training 1.3, 30.6
      peripheral knowledge 30.4
      practice area-specific training 30.3
      required seat 30.3.2
      role models 1.2, 15.12.2, 30.2.2, 36.2.2.4
      writing skills 29.2.1
Training needs analysis 2.3, 3.4
    knowledge/performance gaps
      causes of 3.4.2
      firm-wide gaps 3.4.1
      group-specific gaps 3.4.1
      identifying 3.4.1
      individual gaps 3.4.1
      practice area-specific gaps 3.4.1
Training Principal 2.2, 15.6
Training programme
    delivering *see* Delivering training
    developing 3.6
    preparing 3.6.1
      responsibility for identifying training needs 3.6.1.1
    see also Training needs
Training strategy
    developing a competence framework 3.3
    developing and implementing 3.1–3.7
    evaluating effectiveness of training 3.7
    management responsibility 2.4
    responsibility of the training function 2.5
    Solicitors Regulation Authority 5.4.2
    training needs analysis 3.4
    training programme development 3.6
    understanding firm's business strategy and objectives 3.2
    writing the strategy 3.5
Training for Tomorrow: A Competence Statement for Solicitors 6.4.4, 6.5.1
Training for Tomorrow: A New Approach to Continuing Competence 6.4.2

Training for Tomorrow: Assessing Competence 6.4.6, 7.6, 9.9, 10.6, 11.5, 12.5, 13.5, 14.8, 15.5, 17.4, 21.5
Training for Tomorrow: Regulation Review 6.2.2, 6.4.1
Training for Tomorrow (T4T) website 2.5, 6.2.2
Tutor guides 38.2.2.2
Tutor instructions 38.2.2.2

Venue and accommodation 38.2.4
    client training 35.4
    delivery of PSC 16.5.6.2
    e-learning 36.3.5
    external venue 38.2.4.1
    internal venue 38.2.4.1
    refreshments 38.2.4.2
    room set-up 38.2.2.1, 38.2.5
    soundproofing 38.2.4.3
Video camera 38.2.2.3
Video conferencing 34.3.3.4, 36.3.1, 36.3.3
Video recordings 34.3.3.4, 36.2.2.1, 36.2.2.3, 36.3.1, 36.3.4
Visualiser 38.2.2.3
Visualisers 38.2.2.3
Vocational stage of training
    barristers 23.4.2
    completion of 17.2.1
    definition 17.2.1
    see also Legal Practice Course; Period of Recognised Training; Professional Skills Course

Webinars 34.3.3.4, 36.2.5.3, 36.3.1, 36.3.3, 36.3.4
    CPD hours 20.8.8
    induction 15.10.2, 30.2.1
    T4T 6.2.2
White board 38.2.2.3
Work-based Learning
    Chartered Legal Executive 24.4.3.1, 24.4.4
Work experience
    costs lawyers 27.4
    mature applicants 10.4.3
    PRT reduction 15.7.7
    SQE and 6.5.1
Worshipful Company of Scriveners 28.2.2, 28.3, 28.4.3
Writing skills 29.2.1